COUNTERTERRORISM: DEMOCRACY'S CHALLENGE

Terrorist violence is no novelty in human history and, while government reactions to it have varied over time, some lessons can be learned from the past. Indeed, the debate on when and how a state should use emergency powers that limit individual freedoms is nearly as old as the history of political thought. After reviewing some history of state responses to terrorist violence and their efficacy, this book sets out to assess the effects of contemporary counterterrorism law and policies on democratic states. In particular, it considers the interaction between national and international law in shaping and implementing anti-terror measures, and the difficult role of the judiciary in striking a balance between security concerns and fundamental rights. It also examines the strains this has caused on some democracies, especially a blurring in the separation of powers between the legislative, executive and judicial branches of government, giving reason to inquire afresh whether new paradigms are needed. Finally, the issue of whether the doctrine of constitutionalism can provide an appropriate frame of analysis to encapsulate current developments in international law in response to terrorism is broached.

By drawing on the expertise of historians, political scientists and lawyers, this book promotes transdisciplinary dialogue, recognising that counterterrorism is an issue at the intersection of law and politics that has profound implications for democratic institutions and practices.

Studies in International Law: Volume 19

Studies in International Law

Counterterrorism: Democracy's Challenge

Edited by
Andrea Bianchi and Alexis Keller

with the editorial assistance of
Steven J Barela

·HART·
PUBLISHING

OXFORD AND PORTLAND, OREGON
2008

Published in North America (US and Canada) by
Hart Publishing
c/o International Specialized Book Services
920 NE 58th Avenue, Suite 300
Portland, OR 97213–3786
USA
Tel: +1–503–287–3093 or toll-free: (1)-800–944–6190
Fax: +1 503 280 8832
E-mail: orders@isbs.com
Website: www.isbs.com

Hart Publishing, 16C Worcester Place, Oxford, OX1 2JW
Telephone: +44 (0)1865 517530 Fax: +44(0)1865 510710
E-mail: mail@hartpub.co.uk
Website: http://www.hartpub.co.uk

British Library Cataloguing in Publication Data

Data Available

ISBN: 978–1-84113–818–3

Typeset by Columns Design, Reading
Printed and bound in Great Britain by
TJ International Ltd, Padstow, Cornwall

Preface

The resurgence of international terrorism on a grand scale after 11 September 2001 caused democracies and the international community to inquire afresh whether the tools at their disposal were suitable to face such a threat. The response in the past few years has consisted of a panoply of policies and specific measures of different origin and content which are described, increasingly, as 'counterterrorism'. The conciseness of the term barely hides its underlying complexity and heterogeneous nature. Counterterrorism includes laws, policies, tactics and techniques used to fight terrorism at the national and international level. It is an oddity of sorts that the fuzzy term coined to encapsulate responses to international terrorism mirrors the way in which terrorism itself blurs our traditional legal and political categories. Be that as it may, 'counter-terrorism' aptly conveys, in an almost intuitive fashion, the notion that a set of measures and policies has been put in place expressly to counter one of the most dangerous threats to national and international security we have faced in our times. The line of inquiry pursued in this study focuses on the impact of counterterrorism on democracies and its implications for national and international modes of governance.

Democracies have become increasingly aware of their own vulnerability. The irony is that their distinguishing traits and foundational tenets in many ways constitute fertile ground for international terrorism. The open character of democratic societies, their diversity and the myriad of social interactions that take place freely within them are all elements that make the attainment of an acceptable level of security a daunting task. Undoubtedly, security is thought to be at the core of the social compact that lies at the basis of modern states, but it is also true that liberty and other fundamental rights and freedoms represent the quintessential elements of democratic governance. Likewise, there is a risk that counter-terrorism will strain the institutional equilibrium shaped by the doctrine of constitutionalism and its corollaries (separation of powers, checks and balances and so on). The uncertainty about which branch of government should strike the balance between security and the protection of fundamental freedoms, and according to what criteria, is an ongoing challenge. Some look at this challenge as an opportunity for democracies to reaffirm their commitment to their fundamental rules and underlying values. Others perceive it as potentially disruptive of the main tenets of democratic governance.

As is well known, terrorist violence is no novelty in human history and some useful lessons can be learned from the past. Although government reactions to it have varied over time, history provides useful examples of how terrorist violence has been countered. The records show that the debate on when and how a state should use emergency powers that limit individual freedoms is a very old question. Groups using violence against the state or the civilian population have been defeated in the past, and it is surely a useful exercise to examine the circumstances and factors that led to their demise. The first part of the book reviews and evaluates, in historical perspective, some of the responses states have made to earlier forms of terrorist violence. Part two is taken up with assessing the effects on democratic states of contemporary counterterrorism laws and policies. In particular, it considers the interaction between national and international law in shaping and implementing anti-terror measures, and the difficult role for the judiciary in striking a balance between security concerns and fundamental rights. It also examines the strains this has caused within some democracies, especially a blurring in the separation of powers between the legislative, executive and judicial branches of government, giving reason to inquire whether new paradigms are needed. Part three addresses this particular issue from a twofold perspective. On the one hand it uses a comparative constitutional law perspective to evaluate whether current judicial approaches are appropriate to deal with the threat of international terrorism. Second, it broaches the issue of whether the doctrine of constitutionalism can provide an appropriate frame of analysis to encapsulate current developments in international law in response to terrorism.

The book draws on the expertise of historians, political scientists and lawyers. In this respect it is an attempt to promote trans-disciplinary dialogue at a time when the self-referential and self-contained character of most epistemological academic communities confines the debate to the narrow boundaries of disciplinary approaches. The topic of counterterrorism, admittedly an issue at the intersection of law and politics that has profound implications for democratic institutions and practices, seems to provide a good opportunity to test the viability of a trans-disciplinary approach. The attempt is to provide readers with a set of insights into the ways in which counterterrorism affects the orderly functioning of democratic modes of governance and how it impacts on international law and politics. This is not done in a thorough and systematic way but, rather, by selectively looking at some areas or case-studies from distinct disciplinary perspectives. Looking sparingly into such a complex topic might be tainted with arbitrariness and superficiality. By selecting some areas or topics to the detriment of others, by focusing on some perspectives while neglecting others, one inevitably exposes oneself to criticism. Yet, impressions drawn from a look at separate parts of the whole can capture an essential reality of the entire object of observation. Like the impressionist's paintbrush taken up with the object of giving the general effect without elaborate detail, this book aspires to convey the general impression one is left with after examining the normative and political responses to international terrorism in the aftermath of 11 September 2001: counterterrorism looms as one of democracy's main challenges.

Andrea Bianchi
Alexis Keller
Geneva, November 2007

Acknowledgments

Every book has a story behind it and, avowedly, not all stories are worth telling the reader. The story behind this book is one of intellectual φιλία between two academics who ran into each other, almost haphazardly, in the course of their professional itineraries. Our belonging to different disciplines, and our affiliation to distinct epistemological communities, could have been a cause for us to acknowledge politely our respective research interests and wish each other goodbye. However, intellectual curiosity and mutual esteem prompted us to venture into this common research project on a topic which, by its very nature, requires a much broader analytical framework than any single discipline is able to offer. Perhaps this is what makes the story worth telling: novel human and professional solidarities develop only if one is receptive to challenge.

This edited volume was conceived as part of a wider project on 'Democracy and Terrorism', sponsored by the Geneva-based foundation *Société Académique*. We are particularly grateful to its President, Pierre Buri, and to the other members of its Committee, Monique Caillat, Renaud Gagnebin and Patrizia Lombardo, for their constant support and encouragement. Caroline Baltzinger, the administrative officer of the *Société Académique*, who liaised with us and organised the regular meetings also deserves our thanks. It is not always easy to meet the expectations of donors, but the *Société Académique* invariably supported our initiatives within the project, including this one.

It is no easy task to bring to completion a collection of essays such as this, and the editors are indebted to many people. First and foremost, we are grateful to our collaborators who have provided help and support throughout the project. Steven Barela, Sylvie Guichard, Frederic Esposito, Till Hanisch, Benoit Pelopidas, Mélanie Samson and Fouad Zarbiev provided assistance well beyond the call of duty. The lively atmosphere and cooperative spirit in which the project has been carried out bears witness to the fact that teamwork can be an effective and pleasant way of working, even in the highly individualistic and atomised academic world.

The papers included as chapters in this volume were given at a conference held in Geneva on 19–20 November 2006. The conference, hosted by the Graduate Institute of International and Development Studies, provided a good opportunity to receive feedback on each and every work. Our gratitude goes to the speakers, chairs and interveners at the conference, who were far more numerous than the authors whose written work is published in this collection. To those who still believe that academia is a forum for intellectual freedom the conference was a reassuring event. Specialists from different disciplines interacted with one another constructively, and intellectual curiosity prompted animated discussions that often extended to the dinner table.

Our heartfelt thanks go to Steven Barela, who provided invaluable assistance in the editing process. His unconditional commitment to the project has made publication possible within the timeframe that was originally envisaged. Most volume editors know that this is a remarkable achievement. Finally, we would like to thank Richard Hart for his belief in this book, despite its eclectic character and the fact that it is not exclusively legal. We join him in hoping that readers will understand and appreciate the effort of providing a trans-disciplinary perspective on such a topical issue.

Andrea Bianchi
Alexis Keller

Contents

Part Three: Is There a Need for New Legal Paradigms?

List of Contributors

Eyal Benvenisti

Professor of International Law, Faculty of Law, Tel Aviv University, Israel.

Andrea Bianchi

Professor of Public International Law, Graduate Institute of International and Development Studies, Geneva, Switzerland; Professor of International Law, Catholic University of Milan, Italy.

David Cole

Professor of Law, Georgetown University, United States.

Ian Johnstone

Associate Professor of International Law, Fletcher School of Law and Diplomacy, Tufts University, United States.

Alexis Keller

Professor of History of Legal and Political Thought, Faculty of Law, University of Geneva, Switzerland.

Audrey Kurth Cronin

Professor of Strategy, US National War College; Senior Research Associate, Changing Character of War Programme, Oxford University, United Kingdom.

Dominic McGoldrick

Professor of Public International Law, Liverpool Law School, University of Liverpool, United Kingdom.

Adam Roberts

Emeritus Fellow of Balliol College, Oxford, United Kingdom.

Michel Rosenfeld

Justice Sydney L Robins Professor of Human Rights and Director of the Program on Security, Democracy and the Rule of Law, Cardozo School of Law, United States.

Iain Scobbie

Sir Joseph Hotung Research Professor in Law, Human Rights and Peace-building in the Middle East, School of Oriental and African Studies, University of London, United Kingdom.

Christian Tams

Lecturer, Walther Schücking Institute for International Law, Christian Albrechts University, Kiel.

Paul Wilkinson

Professor of International Relations and Chairman of the Advisory Board of the Centre for the Study of Terrorism and Political Violence (CSTPV), University of St Andrews, United Kingdom.

Part One

The Fight against Terrorism in Historical Perspective

1

Countering Terrorism: A Historical Perspective*

ADAM ROBERTS

WHAT CONCLUSIONS CAN be drawn from the long history of terrorist and counterterrorist campaigns? And what directions does this history suggest for the ongoing international campaign against terrorism? Today's international terrorism has assumed organisational forms and means of operating that are historically new. The shadowy entities labelled 'Al Qaeda' are different from earlier terrorist movements in the extremism of their aims and in the far-flung, co-ordinated and ruthless character of their operations. No less novel is the contemporary US and international campaign against international terrorism. And yet, despite all the unprecedented aspects of this conflict, there are dangers in neglecting the history of terrorism and counterterrorism. These dangers include the repetition of mistakes made in earlier eras. The long and tangled history of terrorism and counterterrorism suggests a number of conclusions about the nature of terrorist and counterterrorist campaigns that need to be taken into account in policymaking.

This survey has three sections. *Section I* glances at the history of attempts at defining terrorism. It notes not only the unavoidable difficulties in international discussions of this topic, but also the degree of progress that there has been in defining and prohibiting terrorism. Above all, this section is a warning against over-simple use of this necessary but troublesome term. *Section II* is about the history of terrorism and counterterrorism, seeking to distil some general conclusions about a phenomenon that is always, in reality, deeply rooted in time, place and circumstance. It indicates how debates on terrorism and counterterrorism

---

* This text is an extensively revised, expanded and updated version of the author's article 'The "War on Terror" in Historical Perspective', which appeared in (Summer 2005) 47(2) *Survival* (London), 101–30.

have often lacked an all-important historical dimension. It offers some inevitably simplified propositions derived from the history of terrorist campaigns, starting with the critical issue of whether terrorism is properly seen as an external threat to democracies. *Section III* is about the 'war on terror' itself, looking particularly at the marshalling of international support for it, and at the emphasis on military intervention that has been part of that war. In the conclusions, six main lines of criticism of the US-led campaign are advanced. This Section suggests that the US doctrine on the 'war on terror' is vulnerable to the charge that it takes too little account of the history of the subject. There is a need to articulate what might be called a British (or, more ambitiously, a European) perspective on terrorism and counterterrorism – one that is more historically informed, encompassing certain elements distinctive from the US doctrine.

Before proceeding, it is necessary to say a brief word about the difficult topic of the causes of terrorism. In most areas of life – including crime, sickness and war – it is possible to discuss causes without inviting the degree of controversy that arises in the case of terrorism. Unfortunately, discussion of the 'causes of terrorism' has become emotionally charged. The principal reason for this sorry state of affairs is that any discussion of causes is easily interpreted as amounting to a justification of terrorism.

The demonstrable historical fact is that terrorist campaigns have arisen in response to several types of situation. They have had as stated purposes the overthrowing of what are perceived as autocratic regimes, including that of the Tsars in Russia in the nineteenth century. They have arisen, even in democracies such as Spain, Sri Lanka and the United Kingdom, as a response to one part of a population's alleged dominance over another. They have also frequently arisen in response to colonial rule, and to foreign occupation. The common thread in the growth of suicide bombing since the attack on the US Embassy in Beirut in 1983 is not just religious extremism but the presence of foreign military occupation. As Robert Pape has written, 'the close association between foreign military occupations and the growth of suicide terrorist movements in the occupied regions should give pause to those who favor solutions that involve conquering countries in order to transform their political systems'.[1] This clear view, that terrorist campaigns are a response to particular types of situation, does not mean that such campaigns are either inevitable or justified. Even in the most difficult circumstances there are moral and strategic choices, and it is far from self-evident that terrorism

---

[1] R Pape, 'The Strategic Logic of Suicide Terrorism' (August 2003) 97(3) *American Political Science Review* 357.

has superior claims over other forms of action. The attempt to define terrorism arises in part from a desire to underline this point.

I. DEFINING 'TERRORISM'

The word 'terrorism', like many abstract political terms, is confusing, dangerous and indispensable. Confusing, because it means very different things to different people, and its meaning has also changed greatly over time. Dangerous, because it easily becomes an instrument of propaganda, and a means of avoiding thinking about the many forms and causes of political violence. Indispensable, because there is a real phenomenon out there that poses a threat to many societies.

A case can be made that a better generic term to cover the phenomenon under discussion would be 'political violence'. It is less emotion-laden, less condemnatory and certainly wider in scope than 'terrorism'. Yet there is a continuing need for a term that distinguishes some forms of political violence from others. Violence used or threatened by those manning an insurrectionary barricade, or defending an area from police or army incursion, is hardly in itself terrorism. By contrast, violence intended to spread terror much more generally, especially when involving attacks on civilians and/or based on the idea of violence as transforming the political landscape, is a distinct category. In short, and despite a large area of debatable borderland between the two, terrorism can in principle be distinguished from certain other forms of political violence.

The problem of defining 'terrorism' is similar to that of defining many other political abstract terms, such as 'imperialism' and 'war': the core meaning may be clear enough, and it may be possible to secure agreement that certain cases fit that meaning. At the edges, however, there is often scope for genuine debate about whether particular acts, or types of action, really deserve to be included in the category.

Even within certain countries there can be different legal definitions of terrorism. For example, different US government agencies have had different understandings of the term, and this has sometimes complicated intra-governmental cooperation. That there should be international disagreement on the meaning of the term is not surprising: what is remarkable is that there has been significant progress towards a definition.

There are traps in most attempted definitions of terrorism, and in the uses made of the term. The most serious is that the label 'terrorist' has sometimes been applied to the activities of movements which, even if they did resort to violence, had serious claims to political legitimacy, and also exercised care and restraint in their choice of methods. Famously, in

1987–88 the UK and US governments labelled the African National Congress of South Africa 'terrorist': a shallow and silly attribution even at the time, let alone in light of Nelson Mandela's later emergence as statesman.

In certain circumstances, the repeated use of the term 'terrorist' to describe a particular class of adversaries can conceal rather than clarify key aspects of the political environment. In particular, the description of a group as 'terrorist' may obscure the fact that its opponents also use terror; and it may also obscure the fact that the so-called terrorist group has a moral, political and economic basis for its power, and does not rely exclusively on terror to maintain its influence. For example, in the 1960s many writers and journalists freely used the word 'terrorist' to describe a member of the Vietcong, the military arm of the National Liberation Front of South Vietnam. The Vietcong did undoubtedly use the weapon of terror ruthlessly and systematically against the South Vietnamese population. However, serious studies suggested that terror was not on its own an adequate basis of control: a sense of the moral justice of the cause was also present. The two factors were mutually reinforcing – and this helped to explain the capacity of the Vietcong to endure.[2]

The problem of defining 'terrorism' is especially difficult as it is generally seen as a pejorative term: all diplomatic attempts to define it have been combined with attempts to prohibit it. This brief exploration of the difficult issue of definition looks at international negotiations on the topic, especially those within a UN framework; and it then offers a short working definition indicating how the term is used in this chapter.

A. Negotiating towards a Definition

The UN General Assembly, which has addressed the problem of terrorism since the early 1970s, has adopted 13 treaties prohibiting particular terrorist acts from air piracy to acts involving nuclear reactors; but it has been able to reach only a limited measure of agreement on a general definition of terrorism.[3] The General Assembly's ad hoc committee on terrorism, established in 1996, has not yet been able to agree all parts of a definition which would form part of the draft comprehensive convention. One problem has been that many post-colonial states in the General

---

[2]   This is the conclusion, for example, of two exceptionally thorough and impressive US studies of the Vietcong published during the war: D Pike, *Vietcong: The Organization and Techniques of the National Liberation Front of South Vietnam* (Cambridge, MA, MIT Press, 1966); and N Leites, *The Vietcong Style of Politics*, Rand Memorandum RM-5487-1-ISA/ARPA (Santa Monica, CA, Rand, 1969).

[3]   For information on the wide range of General Assembly activities on terrorism, see the UN website at <http://www.un.org/terrorism/ga.html>.

Assembly claim origins in national liberation struggles that colonial powers called terrorist campaigns. Such states have been at the forefront of demands to incorporate in any text defining terrorism a pledge to address the root causes of terrorism – which seemed to the United States and others as a backdoor justification of terrorism. There have been parallel difficulties in working out an acceptable generic distinction between terrorists and freedom fighters. Yet there has been some modest progress towards a definition of terrorism.

Partly this has been due to the focus on a particular aspect of contemporary terrorism – the fact that it often involves deliberate attacks on civilians. Progress has been made in the UN Security Council – where there has been less concern than in the General Assembly about referring to the root causes. A Security Council resolution in October 2004, after condemning 'all acts of terrorism regardless of their motivation', came close to a definition of terrorism when it stated that the Council:

> *Recalls* that criminal acts, including against civilians, committed with the intent to cause death or serious bodily injury, or taking of hostages, with the purpose to provoke a state of terror in the general public or in a group of persons or particular persons, intimidate a population or compel a government or an international organization to do or to abstain from doing any act, which constitute offences within the scope of and as defined in the international conventions and protocols relating to terrorism , are under no circumstances justifiable by considerations of a political, philosophical, ideological, racial, ethnic, religious or other similar nature, and *calls upon* all States to prevent such acts and, if not prevented, to ensure that such acts are punished by penalties consistent with their grave nature.[4]

Similarly, the UN High-level Panel on Threats, Challenges and Change, which issued its report in December 2004, focused on civilians in its suggested definition of terrorism:

> any action, in addition to actions already specified by the existing conventions on aspects of terrorism, the Geneva Conventions and Security Council resolution 1566 (2004), that is intended to cause death or serious bodily harm to civilians or non-combatants, when the purpose of such an act, by its nature or context, is to intimidate a population, or to compel a Government or an international organization to do or to abstain from doing any act.[5]

A limitation of both these definitions put forward in 2004 (and especially of the second one) should be noted. The emphasis being largely on the threat to civilians or non-combatants, they might appear not to encompass certain acts such as attacks on armed peacekeeping forces, attacks

---

[4] SC Res 1566 of 8 October 2004, operative para 3.
[5] UN High-level Panel on Threats, Challenges and Change, *A More Secure World: Our Shared Responsibility*, UN doc A/59/565, 2 December 2004, para 164(d).

on police or armed forces, or assassinations of heads of state or government. They might not include the attack on the Pentagon on 11 September 2001, but for the fact that it involved the hijacking of a civilian airliner.

The UN General Assembly's World Summit Outcome document of September 2005 condemned 'terrorism in all its forms and manifestations, committed by whomever, wherever, and for whatever purposes'.[6] However, this document did not attempt to define terrorism. Subsequently, in September 2006, the General Assembly approved a resolution entitled 'UN Global Counter-terrorism Strategy' the preamble of which contained some elements of a definition when it reaffirmed 'that acts, methods and practices of terrorism in all its forms and manifestations are activities aimed at the destruction of human rights, fundamental freedoms and democracy, threatening territorial integrity, security of States and destabilizing legitimately constituted Governments'. The document promised support for a future comprehensive convention on international terrorism, which would contain a legal definition.[7] Then in December 2006, in much the same vein, the General Assembly passed a resolution on 'Measures to Eliminate International Terrorism' in which it stated that the General Assembly:

> *Reiterates* that criminal acts intended or calculated to provoke a state of terror in the general public, a group of persons or particular persons for political purposes are in any circumstances unjustifiable, whatever the considerations of a political, philosophical, ideological, racial, ethnic, religious or other nature that may be invoked to justify them.[8]

The 2005 Council of Europe Convention on the Prevention of Terrorism defines terrorism in a similar fashion in a preambular clause:

> Recalling that acts of terrorism have the purpose by their nature or context to seriously intimidate a population or unduly compel a government or an international organisation to perform or abstain from performing any act or seriously destabilise or destroy the fundamental political, constitutional, economic or social structures of a country or an international organisation;

In sum, although there is agreement on elements of a definition, there is as yet no agreement on a formal legal definition. This is why the nearest things there are to a definition tend to be found in preambular clauses, where their incompleteness is less worrisome than it would be if they

---

[6]   GA Res 60/1 of 16 September 2005, '2005 World Summit Outcome', UN doc A/Res./60/1 of 24 October 2005, para 81.

[7]   GA Res 60/288 of 8 September 2006.

[8]   GA Res 61/40 of 4 December 2006.

were presented as a formal definition. It is also why it has been easier to draw up conventions prohibiting specific terrorist acts than to prohibit terrorism in general.

B. Defining 'Terrorist Acts'

A category that is easier to define than the grand abstraction of terrorism is *terrorist acts*. While still surrounded by a dense thicket of thorny problems, this term has the merit of keeping the focus on specific types of action. It encompasses certain violent acts that can be judged to be unlawful by well-established criteria. The category of 'terrorist acts' can encompass actions that contravene any or all of the following bodies of law:

- certain national laws relating to terrorism;
- regional international agreements on terrorism. Examples include the 2005 Council of Europe Convention on the Prevention of Terrorism;
- global international agreements on terrorism – that is, the 13 conventions approved by the UN General Assembly prohibiting particular terrorist acts;
- the basic principles and specific provisions of the laws of war. However, the question of whether this body of law is formally applicable to particular terrorist acts would depend on whether the acts concerned are part of an ongoing armed conflict (and, if so, on whether the conflict is international or non-international in character).

On the basis of criteria contained in such bodies of law it is possible, at least sometimes, to draw a distinction between prohibited acts and other types and forms of armed resistance. That is why the adage 'one man's terrorist is another man's freedom fighter', while it contains more than a grain of truth (especially that the same act can be seen differently by different people), is too simple: it reflects a lack of awareness that there are some established criteria for distinguishing between the two.

C. Towards a Provisional Definition of 'Terrorism'

A feature of several of the UN attempts at definition is the implication that terrorism is essentially a non-state or even anti-state activity, aimed at undermining governments and/or international organisations. This approach may be unavoidable in the process of narrowing down a broad subject into a specific criminalisation of particular activities. It reflects the fact that, being a form of action in which individuals and small groups can engage, terrorism has often been a weapon of non-state bodies, from anarchists in the nineteenth century to Al Qaeda in the twenty-first. Moreover, the terrorism of non-state groups is of special concern to governments because it threatens their monopoly of the instruments of violence and coercion within a state. This is a perfectly legitimate concern, which many citizens share: to have more than one wielder of violence within a state can be a recipe for anarchy and civil war. Thus it is not surprising that some attempts at definition focus on terrorism's non-state character.

However, many states have also used terror – whether against their own population, expatriates whom they wish to silence or foreign adversaries. While it would be wrong to characterise all state coercion as terrorism, there have been instances in which states have resorted to terrorism through their own armed services, police forces and other state agents, or by secretly supporting non-state terrorist groups. Sometimes they have used *agents provocateurs* to discredit their opponents by falsely attributing terrorist acts to them. A serious definition of terrorism needs to take account of this fact.

In light of the multi-faceted nature of past uses of terrorism, and the many ways in which terrorism overlaps with and shades into other activities, this survey suggests a broad definition – and one that is certainly not definitive granted the controversies that necessarily surround the subject. 'Terrorism' is used here mainly to refer to: *the systematic use of violence and threats of violence – often but not exclusively by non-state groups, and generally clandestine in its organisation and modes of action – designed to cause dislocation, consternation, and submission on the part of a target population, government or international organisation*. This is no more than a provisional working definition indicating how the term is used in this chapter. It is offered because of the continuing absence of an authoritative international definition. In what follows, the focus is mainly on the terrorism of non-state groups.

II. HISTORY OF TERRORISM AND COUNTER-TERRORISM

A. Denial of History

Since 11 September 2001, statements by the principal Western leaders on the subject of the 'war on terror' have contained few references to the previous experience of governments in tackling terrorist threats, or to the ways in which certain international wars of the twentieth century were sparked off by concerns about terrorism. This appears to be true also of their inner deliberations, as revealed by Bob Woodward, Seymour Hersh and others. In particular, Woodward's *Plan of Attack* shows that there was little reference to historical precedents in the two years of decision-making leading up to the invasion of Iraq. An honourable exception occurred when Secretary of State Colin Powell, at a planning meeting on Iraq, asked sarcastically: 'Are we going to be off-loading at Gallipoli?'.[9]

General Bernard Montgomery's first rule of warfare was 'Don't march on Moscow.'[10] Regarding terrorism and counterterrorism there is no such straightforward rule. The history of these matters repays study, not because it offers a single recipe for action, but rather because it enriches our understanding of a peculiarly complex subject. It indicates a range of possibilities for addressing it, and a number of hazards to avoid. Historians are neither agreed nor infallible in addressing this subject, any more than are my own colleagues in the field of international relations. A profession that encompasses both Professor Sir Michael Howard and Professor Bernard Lewis is not about to reach a unanimous party line on a subject as contentious as what to do about terrorism.

Yet it remains odd that since 2001 much writing on terror, particularly in the United States, has tended to neglect the long history of terrorism and counterterrorism. This is true even of historians and historically informed writers: some, such as John Gaddis and Walter Mead, have written books about the war on terror that contain much important insight into US history and the US role in the world, but say almost nothing about the history of terror and counterterror.[11] On the other hand, since 2001 there has been a good deal of writing touching on the history of these matters. A few works have covered only the last few decades.[12] Some works, however, have taken into account experiences of terrorism and counterterrorism from the nineteenth century to the twenty-first – an excellent example being that of Michael Ignatieff.[13]

---

[9]   Bob Woodward, *Plan of Attack* (New York, Simon & Schuster, 2004) 324.

[10]   General Bernard Montgomery said of US policy in Vietnam: 'The US has broken the second rule of war. That is, don't go fighting with your land army on the mainland of Asia. Rule One is don't march on Moscow. I developed these two rules myself': A Chalfont, *Montgomery of Alamein* (London, Weidenfeld & Nicolson, [1976]) 318.

[11]   JL Gaddis, *Surprise, Security, and the American Experience* (Cambridge, MA, Harvard University Press, 2004); and WR Mead, *Power, Terror, Peace, and War: America's Grand Strategy in a World at Risk* (New York, Alfred A Knopf, 2004). See also JL Gaddis, 'And Now This: Lessons from the Old Era for the New One', in S Talbott and N Chanda (eds), *The Age of Terror: America and the World After September 11* (Oxford, Perseus Press, 2001) 1–22.

[12]   B Maxwell, *Terrorism: A Documentary History* (Washington DC, CQ Press, [2003]). The documents in this book cover only a 30-year period, 'from 1972, when international terrorism bust into the public consciousness with live TV pictures of Palestinian terrorists holding Israeli athletes hostage at the Munich Olympics'. In some countries the public was aware of terrorism decades, or even centuries, earlier.

[13]   M Ignatieff, *The Lesser Evil: Political Ethics in an Age of Terror* (Edinburgh, Edinburgh University Press, 2004).

In practice, the response of each country to the 'war on terror' has been deeply influenced by its own particular experience of terrorism and counterterrorism. In the United Kingdom there has been frequent reference to the experience of countering terrorism in Northern Ireland. British Ministers and officials, however, have refrained from pointing out bluntly, and in public, that almost everything about the language and manner in which terror in Northern Ireland has been opposed, and about the attempts at underwriting its end through mediation and even negotiation, has been very different from the US approach to the 'war on terror'. Partly, of course, this is because the problems faced have been different: the Irish Republican Army (IRA) is far removed from Al Qaeda in ideology, in political goals and in methods. Yet the British may have been too reticent about their experience of terrorism.

The tendency to approach terrorism without benefit of history has, itself, a long history. Political debates about terrorism have perennially been ahistorical. Both terrorists and their adversaries tend to talk and write publicly about their campaigns with little reference to the centuries-long history of terrorism and counterterrorism. This is not to say that they do not articulate a view of history more generally. Terrorists, for example, often focus on deep resentments based on perceptions of alien domination of the societies they claim to defend. When terrorists have put pen to paper, either at the time of their activism or subsequently, they have sometimes shown considerable awareness of international developments and the history of their own and earlier epochs.[14] At the same time, the long and tangled history of both terrorism and counterterrorism is frequently airbrushed out of the picture. The publicly articulated world-view of terrorists and their adversaries is often a world of moral and political absolutes, in which terrorism, or the war against it, is seen as an essentially new means of ridding the world of a unique and evil scourge. On both sides, the favoured form of argument is phrased in terms of morality – and a relatively simple morality at that, in which the adversary's actions are seen as such a serious threat as to create an overwhelming necessity for the use of counter-violence.

Many specialists in counter-insurgency have seen their subject more as a struggle of light versus darkness than as a common and recurrent theme of history. A fine example of such an ahistorical approach to the subject is the French group of theorists writing in the 1950s and early 1960s about *la guerre révolutionnaire*. These theorists denied the complexities – especially the mixture of material, moral and ideological factors – that are keys to understanding why and how terrorist movements come

---

[14]   See eg D Rapoport, 'The International World as Some Terrorists Have Seen It: A Look at a Century of Memoirs' (December 1987) 10(4) *The Journal of Strategic Studies* 32–58.

into existence. Colonel Lacheroy, a leading figure in this group and head of the French Army's *Service d'Action Psychologique*, famously stated: 'In the beginning there is nothing.'[15] Terrorism was seen as having been introduced deliberately into a peaceful society by an omnipresent outside force – namely international communism. It is a demonological vision of a cosmic struggle in which the actual history of particular countries and ways of thinking has little or no place. These French theories – no doubt because they date from a period of failed military campaigns, attempted military *coups d'état*, systematic use of torture against insurgents, and a generally disastrous period in French history – are now almost entirely forgotten, even in France itself. They are also ignored in the United States, even though they, and the events with which they are connected, provide object-lessons in how not to conduct a counterterrorist campaign.

If terrorists and counter-terrorists have often forgotten history, history has not entirely forgotten them. Many historians have written subtly and interestingly about the evolution of terrorism (which, like so much else, has significant European as well as extra-European origins), about its ever-changing philosophy, about its sociology and its consequences. Those historians who have combined historical analysis of terrorism with advocacy have tended to favour a tough line against terrorism, but biased more towards a strong police response than towards military interventions.[16]

In present circumstances there are powerful reasons to buttress the claim that the threat faced is totally new, and needs to be tackled in new ways. Today's terrorist incidents can involve a combination of elements, many of which are new: elaborate planning carried out far from the location of the attack; a suicide mission; an assault on a nuclear-armed power; the destruction of major buildings and the killing of hundreds or even thousands of people, usually civilians. Such an attack may be on behalf of a movement many of whose demands are probably unachievable and certainly non-negotiable. Something new is undoubtedly happening, whether at the World Trade Center in Manhattan or at Beslan in North Ossetia. The difference between the scale of carnage now and what

---

[15] Col C Lacheroy, 'La Guerre Révolutionnaire', Talk given on 2 July 1957, reprinted in *La Défense Nationale* (Paris, 1958) 322, cited in P Paret, *French Revolutionary Warfare from Indochina to Algeria: The Analysis of a Political and Military Doctrine* (London, Pall Mall Press, 1964) 15. Paret comments that 'nothing', in this case, means 'the secure existence of the *status quo*'.

[16] See eg W Laqueur, *The Age of Terrorism* (London, Weidenfeld & Nicolson, 1987). See also M Howard, 'What's in a Name? How to Fight Terrorism' (January/February 2002) *Foreign Affairs* 9–13.

resulted from earlier phases of terrorism brings to mind the grim biblical statement that is inscribed on the Machine Gun Corps monument in London:

> Saul hath slain his thousands
>
> but David his tens of thousands.[17]

So sharp is the distinction from earlier eras that, from today's grim perspective, it would be easy to implore earlier terrorists: 'Come back: all is forgiven.' Former terrorists themselves, in the manner of old soldiers, have often deplored the terrible things that later generations of terrorists did, and the impurity of their motivations.[18] Because the changes have been so great, it would also be easy to brush aside earlier historical experience of terrorism on the grounds of diminished relevance – and this indeed appears to have happened in much contemporary analysis. It is a huge mistake.

B. Ten Propositions based on Earlier Campaigns

At the risk of over-simplification, the following ten propositions can be drawn from the long history of terrorism, and action against it. These propositions all have a bearing on the conduct of, and language regarding, today's international campaign against terrorism.

1. The Relation between Terrorism and Democracy is Complex

Terrorism has long been seen as a threat to democracies. The illustration below, from a novel published in 1893, shows this view of the threat more eloquently than any words can.

---

[17]   Monument 'erected to commemorate the glorious heroes of the Machine Gun Corps who Fell in the Great War (1914–1918)', Hyde Park Corner, London. As the monument's inscription notes, the Machine Gun Corps was formed on 14 October 1915, and its last unit was disbanded on 15 July 1922. The quotation is from I Samuel 18: 7.

[18]   A good example is Ratko Parezanin, a member of the Young Bosnia movement in 1914 and a friend of Gavril Princip, the assassin of Archduke Ferdinand in 1914. Parezanin's memoirs, published in 1974, are mentioned below, n 20.

SHELLING THE HOUSES OF PARLIAMENT.   *See page 14?*

Source: E Douglas Fawcett, Hartmann the Anarchist: or, The Doom of the Great City (London, Edward Arnold, 1893) frontispiece.[19]

This vision of the mother of parliaments going down shows just how enduring is the image of terrorism as a threat to democracy. In recent years this tradition of thought has continued, with many seeing contemporary terrorist campaigns as part of a totalitarian attack on the whole idea of democracy. Many, too, have seen democracy as constituting the antidote or prophylactic for terrorism. The historical record suggests that the connections between democracy and terrorism are more complex.

The proposition that democracies are attacked simply because they are democracies has obvious strengths. It is usually associated with the idea that the ideologues leading terrorist campaigns see democracy as their enemy because their whole scheme is about imposing a vision upon society. There is also an argument that democracies are attacked because

---

[19] Also shown in B Porter, 'Oo Let 'Em In? Asylum Seekers and Terrorists in Britain, 1850–1914', in R Louis (ed), *Yet More Adventures with Britannia* (London, IB Tauris, 2005) 21. This shows the Attila, an airship (or 'aëronef') with powerful engines and a 'projecting aëroplane', shelling the Houses of Parliament at an imagined future date in 1920. When it was published, flight was still in its infancy. The first powered heavier-than-air aeroplane flight would be 10 years later, by Orville and Wilbur Wright on 17 December 1903, at Kitty Hawk.

they represent an easier target than autocracies – their very liberalism being used against them. Yet there are other explanations for the occurrence of terrorist attacks in democracies. In particular, because they have a free press, democracies give far more publicity to terrorists than do more autocratic systems of government; and they may also offer them easier chances to gather like-minded people together to initiate a campaign. There is a long history of violent campaigns of various kinds, including terrorist struggles, being supported in democratic countries while having as their main targets governments elsewhere: this is part of the explanation of why London came to be seen by nineteenth-century autocrats as a haven for terrorists – a precursor of its twenty-first century characterisation as 'Londonistan'.

The vision of democracies as simply the innocent victims of terrorism also falls foul of other historical considerations. It risks leaving out of the picture some grievance-based elements in the politics of terrorism. The involvements of democratic states in what are perceived as oppressive policies at home or abroad, including supporting military occupations, are frequently cited as supposed 'justifications' of terrorism. Moreover, the process of democratisation within a hitherto non-democratic society – whether it is brought about by intervening forces or purely domestic ones – can be deeply disruptive and may provoke a violent, even terrorist, response from sections of the population whose rights or privileges appear to be threatened. The nervousness of a large ethnic minority about dominance by a local majority is part of the explanation of why terrorist campaigns have developed and have proved persistent in a number of democratic political systems, including Northern Ireland for well over a generation from 1971, and Sri Lanka from 1983. Not only did they originate within formal democracies, but for long periods both rebellions received significant assistance from ethnic kin support groups in well-established Western democracies – the United States in the case of Northern Ireland, and the United Kingdom and Canada in the case of Sri Lanka.

None of this challenges the view that in the long run a mature and inclusive democracy, recognising rights of minorities, may be an effective means of reducing the likelihood of terrorism. What is called into question is the frequently asserted assumption that democracy in all its forms is the enemy of terrorism.

2. Terrorist Action often has Unintended Consequences

Most terrorist movements and individuals have notions of change with two main strands: (1) a spectacular act of violence will transform the political landscape, particularly by mobilising and radicalising the dormant masses; (2) a long terrorist campaign will wear down the adversary, leading to demoralisation, doubt and withdrawal. These are the terrorist equivalents of *blitzkrieg* and war of attrition, and just as conventional warfare often has unintended consequences, so does terrorism.

There is no doubt that some terrorist campaigns have achieved significant objectives. Certain temporary international presences have proved vulnerable to terrorist campaigns, including especially those of over-stretched colonial powers, and, more recently, of international bodies such as the United Nations. One common consequence of a sustained terrorist campaign in a particular area is that it is bad for tourism – especially when, as has happened in several attacks in the past decade, from Egypt to Indonesia, it is the tourists themselves who are targets. Yet only rarely has the discouragement of tourism been the principal goal of a terrorist movement.

Other consequences of terrorist campaigns are much more unpredictable. For example, political assassinations have very seldom had the effects for which the terrorists hoped, and more often have led to a strengthening of the regime against which they were fighting. An exhaustive study concentrating particularly on the effects of 56 assassinations of heads of government or state in the period 1919–68 concluded:

> We are dismayed by the high incidence of assassination indicated by our collected data ... We are also surprised by the fact that the impact of any single assassination, even of a chief executive or dictator, normally tends to be low.[20]

Sometimes terrorist actions lead to major consequences that are different from what the terrorists anticipated. They may lead to vigorous political or military campaigns against the terrorists, and even to the outbreak of international wars, as in Europe in 1914. According to a friend who was close to him, Gavril Princip, the 19-year-old Bosnian Serb student who killed Archduke Ferdinand in Sarajevo in June 1914, had no idea that the result of the assassination would be war, let alone world war.[21]

In some cases terrorist action has been so callous that it has aroused antagonism even among the population that has some sympathy with, even involvement in, the terrorist cause. For example, in August 1949, when communist terrorists in the Philippines murdered the popular widow of President Quezon, for the first time there was widespread

---

[20] MC Havens, C Leiden and K Schmitt, *The Politics of Assassination* (Engelwood Cliffs, NJ, Prentice-Hall, [1970]) 153.

[21] See the remarkable and detailed memoir by a fellow-student in the Young Bosnia movement who was a friend of Princip, Ratko Parezanin, *Mlada Bosna I prvi svetski rat* [*Young Bosnia and the First World War*] (Munich, Iskra, 1974). The book was published on the sixtieth anniversary of the Sarajevo assassination. A useful short report is I Macdonald, 'Sarajevo: When a Teenager with a Gun Sent the World to War', *The Times* (London), 28 June 1974, 18.

popular wrath against the insurgents.[22] Such actions can contribute to the isolation of terrorist groups. Indeed, the terrorist dream of awakening the masses through their actions has almost never worked in the way in which terrorists have perennially hoped.

Sometimes terrorists may secretly intend what appear to be unintended and even unwelcome consequences. A terrorist leader may seek to provoke a repressive response from the adversary's regime, thus exposing its supposedly true nature – the iron fist inside the velvet glove. As Lawrence Durrell wrote in *Bitter Lemons*, his rich and subtle account of the Eoka insurgency in Cyprus:

> [H]is primary objective is not battle. It is to bring down upon the community in general a reprisal for his wrongs, in the hope that the fury and resentment roused by punishment meted out to the innocent will gradually swell the ranks of those from whom he will draw further recruits.[23]

In some cases an aim may be to provoke not just government repression, but foreign military intervention. The possibility that these may be prime terrorist aims confirms the need for caution in crafting a counterterrorist policy.

3. Terrorism's Tendency to become Endemic

One of the most pernicious aspects of terrorism is its capacity to become endemic in particular regions, cultures and societies. Because of its unofficial and clandestine character, and because of the extreme bitterness it engenders within and between communities, it becomes a habit much more easily than does regular state-based warfare. The experience of terrorism suggests that, after it has been taken up in one cause, it gets adopted by others, and by splinter groups; and that it is difficult to reach a definitive end to terrorist activities. Started by the Right, it gets taken up the Left, or vice versa. Started by nationalists, it may get taken up by so-called religious fundamentalists. Started by the Stern Gang, it gets taken up by the PLO. Started by the high-minded, it gets taken up by criminals, drug-smugglers and Mafiosi. Moreover, it can be difficult to call off terrorist struggles. A hard-core splinter group within a movement may refuse all compromise; and may be able to continue the struggle because the decentralised nature of terrorist organisation and action makes that easy.

This view of terrorism as damaging to the societies in which it takes place is confirmed by the history of the Middle East, Latin America, the

---

[22]   R Asprey, *War in the Shadows: The Guerrilla in History* (London, Macdonald and Jane's, 1976) 811; drawing on ND Valeriano and CTR Bohannan, *Counter-Guerrilla Operations: The Philippine Experience* (New York, Praeger, 1962).

[23]   L Durrell, *Bitter Lemons* (London, Faber & Faber, 1956) 216.

Balkans and Ireland over the past two centuries. It forms an important buttress to moral condemnations of terrorism. An understanding of its destructive character within the societies that produce terrorist movements – which are of course the very societies that they purport to save – provides a better basis for securing international action against terrorism than do certain views of terrorism that focus on it as a threat principally to the democratic states of the West in general, or indeed to the United States in particular.

4. Capacity of Counterterrorism to Achieve Results

Contrary to myth, counterterrorist activities and policies can sometimes succeed – at least in the sense of contributing to a reduction or ending of the activities of terrorists without yielding power to them. For example, the forces opposed to terrorists/guerrillas were successful in this sense in the Huk Rebellion in the Philippines in 1946–54; in the long-running Malayan 'emergency' of 1948–60; and against the 'Red Brigades' that were active in Italy and Germany in the early 1970s. Arguably, they had a measure of success in the troubles in Northern Ireland over three decades from 1969.

Perhaps 95 per cent of the important action in any campaign against terrorism consists of intelligence and police work: identifying suspects, infiltrating movements, collaborating with police forces in other countries, gathering evidence for trials and so on. This underlying truth is far from being denied by President Bush or other leading figures involved in the 'war on terror'. However, their rhetoric, being much more that of open war and of victory, has sometimes obscured this basic fact.

5. Need to Address Underlying Grievances

While there is no simple formula for how terrorism can be undermined or defeated, the process often, perhaps even generally, requires action that is sensitive to the political environment. Where counterterrorist strategies have succeeded, success has often been in combination with a political package that either responded to certain terrorist demands while rejecting others, or undercut the terrorists by reducing their pool of political support, or both. In Malaya, for example, the promise, and the actuality, of unqualified national independence was crucial to containing the terrorist threat.

Apropos the 'war on terror', John Gaddis has reminded us that during the Cold War it was perfectly well accepted that there was a need to address social issues on which Communist propaganda played:

With the rehabilitation of Germany and Japan after World War II, together with the Marshall Plan, we fought the conditions that made the Soviet alternative attractive even as we sought to contain the Soviets themselves.[24]

It is sometimes suggested that making changes that respond in some way to terrorist demands constitutes appeasement, or at least implies recognition that a campaign of terrorism is justified. Such a suggestion is flawed. To say that a movement responds to real grievances – as for example over Palestine – is not to say that it is justified in resorting to terror, but it is to say that the terrorist movement reflects larger concerns in society that need to be addressed in some way. The exact way in which they are addressed may not be the way the movement is demanding. To refuse all changes on an issue because a terrorist movement has embraced that issue is actually to allow terrorists to dictate the political agenda.

6. Respect for a Legal Framework

Respect for law has been an important element in many operations against terrorists. One of the key figures involved in the Malayan campaign in the 1950s, Sir Robert Thompson, distilling five basic principles of counter-insurgency from this and other cases, wrote of the crucial importance of operating within a properly functioning domestic legal framework:

> The government must function in accordance with law.

> There is a very strong temptation in dealing both with terrorism and with guerrilla actions for government forces to act outside the law, the excuses being that the processes of law are too cumbersome, that the normal safeguards in the law for the individual are not designed for an insurgency and that a terrorist deserves to be treated as an outlaw anyway. Not only is this morally wrong, but, over a period, it will create more practical difficulties for a government than it solves.[25]

It is not only national legal standards that are important, but also international standards, including those embodied in the laws of war. A perception that the states involved in a coalition are observing basic international standards may contribute to public support for military operations within the member states; support (or at least tacit consent) from other states for coalition operations; and avoidance of disputes within and between coalition member states. In short, there can be strong

[24] Gaddis, 'And Now This', n 11 above at 20.

[25] R Thompson, *Defeating Communist Insurgency: Experiences from Malaya and Vietnam* (London, Chatto & Windus, 1966) 52. From 1957 to 1961 the author was successively Deputy Secretary and Secretary for Defence in Malaya. As his and other accounts make clear, in the course of the Malayan Emergency there were certain derogations from human rights standards, including detentions and compulsory relocations of villages.

prudential considerations (not necessarily dependent on reciprocity in observance of the law by all the parties to a war) that militate in favour of observing the laws of war.

There are some well-known difficulties in applying the laws of war to terrorist and counterterrorist activities. Most terrorists do not conform to the well-known requirements for the status of lawful belligerent, entitled to full prisoner-of-war (PoW) status. Further, few states could accept application of the law if it meant that all terrorists were deemed to be legitimate belligerents on a par with the regular uniformed forces of a government. However, application of the law does not require acceptance of either of these doubtful propositions. Rather it means recognition that, even in a war against ruthless terrorists, the observance of certain restraints may be legally obligatory and politically desirable – especially as regards treatment of detainees. Understandable doubt over the formal applicability of some provisions of existing law should not be turned into a licence to flout basic norms.[26]

7. Treatment of Detainees

The treatment of detainees is an issue of crucial importance in the history of terrorism and counterterrorism. Indeed, the defining moment in the birth of modern terrorism was an event in Russia in 1878 in response to the flogging of a political prisoner. This was what led a young woman, Vera Zasulich, to shoot and seriously wound General Trepov, the Police Chief of St Petersburg who had had the prisoner flogged.[27] Walter Laqueur has said of this event: 'Only in 1878, after Vera Zasulich's shooting of General Trepov, the governor of the Russian capital, did terrorism as a doctrine, the Russian version of "propaganda by the deed", finally emerge.'[28] Likewise, torture meted out in Egyptian jails from Nasser's time onwards has often been cited as part of the explanation for the emergence of radical purportedly Islamic terrorism.

When fighting an unseen and vicious enemy, who may have many secret sympathisers, all societies encounter difficulties. In such circumstances, most states, even democratic ones, resort to some form of detention without trial. This is an understandable and even necessary response, but it involves huge risks. First, there is a risk of arresting and

---

[26] For a fuller account, see A Roberts, 'The Laws of War in the War on Terror', in P Wilson (ed), *International Law and the War on Terrorism*, US Naval War College, International Law Studies, vol 79 (Newport, RI, Naval War College, 2003) 175–230.

[27] R Gaucher, *The Terrorists: From Tsarist Russia to the OAS*, trs Paula Spurlin (London, Secker & Warburg, 1968) 10–11.

[28] Laqueur, *Age of Terrorism*, n 16 above at 33.

convicting the wrong people; and second, the maltreatment of detainees. Both tend to create martyrs and to give nourishment to the terrorist campaign.

The United Kingdom's long engagement against terrorism in Northern Ireland from 1969 onwards affords ample evidence for both these propositions, and it also points in the direction of a possible solution. This was one of many conflicts in which those deemed to be 'terrorists' were aware of the value, including propaganda value, of making claims to PoW status and publicising claims of ill-treatment. While denying that there was an armed conflict, whether international or otherwise, and strongly resisting any granting of PoW status to detainees and convicted prisoners, the United Kingdom did slowly come to accept that they had a distinct status, and that international standards had to apply to their treatment. After initially using methods that were legally questionable and highly controversial, from March 1972 onwards the United Kingdom adopted a different approach, in effect applying basic legal principles derived from the laws of war. This helped in the long and difficult process of taking some of the political sting out of the emotionally charged issue of treatment of detainees.[29]

The treatment of detainees and prisoners has been one of the major failures of the 'war on terror' ever since it began in late 2001. In January 2002 US Secretary of Defense Donald Rumsfeld infamously said of the prisoners in Guantanamo:

> I do not feel even the slightest concern over their treatment. They are being treated vastly better than they treated anybody else over the last several years and vastly better than was their circumstance when they were found.[30]

Needless to say, this and similar remarks were widely broadcast on radio and TV stations critical of the United States. The episodes of maltreatment and torture in Iraq since April 2003 have reinforced the damage. Those who suggest that humane treatment is a relatively unimportant issue – and those far fewer individuals who argue that torturing prisoners is a way to combat terrorism – do need to address the criticism that ill-treatment and torture have in the past provided purported justifications for the resort to terrorism, and also discredited the anti-terrorist cause.

---

[29]   The key document in this process was Lord Gardiner's minority report in *Report of the Committee of Privy Counsellors Appointed to Consider Authorized Procedures for the Interrogation of Persons Suspected of Terrorism*, Cmnd 4901 (London, HMSO, March 1972). His minority report was accepted by the government, as announced by Prime Minister Edward Heath in the House of Commons on 2 March 1972: *Hansard*, House of Commons, 2 March 1972, cols 743–4.

[30]   Donald Rumsfeld roundtable with radio media, 15 January 2002, available at <http://www.defenselink.mil /transcripts/2002/t01152002_t0115sdr.html>.

8. Evil versus Error

In the history of both terrorism and counterterrorism there has long been a temptation to depict the adversary as evil. In terrorist movements, many otherwise decent and serious individuals have been seduced by the simple and attractive notion of the power of the deed: that a cleansing act of violence can rid the world of uniquely evil forces. This belief of many terrorists that their goals will be achieved by spectacular acts of violence is the central error of their philosophy.

In counterterrorist operations, the depiction of the adversary as evil, while it may faithfully reflect understandable feelings in a society under terrorist assault, poses severe practical problems. One hazard of treating terrorism as a problem of evil is that many people in the population from whom the terrorists come will know that such an explanation is too simple. They will have a broader idea of the mixture of characteristic traits that can make a terrorist: idealism, self-sacrifice, naiveté, hope, despair, ignorance, short-sightedness, thuggishness, hatred, sadism, cleverness and stupidity. The population may have sympathy with the cause for which the terrorists stand but not with the method. If the terrorist group is described as simply 'evil', the population will therefore be further alienated from the anti-terrorist cause, which they will see as depending on a caricature that they do not recognise.

In the struggle against terrorism, it may be most useful to conceive of terrorism as a problem not so much of extreme evil (although it may involve that), but rather of dangerously wrong conduct and ideas. The difference in approach – the view of terrorism more as a dangerous idea and as morally reprehensible than as absolute evil – has significant implications for how terrorist campaigns may be opposed, and how they may end.[31]

9. Similarities between Terrorists and Some of their Opponents

A student of the history of terrorism cannot help being struck by certain similarities between terrorists and at least some of their opponents. Both share not only a vision of the world as a struggle of good versus evil, but also a belief that particular new weapons and tactics now give an opportunity to strike directly at the heart of the adversary's power. Russian terrorists in the nineteenth century believed that their new and

---

[31] The problematic character of defining the 'war on terror' as one of good versus evil is recognized in Talbott and Chanda, *The Age of Terror*, n 11 above at xiv.

quite accurate weapons – the pistol, the rifle and the bomb – could enable them to attack the source of all evil (namely the Tsar) directly and with limited side-effects.[32]

The similarity between so-called terrorists and their adversaries was noted by Régis Debray in his little-known novel *Undesirable Alien*. In this remarkably unsentimental view of his fellow revolutionaries in Latin America, he mocks his comrades in the struggle for having a taste for cowboy films, and suggests that red revolutionaries may be propounding nothing more than the ideology of the American western.[33] Sadly, events have moved on since then, and it is the Hollywood disaster movie that is emulated by Osama bin Laden and his colleagues.[34] The general philosophy of radical Islam also has Californian roots due to the presence there in the 1950s of its founding father, Sayyid Qutb.[35]

In the 'war on terror', a vision of clean and well-targeted war against dictatorial regimes has informed much US policy-making. As George Bush put it in his infamous (because premature) 'Mission Accomplished' speech on 1 May 2003:

> In the images of falling statues, we have witnessed the arrival of a new era. For a hundred of years of war, culminating in the nuclear age, military technology was designed and deployed to inflict casualties on an ever-growing scale. In defeating Nazi Germany and Imperial Japan, Allied forces destroyed entire cities, while enemy leaders who started the conflict were safe until the final days. Military power was used to end a regime by breaking a nation.

> Today, we have the greater power to free a nation by breaking a dangerous and aggressive regime. With new tactics and precision weapons, we can achieve military objectives without directing violence against civilians. No device of man can remove the tragedy from war; yet it is a great moral advance when the guilty have far more to fear from war than the innocent.[36]

---

[32]   Laqueur, *Age of Terrorism*, n 16 above at 36–8.

[33]   R Debray, *Undesirable Alien*, trs Rosemary Sheed (London, Allen Lane, 1978) 121, 123 and 172; first published as *L'Indésirable* (Paris, Editions du Seuil, 1975).

[34]   This may be literally true, although reports of information by detainees given during interrogation need to be treated with extreme caution. According to numerous reports, Abu Zubaydah (a Palestinian captured in Pakistan in 2002 who was allegedly Osama bin Laden's chief of operations) told his interrogators in Guantanamo that terrorists might be taking clues from the film *Godzilla*, which had been remade in 1998 and showed a monster attack on Brooklyn Bridge and the Statue of Liberty: T Maier, 'Has FBI Cried Wolf Too Often?' *Insight on the News*, 5 August 2002, available at <http://www.insightmag.com/news/2002/08/26>.

[35]   On possible connections between southern California and religious radicalism see the brief references in M Ruthven, *Fundamentalism: The Search for Meaning* (Oxford, Oxford University Press, 2004) 10 and 38. Sayyid Qutb (1906–66), when he was in California in the 1950s, was deeply influenced by the Western culture that he opposed as degenerate and corrupt.

[36]   President George W Bush, Remarks from the *USS Abraham Lincoln* at sea off the coast of San Diego, California, 1 May 2003.

This vision of the 2003 Iraq War as a more or less clinical excision of an evil regime looks to have been a desert mirage – just as many terrorist visions of achieving change through violence have also led to disappointment.

10. How Past Terrorist Campaigns Ended

A decisive result is seldom encountered in counterterrorist struggles. There is a need for much broader understanding, based on historical evidence, of how terrorist campaigns do in fact end.[37] The processes – some of them deeply flawed – by which terrorist campaigns end usually include debilitating losses to the terrorist movement caused by military action, arrests and trials. However, they can also involve any or all of the following five elements:

First, *awareness on the part of terrorist movements that they are being defeated politically, or at least are not making gains.* The actions of terrorists usually fail to arouse the masses: indeed, they frequently cause antagonism in the very population whose support is sought. Such failures can often lead to defections and splits, and to a political decision by all or part of a terrorist movement or its political allies to move to a different phase of struggle or of political action. For example, on 1 October 1951 the Malayan Communist Party formally decided to end the armed struggle – an important moment in the long process of the winding-down of the terrorist campaign that had started in 1948. A more indecisive indication of the end of a campaign occurred in Spain in 2004–7. In November 2004 it was reported that six senior members of the Basque separatist group ETA had called on the organisation from their prison cells to lay down its arms. In their letter they stated: 'Our political-military strategy has been overcome by repression ... It is not a question of fixing the rear-view mirror or a burst tyre. It is the motor that does not work.' This letter was 'the closest ETA members had come to recognising that, after more than 30 years in which it has killed more than 800 people, the group is facing defeat'.[38] On 24 March 2006 ETA announced a 'permanent ceasefire' to end its campaign of violence, but on 6 June 2007 it declared this ceasefire over: this is a typical example of the twists and turns that are often involved in the ending, or otherwise, of terrorist campaigns.

---

[37] A useful distillation of conclusions on how terrorist campaigns end may be found in A Guelke, *The Age of Terrorism and the International Political System* (London, IB Tauris, 1995) 180–81. See also A Kurth Cronin, *How Terrorism Ends: Lessons from the Decline and Demise of Terrorist Campaigns* (Princeton, NJ, Princeton University Press, forthcoming, late 2008).

[38] G Tremlett, 'Old Guard Urges End to Eta Terror', *The Guardian* (London), 3 November 2004, 15.

Second, *recognition by governments which organised or assisted terrorism that they must renounce this method of pursuing a cause.* Such recognition may sometimes (as in the case of Libya in 2003) be coupled with compensation to the families of victims of terrorist acts.

Third, *the amelioration of conditions in order to weaken the strength and legitimacy of the terrorist movement's support.* Such amelioration is something in which Messianic terrorists have no interest. It may include a change in the political context, which sidesteps some of the issues that provided grist to the mill of the terrorist movement, provides new opportunities for pursuing its aims in a different manner, or emphasises a new range of attainable goals of general appeal, for example in the field of human rights.

Fourth, *the holding of genuine multi-party elections.* Democratic procedures, especially where there are safeguards for minorities, can undercut terrorist claims to speak for a specific nation or section of society.

Fifth, *a shared awareness of stalemate, giving both sides a possible incentive to reach a negotiated or tacit settlement involving mutual concessions.* This may encompass a recognition by its adversaries that the terrorist movement, however criminal its actions, did represent a serious cause and constituency – leading to a reluctant acceptance that certain concessions should be made to some positions held by terrorists.

Sometimes terrorist campaigns wind down rather than end. They may degenerate into mafia-like activities, including kidnappings for ransom, drug trafficking and bank robberies. Or a few terrorist leaders, hidden in a jungle or a city, maintain their faith, even continue to plot or to detonate the occasional bomb, but lose completely their following and their impact.[39]

In some cases the combatants, or at least a proportion of them, may be retrained. This happened in Guatemala following the civil war of the 1980s and 1990s. The former Marxist guerrillas, who had been called terrorists by their enemies, received extensive retraining at a centre in Quetzaltenango. When I visited it in 1997, the work of the centre, supported mainly by European funds, appeared to be effective, the main concern being whether there would be jobs for the suitably retrained guerrillas.

A general conclusion follows: that terrorist campaigns, while they may go on for a long time, do eventually end; and do so not because every last terrorist is captured or killed, or because they are comprehensively

[39]   In 1987, nearly 40 years after the declaration of a state of emergency in Malaya, and over 35 years after the Malayan Communist Party had publicly announced its decision to end the armed struggle, some 600 guerrillas laid down their arms and started a new life as farmers in southern Thailand. M Fathers, 'Communist "Bandits" Lay Down Arms in Malaysia' *The Independent* (London), 8 June 1987.

defeated in military operations, or because there is a clear victory, but rather because terrorism is seen for what it is: a highly problematic means of bringing about change. It cannot be the sole basis for a movement, it often damages the very people in whose name it is waged, and it may burn itself out or backfire on its own authors.

III. THE 'WAR ON TERROR'

The major pronouncements of what has been variously termed in official US speeches the 'war against terrorism' and the 'war on terror' have been self-consciously historic in character; they have enunciated historically novel and ambitious goals; but have contained only limited reference to the history of terrorism and counterterrorism. In his address to Congress nine days after the destruction of the Twin Towers in New York, President George W Bush stated:

> Our war on terror begins with al Qaeda, but it does not end there. It will not end until every terrorist group of global reach has been found, stopped and defeated …
>
> Americans are asking: 'How will we fight and win this war?' We will direct every resource at our command – every means of diplomacy, every tool of intelligence, every instrument of law enforcement, every financial influence, and every necessary weapon of war – to the disruption and to the defeat of the global terror network.[40]

At the end of September 2001 President Bush added, in a radio address:

> Our war on terror will be much broader than the battlefields and beachheads of the past. This war will be fought wherever terrorists hide, or run, or plan. Some victories will be won outside of public view, in tragedies avoided and threats eliminated. Other victories will be clear to all.[41]

The term 'war' is not being used here in a purely rhetorical sense, as in the 'war on drugs' or 'war on poverty'. It has such a rhetorical side, but is being used to describe a notably broad and multi-faceted overall campaign of a type that is essentially new, and that includes major military operations (starting with Afghanistan) as one important aspect. In respect of both aspects of the war – the visible and the invisible – what is sought is 'victory'.

---

[40] President George W Bush, Speech to Congress, 20 September 2001.
[41] President George W Bush, 'Radio Address to the Nation', 29 September 2001, available at <http://www.whitehouse.gov/news/releases/2001/09/>.

The most important subsequent articulation of the 'war on terror' was the February 2003 White House document, *National Strategy for Combating Terrorism*. This began by emphasising the unique nature of the current threat:

> The struggle against international terrorism is different from any other war in our history. We will not triumph solely or even primarily through military might. We must fight terrorist networks, and all those who support their efforts to spread fear around the world, using every instrument of national power – diplomatic, economic, law enforcement, financial, information, intelligence, and military.[42]

The oft-repeated claim of uniqueness has provided a justification for much of the rhetoric and strategic direction of the 'war on terror', and has provided, too, an implied justification for making little more than ritual reference to earlier history. However, the February 2003 document did contain at least a nod to history: 'Americans know that terrorism did not begin on September 11, 2001.' It continued: 'For decades, the United States and our friends abroad have waged the long struggle against the terrorist menace. We have learned much from these efforts.' In particular, past successes in destroying or neutralising various movements that had been active in the 1970s and 1980s 'provide valuable lessons for the future'.[43], the document was unclear about exactly what terrorist movements were being referred to, and about what lessons had been learned.

Subsequent articulations of US doctrine offered little further reference to the history of terrorism and counterterrorism.[44] The most extraordinary omission in most US statements in the 'war on terror', at least up to 2006, is the lack of reference to the existing US counter-insurgency doctrine, and the reluctance to embrace it even when faced with an insurgency in Iraq. By contrast, the UK military view tends to be that counter-insurgency doctrine is a principal basis of addressing terrorism.

Has the international campaign against terrorism achieved the historically unique breadth of international support that Bush has sought? It was framed from the start as a campaign on a broad front, involving a large number of countries – but at the same time it was always as a US-led operation. Bush's words in his 20 September 2001 speech reflected this duality:

---

[42] The White House, *National Strategy for Combating Terrorism* (Washington, DC, February 2003) at 1.

[43] *Ibid* at 5.

[44] See eg the subsequent version of The White House, *National Strategy for Combating Terrorism* (Washington, DC, September 2006).

Every nation, in every region, now has a decision to make. Either you are with us, or you are with the terrorists. From this day forward, any nation that continues to harbor or support terrorism will be regarded by the United States as a hostile regime.[45]

In 2001–02 the variety and extent of international support for the campaign against terrorism was remarkable. As the US State Department pointed out in March 2002, 136 countries offered some form of military assistance, 46 multilateral organisations issued declarations of support, and three treaty bodies (NATO, the OAS and ANZUS) invoked their collective defence treaty obligations with the United States.[46]

Despite the extensive evidence of international support, including in such delicate matters as sharing intelligence and cooperation between police forces, the idea that the 'war on terror' was a universal project, in which all states could join the United States, ran into trouble. First was the awkward and unavoidable fact that different countries see the world differently. Many had doubts about a war on terror that relied so extensively on military force and did not, at least in its early stages, address underlying grievances with the same level of determination. Second, there was a major difficulty in the particular way in which the US leadership in this struggle was presented. Many were antagonised by the blunt and US-centred approach of: 'Either you are with us, or you are with the terrorists.' Third, several NATO members were offended by aspects of US policy: in 2001, the apparent lack of US response to NATO's unprecedented invocation of Article V, bringing collective self-defence into play; from 2001 onwards, growing concern about the US handling of questions regarding the status and treatment of detainees; and from 2003 onwards, increasing dissatisfaction with US policy on Iraq.

A. Can Military Interventions be Effective against Terrorism?

In countries faced with terrorist attacks, there are often strong reasons for attacking terrorism at what is seen as its source. A state that allows terrorists to organise on its territory to wage operations elsewhere is naturally the object of suspicion, and may well be thought to deserve whatever it gets. Yet in the 'war on terror' the question of military intervention has proved extremely divisive.

---

[45] President George W Bush, Address to a Joint Session of Congress and the American People, Washington, DC, 20 September 2001. The peroration added that 'God is not neutral'.

[46] US State Department, 'Boucher Summarizes International Support for War on Terrorism', 1 March 2002; cited in M Sheehan, 'Diplomacy', in A Kurth Cronin and J Ludes (eds), *Attacking Terrorism: Elements of a Grand Strategy* (Washington, DC, Georgetown University Press, 2004) 107.

Counterterrorist operations, when taking the form of open war and a conventional military response, have often led to tragedy. The First World War began when the assassination of Archduke Ferdinand in Sarajevo in June 1914 by a young Serbian nationalist led to an Austrian determination to root out the 'hornet's nest' that was Serbia. Similarly, Israel's disastrous intervention in Lebanon in 1982 was explicitly a response to a persistent and intense pattern of terrorist attacks on Israeli and Jewish targets not only in Israel but also internationally.

It is not surprising, therefore, that historians have generally been sceptical about waging war as a response to terrorist acts. However, they tend to be admirably discriminate: more sceptical than dogmatic. Two or three months after 11 September 2001, the American historian Paul Schroeder wrote:

> Three lessons emerge from reasoning by historical analogy from the early summer of 1914 to the late summer of 2001. The first is that a great power must avoid giving terrorists the war they want, but that the great power does not want. The second is that a great power must reckon the effects of its actions not only on its immediate circumstances, but also with regard to the larger structure of international politics in which it clearly has a significant stake. The third is that a great power must beware the risks of victory as well as the dangers of defeat. If it is not careful and wise, the United States could find itself enmeshed even deeper in the Middle East and Southwest Asia than it is today, and risk generating greater prospective dangers in the process of containing smaller near-term ones.[47]

He drew a crucial distinction between Afghanistan, where the war had a legitimate objective and was widely understood internationally, and other possible target countries, including Iraq.[48] Within 18 months of this warning, the United States was deeply involved in Iraq in exactly the way he had feared, with no prospect of an early exit. He was right that the two cases, and the nature of the US involvements in them, were very different, both in the justifiability of the intervention and in the consequences that followed.

1. Afghanistan: War and its Aftermath

The first major engagement of the 'war on terror', *Operation Enduring Freedom*, which encompassed the US-led coalition military operations in and around Afghanistan that began on 7 October 2001, was widely

[47]   P Schroeder, 'The Risks of Victory: An Historian's Provocation' (Winter 2001–2) 66 *The National Interest* (Washington, DC) at 22.
[48]   *Ibid* at 28–9. See also his article warning against the likely effects of an attack in the Middle East, 'Iraq: The Case Against Preemptive War' (October 2002) 8(20) *The American Conservative*, available at <http://www.amconmag.com/10_21/iraq.html>.

viewed as a justifiable use of force – a term greatly preferable to the more familiar term 'just war'. It had a great deal of diplomatic support, and received significant legitimation from resolutions passed at the United Nations.[49] There appeared to be no other means of stopping the activities of Al Qaeda, protected as they were by the Taliban regime. The war did result in a victory – at least of sorts. By the end of the year, the Taliban regime had gone, replaced by the Afghan Interim Authority, and then in June 2002 by the Afghan Transitional Government. Between January 2002 and mid-2007, according to the UN High Commissioner for Refugees (UNHCR), more than 4.8 million refugees have returned to Afghanistan (mainly from Pakistan and Iran), and in addition another half million internally displaced have returned to their homes. This is an astonishing achievement. Afghanistan has been UNHCR's largest repatriation operation worldwide for five consecutive years.[50] Although the return of refugees was not the main objective of the campaign – and the capture of the main Al Qaeda leaders, which was an objective, was *not* achieved – this huge refugee return was evidence that the 'war on terror' could achieve at least some positive effects, by helping to depose a reactionary, oppressive and thoroughly dangerous regime. The remarkably successful presidential election on 9 October 2004 provided a further small sign of progress in post-war Afghanistan.

On the first day of the US bombing campaign in Afghanistan, Donald Rumsfeld said of the Taliban: 'Ultimately they're going to collapse from within. That is what will constitute victory.'[51] That is what happened in November and December 2001. Some were critical of the fact that the main achievement was regime change. Richard Clarke, the White House counterterrorism specialist, criticised the otherwise successful handling of the Afghan war on the grounds that 'we treated the war as a regime change rather than as a search-and-destroy against terrorists'.[52]

---

[49] While no UN Security Council resolution specifically authorised the US-led military operations in Afghanistan, several resolutions passed both before and after 11 September 2001 provided a significant degree of support for such action. Resolution 1189 of 13 August 1998 had emphasised the responsibility of Afghanistan to stop terrorist activities on its territory. Resolution 1368 of 12 September 2001 recognised 'the inherent right of individual or collective self-defence in accordance with the Charter', condemned the attacks of the previous day, and stated that the Council 'regards such acts, like any act of international terrorism, as a threat to international peace and security'. It also expressed the Council's 'readiness to take all necessary steps to respond to the terrorist attacks of 11 September 2001, and to combat all forms of terrorism'. These key points were reiterated in Resolution 1373 of 28 September 2001, which additionally placed numerous requirements on all states to bring the problem of terrorism under control.

[50] See <ww.unhcr.org/afghan.html>, visited 8 August 2007.

[51] Rumsfeld, cited in news report by B Knowlton, *International Herald Tribune* (London), 8 October 2001, 1.

[52] R Clarke, *Against All Enemies: Inside America's War on Terror* (London, Simon & Schuster UK, 2004) 274.

Three unique facts enabled the Afghan campaign to succeed: (1) the Taliban regime was weak both within Afghanistan and internationally; (2) the fanatical character of the bombing of the World Trade Centre, and the persuasive evidence of links to Afghanistan, contributed to the Taliban's loss of allies, especially Pakistan, and also meant that the world accepted the legitimate element of self-defence in the US-led campaign; and (3) the role on the ground of the US-supported forces of the Northern Alliance enabled the US-led bombing campaign to be effective rather than merely punitive, and then provided a basis for post-war administration.

In respect of Afghanistan some historians doubted whether any positive result could be achieved in the US-led campaign in late 2001. They could and in some cases did point out, very reasonably, that Afghanistan is not a country in which foreign armed forces have ever had a happy time; that there is good reason to be cautious about the prospects of changing Afghanistan's violent political culture; and that there are problems in waging a bombing campaign against so devious and elusive a target as a terrorist movement.

Sir Michael Howard, former Regius Professor of History at Oxford, criticised the Afghan war during its opening phase, when its main aspect was bombing rather than support for ground forces. In a lecture in London on 30 October 2001 (and subsequently published in *Foreign Affairs*) he said that it would be 'like trying to eradicate cancer cells with a blow-torch'.[53] Three months later, in a thoughtful reappraisal, he said: 'I got it wrong, and I apologize.'[54] Yet in a broader sense he did not get it entirely wrong. Historians have good reasons to be sceptical about the efficacy of military interventions as a response to terrorist campaigns. Howard's vivid image of hazardous use of the blow-torch may fit other cases, including Iraq since 2003, better than it fitted Afghanistan. Moreover, by 2007 Afghanistan itself was the scene of a growing insurgency movement in the South that threatened to undo some of the achievements of the period since the 2001 intervention.

2. Iraq: War and its Aftermath

The Iraq war of 2003 provides a very different context for exploring the question of whether invasion of states believed to assist terrorism is an effective way to achieve the aims of a counterterrorist policy. The rhetoric

---

[53]   M Howard, Lecture in London on 30 October 2001, reported in T Branigan, 'Al-Qaida is Winning War, Allies Warned', *The Guardian* (London), 31 October 2001. The lecture was the basis of M Howard, 'What's in a Name?', n 16 above.

[54]   His reappraisal was in 'September 11 and After: Reflections on the War Against Terrorism', Lecture at University College London, 29 January 2002.

of the 'war on terror', with its emphasis on open war, may be part of the explanation of the US-led assault on Iraq in 2003. In his television address of 17 March 2003 presenting Saddam Hussein with an ultimatum to get out of Iraq within 48 hours, President Bush included the statement that Iraq had 'aided, trained and harbored terrorists, including operatives of al-Qaeda'.[55] Yet in reality Iraq's links to Al Qaeda up to March 2003 appear to have been very limited. There were some Iraqi connections with terrorists, especially those involved in the Arab–Israel conflict, but Iraq does not appear to have had any significant part in the ruthless campaign of international terrorist attacks for which Al Qaeda had been seen as responsible. Within the US government, there was already in early 2003 some official awareness that the accusation of the link between Iraq and al-Qaeda was weak. When on 20 March 2003 the US government gave to the UN Security Council a letter containing its justification for attacking Iraq, the letter dealt exclusively with Iraq's non-compliance with a range of UN Security Council resolutions on weapons issues. Terrorism was not even mentioned.[56]

Against this background, it is peculiar that the US government called the war in Iraq part of the 'war on terror', and issued medals for both the Afghanistan and Iraq campaigns which are called 'the Global War on Terrorism Expeditionary Medal' (for those who served in Afghanistan or Iraq) and 'the Global War on Terrorism Service Medal' (for those whose service was elsewhere). Naturally, critics objected that the administration was 'subtly using the single campaign medal to buttress its contention that the war in Iraq was undertaken as part of the worldwide battle against al Qaeda and other Islamic extremists'.[57]

Overall, the Iraq war has done more harm than good to the US and UK efforts to combat terrorism. The principal criticisms of the use of force in Iraq are that certain of the stated grounds for going to war (especially violations of the UN resolutions on disarmament) have proved to be weak; that the planning for the aftermath of war was so feeble; that the results of the war have proved so violent; and that a perception has arisen that Western countries seek to force Muslim populations into a single, externally imposed political template: a perception that damages efforts at coalition building.[58] Historians were right to warn, as Professor

---

[55] President George W Bush, Speech from the White House, 17 March 2003.

[56] The stated reason for going to war in March 2003 was 'Iraq's continued material breaches of its disarmament obligations under relevant Security Council resolutions': Letter dated 20 March 2003 from the Permanent Representative of the USA, John Negroponte, to the President of the UN Security Council.

[57] V Loeb, 'Medals Couple Two Conflicts: Critics Seek Separate Awards for Afghanistan, Iraq Fighting' *Washington Post*, 6 January 2004.

[58] J Stevenson, *Counter-Terrorism: Containment and Beyond*, IISS Adelphi Paper 367 (Oxford, Oxford University Press, October 2004) 108–13.

Michael Howard did in interviews in March 2003, that Iraq might be easy to defeat in a military campaign, but would be difficult to occupy and administer. At least in terms of the struggle against terrorism, the results so far of the Iraq war appear to be distressingly negative. There is much force in the criticism of Robert Tucker and David Hendrickson:

> The pattern of the first Iraq war, in which an overwhelming victory set aside the reservations of most skeptics, has failed to emerge in the aftermath of the second. If anything, skepticism has deepened.[59]

The presence and role of foreign (mainly US) armed forces in Iraq is regularly cited as justification for terrorist bombings, kidnappings and executions there, and also in other countries. Critics seized on this point. As Richard Clarke argued, Bush 'launched an unnecessary and costly war in Iraq that strengthened the fundamentalist, radical Islamic terrorist movement worldwide'.[60]

There are, to be sure, grounds for questioning the generally negative picture of the results of the Iraq war. Within Iraq, the removal from office of Saddam Hussein was widely welcomed, and some still retain the hope that a stable democratic order can emerge slowly from the twisted wreckage of his brutal regime. The elections in January 2005, with participation of close to 60 per cent of those entitled to vote, strengthened hopes that something could be salvaged from the country's disasters. Outside Iraq, the war may have helped to induce an element of prudence in the conduct of policy of some governments.

One possible case is Libya. In December 2003 Colonel Gaddafi made his decision to bring Libya in from the cold, confirming his renunciation both of terrorism and of ambitions to develop nuclear weapons. Whether his decision owed anything to the Iraq war is debated. Although the process which bore fruit in December had begun long before the initiation of hostilities in Iraq in March 2003, it is possible that seeing a fellow Arab leader unceremoniously deposed may have helped to concentrate Gaddafi's mind. At the very least the Iraq war did not foreclose a highly significant policy development in Libya. That is a small and somewhat speculative consolation for a war whose effects have been so overwhelmingly negative.

3. UK and US Doctrine on Military Intervention

The sobering consequences of the 2003 intervention in Iraq suggest a need to revisit the argument that attack is the best form of defence – an

---

[59]   R Tucker and D Hendrickson, 'The Sources of American Legitimacy' (November/December 2004) 83(6) *Foreign Affairs* 18.
[60]   Clarke, *Against All Enemies*, n 52 above at x.

argument that had been expressed in two key documents of the 'war on terror', both issued in 2002. The UK *Strategic Defence Review: A New Chapter* said: 'Experience shows that it is better where possible, to engage an enemy at longer range, before they get the opportunity to mount an assault on the UK.'[61] There has never been any indication that this statement was based on consideration of any actual cases. As for the US government, *The National Security Strategy of the United States* commits it to attack terrorist organisations by 'convincing or compelling states to accept their sovereign responsibilities'.[62] The implication here is that states will not get rid of terrorists on their soil, the United States will do it for them. The argument is buttressed by the more fundamental ideas that lack of democracy is a principal cause of terrorism, and that a forcible intervention could lead to the growth of a stable democratic system.

In addition to the questions about the circumstances in which democracy can be imposed from outside, there are three serious grounds of criticism of the proposition that terrorism should be attacked at source rather than warded off defensively.

First, *it is a false choice.* However desirable it may be to engage the enemy at longer range, there is no substitute for defensive anti-terrorist and counterterrorist activities. Granted the imperfections of intelligence, the multiplicity of possible sources of attack, and the hazards of taking military action against sovereign states, it may not always be possible, or sensible, to attack terrorism at its source. Meanwhile, much can be done at home to reduce the risk of terrorist attack. The astonishing casualness of US airport security before 11 September 2001 illustrates the point.

Second, *the history of counterterrorist operations suggests no such simple conclusion.* True, some counterterrorist operations have involved military action in states perceived to be the sources of, or providers of support to, terrorist movements. However, by no means all have been successful. Furthermore, many counterterrorist campaigns have been effectively conducted with only limited capacity to engage the enemy at longer range. For example, the UK and Malayan governments had to engage in the long struggle against terrorism without attacking the People's Republic of China (PRC), despite the fact that the PRC was aiding and abetting the Communist Terrorist movement in Malaya from 1949 onwards. Similarly, the UK government had to deal with terrorism in Northern Ireland without resorting to military action in the Republic of Ireland,

[61] UK Ministry of Defence, *The Strategic Defence Review: A New Chapter*, Cm 5566, vols I and II (London, HMSO, July 2002) vol I at 9.
[62] The White House, *The National Security Strategy of the United States of America* (Washington, DC, September 2002) at 6.

despite claims that the Provisional IRA was deriving benefit from resources and support there – not to mention from communities in the United States.

Third, *it is a recipe for a revival of imperialism*. Military intervention in states in order to eliminate the sources of terrorism must inevitably mean, in many cases, exercising external domination for a period of decades. This was the pattern of much European colonialism in the nineteenth century, including in Egypt. By a perverse paradox, external control, intended to stop terrorism in its tracks, frequently has the effect of provoking it and providing a ready-made justification for it.

Paul Schroeder has argued persuasively that the United States can legitimately and sensibly aim to exercise hegemony, but it is ill advised to lunge, on the basis of blinkered historical ignorance, into the mirage of empire. His conclusion is that America's leaders, because they are ignorant of the past, are actually stumbling backwards into it:

What they are now attempting therefore is not a bold, untried American experiment in creating a brave new world, but a revival of a type of nineteenth and early-twentieth century imperialism that could succeed for a time then (with ultimately devastating consequences) only because of conditions long since vanished and now impossible to imagine reproducing. Launched now, this venture will fail and is already failing. Its advocates illustrate the dictum that those unwilling to learn from history are doomed to repeat it.[63]

Any assessment of the US and UK doctrines of intervention in response to terrorism has to differentiate between cases. On both legal and prudential grounds, there was a stronger case for intervention in Afghanistan than in Iraq. In particular, there was a real chance of reducing by such means Afghanistan's involvement in terrorism. Any assessment must also be provisional, as eventual outcomes will necessarily affect judgements of the interventions. However, what is clear is that there was a curious and historically uninformed optimism about the Iraq venture, which led to a lack of planning for those traditional consequences of distant empires – military occupation and counter-insurgency.

---

[63]   P Schroeder, 'The Mirage of Empire Versus the Promise of Hegemony', in P Schroeder, *Systems, Stability and Statecraft: Essays on the International History of Modern Europe*, D Wetzel, R Jervis and J Levy (eds) (New York and Basingstoke, Palgrave Macmillan, 2004) 305.

B. How is the 'War on Terror' supposed to End?

1. The Bush Administration's Vision

The advocates of the 'war on terror' offer a limited vision of how the war might end. The focus is more on victory than other visions of possible endings, but it is victory of a special kind. Some elements of it were outlined in the White House *National Security Strategy* document of September 2002[64]; and they were further elaborated in the White House doctrinal statement of February 2003:

> Victory against terrorism will not occur as a single, defining moment. It will not be marked by the likes of the surrender ceremony on the deck of the USS Missouri that ended World War II. However, through the sustained effort to compress the scope and capability of terrorist organizations, isolate them regionally, and destroy them within state borders, the United States and its friends and allies will secure a world in which our children can live free from fear and where the threat of terrorist attacks does not define our daily lives.

> Victory, therefore, will be secured only as long as the United States and the international community maintain their vigilance and work tirelessly to prevent terrorists from inflicting horrors like those of September 11, 2001.[65]

In his State of the Union address on 3 February 2005, President Bush, while referring to the importance of 'eliminating the conditions that feed radicalism and ideologies of murder', reiterated the key central conception of offensive action as the main way to defeat terrorism: 'Our country is still the target of terrorists who want to kill many, and intimidate us all – and we will stay on the offensive against them, until the fight is won.'

Such glimpses of how victory might come about are essentially schematic and prescriptive rather than historical. They have an abstract and euphemistic quality. Because they leave little room for complexity, they have enabled some individuals to focus on the idea of destruction more than other possible mechanisms. When Timothy Garton Ash asked a very high US administration official how the 'war on terror' would end, he received the answer: 'With the elimination of the terrorists.'[66]

Such simple prescriptive views of how a terrorist campaign should end are also to be found in a book by two supporters of the Bush administration, David Frum and Richard Perle. Published in 2003, *An End to Evil: How to Win the War on Terror* is modestly described by its authors as 'a

---

[64] The White House, *National Security Strategy of the United States*, 2002 version, at 5–7.

[65] The White House, *National Strategy for Combating Terrorism*, 2003 version, at 12. This was the text under the heading 'Victory in the War against Terror'.

[66] This *answer* was given by a senior administration official in Washington, DC, on 10 December 2002, as reported in T Garton Ash, *Free World: Why a Crisis of the West Reveals the Opportunity of our Time* (London and New York, Allen Lane, 2004) 126.

manual for victory'.[67] This paean of praise for Bush's anti-terrorist policy is also a diatribe against all those allies and bureaucrats who fail to support it properly: 'While our enemies plot, our allies dither and carp, and much of our government remains ominously unready for the fight.'[68] What does it say about how terrorist campaigns end? Virtually nothing. In true American fashion, this is a 'How to' book which is full of hectoring instruction but which gives no clue about how terrorist campaigns actually end.

2. UK Policy to Eliminate Terrorism as a Force in International Affairs

On the ending of terrorist campaigns, UK policy is subtly different from that of the United States. It is also flawed, but in a different way. The key UK statement of doctrine about terrorism, published in July 2002, *The Strategic Defence Review: A New Chapter*, says that the goal of the government's efforts is 'to eliminate terrorism as a force in international affairs'.[69] This is a carefully thought-out phrase, and of course it is properly recognised that 'countering terrorism is usually a long-term business requiring the roots and causes to be addressed as well as the symptoms'.[70] Nonetheless, there are two main disadvantages to proclaiming as a goal 'the elimination of terrorism as a force in international affairs'.

First, *terrorism is notoriously difficult to 'eliminate'*. The proclamation of this goal is not only unrealistic, but it also undermines one of the strongest arguments against terrorism – namely that, once started, it easily becomes endemic. The unofficial, decentralised, and hydra-headed character of terrorism provides the main explanation for the difficulty of eliminating it.

Second, *if 'elimination' is the proclaimed goal, then every subsequent terrorist incident represents a victory for the terrorists*. The United Kingdom faced this problem in Northern Ireland. A number of government pronouncements in the 1970s and early 1980s had indicated the United Kingdom's aim was the complete ending of terrorist activity. Thereafter, every terrorist assault, including the IRA's mainland campaign, had a possible added bonus of 'proving' that the government had failed to achieve its proclaimed goal. Eventually the United Kingdom's aims were restated in more modest terms as being the reduction of terrorist activities: this was

---

[67]   D Frum and R Perle, *An End to Evil: How to Win the War on Terror* (New York, Random House, [2003]) 9.

[68]   *Ibid* at 4.

[69]   UK Ministry of Defence, *New Chapter*, n 61 above, vol I, at 4 and 7.

[70]   *Ibid* at 10.

accepted by the public with remarkably little complaint, and may have helped in the slow winding-down of the conflict in Northern Ireland.

C. Six Lines of Criticism of the 'War on Terror'

Any conclusions about how a historical perspective may affect views of the 'war on terror' must begin by acknowledging that this extraordinary 'war' is unique in having achieved something, however incomplete, in military operations in Afghanistan; in having put the full weight and ingenuity of the United States into the struggle; and in having involved a remarkable degree of international collaboration, some of which has survived the fall-out over Iraq. This struggle is not a single campaign, but is highly variegated. The responses to certain events, such as the Bali, Madrid and London bombings, have been much less military in character than the responses to other outrages. There has been slowly growing recognition that the war on terror involves not just a battle of arms, but a 'battle of ideas'.[71] The overall verdict is not entirely negative.

Yet, against a background of the long historical record of the subject, six main lines of criticism of the US-led international campaign arise.

First, the title and language of the so-called 'war on terror' is misleading. It conjures up the image and expectation of open war being a major and recurrent part of the action against international terrorist movements; and it suggests the unrealisable aim of the complete elimination of terrorist movements. There is a need for words to describe the overall policy with regard to terrorism that convey toughness but do not rely so heavily on the imagery of war. The core idea has to be a vigorous and sustained countering of terrorist threats, involving action at many levels, and aimed at achieving a significant reduction and marginalisation of terrorist activities. A better term, more accurate if less dramatic, would be 'international campaign against terrorism'. It may not be too late to use this term in at least partial substitution for 'war on terror'.

Second, the 'war on terror' risks becoming an exercise in latter-day imperialism. There is a need for intervention in certain societies, but it needs to be handled with extraordinary skill and care. The risk of stumbling into a colonial role is especially great because in US political culture there is a caricatured vision of European colonialism of the nineteenth and twentieth centuries. In consequence it is believed, erroneously, that nothing the United States does today could remotely resemble such deplorable European practices. Yet to many the similarities are all

---

[71] The phrase 'battle of ideas' is used six times in the September 2006 version of the White House document *National Strategy for Combating Terrorism*. In the 2003 version it had not appeared at all.

too real. The irony of the situation is that foreign rule, especially foreign military occupation, is notoriously a producer of terrorist movements.

Third, some official statements made in the course of the 'war on terror' have inadvertently credited terrorist movements with a greater capacity to achieve intended results than can be justified on the basis of the record. For example, in several passages the UK *Strategic Defence Review* states or implies that international terrorist attacks have 'the potential for strategic effect'.[72] This phrase is used for a good reason – to avoid implying that it is essential to tackle absolutely all terrorist movements everywhere simultaneously and with equal vigour – but it is flawed. It ignores the important distinction between *intended* and *actual* strategic effect. Although terrorist actions frequently have major effects, they are seldom those that the terrorists intended. It does not make sense to give terrorists more credit than they deserve for the size and capacity of their organisations, for the accuracy of their political calculations or for the effectiveness of their actions.

Fourth, the history of counterterrorist operations in the twentieth century suggests that in the long struggle against terrorism, four assets are important:

(1)   public confidence in official decision-making;
(2)   public confidence in the intelligence on which that decision-making is based;
(3)   an understanding that operations are conducted with respect for a framework of law;
(4)   a willingness to address some of the problems that have contributed to the emergence of terrorism.

Tragically, all of these assets risk being undermined by many events connected with the 'war on terror', especially the 2003 intervention in Iraq and the subsequent insurgency.

Fifth, the torture and ill-treatment of detainees, of which there has been much evidence in the war on terror, is, to quote Talleyrand, worse than a crime: it is a mistake. Guantanamo and Abu Ghraib have provided propaganda gifts to adversaries.

Sixth, the international campaign against terrorism stands in need of a more realistic vision of how terrorist campaigns end than the simple picture of the elimination or incarceration of terrorists.

On the basis of the historical record, some positive recommendations can be advanced about the most appropriate basic aims and character of the international campaign against terrorism. The struggle should be presented, not just as a fight against evil or as a defence of free societies,

---

[72]   UK Ministry of Defence, *New Chapter*, n 61 above, vol I, at 7.

but also as a fight against tragically erroneous ideas. It should be seen as a means of ensuring that the societies from whence terrorism comes do not succumb to endemic violence. An important aim must be not the capture of every last terrorist leader, but their relegation to a status of near-irrelevance as life moves on, long-standing grievances are addressed and peoples can see that a grim terrorist war of attrition is achieving little and damaging their own societies. It needs to encompass close attention to after-care in societies that have been torn apart by terrorism.

The problem of terrorism can diminish over time. Such diminution will require continued resolution and toughness, including arrests, trials and a willingness to take military action where appropriate. It will also require a patient and more prudent approach that would mark a departure from certain major aspects of what we have seen so far in the 'war on terror'. Above all, the international campaign against terrorism needs to take account of the long history of terror and counterterror – and of the way historians have understood it.

2

Constitutionalising Emergency Powers in Modern Europe

The English and the Roman Model

ALEXIS KELLER

I. RETHINKING CONSTITUTIONAL THEORIES OF EMERGENCY POWER IN HISTORICAL PERSPECTIVE

TERRORIST ATTACKS IN New York (11 September 2001), Madrid (11 March 2004) and London (7 July 2005) have revived debates present across the entire Western world since Roman antiquity on the balance between security and order on the one hand and safeguarding the very justification of government's existence – individual rights – on the other hand. In his dissenting opinion on the famous *Korematsu v United States* ruling (1944), US Supreme Court Judge Robert H Jackson flagged the dangers inherent in granting legal force to a measure taken under emergency circumstances.[1] The crux is the extent to which a political community is willing to sacrifice individual rights when confronted with external or internal threats liable to destroy its society.

---

[1] 'A judicial construction of the due process clause that will sustain this order is a far more subtle blow to liberty than the promulgation of the order itself. A military order, however unconstitutional, is not apt to last longer than the military emergency. Even during that period, a succeeding commander may revoke it all. But once a judicial opinion rationalizes such an order to show that it conforms to the Constitution, or rather rationalizes the Constitution to show that the Constitution sanctions such an order, the Court for all time has validated the principle of racial discrimination in criminal procedure and of transplanting American citizens. The principle then lies about like a loaded weapon, ready for the hand of any authority that can bring forward a plausible claim of an urgent need. Every repetition imbeds that principle more deeply in our law and thinking and expands it to new purposes ... I should hold that a civil court cannot be made to enforce an order which violates constitutional limitations even if it is a reasonable exercise of military authority': Justice Jackson, Dissenting Opinion, *Korematsu v United States*, 323 US 214, (1944), 245–7.

Consequently, a fundamental tension exists in any constitutional order between the basic premise of government constrained by law and the perceived need for discretionary power to face disastrous emergencies and crisis. Historically, that tension has been expressed in various forms. Oliver Cromwell already articulated it in 1654 when he stated before Parliament: 'I would it had not been needful for me to have called you hither to have expostulated these things [concerning the militia, and so on] with you, and in such a manner as this is! *But necessity hath no law.* Feigned necessities, imaginary necessities, are the greatest cozenage that men can put upon the providence of God, and make pretences to break known rules by. But it is as legal and as carnal and as stupid, to think that there are no necessities that are manifest necessities, because necessities may be abused or feigned.'[2] In 1861, Abraham Lincoln asked whether a government must 'of necessity, be too *strong* for the liberties of its own people, or too *weak* to maintain its own existence'.[3] The continuing debate over whether the perceived requirements of national security can be combined with traditional civil liberties and separation of powers reflects both Cromwell's and Lincoln's concerns.

Among legal scholars and political theorists, an extensive body of literature has been devoted to analysing the historical expansion of the executive's emergency power to confront foreign dangers, from its philosophical roots to the demise of traditional limiting devices. For example, Rossiter's famous book, *Constitutional Dictatorship* (1948), outlined the historical roots of the idea of the state of exception during the Cold War and called for US legislation to respond to the new crisis conditions. Rossiter advocated tightening, limiting and simultaneously strengthening emergency powers and concluded that in the atomic age 'the use of constitutional emergency powers may well become the rule and not the exception'.[4] Edwin Corwin's *The President, Office and Powers* and Carl Friedrich's *Constitutional Reason of State* each, in their own distinctive way, reiterated Rossiter's theme in the 1950s by showing that mortal threats to the political community have been debated since the origin of modern states.[5] More recently, some scholars have focused on the varieties of responses to emergencies according to a nation's pattern of political experience and institutions. They have analysed and compared

---

[2] O Cromwell, in W Cortez Abbot (ed), *The Writings and Speeches of Oliver Cromwell* (Cambridge, MA, Harvard University Press, 1947) vol 4, 460.

[3] 'Lincoln's message to Congress', 4 July 1861, in J Richardson (ed), *Messages and Papers of the Presidents* (published by the authority of Congress, Washington, 1897) vol 6.

[4] C Rossiter, *Constitutional Dictatorship. Crisis Government in the Modern Democracies* (Princeton, NJ, Princeton University Press, 1948) 297.

[5] E Corwin, *The President, Office and Powers 1787–1957*, 4th edn (New York, New York University Press, 1957); C Friedrich, *Constitutional Reason of State. The Survival of the Constitutional Order* (Providence, Brown University Press, 1957).

the range of authority available to the executive in modern constitutional democracies and the relationships between the executive, the legislature and the courts in times of emergency.[6]

According to Jules Lobel, three frameworks of emergency power have been present throughout US constitutional history: the 'absolutist', 'relativist' and 'liberal'.[7] The first perspective suppresses the tension between law and necessity 'by denying that such a necessity exists in time of crisis'.[8] It argues that even if such necessity does exist, the preservation of a nation would not be worth the sacrifice of liberty. In *Ex Parte Milligan* in 1866, the US Supreme Court adopted such position, by asserting that the Constitution granted the government sufficient power to preserve its existence without resorting to suspending rights or extraordinary emergency power.[9] In contrast to the absolutist's denial of the need for emergency power, the second, 'relativist', position argues that a constitution is a flexible document that allows the executive to take whatever measures are necessary in a crisis situation. In 1942, US President Franklin Roosevelt articulated that view by stating that the President has the constitutional power to ignore statutory provisions when 'necessary to avert a disaster which would interfere with the winning of the war'.[10] According to Lobel, both the absolutist and the relativist view have an underlying philosophical unity, as both tend to abolish the dichotomy between constitutional normalcy and extra-constitutional emergency.

The third perspective, which Lobel terms as 'liberal', seeks to resolve the tension between law and necessity through another approach, one that preserves the dichotomy between ordinary and emergency power. Emergency and normal times are opposed, resulting in distinct legal regimes. As he explains:

> Normalcy permitted a governmental structure based on separation of powers, respect for civil liberties and the rule of law, while emergencies required strong executive rule, premised not on law and respect on civil liberties, but rather on discretion to take a wide range of actions to preserve the government.[11]

---

[6] See, among others, C Cotter, 'Constitutionalizing Emergency Powers: The British Experience' (1953) 5 *Stanford Law Review* 382–417; CC Schweitzer, 'Emergency Powers in the Federal Republic of Germany' (1969) 22 *Western Political Quarterly* 112–21; W Fisch, 'Emergency in the Constitutional Law of the United States' (1990) 38(suppl) *American Journal of Comparative Law* 389–420; KL Scheppele, 'Law in a Time of Emergency: States of Exception and the Temptations of 9/11' (2004) 6 *University of Pennsylvania Journal of Constitutional Law* 1001–83.

[7] J Lobel, 'Emergency Power and the Decline of Liberalism' (1989) 98 *Yale Law Journal* 1385–433.

[8] *Ibid* at 1387.

[9] *Ex Parte Milligan*, US Supreme Court, 71 US 2 (1866), 120–26.

[10] Roosevelt's Speech to Congress, 7 September 1942, quoted in E Corwin, n 5 above at 250–51.

[11] J Lobel, n 7 above at 1388.

There is no doubt that Lobel's categorization is of great importance to frame constitutional theories of emergency power, especially in the United States. But, from a historical point of view, it rests on one flaw: it dismisses the republican tradition, a tradition of thought that played a crucial role in shaping modern constitutionalism. It is certainly right to say that the liberal paradigm of emergency power is built upon John Locke's doctrine of the executive's prerogative. It is also true that this theory was of utmost importance for eighteenth-century constitutional-ism, notably in the United States and in France.[12] But when Locke thought extra-legal powers necessary for the maintenance of a govern-ment in time of crisis, he was sustaining a line of thought that went back to the Roman Republic and to its system of temporary dictatorship. And this kind of temporary, delegated dictatorship to preserve the state has always been a feature of *republican* thought. Rome provided a way to handle severe threats to the institutions of the Republic by creating and following established procedures for doing so. Later, Machiavelli insisted in his *Discourses* (Book I, chapter 34) that

> all republics should have some institutions similar to the dictatorship ... Truly, of all the institutions of Rome, this one deserves to be counted amongst those to which she was most indebted for her greatness and dominion. For without some such an institution Rome would with difficulty have escaped the many extraordinary dangers that befell her.[13]

Thus, historically, modern constitutional theories of emergency power rely not only on a *liberal* but also on a *republican* paradigm of executive prerogative. Since the dictatorship was created under the Roman Repub-lic, republican constitutional thought has been unrelenting in its exami-nation of the conditions surrounding the state of emergency (Cicero, in a landmark text, envisaged the possibility of 'derogare'[14]) and its trade-mark 'exceptional circumstances'. It is a popular modern-day misconcep-tion that the Roman tradition was alone in making political use of emergency measures. Medieval and Renaissance republics in Italy did so as well. In Florence, home to Machiavelli and intellectual heartland of civic humanism and republicanism, the state of emergency was central to the republican regime.[15] Also, as underlined by Machiavelli himself in his

---

[12] For a seminal account of John Locke's influence on French conception of emergency power between 1789 and 1794, see P Gueniffey, *La politique de la terreur. Essai sur la violence révolutionnaire 1789–1794* (Paris, Gallimard, 2000) 163–96.

[13] Machiavelli, 'Discourses on the First Decade of Titus Livius', in C Detmold (trs and ed) *The Historical, Political, and Diplomatic Writings of Niccolo Machiavelli* (Boston, James R. Osgood, 1882) vol II, at 170–71.

[14] Cicero, *De Republica*, III, 22. 'Derogare' here translates as *remove*.

[15] See, among others, N Rubinstein, 'Politics and Constitution in Florence at the End of the Fifteenth Century', in EF Jacobs (ed), *Italian Renaissance Studies* (New York, Barnes & Noble, 1960); N Rubinstein, 'Florentine Constitutionalism and Medici's Ascendancy in the

Discourses (Book I, chapter 34), the Republic of Venice, whose staying power fascinated observers, used mechanisms that could be compared to a state of emergency of sorts throughout its history until its fall in 1797.[16]

As we know, these republican ideas were propagated in England in the mid-seventeenth century, especially in the works of James Harrington.[17] They were revived, in somewhat modified form, by a group of Whig 'neo-Harringtonians' – including Andrew Fletcher, John Trenchard, John Toland, Walter Moyle, Edmund Ludlow and Algernon Sidney – at the turn of the century.[18] In the eighteenth century, Montesquieu and Rousseau also participated in the propagation of this pattern of ideas. Montesquieu concluded that republics were a thing of the past and that the future belonged to monarchies or regimes similar to that found in England. But he was clearly fascinated by Roman institutions and his conclusion was only reached after a meticulous study of republican systems. On the other hand, Rousseau was adamant to remind people that he was a republican citizen with an enduring attachment to Roman model, which led him to provide an elaborated analysis of the 'dictatorship'.

All these authors boasted in-depth knowledge of republican constitutional thought, and they did not see the state of emergency to be a uniquely Roman oddity. Rather, they viewed it as an institution that could be described and analysed on a broader basis, in other cultures and regimes.

Fundamentally, as Michael Ignatieff put it,

Fifteenth Century', in N Rubinstein (ed), *Florentine Studies. Politics and Society in Renaissance Florence* (London, Faber and Faber, 1968); F Gilbert, *Machiavelli and Guicciardini. Politics and History in Sixteenth-Century Florence* (Princeton, NJ, Princeton University Press, 1965) especially chs 1 and 2; G Silvano, 'Florentine Republicanism in the Early Sixteenth Century', in G Bock, Q Skinner and M Viroli (eds), *Machiavelli and Republicanism* (Cambridge, Cambridge University Press, 1990) 41–70.

[16] See WJ Bouwsma, *Venice and the Defense of Republican Liberty* (Berkeley, University of California Press, 1968); G Maranini, *La Costituzione di Venezia*, 2 vols [1927], (Firenze, La Nuova Italia, 1974); see also, from a somewhat different perspective, J Walker, 'Legal and Political Discourse in Seventeenth-Century Venice' (2002) *Society for Comparative Study of Society and History* 800–26.

[17] For a good discussion of Machiavelli's apparent influence on Harrington, see F Raab, *The English Face of Machiavelli* (London/Toronto, Routledge & Kegan Paul/University of Toronto Press, 1964) 185–217; For an excellent treatment of English republicanism, see M Peltonen, *Classical Humanism and Republicanism in English Political Thought, 1570–1640* (Cambridge, Cambridge University Press, 1995); B Worden, 'English Republicanism' in JH Burns and M Goldie (eds), *The Cambridge History of Political Thought 1450–1700* (Cambridge, Cambridge University Press, 1991) 443–75.

[18] See Q Skinner, 'The Principles and Practice of Opposition: The Case of Bolingbroke versus Walpole', in N McKendrick (ed), *Historical Perspectives. Studies in English Thought and Society* (London, Taylor & Francis, 1974) 93–128; JGA Pocock (ed), *The Varieties of British Political Thought, 1500–1800* (Cambridge, Cambridge University Press, 1993).

there is ... a conflict between a *republican* and a *liberal* theory of emergency powers. A republican account could envisage a democratic rationale for rights abridgments in emergency based on the need for executive decisiveness to protect majority interests, while a liberal view would fear that such a majoritarian rationale would risk permanent damage both to rights and to the system of checks and balances.[19]

Both republicans and liberals have tried to resolve the tension between law and necessity by positing a boundary line protecting the normal constitutional order from the dark world of crisis government. But liberals have been much more reluctant to accept the exceptional use of executive prerogative. They have always feared that an executive power might use the pretext of emergency to seize power and abolish constitutional liberty whereas republicans have been more tempted by the use of emergency suspensions of liberties.[20]

In my chapter, I will expose this distinction by exploring some arguments of the *liberal* and the *republican* theory of emergency powers. I will especially emphasise how the republican tradition, deeming the state liberty and the balance of powers to be prerequisites for citizens to enjoy freedom, addressed the issue of emergency powers.[21] My purpose here is

---

[19] M Ignatieff, *The Lesser Evil. Political Ethics in an Age of Terror* (Princeton, NJ, Princeton University Press, 2004) 27. On the distinction between liberal and republican attitudes to prerogative power, see also G Negretto and J Aguilar Rivera, 'Liberalism and Emergency Powers in Latin America: Reflections on Carl Schmitt and the Theory of Constitutional Dictatorship' (2000) 21 *Cardozo Law Review* 1797.

[20] One of the most pertinent defences of the republican theory of emergency powers was made by Abraham Lincoln in a letter in 1863 justifying his suspension of habeas corpus and indefinite detention of opponents of the draft laws, during the American Civil War. In this famous text, Lincoln speaks directly to the central issue: whether temporary abridgments of freedom do permanent damage to constitutional liberty. He explained: 'The Constitution is not, in its application, in all respects the same, in case of rebellion or invasion involving the public safety, as it is in times of profound peace and public security. The Constitution itself makes the distinction; and I can no more be persuaded that the Government can constitutionally take no strong measures in time of rebellion, because it can be shown that the same could not be lawfully taken in time of peace, than I can be persuaded that a particular drug is not good medicine for a sick man, because it can be shown to not be good food for a well one. Nor am I able to appreciate the danger apprehended by the meeting that the American people will, by means of military arrests during the Rebellion, lose the right of Public Discussion, the Liberty of Speech and the Press, the Law of Evidence, Trial by Jury and Habeas Corpus, throughout the indefinite peaceful future, which I trust lies before them, any more than I am able to believe that a man could contract so strong an appetite for emetics during temporary illness as to persist in feeding upon them during the remainder of his healthful life.' See Abraham Lincoln, letter to Erastus Corning and others, 12 June 1863, in M Johnson (ed) *Abraham Lincoln, Slavery and the Civil War: Selected.Writings and Speeches* (Boston, Bedford/St Martin's, 2001) 247.

[21] There is surprisingly little research on republican ideas about emergency powers. For example, Philip Pettit, the leading contemporary republican philosophers, completely ignores the question of emergency powers in his book *Republicanism. A Theory of Freedom and Government* (Oxford, Clarendon Press, 1997). He focuses on the hallmark excesses of emergency situations: tyranny of the majority/tyranny of the elite; breakdown in the system of checks and balances. In ch 6, he recognises the vital role of institutional

not to contend that the republican theory of emergency powers is superior to its liberal alternative; nor to portray liberalism and republicanism as conflicting philosophies since they have both tried to address the tension between law and necessity by demarcating separate spheres of emergency versus non-emergency governance.[22] I shall not either provide a history of the idea of the state of emergency. Instead, I shall seek to pinpoint some specifically *liberal* and *republican* claims in the debate about emergency powers by focusing on Montesquieu's and Rousseau's constitutional theory and by considering their definition of what I would term *legitimate emergency*.

Indeed, there is no reason to assume that these two eighteenth-century philosophers viewed their own observations on the state of emergency as incidental. It might be easy for those of us living in constitutional democracies to dismiss their analyses because the political and historical contexts in which they wrote were so different. In particular, the rise of secular, democratic, and constitutional government at the end of the nineteenth century seems to have created a different dilemma of justification, precisely because executive power in modern democracies is supposed to be accountable to and removable by elections. However, if both republican and liberal traditions do contain visionary resources of use to modern constitutionalism, we need to draw upon those resources in order to propose new directions for thinking about emergency powers in our changing international context.

Before I develop my arguments, I want to make one final remark about my use of terminology. I have chosen to make no distinction between the state of emergency (*gouvernement d'exception*) and the state of exception (*état d'exception*), using them interchangeably to refer to a set of factors linked to extraordinary circumstances. My decision is chiefly based on the uncertainty surrounding the term 'state of exception'. It is widespread in German doctrine (*Ausnahmezustand*, although *Notstand*, state of necessity, also exists), but quite rare in Italian and French doctrine, which instead refer to emergency decrees and *état de siège*. The terms most

---

architecture in guaranteeing liberty, defined as non-domination [as opposed to liberty defined as non-interference]. He discusses restrictions to the principle of separation of powers, but makes no mention of the state of emergency or attendant theory, while the domestic and external defence of his republican state merits no more than a few short pages (150–57). A noticeable exception, and in my view a very perceptive one, is to be found in P Pasquino, 'Urgence et Etat de droit. Le gouvernement d'exception dans la théorie constitutionnelle' (2003) 51 *Les Cahiers de la sécurité intérieure* 9–27.

[22] For a general discussion of the ways liberalism and republicanism have overlapped historically, see J Isaac, 'Republicanism vs Liberalism: a Reconsideration' (1998) 9 *History of Political Thought* 349–77.

widely used in the English-speaking world are martial law and emergency powers. Admittedly, each of these expressions reflects different contexts and legal traditions, but they can largely be subsumed into the phrase 'state of emergency'.[23]

II. EMERGENCY POWERS IN MODERN EUROPE: THE ENGLISH AND THE ROMAN MODEL

In seventeenth- and eighteenth-century Europe, both republican and liberal philosophers were tied to the idea that emergency powers led to a shift in the relationship of power between citizens (as individuals) and the government (as the body in charge of political life). Their theories were rooted in a *dualist* vision of power, deriving from the dichotomy between the state of normalcy (1) and the state of emergency (2) as two distinct constitutional moments. Normalcy permitted a governmental structure based on separation of powers, respect for civil liberties and the rule of law; whereas emergencies required strong executive rule with the possibility to take a wide range of actions to preserve the state. In this sense, these thinkers not only had a specific 'political' position, but a world-view that sought to resolve societal tensions by creating a legally significant dividing line between the two poles of the tension.

As such, they disagreed strongly with their *monist* rivals, who argued that there was no difference between (1) and (2), either because everything could be traced back to the legal rationale underpinning the state of normalcy – like the German philosopher Leibniz – or because government action could be equated with the principle of *'salus populi suprema et sola lex est'* ('the welfare of the people is the highest law'), as advocated by Thomas Hobbes, their fiercest opponent. The state of emergency had no place in the Hobbesian world, in which exception and norm coincided. The extreme nature of conflict and the threat lurking in his perception of society made this *reductio ad unum* of normalcy and emergency possible, as illustrated in chapter 30 of *Leviathan* (1651). Here, Hobbes explained that:

---

[23] For a terminological fine-tuning, see J Fitzpatrick, *Human Rights in Crisis: The International System for Protecting Rights During States of Emergency* (Philadelphia, PA, University of Pennsylvania Press, 1994).

The Office of the Soveraign, (be it a Monarch, or an Assembly,) consisteth in the end, for which he was trusted with the Soveraign Power, namely the procuration of *the safety of the people*; to which he is obliged by the Law of Nature, and to render an account thereof to God, the Author of that Law, and to none but him.[24]

For Hobbes, 'the safety of the people' was the norm, rather than a rule that justified a suspension of the state of normalcy.

Depending on how they structure the relationship between (1) and (2), the liberal and the republican theory of emergency powers in modern Europe can be typified by what I shall call the *English* model, represented by Montesquieu, and what I shall describe as the *Roman* model, with Rousseau as its most illustrious champion.[25]

Nothing has been more hotly disputed than the interpretation of Montesquieu's Book XI, Chapter 6, of *The Spirit of the Laws* (1748). To truly grasp its doctrine, one must simultaneously bear in mind English constitutional history and the reclassification of systems or government forms proposed by Montesquieu therein. Whereas the ancients based their philosophy on a three-way split of power between monarchy, aristocracy and mixed government (democracy), Montesquieu introduced a new category rooted in the trade-off between moderate and despotic governments. He saw the separation of power as the most perfect representation of moderate government. As he put it, 'Any moderate government, in which one power is offset by another, calls for an abundance of wisdom, for it to be established and sustained'.[26]

At this point, it is worth underscoring that the term 'separation of power' has several meanings that are not necessarily compatible: 'pure'

---

[24] T Hobbes, *Leviathan*, R Tuck (ed) (Cambridge, Cambridge University Press, 1996) ch 30, p 231.

[25] I do not want to suggest here that Montesquieu's theory was *only* inspired by the language of natural law on which liberalism drew heavily; nor do I want to imply that Rousseau *only* used the language of classical and modern republicanism in trying to bring the egalitarian ethos of the republican regimes back into modern political theory. The two philosophers relied equally on both these traditions and the attempts by some scholars to diminish the importance of the two discourses in their writings are, in my view, mistaken. Nevertheless, they clearly differ on the model used to define modern politics. For Montesquieu, the classical republic was not only gone for ever, it was for all its many remarkable qualities not to be regretted. The model for Europe now was a commercial, extensive, non-military representative regime like England, ruled by legislation, not mores. To Rousseau, Montesquieu's new political science was nothing but an intellectual obstacle. Not because it was untrue, far from it. But because it implied the elimination of classical republicanism from modern political discourse. That explains why Rousseau used an idealised republican antiquity – mainly Sparta and Rome – as a critical mirror for modern society as a whole. This point is well emphasised in J Shklar, 'Montesquieu and the new Republicanism', in G Bock, Q Skinner and M Viroli (eds), *Machiavelli and Republicanism* (Cambridge, Cambridge University Press, 1990) 265–80.

[26] Montesquieu, *Pensées* n° 1795 (my translation).

separation of powers, balance of power, the checks and balances principle and the mixed government theory.[27] In many ways, the goal of the
'pure' doctrine was linked to the wish in seventeenth-century English
political thought to move from a monarchy to a republic, a step that
required a distinction between legislative and executive power, with the
former in control, while the latter's role was that of loyal magistrate.
Later on, when the supremacy of the legislative power was firmly
established, the first English revolution (the Long Parliament) saw calls
for a separation of powers to prevent a potentially damaging concentration in the hands of the legislative power. The history of pure separation
of powers is a complex one because it is linked to two other concepts that
inspired republican theorists, the idea of mixed government and balance
of powers.

The first idea can largely be attributed to Polybius, a Greek writer who
lived in Rome in the second century BC.[28] According to Polybius, the
constitution of Rome was a blend of monarchical, aristocratic and democratic elements. The consuls and magistrates were the monarchical one,
the senate the aristocratic one and the popular assemblies (*comitia*) the
democratic one. Polybius argued that the balance between these three
powers was the key to the extraordinary stability enjoyed by the Roman
Constitution. All three powers were ring-fenced, balancing each other
out and precluding the abuse of authority that ultimately destroyed all
single-strand systems (monarchies, aristocracies and democracies)
whereupon they were replaced by another as part of a relentless constitutional cycle.[29]

Later, in the seventeenth and eighteenth centuries, Polybius' analysis
became widespread in English republican discourse, as can be seen in the
writings of Harrington (prior to *Oceana*), Molesworth, Trenchard and
Toland.[30] Thus, the doctrine of mixed government was commonplace by
the time of Locke's seminal analysis of the 'powers of government' in the

---

[27] See MJC Vile, *Constitutionalism and the Separation of Powers* (Oxford, Clarendon Press, 1967).

[28] See Polybius, *The Rise of the Roman Empire*, I Scott-Kilvert (trans), FW Walbank (ed) (Harmondsworth, Penguin, 1979) especially book VI, chs 10 [1–14], 11–18. For a clear discussion of book VI, see FW Waldbank, *Polybius* (Berkeley, CA, University of California Press, 1972) ch 5.

[29] As W Nippel has remarked, Polybius' conception of mixed government did not involve 'normative ideas of a necessary differentiation of governmental functions'. Its prime purpose was to ensure that the exercise of political power reflected the natural balance of the different social classes and interests within the political 'body', and to provide mechanisms whereby each could check the other. Nippel also rightly points out that, although the Polybian version of the argument came to predominate, it diverged in important respects from the Aristotelian account. See W Nippel, 'Ancient and modern republicanism: *mixed constitution* and *ephors*' in B Fontana (ed), *The Invention of the Modern Republic* (Cambridge, Cambridge University Press, 1994) 7–9.

[30] See Skinner, n 18 above at 113–21.

Second Treatise (1690) discussed in the last section. By this time, however, the English Restoration (1660) had led to it being reworked from a perspective that upheld the English constitution as a model of the *balance* to be achieved in mixed monarchy. Although present in Locke and other writers, notably Bolingbroke, this thesis only gained its paradigmatic form with Montesquieu. Based on a discussion of the English constitution, he synthesised the three doctrines, namely *mixed government, balance of power*, and the *theory of checks and balances*.

Montesquieu combines all of them in Book XI, Chapter 6, outlining a typology similar to Locke's: 'In each state there are three sorts of powers: legislative power, executive power over the things depending on the right of nations, and executive power over the things depending on civil right.'[31] Montesquieu adds that freedom will be destroyed if all three powers are concentrated in the same hands, as illustrated by the Ottoman Empire and the Italian republics. In the course of Chapter 6, however, Montesquieu returns to the usual distinction between legislative and executive power. He decides that judicial power 'is in some fashion, null' and blends it with what is clearly a version of mixed government in that legislative power is split between two assemblies (popular and aristocratic) while executive power is entrusted to a hereditary monarch. In turn, these powers are interlinked to the extent that they constitute a forerunner to the system of checks and balances: 'As its legislative body is composed of two parts, the one will be chained to the other by their reciprocal faculty of vetoing. The two will be bound by the executive power, which will itself be bound by the legislative power.'[32] This view bears little resemblance to the 'pure' doctrine of separation of powers, which is what prompted a long line of historians like Eisenmann to claim that Montesquieu made no contribution to the theory of separation of powers, seen as akin to a liberal myth.[33] They were wrong.

While Chapter 6 does not tease out a theory on the separation of powers, it does clearly propose a system to *balance* powers, famously summed up in the following sentence:

> It has eternally been observed that any man who has power is led to abuse it; he continues until he finds limits ... So that one cannot abuse power, power must check power by the arrangement of things.[34]

In other words, all three forms of power can never be entrusted to one man or one body, as confusion would ensue. To prevent this happening,

---

[31] Montesquieu, *The Spirit of the Laws*, A Cohler, B Miller and H Stone (trans and eds) (Cambridge, Cambridge University Press, 1989), Book XI, ch 6, p 156.

[32] *Ibid* at 164.

[33] See C Eisenmann, 'L'Esprit des lois et la separation des pouvoirs', in C Pfister (ed) *Mélanges Carré de Malberg* (Paris, Sirey, 1933) 162–92.

[34] Montesquieu, n 31 above, Book XI, ch 4, p 155.

the three powers must be shared out amongst distinct bodies capable of cooperating to exercise government authority. Powers should not encroach on each other's territory. The crux therefore is not that powers must be kept separate, but rather that their division must ensure balance.

Blending the separation of powers and mixed government theory produces a socially and politically *balanced constitution with mutual checks in place.* Although this type of arrangement might lead to 'inaction', Montesquieu claimed that the 'necessary movement of things' forced them to work together. The system served to distil public interest out of disparate private interests and to gain the advantage of the better elements in society in its enactment as law.[35]

Paradoxically, this analysis enabled Montesquieu to propose a theory of emergency powers. Prompted by his in-depth knowledge of English constitutional thinking, particularly the 'royal prerogative' doctrine, and the Roman institution of *dictatorship,* Montesquieu accepted the very principle of state of emergency. Admittedly, he never used the term, but his description of the way in which individual rights may be restricted leaves little room for doubt. He writes in Book XII, Chapter 19:

> I admit, however, that the usage of the freest peoples that ever lived on earth makes me believe that there are cases where a veil has to be drawn, for a moment, over liberty, as one hides the statues of the gods.[36]

Locke had already foreseen a departure from the state of normalcy, one that he believed should be based on the separation of powers. In Chapter 14 of his *Second Treatise of Government,* he advocates what he terms 'prerogative', or the 'power to act according to discretion, for the publick good, without the prescription of the Law, and sometimes even against it'.[37] Locke is not the first among early modern English political theorists to speak about the king's prerogative since this question was the central

---

[35] It could be said that the judicial power remained hard to assimilate to this scheme, since it added a potential fourth department within the theory of mixed government. Montesquieu, however, believed this power would be especially dangerous if linked to either of the other two. He thought its independence was best achieved through the jury system and lay magistrates so that it did not become attached to any estate or profession. This lack of a social base rendered it the weakest power. It became 'invisible', 'in a sense, no force' at least in the political sense.

[36] Montesquieu, n 31 above, Book XII, ch 19, p 204.

[37] J Locke, *Two Treatises of Government,* P Laslett (ed) (Cambridge, Cambridge University Press, 1988) 375. Most interpreters pay little attention to this chapter. MJC Vile, *Constitutionalism and the Separation of Powers* (Oxford, Clarendon Press, 1967) barely refers to it. In his excellent chapter on John Locke published in JH Burns (ed), *The Cambridge History of Political Thought 1450–1700* (Cambridge, Cambridge University Press, 1991) 616–52, J Tully makes no mention of it. Three noticeable exceptions are J Dunn, *The Political Thought of John Locke* (Cambridge, Cambridge University Press, 1969) especially ch 11; J Roy, 'La prérogative chez Locke' (1985) 5 *Cahiers de philosophie politique et juridique de l'Université de Caen* 149–55; and, above all, P Pasquino, 'Locke on King's Prerogative' (1998) 26(2) *Political Theory* 198–208, an excellent outline to which I am much indebted.

issue of English constitutional debate under the Stuarts.[38] But he is the only one, among the major advocates of limited monarchy, to make prerogative a central element of his constitutional theory. It is therefore not surprising that Montesquieu and Rousseau backed up their claims by referring to this often overlooked chapter penned by a writer better known for his liberal political philosophy.

Locke defines prerogative as the power of discretionary action which, in the interests of society as a whole, must be yielded to those in executive office, primarily because legislators are not able 'to foresee, and so by laws to provide for, all Accidents and Necessities, that may concern the publick'.[39] Prerogative is required in all political regimes, regardless of the nature of the underlying institutions, but the need is even greater in 'moderate monarchy and well-framed governments'. In that case, laws are not adopted by those who enforce them, and the legislative authority, which is responsible for meeting society's needs, has not always direct knowledge of those needs. Moreover, the people entrust legislative power to a large, unwieldy and plodding assembly. The upshot is a paradox in which the more rules that constrain those in power, the greater their leeway must be to discard those same rules in the interests of the people. The 'public good' imperative does not necessarily slot into a parliamentary timeline. Hence, 'where the municipal Law has given no direction', it is vital that the government be allowed to adopt requisite measures, at least provisionally, pending a meeting of the legislative power to plug this gap by adopting new legislation.

Furthermore, the 'executor of the laws' needs to be able to construe the legislation it is bound to enforce. In certain cases, application may trigger hurdles that the legislator could not have foreseen. According to Locke, enforcing a law may end up undermining the purpose of civil government, which is 'the preservation for all'. Faced with an infinite range of specific circumstances, government must know how to adjust a generic rule to fit the context and indeed ignore provisions that do more harm than good. Locke went so far as to say that 'even the guilty are to be spared, where it can prove no prejudice to the innocent'.[40] Executive power should be given maximum leeway to tackle emergencies, even if that means contravening legal provisions. In Locke's words, 'many accidents may happen, wherein a strict and rigid observation of the Laws may do harm, (as not to pull down an innocent Man's House to stop the Fire, when the next to it is burning)'.[41]

---

[38] See P Pasquino, n 37 above at 199–200.
[39] Locke, n 37 above at 375.
[40] *Ibid* at 375.
[41] *Ibid.*

It is wrong to destroy the man's home because doing so violates one of the most fundamental rights of all citizens, the right of property. Yet, its destruction is justified by the need to halt the fire's spread, in the interests of society as a whole. The government must break the law for the good of all and, while a citizen's rights are indeed violated, the ultimate goal, as Montesquieu would later argue, is to safeguard all rights for all citizens.

Locke cannot avoid the question that inevitably arises when discussing emergency powers: who decides that it is an emergency? Who is responsible for furnishing the proof, ascertaining whether the circumstances do actually warrant prerogative and whether it is exercised in the interests of public welfare? One might assume that only a genuine risk that the fire will spread could justify the decision to pull down surrounding homes. However, Locke argues that 'there can be no Judge on Earth'. In other words, the action taken by government cannot be judged by *one of the constitutional powers* or even by the people.

The main reason is that Locke's prerogative falls completely *outside* the scope of a constitution. It belongs to a category of government action that cannot be ring-fenced at the outset or constrained by rules that would hamper its success. Nevertheless, this discretionary authority is not absolute, and there are two reasons for this. First, prerogative is an *attribute* of government, not a *right* enjoyed by holders of that office, entitling them as such to wilfully take action 'harmful to the people'. Second, the exercise of prerogative is bound by the overarching goal of civil association, which is to derive mutual benefit for all citizens. Consequently, Locke's prerogative is a discretionary power to be used for the common good – and only for the common good.

It is not so much the power to act beyond the rules that spawn it, with no set timeframe or scope. It is more an *authorisation* that remains valid until it is revoked or restricted. Prerogative is not an explicit, structured act of delegation – unlike the handover of legislative power to elected representatives. The government enjoys a right of initiative; the people endorse this authority since they are supposed to tacitly approve anything they do not explicitly condemn. As such, the act of *delegation is purely negative:* the people do not grant authority, but they may withdraw it. Locke dwells on this point, stressing that the people may allow their governments completely free reign and decide not to circumscribe prerogative, or they may explicitly revoke it and limit its scope in areas that infringe their interests.

As far as Locke is concerned, governments should be free to take whatever action is necessary at the appropriate time. However, the people will withdraw their backing if the government exploits the means tacitly entrusted to it to instead attack its own enemies, promote individual interests or repress peaceful citizens. The scope of Locke's prerogative can therefore be extended or indeed eliminated completely. It is not a 'power' whose delegation or conditions can be circumscribed by rules; it is a *delegation of authority accountable only to the people.*

Montesquieu adopts a similar take in his writings. He accepts Locke's view that fundamental rights may be temporarily curtailed. In clearly defined circumstances, judicial authority may have to be wielded by other powers and its prerogatives infringed. Accordingly, the legislative power allows the executive power to arrest forthwith any person accused of a capital offence. In very serious cases (national conspiracy, external threat), the legislative power may, 'for a brief, limited time' authorise the executive power to apprehend suspect citizens. Parliament can suspend habeas corpus. While the judge has a duty to judge according to the law, he is ultimately merely a cog in a soulless judicial machine. Hence, part of the legislative power must be able to 'moderate the law in favor of the law itself by pronouncing less rigorously than the law'.[42]

Montesquieu lists a number of other exceptions which I shall not go into here. The point is that his discourse is *extremely cautious*. He acknowledges the existence of 'exceptional situations' – although he never describes them in detail – but he remains firmly attached to the idea of individual liberty, be it objective (enshrined in law) or subjective (an individual's sense of security). That is why he refuses to address the issue of *full powers*. He is less concerned about the risks emergencies pose for the constitutional system than about potential abuse by executive power. He therefore argues against tying the state of emergency to the constitution. He favours *ex post* checks on the exercise of emergency powers. Special laws and specific measures adopted by the executive are sufficient to tackle crises.

The *Roman* model of emergency powers, championed by Rousseau, crafts its theory from a radically different perspective. Although influenced by Locke's view, its starting point is two Roman institutions: *dictatorship* and *senatus consultum ultimum* (ultimate decree of the Senate).

For three centuries, Rome overcame crises through constitutional mechanisms by which one organ, the Senate in the Roman Republic, invested another, the dictator, with emergency powers. This institution – the dictatorship – defies modern-day classification. It was not anti-constitutional since no law forbade the appointment of the dictator, nor was it a derogation because no text defined its powers. It was not exceptional given that it did not deviate from the established rule, nor legally irregular for the same reason, nor indeed in any way irregular

---

[42] Montesquieu, n 31 above, Book XI, ch 6, p 163.

because the office was deemed part of the normal system. It was, however, extraordinary or intermittent in that a dictator was not necessarily appointed each year and his post was limited to six months. In the words of Claude Nicolet, the Roman dictatorship involved 'exceptional, albeit normal and quasi-constitutional power being conferred on a magistrate in accordance with precise conventions ... and in critical circumstances, to address an external or domestic threat and thus preserve public safety'.[43]

The other institution that shaped the *Roman* theory of emergency powers was the *senatus consultum ultimum*, also deemed a dictatorship, albeit one in the Senate's favour. In light of the context for its implementation, it is difficult to dissociate the legal and political issues. Matters have been obscured by the dispute between *populares* and *optimates*. Each camp defended its own perception of public law, ultimately giving the latter an artificial hue, with legality a mere argument used to political ends. Corrado Barbagallo defined the *senatus consultum ultimum* as an 'exceptional public safety measure through which the senate delegated equally exceptional powers to consuls ... generally using the words *videant consules ne quid respublica detrimenti capiat* (let the consuls see to it that no harm comes to the republic)'.[44]

Rousseau is undoubtedly the true heir of this *Roman* – or republican – theory of emergency powers, not merely because he describes the two aforementioned institutions at length, but because he defines emergency measures that echo Roman practices.

His theory of emergency powers is rooted in a new concept of *government*. It is widely known that Rousseau views laws as general rules applicable to the entire political body, making no distinction between citizens. Conversely, state administration calls for rulings on specific matters and individual cases. By its very nature, the 'general will' cannot determine administrative affairs, and its sphere of influence should be limited to legislation. Since sovereignty is an expression of the general will, a sovereign cannot enforce laws. That role is distinct from sovereignty and described by Rousseau as *government*: 'I therefore call Government or supreme administration the legitimate exercise of the executive power, and Prince or Magistrate the man or the body charged with that administration'.[45] In other words, Rousseau sees legislation and administration as two separate tasks to be carried out by two different bodies.

---

[43]   See C Nicolet, 'La dictature à Rome', in M Duverger (ed), *Dictatures et légitimité* (Paris, PUF, 1982) 69 (my translation).

[44]   See C Barbagallo, *Una misura eccezionale dei romani. Senatus-Consultum Ultimum* (Rome, Jovene, 1980) 1.

[45]   J-J Rousseau, *The Social Contract and other later Political Writings*, V Gourevitch (ed) (Cambridge, Cambridge University Press, 1997) Book III, ch 1, p 83.

Legislative power belongs to the people as sovereign, whereas executive power must be vested in a body of magistrates mediating between subjects and sovereign.

It does not follow that the people can never theoretically merge the tasks of government and sovereignty or enforce their own laws, since that is the very crux of democracy according to Rousseau. Nonetheless, Rousseau opposed the idea, stating:

> It is not good that he who makes the laws executes them, nor that the body of the people turn its attention away from general considerations, to devote it to a particular objects. Nothing is more dangerous than the influence of private interests on public affairs, and abuse of the laws by the Government is a lesser evil than the corruption of the Lawgiver, which is the inevitable consequence of particular considerations.[46]

A few pages later, he adds:

> Once the legislative Power is well established, it remains likewise to establish the Executive power; for this latter, which operates only by particular acts, inasmuch as it is not of the essence of the former, is naturally separate from it. If it were possible for the Sovereign, considered as such, to have the executive power, right and fact would be so utterly confounded that one could no longer tell what is law and what is not, and the body politic thus denatured would soon fall prey to the violence against which it was instituted.[47]

Rousseau's key concern, therefore, was how to set the right balance between legislative and executive powers. Yet, his understanding on this matter differed from that of Montesquieu. On this point, Rousseau was diametrically opposed to his predecessor.[48] His goal was not to 'separate' the constitutional powers but rather thoroughly and permanently to subordinate the executive to the legislative. Clearly, if the sovereign wished to govern, his power would be much greater than that of the government and if the government wished to legislate, its abusive power would make it stronger than the sovereign.

In moving from a broad to a modern definition of *government*, Rousseau provided the first rigorous analysis of the rules of government. The subtle study he carries out in Book III of *The Social Contract* (1762) offers a fresh take on a concept that had previously been ill-defined. More importantly, this new definition enabled him to address the issue of emergency powers.

In *The Social Contract* (Book IV, chapter 6), emergency situation is examined in connection with the Roman dictatorship. The references to it

---

[46] *Ibid*, Book III, ch. 4, p 91.
[47] *Ibid*, Book III, ch 16, p 116.
[48] See J-J Derathé, *Jean-Jacques Rousseau et la science politique de son temps* (Paris, Vrin, 1995) 294–307.

are designed merely to illustrate a point. As Rousseau states at the outset: 'The inflexibility of the laws, which keeps them from bending to events, can in some cases render them pernicious, and through them cause the ruin of a State in crisis.'[49] This abrupt statement seems to be a colossal blow to Rousseau's philosophy, in which 'the supreme law is that all laws must be obeyed'.[50] Yet, he levels criticism at the procedure under which laws are proclaimed, since they may sometimes be protracted or fail to provide for all eventualities. It is still important to legislate but, in certain circumstances, the drawbacks may outweigh the benefits: 'One should therefore not try to consolidate political institutions to the point of depriving oneself of the power to suspend their effect. Even Sparta let its laws lie dormant.'[51]

Be that as it may, Rousseau says little about the exceptional circumstances that endanger the nation (war, sedition, rebellion, and so on). All he refers to is a public security threat, which he fails to define. If such a situation arises, in keeping with the *Roman* model, Rousseau suggests that power be entrusted to the worthiest holder, either by bolstering government activity or by appointing a 'dictator' who would 'override all laws' and 'temporarily suspend sovereign power'. In the first scenario, executive authority would be placed in the hands of one or two government members, which 'would not change the authority of laws, but the way in which they are enforced'. The second scenario would see the sovereign mandate a 'dictator' to make decisions and report to 'extraordinary assemblies which may be required by unforeseen circumstances'.[52] Whatever option is chosen, unlike Locke's theory, the initiative of emergency measures does not lie with the party entrusted with full powers.

Fundamentally, Rousseau sees nothing strange in the sovereign authority removing itself from the equation, since 'the general will is not in doubt'. Indeed,

> it is obvious that the people's foremost intention is that the State not perish. This way the suspension of the legislative authority does not abolish it; the magistrate who silences it cannot make it speak, he dominates it without being able to represent it; he can do everything, except make laws.[53]

While suspended, legislative activity is merely put on hold. Dictators – or government members – draw their authority solely from a *mandate*, and *hold no sovereign powers*. A decision by the legislative authority to suspend

[49] Rousseau, n 45 above, Book IV, ch 6, p 138.
[50] J-J Rousseau, 'Discours sur l'économie politique', in *Œuvres complètes* (Paris, éd La Pléiade, 1964) tome III, p 249 (my translation).
[51] Rousseau, n 45 above, Book IV, ch 6, p 138.
[52] *Ibid*, Book III, ch 13, p 111.
[53] *Ibid*, Book IV, ch 6, pp 138–9.

its office does not therefore pose any major legal difficulty since it is nothing more than an extraordinary recess. If the legislative power alone decides how often it meets and empowers the magistrate to convene extraordinary legislative sessions, it is also entitled to waive its own rules. Moreover, Rousseau sees the mandate as limited in time. He considers how to safeguard the sovereign against dictators taking liberties and, to this end, examines the lessons learnt from history. He points out the excellent standards upheld by the Romans, which deteriorated under Sylla and Cesar. Basically, however, if the choice comes down to the state's survival or compliance with its laws, *the former should prevail.* The decision is to be taken by the sovereign, whose general will can not be doubted, since the state of emergency must be *blatant.* If the circumstances clearly require action, what counts is the goal pursued by the general will (common good), not its scope (unanimity).

There is no logical conflict inherent in the legal mechanisms governing the implementation of emergency powers. Sovereign power cannot be limited by positive law. Instead, it is circumscribed by its own preservation, a veto on self-destruction. According to Rousseau,

> the body politic or Sovereign, since it owes its being solely to the sanctity of the contract, can never obligate itself, even toward another, to anything that detracts from that original act, such as to alienate any part of itself or to subject itself to another Sovereign. To violate the act by which it exists would be to annihilate itself, and what is nothing produces nothing.[54]

The underlying principle here is that sovereignty must last. *The sovereign can and must do all* within its power to survive, even if its action is iniquitous, violent or downright criminal. In the face of extreme danger, the law can be bent infinitely. The mandate that gives rise to a dictator does not redefine the sovereign; it merely stretches its meaning for as long as the dictatorship lasts. Here, Rousseau draws a distinction between suspending legislative authority and suspending sovereign authority. In a dictatorship, the sovereign no longer legislates, but it does not relinquish its authority. Moreover, the dictator is empowered by a *mandate*, not through a *transfer* of sovereignty.

Rousseau sidesteps the Lockean possibility of an *'appeal to heaven'* because 'since the alienation is made without reservation, the union is as perfect as it can be, and no associate has anything further to claim'. Indeed,

> for if individuals were left some rights, then, since there would be no common superior who might adjudicate between them and the public, each, being judge

---

[54] *Ibid*, Book I, ch 7, p 52.

of his own case on some issue, would soon claim to be so on all, the state of nature would subsist and the association necessarily become tyrannical or empty.[55]

On this count, Rousseau is as categorical as Hobbes: sovereignty is either absolute or it does not exist. That does not mean that the sovereign must constantly intervene in the lives of subjects. Under the social pact, individuals only relinquish the part of their authority, assets and freedom that is important to the community. However, as Rousseau insists, 'the Sovereign is alone judge of that importance'.[56]

Rousseau tested out his emergency model in *The Government of Poland* (1772), published ten years after *The Social Contract*. Under the Polish system, only nobles enjoyed political rights. The Parliament – the Diet – was made up of a senate (largely aristocrats) and a chamber of deputies (elected by noblemen in provincial assemblies). Ultimate power laid with the Diet, and the King could not act without its blessing. In Rousseau's day, it was frequently hamstrung by dissent amongst the nobles, as *liberum veto* meant that just one opposing vote could stifle a decision within the assembly. Against this backdrop, noblemen came together to form *confederations* or leagues in a bid to safeguard the state and its constitution. Rousseau approved, although this was 'a violent state in the Republic; but there are extreme evils which render violent remedies necessary'. He compared confederations to Roman dictatorships – 'both silence the laws in times of pressing peril' – and praised them as a 'masterpiece of politics'.[57]

As in *The Social Contract*, Rousseau accepts that in times of peril, laws may be silenced and power concentrated. He recommends an appraisal of the cases in which these *confederations* might legitimately be required (without actually mooting a list of probable triggering factors). He adds that one should 'then carefully regulate their form and function, so as to give them legal sanction as far as it is possible to do so without interfering with their formation or their activity'. No further guidance is provided however. Realism or fatalism spurs Rousseau on to point out that 'there are even situations the very occurrence of which should lead to an immediate confederation of the whole Poland'.[58] Examples include foreign invasion or suspension of the Diet by force. A confederation may be formed without prior authorisation or defined scope. In that case, it has no legal basis. In *The Social Contract*, Rousseau, who refuses to split the scope or exercise of sovereignty, effortlessly addressed the issue of

[55]   *Ibid*, Book I, ch 7, p 50.
[56]   *Ibid*, Book II, ch 4, p 52.
[57]   J-J Rousseau, *Considerations on the Government of Poland*, V Gourevitch (ed) (Cambridge, Cambridge University Press, 1997) 219–20.
[58]   *Ibid* at 220.

preserving the state. Faced with a real-life situation in *The Government of Poland*, he struggled to provide legal justification for the absolute imperative of safeguarding the state.

It may appear strange that a philosopher could theorise so easily about what he most feared, that is the suspension of the laws. To understand his reasoning, we must begin with Rousseau's conversion of men into citizens, which in a sense subjugates laws to what I shall call the *patriotic imperative*.[59] Ultimately, the state must prevail and the very valid pursuit of its survival justifies the state of emergency. Under the social pact, the whole takes precedence over the parts: natural man ceases to exist and citizens are born, existing through their participation in a society whose purpose is its own preservation. One of the fundamental rights that citizens enjoy is the right to participate in lawmaking, and laws may be suspended if the sovereign so decides. This 'collective body' is to be protected at all costs; any enemy of the state is an enemy of the people. According to this line of reasoning, the sovereign is fully entitled to eliminate someone who does not threaten its integrity or unity but has been deemed a 'public enemy'. Here Rousseau is close to a permanent theory of the state of emergency, as evidenced by his choice of words, gradually moving from the clear-headed preservation of the state to 'homeland safety'.

Besides the *patriotic imperative*, there is another reason for Rousseau to support such vision of emergency powers, which, at this point, I shall briefly lay out: his *republican* conception of liberty.

As demonstrated by Quentin Skinner, the debate on civil liberty in the republican tradition was generally bound to an analysis of the link between the liberty of subjects and the powers held by the state. The central question was always to identify the prerequisites for reconciling the opposing demands of civil liberty and political duty in the most harmonious way possible.[60] This view largely stemmed from Roman moral philosophy and, in particular, from writers who admired the ancient Roman Republic, such as Titus Livy, Sallust and, above all, Cicero. They drew heavily on the Roman legal tradition as set out in the *Digest* of Roman law.

---

[59] See J Shklar, *Men and Citizens* (Cambridge, Cambridge University Press, 1969).

[60] Quentin Skinner has developed his account of republicanism in a number of different articles since the early 1980s. They include: 'Machiavelli on the Maintenance of Liberty' (1983) 18 *Politics* 3–15; 'The Paradoxes of Political Liberty', in S McMurrin (ed), *The Tanner Lectures on Human Values* (Cambridge, Cambridge University Press, 1986) vol VII, pp 225–50; 'The Republican Ideal of Political Liberty', in G Bock, Q Skinner and M Viroli (eds), *Machiavelli and Republicanism* (Cambridge, Cambridge University Press, 1990) 293–309; For a most recent account to which I am much indebted, see *Liberty before Liberalism* (Cambridge, Cambridge University Press, 1998).

In Roman private law, a citizen's freedom was defined as the individual liberty of one who was not a slave. Slavery was first examined in the *Digest* under the heading *De statu hominis*, which explained that the most fundamental legal distinction was that drawn between a free man and a slave. The latter was described as 'property'. A slave belonged to someone else. While he might have limited ability to take action, he was at all times *in potestate domini*, under his master's authority. The defining feature of slavery and, by extension, the loss of individual liberty, was therefore the fact of being *in potestate*, under someone else's rule.[61]

Roman moralists and historians drew extensively on this definition of slavery when analysing freedom or the lack thereof in a civil or political association. Titus Livy's *History of Rome* is a case in point. The first few books by and large set out how the people of Rome freed themselves from their former rulers to found a free state. According to Titus Livy, a free state is one in which magistrates are elected each year and all citizens are equal in the eyes of the law. It is an autonomous community in which 'laws [*imperium*] take precedence over any man'.[62] When Titus Livy moves on to examine how free states lose their liberty, he inevitably equates this risk with that of 'reverting to slavery'. He uses the terminology of liberty versus slavery to elucidate the idea of political servitude, portraying communities without freedom as living *in potestate*, under the power of another state, or being *dependent* on the will of another. The same 'neo-Roman' theory of liberty re-emerged in the Renaissance, chiefly in the writings of Machiavelli, and became commonplace in seventeenth- and eighteenth-century republicanism, including that of Rousseau.

When analysing civil or political liberties, modern republican theorists made three claims, which are each of constitutional relevance for our purpose. The first claim may be summed up as follows: individual freedom is only available to citizens of a free state. There is no point discussing the freedom of individuals if we do not first examine what Harrington called the 'the liberty of a commonwealth'. A free state can be characterised as one that is not prevented from implementing its own will. In a free state, citizens are free because they are never bent to the arbitrary will of another person. The only authority to which they must answer is that represented by laws. Since no one – not even a magistrate

---

[61]   See, for example, *Digest*, 1985, 2.9.2, vol I, p 52; 9.4.33, vol I, p 303; 11.1.16, vol I, p 339. For the fullest later discussion, see Book 41 on the acquisition of the ownership of things, especially 41.1.10, vol IV, p 491.

[62]   Livy 2. 1. para 1, in Livy, 1919, p 218: 'Imperiaque legum potentiora quam hominum.' For similar phrases in Cicero and Sallust, see C Wirszubski, *Libertas as a Political Idea at Rome during the Late Republic and Early Principate* (Cambridge, Cambridge University Press, 1960) 9.

– is above the laws adopted by the majority, there can be no arbitrary action and no domination. Clearly, *individual freedom and freedom of the state are linked*.

The second assumption follows on closely from the first. A free state can lose its liberty, thereby depriving individuals of theirs. As a result, their situation changes, to become one of servitude. Machiavelli, Harrington and Rousseau all agree on the trade-off between liberty and servitude in their analysis of political systems. On the one hand, there are free states and, on the other, states in servitude. There is no middle ground, and it is a short path to servitude. All it takes is an incident where the political body is subjugated to the will of a third party, say a royal veto, for arbitrary power to take hold. In the ensuing scenario, individual security is jeopardised, there are people above the law and the system teeters on the brink of tyranny.

The third republican claim flows logically from the first two. If liberty is only achieved by living in a free state, there is the need for a political system untainted by discretionary power, one in which civil rights do not hinge on the good will of a sovereign, oligarchy or any other representative of the state. In other words, what is called for is a legal system defined by Titus Livy and translated by Harrington in 1656 as 'the empire of laws and not of men'.[63] Only in this way is it possible to safeguard citizens' action through rights enshrining their liberty. The only free system is one in which liberty and law are interlinked, creating a symbiotic relationship between the two. Freedom exists through laws, not in spite of them.

Most of the elements of this republican conception of liberty are to be found in Rousseau's theory. Since we can only hope to enjoy freedom if we live as members of a free state, it is thus vital to take any necessary steps to maintain such a free state. This is clearly for Rousseau one of the reason to support emergency measures as part of a set of constitutional arrangements under which it might be claimed that the *res* (the government) genuinely reflects the will and promotes the good of the *publica* (the community as a whole). Indeed, when the state dissolves, the people become a multitude, and individual liberty degenerates into servitude. There is no longer a 'republic'; both the community and the individual become enslaved. Thus, the preservation of liberty requires the preservation of a 'well-ordered society'. As Maurizio Viroli points out:

> Although it might be almost impossible to achieve, the republic is the only alternative to disorder. For Rousseau, to live in a well-ordered community is the principal condition for happiness and personal dignity. When men feel

---

[63] J Harrington, *The Commonwealth of Oceana* and *A System of Politics*, JGA Pocock (ed) (Cambridge, Cambridge University Press, 1992) 8, 20.

themselves to be in their proper place and all about them to be in its proper place, then their existence becomes *douce*. By contrast it is better to live alone than to live in a disordered society, for there is no condition so onerous as the absence of liberty.[64]

As could be expected, Rousseau favours placing the state of emergency within the constitution. It must be regulated *ex ante*, with specific constitutional rules on how and when it may be triggered, how long it can last and the powers that may be invoked. Unlike Montesquieu, Rousseau still believed that the constitutional regulation of emergency powers would make it easier to deal with emergencies and crisis, as well as preventing such powers from being misused. If a specific form of government was triggered to overcome an uncharacteristic threat, citizens, and thus the sovereign, should have the legal means to monitor emergency powers.

III. THE LEGACY OF THE TWO MODELS

In his famous *Decline and Fall of the Roman Empire* (1776–1788), Edward Gibbon restated the story of how the Romans slaughtered defenceless aliens in their eastern cities in 395 AD as a pre-emptive warning to the barbarians massing at the gates of their empire:

> On the appointed day, the unarmed crowd of the Gothic youth was carefully collected in the square, or Forum; the streets and avenues were occupied by the Roman troops; and the roofs of the houses were covered with archers and slingers. At the same hour, in all the cities of the East, the signal was given of indiscriminate slaughter; and the provinces of Asia were delivered, by the cruel prudence of Julius, from a domestic enemy, who, in a few months, might have carried fire and sword from the Hellespont to the Euphrates. The urgent consideration of the public safety may undoubtedly authorise the violation of every positive law. How far that, or any other, consideration may operate to dissolve the natural obligations of humanity and justice is a doctrine of which I still desire to remain ignorant.[65]

Gibbon declined to answer to one of the oldest and hardest questions in politics. Had he tried to, he would have faced the two models of emergency powers analysed by Montesquieu and Rousseau.

---

[64] M Viroli, 'The Concept of *ordre* and the Language of Classical Republicanism in Jean-Jacques Rousseau' in A Pagden (ed), *The Languages of Political Theory in Early-Modern Europe* (Cambridge, Cambridge University Press, 1987) 178.

[65] E Gibbon, *The History of the Decline and Fall of the Roman Empire*, JB Bury (ed) (New York, Fred de Fau and Co, 1906) vol IV, ch 26, p 321.

Indeed, these two philosophers adopted widely divergent approaches to emergency powers. Although both ended up with a type of 'monar-chy' in exceptional circumstances, Montesquieu's government drew his authority from the social pact, whereas Rousseau's dictator was assigned it for a limited period of time through a mandate. The two men believed that the state should be preserved, but Montesquieu, like Locke, acknowledged that individuals have the right – sometimes the obligation – to 'oppose' state interference, while Rousseau did not, on account of his idea of sovereignty and his vision of liberty.

Clearly, modern European constitutionalism provides us with two models of the state of emergency: the *English* model promoted by Montesquieu, and Rousseau's *Roman* model, which relied upon classical republicanism. The *English* one is based on a balanced view of powers. The executive can decide to declare a state of emergency and accordingly assigns itself special powers, but ultimately citizens alone – or their representatives – can pass judgement on this prerogative. The body entrusted with increased powers is therefore accountable to a judicial authority, that is, *ex post* checks. I would describe advocates of this model as *sceptics*, on account of their belief that disagreement on the onset and very existence of a state of emergency is inevitable. Hence, they prefer to empower a branch of the constitutional system to proclaim a state of emergency. Their concern is not so much the risk emergencies pose for the constitutional structure, but rather potential misuse by regular state bodies in their recourse to special laws. Since the perception of danger or threat is deeply subjective, they feel that constitutional leeway is required. This path seems to be the one taken by the US constitutional system since the end of the civil war. Admittedly, the US Constitution does stipulate (US Constitution, Article 1, section 9, clause 2) that the privilege of the writ of habeas corpus may be suspended 'when in Cases of Rebellion or Invasion the public Safety may require it', but this Article has not been invoked since the civil war and the *Ex Parte Milligan* ruling (1866). Also, according to some authors, while emergencies may result in a temporary suspension of judicial power, the emergency provisions of the US Constitution do not allow suspension of congressional power. Instead, they seem to require that the President's own power be subordi-nate to that of the Congress at such a time.

The second model is one I described as *Roman*. It is rooted in the *separation* between the body which declares the state of emergency and that which exercises emergency powers. Legal mechanisms are devised to regulate emergency measures, and these measures must be brought within the constitution. To my mind, those who champion this model are *idealists*. They are concerned by the fragility of the constitutional order and believe that the very concept of emergency must be covered by a prior definition. They underline the notion of public safety and argue that we are capable of objectively recognising the presence of a threat or emergency. Their overarching goal is to *legalise* the state of emergency, and they do not tolerate vagueness in the constitution. This approach to emergency powers is common in mainland Europe. For example, French Constitutions of the late eighteenth and nineteenth centuries tentatively began to elaborate the idea of a constitutional state of emergency, leaving some important details to statutes. More recently, in line with General de Gaulle's wishes, Article 16 of the current French Constitution regulates emergency powers, authorising the President of the Republic to take requisite *measures* 'if the institutions of the Republic, the independence of the nation, its territorial integrity or ability to fulfil international commitments are in serious and immediate jeopardy and the normal exercise of constitutional public powers has broken down'. In April 1961, during the Algerian crisis, de Gaulle invoked Article 16, even though there had been no breakdown in public powers. In many ways, a similar path has been adopted in Germany. Article 48 of the Weimar Constitution (1919), which has been described as the *'Diktaturgewalt des Reichpraesidenten'* (dictatorial power of the President), was not included in the current German Constitution, for obvious historical reasons.[66] Nevertheless, on 24 June 1968, the coalition of Social Democrats and Christian Democrats passed a law supplementing the Constitution with the possibility of a 'domestic state of necessity' (*Innere Notstand*).

A more in-depth analysis of emergency powers in the Western legal tradition would undoubtedly provide further proof of the debt owed to both republican and liberal constitutional thought.[67] As I have already posited, republican constitutional thinking viewed the freedom of the state and, by extension, of the *majority of citizens* as its supreme political tenet. As such, it contemplated a theory of emergency that went further than liberal thinking in the emphasis placed on preserving the state.

In a 2005 article entitled 'The Return of Carl Schmitt', Scott Horton compared the US administration's rationale that the President, as 'commander-in-chief', is not bound by international conventions in times of war with Carl Schmitt's arguments in the 1920s that a state could not remain sovereign, if the President could not exempt himself upon necessary occasions from constitutional rules that would prevent him from prevailing in a contest of force with the state's enemies.[68] Whether or not he is right, Scott Horton's article alerts us to the danger of gradually

---

[66] In the early 1930s, the creeping use of the ever-expanding Art 48 of the Weimar Constitution had, in many ways, allowed the Nazis to seize power in Germany.

[67] For a more detailed analysis, see K Lane Scheppele, 'Law in a Time of Emergency: States of Exception and the Temptations of 9/11' (2004) 6 *University of Pennsylvania Journal of Constitutional Law* 1001–83.

[68] S Horton, 'The Return of Carl Schmitt', *Balkanisation*, 7 November 2005, <http:\\balkin.blogspot.com/2005/11/return-of-carl-schmitt.html>.

chipping away at the principles of both liberal and republican constitutional thinking. In its 'war on terror', the United States is using extraordinary provisional powers as if they were part and parcel of a standard model of government. A permanent state of emergency is taking hold, with no distinction between war and peace or domestic and international politics. As Kim Lane Scheppele points out:

> The idea of the state of exception from which the Bush administration has proceeded has met sharp international criticism, precisely because the international community has moved from the Schmittian framework to which the Bush administration's response bears strong resemblance. Carl Schmitt's justification for the state of exception – and by extension the Bush administration's justification for the response to the terrorists attacks of 2001 – presupposes a world that no longer exists.[69]

In eighteenth-century Europe, leading liberal or republican theorists may not necessarily have provided a detailed roadmap for declaring a state of emergency, deploying emergency powers or ascertaining emergency situations, but they did sketch a fairly comprehensive picture of the difficulties linked to the state of emergency. They argued that emergency powers were not inherently dangerous, but their misuse was. According to them, every effort must be made to prevent the line between normalcy and emergency becoming irrevocably blurred. The state of emergency could not become the norm, as this would fundamentally jeopardise the rule of law.

---

[69] Scheppele, n 67 above at 1003. The philosopher Giorgio Agambem takes a similar view by pointing out the danger for modern politics of eviscerating the dichotomy between the norm and the exception: see G Agemben, *Etat d'exception. Homo Sacer* (Paris, Seuil, 2003).

3

Liberal State Responses to Terrorism and Their Limits

PAUL WILKINSON

I. CONCEPT AND TYPOLOGY

THE CONCEPT OF terrorism is often totally misused, as when it is employed as a synonym for political violence in general or when it is used as a pejorative for any insurgent campaign of which we disapprove. It is also frequently used loosely and inconsistently. In this respect it shares the same problem of other key strategic political concepts, such as 'revolution', 'imperialism' and 'democracy'. None of these concepts lends itself to a universally agreed one-sentence definition. Yet all of them are indispensable for political discourse, and there is a sufficiently widely shared acceptance of the core meaning of such concepts for them to play a central role in international political and social scientific debate.

Alex Schmid and Albert Jongman have produced impressive evidence of the extent to which a minimum consensus definition of terrorism has become accepted among the international community of social scientists who study conflict.[1] Equally significant is the development of a whole body of international resolutions, conventions and agreements dealing with aspects of the prevention, suppression and punishment of acts of terrorism[2] in which there is near-universal acceptance of the terminology used to describe the form of behaviour to be condemned or prohibited. Contemporary international academic, diplomatic and juridical debates on terrorism no longer become bogged down in definitional debate. The

---

[1] A Schmid, A Jongman, M Stohl, J Brand, P Flemming, A Van der Poel and R Thijsse (eds), *Political Terrorism: A New Guide to Actors, Authors, Concepts, Data Bases, Theories and Literature*, 2nd edn (Amsterdam, North Holland Publishing Co, 1988) 1–32. This volume also contains an invaluable bibliography.

[2] A useful collection of the texts of these international measures, together with an authoritative commentary, is provided in R Friedlander, *Terrorism: Documents of International and Local Control. Vols 1–48* (Dobbs Ferry, Oceana Publications Inc, 1970–2004).

major disputes that arise concern culpability for specific attacks or for sponsoring or directing them, and over the kind of international measures that should be taken in response.

Terrorism is neither a political philosophy nor a movement, nor is it a synonym for political violence in general. It is a special means or method of conflict which has been employed by a wide variety of factions and regimes. It is premeditated and systematic, and aims to create a climate of extreme fear or terror. The modern words *terror* and *terrorism* are derived from the Latin verbs *terrere*, to cause to tremble, and *deterrere*, to frighten from. *Terrorism* and *terrorist* did not come into use until the period of the French Revolution in the 1790s. The term was used by Edmund Burke in his polemic against the French Revolution,[3] and came to be used to denote those revolutionaries who sought to use terror systematically either to further their views or to govern, whether in France or elsewhere.

A key feature of terrorism is that it is directed at a wider audience and target than the immediate victims. It is one of the earliest forms of psychological warfare. The ancient Chinese strategist, Sun-Tzu, conveyed the essence of the method when he wrote 'kill one, frighten ten thousand'.[4] An inevitable corollary is that terrorism entails attacks on random and symbolic targets, including civilians, in order to create a climate of extreme fear among the wider groups. Terrorists often claim to be carefully selective and discriminating in their choice of targets but to the community that experiences a terrorism campaign, the attacks are bound to seem arbitrary and indiscriminate. In order to create the widespread sense of fear they seek, terrorists deliberately use the weapons of surprise and disproportionate violence in order to create a sense of outrage and general insecurity. As Raymond Aron observes:

> An action of violence is labelled "terrorist" when its psychological effects are out of all proportion to its purely physical result ...The lack of discrimination helps to spread fear, for if no one in particular is a target, no one can be safe.[5]

It is this characteristic which differentiates terrorism from tyrannicide and individual political assassination.

As Hannah Arendt has observed,[6] the belief that one could change a whole political system by assassinating the major figure has clearly been rendered obsolete by the transition from the age of absolutist rulers to an age of government bureaucracy. In all but a handful of regimes today real

[3] E Burke, *Reflections on the Revolution in France* (Stanford, CA, Stanford University Press, 2001).

[4] Sun-Tzu, 'The Art of Warfare' in Sun-Tzu and Karl Von Clausewitz, *The Book of War* (New York, The Modern Library, 2000) 1–248

[5] R Aron, *Peace and War* (London, Weidenfeld and Nicholson, 1966) 170.

[6] H Arendt, 'On Violence' in *Crises of the Republic* (Harmondsworth, Penguin, 1973) 103–98.

power is wielded by bureaucratic elite of anonymous or faceless officials. Arendt provides a powerful explanation for the fact that the age of bureaucracy has coincided with the burgeoning of political terrorism. Terrorism has become for its perpetrators, supporters and sponsors the most attractive low-cost, low-risk but potentially high-yield method of attacking a regime or a rival faction. The bomb plot against Hitler, had it succeeded, would have been an act of tyrannicide, not of terrorism. Who can deny that Hitler was the linchpin of the Nazi system?

The concept of terrorism used in the contemporary academic literature is essentially political. What about the use of terrorist methods in the name of a religious cause? Or for the pursuit of criminal gain? It is true that militant religious fundamentalists have often throughout history waged holy terror as part of a holy war, and there is much concern about the risk of contemporary fanatical Islamist fundamentalist groups such as the Al Qaeda network. But the major reason why moderate Muslim leaders and secular movements see these particular fundamentalist groups as such a threat is precisely because their revolutionary Islamic agenda aims not merely at the 'purifying' of religious practice but at the overthrow of existing governments and their replacement by fundamentalist theocracies. Hence these movements are inherently religious *and* political. The worrying trend whereby powerful criminal gangs, such as the Italian Mafia[7] and the Latin American narco-barons,[8] have adopted some of the tactics and weapons of terrorist groups, does pose grave problems for the relevant law-enforcement authorities. But it does not detract from the value of the core concept of political terrorism. In reality, the overwhelming majority of perpetrators of contemporary terrorism use the weapon to influence political behaviour.

It is important to note that the above defining criteria of political terrorism are broad enough to encompass states' use of terror as well as that performed by groups. Typologically, it is useful to distinguish *state* from *factional* terror. Normally in the literature, a state's use of terror is referred to as *terror*, while sub-state terror is referred to as *terrorism*. This distinction is employed throughout this chapter. Historically, states have employed terror as a weapon of tyranny and repression and as an instrument of war. Another important distinction can be made between *international* and *domestic* terrorism: the former is terrorist violence involving the citizens of more than one country, while the latter is confined within the borders of one country, sometimes within a particular locality in the country. This distinction is useful for analytical and statistical purposes. However, in reality, it is hard to find an example of

---

[7] See, eg, 'Mafia Blows up Judge', *The Guardian* (London), 20 July 1992.
[8] R Clutterbuck, *Terrorism and Guerrilla Warfare* (London, Routledge, 1990).

any significant terrorist campaign that remains purely domestic: any serious terrorist campaign actively seeks political support, weapons, financial assistance and safe haven beyond its own borders.

Once we move beyond these very broad categories it is useful to employ a basic typology of contemporary perpetrators of terrorism based on their underlying cause or political motivation.

A. Nationalist Terrorists

These are groups seeking political self-determination. They may wage their struggle entirely in the territory they seek to liberate, or they may be active both in their home areas and abroad. In some cases they may be forced by police or military action or by threat of capture, imprisonment or execution to operate entirely from their places of exile. Nationalist groups tend to be more capable of sustaining protracted campaigns and mobilising substantial support than ideological groups. Even those nationalist groups that can only claim the support of a minority of their ethnic constituency, for example ETA (Basque Homeland and Liberty), can gain political resonance because of their deep roots in the national culture for which they claim to be the authentic voice.[9]

B. Ideological Terrorists

These terrorists seek to change the entire political, social and economic system either to an extreme Left or extreme Right model. In the 1970s and 1980s studies of ideological terrorism focused on the extreme Left, because of the preoccupation with groups such as the Red Army Faction in Germany and the Red Brigades in Italy. Yet, as Laqueur[10] noted in his magisterial general history of terrorism, the dominant ideological orientation of European terrorism between the world wars was fascist. And it is neo-Nazi and neo-fascist groups which are behind so much of the racist and anti-immigrant violence in present-day Germany and other European countries. The Red Army groups so active in the 1970s and 1980s have now largely faded away, the victims of their own internal

---

[9] E Martinez-Herrera, 'National Extremism and Outcomes of State Policies in the Basque Country, 1979–2001' (2002) 4 *International Journal on Multicultural Studies* 1.

[10] W Laqueur, *Terrorism* (London, Weidenfeld and Nicholson, 1977).

splits, determined law enforcement by their respective police and judicial authorities and changing political attitudes among young people in the post-Cold War era.[11]

C. Religio-political Terrorists

The most frequently cited examples of this type of terrorism are groups such as Hezbollah and Hamas. Al Qaeda is the most dangerous of all these groups and has a political agenda and religious doctrine combined. But it is important to bear in mind that militant fundamentalist factions of major religions other than Islam have also frequently spawned their own violent extremist groups. Striking examples can be found among Sikhs, Hindus and Jews and there is a well-documented link between certain Christian fundamentalist groups and extreme right-wing terrorism in North and Central America.[12]

D. Single Issue Terrorists

These groups are obsessed with the desire to change a specific policy or practice within the target society, rather than with the aim of political revolution. Examples include the violent animal rights and anti-abortion groups.

E. State-sponsored and State-supported Terrorists

States use this type of terrorism as a tool of both domestic and foreign policy. For example, when regimes send hit squads to murder leading dissidents and exiled political leaders they are doing so for domestic reasons, to intimidate and eradicate opposition to the regime. However, when North Korea sent its agents to mount a bomb attack on the South Korean government delegation on its visit to Rangoon, the communist regime was engaging in an act of covert warfare against its perceived 'enemy' government in the South.[13] It was an act designed to further their foreign policy aim of undermining the Republic of South Korea. State sponsors may use their own directly recruited and controlled terror squads, or may choose to act through client groups and proxies. They

[11] R Drake, *The Aldo Moro Murder Case*, (Cambridge, MA, Harvard University Press, 1995).
[12] See P Wilkinson, *Political Terrorism* (London, Macmillian, 1974).
[13] 'A Bomb Wreaks Havoc in Rangoon', *Time Magazine*, October 1983.

almost invariably go to some lengths to disguise their involvement in order to sustain plausible deniability. The ending of the Cold War together with the overthrow of the Eastern European communist one-party regimes and the former Soviet Union certainly removed in one fell swoop the Warsaw Pact's substantial network of sponsorship and support for a whole variety of terrorist groups. But this does not mean that state sponsorship has ceased to be a factor in the international terrorist scene.

F. Differences between Traditional Terrorist Groups and the Al Qaeda Network

A common mistake is to assume that the variety of terrorism which is seen as the predominant threat at any given time is the only type of terrorism the liberal state has to try to prevent and respond to. This can lead governments and counterterrorism agencies to neglect or completely ignore the wider range of terrorists that may cause problems for their own countries and for the international system generally. Over-concentration on the problems posed by the Al Qaeda network of terrorist networks can lead to a 'one-size-fits-all' approach to dealing with terrorism. It is important to remember that almost all liberal states face various types of more traditional terrorism in addition to the so-called 'new terrorism' of the Al Qaeda network and other *jihadi* groups.

The Al Qaeda network is a truly transnational movement with a presence in at least 60 countries. It aims at nothing less that the reordering of the entire international system.[14] They want to force the United States and other Western countries to withdraw their presence from the Middle East and other Muslim lands. The regimes of all Muslim states that trade and cooperate with Western states are to be toppled because they are deemed to be 'apostate' regimes, betraying the 'true Islam' as defined by Osama bin Laden. Ultimately Al Qaeda aims to create a pan-Islamist Caliphate to rule over all Muslims throughout the world. In order to achieve their absolutist aims members of the Al Qaeda network are dedicated to using the weapon of terrorism and are prepared to launch mass killing attacks because they believe that the end justifies the means.

The Al Qaeda attacks on the World Trade Center and the Pentagon on 11 September 2001 and their whole world record of suicide no-warning

[14] See FA Gerges, *The Far Enemy: Why Jihad Went Global* (New York, Cambridge University Press, 2005).

bombings before and since then shows that they have no compunction about the mass murder of civilians including thousands of their co-religionists.

It is true that some more traditional terrorist groups, both past and present, have killed many hundreds of civilians. However, unlike Al Qaeda, which has explicitly urged Muslims to kill as many of their designated 'enemy' civilians as possible,[15] the more traditional groups have aimed, in Brian Jenkins' words, to have 'a lot of people watching, not a lot of people dead'.[16]

Most traditional terrorist groups have directed their attacks against a single chosen 'enemy' state in order to pursue a more specific and limited agenda. For example, although the Tamil Tigers (LTTE)[17] have established a worldwide network for obtaining funds, weaponry and political support, almost all their violence has been directed at the Sri Lankan government and citizens inside Sri Lanka itself. The same is true of the Basque terrorist group, Basque Homeland and Liberty (ETA),[18] and other ethno-nationalist groups, although in some cases they have chosen to target foreign tourists and businesses in order to damage the economy of their target state and gain international publicity for their cause.

Traditional terrorist groups usually have a vertical command and control structure under the tight control of a single leader or a small directorate. However, it is also quite common, especially in the case of ethno-nationalist groups, to have a political wing which concentrates on winning the propaganda war against the government and, if they are permitted, on winning electoral support by running candidates for national and local representative institutions.[19] These features can, in some cases, open up the prospect of more pragmatic elements in the movement successfully building a political support base among the general population and discarding the weapon of terrorism and choosing the political pathway to achieve their objectives (for example the IRA).[20] In other words, in some cases the violent conflict which spawns increasing terrorism may be terminated when leaders and the government they oppose see a common interest in seeking a ceasefire[21] and following this up with a peace process. In these circumstances a terrorist campaign

---

[15] Fatwa issued by bin Laden and others, February 1998, in W Laqueur (ed), *Voices of Terror* (New York, Reed Press, 2004).

[16] B Jenkins, 'Will Terrorists Go Nuclear?' (1975) P-5541 *Rand Paper* 4.

[17] See R Gunaratna, 'War and Peace in Sri Lanka' (1987) *Colombo Institute of Fundamental Studies*.

[18] See FS Leera, JM Mata and C Irwin, 'ETA: From Secret Army to Social Movement' (Autumn 1993) 5(3) *Terrorism and Political Violence* 123.

[19] See useful analysis in A Richards, 'The Role and Utility of Terrorist Political Fronts in the "Northern Ireland Context"' (unpublished Ph D thesis, University of St Andrews, 2003).

[20] *Ibid*.

[21] *Ibid*.

becomes potentially corrigible. One of the features of Al Qaeda which makes it so dangerous is that it shows no pragmatic tendencies of this kind. Its absolutist and fanatical commitment to mass slaughter of civilians continues unabated, indicating that it is essentially incorrigible in nature. In other words, democratic states do not have the option of attracting it into a political route out of terrorism.[22] Hence liberal states committed to upholding democracy, the rule of law and human rights must find other forms of response which can deal effectively with the task of protecting the public from Al Qaeda terrorism. This must be done while ensuring that the basic values and principles on which a democratic way of life is based are not sacrificed in the process.[23] After all, let us be quite clear that the overriding aim of the liberal state's response to terrorism is to preserve free and open societies.

If we start to demolish or undermine our freedom in the name of state security we will unwittingly be doing the terrorists' job for them, far more rapidly and effectively than they could ever hope to achieve. The public are repeatedly being reminded by government ministers that we need a tougher response to terrorism, more legislation to give the state security authorities yet more powers on the grounds that otherwise the state will be too weak to deal effectively with the threat posed.[24] It is all too rarely the case that legislators pose the important question about these endless demands for extra powers. How *effective* are the new measures likely to be? Have they been tried before? If so, with what degree of success, if any? Is there a real risk that the more Draconian measures will increase the threat by alienating people within minority communities and serving as a recruiting sergeant for terrorists groups? The dangers of a response which is an overreaction may be just as great or even greater, than the risk of underreaction.[25]

To be successful at dealing with the challenges of modern terrorism while remaining true to its own values, the liberal state must seek to achieve a measured and proportionate response which preserves the balance between the protection of civil liberties and the duty of government to maintain national security.

[22] See Gerges, n 14 above, for an expert analysis of the implications of Al Qaeda ideology.
[23] See P Wilkinson, *Terrorism Versus Democracy – The Liberal State Response*, 2nd edn (London, Routledge, 2006).
[24] *Ibid.*
[25] *Ibid* at chs 5, 6 and 12.

II. POSSIBLE MODELS OF LIBERAL DEMOCRATIC RESPONSE

There are two possible responses which we should discount at the outset because both would almost inevitably lead to the destruction, or, at best, a prolonged suspension, of liberal democracy. At one extreme there is a response of complete acquiescence to terrorist violence, threats and demands, leading to a situation where the terrorists win their aims entirely on their terms. In a number of colonial independence struggles in the 1950s and 1960s (for example in Algeria, Cyprus and Aden) some-thing very close to this did occur. But the conditions of decaying colonialism provided exceptional opportunities for terrorists which no longer exist in the twenty-first century.[26] The colonial regimes lacked the will to maintain their control and were gravely economically and mili-tarily weakened by the exertions of World War Two. The terrorists in such cases had vast popular support from their own populations. How-ever, the resulting regimes set in place by the victorious terrorists could hardly be described as models of liberal democratic governance.

At the other extreme, security forces may employ Draconian military action in an all-out effort to suppress a major terrorist campaign. As is clear from recent experience in Iraq, this is extremely hard to achieve when the terrorism is accompanied by a major insurgency and when it enjoys widespread sympathy and support among the civilian popula-tions. When the terrorist campaign has the support of a small minority, and the majority actively cooperates with the authorities to help suppress the terrorists, security forces may enjoy considerable success in at least significantly reducing, if not entirely eradicating terrorist activity. For example, a Draconian military campaign virtually wiped out the Tupamaros' campaign in Uruguay.[27] But this was at the heavy cost of the virtual suspension of one of the previously most liberal and welfare-minded governments in Latin America and its replacement by an emer-gency regime of an authoritarian character. Extreme overreaction should be rejected because it is potentially totally counterproductive and could result in the undermining of the democratic institutions and constitu-tional and legal foundations one is trying to defend and uphold.

If we rule out these two forms of extreme response for the reasons given above, this leaves four main models of response to terrorism which are open to the liberal state, all of which are currently being employed by a variety of governments.[28]

---

[26] For a valuable historical overview of the types of conflict in former British colonies, see C Townshend, *Britain's Civil Wars* (London, Faber, 1986).

[27] See A Labrousse, *The Tupamaros: Urban guerrillas in Uruguay* (Harmondsworth, Pen-guin, 1973).

[28] For a more detailed discussion of these models see P Wilkinson, n 23 above.

A. Finding a Political Pathway Out of Terrorism

'Peace process' is a much-abused term which has been used in many contexts frequently to denote a predetermined political or ideological 'solution' to a conflict designed and imposed by one party to the conflict. The term can be applied to any sustained political and diplomatic efforts to resolve either international or internal conflicts. Hence it has been used in situations as varied as the Israeli–Palestinian relationship, South Africa, Bosnia, Northern Ireland, Colombia, Nicaragua, El Salvador, Mali, Angola, Mozambique and Cambodia.

Much of my academic work has focused on the relationships between terrorism and liberal democracy,[29] and hence my concern is with the concept of peaceful methods of conflict resolution to prevent or terminate terrorist violence in democratic societies while ensuring that democracy is safeguarded in the process. The new strategic environment with the ending of the Cold War appeared propitious for such peacemaking efforts. For the first time since the establishment of the United Nations the Security Council was no longer completely paralysed by the ideological and strategic conflict between the superpowers. Not surprisingly we have seen a record number of UN peacekeeping and peacemaking efforts during the 1990s. Most of these efforts have involved the extraordinarily difficult problems of terminating and resolving protracted internal ethnic or ethno-religious or ideological wars in which terrorism has played a relatively minor or auxiliary role, or has not been a significant feature. There are very few clear-cut cases where conflict resolution has been used as a means of ending violence by factions using terrorism as their primary weapon. It is salutary realism for us to recognise that to date there have been very few cases of a successful peace process leading to the comprehensive and effective transformation of a terrorist organisation into a democratic party. The IRA's decommissioning of weapons and Sinn Fein's entry into a power-sharing government in Northern Ireland is the most encouraging example.[30] In the 1970s and early 1980s the political wing of ETA did respond very positively to the Spanish government's initiative of 'social reinsertion', which meant that almost all of its members were able to secure their liberty on the clear understanding that they would abandon terrorist violence and participate in purely non-violent democratic politics. This partial achievement is highly encouraging, but we should bear in mind that the hardliners of ETA-militar refused this pathway out of terrorism and continued stubbornly with

[29] See, eg, *ibid*; and P Wilkinson, *Terrorism and the Liberal State*, 2nd edn (Basingstoke, Macmillan, 1986).

[30] See R Monaghan and P Shirlow (eds), 'Northern Ireland 10 Years After the Ceasefires' (2004) Special Issue, 16(3) *Terrorism and Political Violence*.

their campaign of terrorism.[31] It was not until 1998, after it caused outrage by kidnapping and murdering a young councillor, that ETA's hardliners were at last willing to declare a ceasefire and to follow the example of IRA/Sinn Fein by initiating a 'peace process',[32] although the Spanish government and public had grave doubts about ETA's true intentions. These doubts were fully justified by events. In June 2007, ETA ended a brief ceasefire and signalled a return to its terrorist campaign.[33]

The same, sadly, is true of the M19 movement in Colombia. The majority of M19's membership did accept the idea of becoming a peaceful democratic party, but a small hard core continues to believe in violence and is still involved in armed struggles which continue to plague that benighted country.

The recent experience of efforts to pursue peace processes in conflict situations does, however, enable us to reach some tentative conclusions concerning the prerequisites for an effective peace process compatible with democratic principles and values:

- There must be a sufficient political will among both parties to a conflict to initiate and sustain a peace process.
- The role of individual leaders in mobilising and guiding their population/community/movement through the peace process is crucial.
- In many cases, though not invariably, external mediators or brokers for peace may be invaluable in the process, and this may mean a key role for the United Nations, for a regional organisation, or for a major power such as the United States, capable of bringing not only enormous influence but also the substantial economic resources which may be crucial in rehabilitation and recovery following severe conflict.
- Patience and a spirit of compromise together with the courage to take risks for peace are essential qualities for the leaders and negotiators on both sides if they are going to avoid being blown off course by inevitable crises and setbacks during what is likely to be a very protracted and highly complex process.[34]
- A key requirement is for at least a minimal degree of bipartisan consensus in favour of the peace process among the major political parties in the legislature. This proved an essential element in the

---

[31] See RP Clarke, *The Basques: The Franco Years and Beyond* (Reno, NV, University of Nevada Press, 1979); and SG Payne, 'Madrid: ETA–Basque terrorism' (1979) 2(2) *Washington Quarterly* 109–13.

[32] *Ibid.*

[33] L Crawford, 'Spain braced for violence as ETA ends truce', *Financial Times* (London), 6 June 2007.

[34] See R Monaghan and P Shirlow (eds), n 30 above.

long and difficult route to Northern Ireland's Good Friday Agreement.[35] As additionally illustrated by the 1997–98 impasse in the Israeli–Palestinian peace process, if this mainstream consensus is lacking and parties fundamentally opposed to the assumption of the peace process come to power the survival of the process itself is immediately in jeopardy.

Lastly, but every bit as important as the other requisites for peace, political advances must go hand in hand with adequate security safeguards to meet the security concerns and fears of both parties to the conflict. If this fails to be delivered there is a real danger of key parties pulling out of the peace process, or alternatively trying to impose a solution entirely on their own terms, if necessary by the resumption of violence. To overcome these security fears and to build vital confidence some degree of properly supervised disarmament and demobilisation of armed forces/groups is normally a vital phase in a successful peace process.

It is extremely important to beware of a 'miracle breakthrough', or a euphoria based perhaps entirely on paper agreements. Reaching an agreed formula or document of agreement is not enough in itself: much care must be taken to monitor the agreement and to ensure that it is comprehensively and fairly implemented. Without proper follow-through, violence can so easily be rekindled and another peace effort may be even more difficult to achieve.

Last, but by no means least, in the process of attempting to mobilise initial support for peace initiatives and in sustaining the momentum crucial to success, a peace movement with genuine mass support, as broadly based as possible, is of inestimable value. It is hard to exaggerate the difficulties of attaining success with the 'political pathways' model, but wherever possible it should be attempted.

B. The Use of the Military to Aid the Civil Power in Combating Terrorism

This concept of a fully militarised response is quite distinct from the use of the military in aid of the civil power (MACP), so clearly exemplified in Northern Ireland since 1969.[36] Under MACP the military's role is strictly limited to support of the police and the civil authorities, and the army is responsible to the Chief Constable of the Police Service of Northern Ireland (PSNI, previously the Royal Ulster Constabulary – RUC) for

---

[35] *Ibid.*
[36] *Ibid.*

assisting in the maintenance of law and order and the protection of the community and can be held accountable for its actions under the criminal and civil laws.[37] This peacekeeping or quasi-constabulary role is a very difficult one for the army to adapt to and sustain for a prolonged period. The armed forces are trained for the external defence role and for the use of maximum force, or for a peacekeeping role facing a hostile military force. In a quasi-constabulary or peacekeeping role the task of the army is to use minimum force in assisting the police to enforce the law and to protect the community. There are very strong reasons why governments of liberal states should only employ troops for internal security purposes with the very greatest reluctance, and that if they are compelled to deploy them they should seek to withdraw them at the earliest opportunity. This is not meant as a criticism of the policy of using the army in aid of the civil power in Northern Ireland. In 1969 the then Labour Home Secretary James Callaghan[38] and his colleagues had no alternative but to commit troops to Northern Ireland: it was essential because of the escalation of sectarian or inter-communal conflict and the total loss of confidence of one section of the community in the police. Despite occasional serious errors of judgement and policy, perhaps unavoidable in such a sensitive and intractable conflict situation, the British Army's overall contribution in support of the police and in reducing the lethality of the IRA's terrorist campaign has been vital. Without it, Northern Ireland would almost certainly have been plunged into all-out civil war.[39]

There is all the difference in the world between the skilful utilisation of the military within a carefully controlled liberal democratic response to terrorism by the civil authorities and a fully militarised response. A fully militarised response implies the complete suspension of the civilian legal system and its replacement by martial law, summary punishments, the imposition of curfews, military censorship and extensive infringements of normal civil liberties in the name of the exigencies of war. By adopting a totally militarised response the government inevitably finds it has removed all constraints of legal accountability and minimum force, enabling the military commanders to deploy massively lethal and destructive firepower in the name of suppressing terrorism. A tragic example of this in a supposedly democratic state was Russia's use of air power to inflict devastation on Grozny, causing between 30,000 and 40,000 deaths among the civilian population.[40] Far from crushing the separatist movement of the Chechens, the brutality of the Russian armed

---

[37] *Ibid.*

[38] For Callaghan's own account see his *A House Divided* (London, Collins, 1973).

[39] See M Dewar, *The British Army in Northern Ireland* (London, Guild, 1985).

[40] See B Lambeth, 'Russia's Air War in Chechnya' (October–December 1996) 19(4) *Studies in Conflict and Terrorism* 365–84.

forces' assault on Chechnya only served to strengthen the determination of the militants, who in 1996 achieved the withdrawal of Russian forces following further acts of political violence, including mass hostage-taking, against the Russians. The final irony is that unleashing a totally militarised response at huge cost in human rights may ultimately prove counterproductive. Sadly, in the summer of 1999 the Russian government repeated these tragic errors in response to a rebellion led by a Chechen, Shamil Basayev, and Moscow apartment bombings in which several hundred people died, blamed on Chechen terrorists.[41]

A switch to a full-scale militarised response has particularly dangerous implications at the international level. The governments of many countries, including the United States, Israel, India, Turkey and South Korea, have frequently blamed foreign states for their role in sponsoring or masterminding acts of terrorism against them. The hawkish politicians, think-tanks and commentators who advocate 'waging war' on terrorism are to be found advocating military reprisal attacks on alleged sponsors.[42] This view became particularly influential in the United States during the second Reagan administration. Indeed, the Reagan administration adopted this policy when it launched bombing raids on Tripoli and Benghazi in April 1986 in retaliation against Libya's role in the La Belle discotheque bombing in West Berlin in which one US serviceman was killed and 230 customers injured. The Gaddafi regime was militarily powerless to prevent the US air attack or to take any direct military action in response. But Gaddafi did use terrorist methods to exact vengeance on both the United States and on Britain (which had given the US government permission to launch the bombing attack on Libya from British air bases).[43]

However, quite aside from the question of whether such actions as the US bombing of Libya actually 'work' in deterring further terrorism from the sponsor states, there are two other major problems about the idea of waging a 'war against terrorism' in the international arena. First, innocent members of the civilian population in the state targeted for retaliation may be killed or injured, as indeed was the case in the US raid on Libya. Given the scale of modern military firepower this is bound to be a risk in any act of military retaliation. Morally most people would find it easier to justify military retaliation if it was aimed at those actually

---

[41]   See Anna Polikovskaya, *A Dirty War: A Russian Reporter in Chechnya* (New York, The Harvill Press, 2001).

[42]   See Christian Reus-Smit, *American Power and World Order* (Cambridge, Polity Press, 2004).

[43]   The destruction of Pan Am flight 103 could have been motivated by the desire to avenge the 1986 US raid on Libya. It has also been widely assumed that Libya's decision to send major consignments of weapons to the IRA was also an act of revenge for British assistance to the US raid on Libya.

responsible for sponsoring and planning terrorism. Second, there is an obvious danger, especially where the state accused of sponsoring terrorism shares a common border with the state launching military retaliation, that the outcome will be full-scale war. This has already happened in the Middle East, when, in 1982, a terrorist attack triggered the Israeli invasion of Lebanon,[44] and in Kashmir where allegations and counter-allegations concerning terrorism helped spark conflict between India and Pakistan and could do so again.[45] Now terrorism is undoubtedly an evil, but war is a far greater evil involving infinitely greater numbers of deaths and far greater destruction, with the attendant dangers of other states being drawn into the conflict. When one poses the basic questions about international consequences of the militarised response to state-sponsored or -supported terrorism, one becomes more aware of the irresponsibility of those who assume that there is a simple 'military solution' of this nature. Surely the only thing that entitles states to call themselves 'civilised' in terms of international relations is behaviour which is consistent with respect for the rights of the innocent and for the basic principles of international law. Those who do not maintain these basic standards put themselves on the same level morally as the terrorist states. These criticisms of the 'war against terrorism' approach do not imply, however, that the military should have no role in the liberal democratic response.

C. The Criminal Justice Model

The criminal justice system is morally and logically the correct institution in a liberal state to take the prime responsibility for dealing with terrorism.

In every liberal democratic state, terrorist attacks and associated activities are regarded as serious crimes.[46] Most democratic states now have anti-terrorism legislation and most have signed up to many or all of the

---

[44] See R Fisk, *Pity the Nation: Lebanon at War*, 2nd edn (Oxford, Oxford University Press, 1992).

[45] Moreover, in the light of nuclear tests by both India and Pakistan in June 1998 and the border war along the Line of Control in the summer of 1999, we must recognise the real danger that an escalation of conflict between India and Pakistan could well lead to the unleashing of missiles with nuclear warheads. In the sub-continent terrorism could potentially trigger a nuclear war.

[46] For a fuller discussion see Wilkinson, n 23 above, ch 5.

international conventions against terrorism established under the authority of the United Nations and regional organisations such as the European Union.[47]

From the perspective of governments and citizens of liberal states, the use of the criminal justice model has considerable advantages and attractions. It should ensure that the basic human rights of individuals are safeguarded. Those suspected of crimes of terrorism will be assumed to be innocent until proved guilty before a properly constituted court of law on the basis of evidence which establishes guilt 'beyond reasonable doubt'. The suspects' rights to a fair trial, to a proper defence and to appeal in the event that they wish to contest the trial verdict are all part of the norms of a proper rule-of-law judicial process. Moreover, if a suspect is convicted on the basis of overwhelming evidence of guilt this will send important messages to the public showing that the authorities will ensure that those guilty of such serious crimes can and will be brought to justice, and to other terrorists or those contemplating participation in terrorism that the arms of the law will reach out and find them and bring them to book if they commit terrorist crimes.

Despite these obvious advantages, above all the reassurances that when terrorists are sentenced to imprisonment they will be precluded from committing further attacks while they are in gaol, there are serious *limits* to the capacity of the criminal justice model in the struggle against terrorism. It is notoriously difficult to identify and capture terrorists and their 'godfathers' or bosses. They are taught how to blend into their surroundings, how to avoid attracting attention and how to keep their communications secure.[48] Al Qaeda network operatives tend to be very well prepared for keeping their activities hidden from the authorities. Moreover, Al Qaeda terrorists who blow themselves up in acts of suicide terrorism, of course, put themselves beyond the reach of any human law.

Another major difficulty is that much of the information which leads to the arrest of suspects is in the form of intelligence from the secret services or from the special branches of the police tasked with gathering intelligence. Converting this intelligence, some of which often turns out to be inaccurate, into evidence that will stand up in a court of law is no easy matter.[49]

Obtaining testimony from witnesses may be very difficult, if not impossible, because of intimidation by terrorist groups. Members of juries, lawyers, even judges, may be threatened or in some cases even

---

[47] See P Wilkinson, 'International Terrorism: The Changing Threat and the EU's Response', Chaillot Paper No 84 (Paris, Institute for Security Studies, October 2005).

[48] See Gerges, n 14 above.

[49] See C Andrew, *For the President's Eyes Only: Secret Intelligence and the American Presidency from Washington to Bush* (London, HarperCollins, 1995).

murdered in order to disrupt the judicial process, and terrorists often use various ploys to disrupt and delay proceedings. For these and many other reasons, criminal justice processes are often extremely cumbersome and the outcomes highly uncertain.

All these difficulties are, of course, made infinitely more complex and intractable in cases of international terrorism in which it may prove impossible to obtain extradition of suspects or to secure key witnesses or information which other state judicial authorities are unwilling to supply.

D. The 'War on Terror' Model

In its response to the 11 September 2001 attacks the Bush administration not only adopted the language of a 'war on terrorism', deploying troops to Afghanistan to topple the Taliban and then moving on to attack Iraq (for reasons which had nothing to do with Al Qaeda). It also decided to circumvent, if not entirely abandon, the criminal justice system as a means of dealing with suspected terrorists.

Prisoners captured in Afghanistan or elsewhere were labelled 'unlawful combatants', and interned without trial in a specially designed prison camp at Guantanamo Bay, Cuba, or at one of the number of US bases abroad.[50]

Instead of indicting prisoners suspected of terrorism for trial in the federal courts, the US government devised a system of military tribunals which are supposed to try the suspects on the basis of evidence of their involvement in terrorism. However, very few detainees have ever had the chance of appearing before a tribunal, the tribunals are conducted by the military, suspects are not allowed to choose their own lawyer, and the standards of proof are much less rigorous than those used in the federal criminal courts.[51] Friends and allies of the United States have been baffled by the way in which the federal criminal justice system has been circumvented. In many famous cases, such as those involving Ramzi Youssef and the four terrorists convicted by a New York court for their involvement in the August 1998 US Embassy bombings in East Africa,[52] the federal courts have shown that they have the capability of dealing with complex terrorism cases and delivering appropriate sentences on the basis of *overwhelming* evidence. In such cases both domestic and

---

[50] See D Cole, *Enemy Aliens* (New York, The New Press, 2005).
[51] *Ibid.*
[52] *United States of America v Ramzi Ahmed Yousef et al*, 327 F 3rd 56 (2nd Circuit, 2003).

international opinion can be satisfied that justice has been done. Guantanamo Bay and extra-judicial procedures only do harm to the traditional reputation of the United States as a champion of the rule of law and individual human rights.

What possible justifications can there be for this abandonment of due process? Those hawks who see themselves as fighting the 'Third World War' argue that the only way to deal with terrorists is to suppress them with crushing military force on the assumption that 'the only good terrorist is a dead terrorist'. They believe that the end, that is crushing the Al Qaeda network, justifies any means and that terrorists have forfeited their human rights. They also argue that the criminal courts are too cumbersome, too slow and too unpredictable in their results, and as they have already decided that the detained suspects are guilty, trials before courts of law would be an expensive waste of time. Those who are in favour of this position, not unexpectedly, also tend to take the view that in some circumstances inhuman and degrading treatment of suspects and even torture may be justified in the name of the 'war on terrorism'.

Those who take the opposite view – including this author – would object that by abandoning the due process under the rule of law and by violations of the human rights of suspects, we betray the very values and principles which are the foundation of the democracies we seek to defend. We are also corrupting our democracies and those public officials, members of the military and others who are ordered to carry out such policies. We perpetrate major injustice in the name of national security. How can the security authorities be sure that the detained suspects are actually guilty of any terrorist crime? Are we to believe that intelligence agencies are always correct in their information? Is it justice to deny captives who may have to suffer decades of imprisonment any opportunity to prove their innocence before a court of law? Surely not. And what effect is such a cruel policy likely to have on Muslim communities around the world? Al Qaeda propaganda, for example dressing captured Western hostages in Guantanamo-style orange clothes and showing pictures of prisoner abuse at Abu Ghraib gaol in Iraq, constantly seeks to exploit these images in their efforts to recruit more alienated, angry young Muslims into the network. In other words, not only are these violations of the rule of law by a leading democracy morally and legally wrong, they are ultimately a gratuitous weapon for the terrorist movement.

The huge advantages of using due process and upholding human rights are well understood by judiciaries, police forces and governments in EU countries. This is not to say that the EU's use of criminal justice systems has always been perfect. Far from it: there have been serious miscarriages of justice in the United Kingdom and elsewhere. Yet there is genuine puzzlement in Europe about their US ally's Draconian departure from the rule of law in its treatment of terrorist suspects. In view of the importance of maximising international judicial and police cooperation, this startling divergence is of considerable concern because it becomes a severe impediment to bringing terrorists to justice before the courts. For example, in the case of el Motassadeq in Hamburg, the German prosecutors were frustrated in their efforts to secure a conviction of the accused for allegedly assisting the 11 September hijackers by the refusal of the US authorities to allow a key witness in US custody to be called to testify before the court in Germany.[53] If all democratic states endeavour to uphold due process and basic human rights norms it helps to maintain solidarity, and it is also a valuable weapon in the battle of ideas against the terrorists. Last but not least, if the United States is sincerely committed to spreading democratic values and processes to countries in the developing world, what kind of example is being set by the suspension of rule-of-law norms and due process in the world's most powerful democracy? Respect for law and fundamental rights is what distinguishes democratic systems from the murky worlds of dictatorship and tyranny.

III. CONCLUSIONS

In my brief overview of the main models of liberal state response to terrorism, it has been emphasised that all of them have severe limits. No single model can possibly provide an adequate response to the serious challenges posed by contemporary terrorism, especially by the *jihadi* terrorism of the Al Qaeda network and its affiliated groups.

In countering international terrorism, the democratic state confronts an inescapable dilemma. It has to deal effectively with the terrorist threat to citizens and to vulnerable potential targets, such as civil aviation, diplomatic and commercial premises, without at the same time destroying basic civil rights, the democratic process and the rule of law. On the one hand, the democratic government and its agencies of law enforcement must avoid the heavy-handed overreaction, which many terrorist groups deliberately seek to provoke. Such a response would only help to alienate the public from the government and could ultimately destroy democracy more swiftly and completely than any small terrorist group ever could. On the other hand, if government, judiciary and police prove incapable of upholding the law and protecting life and property, then their whole credibility and authority would be undermined.

---

[53] D Butler, 'German Judges Order Retrial for 9/11 Figure', *New York Times*, 5 March 2004.

If this balance is to be maintained, the liberal state should seek at all times to combat terrorism using its criminal justice and law-enforcement mechanisms. However, it is clearly the case that some terrorist groups attain a level of firepower that outstrips even the capabilities of elite squads of armed police. It has been proven time and again that in certain circumstances of high emergency, such as the hijacking to Entebbe and the subsequent rescue mission in 1976,[54] and the Iranian embassy siege of 1980,[55] it may be essential to deploy a highly trained military rescue commando force to save hostages. Military, naval or air forces may be invaluable in interdicting a major terrorist assault, as has been seen in the case of Israel's measures against terrorist groups attacking its borders from land and sea. In the more normal conditions enjoyed by democratic states in Western Europe, the occasions when military deployment to tackle international terrorists is required will be very rare.

A number of dangers need to be constantly borne in mind when deploying the army in a major internal terrorist emergency role. First, an unnecessarily high military profile may serve to escalate the level of violence by polarising pro- and anti-government elements in the community. Second, there is a constant risk that a repressive overreaction or a minor error in judgement by the military may trigger further civil violence. Internal security duties inevitably impose considerable strains on the soldiers, who are well aware of the hostility of certain sections of the community towards them. Third, anti-terrorist and internal security duties absorb considerable human resources and involve diverting highly trained military technicians from their primary NATO and external defence roles. Fourth, there is a risk that the civil power may become over-dependent on the army's presence and there may a consequent lack of urgency in preparing the civil police for gradually reassuming the internal security responsibility. Finally, in the event of an international terrorist attack, a military operation to punish a state sponsor or to strike at alleged terrorist bases may trigger an international conflict worse than the the act of terrorism one is seeking to oppose. This danger is exacerbated by the risks posed by the proliferation of chemical, biological, radiological and nuclear (CBRN) weapons in conflict-ridden parts of the world.

Last but not least, we should remind ourselves that the most dangerous form of terrorist threat faced by the international community is Al Qaeda's transnational network of cells and affiliated groups.[56] The most

---

[54] See W Stevenson, *90 minutes at Entebbe* (New York, Bantam Books, 1976).

[55] See B Jenkins, 'Embassies Under Siege: A Review of 48 Embassy Takeovers, 1791–1980'RAND R2651-RC (Santa Monica, CA, 1981).

[56] For an explanation of why Al Qaeda poses the most dangerous threat see P Wilkinson (ed), *Homeland Security in the UK* (London, Routledge, 2007) ch 2.

serious of all the limitations of current anti-terrorism policies and meas-ures is that they are nearly all purely national in character. Despite a welcome improvement in intelligence, police and judicial cooperation there is as yet no widely agreed international strategy on how to tackle the threat from Al Qaeda. As the United States has found to its cost, reliance on unilateralist policies, with heavy dependence on the 'war model', is not working. A truly multilateral and effective strategy com-patible with the rule of law is urgently needed.

4

The Role of Modern States in the Decline and Demise of Terrorism*

AUDREY KURTH CRONIN

I. INTRODUCTION

A LTHOUGH THE TACTIC of terrorism has increased in its profile, lethality and leverage with respect to the state, these developments have been matched by a rich, varied and important state experience with the end of terrorist campaigns. Yet the second half of the equation is virtually ignored. There is an obsession with dissecting the growing threat of terrorism that is not matched by an interest in how it ends. Recent perceptions of terrorism's prospects as a means of political change have been enhanced by the shock of high profile attacks on Western targets, but the resulting exaggeration of terrorism's effectiveness as a coercive tool is overblown and self-defeating. Terrorism is a powerful foe for the democratic state, especially when leaders feed into the counterproductive dynamic of escalating terrorism and counterterrorism; but it is also a challenge that can be intelligently met with time-honoured techniques that have successfully nudged terrorist campaigns toward their demise.

II. TERRORISM'S INCREASING LEGITIMACY, LETHALITY AND LEVERAGE

A growing conviction developed over the course of the twentieth century that terrorism was a promising method of popular resistance to the state

* The views expressed are the author's and do not necessarily reflect the views of the US government, particularly as this work was written while in residence at Oxford University. Portions of this paper are derived from A Kurth Cronin, 'How al-Qaida Ends: The Decline and Demise of Terrorist Groups' (Summer 2006) 31(1) *International Security* 7–48; and A Kurth Cronin, *How Terrorism Ends: Lessons from the Decline and Demise of Terrorist Campaigns* (Princeton, NJ, Princeton University Press, forthcoming, 2008).

and a valid means of rectifying injustice. While some commentators had admired the 'propaganda of the deed' of the anarchists and social revolutionaries in the nineteenth century, that enthusiasm was confined to a relatively small number of elite intellectuals. As the twentieth century unfolded, these altruistic but misguided thinkers had their numbers further diminished on the Left by Lenin's repudiation of 'individual' terrorist tactics, and on the Right by the viciousness and defeat of Nazi Germany. Terrorism was the weapon of the weak; war and popular revolution were the weapons of the strong.

Following the Second World War, however, the sweeping force of decolonisation brought with it a dramatic increase in terrorist attacks against Western targets. The spontaneous emergence of 'wars of national liberation' was accompanied by a transition in international norms from condemning terrorist attacks on innocent civilians (or non-combatants), to popularly viewing terrorism as a romanticised and promising means of pursuing a cause. The argument in defence of terrorist attacks was that they were a lesser evil compared to the abundant evils visited upon civilians by the state, demonstrated by a long list of horrors from strategic bombing, to the holocaust, the brutality of apartheid, Bloody Sunday, the My Lai massacre, and countless more. This argument was true, but it was also irrelevant. While much state violence was indefensible, the leap of logic necessary to legitimise terrorism required abandoning the protection of civilians or non-combatants as a universal good, and replacing it with a belief in the deliberate and symbolic slaughter of some for the benefit of others, in pursuit of a legitimate aim. In other words, if a population were desperate enough, the argument held, they could be excused for using random terrorist attacks against others to pursue their cause.

Thus, in the 1960s and 1970s the growing enthusiasm for free peoples everywhere led to a fateful and deliberate step, expressed particularly in international forums such as the General Assembly of the United Nations, towards believing that terrorism was acceptable if it was enacted in pursuit of the principle of self-determination. For those on both the Right and the Left of the political spectrum, caught up in the excitement of sweeping decolonisation and democratisation, the ends overshadowed the means: the focus on the illegitimacy of the act itself was clouded by enthusiasm for the outcome it was meant to support, and civilians ultimately paid the price.[1]

This crucial change in attitudes towards terrorism, especially the growing tendency to object to it only when your own people were the

---

[1]   A brilliant exploration of this position was argued by journalist P Johnson in 'The Age of Terror', *New Statesman*, 29 November 1974, 763–4.

victims, was accompanied by four other important developments that influenced its frequency and effectiveness. First, terrorism gained popularity alongside a growing public susceptibility to images, transmitted first through television and then through a plethora of other media, of innocent civilians being killed in far-flung places. The ability of terrorist operatives to impress a shocking event upon a wider and wider audience grew exponentially with the dramatic expansion of media technologies. Terrorism has been likened to theatre or 'perverted show business' and modern media brought that show to a world stage.[2] The powerful psychological and emotional effects of those images came to be more important politically than were the military or tactical benefits of the violence itself – or, indeed, the response to the violence. The strategically targeted assassinations or bombings of major figures that were popular in the latter part of the nineteenth century were replaced in the twentieth century by symbolic, increasingly indiscriminate, publicised terrorist attacks on ordinary citizens who were treated as proxies for their states.

The triumph of democratic institutions in the West thus had the perverse effect of making individual civilians symbolic national targets, even when they were utterly ignorant of their government's policies. In the twentieth century, most terrorist attacks either occurred in democratic states or targeted civilians of those states.[3] Terrorism was contrived to be a means of communicating with 'the people' by killing other people, and the media became an instrument of this goal. And the ability to intimidate grew exponentially as popularly elected governments at times took actions that seemed in line with what the operatives had wanted them to do. If kidnappings or gruesome murders could grab the attention of a broad swathe of humanity, the reasoning went, then the organisation's cause could achieve international staying power. The success of these theatrics was trumpeted by the operatives themselves, and the result was a self-perpetuating cycle of violence.

Terrorism in the late twentieth century thus became a repugnantly voyeuristic phenomenon. Reflecting on the 1972 Munich Olympics massacre, for example, surviving Palestinian gunman Abu Daoud claimed that the murder of 11 Israeli athletes before the horrified eyes of millions of viewers 'force[d] our cause into the homes of 500 million people'.[4] The

---

[2] B Jenkins, 'International Terrorism: A New Mode of Conflict', in D Carlton and C Schaer (eds), *International Terrorism and World Security* (London, Croom Helm, 1975) 16; and B Hoffman, *Inside Terrorism* (New York, Columbia University Press, 1998) 134.

[3] For data to support this point, as well as more information on broad trends in global terrorist attacks, see A Kurth Cronin, 'Rethinking Sovereignty: American Strategy in the Age of Terror' (Summer 2002) 44(2) *Survival* 119–39.

[4] A Daoud, quoted by Z Karam in 'For Planner of Assault on Munich Olympics, No Regret Three Decades Later', *Associated Press*, 23 February 2006.

fascination with images often overshadowed the failure to deliver long-term practical results, however: the most common outcome – in the Palestinian case as in most others – was that *everyone* lost ground. Terrorism was the violent incarnation of the increasing democratisation of states in the international system, as it dramatically demonstrated the ability both of the disgruntled individual to kill publicly and of the enfranchised citizen to die publicly.

But terrorism was inexorably tied to the evolving politics and identity of the state in a more direct way, through the close connection between terrorist groups and state sponsors. Particularly during the twentieth century, terrorism was often employed as a secret means of exercising state power and indirectly accomplishing policy aims. The sclerotic international environment of the Cold War resulted in a proliferation of 'proxy' organisations, carrying out campaigns that were underwritten by states from either the so-called Communist Eastern bloc or Western countries. Proxy war was preferable to central war, and illicit organisations sometimes played sponsors off each other. The Soviet Union, Czechoslovakia, Bulgaria, East Germany and Cuba ran training camps and operated an intricate support network for a wide range of terrorist groups; the USSR provided arms to the Popular Front for the Liberation of Palestine (PFLP), the German Democratic Republic (DDR) gave explosives to the Palestinian Liberation Organisation (PLO), and South Yemen (supported by East Germany) provided training and safe haven for the Irish Republican Army (IRA) and Basque separatists, to name a few of many examples.[5] The US government also supported groups that used terrorist tactics, including the *mujahideen* in Afghanistan and the National Union for the Total Independence of Angola (União Nacional para a Independência Total de Angola, or UNITA) in Angola.[6] With the break-up of the Soviet Union, the practice of direct state sponsorship declined internationally, although some states, notably including Iran

---

[5] For documentary evidence of these and many other examples, see D Tucker, *Skirmishes at the Edge of Empire: The United States and International Terrorism* (Westport, CN, Praeger, 1997) 25–7 and *passim*.

[6] A Dershowitz, *Why Terrorism Works: Understanding the Threat, Responding to the Challenge* (New Haven, CT, and London, Yale University Press, 2002) 7–8. Unfortunately, the United States directly or indirectly supported terrorism in a number of ways. Individual Irish Americans sent funds to support the terrorist activities of the IRA with impunity, and Members of the US House of Representatives even gave public support for MEK activities against the Iranian government. (The MEK, or MKO, Mojahedin-e-Khalq organisation, is also known as the National Council of Resistance (NCR) and the People's Mojahedin Organization of Iran (PMOI).) See K Katzman, *Iran: U.S. Concerns and Policy Responses*, Congressional Research Service Report for Congress, No RL32048, 20 January 2006, 6–7.

and Syria, continued to actively support terrorist groups.[7] Yet the damage had already been done. State sponsorship not only increased the frequency of the tactic during the twentieth century but also had a further nefarious effect on the concept's evolution: the popular sentiment that some terrorism might be acceptable was buttressed by clear evidence that certain state governments clearly thought so. This again seriously degraded the legal and moral norm against non-state actors deliberately targeting civilians for political ends. Condemning terrorism was seen as hypocrisy.

A third reason for terrorism's improved prospects was that some of its short-term accomplishments were noteworthy. Terrorism achieved well-publicised concessions from states during the middle and late twentieth century. This was especially the case when it came to kidnappings and exchanges of prisoners. Stories of helpless hostages held to blackmail elected governments exploited the link between the media, public opinion and democratic decision-making. Even when governments stood firm (which was the exception, not the rule), the causes of the terrorist organisations carrying out operations were explained and disseminated by formal and informal news media analysing and speculating about their motivations. As was most dramatically demonstrated with the 1979–80 Iran hostage crisis, which arguably brought down the Carter presidency, it was extremely difficult for democratic governments to withstand the widely broadcast fates of individual citizens in order to pursue the less tangible interests of the nation.[8] Many governments claimed that they would not negotiate with terrorists. In fact, under the pressure of the imminent and widely publicised murder of innocent constituents, most did. The resulting gap between Western governments' public and private policies provided another point of leverage for non-state groups, crowing about the hypocrisy of states.

Likewise, campaigns of suicide attacks played a role in compelling states to make territorial concessions, including the withdrawal of US and French military forces from Lebanon in 1984, the departure of Israeli troops from Lebanon in 1985, the pulling-out of Israeli forces from the Gaza Strip and the West Bank in 1994 and 1995, and the creation of autonomous homelands for the Tamils and the Kurds by the Sri Lankan

---

[7] For an interesting analysis of active and passive sponsorship, particularly by states in the Middle East and South Asia, see D Byman, *Deadly Connections: States that Sponsor Terrorism* (Cambridge, Cambridge University Press, 2005).

[8] B Nacos, *Terrorism and the Media: From the Iran Hostage Crisis to the World Trade Center Bombing* (New York, Columbia University Press, 1994).

and Turkish governments, respectively, in the 1990s.[9] More recently, the March 2004 train bombing in Madrid, the electoral defeat of the conservative Spanish government three days later, and subsequent withdrawal of Spanish troops from Iraq combined to create the impression that terrorism was an effective means of manipulating state behaviour. Although attacks on military targets were not technically 'terrorist', the distinction was blurred in popular perceptions—not least as a result of the intellectual muddle of the concept of a 'war on terrorism' that started off the new century. In contrast to what had previously been the case, the apparent power of the individual operative to coerce a state government, especially to withdraw troops from occupied territories or foreign lands, seemed profound – later emphasised more than ever in the context of increasing numbers of suicide attacks in Iraq.[10]

Finally, terrorism's perceived success with respect to the state was linked to greater access to more lethal means of destruction. Technological advances seemed to favour the use of terrorist violence in the twentieth century, particularly the increasing sophistication and potency of explosives. In a matter of a few decades, bombings went from relatively discriminate attacks on specific targets claimed by specific groups to huge explosives that destroyed entire buildings, often went unclaimed, and killed or injured thousands. The attacks of 11 September 2001 were, again, a logical continuation of established trends toward mass casualty attacks using conventional weaponry, which had become increasingly frequent and lethal from the 1980s to the end of the century.[11] Although there were fewer attacks overall in the 1990s than there had been in the 1980s, the average number of casualties per incident was growing.[12] Notable mass casualty attacks included the downing of planes such as Pan Am 103 (1988; 270 killed) and the French airline UTA (1989; 171 killed), the bombings of Bombay businesses (1993, 317 killed), the truck bomb that obliterated the Alfred P Murrah Building in Oklahoma City (1995; 168 killed), and the explosion of a 500 pound bomb at the US

---

[9] R Pape, *Dying to Win: The Strategic Logic of Suicide Terrorism* (New York, Random House, 2005); and M Crenshaw, 'Coercive Diplomacy and the Response to Terrorism' in RJ Art and PM Cronin (eds), *The United States and Coercive Diplomacy* (Washington, DC, US Institute of Peace Press, 2003).

[10] Unfortunately, this confusion in terminology has been perpetuated by recent scholarship, which now calls any action that uses suicide tactics 'terrorist' regardless of whether the target is military or civilian. Historically, terrorism has been distinguished more by its targeting than by whether or not it involves suicide tactics.

[11] W Laqueur, 'Postmodern Terrorism' (September/October 1996) 75(5) *Foreign Affairs* 24–36. Laqueur makes the same point, also arguing that the nature of the groups and individuals who use those weapons is improving the prospects for success.

[12] Internationally in the 1990s, the number averaged below 400 per year, whereas in the 1980s the number of incidents per year averaged well above 500. See A Kurth Cronin, n 3 above at 123–4 and 128.

embassy in Nairobi, Kenya (1998; 213 killed, over 5,000 injured).[13] Mass casualty attacks were well established before the new century dawned, and the growing death toll gave the impression of a powerful wave of violence that was increasingly effective in its carnage – perhaps moving inexorably to terrorism with chemical, biological or nuclear weapons.

So, terrorist organisations had over the course of the twentieth century gradually shown the ability to kill more people, gain more attention, catalyse government reactions, and act as proxies for powerful sponsors. Many groups were building reputations as formidable, legitimate actors, some even acquiring sufficient strength to launch insurgent attacks on military forces, prompting states to withdraw from territory. On the other hand, few groups were accomplishing their strategic aims. Even though terrorism's successes, in terms of attacks and influence, were more storied than its failures, the response of the state to the challenge of terrorism proved to be formidable. If the survival of the group – like the Weberian imperative for the state – was a fundamental goal of terrorism, then obviously it was proving to be a dubious tactic. According to David Rapoport, 90 per cent of terrorist organisations in the late twentieth century were lasting less than a year, and of those that made it to the one-year point, more than half disappeared within a decade.[14] Political actors could not be effective if they could not endure. As the tactic seemed to be collectively gaining force, why did the vast majority of individual terrorist campaigns nonetheless end?

III. TERRORISM'S PATTERNS OF DEMISE

Very little research has been done in answer to this question. Most of the work focusing on the endings of terrorism groups has consisted of individual case studies drawing lessons relevant to those individual campaigns. While helpful to national or regional specialists, writers have rarely systematically thought about how the lessons of a particular group's end might or might not be applied beyond the local context. Even as rich research into the origins of terrorism has proceeded apace (usually well- funded by governments desperate for answers to unfolding campaigns), there has been almost nothing written about how groups

---

[13] C Quillen, '"A Historical Analysis of Mass Casualty Bombers' (September–October 2002) 25(5) *Studies in Conflict and Terrorism* 279–92; and C Quillen, '"Mass Casualty Bombings Chronology' (September–October 2002) 25(5) *Studies in Conflict and Terrorism* 293–302. Quillen defines mass casualty attacks as those that kill more than 25 people.

[14] D Rapoport, 'Terrorism', in M Hawkesworth and M Kogan (eds), *Routledge Encyclopedia of Government and Politics, Vol 2* (London, Routledge, 1992) 1067. This claim needs to be updated. I am in the process of doing a more comprehensive study of the lifespans of terrorist groups from 1968 to the present, but the results are not yet complete and ready to be shared.

end. The assumption has been that the same factors that lead to the beginning of a group also lead to its demise. Yet, the myriad changes that terrorist groups undergo throughout their lifespan – shifts in such things as aims, tactics, personnel, structure and support that are utterly normal adaptations for groups that use terrorism – are ignored. In truth, how a group starts has very little to do with how it ends.

To understand the patterns of terrorism's demise in recent decades, it is crucial to look at case studies laterally, across different cultural and regional contexts, identifying the point or points where a critical mass of factors led to the demise of the group. Doing so reveals the outline of a rough framework for thinking about the demise of terrorist groups throughout recent history. The relevant factors have been both internal and external: terrorist groups have imploded for reasons that sometimes were and sometimes were not related to the measures taken against them. And the factors of importance in their waning days have not always been separate and distinct: sometimes more than one element has been at play. But a survey of the recent history of terrorism reveals seven broad explanations for, or critical elements in, the decline and ending of twentieth-century terrorist campaigns.

First, terrorist groups have sometimes met their demise following the capture or killing of their leader. The effects of decapitation have varied according to the group, especially whether it was hierarchically organised and oriented toward a charismatic leader. Examples of groups that were heavily damaged by the capture of their leader included the Shining Path (or Sendero Luminoso), the Kurdistan Workers' Party (PKK), the Real IRA, and Aum Shinrikyo. Of course, state targeting of the leader has also sometimes backfired, especially in non-hierarchical groups where a ready successor was found, or where the leader was killed in the operation and became a martyr. Assassination campaigns have resulted in the splintering of groups, a development that can be good or bad depending on the nature of the new leadership and the degree to which the ideological cause endures.

Reviewing the record, there is considerable evidence to indicate that the capture of a leader has been a more effective strategy than the killing of a leader, assuming that the goal was the long-term undermining of a group. However, even high profile arrests have sometimes backfired, when the jailed leader has been allowed to communicate with followers from jail, or when the group members still on the outside have attempted to free him. Examples include Sheikh Omar Abd al-Rahman (the so-called Blind Sheikh), convicted for conspiracy in the 1993 World Trade Center bombing, who continued to communicate and radicalise followers from his cell; and the so-called Baader-Meinhof group, whose comrades attempted to free them from a German jail. Nonetheless, removal of a leader, often the source of inspiration for a group and thus its intellectual engine for violence, has nearly always been a watershed in the evolution of the group one way or another, and often the beginning of its end.

Second and related, unlike states, whose succession procedures are institutionalised, many groups have been unable to pass the cause or vision on to the next generation. Terrorism often reflects generational phases, related to demographic patterns and the growth of radical ideologies internationally.[15] The left-wing groups of the 1970s in Europe were notorious for their inability to articulate a clear vision of their goals that could be handed down to successors after the first generation of leaders was captured or eliminated. Examples include the Red Brigades, the Second of June Movement, the Japanese Red Army and the Weather Underground. Even when a group spawned another generation, it was a pale shadow of its forebears. Again, the Red Army Faction (RAF, also called the Baader-Meinhof group by the media) may have drawn media fascination in its spree of bombings and arsons, but when its leaders were jailed in 1972, the successor generation shifted their fundamental purpose away from the initial goal of attacking symbols of the state to gaining their leaders' freedom—an endeavour unlikely to inspire a durable following. Losing their support, not to mention their connection to reality (particularly after the end of the Vietnam War), the RAF also lost their ability to continue a viable campaign.

Right-wing groups have likewise had difficulty persisting over generations, probably a reflection of their peripatetic nature and their decentralised cell structures, not least the prodigious challenges in tracking their evolution. Some European neo-Nazi groups and right-wing Christian militia groups in the United States fitted this description by the end of the twentieth century. Examples include the Christian Patriots, the Aryan Nations, Combat 18, the German People's Union and the National Front in Europe, among many others. Right-wing groups also regularly engage in criminal behaviour, such as robbing banks, racketeering and counterfeiting, which makes them vulnerable to detection by traditional law enforcement. Unfortunately, their appeal to racist tenets also provides them an avenue to tap into prejudices that may sometimes persist under the surface, inciting violence either by attacking members of minority groups who then respond with counter-attacks against the majority or inflaming the majority by spreading paranoid propaganda. Thus, even

---

[15] For more on this argument, see D Rapoport, 'The Four Waves of Modern Terrorism,' in A Kurth Cronin and J Ludes (eds), *Attacking Terrorism: Elements of a Grand Strategy* (Washington, DC, Georgetown University Press, 2004) 46–73; and A Kurth Cronin, 'Behind the Curve: Globalization and International Terrorism' (Winter 2002/03) 27(3) *International Security* 30–58.

when individual groups die out, in the absence of rigorous efforts at education, there is reason to fear that their cause may be taken up by new groups in the future

Third, a few terrorist groups have succeeded – that is, they have achieved their long-term aims. The achievement of tactical goals, such as the freeing of hostages, increasing attention to their cause, forcing government reaction or intimidating a local population, has occurred regularly through the use of terrorism. This is one reason why the tactic can become a self-perpetuating phenomenon, as populations confuse short-term successes with long-term results.

Achieving strategic goals has been extremely rare, although it has occasionally occurred. Examples of groups that succeeded in achieving major political change, and then either disbanded or transitioned to more legitimate political behaviour, include Irgun Zvai Leumi, the Jewish organisation that fought to protect Jews in the Palestinian Mandate and to advance the cause of the independent state. Irgun attacks such as the 1946 bombing of the King David hotel hastened the British withdrawal and arguably also facilitated the establishment of Israel. Another example is the African National Congress (ANC), which created a military wing (Umkhonto, or MK) and, after nearly five decades of passive resistance, turned to terrorist attacks in 1961. The ANC fought to end apartheid and establish a multi-racial state in South Africa. The MK's last attack occurred in 1989, and the ANC became a legitimate political party in 1990, with its leader, Nelson Mandela, elected first President of post-apartheid South Africa. Yet the question of cause and effect in these examples (as in others) is quite complex: although more work remains to be done, there is a great deal of evidence to indicate that both outcomes were achieved at least as much *despite* the use of terrorism as because of it.

Fourth, negotiations have sometimes led to the decline or end of terrorism. Groups that entered negotiation with the state include the provisional IRA (the 1998 Good Friday Accords), the PLO (progress in the peace process during the 1990s) and the Liberation Tigers of Tamil Eelam (LTTE) (in talks 2002–05). As these cases obviously indicate, however, a process of negotiations is by no means a panacea, with many setbacks along the way. Groups often splinter as the result of talks, which can be either a good or a bad thing depending on the circumstances. There are many examples, including the Real IRA, the PFLP and the Popular Front for the Liberation of Palestine-General Command (PFLP-GC). Dividing terrorist groups into factions either isolates the most radical elements, making them easier to target; or alternatively it increases the violence against civilians in the short term, as radical factions try to demonstrate their viability by carrying out new attacks. The record indicates that expecting terrorism to end while a process of negotiations is under way is naïve: attacks often continue and should even be anticipated. Negotiations shift the dynamic of terrorism and counterterrorism to another plane but they rarely end it immediately.

Since negotiations in the wake of terrorist acts are always controversial, sometimes the splintering has occurred on the status quo or government side instead, especially when the government undertaking talks represented an unstable constellation of political interests. This was the case, for example, in South Africa (with the Afrikaner white power group Farmers' Force, or Boermag) and in Northern Ireland (with the Ulster Volunteer Force). Negotiations can be risky, particularly for democratic governments, potentially dividing the domestic population and threatening vulnerable coalitions. Some publics consider any negotiation with groups that use terrorism to be 'appeasement', although there are often palpable tactical advantages for governments that are strong enough to enter talks either openly or clandestinely. Talks with terrorists, whether or not governments yield concessions, can provide crucial intelligence insights into the structures of groups, the personalities of leaders, the nature of their popular support, and many other vital sources of insight. They can also change the political dynamic in situations where a group's grievances enjoy some support within the population, providing an alternative narrative where the government appears to be 'reasonable'. But the historical record indicates that talks end terrorism only over the long term, with many stops and starts, and often much periodic violence. In short, with negotiations, the long-term goal (a viable political outcome) is often at odds with the short-term goal (a reduction in violence).

Fifth, terrorist campaigns have often ended when they became cut off from their sources of sustenance. Popular support has dissipated for a number of reasons, including intimidation (as in Chechnya), the offer of a better alternative (reform movements, employment programmes or amnesties) or the bankrupting of the ideology of the group (as with many of the Marxist groups supported by the Soviet Union and its Eastern European allies). A key source of marginalisation of a group, however, is the organisation's own errors, especially miscalculations in targeting that backfire. Attacks often cause revulsion among a group's actual or potential political constituency: examples include the Real IRA's Omagh bombing, to which the local community reacted in outrage; and Basque popular revulsion to ETA attacks in Spain. Indeed, there are scores of examples of miscalculations of targeting leading to the ending of groups. A classic Western European case of an operation that seriously hurt the cause was the 1978 killing of Aldo Moro by the Italian Red Brigades (*Brigate Rosse*, or BR). Moro had been a popular politician, and his killing dramatically reversed the upward trajectory of the Red Brigades. The state began a vigorous counterterrorism campaign, popular support dried up, the group began to crumble from within, and by 1982, the Red Brigades had effectively faded.[16]

Another notorious example of counterproductive targeting was the November 1997 killing of 62 tourists in the town of Luxor in Southern Egypt by the Islamist group al-Gama'a al-Islamiyya, or GAI. Among them were Germans, French, Bulgarians, British and other foreigners, snapping pictures of the pyramids, temples and mausoleums, completely defenceless and unaware of the six operatives who drove up in a taxi and ruthlessly killed them all. The Egyptian people were deeply revolted by the attacks, both because of their brutality and also because of the serious impact on the tourist economy upon which many livelihoods depended. According to Lawrence Wright, in the five years before Luxor, Islamist terrorist groups in Egypt had killed more than 1,200 people, many of them foreigners; after Luxor, attacks by Islamists in Egypt abruptly stopped.[17]

Sixth, the use of overwhelming military and police force has sometimes led to the end of terrorism. Examples include Peru's Shining Path and Narodnaya Volya, the small group that arose within the social revolutionary movement in nineteenth-century Russia. Narodnaya Volya devoted its short life to the aim of assassinating the Tsar, so as to shock the people out of their apathy and to force the government to call a constituent assembly and grant a constitution. Members reasoned that the humble Russian peasant was overawed by the Tsar and needed to be prodded into a mass uprising. On their seventh attempt, on 1 March 1881, members of Narodnaya Volya famously succeeded in assassinating Alexander II. In one of history's great ironies, Alexander II was actually in the process of establishing elected committees as an intermediate step toward greater liberalisation; his death prevented him from signing the order that afternoon. The death of Alexander II set off a huge police crackdown in Russia, ending the group and causing the Russian state to become increasingly rigid and inflexible. Within two years Narodnaya Volya had ended; within a few decades so had the tsarist state.[18]

---

[16] Before the Moro case, Italy had no centralised state database on terrorism. See R Meade Jr, *The Red Brigades: The Story of Italian Terrorism* (Basingstoke, Macmillan, 1990) 177. For excellent concise studies of this case, see L Weinberg, 'The Red Brigades' in RJ Art and L Richardson (eds), *Democracy and Counterterrorism: Lessons from the Past* (Washington, DC, US Institute of Peace Press, 2007); and D della Porta, 'Left-Wing Terrorism in Italy' in M Crenshaw (ed), *Terrorism in Context* (Pennsylvania, PA, University of Pennsylvania Press, 1995).

[17] L Wright, *The Looming Tower: Al-Qaeda and the Road to 9/11* (New York, Knopf, 2006) 258. See also G Kepel, *Jihad: The Trail of Political Islam*, 4th edn (London, IB Taurus, 2006) 288–9.

[18] The classic source on Narodnaya Volya is A Yarmolinsky, *Road to Revolution: A Century of Russian Radicalism* (New York, Macmillan, 1959). See also W Moss, *Alexander II and His*

The use of force has also regularly proved to be a temporary solution, resulting in the export of the problem to another country or region, as in the spreading of violence from Chechnya to other parts of the Caucasus, including Dagestan and Ingushetia. It is especially difficult for democracies to engage successfully in military repression over time, since it requires distinguishing individual 'targets' from the rest of the population, often undermines civil liberties, and is a very high-cost strategy. Sometimes the cost is the viability of the government itself: the use of repression against terrorism has not infrequently resulted in the undermining of liberal or liberalising regimes, as with Uruguay's crackdown on the Tupamaros and the takeover of a military government in 1973. Repression is thus a tool that can end terrorism while exacting an enormous cost upon the state.

Finally, groups that used terrorism have at times reoriented, transitioning out of attacks on civilians or non-combatants for political ends, towards either criminality (as with the Colombian Revolutionary Armed Forces of Colombia (Fuerzas Armada Revolucionarias de Colombia, or FARC) or towards full insurgency or conventional war (as with the Algerian National Liberation Front (Front de Libération Nationale, or FLN)). The Philippine Abu Sayyaf Group ('Bearer of the Sword,' or ASG), for example, claimed to be seeking the establishment of an Islamic state separate from the predominantly Catholic Philippines; however, following the 1998 death of its founder, Abdurajak Bubakar Janjalani, the ASG splintered into several factions and transitioned towards criminal behaviour, especially kidnapping for ransom, extortion and drug-trafficking in Manila. The money earned from these activities enabled them to purchase a formidable fleet of quick vessels and other high-tech equipment, giving them a huge tactical boost against the authorities. Some argue that, thus fortified, the ASG then returned to its roots, developing close links to Al Qaeda and becoming a serious Islamist terrorist threat again, although this interpretation is debated by many in the Philippine government.[19] In any case, both the Moro Islamic Liberation Front (MILF) and the Moro National Liberation Front (MNLF) have condemned the ASG's criminal activities and tried to distance themselves from the group, and there is little evidence that the ASG have a widespread popular following

Times: A Narrative History of Russia in the Age of Alexander II, Tolstoy, and Dostoevsky (London, Anthem Press, 2002); E Radzinsky, *Alexander II: The Last Great Tsar* (New York, The Free Press, 2005); and H Seton-Watson, *The Decline of Imperial Russia, 1855–1914* (London, Methuen, 1952).
[19] See Z Abuza, 'Balik-Terrorism: The Return of the Abu Sayyaf' (September 2005) *Strategic Studies Institute Monograph,* US Army War College.

attracted by an ideological vision. Philippine President Gloria Macapagal Arroyo, for example, described them as a 'money-crazed gang of criminals'.[20]

Other terrorist groups have transitioned to becoming insurgent organisations. Terrorism and insurgency admittedly overlap and are cousins, and the same organisations can use both tactics; but they are different phenomena. Reviewing the record of the twentieth century, the success rate for insurgencies (which attack military targets and typically shore up their constituency's support) was higher than the success rate for terrorist organisations (which attack civilian or non-combatant targets and often undermine their own support). Terrorism is indeed the tactic of the weak: used alone it has rarely proved to be a successful approach. Insurgents can seize and hold territory, have more pervasive networks of logistical support among the people, and larger numbers of operatives. When groups become strong enough to be able to carry out attacks on opposing military forces, they often do so. Many groups that use terrorism *aspire* to become insurgencies, which are typically larger in number than terrorist groups, operate as military units and can seize and hold territory (at least temporarily).[21] Transferring the use of violence from civilian to military targets has certain advantages for a state, as it diverts the threat away from its most vulnerable constituents and translates terrorism into a more traditional framework for state use of force. The use of military force in response to attacks on military assets is a paradigm very familiar to the state. When a group transitions to insurgency, 'terrorism' may have ended but from the perspective of a government the transition is a bad outcome and an indication of failure. The ability to attack military assets typically indicates greater strength on the part of the group.

IV. CONCLUSIONS

Major powers regularly relearn a seminal lesson of strategic planning, which is that embarking on a long war or campaign without both a grounding in previous experience and a realistic projection of an end state is folly. This is just as true in response to terrorism as it is with more conventional forms of political violence. Terrorism is an illegitimate tactic

---

[20]   *BBC News Online*, 1 June 2001, <http://news.bbc.co.uk> (accessed 14 April 2007).
[21]   See B Hoffman, *Inside Terrorism* (New York, Columbia University Press, 1998) 41. Some scholars have defined all terrorist behaviour as a subset of insurgency; in which one defines seven types of insurgent movements, including anarchist, egalitarian, traditionalist, pluralist, secessionist, reformist, and preservationist. See B O'Neill, *Insurgency and Terrorism: Inside Modern Revolutionary Warfare* (Washington, DC, Brassey's, 1990) especially ch 2, 13–30. While recognising the huge overlap between the two terms, I argue that they can and should be distinguished.

that by its very nature is purposefully and ruthlessly employed. At the heart of a terrorist's plan is seizing and maintaining the initiative. Policy-makers who have no concept of a feasible outcome are unlikely to formulate clear steps to reach it, especially once they are compelled by the inexorable action/reaction, offence/defence dynamic that all too often drives terrorism and counterterrorism. Although history does not repeat itself, ignoring history is the surest way for a state to be manipulated by the tactic of terrorism.

Although terrorism has evolved over the past century in ways that seem to strengthen its attractiveness and prospects, state experience in responding to it has yielded a parallel body of knowledge that is the key to its demise, notably in the seven patterns of behaviour that have just been briefly described in this chapter. The aim of terrorist attacks is virtually always to undermine the state; the answer to the threat of terrorism lies in the resilience and experience of the state. That experience points most importantly towards shoring up international norms against terrorism, undermining the ties between terrorist groups and their supporters, avoiding actions that feed into the world-view of groups and thereby increase their legitimacy, and turning the abundant missteps of terrorist groups against them.

Part Two

Balancing Security Concerns and Individual Freedoms

5

Terrorism and Human Rights Paradigms

The United Kingdom after 11 September 2001

DOMINIC MCGOLDRICK

'The legacy of the 11 September attacks in the USA haunts government life in the UK.'[1]

'[W]hile terrorism is not new, September 11th changed the legal landscape of terrorism forever.'[2]

I. INTRODUCTION: THE UNITED KINGDOM AND TERRORISM

THE UNITED KINGDOM has a long history of terrorism law and practice both at home, particularly in Northern Ireland,[3] and abroad in its former colonial empire.[4] Since 11 September 2001, however, the 'war on terror' has become a meta-concept that threatens to engulf rational debate about all political and social issues[5] including human rights.[6] The United Kingdom has assumed a leadership role in

---

[1] I Byrne and S Weir, 'Democratic Audit: Executive Democracy in War and Peace' (2004) 57(2) *Parliamentary Affairs* 453–68 at 462.

[2] Attorney-General, Lord Goldsmith, 'UK Terrorism Legislation in an International Context', RUSI Homeland Security and Resilience Department Conference, 10 May 2006, <http://www.the times.co.uk>.

[3] See P Wilkinson (ed), *Terrorism: British Perspectives* (Aldershot, Dartmouth, 1993).

[4] See C Walker, *Blackstone's Guide to the Anti-terrorism Legislation* (Oxford, Oxford University Press, 2002); C Townshend, *Britain's Civil Wars: Counterinsurgency in the Twentieth Century* (London, Faber, 1986).

[5] See C Campbell, '"Wars on Terror" and Vicarious Hegemons: The UK, International Law, and the Northern Ireland Conflict' (2005) 54(2) *ICLQ* 321–56; P Berman, *Terror and Liberalism* (New York, Norton, 2003).

[6] See C Gearty, 'Re-thinking Civil Liberties in a Counter-Terrorism World' (2007) *European Human Rights Law Review* 111–19 at 115, arguing that: 'The change since September

the 'war on terror'.[7] It has been the principal ally of the United States in the 'war on terror' generally, and the wars in Afghanistan and in Iraq in particular.[8] In November 2006, Eliza Manningham-Buller, the Director-General of the Security Service (MI5), took the unusual step of making public that MI5 sought to counter 30 significant terrorist plots, and monitor the activities of 200 terrorist networks, involving some 1,600 suspects.[9] She had previously warned that an erosion of civil liberties might be necessary to stop more British citizens being killed by terrorists.[10] The United Kingdom's domestic anti-terrorism law is wide-ranging and highly sophisticated.[11] UK practice and policy on anti-terrorism continues to attract great interest,[12] as do the leading judicial decisions.[13] In many of the leading cases discussed below, the legal issue was quite specific and/or the legal ruling was quite narrow. However, in many of the cases there was recognition of the 'constitutional' significance of the issues raised: 'It trivialises the issue before the House to treat it as an argument about the law of evidence. The issue is one of

---

[11] has been in the way in which terrorism laws have become generalised and in the flimsiness of the national security claims that have underpinned their expansion.'

[7] A search of the UK Prime Minister's website on 28 November 2006 for 'war on terror' found 4,151 hits, <http://www.pm.gov.uk>. The United States now prefers to describe it as the 'long war'.

[8] See the speeches of T Blair, UK Prime Minister, on 'The Threat of Global Terrorism', 5 March 2004 <http://www.pm.gov.uk/output/Page5461.asp>, and on the 'Clash of Civilisations', 21 March 2006 <http://www.pm.gov.uk/output/Page9224.asp>.

[9] E Manningham-Buller, Director-General of the Security Service (MI5), 'The International Terrorist Threat To The UK', Speech at Queen Mary's College, London, 9 November 2006, <http://www. mi5.gov.uk/output/Page568.html>. By November 2007 the number of suspects had risen to 2,000, see J Evans, MI5 Director-General, 'Intelligence counter terrorism and trust', <http://www.societyofeditors.co.uk>; see also D Foggo and D Leppard, 'MI5 at full stretch as 20 Islamist terror plots revealed', *The Sunday Times* (London), 28 May 2006.

[10] E Manningham-Buller, 'The International Terrorist Threat and the Dilemmas in Countering It', The Hague, 1 September 2005, <http://www.mi5.gov.uk/output/Page387.html>.

[11] Some aspects of domestic law have been required by legal obligations under European and international law. See H Duffy, *The 'War on Terror' and the Framework of International Law* (Cambridge, Cambridge University Press, 2005); F Gregory, 'The EU's Response to 9/11: A Case Study of Institutional Roles and Policy Processes with Special Reference to Issues of Accountability and Human Rights' (2005) 17 *Terrorism and Political Violence* 105–23; P Eeckhout, 'Community Terrorism Listings, Fundamental Rights, and UN Security Council Resolutions: In Search of the Right Fit' (2007) 3 *European Journal of Constitutional Law* 183–206.

[12] See C Walker, 'Policy Options and Priorities: British Perspective', in M van Leeuwen (ed), *Confronting Terrorism: European Experiences, Threat Perceptions and Policies* (The Hague, Kluwer, 2003) 11; A Vercher, *Terrorism in Europe* (Oxford, Oxford University Press, 1992).

[13] '[T]he decision in the *A* case is a landmark decision that will be used as a point of reference by courts all over the world for decades to come, even when the age of terrorism has passed': M Arden, 'Human Rights in The Age of Terrorism' (2005) 121 *LQR* 604–27 at 621.

constitutional principle.'[14] Legal discourse in the United Kingdom is now infused with human rights. Virtually all of the decisions discussed are framed in terms of the human rights of suspects, detainees and so on. However, it is important at the outset to emphasise that human rights obligations require states to take precautions against terrorist attacks.[15] The human rights issues should properly be understood as ones of conflict or balance between human rights claims.[16] Thus the European Court of Human Rights (ECtHR) has recognised that the need to protect a state's citizens from the risk of terrorist attack is one of the most important and pressing competing interests.[17]

This chapter seeks to assess the application of a number of anti-terrorism strategies in the United Kingdom after 11 September 2001. The principal 'terrorist-related' contexts considered are: (i) the detention and control of persons who cannot be tried or deported; (ii) the admission and the standard of proof in relation to evidence which may have been derived from torture; (iii) powers of stop and search; and (iv) the protection of nationals and residents when they are abroad. In each context we can observe and assess the efficacy of the doctrine of the separation of powers as understood in a UK context. In practice this tends to be an assessment of how well each branch (executive, legislative

---

[14] See *A (FC) and others (FC) (Appellants) v Secretary of State for the Home Department (Respondent)* [2005] UKHL 71, [2006] 2 AC 221 at para 51, per Lord Bingham. Similarly, in *R (Gillan and Another) v Commissioner of Police for the Metropolis and Another* [2006] UKHL 12, [2006] UKHRR 740, considered in Section XIV below, Lord Brown observed, at para 71, that the appeal raised points of 'real constitutional importance'.

[15] 'States are under the obligation to take the measures needed to protect the fundamental rights of everyone within their jurisdiction against terrorist acts, especially the right to life', *Guidelines on human rights and the fight against terrorism*, Principle I, Committee of Ministers of the Council of Europe, 11 July 2002, <http://www.coe.int/t/E/Human_Rights/Guidelines%20compendium%20ENG.pdf>. See also *A (FC) and others (FC) v Secretary of State for the Home Department* [2005] UKHL 71, [2006] 2 AC 221 at para 119, per Lord Hope; B Duner, 'Disregard for Security: The Human Rights Movement and 9/11' (2005) 17 *Terrorism and Political Violence* 89–104.

[16] See Lord Falconer of Thoroton, 'Finding the Balance Between Security and Liberty in the Modern World', 3 October 2006 <http://www.dca.gov.uk/speeches>; BJ Goold and L Lazarus (eds), *Security and Human Rights* (Oxford, Hart, 2007), although some authors are wary of the language of balance, see eg LK Donoghue, 'Security and Freedom on the Fulcrum' (2005) 17 *Terrorism and Political Violence* 69–87 (a better way to think about counterterrorism is in terms of a constellation of short- and long-term trade-offs that consider the risks imposed on the state by the suspension – and maintenance – of complex and interconnected rights); J Waldron, (2003) 'Security and Liberty: The Image of Balance' 11(3) *Political Philosophy* 191–210.

[17] See eg, *McCann v UK* (1996) 21 EHRR 97; *Murray v United Kingdom* (1994) 19 EHRR 193; *Chahal v United Kingdom* (1996) 23 EHRR 413. For a comparative analysis see B Goold, L Lazarus and G Swiney, *Public Protection, Proportionality, and the Search for Balance*, UK Ministry of Justice Research Series 10/07, <www.justice.gov.uk/docs/270907.pdf>.

and judicial) has performed, and how they see their respective roles, rather than a concentration on the idea of 'separation' as such.[18]

The doctrine of the 'separation of powers' in the United Kingdom is dealt with briefly in Section II. The most significant legal developments in relation to the doctrine – the Human Rights Act 1998 and the Constitutional Reform Act 2005 – are considered in Sections III and IV, respectively. Section V addresses the principal aspects of anti-terrorist legislation in the United Kingdom since 2000. Sections VI and VII consider the provisions on indefinite detention and the judicial response to them. Section VIII examines the Prevention of Terrorism Act 2005, and in particular the detailed regime of control orders it introduced. Sections IX–XI assess the judicial challenges that have been brought to control orders, and Section XII considers their future use. Section XIII examines the Terrorism Act 2006, in particular its provisions on extended detention. Section XIV assesses some of the extensive stop-and-search powers and the contexts in which they can be used. Section XV considers executive policy and judicial responses to the use of evidence that may be derived from foreign torture. Section XVI considers executive policy and judicial responses to the protection of nationals and residents subject to anti-terrorist measures abroad. Section XVII outlines the major anti-terrorism policy options and how they interrelate. Section XVIII highlights the contemporary political and legal attacks on human rights in the United Kingdom. Finally, Section XIX contains some brief concluding comments. In particular, it articulates the contours of the evolving human rights paradigm in the United Kingdom.

II. THE SEPARATION OF POWERS IN THE UNITED KINGDOM

The meanings and implications of the doctrine of the separation of powers depend on, 'detailed analysis of the constitutional system as a whole'.[19] Moreover, in the United Kingdom's constitutional system the separation of powers is not so much a doctrine of 'separation' but rather one of cooperation and co-existence.[20] Nonetheless the doctrine of separation retains an important place in political discourse and intellectual

---

[18] See R Stevens, 'A Loss of Innocence?: Judicial Independence and the Separation of Powers' (1999) 19 *Oxford Journal of Legal Studies* 365–402. The concepts of judicial independence and the separation of powers are used more as terms of political rhetoric than legal concepts in the British constitution.

[19] TRS Allen, *Constitutional Justice: A Liberal Theory of the Rule of Law* (Oxford, Oxford University Press, 2001) 18.

[20] See G Drewry, 'The Executive: Towards Accountable Government and Effective Governance?' and A Le Sueur, 'Judicial Power in the Changing Constitution', in J Jowell and D Oliver (eds), *The Changing Constitution*, 5th edn (Oxford, Oxford University Press,

critique.[21] Apparently bright doctrinal lines – that the sovereign legislature legislates, the executive governs and the judiciary interprets – appear much more blurred in practice.[22] Membership of the (now) European Union since 1972 bears much responsibility for this blurring but the legal and political consequences of EU membership on the separation of powers are now generally understood and accepted.[23] The most recent challenges to the doctrine of separation have stemmed from the passing of the Human Rights Act in 1998, and the Constitutional Reform Act in 2005. We consider these in turn.

III. THE HUMAN RIGHTS ACT 1998

The Human Rights Act 1998 (the HRA), most of which entered into force in October 2000, was a major constitutional development.[24] The HRA 'incorporates'[25] the European Convention on Human Rights (ECHR) into UK law. All legislation can now be tested for its compatibility with the ECHR. The HRA represents an ingenious construction that impacts on legislative, executive and judicial powers and involves all institutional

---

2004). In the debates on the Constitutional Reform Act 2005, Lord Hobhouse of Woodborough argued that the separation of powers, as opposed to the principle of judicial independence, was not part of our constitution, nor ever had been. The theory of the separation of powers was primarily a French invention. It had never been part of the British constitution, or the Westminster model. If it were, the executive, including the Prime Minister, would have to be removed from the House of Commons. See *Hansard*, HL, col 127 (8 September 2003).

[21] For example, it is a standard part of academic constitutional law and political texts. For a comparative analysis of the doctrine elsewhere than the United Kingdom see B Ackerman, 'The New Separation of Powers' (2000) 113 *Harvard Law Review* 633–729. He argues that the modern separation of powers doctrine is motivated by three great principles – democracy, professionalism and the protection of fundamental rights.

[22] See *Jackson v Her Majesty's Attorney-General* [2005] UKHL 56, [2005] 3 WLR 733, particularly para 102, per Lord Steyn (parliamentary sovereignty was the *general principle* of the constitution, and was a construct of the common law created and subject to revision by the judges), and para 104, per Lord Hope (parliamentary sovereignty is no longer, if it ever was, absolute; the English principle of the absolute legislative sovereignty of Parliament was gradually being qualified); A Young, 'Hunting Sovereignty: *Jackson v Her Majesty's Attorney-General*' [2006] *Public Law* 187–96; T Mullen, 'Reflections on *Jackson v Attorney General*: Questioning Sovereignty' (2007) 27 *Legal Studies* 1–25.. See also *Thoburn v Sunderland DC* [2002] EWHC 195, [2002] 3 WLR 247, per Laws LJ (constitutional statutes, eg the Magna Carta, the Bill of Rights 1689, the Act of Union, the Reform Acts, the Human Rights Act 1998, the Scotland Act 1998, the Government of Wales Act 1998, and the European Communities Act 1972, could not be repealed by implication).

[23] See eg *R v Secretary of State for Transport ex p Factortame (No 2)* [1991] AC 603.

[24] See D McGoldrick, 'The HRA in Theory and Practice' (2001) 50 *ICLQ* 901–53. It is also notable that the HRA was passed in the middle of a constitutional process of devolution.

[25] It is not a technical 'incorporation' as the ECHR is not per se part of UK law.

actors in rights review.[26] Under section 3 of the HRA all legislation must 'so far as it is possible to do so' be read and given effect to in a way that is compatible with the ECHR.[27] If it is not possible, the higher courts can issue a 'declaration of incompatibility' under section 4 of the HRA. In all cases so far, these have been followed by remedial legislation. Finally, under section 6 of the HRA it is unlawful for a public authority to act in a way which is incompatible with a Convention right.[28]

In any historical circumstances the HRA would have represented a significant challenge to the UK constitutional system. The post-11 September context has subjected the HRA to the most searching forensic testing conceivable. As Conor Gearty has observed, 'the events of 11 September 2001 have posed a major challenge to the philosophical and political integrity of the Human Rights Act'.[29] We examine the HRA's effects on the separation of powers in Sections III.A and III.B, and consider the principal judicial decisions in terrorist-related contexts in Sections V–XII below.

A. The HRA and the Legislative–Judicial Relationship

Following the enactment of the HRA, 'British constitutional discourse has become more nuanced and more complicated'.[30] Formally, the HRA acknowledges the sovereignty of Parliament.[31] It is clear that Parliament

---

[26] See D Feldman, 'The Human Rights Act 1998 and Constitutional Processes' [1999] *Legal Studies* 165–206; P Craig, 'The Courts, the Human Rights Act and Judicial Review' (2001) 117 *LQR* 589–603; D Nicol, 'Are Convention Rights a No-Go Area For Parliament' [2002] *Public Law* 438–48.

[27] See A Kavanagh, 'The Role of Parliamentary Intention in Adjudication under the Human Rights Act 1998' (2006) 26(1) *OJLS* 179–206; TRS Allen, 'Legislative Supremacy and Legislative Intention: Interpretation, Meaning and Authority' (2004) 63(3) *Cambridge Law Journal* 685–711; R Ekins, 'Constitutional Law, Judicial Supremacy and the Rule of Law' (2003) 119 *LQR* 127–52; Lady Justice Arden, 'The Changing Judicial Role: Human Rights, Community Law and the Intention of Parliament', 26 November 2007, <http://www.judiciary.gov.uk/docs/speeches/lja_261107.pdf>.

[28] Section 6 details the scope of 'public authority'. It includes the courts but not Parliament.

[29] C Gearty, '11 September 2001, Counter-terrorism, and the Human Rights Act' (2005) 32 *Journal of Law and Society* 18–33 at 18. More generally see D Dyzenhaus, *The Constitution of Law: Legality in a Time of Emergency* (Cambridge, Cambridge University Press, 2006); O Gross and F Ní Aoláin, *Law in Times of Crisis* (Cambridge, Cambridge University Press, 2006).

[30] M Loughlin, 'Introduction to *A v Secretary of State for the Home Department*' (2005) 68(4) *MLR* 654.

[31] 'The HRA is careful to preserve the sovereignty of Parliament': Baroness Hale in *A and Others v Secretary of State for the Home Department* (also referred to as the *A (Belmarsh Detainees)* case) [2004] UKHL 56, [2005] 2 AC 68 at para 220.

can pass legislation that is incompatible with the ECHR.[32] However, the judiciary has used the HRA to give greater substance to the 'principle of legality'. Lord Hoffmann explained the principle in *R v Secretary of State for the Home Department, ex p Simms*:

> Parliamentary sovereignty means that Parliament can, if it chooses, legislate contrary to fundamental principles of human rights. The Human Rights Act 1998 will not detract from this power. The constraints upon its exercise by Parliament are ultimately political, not legal. But the principle of legality means that Parliament must squarely confront what it is doing and accept the political cost. Fundamental rights cannot be overridden by general or ambiguous words. This is because there is too great a risk that the full implications of their unqualified meaning may have passed unnoticed in the democratic process. In the absence of express language or necessary implication to the contrary, the courts therefore presume that even the most general words were intended to be subject to the basic rights of the individual. In this way the courts of the United Kingdom, though acknowledging the sovereignty of Parliament, apply principles of constitutionality little different from those which exist in countries where the power of the legislature is expressly limited by a constitutional document.[33]

In practice, Parliament prefers not to 'squarely confront' what it is doing because it can be politically unpopular. But if it does not do so then it knows that the judiciary will not accept that fundamental rights have been overridden by general or ambiguous words.[34] It is also clear that Parliament could refuse to amend or replace legislation declared by a court to be incompatible with the ECHR. The fact that it has not done so, even in a terrorist/national security context, evidences the political power of such a declaration.[35]

B. The HRA and the Executive–Legislative Relationship

In the United Kingdom's legislative context the executive normally dominates the agenda of Parliament. However, the HRA also introduced

---

[32] 'The 1998 Act did not, and could not, deprive Parliament of its power to legislate inconsistently with the ECHR': *ibid* at para 144, per Lord Scott.

[33] [2000] 2 AC 115 at 131.

[34] For an example see *A (FC) and others (FC) v Secretary of State for the Home Department* [2005] UKHL 71, [2006] 2 AC 221, discussed in Section XV below. For an example of where the wording was clear see *R (Gillan and Another) v Commissioner of Police for the Metropolis and Another* [2006] UKHL 12, [2006] UKHRR 740, discussed in Section XIV below

[35] * Lord Scott has commented that under s 4 of the HRA the courts were being asked to perform a function 'the consequences of which will be essentially political in character rather than legal': *A (Belmarsh Detainees) case* [2004] UKHL 56, [2005] 2 AC 68 at para 144. A point which is often overlooked is that the government needs to respond to declarations of incompatibility with remedial measures to prove that the HRA is, in such circumstances, an effective remedy for the purposes of Article 35 ECHR.

two particularly significant changes that affected that relationship. First, section 19 introduced a new constitutional and parliamentary procedure that requires 'statements of compatibility' by Ministers in relation to parliamentary Bills.[36] Before the Second Reading of a Bill, the Minister introducing it has to make a 'declaration of compatibility' with the ECHR. This could and should operate as a powerful pre-legislative discipline on the government. At least since 1987 there has been a system of 'Strasbourg proofing' in the United Kingdom, but the HRA made this more formalised and systematic. It is therefore likely to be more rigorous. The practice has been that the Minister will make the statement of compatibility where they have received legal advice that, 'at a minimum, the balance of [legal argument] supports the view that the provisions are compatible'.[37] Although legal advice is not to be disclosed, the statement should draw attention to the main ECHR issues and the Minister's conclusions on them, including, if possible, the policy justifications for what is proposed. Statements of compatibility with ECHR rights have been made in respect of successive terrorism Bills even though there were serious concerns about compatibility with the ECHR.[38] There is also a provision for the Minister to state that they cannot say that a Bill is compatible, but that the government wishes to proceed with the legislation nevertheless.[39] The Attorney-General, Lord Goldsmith, has argued that

> section 19 has deepened the analysis and intensified the consideration in a very strong way. It is actually this, in my opinion, which has had the greatest impact on bringing respect for fundamental rights sweeping through Whitehall's corridors – rather than the power of the court to rule on noncompliance. It is not generally understood that proposals are modified, dropped or sometimes never even see the light of day because they would not otherwise be lawful. But any Government lawyer would confirm it.[40]

The second change was the establishment of a new parliamentary Joint Committee on Human Rights (JCHR) composed of six members of each

---

[36]   In force on 24 November 1998, see SI 1998/2882. Section 19 has been described as an 'important provision in balancing the role of the executive, Parliament and the courts': J Wadham, H Mountfeld and A Edmundson, *Blackstone's Guide to the Human Rights Act*, 3rd edn (Oxford, Oxford University Press, 2003) 10.

[37]   See Lord Burlison, *Hansard*, HL, vol 600 (5 May 1999), Written Answer, 93.

[38]   H Fenwick, 'The ATCSA 2001: The "Response" of Great Britain's Legal Order to September 11, 2001: Conflicts With Fundamental Rights', in P Eden and T O'Donnell (eds), *September 11, 2001: A Turning Point in International and Domestic Law?* (Ardsley, NY, Transnational Publishers, 2005) argues that the declarations had the effect of 'casting a legitimizing cloak' over the legislation.

[39]   HRA, s 19(1)(b).

[40]   Lord Goldsmith, 'Government and the Rule of Law in the Modern Age', LSE Clifford Chance Lecture, 22 February 2006, <http://www.timesonline.co.uk>.

House and with a specialist legal adviser.[41] Its terms of reference are to consider and report on matters relating to human rights in the United Kingdom (excluding consideration of individual cases) and proposals for remedial orders under the HRA.[42] The Committee decided to make scrutiny of primary legislation for its compatibility with the ECHR a first priority. In 2001, the Committee issued its first substantive reports questioning the compatibility of a number of Bills with the ECHR, including what became the Anti-terrorism, Crime and Security Act 2001 (ATCSA). It also raised concerns about all of the subsequent terrorism-related Bills, and other Bills, for example on asylum and immigration, that had anti-terrorism aspects. The JCHR has described its role as the 'parliamentary guardian' of human rights.[43] It has operated in a non-partisan manner and the standard of its analysis has been very high.[44] Interestingly, in some cases it has accepted the government's case for measures, even if it has questioned particular definitions or the lack of exceptions or qualifications.[45] That makes it more credible than human rights organisations that see every anti-terrorist measure as a human rights violation.[46] Its reports have been relied upon in the debates in Parliament[47] and by other human rights organisations.[48] They have also been relied upon by the courts. For example, in the *A (Belmarsh Detainees)* case[49] the leading judgment of Lord Bingham relied heavily on the criticisms of the JCHR and the Privy Councillors Review Committee (Newton Committee).[50] He took the view that the government had no effective answer to these criticisms.

[41] Professor David Feldman was the first legal advisor to the Committee, Murray Hunt the second.

[42] In 2006 the JCHR agreed a new strategy for its future work, see JCHR, *The Committee's Future Working Practices*, Twenty-third Report of Session 2005–06, 4 August 2006; F Klug and H Wildbore, 'Breaking New Ground: the Joint Committee on Human Rights and the Role of Parliament in Human Rights Compliance' (2007) *European Human Rights Law Review* 231–50.

[43] JCHR, Second Report of Session 2001–02, HL 37/HC 372, para 5.

[44] See JL Hiebert, 'Parliament and the Human Rights Act: Can the JCHR Help Facilitate a Culture of Rights?' (2006) 4(1) *International Journal of Constitutional Law* 1–38.

[45] See eg, JCHR, *Counter-Terrorism Policy and Human Rights: Terrorism Bill and related matters*, Third Report of Session 2005–06, HL 75-I/HC 561-I (encouragement and glorification of terrorism).

[46] See B Duner, 'Disregard for Security: The Human Rights Movement and 9/11' (2005) 17 *Terrorism and Political Violence* 89–104.

[47] Particularly in the House of Lords: see Hiebert, n 44 above.

[48] Lord Goldsmith, then Attorney-General, described the JCHR as providing a 'vital force' in debates: see Lord Goldsmith, n 40 above at 19.

[49] [2004] UKHL 56, [2005] 2 AC 68, considered in Section VII below.

[50] See *ibid* at paras 23, 32, 34 and 43.

IV. THE CONSTITUTIONAL REFORM ACT 2005

The doctrine of the separation of powers has recently received stronger legislative underpinning in the Constitutional Reform Act 2005 (the CRA). The government's proposals to abolish the Office of the Lord Chancellor, without creating additional constitutional safeguards, and the proposed degree of executive control over judicial appointments, raised strong objections on the basis of their threat to judicial independence.[51] For its part the government claimed that the reforms were actually designed to secure the independence of the judiciary, and to make a clear and transparent separation between the judiciary and the legislature.[52] An important part of the eventual constitutional settlement between Ministers and judges was a detailed *Concordat* between the Lord Chancellor and the Lord Chief Justice about the administration of justice in England and Wales.[53] In the event the CRA reformed the office of Lord Chancellor, transferring his judicial functions to the Lord Chief Justice (who became the Head of the Judiciary of England and Wales) and provided for a new independent Judicial Appointments Commission. It created a new Supreme Court of the United Kingdom that is physically[54] and institutionally separate from the House, and it removed the Law Lords from the legislature.[55]

Perhaps the most remarkable part of the CRA is section 1, entitled 'Rule of Law'. It provides that the CRA 'does not adversely affect the existing constitutional principle of the Rule of Law or the Lord Chancellor's existing constitutional role in relation to that principle'. The Act

---

[51] See Lord Windlesham, 'The Constitutional Reform Act 2005: Ministers, Judges and Constitutional Change' [2005] *Public Law* 806–23. Part of the criticism was that massive constitutional change was being devised 'on the back of an envelope' rather than after proper thought and consultation.

[52] See Lord Falconer of Thoroton, Secretary of State for Constitutional Affairs and Lord Chancellor, *Hansard*, HL, vol 657, col 927 (9 February 2004). See also Lord Windlesham, 'The Constitutional Reform Act 2005: The Politics of Constitutional Reform' [2005] *Public Law* 35–57.

[53] See *The Lord Chancellor's Judiciary-related Function: Proposals (the 'concordat')*, App 6 of the report of the Select Committee on the Constitutional Reform Bill (2003–04 HL 125-i) at 202–24. See also S Prince, 'Law and Politics: Rumours of the Demise of the Lord Chancellor have been Exaggerated' (2005) 58(2) *Parliamentary Affairs* 248–57. Prince has argued that: 'The Concordat is, in itself, a significant constitutional development: in the past, the relationship between these branches of state has been governed by tradition and convention rather than by formal document.'

[54] The chosen location is Middlesex Guildhall, a Grade II listed building, on Parliament Square, opposite the Houses of Parliament and alongside Westminster Abbey and the Treasury Building. After refurbishment, the UK Supreme Court is scheduled to open in October 2009.

[55] Interestingly, there were significant were divisions within the judicial House of Lords on the proposals: see *The Law Lords' response to the Government's consultation paper on Constitutional reform: a Supreme Court for the United Kingdom* (CP 11/03, July 2003), <http://www.parliament.uk/documents/upload/JudicialSCR071103.pdf>.

does not define the 'existing constitutional principle of the Rule of Law'. Speaking extra-judicially, Lord Bingham has suggested that the core of the existing principle is that 'all persons and authorities within the state, whether public or private, should be bound by and entitled to the benefit of laws publicly and prospectively promulgated and publicly administered in the courts'.[56] He proceeded to identify eight sub-rules. His fourth sub-rule was that the law must afford adequate protection to human rights:

> [W]ithin a given state there will ordinarily be a measure of agreement on where the lines are to be drawn, and in the last resort (subject in this country to statute) the courts are there to draw them. The rule of law must, surely, require legal protection of such human rights as, within that society, are seen as fundamental.[57]

The Attorney-General, Lord Goldsmith, has argued that the courts alone are not responsible for upholding the rule of law.[58] Rather, the executive, the legislature and the judiciary have a shared responsibility for upholding it. Hence, the 'courts recognise that in their appreciation of [the balance between the rights of individuals and the right of the majority] they must pay great respect to the views of Parliament and Government'.[59]

Section 3 of the CRA places a duty on Ministers of the Crown, including the Lord Chancellor, and all others with responsibility for matters relating to the judiciary or otherwise to the administration of justice to uphold the continued independence of the judiciary. There is a duty on Ministers of the Crown not to seek to influence particular judicial decisions through any special access to the judiciary. There is a duty on the Lord Chancellor to have regard to the need to defend the continued independence of the judiciary, the need for the judiciary to have proper support necessary to enable them to exercise their functions, and the need for the public interest in matters relating to the judiciary or otherwise to the administration of justice to be properly represented in decisions affecting those matters. As Lord Windlesham has noted, it had never been thought necessary, in modern times at least, to accord

---

[56] Lord Bingham, 'The Rule of Law', The Sixth Sir David Williams Lecture, 16 November 2006, <http://cpl.law.cam.ac.uk>.

[57] *Ibid* at 16–20. The eighth sub-rule was that the existing principle of the rule of law 'requires compliance by the state with its obligations in international law, the law which whether deriving from treaty or international custom and practice governs the conduct of nations': *ibid* at 29–34. Those international obligations would, of course, include international human rights obligations.

[58] Lord Goldsmith, n 40 above.

[59] *Ibid* at 23.

statutory recognition to an independent judiciary as one of the corner-stones of the British constitution. But the tide of events had caused a degree of genuine concern not confined to judges.[60]

One of the other contemporary events that had caused 'concern' was the executive's proposals in what became the Asylum and Immigration (Treatment of Claimants etc) Act 2005. In the Bill the government had proposed an ouster clause, which would have prevented the courts from reviewing the decisions of the new Asylum and Immigration Tribunal.[61] Notwithstanding advice from the judges that the wording was unlikely to be effective, and public expressions of concern by the then Lord Chief Justice, Lord Woolf,[62] and Lord Steyn, the government strengthened the wording. However, in the face of the strong judicial opposition,[63] and anticipated parliamentary opposition, the proposal was withdrawn. The incident can be viewed as evidence of the continuing strength of the rule-of-law principle and another indication of the exertion of judicial power. So too was the striking judgment of the High Court in 2008 to the effect that the Director of the Serious Fraud Office and the government had failed to recognize that the rule of law required that a decision to discontinue bribery investigations by BAE Systems plc had to be reached as an exercise of independent judgment and not in response to a threat from a foreign state.[63a]

V. CONTROLLING THE TERROR THREAT: ANTI-TERRORIST LEGISLATION IN THE UNITED KINGDOM

In the anti-terrorist context a major Act of Parliament, the Terrorism Act 2000, had been passed before 11 September 2001. The aim was to put

---

[60] Lord Windlesham, 'The Constitutional Reform Act 2005: The Politics of Constitutional Reform' [2005] *Public Law* 57. See also House of Lords, Select Committee on the Constitution, *Relations between the executive, the judiciary and Parliament*, 6th Report of Session 2006–07, 26 July 2007, HL Paper 151.

[61] Clause 11 had read: 'No court shall have any supervisory or other jurisdiction (whether statutory or inherent) in relation to this Tribunal'. See A Le Sueur, 'Three strikes and it's out? The UK Government's strategy to oust judicial review from immigration and asylum decision making' [2004] *Public Law* 225–33.

[62] See Lord Woolf, 'The Rule of Law and a Change in the Constitution' (2004) 63 *Cambridge Law Journal* 317–30. He suggested, inter alia, that the provision could be the catalyst for a written constitution.

[63] There was also strong criticism from the JCHR in *Asylum and Immigration (Treatment of Claimants, etc) Bill*, Fifth Report of Session 2003–04, HL 35/HC 304, para 57. Ousting the review jurisdiction of the High Court over the executive is a direct challenge to a central element of the rule of law and sets a dangerous precedent for other areas.

[63a] *R (Corner House Research and Campaign Against Arms Trade) v Director of Serious Fraud Office* [2008] EWHC 714 (Admin).

anti-terrorist legislation on a permanent footing rather than as regularly renewed temporary provisions.[64] The Secretary of State made a statement that the provisions of the Terrorism Bill were compatible with the Convention rights.[65] The Commissioner for Human Rights of the Council of Europe has described the UK's pre-11 September legislation as, 'amongst the toughest and most comprehensive anti-terror legislation in Europe'.[66] However, major terrorist atrocities almost always see new legislative provisions in response to public demand. After 11 September 2001 the Anti-terrorism, Crime and Security Act 2001 (the ATCSA)[67] was passed with great speed – taking just over a month from Bill to Royal Assent.[68] It contained an array of new offences and new powers.[69] It has been argued that the executive used 11 September to get into legislation many measures for which it had not previously been able to secure parliamentary support.[70] While the House of Commons forced no amendments from the government, the House of Lords did force a number of significant amendments.[71] The government had to accept these to secure the passage of legislation it deemed urgent.

The most controversial new measures in the ATCSA were those in Part 4, titled 'Immigration and Asylum', permitting indefinite detention for foreign nationals suspected of being international terrorists.[72] These provisions required the United Kingdom to derogate from Article 5

---

[64] See C Walker, *Blackstone's Guide to the Anti-terrorism Legislation* (Oxford, Oxford University Press, 2002).

[65] The implication was that there was no need to derogate from the ECHR: see C Warbrick, 'The European Response to Terrorism in an Age of Human Rights' (2004) 15 *European Journal of International Law* 989–1018.

[66] Report by Mr Alvaro Gil-Robles, Commissioner for Human Rights, on his visit to the United Kingdom, 4–12 November 2004, CommDH(2005) 6, <http://www.coe.int/t/commissioner/Default_en.asp>.

[67] See A Tomkins, 'Legislating Against Terror: The Anti-Terrorism, Crime and Security Act' [2002] *Public Law* 205.

[68] See PA Thomas, 'September 11th and Good Governance' (2002) 53 *Northern Ireland Legal Quarterly* 366; JL Hiebert, 'Parliamentary Review of Terrorism Measures' (2005) 68 *MLR* 676–80.

[69] Eg there were provisions on the disclosure of information, policing of nuclear and aviation facilities, retention of communications data and EU third pillar provisions. On the latter see D Bonner, 'Managing Terrorism While Respecting Human Rights? European Aspects of the ATCSA 2001' (2002) 8 *European Public Law* 497.

[70] See H Fenwick, 'The ATCSA 2001: The "Response" of Great Britain's Legal Order to September 11, 2001: Conflicts With Fundamental Rights', in P Eden and T O'Donnell (eds), *September 11, 2001: A Turning Point in International and Domestic Law?* (Ardsley, NY, Transnational Publishers, 2005) 542; A Tomkins, n 67 above.

[71] See A Blick, I Byrne and S Weir, 'Democratic Audit: Good Governance, Human Rights and the War against Terror' (2005) 58(2) *Parliamentary Affairs* 408–23.

[72] Eg on a sunset provision and on reviews. For the detailed provisions see H Fenwick, 'The ATCSA 2001: The "Response" of Great Britain's Legal Order to September 11, 2001: Conflicts With Fundamental Rights', in P Eden and T O'Donnell (eds), *September 11, 2001: A Turning Point in International and Domestic Law?* (Ardsley, NY, Transnational Publishers, 2005).

ECHR and Article 9 of the International Covenant on Civil and Political Rights (ICCPR).[73] The speed of ATCSA's passage allowed only very quick reports from the JCHR[74] and other parliamentary committees.[75] The UK government described the measures in Part 4 as 'exceptional immigration powers'. Among a number of concerns, the JCHR doubted whether the derogation order in relation to Article 5 ECHR – (for the indefinite detentions) – was justified. The government did not accept this view, but it did make a number of amendments that reflected the JCHR's concerns.[76]

VI. THE ATSCA PART 4 REGIME FOR INDEFINITE DETENTION

Section 21 of the ATCSA provided that the Home Secretary could certify an individual if he reasonably believed that that person's presence in the United Kingdom was a threat to national security and he suspected that the person was a terrorist. Once certified a range of immigration decisions (which can only be taken against non-nationals), including an order for removal, could be taken even though the person could not be removed for legal or practical reasons. Interestingly, the principal legal reason would normally be that it was contrary to the ECHR to remove an individual who presented substantial evidence that he or she would face a real risk[77] of treatment incompatible with the ECHR.[78] In the anti-terrorist context this would normally be ill-treatment or the death penalty, but in principle it could extend to violation of other rights.[79] persons

[73] See generally C Mikaelson, 'Derogating From International Human Rights Obligations in the "War Against Terrorism" – A British–Australian Perspective' (2005) 17 *Terrorism and Political Violence* 131–55.

[74] See Second and Fifth Reports of JCHR, Session 2001–02, *Anti-terrorism, Crime and Security Bill*, HL 37/HC 372; HL 51/HC 420. For a government perspective stressing that it was the Law Officers' Advice that was critical for the government see the evidence of Rt Hon Harriet Harman, Minister of State, to the JCHR, 16 January 2006, on Human Rights Policy, HL 143/HC 830-i.

[75] There were reports from the HC Home Affairs Committee, the HL Constitution Committee and the HL Delegated Powers and Regulatory Reform Committee.

[76] Eg it introduced a legal requirement for reasonableness relating to the decision to certify a person as a suspected terrorist and modified the definition of a terrorist suspect.

[77] A real risk is more than a mere possibility but something less than on the balance of probabilities or more likely than not: *AS and DD (Libya) v Secretary of State for the Home Department and Another* [2008] EWCA Civ 289 (9 April 2008) at para 60. The examination of the evidence must be rigorous and there must be serious reasons (*motifs sérieux et avères*) to believe in the risk of ill-treatment: *ibid* at para 67.

[78] It could also have been that he or she satisfied the criteria for being granted asylum.

[79] The House of Lords has held that a person may rely not only on Arts 2 and 3 ECHR but also on Arts 5, 6, 8 and possibly 9 to resist a decision to remove them to a state where anticipated ill-treatment would or might result in the complete denial or nullification of those Convention rights: see *R (Razgar) v Secretary of State for the Home Department (No 2)* [2004] UKHL 27, [2004] 2 AC 368; and *R (Ullah) v Special Adjudicator* [2004] UKHL 26, [2004]

were detained under Part 4 regime.[80] Only one person won an appeal against certification. In March 2004, the Special Immigration Appeals Commission (SIAC) ruled that the assessments placed before it for detaining a Libyan man as a 'suspected international terrorist were not reliable' and that reasonable suspicion had not been established. The Court of Appeal upheld the SIAC's decision.[81] There was particular controversy in 2006 when it 'emerged that lawyers discovered that material presented by the intelligence services in his case contradicted evidence given in another appeal. The discrepancy led to severe criticism of the Home Office by SIAC judges'.[82]

According to Amnesty International most of the ATCSA detainees were held in the High Security Unit (HSU) in Belmarsh Prison. The HSU was described as a prison within the prison. The cells were small with restricted natural light. Detainees were kept in their wing and could communicate only with detainees in the same wing, except during religious worship. During their initial detention in the HSU, the ATCSA detainees were locked in their cells for 22 hours a day, and in the two hours out of their cells they were subjected to 'small-group isolation'. Amnesty International considered that many of these aspects of the HSU regime violated international human rights standards: the lack of adequate association time and activities in communal areas; the lack of educational, sport and other meaningful activities and facilities; and the lack of access to open air, natural daylight and exercise in a larger space. In March 2002 the ATCSA detainees were shifted from Category A 'high risk' to Category A 'standard risk', and transferred to House Block 4 in Belmarsh. When Amnesty International delegates visited the detainees in June 2002, the detainees said they were still being locked up for 22 hours a day, that they were denied adequate health care and that they were allowed only 'closed' visits with their families (when a glass screen separates the detainee from family). Amnesty International concluded that those held at Belmarsh were suffering conditions that amounted to

---

2 AC 323. There has been no case in which the ECtHR has recognised a breach of the Convention where extradition or expulsion was resisted on the basis of conduct inconsistent with Art 6 in the receiving state, but the Court has on a number of occasions recognised that such a complaint is maintainable: see, eg, *Mamatkulov and Askarov v Turkey*, 41 EHRR 25 at para 88.

[80] For details of their national origin and the allegations against them see 'Who are the terror detainees?' *BBC News*, 11 March 2005, <http://news.bbc.co.uk>.

[81] See *Secretary of State for the Home Department v M* [2004] EWCA Civ 324, [2004] 2 All ER 863. See also *A and Others v State for the Home Department* [2004] EWCA Civ 1123 on a number of generic issues dealt with by the SIAC. One person was granted bail: see *G v Secretary of State for the Home Department* [2004] EWCA Civ 265.

[82] See S O'Neill, 'Immigration Powers Used To Hold Al-Qaeda Kingpin in Jail' *The Times* (UK), 20 October 2006.

cruel, inhuman and degrading treatment, and that the conditions had led to a serious deterioration of their physical and mental health.[83]

There was also some evidence that the conditions of detention were causing psychiatric problems.[84] One person was detained in a secure mental hospital; another was released on conditional bail because of the deterioration of his mental health while in custody. Another was released on bail, on strict conditions, in April 2004. The Home Secretary revoked his certification of another in September 2004, and he was released without conditions. The remainder were detained in high security jails. The European Committee on the Prevention of Torture twice visited persons detained under Part 4 of ATCSA and made adverse comments on the regime.[85] Amnesty International condemned it as a 'shadow criminal justice system'.[86] Other human rights organisations were heavily critical. In a powerfully reasoned report, a Committee of Privy Councillors (the Newton Committee) 'strongly recommended' that the detention power be terminated 'as a matter of urgency'.[87] As noted, 17 people were subjected to the Part 4 regime. Legally, they could have left at any time (hence it was referred to as a three-wall prison) if they were willing to return to a place where they faced a real risk of serious ill-treatment. Although two individuals did just this, it was not be realistic to expect detainees make this choice. By the time of the decision of the House of Lords in the *A (Belmarsh Detainees)* case, those detained had already been held for three-and-a-half years and faced the prospect of indefinite detention.

VII. THE JUDICIARY AND INDEFINITE DETENTION

The detention system in the ATCSA was challenged in *A and Others v Secretary of State for the Home Department* (the *A (Belmarsh Detainees)* case).[88] While 'Belmarsh [was] not the British Guantanamo Bay',[89] there had been strong judicial criticism of the regime at the US base. Lord Steyn had described it as a 'legal black hole' and made clear that English

---

[83] See Amnesty International Report, 'UK – Human Rights: A Broken Promise', 23 February 2006, <http://web.amnesty.org/library/Index/ENGEUR450042006?open&of=ENG-GBR>.

[84] *Ibid* at 21–3. In a number of cases the Home Office has commissioned independent medical evidence on a controlled individual, including on their mental health. This evidence, and any provided by the controlled person, is taken into account when assessing the necessity and proportionality of the control order and the controlee's obligations.

[85] See CPT/Inf (2003) 18, 9; CPT/Inf (2006), 26, 27, 28 and 29.

[86] See Amnesty International Report, n 83 above at 15.

[87] Privy Counsellor Review Committee, *Anti-terrorism, Crime and Security Act 2001 Review: Report*, House of Commons, HC 100 (2003), paras 185–204.

[88] [2004] UKHL 56, [2005] 2 AC 68.

law would not allow a similar black hole.[90] In 2002 in *R on the Application of Abbasi & Anor v Secretary of State for Foreign and Commonwealth Affairs & Secretary of State for the Home Department*[91] the Court of Appeal had used the same expression in a descriptive sense. Unusually for a high level court, it made comments about the treatment of individuals in another state's jurisdiction. It expressed 'anxiety' about the position of the detainees at Guantanamo Bay and surprise at

> the proposition that the writ of the United States courts does not run in respect of individuals held by the government on territory that the United States holds as lessee under a long term treaty.[92]

A. The Special Immigration Appeals Commission

It is important to understand how the issue of indefinite detention came before the respective courts. In 1997, the UK authorities established the Special Immigration Appeals Commission (SIAC).[93] The SIAC is an immigration tribunal, empowered to hear appeals by foreign nationals against being issued with deportation orders on grounds that they pose a threat to the 'national security' of the United Kingdom, and that their presence in the United Kingdom is not conducive to the public good. The SIAC can conduct 'closed' hearings in which the deportee and counsel are excluded, and at which the Home Secretary is allowed to present secret intelligence information. This is to ensure the protection of 'national security'. Under immigration powers, the UK authorities are entitled to detain people pending deportation.[94]

---

[89] *Ibid* at para 223, per Baroness Hale. See also PA Thomas, 'Emergency and Anti-Terrorist Powers: 9/11: USA and UK' (2003) 26 *Fordham International Law Journal* 1193–233; W Scheuerman, 'Emergency Powers and the Rule of Law After 9/11' (2006) 14 *The Journal of Political Philosophy* 61–84.

[90] Lord Steyn, 'Guantanamo Bay: The Legal Black Hole' (2004) 53 *ICLQ* 1–15. His comments may have meant that he could not sit on the *A (Belmarsh Detainees)* case but they were not the reason formally given by the Treasury Solicitors which related to another lecture. See also J Steyn, '2000–2005: Laying the Foundations of Human Rights Law in the United Kingdom' [2005] *European Human Rights Law Review* 349–62 at 350.

[91] [2002] EWCA Civ 1598, [2003] UKHRR 76 at para 22.

[92] *Ibid* at para 15. The US Supreme Court subsequently held that that federal courts did have jurisdiction to consider challenges to the legality of the detention of foreign nationals held at the Guantanamo Bay Naval Base in Cuba: see *Rasul v Bush* (03–334) 542 US 466 (2004). See also *Hamdan v Rumsfeld*, 548 US 557 (2006).

[93] This was done in response to the adverse judgment of the ECtHR in the case of *Chahal v United Kingdom*, finding that the safeguards advanced by the United Kingdom as affording proper due process standards were inadequate. Neither judicial review by the High Court nor the adviser system satisfied Art 5(4) ECHR, which mandates that the legality of detention must be determined by a 'court'.

[94] See S O'Neill, n 82 above.

The applicant in *Secretary of State for the Home Department v Rehman*,[95] a Pakistani national, had applied for indefinite leave to remain in the United Kingdom. This was refused on the basis that the Secretary of State was satisfied by information he had received from confidential sources that R was involved with an Islamic terrorist organisation. He was satisfied that in the light of R's association with the organisation it was undesirable to permit him to remain and that his continued presence in the country represented a danger to national security. R challenged the decision before the SIAC, which allowed his appeal on the basis that the Secretary of State had not established that R had been, was, and was likely to be a threat to national security. The Court of Appeal allowed the Secretary of State's appeal and this was upheld by the House of Lords. The key focus was on the interpretation of 'national security' and 'in the interests of national security'. The House of Lords accepted that the United Kingdom's national security could be threatened by action targeted at an altogether different jurisdiction, even if no British subjects were directly involved. The determination of the issue of whether something was 'in the interests' of national security was not a question of law, but rather a 'matter of judgment and policy'.[96] Their Lordships' judgments were delivered on 11 October 2001. Lord Hoffmann stated that he had written his speech some three months before 11 September 2001 but he added a postscript in the light of those events:

> They are a reminder that in matters of national security, the cost of failure can be high. This seems to me to underline the need for the judicial arm of government to respect the decisions of ministers of the Crown on the question of whether support for terrorist activities in a foreign country constitutes a threat to national security. It is not only that the executive has access to special information and expertise in these matters. It is also that such decisions, with serious potential results for the community, require a legitimacy which can be conferred only by entrusting them to persons responsible to the community through the democratic process. If the people are to accept the consequences of such decisions, they must be made by persons whom the people have elected and whom they can remove.[97]

This was a strong assertion that the judiciary should not undermine the executive's decision on whether particular individuals were a threat to national security. In particular, such decisions needed the democratic legitimacy that they were afforded if taken by persons responsible to the electorate. That meant members of the executive rather than members of

---

95   [2001] UKHL 47, [2003] 1 AC 153.
96   *Ibid* at para 50, per Lord Hoffmann.
97   *Ibid*, para 62.

the judiciary.[98] In response, Feldman has argued that concentrating on the democratic accountability of politicians is flawed for two reasons:

> The first relates to legitimacy: democratic accountability is not the only or predominant basis for legitimacy of policy-related decision-making. The second relates to competence: the judiciary is not notably less competent than Parliament, or even perhaps the government, to make risk assessments in relation to terrorism and security.[99]

Lord Steyn has also rejected Lord Hoffmann's approach that the lack of democratic legitimacy of judges was a legal principle that introduced limits on the jurisdiction of the court. Rather, deference was to be treated as a matter of the exercise of a wise discretion by a court.[100]

The ATCSA gave the SIAC new powers. These included provision for the grant of bail (section 24), to hear appeals against certification by a certified suspected international terrorist (section 25) and to hold periodic reviews of certification (section 26) and periodic reviews of the operation of sections 21 to 23 (section 28). Section 29 provided for the expiry (subject to periodic renewal) of sections 21 to 23 and for the final expiry of those sections, unless renewed, on 10 November 2006. By section 21(8), legal challenges to certification were reserved to the SIAC. Habeas corpus was thus excluded. Section 30 gave the SIAC exclusive jurisdiction on 'derogation matters', which covered the derogation from Article 5(1) ECHR made by the United Kingdom. The SIAC was designated as the appropriate tribunal to hear a challenge under the HRA to the compatibility of the use of derogation power with an applicant's Convention right. The SIAC was constituted as a superior court (section 35) and appeals from its decisions under the ATCSA lay to the Court of Appeal and House of Lords.

With respect to certification the only remedy was cancellation of the certificate if either the SIAC considered that there were no reasonable grounds for the belief or suspicion required under section 21(a) or (b) or 'for some other reason' (section 25(2)). The SIAC could appoint an independent lawyer – a Special Advocate – to represent an applicant's interests when considerations of national security meant that the applicant and his lawyers had to be excluded from the proceedings while the

---

[98] See A Tomkins, 'Defining and Delimiting National Security' (2002) 118 *Law Quarterly Review* 200–203.
[99] See D Feldman, 'Human Rights, Terrorism and Risk: The Roles of Politicians and Judges' [2006] *Public Law* 364–84 at 374.
[100] See J Steyn, 'Deference: A Tangled Story' [2005] *Public Law* 346–59.

sensitive evidence was put.[101] The Special Advocate represents the interests of, but is not responsible for, an appellant. This significantly modifies the ordinary lawyer–client relationship. The Special Advocate is precluded from communicating highly pertinent information, namely the closed case, to the appellant and, as a result, the scope of the Special Advocate to receive meaningful instructions is limited. Thus, the ability of the appellant, or his solicitor, to make informed decisions as to how best to proceed is constrained. At any closed session, neither the appellant nor his lawyers are permitted to be present and the Special Advocate takes over entirely as the appellant's representative. Special Advocates have no power to call witnesses.[102]

B. *Re A and others v Secretary of State for the Home Department* (the *A (Belmarsh Detainees)* case)

The nine appellants had been certified by the Home Secretary under section 21 and detained under section 23 of the ATSCA.[103] They shared certain common characteristics that were central to their appeals. All were foreign (non-UK) nationals. None had been the subject of any criminal charge.[104] In none of their cases was a criminal trial in prospect. The United Kingdom had derogated from Article 5(1)(f) ECHR.[105] The applicants challenged the lawfulness of their detention as inconsistent with the ECHR. They argued that the United Kingdom was not legally entitled to derogate from its ECHR obligations; that, if it was, its derogation was nonetheless inconsistent with the ECHR and therefore ineffectual to justify the detention; and that the statutory provisions under which they had been detained were incompatible with their Convention rights.

The SIAC considered a body of closed material, that is, secret material of a sensitive nature not shown to the parties. The Court of Appeal was

---

[101] For critiques see HC Constitutional Affairs Committee, *The Operation of the SIAC and the Use of Special Advocates*, Seventh Report of Session 2004–05, HC 323–1; JCHR, *Counter-Terrorism Policy and Human Rights: 28 days, intercept and post-charge questioning*, Nineteenth Report of Session 2006–07, HL 157/HC 304, paras 183–212 and Ev 10–21.

[102] The Special Advocate system was also imported into the PTA 2005. See Section IX below.

[103] Two of the eight December 2001 detainees exercised their right to leave the United Kingdom: one went to Morocco on 22 December 2001; the other (a French as well as an Algerian citizen) went to France on 13 March 2002. One of the December 2001 detainees was transferred to Broadmoor Hospital on grounds of mental illness in July 2002. Another was released on bail, on strict conditions, in April 2004. The Home Secretary revoked the certification of another in September 2004, and he was released without conditions.

[104] Although one of the detainees has previously been tried and acquitted of a terrorist offence.

[105] See *A (Belmarsh Detainees)* case [2004] UKHL 56, [2005] 2 AC 68 at para 11.

not asked to read this material. Nor was the House of Lords. Before the SIAC and the Court of Appeal, the applicants lost on the issue of whether there was a public emergency. Before the SIAC they were successful in their argument that the provisions of section 23 were discriminatory and so in breach of Article 14 of the Convention:

> If there is to be an effective derogation from the right to liberty enshrined in Article 5 in respect of suspected international terrorists – and we can see powerful arguments in favour of such a derogation – the derogation ought rationally to extend to all irremovable suspected international terrorists. It would properly be confined to the alien section of the population only if, as [counsel for the appellants] contends, the threat stems exclusively or almost exclusively from that alien section.
>
> But the evidence before us demonstrates beyond argument that the threat is not so confined. There are many British nationals already identified – mostly in detention abroad – who fall within the definition of 'suspected international terrorists', and it was clear from the submissions made to us that in the opinion of the [Secretary of State] there are others at liberty in the United Kingdom who could be similarly defined. In those circumstances we fail to see how the derogation can be regarded as other than discriminatory on the grounds of national origin.[106]

The Court of Appeal rejected this view.[107] Lord Woolf CJ referred to a tension between Articles 14 and 15 ECHR.[108] He held that it would be 'surprising' if Article 14 prevented the Secretary of State from restricting his power to detain to a smaller rather than a larger group. He held that there was objective and reasonable justification for the differential treatment of the appellants.[109] Brooke LJ similarly found good objective reasons for the Secretary of State's differentiation, although he also relied on rules of public international law.[110] Chadwick LJ found that since the Secretary of State had reached his judgment on what the exigencies of the situation required, his decision had to stand. He stated that:

> The decision to confine the measures to be taken to the detention of those who are subject to deportation, but who cannot (for the time being) be removed, is not a decision to discriminate against that class on the grounds of nationality.[111]

---

[106] *A v Secretary of State for the Home Department* [2002] HRLR 45, [2002] ACD 98 (Sp Imm App Comm) at paras 94–5.
[107] *A, X and Y, and Others v Secretary of State for the Home Department* [2002] EWCA Civ 1502, [2004] QB 335.
[108] *Ibid* at para 45. Art 15 ECHR deals with derogations.
[109] *Ibid* at para 56.
[110] *Ibid* at paras 112–32.
[111] *Ibid* at paras 152–3.

C. The Decision of the House of Lords

In *A and others v Secretary of State for the Home Department*[112] the appeal was exceptionally heard by a nine-member panel.[113] The judgment has been described as 'one of the most constitutionally significant ever decided by the House of Lords'.[114] All nine made some reference to 11 September 2001. The Senior Law Lord, Lord Bingham, delivered the leading judgment.[115] A notable feature of his opinion was its strong internationalist focus. Along with UK decisions of UK courts and the Privy Council, he cited extensively from decisions of the European Commission and ECtHR, and from Canadian and US Supreme Courts. That has been a normal feature of post-HRA jurisprudence. Rather more striking is the range of other European and international materials cited by Lord Bingham: Opinion 1/2002 of the Council of Europe Commissioner for Human Rights; the Siracusa Principles on the Limitation and Derogation Provisions in the International Covenant on Civil and Political Rights; the parliamentary Joint Committee on Human Rights; the International Covenant on Civil and Political Rights 1966; the General Comments of the United Nations (UN) Human Rights Committee; the European Commission against Racism and Intolerance; the UN Commission on Human Rights; Resolutions of the Security Council of the United Nations; the International Convention on the Elimination of All Forms of Racial Discrimination 1966; General Recommendations of the Committee on the Elimination of All Forms of Racial Discrimination; and the International Law Association's Paris Minimum Standards of Human Rights Norms in a State of Emergency.[116] Dickson has observed that: 'For a Law Lord to rely to such an extent on "soft law" standards is rare indeed and it will certainly add to the status of these standards internationally.'[117]

---

[112] [2004] UKHL 56, [2005] 2 AC 68. See M Elliott, 'UK: Detention Without Trial and the "War on Terror"' (2006) 4 *International Journal of Constitutional Law* 553–66; R O'Keefe, 'Decisions of British Courts During 2004' (2004) 75 *British Yearbook of International Law* 518–35.

[113] This evidenced its constitutional importance.

[114] M Loughlin, 'Introduction to *A v Secretary of State for the Home Department*' (2005) 68(4) *MLR* 654.

[115] Lord Nicholls, Lord Scott, Lord Rodger, Lord Carswell and Baroness Hale all made approving references to Lord Bingham's speech.

[116] It is interesting to compare the judgment of Lord Bingham with that of Lord Hoffmann, who has a much more nationalist focus: see T Poole, 'Harnessing the Power of the Past? Lord Hoffmann and the Belmarsh Detainees Case' (2005) 32(4) *Journal of Law and Society* 534–61.

[117] B Dickson, 'Law Versus Terrorism: Can Law Win?' [2005] *European Human Rights Law Review* 11–28 at 23; M Arden, 'Human Rights in The Age of Terrorism' (2005) 121 *LQR* 604–27 at 616. This describes the judgment as remarkable for the use it makes of such materials. There was similarly extensive use of international materials in *A (FC) and others*

Lord Bingham began by stressing that: 'The duty of the House, and the only duty of the House in its judicial capacity, is to decide whether the appellants' legal challenge is soundly based.'[118] His account of the background to the case refers to the events of 11 September 2001 and the fact that: 'Before and after 11 September Usama bin Laden, the moving spirit of Al-Qaeda, made threats specifically directed against the United Kingdom and its people.'[119] As noted above, an important aspect of the case was that the difficulty the United Kingdom found itself in was because of its efforts to comply with the rulings of the ECtHR and in particular the *Chahal* case.[120] The practical effect of that jurisprudence was that

> a non-national who faces the prospect of torture or inhuman treatment if returned to his own country, and who cannot be deported to any third country and is not charged with any crime, may not under Article 5(1)(f) of the [ECHR] and Schedule 3 to the Immigration Act 1971 be detained here even if judged to be a threat to national security.[121]

It was this jurisprudence that had necessitated that the United Kingdom's derogation from Article 5 to cover the detention powers in Part 4 of ATCSA.

D. The Threshold Question – Was there a Public Emergency?

All but one member of the House of Lords rejected the challenge to the existence of a public emergency.[122] Lord Bingham gave three reasons. First, the SIAC had considered a body of closed material, that is, secret material of a sensitive nature not shown to the parties. The Court of

---

(FC) v Secretary of State for the Home Department [2005] UKHL 71, [2006] 2 AC 221, [2006] HRLR 6 (otherwise known as *Re A (Foreign Torture Evidence)*), considered in Section XV below.

[118] *A (Belmarsh Detainees)* case at para 3.

[119] *Ibid* at para 6.

[120] *Chahal v United Kingdom* (1996) 23 EHRR 413.

[121] *A (Belmarsh Detainees)* case at para 9, per Lord Bingham. The United Kingdom has supported a challenge to *Chahal* in *Ramzy v Netherlands*, A/25224/05, currently before the ECtHR. It relies on the minority judgment of judges Gölcüklü, Matscher, Sir John Freeland, Baka, Mifsud Bonnici, Gotchev and Levits in *Chahal* that 'a Contracting State which is contemplating the removal of someone from its jurisdiction to that of another State may legitimately strike a fair balance between, on the one hand, the nature of the threat to its national security interests if the person concerned were to remain and, on the other, the extent of the potential risk of ill-treatment of that person in the State of destination': (1996) 23 EHRR 413 at para 1. See also the intervention by Liberty and Justice, <http://www.icj.org/IMG/pdf/Ramzy_intervention_Justice.pdf>. The United Kingdom also put the arguments in *Saadi v Italy*, A/37201/06 (unreported), which reached the ECtHR first.

[122] Although there were some misgivings, see eg Lord Bingham at para 26; Lord Scott at para 154.

Appeal had not been asked to read this material. The Attorney-General had expressly declined to ask the House of Lords to read the closed material. It was not shown that SIAC misdirected itself in law on the issue, and the view that it accepted was one it could reach on the open evidence in the case. Nor had the Court of Appeal misdirected themselves on this issue. Second, if it was open to the Irish government in the *Lawless* case[123] to conclude that there was a public emergency threatening the life of the Irish nation in a situation of 'low-level IRA terrorist activity', the British government could scarcely be faulted for reaching that conclusion in the much more dangerous situation which arose after 11 September 2001. However, it is Lord Bingham's third reason that is of the greatest interest in the context of this chapter:

> I would accept that great weight should be given to the judgment of the Home Secretary, his colleagues and Parliament on this question, because they were called on to exercise a pre-eminently political judgment. It involved making a factual prediction of what various people around the world might or might not do, and when (if at all) they might do it, and what the consequences might be if they did. Any prediction about the future behaviour of human beings (as opposed to the phases of the moon or high water at London Bridge) is necessarily problematical. Reasonable and informed minds may differ, and a judgment is not shown to be wrong or unreasonable because that which is thought likely to happen does not happen. It would have been irresponsible not to err, if at all, on the side of safety. As will become apparent, I do not accept the full breadth of the Attorney General's argument on what is generally called the deference owed by the courts to the political authorities. It is perhaps preferable to approach this question as one of demarcation of functions or what Liberty in its written case called "relative institutional competence". The more purely political (in a broad or narrow sense) a question is, the more appropriate it will be for political resolution and the less likely it is to be an appropriate matter for judicial decision. The smaller, therefore, will be the potential role of the court. It is the function of political and not judicial bodies to resolve political questions. Conversely, the greater the legal content of any issue, the greater the potential role of the court, because under our constitution and subject to the sovereign power of Parliament it is the function of the courts and not of political bodies to resolve legal questions. The present question seems to me to be very much at the political end of the spectrum: see *Secretary of State for the Home Department v Rehman* [2001] UKHL 47, [2003] 1 AC 153, para 62, per Lord Hoffmann. The appellants recognised this by acknowledging that the Home Secretary's decision on the present question was less readily open to challenge than his decision (as they argued) on some other questions. This reflects the unintrusive approach of the European Court to such a

---

[123]   *Lawless v Ireland (No 3)* (1961) 1 EHRR 15.

question. I conclude that the appellants have shown no ground strong enough to warrant displacing the Secretary of State's decision on this important threshold question.[124]

The concept of 'relative institutional competence' has since appeared in a number of decisions under the HRA.[125] Lord Bingham's citation of Lord Hoffmann in *Rehman* is somewhat ironic given that the latter was more strongly against the government's case, for example on the public emergency issue.[126] All of the other members of the House, except Lord Hoffmann, accepted that there was a public emergency for the purposes of Article 15 ECHR.

E. The Standard of Review

The appellants had argued that

> Since the right to personal liberty is among the most fundamental of the rights protected by the European Convention, any restriction of it must be closely scrutinised by the national court and such scrutiny involves no violation of democratic or constitutional principle.[127]

Lord Bingham considered that the weight of the Attorney-General's submission in response was directed to challenging the 'standard of judicial review' for which the appellants contended:

> He submitted that as it was for Parliament and the executive to assess the threat facing the nation, so it was for those bodies and not the courts to judge the response necessary to protect the security of the public. These were matters of a political character calling for an exercise of political and not judicial judgment. Just as the European Court allowed a generous margin of appreciation to member states, recognising that they were better placed to understand and address local problems, so should national courts recognise, for the same reason, that matters of the kind in issue here fall within the discretionary area of judgment properly belonging to the democratic organs of the state. It was not for the courts to usurp authority properly belonging elsewhere. The

---

[124] *A (Belmarsh Detainees)* case at para 29.

[125] Reference to this concept was also made in *R (Gillan and Another) v Commissioner of Police for the Metropolis and Another* [2006] UKHL 12, [2006] UKHRR 740, see Section XIV below, and *R (on the application of Al Rawi and others) v Secretary of State for Foreign and Commonwealth Affairs* [2006] EWCA 1279, see Section XVI.B below. See also J Jowell, 'Judicial Deference: Servility, Civility or Institutional Capacity' [2003] *Public Law* 592; M Hunt, 'Sovereignty's Blight: Why Contemporary Public Law Needs the Concept of 'Due Deference' in N Bamforth and P Leylands (eds) *Public Law in a Multilayered Constitution* (Oxford, Hart, 2003) 337–70.

[126] See Section VII.F and text at n 163 below.

[127] *A (Belmarsh Detainees)* case at para 31.

Attorney General drew attention to the dangers identified by Richard Ekins in 'Judicial Supremacy and the Rule of Law' (2003) 119 LQR 127.[128]

Lord Bingham acknowledged that where the conduct of government was threatened by serious terrorism, difficult choices had to be made and the terrorist dimension could not be overlooked. Any decision made by a representative democratic body commanded respect but the degree of respect would be conditioned by the nature of the decision. However, he stressed that the ECHR regime for the international protection of human rights required national authorities, including national courts, to exercise their authority to afford effective protection. That was part of the rationale for the margin of appreciation in relation to derogations. He recalled the observation of Simon Brown LJ in *International Transport Roth GmbH v Secretary of State for the Home Department* that 'the court's role under the 1998 Act is as the guardian of human rights. It cannot abdicate this responsibility'.[129] From this analysis Lord Bingham deduced that

> the appellants are in my opinion entitled to invite the courts to review, on proportionality grounds, the Derogation Order and the compatibility with the Convention of section 23 and the courts are not effectively precluded by any doctrine of deference from scrutinising the issues raised. It also follows that I do not accept the full breadth of the Attorney General's submissions. I do not in particular accept the distinction which he drew between democratic institutions and the courts. It is of course true that the judges in this country are not elected and are not answerable to Parliament. It is also of course true ... that Parliament, the executive and the courts have different functions. But the function of independent judges charged to interpret and apply the law is universally recognised as a cardinal feature of the modern democratic state, a cornerstone of the rule of law itself. The Attorney General is fully entitled to insist on the proper limits of judicial authority, but he is wrong to stigmatise judicial decision-making as in some way undemocratic. It is particularly inappropriate in a case such as the present in which Parliament has expressly legislated in section 6 of the 1998 Act to render unlawful any act of a public authority, including a court, incompatible with a Convention right, has required courts (in section 2) to take account of relevant Strasbourg jurisprudence, has (in section 3) required courts, so far as possible, to give effect to Convention rights and has conferred a right of appeal on derogation issues. The effect is not, of course, to override the sovereign legislative authority of the Queen in Parliament, since if primary legislation is declared to be incompatible the validity of the legislation is unaffected (section 4(6)) and the remedy lies with the appropriate minister (section 10), who is answerable to Parliament. The 1998 Act gives the courts a very specific, wholly democratic, mandate.[130]

---

[128]   *Ibid* at para 37.

[129]   [2003] QB 728 at para 27.

[130]   *A (Belmarsh Detainees)* case at para 42. He cited Jeffrey Jowell's comment that: 'The courts are charged by Parliament with delineating the boundaries of a rights-based

It is important to note that Lord Bingham considers that, as a general proposition, judicial decision-making is democratic. The HRA made the argument against the proposition inappropriate in this context, but even absent the HRA the general proposition would remain.

Lord Rodger drew attention to the fact that section 30 of the ATCSA specifically provided that derogation from Article 5(1) ECHR, relating to the detention of a person where there was an intention to remove or deport him from the United Kingdom, or the designation of that derogation in terms of section 14(1) of the HRA, could be questioned in legal proceedings before the SIAC and in an appeal from the SIAC's decision. Parliament had thereby conferred on those detained under the 2001 Act this special right to challenge the derogation from their Article 5(1) Convention rights. If that right was to be meaningful, 'the judges must be intended to do more than simply rubber-stamp the decisions taken by ministers and Parliament'.[131] Parliament had given the courts a specific mandate to perform a function that the executive and the legislature could not perform for themselves. In those circumstances: 'The legitimacy of the courts' scrutiny role cannot be in doubt.'[132]

Lord Hope accepted that the executive and the legislature were to be accorded a wide margin of discretion in matters relating to national security, especially where the Convention rights of others, such as the right to life, might be put in jeopardy. However, the width of the margin depended on the context and the right to liberty, and the responsibility that rested on the court to give effect to the guarantee to minimise the risk of arbitrariness and to ensure the rule of law provided the context. The margin of the discretionary judgment that the courts would accord to the executive and to Parliament where this right was in issue was narrower than would be appropriate in other contexts:

> We are dealing with actions taken on behalf of society as a whole which affect the rights and freedoms of the individual. This is where the courts may legitimately intervene, to ensure that the actions taken are proportionate. It is an essential safeguard, if individual rights and freedoms are to be protected in a democratic society which respects the principle that minorities, however unpopular, have the same rights as the majority. The intensity of the scrutiny will nevertheless vary according to the point that has to be considered at each stage as one examines the question that was referred to [SIAC][133]

---

democracy' (in 'Judicial Deference: Servility, civility or institutional capacity?' [2003] *Public Law* 592 at 597); and R Clayton, 'Judicial deference and "democratic dialogue": The legitimacy of judicial intervention under the Human Rights Act 1998' [2004] *Public Law* 33.

[131] *A (Belmarsh Detainees)* case, para 164 at per Lord Rodger.

[132] *Ibid* at para 176.

[133] *Ibid* at para 108, per Lord Hope.

Lord Roger also thought that the lesson of history was that judicial scrutiny was appropriate as national security could, even in good faith, be used as a pretext for repressive measures that were really taken for other reasons.[134] In discharging that duty to check whether the measures were strictly required by the exigencies of the circumstances, British courts were performing their 'traditional role of watching over the liberty of everyone within their jurisdiction, regardless of nationality'.[135] The reference to a traditional role suggests that the role was not dependent on the HRA.

Lord Hope was content to accept that the questions of whether there was an emergency and whether it threatened the life of the nation were 'pre-eminently for the executive and for Parliament. The judgment that has to be formed on these issues lies outside the expertise of the courts'.[136] However, he also explained that the United Kingdom was only accorded a margin of appreciation on the question whether the measures taken to interfere with the right to liberty did not exceed those 'strictly required by the exigencies of the situation' on the understanding that domestic courts would provide effective judicial review of such measures. The 'proper function of the judiciary' was to subject the government's reasoning on these matters in this case to very close analysis.[137]

For Baroness Hale, any sensible court recognised the limits of its expertise:

> Assessing the strength of a general threat to the life of the nation is, or should be, within the expertise of the Government and its advisers. They may, as recent events have shown, not always get it right. But courts too do not always get things right. It would be very surprising if the courts were better able to make that sort of judgment than the Government. Protecting the life of the nation is one of the first tasks of a Government in a world of nation states. That does not mean that the courts could never intervene. Unwarranted declarations of emergency are a familiar tool of tyranny. If a Government were to declare a public emergency where patently there was no such thing, it would be the duty of the court to say so.[138]

F. Proportionality

Lord Bingham accepted the proportionality challenge to the Derogation Order and to section 23 of the ATCSA. Central to this view was the argument that the choice of an immigration measure to address a security

---

[134]   *Ibid* at para 177, per Lord Rodger.
[135]   *Ibid* at para 178.
[136]   *Ibid* at para 116, per Lord Hope.
[137]   *Ibid.*
[138]   *Ibid* at para 226, per Baroness Hale.

problem had the inevitable result of failing adequately to address that problem.[139] It allowed non-UK suspected terrorists to leave the country with impunity and left British suspected terrorists at large, while imposing the severe penalty of indefinite detention on persons who, even if reasonably suspected of having links with Al Qaeda, might harbour no hostile intentions towards the United Kingdom.[140] He robustly rejected the approach of the SIAC and the Court of Appeal:

> I do not consider SIAC's conclusion as one to which it could properly come. In dismissing the appellants' appeal, Lord Woolf CJ broadly considered that it was sensible and appropriate for the Secretary of State to use immigration legislation, that deference was owed to his decisions (para 40) and that SIAC's conclusions depended on the evidence before it (para 43). Brooke LJ reached a similar conclusion (para 91), regarding SIAC's findings as unappealable findings of fact. Chadwick LJ also regarded SIAC's finding as one of fact (para 150). I cannot accept this analysis as correct. The European Court does not approach questions of proportionality as questions of pure fact: see, for example, *Smith and Grady v United Kingdom* ... Nor should domestic courts do so. The greater intensity of review now required in determining questions of proportionality, and the duty of the courts to protect Convention rights, would in my view be emasculated if a judgment at first instance on such a question were conclusively to preclude any further review. So would *excessive deference*, in a field involving indefinite detention without charge or trial, to ministerial decision. In my opinion, SIAC erred in law and the Court of Appeal erred in failing to correct its error.[141] (emphasis added)

Lord Scott was unable to accept that the Secretary of State had established that section 23 was 'strictly required' by the public emergency. He should, at the least, have shown that monitoring arrangements or movement restrictions less severe that incarceration in prison would not suffice.[142] For Baroness Hale, if it was not necessary to lock up the nationals it could not be necessary to lock up the foreigners. It was not strictly required by the exigencies of the situation.[143] Finally, a number of their Lordships also made the point that it was hard to see that the

---

[139] *Ibid* at para 43, per Lord Bingham. See also Lord Hope at para 103 (serious error to regard the case as being about the right to control immigration; rather it was an issue about the aliens' right to liberty), para 129 (indefinite detention without trial of foreign nationals cannot be said to be strictly required to meet the exigencies of the situation, if the indefinite detention without trial of those who present a threat to the life of the nation because they are suspected of involvement in international terrorism is not thought to be required in the case of British nationals) and para 133 (s 23 of ATCSA not rationally connected to the legislative objective).

[140] *Ibid* at para 43.

[141] *Ibid* at para 44.

[142] *Ibid* at para 155, per Lord Scott.

[143] *Ibid* at para 231, per Baroness Hale.

detainees were so very dangerous given that the government was happy to let them go to any country that would take them.[144] This pointed to the disproportionality of the measures.

G. Discrimination

The appellants also attacked section 23 as discriminatory on the basis of nationality. The Home Secretary had argued that the threat to the life of the nation, 'came predominantly, but not exclusively from foreign nationals and that foreign nationals were using the UK as a base for international terrorist activities'.[145] Although there was a threat from British nationals, extending the ATCSA detention powers to them would be disproportionate:

> While it would be possible to seek other powers to detain British citizens who may be involved in international terrorism it would be a very grave step. The Government believes that such draconian powers would be difficult to justify.[146]

The SIAC had concluded that section 23 was discriminatory because the threat did not stem solely from foreign nationals. The Court of Appeal disagreed, but the House of Lords reversed this. The critical issue, as often in discrimination analysis, was in determining the appropriate comparator. The Attorney-General submitted that the position of the appellants should be compared with that of non-UK nationals who represented a threat to the security of the United Kingdom but who could be removed to their own or to safe third countries. The relevant difference between them and the appellants was that the appellants could not be removed. A difference of treatment of the two groups was accordingly justified and it was reasonable and necessary to detain them. The Court of Appeal had accepted this on the basis that 'the nationals have a right of abode in this jurisdiction but the aliens only have a right not to be removed'.[147] However, Lord Bingham rejected this approach because it meant accepting, 'the correctness of the Secretary of State's choice of immigration control as a means to address the Al-Qaeda security problem, when the correctness of that choice is the issue to be

---

[144] *Ibid* at para 33, per Lord Bingham; at para 85, per Lord Nicholls; at para 133, per Lord Hope; at para 140, per Lord Scott; at para 230, per Baroness Hale; and at para 240, per Lord Carswell.

[145] See David Blunkett *et al, Counter-terrorism Powers: Reconciling Security and Liberty in an Open Society*, Cm 6147 (February 2004), <http://www.statewatch.org/news/2004/feb/uk-CT-discussion-paper.pdf> at para 24.

[146] *Ibid* at para 36, cited by Lord Bingham in *A (Belmarsh Detainees)* case at para 64.

[147] *A, X and Y, and Others v Secretary of State for the Home Department* [2002] EWCA Civ 1502, [2004] QB 335 at para 56, per Lord Woolf.

resolved'.[148] In his view the proper comparators were suspected international terrorists who were UK nationals. The appellants shared with this group the most relevant characteristics: (a) of being suspected international terrorists and (b) of being irremovable.[149] Although he accepted that the Attorney-General's comparison might be reasonable and justified in an immigration context, it could not be so 'in a security context, since the threat presented by suspected international terrorists did not depend on their nationality or immigration status'.[150] Baroness Hale also followed this approach. She was particularly scathing about the Attorney-General's efforts to justify the measures:

> No one has the right to be an international terrorist. But substitute 'black', 'disabled', 'female', 'gay', or any other similar adjective for 'foreign' before 'suspected international terrorist' and ask whether it would be justifiable to take power to lock up that group but not the 'white', 'able-bodied', 'male' or 'straight' suspected international terrorists. The answer is clear.[151]

The Attorney-General also made a more far-reaching submission that 'international law sanctions the differential treatment, including detention, of aliens in times of war or public emergency'.[152] After considering a range of European and international materials, Lord Bingham asserted that there was no European or other authority for the Attorney-General's view. Moreover, there were a number of international treaties and materials that were 'inimical to the submission that a state may lawfully discriminate against foreign nationals by detaining them but not nationals presenting the same threat in a time of public emergency.[153] A decision to detain one group of suspected international terrorists, defined by nationality or immigration status, and not another, could not be justified. It was a violation of Article 14 ECHR. It was also a violation of Article 26 of the ICCPR and so inconsistent with the United Kingdom's 'other obligations under international law' within the meaning of Article 15 ECHR. A range of international instruments and US authorities was considered, but none was considered to support the Attorney-General's view.[154]

Lord Nicholls similarly thought that the government had misconceived the human rights of non-nationals in this situation.[155] For Lord

---

[148]   *A (Belmarsh Detainees)* case at para 53.
[149]   *Ibid* at paras 51–2. Similarly, at para 138, per Lord Hope.
[150]   *Ibid* at para 54. See also Lord Rodger at para 166.
[151]   *Ibid* at para 238, per Baroness Hale.
[152]   *Ibid* at para 55, per Lord Bingham.
[153]   *Ibid* at para 63.
[154]   See also D Wilsher, 'The Administrative Detention of Non-Nationals Pursuant to Immigration Control: International and Constitutional Law Perspectives' (2004) 53 *ICLQ* 897–934.
[155]   *A (Belmarsh Detainees)* case at para 84.

Scott, a difference based on the right to residence was 'irrelevant to the issue as to what measures are required in order to combat the threat of terrorism that their presence in this country may be thought by the Secretary of State to present'.[156] If the measures were really necessary they would logically have been applicable to nationals and non-nationals. The measures were as irrational as if they had been confined to Muslims only, or to men only.[157] It was irrational and discriminatory to restrict the application of the measures to suspected terrorists who had no right of residence in this country. Some suspected terrorists might well be home-grown.[158] course, the truth of this last comment became evident in July 2005 when there was a series of suicide attacks in London by UK nationals.

Lord Nicholls stressed that the courts were 'acutely conscious' that the government alone was able to evaluate and decide what counter-terrorism steps were needed and what steps would suffice to protect the security of this country and its inhabitants. He accepted that courts were not equipped to make such decisions, nor had they been charged with that responsibility. However, Parliament had charged the courts with a particular responsibility to check that legislation and ministerial decisions did not overlook the human rights of persons adversely affected. The courts would accord to Parliament and ministers, the 'primary decision-makers', an appropriate degree of latitude. As the latitude would vary according to the subject matter under consideration, the importance of the human right in question, and the extent of the encroachment upon that right, the courts would only intervene when it was apparent that, in balancing the various considerations involved, the primary decision-maker must have given insufficient weight to the human rights factor. For Lord Nicholls that was the situation in this case.[159]

Although this was a national security case where Parliament would normally have substantial latitude to make decisions, that was under-mined because security considerations had not prompted a similar negation of the right to personal liberty in the case of nationals who posed a similar security risk. The government had described such a 'draconian' power as 'difficult to justify'.[160] But, in practical terms, it was equally draconian for a non-national who, in practice, could not leave the country for fear of torture abroad.[161]

---

[156]   *Ibid* at para 157, per Lord Scott.
[157]   *Ibid* at para 158.
[158]   *Ibid.*
[159]   *Ibid* at paras 79–81, per Lord Nicholls.
[160]   Blunkett *et al*, n 145 above at para 36. The discussion paper was a direct response to the report of the Newton Committee, n 87 above.
[161]   *A (Belmarsh Detainees)* case at para 83, per Lord Nicholls.

Lord Hoffmann's opinion attracted the greatest publicity because of its language and tenor. It was also firmly grounded in English law and domestic considerations rather than in the international and European sources that underlay Lord Bingham's opinion.[162] Lord Hoffmann did not accept the case that there was a threat to the life of the nation for the purposes of Article 15 ECHR. Indeed, he was of the view that:

> The real threat to the life of the nation, in the sense of a people living in accordance with its traditional laws and political values, comes not from terrorism but from laws such as these. That is the true measure of what terrorism may achieve. It is for Parliament to decide whether to give the terrorists such a victory.[163]

However, it is worth remembering that Lord Hoffmann's view on the existence of a public emergency was not shared by any other member of the House. It has also been criticised extra-judicially by Arden LJ on the basis that the Law Lords had not seen the closed material in the case.[164] It is somewhat ironic that the leading opinion of Lord Bingham and a number of the other opinions actually cited Lord Hoffmann's opinion in *Secretary of State for the Home Department v Rehman*[165] in support of the argument that a decision on the very existence of an emergency was very much at the political end of the spectrum and required legitimation through the democratic process.

For completeness it is necessary to briefly note Lord Walker's dissent. He did not consider the measures to be discriminatory. He reasoned that there were sound, rational grounds for different treatment and that the measures were not disproportionate, given the safeguards against oppression and the possibilities for judicial and parliamentary review.[166]

H. Concluding Comments on the *A (Belmarsh Detainees)* Case

The House of Lords decision in the *A (Belmarsh Detainees)* case was greeted with acclaim by human rights lawyers and with shock by the government.[167] It is particularly significant in terms of how it saw the relative institutional competence of the executive and the judiciary. It asserts a relatively strong role for the judiciary in the protection of the

---

[162] For an excellent analysis see Poole, n 116 above.

[163] *A (Belmarsh Detainees)* case at para 97, per Lord Hoffmann. See also S Jenkins, 'Judges Cut Through the Hysteria of Rulers Made Tyrants By Fear', *The Sunday Times* (UK), 22 July 2006.

[164] M Arden, 'Human Rights In The Age of Terrorism' (2005) 121 *LQR* 604–27 at 616.

[165] [2001] UKHL 47, [2003] 1 AC 153 at para 62, cited in text at n 95 above.

[166] *A (Belmarsh Detainees)* case at paras 191–218, per Lord Walker.

[167] See Arden, n 164 above; T Hickman, 'Between Human Rights and the Rule of Law: Indefinite Detention and the Derogation Model of Constitutionalism' [2005] 68 *MLR* 655–68;

rule of law in general and of fundamental human rights in particular. The decision can be read to support the argument of those who claim that parliamentary sovereignty in the United Kingdom is gradually being replaced by a system of constitutional supremacy under which fundamental rights are not subject to executive or even parliamentary removal.[168] However, it can be read more narrowly as simply following Parliament's own direction in the HRA and applying it to the narrow technical legal issue of discrimination – an area where courts traditionally feel they have proper expertise.[169] Fundamental to the House of Lords decision was its conception that what was at issue was not an 'immigration' matter but a 'security' one. Conceived in security terms, the government's position was illogical and irrational because British nationals could present an equal security threat but were not subject to detention. In rule of law terms, the ATCSA violated the rule that laws should apply equally to all save to the extent that objective differences justify differentiation.[170] In an emergency situation, states have commonly resorted to measures against aliens and subsequently sought to extend them to citizens.[171] The House of Lords stood up for a small number of politically (and largely legally) powerless individuals. As Dickson has rightly observed, '[t]he House of Lords, much to its credit, has ensured that the rule of law prevails even when very few people, including non-British nationals, have their fundamental rights breached'.[172]

Steyn (2005), n 90 above at 351–2. *Cf* the acceptance of the High Court of Australia of the lawfulness of indefinite detention of non-citizens in a migration context, *Al-Kateb v Goodwin* [2004] HC 37.

[168] See the discussion in *International Transport Roth GMBH and Others v Secretary of State for the Home Department* [2002] UKHRR 479.

[169] For a leading example see *Ghaidan v Godin-Mendoza* [2004] UKHL 30, [2004] 2 AC 557 (housing legislation regulating surviving tenancies discriminatory on grounds of sexual orientation). See also S Fredman, 'From Deference to Democracy: The Role of Equality Under the Human Rights Act 1998' (2006) 122 *Law Quarterly Review* 53–81.

[170] See Lord Bingham, n 56 above at 12–15.

[171] See D Cole, *Enemy Aliens* (New York, New Press, 2003).

[172] B Dickson, 'Law Versus Terrorism: Can Law Win?' [2005] *EHRLR* 11–28 at 24. Eleven individuals detained under ATCSA have brought an application to the European Court of Human Rights alleging violations of Articles 3, 5, 6, 13 and 14. See *A and Others v UK*, A3455/50. Cf the decision of the Canadian Supreme Court in *Charkaoui v Canada (Citizenship and Immigration)* [2007] 1 SCR 350 that since s 6 of the *Canadian Charter of Rights and Freedoms* specifically provided for differential treatment of citizens and non-citizens in deportation matters, a deportation scheme that applied to non-citizens, but not to citizens, did not for that reason alone infringe s 15 of the Charter. Even though the detention of some of the appellants had been long, the record did not establish that the detentions at issue had become unhinged from the state's purpose of deportation: paras 129, 131.

Legally, under the structure of the HRA, the government did not have to accept the declaration of incompatibility.[173] However, it was in a difficult legal and political position. As Bonner has observed:

> Ignoring it would have devalued the constitutional settlement embodied in the HRA and constituted a further sign of the weak rooted nature of our human rights' culture. Not doing so would have meant that it would have been nigh impossible to get the House of Lords as a legislative chamber to renew the detention without trial provisions of ATCSA Part 4 in March 2005. Furthermore, not doing so at all would have enhanced the risk of adverse comment by the European Court of Human Rights to which the case would be taken in due course, on the efficacy of a Declaration of Incompatibility as a remedy, thus necessitating consideration of again redrawing the constitutional balance between lawmakers and judiciary over the validity of legislation.[174]

In January 2005 the government announced that it accepted the declaration of incompatibility and that new legislation would replace indefinite detention in prison.[175] The new provisions were contained the Prevention of Terrorism Act 2005. We proceed to examine them, but it is important to bear in mind that they were resorted to because human rights jurisprudence was restricting the government from its preferred option for the deportation or indefinite detention of non-nationals.

VIII. THE PREVENTION OF TERRORISM ACT 2005

After the measures in Part 4 of the ATCSA were held incompatible with the ECHR in the *A (Belmarsh Detainees)* case, the executive proposed a new system of control orders.[176] The proposals applied to both British nationals and non-nationals, and were considered very controversial.[177] The government accepted that they represented a 'very substantial increase in the executive powers of the State in relation to British citizens'.[178] There was a major rebellion by backbench Labour MPs in the House of Commons and strong opposition in the House of Lords.[179] The parliamentary process had to be dealt with very quickly because the previous powers to detain the individuals were due to expire on 14

---

[173] See P Naughton, 'Clarke Stands Firm Over Terror Detainees After Ruling', *The Times* (UK), 16 December 2004.

[174] D Bonner, 'Checking the Executive? Detention Without Trial, Control Orders, Due Process and Human Rights' (2006) 12(1) *European Public Law* 45–71 at 59.

[175] See Home Secretary, HC Deb, vol 430, cols 306–309 (26 January 2005).

[176] The essential idea of these had been proposed by the Newton Committee, n 87 above, which described them as 'restrictions': para 251.

[177] See Bonner, n 174 above.

[178] HC Deb, vol 430, col 309 (26 January 2005).

[179] See M Bright and G Hinslif, 'Chaos: How War On Terror Became A Political Dogfight', *The Observer* (UK), 13 March 2005.

March 2005. In the event, the Prevention of Terrorism Act 2005 (the PTA) took just 18 days between introduction and Royal Assent. The first control orders, to deal with the ten suspects previously interned in Belmarsh, were issued by the Home Secretary immediately.

The JCHR produced, at great speed, a critical report on the Bill.[180] The Bill sought to authorise the Secretary of State to make 'control orders' that would allow a suspected terrorist to be placed under house arrest, and thereby derogate from the right to liberty under Article 5 ECHR, without prior judicial authorisation. The Bill would also authorise a wide range of restrictions on suspects' movements, association, expression, and travel, again without prior judicial involvement. The JCHR conducted a rigorous rights review of the proposed measures within days of the Bill's introduction. It questioned why house arrest was being contemplated, particularly in light of the Home Secretary's admission that 'there is currently no need' to derogate from Article 5 ECHR. The JCHR also expressed doubt about the legitimacy of denying liberty without prior judicial involvement.[181] The reason given for refusing prior judicial authorisation was that the government had 'prime responsibility to protect the nation's security' and that to abdicate this responsibility to the judiciary would be inappropriate.[182] The JCHR characterised this explanation as an 'eccentric interpretation of the constitutional doctrine of the separation of powers', and reminded the government that the 'judiciary's responsibility for the liberty of the individual' had long been accepted and respected. Therefore, to, 'invoke national security to deny that role' would be to 'subvert' the nation's 'traditional constitutional division of powers'.[183] This is very strong language and reflects a real difference in the perception of executive and judicial roles.

After strong opposition, in the House of Lords in particular, the government accepted amendments under which judges authorised control orders (except for temporary emergency orders) and that there would be a review of the legislation after one year.

A. Control Orders

The PTA 2005 provides 'legislative power to subject to a "control order" any terrorist suspect whatever his/her citizenship and whatever the

---

[180]   JCHR, *Prevention of Terrorism Bill: Preliminary Report*, Ninth Report of Session 2004–05, HL 61/HC 389.

[181]   *Ibid* at paras 5, 13, 15–17.

[182]   Charles Clarke, Secretary of State for the Home Department, HC Deb, vol 431 cols 151–5 (22 February 2005).

[183]   JCHR, Ninth Report of of Session 2004–05, n 180 above at para 12.

terrorism involved'.[184] It was designed therefore to avoid dealing with nationals and non-nationals differently. The ATCSA provisions on detention without trial were repealed with effect from 14 March 2005. Two forms of control orders replaced them: 'non-derogating' and 'derogating' orders. The intended distinction was that the conditions in a derogating control order would constitute an interference with the right to liberty and security of person enshrined in Article 5 ECHR and would not fall within the exhaustive range of permissible heads of legitimate interference. An example would be if the person were effectively under house arrest. A derogating control order would require parliamentary approval via an Article 15 ECHR designated derogation order under the HRA[185] and could be authorised only by a judge. Derogating control orders can be imposed on application to a judge where there is a belief that it is more likely than not that someone is or has been involved in terrorism-related activities. As of April 2008 no such orders had yet been made, although, as explained below, it is arguable that a derogation should have been made because of the scope of the restrictions that have been contained in control orders.

A 'control order' is an order against an individual that imposes obligations on him for purposes connected with protecting members of the public from a risk of terrorism.[186] The Secretary of State may make a control order against an individual if he: (a) has reasonable grounds for suspecting that the individual is or has been involved in terrorism-related activity; and (b) considers that it is necessary, for purposes connected with protecting members of the public from a risk of terrorism, to make a control order imposing obligations on that individual.[187] The obligations that may be imposed by a non-derogating control order are, 'any obligations that the Secretary of State . . . considers necessary for purposes connected with preventing or restricting involvement by that individual in the terrorism-related activity'.[188] A non-exhaustive list includes: a prohibition or restriction on his possession or use of specified articles or substances; a prohibition or restriction on his use of specified services or specified facilities, or on his carrying on specified activities; a restriction in respect of his work or other occupation, or in respect of his business; a restriction on his association or communications with specified persons or with other persons generally; a restriction in respect of his place of residence or on the persons to whom he gives access to his place

---

[184] See Bonner, n 174 above at 61.
[185] See HRA, s 14(1).
[186] PTA, s 1(1).
[187] *Ibid*, s 2(1). See Part 76 of the Civil Procedural Rules. The terrorist activity can be domestic or international.
[188] *Ibid*, s 1(3).

of residence; a prohibition on his being at specified places or within a specified area at specified times or on specified days; a prohibition or restriction on his movements to, from or within the United Kingdom, a specified part of the United Kingdom or a specified place or area within the United Kingdom; a requirement on him to comply with such other prohibitions or restrictions on his movements as may be imposed, for a period not exceeding 24 hours, by directions given to him in the specified manner, by a specified person and for the purpose of securing compliance with other obligations imposed by or under the order; a requirement on him to surrender his passport, or anything in his possession to which a prohibition or restriction imposed by the order relates, to a specified person for a period not exceeding the period for which the order remains in force; a requirement on him to give access to specified persons to his place of residence or to other premises to which he has power to grant access; a requirement on him to allow specified persons to search that place or any such premises for the purpose of ascertaining whether obligations imposed by or under the order have been, are being or are about to be contravened; a requirement on him to allow specified persons, either for that purpose or for the purpose of securing that the order is complied with, to remove anything found in that place or on any such premises and to subject it to tests or to retain it for a period not exceeding the period for which the order remains in force; a requirement on him to allow himself to be photographed; a requirement on him to cooperate with specified arrangements for enabling his movements, communications or other activities to be monitored by electronic or other means; a requirement on him to comply with a demand made in the specified manner to provide information to a specified person in accordance with the demand; a requirement on him to report to a specified person at specified times and places.[189] The intention was that each order would be tailored to the particular risk posed by the individual concerned. In fact many of the early orders appeared to follow a standard format.[190] However, gradually there were more variations. Before making, or applying for the making of, a control order against the individual, the Secretary of State must consult the chief officer of the police force about whether there is evidence available that could realistically be used for the purposes of a prosecution of the individual for an offence relating to terrorism.[191]

---

[189]   *Ibid*, s 1(4). See also ss 1(5)–(7).

[190]   See T de la Mare, 'Control Orders and Restrictions on Liberty', <http://www.blackestonechambers.com /papers/asp>. De la Mare also examines potential conflicts with EU law.

[191]   PTA, s 8(2). If a control order is imposed the possibility of prosecution must be kept under review: *ibid*, s 8(4). See *Secretary of State for the Home Department v E and S* [2007] EWCA Civ 459, discussed in Section XI below.

The PTA 2005 thus permits a range of conditions from house arrest, tagging, curfews, controlling access to visitors, and restrictions on meetings and communications. As of the end of January 2008 a total of 31 individuals had been the subject of a 'non-derogating' control order, of which 15 such orders were still in force.[192] The subjects of these orders were all male. They are normally protected by an anonymity order.[193] One was a UK national; all the rest were non-UK nationals. Modifications of control order obligations are now more frequently made, and there are an increasing number of requests for modifications.[194] The first was made using the urgency procedures under section 3(1)(b) of the PTA 2005 in February 2007.[195] Seven individuals subject to a control order have absconded,[196] as has another individual in relation to whom a control order had been made (that is, signed), but before the order was served. This order was therefore not in operation. Three orders have been revoked and six individuals have been deported.

The Minister can impose such an order when he or she has 'reasonable grounds' to suspect that someone is or has been involved in terrorism-related activities, and considers it necessary to do so 'for purposes connected with protecting members of the public from a risk of terrorism'. Where the Secretary of State makes an application for permission to make a non-derogating control order against an individual, the application must set out the order for which he or she seeks permission, and the function of the court is to consider whether the Secretary of State's decision that there are grounds to make that order is 'obviously flawed'. If it gives permission, the court must give directions for a hearing in relation to the order as soon as reasonably practicable after it is made.

---

[192] *Third Report of the Independent Reviewer Pursuant to Section 14(3) of the Prevention of Terrorism Act 2005*, 18 February 2008, <http://security.homeoffice.gov.uk> at para 11. The independent reviewer stressed that the key to the obligations under control orders was proportionality: *ibid* at para 45.

[193] Anonymity is based on the operational advice of the police. '[F]or the controlee it avoids publicity that might lead to harassment in the community where he/she lives, or that might prejudice a fair trial if criminal charges are brought later, as has occurred and may well happen with increasing frequency': *ibid* at para 20.

[194] In *Mahmoud Abu Rideh v Secretary of State for the Home Department* [2007] EWHC 2237 (Admin), Beatson J held that modifications made by the Secretary of State to the appellant's control order were proportionate and necessary for purposes connected with preventing or restricting the appellant's involvement in terrorism-related activity.

[195] 'Update on control orders', Written Ministerial Statement by the Secretary of State for the Home Department, 22 March 2007, <http://www.publications.parliament.uk>.

[196] The independent reviewer submitted that 'the disappearance of a small minority does not necessarily undermine the benefits of the orders in relation to the majority. It is plainly doubtful that any well-organised terrorism cell would wish to rely in a significant way on someone who is being sought by police internationally, so the absconders probably present little risk provided that they are sought diligently': *Second Report of the Independent Reviewer Pursuant to Section 14(3) of the Prevention of Terrorism Act 2005*, 19 February 2007, <http://security.homeoffice.gov.uk> at para 59.

The Secretary of State may make a non-derogating control order against an individual without the permission of the court but must immediately refer the order to the court, and the court's consideration must begin no more than seven days after the day on which the control order in question was made. The court may quash a certificate if it determines that the Secretary of State's decision that the certificate should be contained in the order was 'flawed'. Individuals subject to these control orders can appeal against them, and the conditions in them, on the principles of judicial review.[197] The High Court may consider the case in open or closed session. Where national security requires a closed session in the absence of the controlee and his chosen legal advisers, a trained and security-cleared independent lawyer described as a Special Advocate represents the interests of the controlee in the closed sessions. Non-derogating control orders are limited to 12 months' duration. A fresh application has to be made if it is desired that the person concerned should remain a controlee at the end of each 12-month period. Breach of any conditions without reasonable excuse is a criminal offence punishable on indictment by imprisonment of up to five years, or an unlimited fine.[198] Controlees and the government both have the option of applying to the court for anonymity to apply to the identity of the controlee. For the controlee this avoids publicity that might lead to harassment in the community where he or she lives, or that might prejudice a fair trial if criminal charges are brought later. Finally, section 14(1) of the PTA requires the Secretary of State for Home Affairs to report to Parliament as soon as reasonably practicable after the end of every relevant three-month period on the exercise of the control order powers during that period.

B. The Distinction Between Derogating and Non-derogating Control Orders

The distinction between the two forms of control orders is obviously one of degree. Lord Carlile of Berriew QC, the independent reviewer of the legislation, has noted that:

---

[197]   PTA, s 3(11).

[198]   In January 2007 one controlee was convicted on his plea of guilty of offences of breach, founded on persistent late reporting and unauthorised change of residence. He was sentenced to five months' imprisonment. In 2007 another four individuals were charged with breach of conditions. The Counterterrorism Bill 2008 provides constables with the power to enter and search the premises of individuals subject to control orders who are reasonably suspected of absconding or of failing to grant access to premises when required to do so.

The intention is that conditions imposed under a control order should be specific and tailored to the individual. The aim is to secure the safety of the State by the minimum measures needed to ensure effective disruption and prevention of terrorist activity.[199]

He also observed how restrictive the orders could be:

> On any view those obligations [the restrictions imposed under non-derogating control orders] are extremely restrictive. They have not been found to amount to the triggering of derogation, indeed there has been no challenge so far on that basis – but the cusp is narrow ... The obligations include an eighteen hour curfew, limitation of visitors and meetings to those persons approved by the Home Office, submission to searches, no cellular communications or internet, and a geographical restriction on travel. They fall not very far short of house arrest, and certainly inhibit normal life considerably.[200]

The JCHR has continued to express strong doubts about the ECHR compatibility of the control orders system in the PTA:

> we seriously question renewal without a proper opportunity for a parliamentary debate on whether a derogation from Articles 5(1), 5(4) and 6(1) ECHR is justifiable, that is, whether the extraordinary measures in the Prevention of Terrorism Act 2005, which the Government seeks to continue in force, are strictly required by the exigencies of the situation. It would be premature for us to express a view on that question. We merely conclude at this stage that we cannot endorse a renewal without a derogation and believe that Parliament should therefore be given an opportunity to debate and decide that question.[201]

The then Home Secretary, Charles Clarke, had agreed to table legislation in the spring of 2006 to allow Parliament to consider amendments to the PTA following the first report of the independent reviewer, Lord Carlile. He reported on 2 February 2006 but the Home Secretary announced that he would not be introducing fresh legislation, given that a Terrorism Bill was already under consideration. Instead, the government indicated that it would allow amendment to the Act in consolidating counter-terrorism legislation scheduled for 2007. In any event, sections 1–9 of the PTA were subject to annual renewal by affirmative resolution of both Houses of Parliament. The provisions were renewed from 11 March 2006.[202] A year later there was still no Terrorism Consolidation Bill and the provisions

---

[199] *First Report of the Independent Reviewer Pursuant to Section 14(3) of the Prevention of Terrorism Act 2005*, 2 February 2006, para 10. For the view of a person subject to an order see A Gillan and F al Yafai, 'Control Order Flaws Exposed', *The Guardian* (UK), 24 March 2005.

[200] *Ibid*. See also de la Mere, n 190 above.

[201] See JCHR, *Counter-terrorism Policy and Human Rights: Draft Prevention of Terrorism Act 2005 (Continuance in force of sections 1 to 9) Order 2006*, Twelfth Report of Session 2005–06, HL 122/HC 915, para 89.

[202] See Prevention of Terrorism Act 2005 (Continuance in force of sections 1 to 9) Order 2006, SI 2006/512. For the debate on renewal see *Hansard*, HC Deb, vol 442, cols 1499–523 (15 February 2006).

were again renewed until 10 March 2008.[203] A year later a Counterterrorism Bill was introduced, but too late (24 January 2008) to obviate another annual renewal until 10 March 2009.[204] The JCHR has been strongly critical of the parliamentary procedure used:

> [A] debate on a motion to approve an affirmative resolution is a wholly inappropriate procedure for renewal of provisions of such significance. To fail to provide an opportunity to amend the legislation is also, for the second year running, a serious breach of commitments made to Parliament. Parliament is being deprived once again of an opportunity to debate in detail and amend the control orders regime in the light of experience of its operation and concerns about its human rights compatibility.[205]

Moreover, Parliament was being asked to be complicit in a *de facto* derogation from Article 5, without an opportunity to debate whether such a derogation was justified.[206] The government maintains that the affirmative resolution procedure is the appropriate mechanism for annual renewal of the PTA, providing both Houses with the opportunity to debate renewal and the legislation.[207] In addition, the JCHR has observed the failure to ensure the timely availability of Lord Carlile's annual report (all the reports have been published in mid-February) frustrates effective parliamentary review of the operation of the control order legislation. In 2008, for example, the Home Secretary laid before both Houses a draft Order to renew the control order legislation – the third annual extension of the control order regime – on 30 January 2008. Lord Carlile's report was published three days before the renewal order was due to be debated in the House of Commons. The JCHR has recommended measures to strengthen parliamentary oversight in future. These include that the independent reviewers report to Parliament rather than the Secretary of State and that their report should be published a month before the debate on renewal.[208]

---

[203] See Prevention of Terrorism Act 2005 (Continuance in force of sections 1 to 9) Order 2007, SI 2007/706. For the debate on renewal see *Hansard*, HC Deb, vol 457, cols 434–60 (22 February 2007); *Hansard*, HL Deb, vol 690, cols 12–42 (5 March 2007).

[204] Prevention of Terrorism Act 2005 (Continuance in force of sections 1 to 9) Order 2008. SI 2008/559.

[205] JCHR, *Counter-Terrorism Policy and Human Rights: Draft Prevention of Terrorism Act 2005 (Continuance in force of sections 1 to 9) Order 2007*, Eighth Report of Session 2006–07, HL 60/HC 365 (28 February 2007), para 15.

[206] *Ibid* at paras 17–29.

[207] *Government Response to the JCHR's Eighth Report*, Session 2006–07, JCHR, Fourteenth Report of 2006–07, HL 106/HC 539, p 4.

[208] JCHR, *Counter-Terrorism Policy and Human Rights (Ninth Report): Annual Renewal of Control Orders Legislation 2008*, Tenth Report of Session 2007–08, HL Paper 57/HC 356, paras 19–34. The government robustly disagreed with every recommendation by the JCHR. See *Government Reply*, Cm 7368 (2008).

C. Judicial Control of Control Orders

Non-derogating control orders, once made by the Secretary of State under section 2, and derogating control orders, once made by the court under section 4, go their wholly separate and very different procedural ways.[209] In particular, in the former case the court's role is supervisory, and the standard of proof is a reasonable suspicion, whereas in the latter case the court decides whether to confirm its order on the balance of probabilities.

Under section 3(2) of the PTA, where the Secretary of State makes an application for permission to make a non-derogating control order against an individual,

> the application must set out the order for which he seeks permission and—
>
> (a) the function of the court is to consider whether the Secretary of State's decision that there are grounds to make that order is obviously flawed;
>
> (b) the court may give that permission unless it determines that the decision is obviously flawed; and
>
> (c) if it gives permission, the court must give directions for a hearing in relation to the order as soon as reasonably practicable after it is made.

Under section 3(10) on a hearing in pursuance of directions under s 3(2)(c) the function of the court is to determine whether any of the following decisions of the Secretary of State were flawed: (a) his decision that the requirements of section 2(1)(a) and (b) were satisfied for the making of the order; and (b) his decisions on the imposition of each of the obligations imposed by the order:

> In determining (a) what constitutes a flawed decision for the purposes of subsection (2) . . . or (b) the matters mentioned in subsection (10), the court must apply the principles applicable on an application for judicial review.[210]

The House of Commons Constitutional Affairs Committee had expressed concern that under the PTA the appeal mechanism used under the ATCSA has been transposed into potential challenges to control orders:

> Under the new provisions, Parliament had accepted that the Home Secretary need only demonstrate a 'reasonable suspicion' that someone is engaged in prescribed activity. The judicial review then only considers whether the Home Secretary's decision was reasonable and does not adequately test whether there was sufficient evidence to justify that suspicion. This test is one step further removed from whether there was objectively a 'reasonable suspicion'.

---

[209] See *Re MB*, discussed in Part IX below.
[210] PTA, s 3(11). See M Zander, 'The Prevention of Terrorism Act 2005' (2005) 155 *New Law Journal* 438.

The Home Secretary merely has to show to a judge that he had 'reasonable grounds to suspect' not that such a belief was reasonable to any objective standard. We believe that this system could be made fairer through a variation of the current test, whereby the Home Secretary would have to prove that the material objectively justified his 'reasonable suspicion'.[211]

The Committee recommended that the government 'moves from a judicial review on non-derogating control orders to an objective appeal considering whether or not there is a "reasonable suspicion" that an appellant is involved in terrorist related activities'.[212]

In the *A (Belmarsh Detainees)* case the House of Lords focused exclusively upon the issue of whether or not detention without trial was justified. Little or no attention was focused upon the particular means by which an individual's case was assessed by the SIAC on appeal, or upon the mechanics and procedures used by the SIAC to conduct secret hearings. In particular, the House of Lords declined to rule (either way) upon the arguments advanced by the appellants based upon the criminal aspects of Article 6 ECHR relating to fair trial provisions.[213] It was perhaps inevitable that there would be a judicial challenge to the orders.

IX. JUDICIAL CHALLENGES TO CONTROL ORDERS: PROCEDURES

A. The High Court in *Re MB*

In April 2006, in *Re MB*,[214] the High Court held the first hearing under section 3(10) of the PTA in relation to a non-derogating control order made under section 2(1) of the Act. On 1 September 2005, on an application by the Home Secretary, the court had made a non-derogating control order against MB. The basis for the decision was that the Home Secretary believed that MB intended to go to Iraq to fight against coalition forces. The open statement asserted that MB was an Islamic extremist and that the Security Service considered that he was involved in terrorism-related activities The control obligations on MB were as follows:

(1) You will reside at [address given] ('the residence') and shall give the Home Office at least 7 days prior notice of any change of residence.

(2) You shall report in person to your local police station (the location of which

---

[211] HC Constitutional Affairs Committee, *The Operation of the SIAC and the Use of Special Advocates*, Seventh Report of Session 2004–05, HC 323–1, para 105.

[212] *Ibid* at para 112.

[213] *A (Belmarsh Detainees)* case at para 71, per Lord Bingham.

[214] [2006] EWHC 1000 (Admin), [2006] HRLR 29.

will be notified in writing to you at the imposition of this order) each day at a time to be notified in writing by your contact officer, details to be provided in writing upon service of the order.

(3) You must surrender your passport, identity card or any other travel document to a police officer or persons authorised by the Secretary of State within 24 hours. You shall not apply for or have in your possession any passport, identity card, travel document(s) or travel ticket which would enable you to travel outside the UK.

(4) You must not leave the UK.

(5) You are prohibited from entering or being present at any of the following:
(a) any airport or sea port;
(b) any part of a railway station that provides access to an international rail service.

(6) You must permit entry to police officers and persons authorised by the Secretary of State, on production of identification, at any time to verify your presence at the residence and/or to ensure that you can comply with and are complying with the obligations imposed by the control order. Such monitoring may include but is not limited to:
(a) a search of the residence;
(b) removal of any item to ensure compliance with the remainder of the obligations in these orders; and
(c) the taking of your photograph.[215]

There was no argument to the effect that the controls on MB were incompatible with Article 5 ECHR. Two Special Advocates were appointed. They agreed with counsel for the Home Secretary that it would not be possible to serve a summary of the closed material on the respondent or his legal advisers which would not contain information or other material the disclosure of which would be contrary to the public interest. Sullivan J endorsed this view. Therefore, MB had not been provided with even a summary of the closed evidence against him.

The key focus in *Re MB* was on whether, in discharging its role in hearings under section 3(10), the court was able to give MB a fair hearing for the purposes of Article 6 ECHR. Sullivan J thought not. He issued a declaration under section 4 of the HRA that section 3 of the PTA was incompatible with the right to fair hearing under Article 6. He identified the features of the decision-making process:

(1) the order was made by the executive, not by the court;
(2) although the order was made with the permission of the court, the ability of the court to exercise a supervisory role at the section 3(2) stage was very limited indeed;
(3) the standard of proof to be applied by the decision-taker in making

---

[215] *Ibid* at para 18. The open evidence against MB is reproduced in para 20.

the decision subject to review was very low (reasonable grounds for suspicion), even though the allegation made against the respondent, that he was or had been involved in terrorism-related activity, was a very serious one and may in some cases amount to an allegation that he had committed very serious crimes which would be punishable upon conviction in a criminal court with life imprisonment;

(4)   in proceedings under section 3 the Secretary of State was able to deploy the whole of his case, relying on evidence which would not be admissible in ordinary criminal or civil proceedings, and he may adduce any 'sensitive' intelligence material in closed documents and closed session.

(5)   Not merely did the Secretary of State have to meet a very low standard of proof whilst being able to deploy the whole of his case, including evidence that would otherwise be inadmissible, the procedure enabled to the Secretary of State to place a significant part, and in some cases *the* significant part of his case, before the court in the absence of the respondent and his legal representatives.

Sullivan J referred to the provisions relating to closed material, the court's power to exclude the respondent and his legal advisers, and the appointment and duties of the Special Advocate contained in Part 76 of the CPR.[216]

The central issue was whether the use of a Special Advocate could sufficiently reduce the unfairness of using closed material against a respondent in cases where the court was not coming to its own judgment upon the totality of the evidence, open and closed, but was merely reviewing the lawfulness of the Secretary of State's decision based upon the open and closed material before the Secretary of State at an earlier stage. Sullivan J concluded that, in the absence of a merits review at the section 3(10) stage, the overall procedure was 'manifestly ineffective and unfair'.[217] Moreover:

nothing short of an ability to re-examine and reach its own conclusions on the merits of the case (applying the higher civil standard of proof ...) would be sufficient to give the court "full jurisdiction" for the purposes of determining the respondent's rights under Article 8 ECHR in compliance with Article 6(1) of the ECHR.[218]

Sullivan J was particularly damning in his overall criticism:

To say that the Act does not give the respondent in this case, against whom a non-derogating control order has been made by the Secretary of State, a fair

---

[216]   *Ibid* at paras 51–87.
[217]   *Ibid* at para 86.
[218]   *Ibid* at para 87.

hearing in the determination of his rights under Article 8 of the Convention would be an understatement. The court would be failing in its duty under the 1998 Act, a duty imposed upon the court by Parliament, if it did not say, loud and clear, that the procedure under the Act whereby the court merely reviews the lawfulness of the Secretary of State's decision to make the order upon the basis of the material available to him at that earlier stage are *conspicuously unfair*. The *thin veneer of legality* which is sought to be applied by section 3 of the Act cannot disguise the reality. That controlees' rights under the Convention are being determined not by an independent court in compliance with Article 6.1, but by executive decision-making, untrammelled by any prospect of effective judicial supervision.[219] (emphasis added)

Sullivan J was unable to envisage any circumstances in which it would realistically have been possible for the court to conclude that the Secretary of State's decisions were legally flawed upon the basis of the one-sided information then available to him. It followed that the control order was to continue in force. However, he made a declaration under section 4 of the HRA that the procedures under section 3 of the PTA relating to the supervision of the court of non-derogating control orders made by the Secretary of State were incompatible with the respondent's right to a fair hearing under Article 6(1) ECHR.[220]

B. The Court of Appeal in *Re MB*

In *Secretary of State for the Home Department v MB*[221] the Court of Appeal 'unravelled' each strand of Sullivan J's reasoning.[222] Interestingly, before the Court of Appeal the executive was in an interesting position of having to argue that the High Court's powers of review of the Secretary of State's decision were more extensive than Sullivan J had considered them to be. He had argued, first, that given the appropriate purposive construction, section 3(10) of the PTA required the court to review the Secretary of State's decision having regard to the evidence before the court at the time of conducting the review and not solely at the time of the original decision. Second, section 1(2) of the PTA required the court to consider whether, as at the time of the review, there was any interference with the suspect's human rights.[223] The Court of Appeal agreed with

---

[219]   *Ibid* at para 103.
[220]   *Ibid* at para 104.
[221]   [2006] EWCA Civ 1140, [2006] 3 WLR 839, [2006] HRLR 37. The Court of Appeal was composed of the Lord Chief Justice, the Master of the Rolls and the President of the Queen's Bench Division.
[222]   *Ibid* at para 87.
[223]   PTA, s 1(2) provides that: 'The court is the appropriate tribunal for the purposes of section 7 of the Human Rights Act 1998 (c 42) in relation to proceedings all or any part of which call a control order decision or derogation matter into question.'

these submissions. It considered that, in accordance with section 3 of the HRA, section 3(1) of the PTA 'can and should be "read down" so as to require the court to consider whether the decisions of the Secretary of State in relation to the control order are flawed as at the time of the court's determination'.[224]

As for the standard of review, the Court of Appeal did not consider that the terms of section 3(10), when read in the light of section 1(2), restricted the court to a standard of review that fell short of that required to satisfy Article 6. Proceedings under section 3 of the PTA did not involve the determination of a criminal charge. The Court of Appeal took a sophisticated approach to the courts' powers of review by focusing on the distinction

> between a finding of fact and a decision which turns on a question of policy or expediency. So far as the former is concerned, Article 6 may require the factual evaluation to be carried out by a judicial officer. So far as the latter is concerned, the role of the court may be no more than reviewing the fairness and legality of the administrator to whom Parliament has entrusted the policy decision.[225]

The first requirement in section 2 of the PTA was that the Secretary of State must have reasonable grounds for suspecting that the controlled person is or has been involved in terrorist-related activity. For the Court of Appeal this element involved an assessment of fact. As involvement in terrorist-related activity was likely to constitute a serious criminal offence, this suggested that when reviewing a decision by the Secretary of State to make a control order, the court must make up its own mind as to whether there were reasonable grounds for the necessary suspicion.[226] Whether there were reasonable grounds for suspicion was an objective question of fact. A court could not review the decision of the Secretary of State without itself deciding whether the facts relied upon by the Secretary of State amounted to reasonable grounds for suspecting that the subject of the control order 'is or has been involved in terrorism-related activity'.[227]

The second requirement in section 2 of the PTA was that the Secretary of State must consider that it was necessary, for purposes connected with protecting members of the public from a risk of terrorism, to make the order. For the Court of Appeal this second element required a value judgment as to what was necessary by way of protection of the public. In reviewing this second element different considerations applied:

---

[224] [2006] EWCA Civ 1140 at para 46.
[225] *Ibid* at para 56.
[226] *Ibid* at para 58.
[227] *Ibid* at para 60.

Whether it is necessary to impose any particular obligation on an individual in order to protect the public from the risk of terrorism involves the customary test of proportionality. The object of the obligations is to control the activities of the individual so as to reduce the risk that he will take part in any terrorism-related activity. The obligations that it is necessary to impose may depend upon the nature of the involvement in terrorism-related activities of which he is suspected. They may also depend upon the resources available to the Secretary of State and the demands on those resources. They may depend on arrangements that are in place, or that can be put in place, for surveillance.

The Secretary of State is better placed than the court to decide the measures that are necessary to protect the public against the activities of a terrorist suspect and, for this reason, a degree of deference must be paid to the decisions taken by the Secretary of State. That it is appropriate to accord such deference in matters relating to state security has long been recognised, both by the courts of this country and by the Strasbourg court, see for instance: *Secretary of State for the Home Department v Rehman* [2001]UKHL 47; [2003] AC 153; *The Republic of Ireland v the United Kingdom* (1978) 2 EHRR 25.

Notwithstanding such deference there will be scope for the court to give intense scrutiny to the necessity for each of the obligations imposed on an individual under a control order, and it must do so. The exercise has something in common with the familiar one of fixing conditions of bail. Some obligations may be particularly onerous or intrusive and, in such cases, the court should explore alternative means of achieving the same result. The provision of section 7(2) for modification of a control order 'with the consent of the controlled person' envisages dialogue between those acting for the Secretary of State and the controlled person, and this is likely to be appropriate, with the assistance of the court, at the stage that the court is considering the necessity for the individual obligations.[228]

As for the low standard of proof for the requirement to find that the controlled person was or had been involved in terrorism-related activities, the Court of Appeal considered that Sullivan J had confused substance, relevant to the substantive Articles of the Convention, and procedure, relevant to Article 6:

The PTA authorises the imposition of obligations where there are reasonable grounds for suspicion. The issue that has to be scrutinised by the court is whether there are reasonable grounds for suspicion. That exercise may involve considering a matrix of alleged facts, some of which are clear beyond reasonable doubt, some of which can be established on balance of probability and some of which are based on no more than circumstances giving rise to suspicion. The court has to consider whether this matrix amounts to reasonable

---

[228] *Ibid* at paras 63–5. In the *E and S* case, considered below, that Court of Appeal stated, at para 70, that: 'The jurisdiction to give such directions has not been challenged on the hearing of this appeal. While the point has not been fully argued, we are inclined to the view that the court has jurisdiction to direct modifications of the obligations in the order.'

grounds for suspicion and this exercise differs from that of deciding whether a fact has been established according to a specified standard of proof. It is the procedure for determining whether reasonable grounds for suspicion exist that has to be fair if Article 6 is to be satisfied.[229]

The aspect of the case that caused the Court of Appeal most concern was the use of closed material but it accepted that both Strasbourg (that is, the ECtHR) and domestic authorities had accepted that there were circumstances where the use of closed material was permissible and might not be incompatible with Articles 5(4), 6 and 13 ECHR.[230] For the Court of Appeal the issue was whether Article 6 required an absolute standard of fairness to be applied, or whether, in a case such as that before it, some derogation from that standard was permissible in the interests of national security. It considered that the Strasbourg jurisprudence accepted the latter approach. In particular:

> If one starts with the premise that the risk of terrorism may justify such measures [powers conferred on the executive to interfere with individual rights in order to protect the public against the risk of terrorism], we consider that it must follow that Article 6 cannot automatically require disclosure of the evidence of the grounds for suspicion. Were this not so, the Secretary of State would be in the invidious position of choosing between disclosing information which would be damaging to security operations against terrorists, or refraining from imposing restrictions on a terrorist suspect which appear necessary in order to protect members of the public from the risk of terrorism.

> If one accepts, as we do, that reliance on closed material is permissible, this can only be on terms that appropriate safeguards against the prejudice that this may cause to the controlled person are in place. We consider that the provisions of the PTA for the use of a special advocate, and of the rules of court made pursuant to paragraph 4 of the Schedule to the PTA, constitute appropriate safeguards, and no suggestion has been made to the contrary.[231]

In conclusion the Court of Appeal found the provisions for review by the court of the making of a non-derogating control order complied with the requirements of Article 6.

[229]   *Ibid* at para 67.
[230]   *Ibid* at paras 70–78, citing *Chahal v UK* (1996) 23 EHRR 413 ay paras 131, 144; *Tinnely and McElduff v UK* (1999) 27 EHRR 249 ay para 78; *Rowe v United Kingdom* (2000) 30 EHRR 1 at para 61; *R v H* [2004] UKHL 3; [2004] 2 AC 134; *A v Secretary of State for the Home Department* [2002] EWCA Civ 1202; [2004] QB 335 at para 57: *A v Secretary of State for the Home Department (No 2)* [2004] EWCA Civ 1123; [2005] 1 WLR 414 at paras 51, 235; *R (Roberts) v Parole Board* [2005] UKHL 45; [2005] 2 AC 738.
[231]   *Ibid* at paras 85–6.

C. The *MB and AF* case in the House of Lords

When the *MB* case reached the House of Lords it was joined with another case, that of *AF*.[232] One issue in the *AF* case was whether a non-derogating control order imposed under the PTA constituted a 'criminal charge' for the purposes of Article 6 ECHR. AF contended that they did or, alternatively, that if they fell within the civil limb only, they should nonetheless, because of the seriousness of what was potentially involved, attract the protection appropriate to criminal proceedings. The House unanimously held that a review of a non-derogating control order was not a determination of a criminal charge.[233] For Lord Bingham it was significant that:

> Parliament has gone to some lengths to avoid a procedure which crosses the criminal boundary: there is no assertion of criminal conduct, only a foundation of suspicion; no identification of any specific criminal offence is provided for; the order made is preventative in purpose, not punitive or retributive; and the obligations imposed must be no more restrictive than are judged necessary to achieve the preventative object of the order.[234]

However, he accepted the substance of AF's alternative submission that in any case in which a person is at risk of an order containing obligations of the stringency found in this case (or the cases of *JJ and others* and *E* (considered below)), the application of the civil limb of Article 6(1) entitled such person to such measure of procedural protection as was commensurate with the gravity of the potential consequences. He considered this to have been the approach of the UK domestic courts and to reflect the spirit of the Convention.[235] Lord Brown and Baroness Hale specifically agreed with Lord Bingham's approach.

A second issue in AF's case was whether the procedures provided for by section 3 of the PTA and the Rules of Court were compatible with Article 6 ECHR in circumstances where they had resulted, for example, in the case made against AF being in its essence entirely undisclosed to him and in no specific allegation of terrorism-related activity being contained in open material. MB's case raised the same issue of principle. Two of the leading UK human rights organisations, JUSTICE and Liberty,

---

[232] See *Secretary of State for Home Department v MB and AF* [2007] UKHL 46, [2007] 3 WLR 681 (the *MB and AF* case). The facts of the *AF* case are considered in Section X.G below.

[233] The position with respect to a derogating order was not argued but Lord Bingham noted that it might be criminal and that this was the unequivocal view of the JCHR: see *ibid* at para 16.

[234] *MB and AF* case at para 24.

[235] *Ibid*, citing *B v Chief Constable of Avon and Somerset Constabulary* [2001] 1 WLR 340; *Gough v Chief Constable of the Derbyshire Constabulary* [2002] EWCA Civ 351, [2002] QB 1213; *R (McCann) v Crown Court at Manchester* [2002] UKHL 39, [2003] 1 AC 787.

also supported this argument. The JCHR view is that 'due process standards should apply to control orders in view of the severity of the restrictions they contain'.[236]

The majority view in the House of Lords was that the relevant provisions should be read down under section 3 of the HRA so that they would take effect only when it was consistent with fairness for them to do so. For Baroness Hale, with strenuous efforts from all the personnel involved it would usually be possible to accord the controlled person a substantial measure of procedural justice[237]:

> Everyone involved will have to do their best to ensure that the 'principles of judicial inquiry' are complied with to the fullest extent possible. The Secretary of State must give as full as possible an explanation of why she considers that the grounds in section 2(1) are made out. The fuller the explanation given, the fuller the instructions that the special advocates will be able to take from the client before they see the closed material. Both judge and special advocates will have to probe the claim that the closed material should remain closed with great care and considerable scepticism. There is ample evidence from elsewhere of a tendency to over-claim the need for secrecy in terrorism cases: see Serrin Turner and Stephen J Schulhofer, *The Secrecy Problem in Terrorism Trials*, 2005, Brennan Centre for Justice at NYU School of Law. Both judge and special advocates will have stringently to test the material which remains closed. All must be alive to the possibility that material could be redacted or gisted in such a way as to enable the special advocates to seek the client's instructions upon it. All must be alive to the possibility that the special advocates be given leave to ask specific and carefully tailored questions of the client. Although not expressly provided for in CPR r 76.24, the special advocate should be able to call or have called witnesses to rebut the closed material. The nature of the case may be such that the client does not need to know all the details of the evidence in order to make an effective challenge.[238]

The best judge of whether the proceedings had afforded a sufficient and substantial measure of procedural protection is likely to be the judge who conducted the hearing. Any appeal court should be slow to interfere with their judgment. Baroness Hale identified a particular problem with paragraph 4(3)(d) of the schedule to the 2005 Act, which provides that:

> the relevant court is required to give permission for material not to be disclosed where it considers that disclosure of the material would be contrary to the public interest.

---

[236] JCHR, Eighth Report of Session 2006–07, n 205 above at paras 30–38. See also JCHR, Nineteenth Report of Session 2006–07, n 101 above at paras 176–205 (declaring that Special Advocate system does not afford the individual a fair hearing, and recommending changes).

[237] *MB and AF* case at para 66.

[238] *Ibid.*

This could mean that the judge was precluded from ordering disclosure even where he considered that this was essential in order to give the controlled person a fair hearing. The judge might not be able to refuse to uphold the order because unless the decision of the Secretary of State was flawed the court must decide that the control order is to continue in force.[239] In Baroness Hale's view the procedures could be made to work fairly and compatibly in many cases. It was not, therefore, appropriate to make a declaration of incompatibility. Rather, resort was to be had to section 3 of the HRA, and schedule I, paragraph 4(3)(d) should be read and be given effect 'except where to do so would be incompatible with the right of the controlled person to a fair trial'.[240] The practical consequences were as follows:

> Where the court does not give the Secretary of State permission to withhold closed material, she has a choice. She may decide that, after all, it can safely be disclosed (experience elsewhere in the world has been that, if pushed, the authorities discover that more can be disclosed than they first thought possible). But she may decide that it must still be withheld. She cannot then be required to serve it. But if the court considers that the material might be of assistance to the controlled person in relation to a matter under consideration, it may direct that the matter be withdrawn from consideration by the court. In any other case, it may direct that the Secretary of State cannot rely upon the material. If the Secretary of State cannot rely upon it, and it is indeed crucial to the decision, then the decision will be flawed and the order will have to be quashed.[241]

Baroness Hale supported her view with three arguments. First, the courts were required by Parliament to take this course if it was possible. When Parliament passed the PTA, it must have thought that the provisions were compatible with the Convention rights. In interpreting the Act compatibly the House was doing its best to make it work. This gave the greatest possible incentive to all parties to the case, and to the judge, to conduct the proceedings in such a way as to afford a sufficient and substantial measure of procedural justice. This included the Secretary of State, who would be anxious that the control order be upheld. A declaration of incompatibility, on the other hand, would have allowed all of them to conduct the proceedings in a way which they knew to be incompatible. Second, there was good reason to think that Strasbourg would find proceedings conducted in accordance with the Act and rules compatible in the majority of cases. Inviting a derogation in order to cater

---

[239]   PTA, s 3(13).
[240]   *MB and AF* case, para 72. Baroness Hale cited use of the same technique in *R (Hammond) v Secretary of State for the Home Department* [2005] UKHL 69, [2006] 1 AC 603, and *R v A (No 2)* [2001] UKHL 25, [2002] 1 AC 45.
[241]   *MB and AF* case at para 72.

for the minority where it might not so find may risk even greater incursions into the fundamental requirements of a fair trial, which had not yet been shown to be necessitated by the exigencies of the situation. Third, there were powerful policy reasons in support of procedures which enable cases to be proven through the evidence of infiltrators and informers rather than upon evidence which may have been obtained through the use of torture. Not only was the latter abhorrent, there was good reason to believe that it was generally unreliable and counterproductive. The House had ruled that such evidence was always inadmissible, but had placed the burden of proving this upon the person who wished to challenge it.[242] It was particularly difficult for a person subject to control order proceedings to do this. Devising a sufficient means of challenging the evidence was an incentive to the authorities to rely on better and more reliable sources of intelligence. That might sometimes mean keeping the identity of informants, and sometimes some of the surrounding circumstances, secret. But that was an overall price worth paying for the good of all.[243] The use of Special Advocates could comply with Article 6 ECHR, as could the procedure in the *MB* and *AF* cases. The two cases were to be reconsidered in the light of the majority opinions in the House. Lord Carswell and Lord Brown agreed with Baroness Hale's approach. For Lord Carswell the judge who had seen both the open and the closed material and had had the benefit of the contribution of the Special was in much the best position to make the decision. However, he considered that there was a fairly heavy burden on the controlee to establish that there had been a breach of Article 6, for the legitimate public interest in withholding material on valid security grounds should be given due weight. The courts should not be too ready to hold that a disadvantage suffered by the controlee through the withholding of material constituted a breach of Article 6.[244] For Lord Brown a suspect's entitlement to an essentially fair hearing was not merely a qualified right capable of being outweighed by the public interest in protecting the state against terrorism. On the contrary, it was not merely an absolute right but one of altogether too great importance to be sacrificed on the altar of terrorism control.[245] So closed material should be rejected if reliance on it would necessarily result in a fundamentally unfair hearing.

For Lord Bingham the task of the court in any given case was to decide, looking at the process as a whole, whether a procedure had been used

---

[242] See *A and others v Secretary of State for the Home Department (No 2)* [2005] UKHL 71, [2006] 2 AC 221, discussed in Section XV below.
[243] *MB and AF* case at para 73.
[244] *Ibid* at para 85.
[245] *Ibid* at para 91.

which involved significant injustice to the controlled person.[246] He noted that the Court of Appeal had considered that the justification for the obligations imposed on MB lay in the closed material. MB was confronted by a bare, unsubstantiated assertion which he could do no more than deny. In these circumstances he had difficulty in accepting that MB had enjoyed a substantial measure of procedural justice, or that the very essence of the right to a fair hearing had not been impaired.[247] AF's case was even stronger case than MB's. The concept of fairness imported a core, irreducible minimum of procedural protection and, on the judge's findings, such protection had not been afforded to AF. The right to a fair hearing was fundamental. In the absence of a derogation (where that was permissible) it had to be protected.[248] Although Lord Bingham thought there should have been a declaration of incompatibility under section 4 of the HRA he accepted the argument of the majority that the relevant provisions should be read down under section 3 of the HRA so that they would take effect only when it was consistent with fairness for them to do so.[249] Thus a majority of four Lords approved this approach. Only Lord Hoffmann took the view that in principle the Special Advocate procedure provided sufficient safeguards to satisfy Article 6 in all cases, and so would have dismissed the appeals.[250] A decision that Article 6 did not allow the Secretary of State to rely on closed material would create a dilemma: either he must disclose material which the court considers that the public interest requires to be withheld, or he must risk being unable to justify to the court an order which he considers necessary to protect the public against terrorism. There was no Strasbourg or domestic authority which had gone to the lengths of saying that the Secretary of State cannot make a non-derogating control order (or anything of the same kind) without disclosing material which a judge considers it would be contrary to the public interest to disclose. He did not think that the House should put the Secretary of State in such an impossible position.

A number of the principles relating to the disclosure of evidence were expounded in *Re Bullivant (AG)*.[251] Collins J held that when the court was considering a control order, the Secretary of State should only seek to withhold material that it was clearly in the public interest not to disclose. Before seeing the closed material, the Special Advocate appearing on behalf of the individual could be involved with the controlee and his representatives so as to understand such defence as might be put

---

[246] *Ibid* at para 35.
[247] *Ibid* at para 41.
[248] *Ibid* at paras 42–3.
[249] *Ibid* at para 44.
[250] *Ibid* at paras 50–55.
[251] [2007] EWHC 2938 (Admin), Collins J.

forward. The Special Advocate should identify those matters regarded by him or her as crucial and could in due course submit that a failure to disclose had rendered the proceedings unfair and in breach of Article 6 ECHR. Save in the most exceptional cases, the courts would not make a finding that the withholding of material had rendered the proceedings unfair before the evidence had been tested in open and closed hearings. There was also an ongoing duty to consider whether there should be further disclosure, and the court could make an order accordingly. It was only in exceptional circumstances that a court would order disclosure based on fairness grounds alone prior to the testing of the evidence through the open and closed hearings. At the conclusion of the hearing the court must decide whether there was a breach of Article 6, and give the Secretary of State the opportunity to remedy the breach by further disclosure.[252] The decision stresses once more the central role of the trial judge in ensuring that the requirements of a fair trial are met. For example, when the *AF* case returned to the High Court it was held that there had been insignificant disclosure to enable an effective challenge to be made. The Home secretary was put to election as to whether she wished to disclose any further allegations or evidence.[252a]

Interestingly, there was quite a negative response to the House of Lords' decision in *MB* from the JCHR. It considered that

> it would have been more consistent with the scheme of the Human Rights Act for the House of Lords to have given a declaration of incompatibility, requiring Parliament to think again about the balance it struck in the control order legislation between the various competing interests. In any event, we think it is now incumbent on Parliament to consider again, in detail, exactly what a 'fair hearing' requires in this particular context, in light of the House of Lords judgment, and to amend the control order legislation accordingly.[253]

The JCHR made a series of recommendations for amendments to the control order regime in order to ensure that, in future, hearings are much more likely to be fair. These were:

(i) that the relevant provisions in the statutory framework, which expressly required non-disclosure, even where disclosure would be essential for a fair hearing, be amended by the insertion of qualifying words, such as 'except where to do so would be incompatible with the right of the controlled person to a fair hearing';

---

[252] The court subsequently quashed the control order in B's case: see *R. (on the application of Secretary of State for the Home Department) v Bullivant* [2008] EWHC B2 (Admin), 29 January 2008.

[252a] *Secretary of the State for the Home Office Department v AF* [2008] EWHC 453 (Admin).

[253] JCHR, *Counter-Terrorism Policy and Human Rights (Eighth Report): Counter-Terrorism Bill*, Ninth Report of Session 2007–08, HL 50/HC 199, 7 February 2008, para 47.

(ii) that the relevant power for making rules of court in the control orders regime be amended to make explicit reference to the right to a fair hearing in Article 6 ECHR, in the same way as the Counter-terrorism Bill 2008 itself qualified the power to make rules of court for asset freezing;

(iii) that an obligation on the Secretary of State to give reasons for the making of a control order be inserted into the statutory framework;

(iv) that the statutory framework be amended to provide that rules of court for control order proceedings 'must require the Secretary of State to provide a summary of any material which fairness requires the controlled person have an opportunity to comment on';

(v) that the statutory framework be amended to enable the controlled person to give meaningful instructions about the allegations against him, where it was possible to do so;

(vi) that Special Advocates be given the power to apply ex parte to a High Court judge for permission to ask the controlee questions, without being required to give notice to the Secretary of State;

(vii) that the PTA be amended to provide that, in a hearing to determine whether the Secretary of State's decision was flawed, the controlled person is entitled to such measure of procedural protection (including, for example, the appropriate standard of proof) as is commensurate with the gravity of the potential consequences of the order for the controlled person; and

(viii) that the PTA be amended to provide that, where permission is given by the relevant court not to disclose material, Special Advocates may call witnesses to rebut the closed material.[254]

X. JUDICIAL CHALLENGES TO CONTROL ORDERS: SUBSTANCE – THE RIGHT TO LIBERTY

A. The High Court in *JJ and others*

In June 2006, in *Secretary of State for the Home Department v JJ and others*[255] Sullivan J also heard an application from six individuals subject to control orders. The obligations on them were far more restrictive than those imposed on MB. They related to: electronic tagging (to be worn at all times); residence (being required for 18 hours per day and, for five of the controlees, in areas with which they had no previous connection); reporting to a monitoring company; visitors to the residence; pre-arranged meetings outside the residence; identified individuals with

---

[254] *Ibid* at paras 54–73.
[255] [2006] EWCA 1623 (Admin), [2006] 103 (28) *Law Society Gazette* 27 (*JJ and others*).

whom any association or communication was prohibited; police searches (in each case there had been a number of searches); further prohibitions or restrictions; communications equipment (only one fixed telephone line permitted); Mosque attendance; restriction to the geographical area; notification of international departure and arrival; Bank account; transfer of money sending of documents or goods; passport or identity card and so on; and prohibition from entering air or sea port, and so on.[256] In *JJ and others* the only issue considered was whether the cumulative impact of the obligations imposed by the orders amounted to a deprivation of the respondents' liberty in breach of Article 5(1) ECHR? If so, the Secretary of State had made a derogating control order which he had no power to do (and which the court had no power to do in the absence of a designated derogation). Sullivan J emphasised that the restrictions had not been imposed to protect the interests of the individuals. Rather, they had been imposed to protect the public. In the absence of a derogation under Article 15 ECHR the respondents were entitled to the full protection of Article 5, and there was no justification for any attempt to water down that protection in response to the threat of terrorism. He considered that the respondents' liberty to lead a normal life in their residences during the 18-hour curfew period was so curtailed as to be non-existent for all practical purposes. He also observed that the restrictions on social contacts significantly affected their liberty to lead a normal life. Overall he concluded that:

> bearing in mind the type, duration, effects and manner of implementation of the obligations in these control orders, I am left in no doubt whatsoever that the cumulative effect of the obligations has been to deprive the respondents of their liberty in breach of Article 5 of the Convention. I do not consider that this is a borderline case. The collective impact of the obligations in Annex I could not sensibly be described as a mere restriction upon the respondents' liberty of movement. In terms of the length of the curfew period (18 hours), the extent of the obligations, and their intrusive impact on the respondents' ability to lead anything resembling a normal life, whether inside their residences within the curfew period, or for the 6-hour period outside it, these control orders go far beyond the restrictions in those cases where the European Court of Human Rights has concluded that there has been a restriction upon but not a deprivation of liberty. The respondents' 'concrete situation' is the antithesis of liberty, and is more akin to detention in an open prison … the respondents' lives are not free, but are for all practical purposes under the control of the Home Office.[257]

---

[256] They are set out in Annex I to the judgment, *ibid*. Annex II contains a statement of agreed facts on each individual.

[257] *Ibid* at paras 73–4. The same conclusion was reached for the one individual, GG, who continued to reside at his home: *ibid* at para 60.

Sullivan J then considered whether he should defer to the Home Secretary's opinion that the control orders were not incompatible with Article 5 ECHR. He saw no reason for such deference:

> While the court will defer, to the extent that it is appropriate, to the Secretary of State's views on certain matters, including, for example, what obligations are necessary under subsection 1(3) of the Act, there is no reason for such deference in respect of the Secretary of State's view that the obligations in these control orders merely restrict the respondents' liberty, but do not deprive the respondents of their liberty: see paragraph 221 of the speech of Baroness Hale in [*A (Belmarsh Detainees)* case]. The Secretary of State's view on that question is only as good as the analysis of the Strasbourg jurisprudence that was carried out on his behalf before he made the orders. Naturally, I have not seen that analysis, but insofar as it is reflected in the submissions made on behalf of the Secretary of State in these proceedings, I have explained why I have found them unpersuasive. In saying that I intend no disrespect to Mr Eicke, whose ability to construct a silk purse out of a sow's ear was, as always, most impressive.[258]

Sullivan J noted that his view accorded with that of the JCHR, cited above,[259] and with the concerns of Mr Alvaro Gil-Robles, the Council of Europe's Commissioner for Human Rights, in his report to the Committee of Ministers and the Parliamentary Assembly on his visit to the United Kingdom on 4–12 November 2004.[260] As to the appropriate remedy, the Home Secretary argued that the court should direct the Home Secretary to revoke or modify the orders rather than quash them. Sullivan J expressed concern at this view because the United Kingdom had previously given an assurance to the Committee of Ministers of the Council of Europe that the court could quash such an order. Sullivan J regarded this change of position as having the

> the potential to undermine confidence in the integrity of public administration. The United Kingdom government's comments in 2005 would have left the Committee of Ministers of the Council of Europe with the reassuring impression that if a control order made by the Secretary of State did constitute a deprivation of liberty, then the court could be expected to use its powers to quash that order, but now that the crunch has come in 2006, the Secretary of State is strenuously seeking to persuade the court that it would not be appropriate to exercise that power. One would have thought that public assurances given by the UK government in response to concerns expressed in an official report could be relied upon, particularly where a Convention right of 'fundamental importance' was in issue.[261]

---

[258] *Ibid* at para 79.
[259] See JCHR, Ninth Report of Session 2004–05, n 180 above.
[260] See n 66 above. Gil-Robles noted that 'Control orders raise ... general points of constitutional principle concerning the rule of law and the separation of powers': para 16.
[261] *JJ and others* at para 87.

Sullivan J considered that the proper course was to quash the control orders.

Unsurprisingly, the decisions of Sullivan J on control orders attracted wide publicity.[262] They were attacked by the new Home Secretary, John Reid, and appealed.[263]

B. The Court of Appeal in *JJ and others*

In *Secretary of State for the Home Department v JJ and Others*,[264] decided on the same day and with the same composition as the appeal in *Re MB*, the Court of Appeal upheld the decision of Sullivan J that the control orders amounted to a deprivation of liberty contrary to Article 5 ECHR. In the Court of Appeal's view they, 'clearly fell on the wrong side of the dividing line'.[265] The Court also held that Sullivan J was correct to conclude that he had jurisdiction to quash the orders and that the reasons he gave for quashing them were compelling. It gave an additional reason, namely that if the Secretary of State decided to make new control orders to replace those that had been quashed, he would have to devise a new package of measures imposing control on the respondents. In the Court's view that was an exercise that the Secretary of State was 'very much better placed to perform than the courts'.[266] The response of the Secretary of State was that he would appeal the matter to the House of Lords. In the meantime some of the conditions have been relaxed, for example in one case by reducing the curfew from 18 hours to 14 hours. There was further political controversy over control orders in October 2006 when it eme7rged that two people subject to orders had escaped and were missing.[267] They had been missing for a month but the government had not informed the public.

---

[262] R Ford, 'Key anti-terror law is a Breach of Human Rights, Judge Rules', *The Times* (UK), 29 June 2006; F Gibb, 'Anti-terror Law "Sinister" Says Judge', *The Times* (UK), 9 June 2006. There you will find discussion of the more general criticisms of Lord Lloyd.

[263] See A Travis, 'Judge "Misunderstood" Anti-Terror Legislation', *The Guardian* (UK), 4 July 2006.

[264] [2006] EWCA Civ 1141, [2006] 3 WLR 866, [2006] HRLR 38.

[265] *Ibid* at para 23.

[266] *Ibid* at para 27.

[267] See R Ford and S Tendler, 'Terror Suspect Fled As His Curfew Order Was Quashed', *The Times* (UK), 18 October 2006; A Travis and A Kumi, 'Manhunt as Terror Suspect Escapes Control Order', *The Guardian* (UK), 17 January 2007.

C. The House of Lords in *JJ and others*

In *Secretary of State for the Home Department v JJ and Others*[268] a majority of the House of Lords (Lords Bingham and Brown, and Baroness Hale) rejected the appeal and held that the control orders imposed on six individuals concerned constituted a deprivation of liberty contrary to Article 5 ECHR. Lord Bingham stressed that the ECHR jurisprudence was to be used as laying down principles and not mandating solutions to particular cases. There was no comparable ECHR case but the guiding principle under the ECHR was that the national court was to assess the impact of the measures in question on a person in the situation of the person subject to them.[269] No legal error in the reasoning of the judge or the Court of Appeal had been shown, and it was not for the House to make a value judgment of its own. However, he added that on the agreed facts of these individual cases he would have reached the same conclusion:

The effect of the 18-hour curfew, coupled with the effective exclusion of social visitors, meant that the controlled persons were in practice in solitary confinement for this lengthy period every day for an indefinite duration, with very little opportunity for contact with the outside world, with means insufficient to permit provision of significant facilities for self-entertainment and with knowledge that their flats were liable to be entered and searched at any time. The area open to them during their six non-curfew hours was unobjectionable in size, much larger than that open to Mr Guzzardi.[270] But they were (save for GG) located in an unfamiliar area where they had no family, friends or contacts, and which was no doubt chosen for that reason. The requirement to obtain prior Home Office clearance of any social meeting outside the flat in practice isolated the controlled persons during the non-curfew hours also. Their lives were wholly regulated by the Home Office, as a prisoner's would be, although breaches were much more severely punishable. The judge's analogy with detention in an open prison was apt, save that the controlled persons did not enjoy the association with others and the access to entertainment facilities which a prisoner in an open prison would expect to enjoy.

Baroness Hale agreed with Lord Bingham, and she was hesitant to suggest, in the abstract, what length of curfew would fall on the other

---

[268] [2007] 3 WLR 642.

[269] *Ibid* at para 15.

[270] *Ibid*. Mr Guzzardi, a suspected Mafioso, was the applicant in the leading ECHR case of *Guzzardi v Italy* [1983] 3 EHRR 333, He was detained within a 2.5 km² area on an Italian island.

side of the line.[271] Lord Brown agreed with Lord Bingham and Baroness Hale but he sought to be more specific on the permissible limits. For him 12- or 14-hour curfews (those at issue in two of the related appeals before the House) were consistent with physical liberty. He regarded the acceptable limit to be 16 hours, leaving the suspect with 8 hours' (admittedly in various respects controlled) liberty a day.[272] This should be regarded as the absolute limit. He added that any curfew regime exceeding 16 hours really ought not to be imposed unless the court could be satisfied of the suspect's actual involvement in terrorism, the higher threshold that would apply to the making of a derogating control order.[273]

For the two dissentients, Lords Hoffmann and Carswell, deprivation of liberty had to be narrowly interpreted.[274] Lord Hoffmann restated his opinion in *A v Secretary of State for the Home Department*[275] that the power to derogate in peacetime was a narrow one and that politically or religiously motivated violence, even threatening serious loss of life, did not necessarily 'threaten the life of the nation' within the meaning of the Convention. The liberty of the subject and the right to habeas corpus were too precious to be sacrificed for any reason other than to safeguard the survival of the state. However, he added that this position could only be maintained if one confined the concept of deprivation of liberty to actual imprisonment or something which was for practical purposes little different from imprisonment. Otherwise the law would place too great a restriction on the powers of the state to deal with serious terrorist threats to the lives of its citizens. In the case of anything less than actual deprivation of liberty, the other rights which were engaged were adequately protected by the requirement that any interference with them must be necessary and proportionate in the interests of national security.[276] For Lord Hoffmann it was it impossible to say that a person under the most restrictive conditions imposed (LL) was for practical purposes in prison.[277] Lord Carswell agreed.

As for the appropriate remedy, four of their Lordships considered that the order had to be quashed because the Home Secretary had no power to make a derogating order.[278]

---

[271] *Ibid* at paras 57–63.
[272] *Ibid* at para 105.
[273] *Ibid*.
[274] *Ibid* at paras 30–46, per Lord Hoffmann; at paras 65–84, per Lord Carswell.
[275] See text at n 163 above.
[276] *JJ and others*, HL, at para 44.
[277] *Ibid* at para 45.
[278] *Ibid* at paras 25–7, per Lord Bingham; at para 64, per Baroness Hale; at para 85, per Lord Carswell; and at para 109, per Lord Brown. Lord Hoffmann dissented: *ibid* at paras 47–55.

D. The High Court in the *E* case

The third major judicial challenge to control orders came in *E v Secretary of State for the Home Department*.[279] This was the first full hearing with evidence about the relevant factual issues. In the *E* case the High Court considered whether a less restrictive control order amounted to a deprivation of liberty. The subject of the control order was a Tunisian national who had been in the United Kingdom since 1994. He had been convicted in his absence by a Tunisian military court for various terrorism offences under Tunisian law. His claim for asylum in the United Kingdom had been refused but he had been granted exceptional leave to remain in the United Kingdom until 2005. He was married with four young children under the age of seven, and, at the time of High Court hearing, E's wife (S) was five months' pregnant. E lived in his own home. It is helpful to set out the terms of the control order and the justification for it. E was required to reside in his home and remain there, save between 7 am and 7 pm, or as specified in written directions. By a variation, the residence included the garden. He was required to report to a monitoring company by telephone each day on the first occasion he left the residence and on the last occasion he returned to it. Except by prior agreement with the Home Office, he could not permit any person to enter the residence, apart from his wife and children, his nominated legal representative, members of the emergency services or health care or social work professionals, any person aged 10 or under and any person required to be given access under the tenancy agreement. When seeking agreement for the entry of other persons, E was required to supply the name, address, date of birth and photographic identity of the individual to be admitted. The prior agreement of the Home Office was not required for subsequent visits by an agreed individual unless the existing agreement was withdrawn. E could not, outside the residence, meet any person by prior arrangement other than his wife and children or his legal representative, except for health and welfare purposes at establishments to be agreed by the Home Office, or for educational purposes at establishments similarly agreed. He could not attend any pre-arranged meetings or gatherings, other than attending group prayers at a mosque, save, in all the above cases, with the prior agreement of the Home Office. E had to permit entry to his residence to police officers and persons authorised by the Secretary of State or by the monitoring company, on production of identification, to verify his presence at the residence and to ensure that he could comply and was complying with the obligations imposed by the order. Monitoring could include searches of the residence, inspection and removal of

---

[279] [2007] EWHC 233 (Admin).

articles to ensure that they did not breach obligations imposed by the order, and the installation of equipment considered necessary to ensure compliance with the obligations. E could not bring or permit into the residence, or use, whether in or outside the residence, any communications equipment (including mobile phones) other than one fixed telephone line in the residence and one or more computers. The computer had to be disabled from connecting to the internet. Other persons entering the residence could bring in a mobile phone, provided it was switched off while E was in the residence. E had to notify the Home Office of any intended departure from the United Kingdom and report to the Home Office immediately upon arrival on return. He could not hold more than one bank account. He could not transfer any money, or send any documents or goods, to a destination outside the United Kingdom, without the prior agreement of the Home Office.

The justification for the order was set out by the Secretary of State in an open statement made in March 2005:

> E was detained under the ATCSA in December 2001 on the basis of his current involvement with, and activities in support of, terrorist groups and networks which pose a direct threat to the national security of the UK. The Secretary of State assesses that unless stringent bail conditions are imposed upon him, E would resume his extremist activities in connection with these groups and networks, and would continue to pose a threat to the UK's national security.

The justification for restrictions relating to meetings, contacts and visitors was stated to be that much of E's terrorism-related activity necessarily involved regular contact with associates who were themselves involved in the same or other terrorism-related activity. Restrictions on E's capacity to contact such persons or to share his expertise and contacts reduced the risk that he would involve himself again in those activities.

The High Court concluded that, although this was more finely balanced than the *JJ and others* cases, the cumulative effect of the restrictions deprived E of his liberty in breach of Article 5 ECHR. It was the subjection to police and other searches of E's home and the requirement that all visitors (and pre-arranged meetings outside the house) be approved in advance which made the requirements particularly intense. The restrictions that applied within the house give E's home some of the, 'characteristics of prison accommodation in which the prisoner has no private space and his visitors are all vetted'.[280]

---

[280] *Ibid* at para 240, per Beatson J. On similar facts, the same judge reached the same conclusion in *Secretary of State for the Home Department v Abu Rideh and J* [2007] EWHC 804 (Admin) at para 147.

E. The Court of Appeal in the *E* case

The Court of Appeal reversed the decision.[281] By reference to the ECHR jurisprudence in *Engel & Ors v Netherlands (No 1)*,[282] *Guzzardi v Italy*,[283] *Ciancimino v Italy*,[284] and *Trijonis v Lithuania*[285] it set out the principles by which it approached the issue. The starting point was to consider the 'physical liberty' of the person: individual liberty in the classic sense. Article 5(1) was not concerned with mere restrictions on liberty of movement which are governed by Article 2 of Protocol No 4 and which had not been ratified by the United Kingdom. The effect of the physical restraint had to be considered in the context of restrictions applied when the restraint was not operating. Whether the confinement was in the individual's own home could be very relevant but the inviolability or otherwise of the home was a relevant consideration. The opportunity for social contacts was also a factor. The difference between deprivation of liberty, contrary to Article 5(1), and restriction upon liberty was one of degree or intensity. The court was concerned with the 'effect', 'duration' and 'manner of implementation' of the restrictions, as well as the 'type' of restriction.[286] The state of a controlled person's health, whether the disability was physical or mental, and possibly other 'person specific' characteristics, might have an impact upon the severity of the effect, in his case, of restrictions imposed. In this case, only very limited weight could be given to this factor.[287] With respect to some of the restrictions imposed by this and other orders, and said to contribute to the breach of Article 5, their duration, and their intensity, may be relevant to whether the overall restrictions amounted to a deprivation of liberty.[288] The restrictions were to be considered on the basis that they were likely to be renewed.[289] That restrictions engaged other Articles in the Convention, such as Article 8, did not mean that they should be disregarded in an Article 5 context, but it had to be kept in mind that it was deprivation of liberty, and not some other right, which was under consideration.

Applying these principles to the facts, the Court of Appeal stressed that E was free to practise a range of activities, during the daytime, in an area with which he was very familiar, and beyond it. He could attend the mosque and educational courses where he was likely to meet a range of

---

[281] *Secretary of State for the Home Department v E and S* [2007] EWCA Civ 459.
[282] [1976] 1 EHRR 647.
[283] [1983] 3 EHRR 333.
[284] (1991) 70 *Decision & Reports of the European Commission on Human Rights* 103.
[285] Application No 2333/02, 17 March 2005 (unreported).
[286] *Secretary of State for the Home Department v E and S* at para 52.
[287] *Ibid* at para 55.
[288] *Ibid* at para 56.
[289] *Ibid* at para 57.

persons and to do so regularly. The facts were very different from the cases in *JJ and others* in that: (a) the period of curfew in the present case was substantially shorter, 12 hours out of 24 as against 18; (b) E was living with his family in his own home, with garden, whereas the specified residences in the *JJ* cases were one-bedroom flats away from areas in which the controlled persons had previously lived; (c) the controlled persons in the *JJ* cases were confined to restricted urban areas which, save in one case, did not extend to any area in which they had previously lived. The physical liberty of E, that is individual liberty in its classic sense, was both the starting point and the central issue. E was deprived of the right to leave his home, and was detained in it, for 12 hours a day, the overnight hours. It was, however, his own home (and garden) and he could live there with his wife and young family. During the remaining 12 hours, the daytime hours, not only was there no geographical restriction on where he might go but his starting point, his home, was in the area he knew well as a result of having lived there for four years. That degree of physical restraint upon liberty was 'far from a deprivation of liberty in Article 5 terms'.[290]

The intrusion into E's life at home and the restriction on his outside activities also had to be considered. Combined with a degree of physical restraint, such restrictions might create a breach of Article 5 but it had to be kept in mind that it was the concept of individual liberty in its classic sense which was in issue, a different concept from, for example, respect for private and family life. Intrusions into home and family life might contribute to a loss of liberty but their impact and effect on liberty required analysis. While the intrusion, under the control order, was potentially substantial, and applied for 24 hours a day, the Court of Appeal did not consider that it led to a finding that the home thereby acquired the characteristics of 'prison accommodation' in which E was detained, as had been suggested in the High Court.[291] It retained the attributes of a family home where domestic life could be enjoyed at all times.[292] As to the alleged 'chilling effect' of the restrictions on people visiting the premises, it was the control order itself which essentially created the chill. In *AF* (considered below), there was evidence to that effect and Ouseley J so found, but for the Court of Appeal an inference could readily be drawn that people would be less ready to visit the home of someone subject to a control order, the existence of which was likely to

---

[290]   *Ibid* at para 63. The Court of Appeal (and subsequently the House of Lords) cited the decision in *Trijonis v Lithuania* Application No 2333/02, 17 March 2005, where the 'home arrest' included an obligation to remain at home throughout weekends, and the complaint was held inadmissible.

[291]   See text at n 283 above.

[292]   *Secretary of State for the Home Department v E and S* at para 64.

be known. The requirement to 'register' visitors might add to the reluctance to visit but was unlikely to be the sole or main cause, and the restriction should be viewed in that light. The restrictions on E's outside activities and contacts were also significant and their effect on E had to be considered. Keeping in mind that protection of physical liberty was at the heart of any consideration of Article 5, they did not make a substantial or decisive contribution to a complaint of deprivation of liberty. Restrictions were placed upon E's activities in that he could not, without the Secretary of State's agreement, make prior arrangements to meet people or attend pre-arranged meetings or gatherings. He was, however, left with wide opportunities, and in fact did engage in everyday activities, including religious observance and practices. He could take up educational opportunities at agreed establishments. Not only could he engage in these activities, but they provided considerable opportunity to make a wide range of social contacts in an area with which he was very familiar, and beyond. Finally, the court also had to have regard to the 'manner' in which restrictions were implemented. Save that there were teething troubles, there was no evidence that the restrictions were being implemented, or the powers granted exercised, in an oppressive manner, or a manner beyond that contemplated by the stated justification for them, or as significantly interfering with domestic life or outside activities. The Court of Appeal's conclusion was that

> [b]earing in mind the 'type, duration, effects and manner of implementation' of the order, no deprivation of liberty, within the meaning of Article 5 was established. E's case was in material respects plainly distinguishable from the *JJ* cases. The facts of E's case fell on the right side of the dividing line.[293]

Finally, the Court of Appeal dismissed three other sets of arguments alleging: (1) a lack of sufficient scrutiny by the judge of the individual obligations imposed on the respondent; (2) a lack of procedural fairness in the making and/or the renewing of the control order; and (3) on behalf of S and the children, alleged breaches of Articles 3 and 8 ECHR so far as E's family were concerned.[294]

F. The House of Lords in the *E* case

In *Secretary of State for the Home Department v E and Another*[295] the House of Lords unanimously upheld the decision of the Court of Appeal. Lord Bingham inferred that the Court of Appeal found the judge to have erred

---

[293] *Ibid* at para 69.
[294] *Ibid* at paras 108–22.
[295] [2007] 3 WLR 720.

in law in failing to focus on the extent to which E was actually confined, an overnight curfew of 12 hours, a period accepted by the Strasbourg authorities, as compared with the very much more stringent restriction in *JJ and others*. The matters which particularly weighed with the judge were not irrelevant, but they could not of themselves effect a deprivation of liberty if the core element of confinement, to which other restrictions (important as they may be in some cases) were ancillary, was insufficiently stringent. That was a sound criticism of the judge's approach, and the Court of Appeal was right to regard the case, on its special facts, as distinguishable from *JJ and others*.[296] Similarly for Baroness Hale, the starting point in any consideration of deprivation of liberty was the 'core element' of confinement. The length of the curfew in this case was within the range which Strasbourg had accepted as merely restricting liberty. Nor was there anything to make it more severe.[297] For Lord Brown the length was within the period he considered acceptable in the *JJ and others* case.[298] For Lords Hoffmann and Carswell, on the basis of their stricter interpretation of deprivation of liberty, there had been no deprivation.[299]

G. The High Court in the *AF* case

Before the Court of Appeal decision on the *E* case, another breach of Article 5 was found in *Secretary of State for the Home Department v AF*.[300] The facts were different from those in other cases considered. Ouseley J cited the Court of Appeal's decision in *JJ and others* and the High Court judgment in the *E case*. He recognised the 'quite intrusive process' involved in a restriction on receiving guests without prior approval. He accepted the 'chilling effect' of the control order upon the controlled person meeting with other people, in the home and outside. The curfew in this case was of 14 hours' duration. AF, a dual UK and Libyan national, was able to meet almost whomever he liked either in his home or outside it provided he remained in the permitted area. The real restriction outside curfew hours, the judge held, was in the extent of the permitted area. Within the area from which the controlled person was excluded were all three mosques to which he used to go. He was permitted to attend only a specific Urdu-speaking mosque, and he was not Urdu. The restrictive area prevented him from going into any significant educational establishment where he could study English because there were no

---

[296]   *Ibid* at para 11.
[297]   *Ibid* at para 25.
[298]   *Ibid* at para 36.
[299]   *Ibid* at para 23, per Lord Hoffmann; at para 31, per Lord Carswell.
[300]   [2007] EWHC 651 (Admin).

places at the relevant college. Ouseley J concluded that taken by them-selves, any one of the restrictions which flowed from the way in which the area had been delineated would not amount to a deprivation of liberty. AF was not prevented from rearranging many parts of his life within this area. But together they cut him off to a large extent from his previous life. Ouseley J attributed particular significance to the cumula-tive restrictions on mosques and educational establishments or employ-ment opportunities in judging whether there was a deprivation of AF's liberty. These restrictions had to be seen as additional to those which applied during curfew hours.[301] The judge concluded that, although as with the *E case* the decision was quite finely balanced, the restrictions cumulatively amounted to a deprivation of liberty. They were markedly less severe than those in *JJ and others* but broadly they were of compara-ble severity to those in the *E* case, overall. In the *E* case the requirement for prior approval for all visitors to the home and for prior approval for any pre-arranged meetings, and the requirement for approval to attend any meetings were very real restrictions which tipped the balance towards there being a deprivation of liberty. Those serious features were not present in that way in the *AF* case. Outside, curfew hours AF could have visitors to his flat and he could meet them outside, both without prior approval. But instead AF had a longer curfew, and a geographical area which had specific effects in relation to attendance at his preferred mosque and his pursuit of education in English, as well as other specific and more general impacts on what AF used to do. There was no issue over the mosque in the *E* case, and E had a larger family group, including his children, with whom he had unrestricted contact. Ouseley J permitted AF to adopt a 'leapfrog' procedure and petition the House of Lords for leave to appeal, which the House granted.

H. The House of Lords in the *AF* case

In *Secretary of State for the Home Department v AF*[302] the House unani-mously held that there had been no deprivation of liberty. For Lord Bingham, if the judge had had the benefit of the Court of Appeal's decision in *Secretary of State for the Home Department v E and S* [303] then he would probably have found no deprivation of liberty.[304] Baroness Hale agreed with Lord Bingham. For Lord Hoffmann the restrictions did not

---

[301] *Ibid* at para 88.
[302] [2007] 3 WLR 681.
[303] See Section X.E above. As noted in Section X.F above, the House of Lords upheld that decision.
[304] *Secretary of State for the Home Department v AF* at para 11.

come anywhere near amounting to a deprivation of liberty.[305] Lord Carswell came to the same conclusion.[306] For Lord Brown the 14-hour curfew did not involve a sufficient degree of physical confinement to constitute a deprivation of liberty as opposed to a restriction of AF's freedom of movement.[307]

XI. JUDICIAL CHALLENGES TO CONTROL ORDERS: THE POSSIBILITY OF PROSECUTION

In *E v Secretary of State for the Home Department*[308] even if the High Court had not found there to be a deprivation of liberty and a breach of Article 5 ECHR, it would have quashed the control order in question because of a failure by the government to keep the possibility of prosecution under review after the control order was made. Under s 8 of the PTA the Home Secretary is under a continuing duty to keep the decision to impose and maintain a control order under review, and the High Court held that this included keeping the matter of prosecution under review. On the facts in the *E* case, the court found that significant new material had become available since the making of the control order, in the form of two Belgian court judgments in cases in which associates of E were successfully prosecuted for terrorism offences, and in which there were references to their association with E and to his activities. In those Belgian proceedings, intercept evidence from Spain and the Netherlands had been admitted, and that evidence would in principle be admissible in England because it originated from abroad.[309] The High Court found that the possibility of prosecuting E in the light of the material about him identified in the Belgian judgments needed to be considered by the Home Secretary. The High Court therefore found as a fact that at no point was the question of prosecution reviewed in the light of the Belgian judgments. This failure to consider the impact of significant new material on the prospects of prosecuting E meant that the Home Secretary's continuing decision to maintain E's control order was flawed, and would have been quashed on this basis.

The Court of Appeal agreed in part but saw the matter differently. When properly considered in its statutory context, the duty under section 8(2) was not a condition precedent. Once it was accepted that there was a

---

[305]   *Ibid* at para 47.
[306]   *Ibid* at para 78.
[307]   *Ibid* at para 89.
[308]   See Section XI above.
[309]   This is so under the Regulation of Investigatory Powers Act 2000: see *R v P* [2002] 1 AC 146. The judgments were at the core of the Secretary of State's open national security case against E.

continuing duty to review pursuant to the *MB* case, it was implicit in that duty that the Secretary of State must do what he reasonably could to ensure that the continuing review was meaningful. There could be no properly considered answer to the question about the prospect of prosecution unless and until the police were provided with the Belgian judgments. That had not occurred by February and March 2006. There had been a breach by the Secretary of State of his *MB* duty to keep the question of possible prosecution under review, not in the sense that the decision to prosecute was one for him (for clearly it was not), but in the sense that it was incumbent upon him to provide the police with material in his possession which was or might be relevant to any reconsideration of prosecution. The duty extended to a duty to take reasonable steps to ensure that the prosecuting authorities are keeping the prospects of prosecution under review. The duty did not, however, extend to the Secretary of State becoming the prosecuting authority. The decision whether to prosecute lay elsewhere.[310] The breach arose from the omission of the Secretary of State himself to provide the police with the Belgian judgments so as to prompt and facilitate a reconsideration. That failure rendered nugatory the negative responses of the police at meetings of the Control Orders Review Group (CORG) when asked about prosecution.[311]

However, the Court of Appeal differed on the appropriate relief. It did not regard the breach as 'technical'. Beatson J had concluded that the identified breach led inexorably to a finding of a flawed decision and to the quashing of the order. He had stated the question as being 'whether there is now *evidence* which gives rise to a realistic possibility of prosecuting E'. The Court of Appeal considered this to be an error as the findings of the Belgian courts were not in themselves evidence capable of supporting a successful prosecution in this country. When properly considered, they may or may not enable investigators and prosecutors to assemble a case with a realistic prospect of success. However, even if the Secretary of State had acted diligently and expeditiously in relation to the Belgian judgments, the Court was satisfied that, again taken at their highest, they could not have given rise to a prosecution at any time material to the case. A prosecution in this jurisdiction had to conform with domestic procedural and evidential requirements. The Belgian judgments were not in themselves capable of being evidence in an English trial. At best, they

---

[310] *Secretary of State for the Home Department v E and S* [2007] EWCA Civ 459 at para 97.

[311] *Ibid* at para 99. The CORG was set up by the Home Secretary. Its general purpose is to bring together all departments and agencies involved in making and maintaining control orders on a quarterly basis to keep all orders under frequent, formal and audited review. Its establishment was recommended by the independent reviewer: see First Report, n 199 above at para 16, Second Report, n 196 above at para 43, and Third Report, n 192 above at paras 46–8.

were in a form which might ultimately enable investigators and prosecutors to adduce evidence from relevant and appropriate witnesses. The Court of Appeal had seen no material to suggest that the material could realistically have been reduced to a form appropriate for prosecution within the relevant timescale. Not every breach of an obligation rendered a subsequent decision flawed. The Court of Appeal considered that the refusal of Ouseley J to quash a control order by reference to one of the breaches he found in the *AF* case was undoubtedly correct. It supported his view that not every breach necessarily made a control order a nullity and required it to be quashed. For the Court of Appeal, the critical question was whether a particular breach materially contributed to and vitiated the decision to make the control order. In the *E* case, the breach delayed the process of review by the police and the Crown Prosecution Service but that, absent the breach, no different decision about the maintenance and renewal of the control order would have been taken or required at any material time. It was an error of law to hold that the breach justified the remedy. It was wrong to describe the Belgian judgments as 'evidence' giving rise to a realistic possibility of prosecution. Further analysis of the consequences of the breach was required. More generally, the question, on an appeal under section 10(4) of the PTA, was to decide whether the decision of the appellant was flawed. In deciding that, the duty to be considered was the duty to keep the prosecuting authorities informed and to take reasonable steps to ensure that they were keeping the controlled person's conduct, with a view to his prosecution for an offence, under review. The duty was not to assume the role of prosecuting authority or to assume responsibility for every decision taken by that authority.[312]

In *Secretary of State for the Home Department v E and Another*[313] the House of Lords unanimously upheld the decision of the Court of Appeal. The duty to consult under section 8(2) was not a condition precedent but was relevant to whether a control order was necessary.[314] By the time of the hearing in the House of Lords the Secretary of State had accepted that it was implicit in the duty of continuing review under section 8(4) that the Secretary of State must do what he or she reasonably can to ensure that the continuing review is meaningful and it was incumbent upon him to provide the police with material in his possession which was or might be relevant to any reconsideration of prosecution. All of their Lordships

---

[312] *Secretary of State for the Home Department v E and S* [2007] EWCA Civ 459 at paras 102–6.

[313] [2007] 3 WLR 720.

[314] *Ibid* at paras 15–16, per Lord Bingham.

endorsed that approach.[315] They also agreed with the Court of Appeal's approach to the appropriate remedy.[316]

The JCHR considered that the High Court decision in the *E case* and the second report of the independent reviewer cast serious doubt on the seriousness of the government's commitment to prosecution as its first preference. Its evidence supported fears that once a control order was imposed it relieved the pressure on the police and the Home Office to bring a criminal prosecution.[317] It remained the JCHR's view that the only human rights-compatible answer was to find ways of prosecuting such individuals.[318] In its report on the continuance of control orders in February 2008, the JCHR considered it significant that no individual who had been made the subject of a control order had subsequently been prosecuted for a terrorism offence, other than for breach of a control order. It suggested that the government's professed policy of preferring to prosecute as a first resort could be more effectively underpinned by a number of amendments to the control orders framework. It recommend that the PTA should be amended: (i) to provide that, except in urgent cases, the Secretary of State may make a control order only where he or she is satisfied that there is no reasonable prospect of successfully prosecuting the subject of the order for a terrorism-related offence; (ii) to impose an express duty on the Secretary of State, throughout the period during which a control order has effect, to ensure that the question of whether there is a reasonable prospect of successfully prosecuting the subject of the order for a terrorism-related offence is kept under review at least every three months; (iii) to provide that the Secretary of State should be placed under a duty to consult the police prior to his or her regular review of the prospects of prosecution and to share with the police such information (including intelligence information) as is available to him or her which is relevant to the prospects of a successful prosecution; and (iv) to impose a duty on the Chief Officer of Police to provide reasons when advising the Secretary of State that there is no realistic prospect of prosecution, and to provide that those reasons shall be disclosed to the controlled person to the extent that such disclosure would not be contrary to the public interest.[319]

---

[315] *Ibid* at para 18.
[316] *Ibid* at para 21.
[317] JCHR, Eighth Report of Session 2006–07, n 205 above at para 48.
[318] In support of its view, the JCHR cited *Security and Rights*, public lecture to the Criminal Law Bar Association by Sir Ken Macdonald QC, Director of Public Prosecutions, 23 January 2007, <http://www.cps.gov.uk /news/nationalnews/security_rights.html>.
[319] JCHR, Tenth Report of Session 2007–08, n 208 above at paras 65–6.

XII. THE FUTURE FOR CONTROL ORDERS

The government's view was that the control order regime, as it was currently being implemented, did not breach Article 5 ECHR.[320] It did not accept that any of the control orders made thus far were derogating control orders or deprived any individual of their liberty. Consequently, it did not believe either that a derogation was necessary or that Parliament was being asked to be complicit in a *de facto* derogation.[321] In its view these were civil procedures with civil procedure rules. It did not accept that non-derogating control order proceedings amount to a criminal charge.[322] The result of the series of judgments in the House of Lords in October 2007 was a mixed success for the government. The regime was upheld and orders could continue to be issued largely as they had been. They did not involve the determination of a criminal charge. Eighteen-hour curfews had to be reviewed but the Home Office fastened onto the argument of Lord Brown that 16 hours might be the acceptable limit.[323] The Home Secretary therefore increased the curfews in four cases from 12 to 16 hours The net effect of the litigation has therefore been to reduce the curfew period in the most onerous control orders from 18 to 16 hours. The role of the Special Advocates was approved but the disclosure regime had to be read and given effect to except where to do so would be incompatible with the right of the controlled person to a fair trial. That was a bold and imaginative interpretation.[324] It returns the matter to the judge in the SIAC to make the determination on fairness. There may now be exceptional cases where the Secretary of State will have to choose between disclosing material and not obtaining a control order.

The government took the view that the House of Lords judgments on control orders upheld the control orders regime and that no amendments

---

[320] *Government Response to JCHR's Eighth Report*, n 207 above at 5. *Cf* The Australian High Court has upheld the constitutionality of control orders, *Thomas v Mowbray* [2007] HCA 33.

[321] *Ibid.*

[322] *Ibid* at 6.

[323] See Home Secretary's statement on Control Orders, 1 November 2007, <http://www.homeoffice.gov.uk/about-us/news/control-orders-decision>; R. Ford, 'Home Office relief over control orders, but other measures are in pipeline', *The Times* (UK), 31 October 2007.

[324] *Cf* the decision of the Canadian Supreme Court in *Charkaoui v Canada (Citizenship and Immigration)* [2007] 1 SCR 350 (right to fair hearing violated in certification and detention review procedures; Canadian legislation did not make provision for a special counsel to be appointed to test the secret evidence), paras 23, 27–31, 38, 45, 50–52, 61, 65. This court's declaration was suspended for one year from the date of the judgment. The Canadian Parliament's Bill C-3, amending the Immigration and Refugee Protection Act 2000, came into force on 22 February 2008, just one day before the Supreme Court deadline expired. A certificate under it was issued against Charkaoui. The Act provides for the introduction of a special advocate who has security clearance and can review secret information: see T Poole, 'Recent developments in the "war on terrorism" in Canada' (2007) 7 *Human Rights Law Review* 633–42.

to the legal framework were necessary following those judgments. The JCHR disagreed and considered it imperative for the government to amend counterterrorism laws where experience had shown those laws to lead to breaches of human rights. In its view, control orders would continue to cause breaches of rights unless the legislation was modified in a number of important respects. It put forward amendments intended to make the control orders regime compatible with human rights in its report on the Counterterrorism Bill.[325] The JCHR recommended that Parliament should amend the control orders framework to clarify what measures may amount to a deprivation of liberty and to impose a maximum limit on the length of curfews of 12 hours a day.[326] It also recommended changes to help ensure fairer hearings in control order cases.[327]

Lord Carlile, the statutory reviewer of the PTA, concluded that the control order system remained necessary, although in some cases the obligations imposed were more cautious and extensive than absolutely necessary.[328] The JCHR has argued that the combination of the degree of restriction imposed by control orders, their indefinite duration, and the limited opportunity to challenge the basis on which they are made carries a very high risk of subjecting those who are placed under control orders to inhuman and degrading treatment contrary to Article 3 ECHR.[329] The government accepted that control orders were less than 100 per cent effective in countering terrorism. There were limitations and problems with the legal framework. The government had to operate under the constraints imposed by Parliament, the courts and the law. The government's view was that, in policy terms, 'Control orders are not even our second – or third – best option for dealing with suspected terrorists. But under our existing laws they are as far as we can go'.[330] It considered that control orders were the best available means of addressing the continuing threat posed by suspected terrorists who could not currently be prosecuted or, in respect of foreign nationals, could not be removed from the United Kingdom.[331] The independent reviewer, Lord Carlile, expressed a similar view in his Second Report in 2007:

---

[325] JCHR, Tenth Report of Session 2007–08, n 208 above at paras 1–18.

[326] *Ibid* at paras 35–49.

[327] *Ibid* at paras 50–59. See also JCHR, Ninth Report of Session 2007–08, n 253 above at paras 39–73.

[328] *Second Report of the Independent Reviewer Pursuant to Section 14(3) of the Prevention of Terrorism Act 2005*, 19 February 2007: see <http://security.homeoffice.gov.uk>.

[329] See JCHR, *Eighth Report of Session 2006–07*, n 205 above at para 59. Alleged violations of Art 3 ECHR were rejected in the *E* case: see Section XI above.

[330] 'Control Order Update', Written Ministerial Statement by the Minister for Security, Counter-terrorism and Police, 21 June 2007.

[331] *Government Response to JCHR's Eighth Report*, n 207 above at 9.

I would prefer it if no control order system was necessary. However, in my view it remains necessary given the nature of the risk of terrorist attacks and the difficulty of dealing with a small number of cases. Control orders provide a proportional means of dealing with those cases, if administered correctly.[332]

The Security Service view is that control orders have been successful in preventing or limiting individuals' involvement in terrorism-related activity.[333] The independent reviewer and the JCHR have referred to the need for an 'exit strategy' from the control order regime. The main potential exit strategies for individuals are prosecution, deportation (in the case of foreign nationals), modification of the obligations in the control order, non-renewal or revocation of the control order, de-radicalisation and rehabilitation programmes. In his Third Report in 2008 the independent reviewed submitted:

It is now my view that it is only in rare cases that control orders can be justified for more than two years. After that time, at least the immediate utility of even a dedicated terrorist will seriously have been disrupted. The terrorist will know that the authorities will retain an interest in his or her activities and contacts, and will be likely to scrutinise them in the future. For those organising terrorism, a person who has been subject to a control order for up to two years is an unattractive operator, who may be assumed to have the eyes and ears of the State upon him/her. Many terrorists prefer to use for operational purposes 'clean skins', persons who are not known ever to have been arrested, as largely has been evident from terrorism plots uncovered in the UK since September 2001, and indeed well before in a context different from violent jihad. A controlee most certainly does not fall into the category of a 'clean skin'.[334]

He advised that there should be a recognised and possibly statutory presumption against a control order being extended beyond two years, save in genuinely exceptional circumstances. However, if a former controlee brought themselves within the legislation thereafter, they could be made the subject of a fresh control order, on the basis of new material and a change in the circumstances.[335] The JCHR similarly recommended that the law be amended to impose a duty on the Secretary of State to keep the need for a control order under review and to impose a maximum limit on the duration of a control order.[336] As of February 2008, seven of the 15 individuals who were then the subject of control orders had been so for more than two years, and of those seven, two had been on control

---

[332] See n 328 above at para 7. Similarly in his Third Report, n 192 above at paras. 27, 76.
[333] *Ibid.*
[334] See n 192 above at para 50.
[335] *Ibid* at para 41.
[336] See Tenth Report of Session 2007–08, n 208 above at paras 77–87.

orders for three years and before that were probably detained for more than three years in Belmarsh Prison under the ATCSA.

XIII. THE TERRORISM ACT 2006

A. New Offences and New Powers

After the 7 July 2005 bombings in London[337] the executive introduced a new Terrorism Bill. By the time of its parliamentary consideration, the cross-party consensual approach had broken down badly and the government suffered major retreats and defeats, particularly over the length of detention without charge. To its credit the legislature withstood the pressures from the executive on the issue of extended detention.

The Terrorism Act 2006 (TA 2006) created a number of new offences. One of the most controversial and complex was the offence of encouragement of terrorism. Encouragement can include making statements which glorify the commission or preparation (whether in the past, in the future or generally) of such acts of terrorism or Terrorist Convention (Council of Europe Convention on the Prevention of Terrorism 2005) offences and making a statement from which members of the public could reasonably be expected to infer that what is being glorified is being identified as conduct that should be emulated by them in existing circumstances. The JCHR considered that the main problem was that the new encouragement offence was capable of application to speech or actions concerning resistance to an oppressive regime overseas. It expressed concern that the new offence would, 'criminalise any expression of a view that armed resistance to a brutal or repressive anti-democratic regime might in certain circumstances be justifiable, even where such resistance consists of campaigns of sabotage against property, and specifically directed away from human casualties'.[338]

There are other offences in the TA 2006 relating to bookshops and other disseminators of terrorist publications, the preparation of terrorist acts,[339] and terrorist training. The Act also created a number of offences relating to radioactive material or devices, and nuclear facilities, and amended

---

[337] Fifty-two people were killed and hundreds were injured in four bomb attacks on London's transport system. See 'Applied Intelligence – The Three Fatal Security Mistakes Leading to 7/7', *The Times* (UK). 4 July 2006.

[338] JCHR, *Counter-Terrorism Policy and Human Rights: Terrorism Bill and related matters,* Third Report of Session 2005–06, HC 561-I, para 12.

[339] 'The creation of the new offence of "preparation of acts of terrorism" has been a useful instrument for bringing action against suspected terrorists and disrupting or preventing violent conspiracies within the criminal justice system early enough to protect the public – and also for providing a workable alternative to more preventive detentions': A

the penalty for certain offences relating to nuclear material. The Act amended the TA 2000 in a number of ways. First, it made some changes to terrorist offences (for example raising the penalty for the offence of possession for terrorist purposes). Second, it extended powers currently available to the Secretary of State relating to proscription, to allow for the proscription of groups which glorify terrorism or the activities of which associate it with acts that glorify terrorism, and to deal with proscribed organisations that change their names. The Act also extended police and investigatory powers in relation to terrorism (most controversially by allowing the extension of detention of terrorist suspects with judicial approval for up to 28 days, and enabling all premises search warrants to be issued). With reference to the powers of the security and intelligence services, the Act also amended the Intelligence Services Act 1994 with respect to warrants to carry out acts both overseas and in the United Kingdom. It also amended the Regulation of Investigatory Powers Act 2000 in a number of ways. First, it increased the penalties for refusal to obey a notice to provide an encryption key, as set out in Part 3 of that Act. Second, it amended investigatory powers, extended the period that warrants for intercept (and related authorisations) under that Act were issued for, and further delegated the authority to modify warrant schedules. Finally, the Act made a small but important amendment to the definition of terrorism as contained in the TA 2000.

B. The Definition of Terrorism

The TA 2000 contained a very broad definition of terrorism. 'Terrorism' was defined as the use or threat of action where the action is designed to influence the government or advance a political, religious or ideological

Blick, T Choudhury and S Weir, 'The Rules of the Game: Terrorism, Community and Human Rights', Joseph Rowntree Report, November 2006, <http://www.jrrt.org.uk/Terrorism_final.pdf> at 66.

cause.[340] Section 34 of the TA 2006 amends the definition in the TA 2000 to include cases where the use or threat is designed to influence an international governmental organisation. The UK government considered that the definition of terrorism remained appropriate, but the Home Secretary asked Lord Carlile of Berriew QC, the independent reviewer of the anti-terrorism legislation, to conduct a review of the definition of terrorism within a year from the coming into force of the TA 2006. He consulted widely.[341] There is no agreed definition of terrorism in international law.[342] There are narrower definitions in the EU Council Framework Decision of 13 June 2002,[343] and in UN Security Council Resolution 1566.[344]

C. Extended Detention

The TA 2006 amended the powers to detain terrorist suspects under the TA 2000, and the grounds on which such detention may be authorised. The provisions extending the maximum length of time a person may be

[340] See C Walker, *Blackstone's Guide to the Anti-terrorism Legislation* (Oxford, Oxford University Press, 2002) 20–30.

[341] His report was published in 2007: see <http://security.homeoffice.gov.uk>. The Counter-terrorism Bill 2008 Part 7 ('Miscellaneous') amends the definition of terrorism in s 1 of the Terrorism Act 2000 (and various other pieces of terrorism legislation) by inserting a reference to a racial cause. This Part also creates an offence of eliciting, publishing or communicating information relating to members of the armed forces which is likely to be of use to terrorists, and amends the offence of failing to disclose information about a suspected terrorist offence.

[342] There is no agreed definition of terrorism in international law. See CA Gearty, 'Terrorism and Human Rights' [2005] *EHRLR* 1–6; T Meisels, 'The Trouble With Terror: The Apologetics of Terrorism – A Refutation' (2006) 18 *Terrorism and Political Violence* 465–83. For a working international law definition see *A More Secure World: Our Shared Responsibility – Report of High Level Panel on Threats, Challenges and Change*, UN doc A/59/565 (29 November 2004): 'attacks that specifically target innocent civilians and non-combatants'.

[343] '1. Each Member State shall take the necessary measures to ensure that the intentional acts referred to below in points (a) to (i), as defined as offences under national law, which, given their nature or context, may seriously damage a country or an international organisation where committed with the aim of: seriously intimidating a population, or unduly compelling a Government or international organisation to perform or abstain from performing any acts, or seriously destabilising or destroying the fundamental political, constitutional, economic or social structures of a country or an international organisation, shall be deemed the terrorist offences.'

[344] '*Recalls* that criminal acts, including against civilians, committed with the intent to cause death or serious bodily injury, or taking of hostages, with the purpose to provoke a state of terror in the general public or in a group of persons or particular persons, intimidate a population or compel a government or an international organization to do or to abstain from doing any act, which constitute offences within the scope of and as defined in the international conventions and protocols relating to terrorism, are under no circumstances justifiable by considerations of a political, philosophical, ideological, racial, ethnic, religious or other similar nature, and *calls upon* all States to prevent such acts and, if not prevented, to ensure that such acts are punished by penalties consistent with their grave nature'.

detained under the TA 2000 from 14 to 28 days have effect for one year after their commencement but they can be extended by Order made by the Secretary of State for periods of up to a year each. A report from the Home Affairs Committee (HAC), *Terrorism Detention Powers*, in July 2006 contained a damning indictment of the executive's approach to this issue.[345] The executive (effectively the government in this context), strongly supported by the Prime Minister, proposed a 90-day maximum detention period.[346] It stressed that it was doing so on the advice of the police and security services. Indeed, it refused to countenance amendments that would have permitted, for example, maximum detention of 60 days.[347] The end result was a period of 28 days and bitter political recriminations between the political parties. The HAC considered that the process of the Terrorism Bill 2005 through Parliament was 'divisive' and 'did not increase public trust in the police or the Government'.[348] It found the case for extending the maximum detention period to 28 days was 'convincing', but did not find the arguments for the 90-day period 'compelling'.[349] However, it was heavily critical of the executive's approach:

> On such a major issue, with very significant human rights implications, we would have expected the case made by the police to have been better developed. *The police should have been able to present an evidence-based analysis of the type we have endeavoured to undertake.* It is clear that this was not done, despite their reliance on their 'professional judgement'. We think it is reasonable for the Prime Minister and Home Secretary to rely on advice from the police on such issues, but *we would also expect them to have challenged critically that advice in order to assure themselves of the case that was being made.* We heard no evidence that this had happened: this is unsatisfactory ... in our view the primary origin of the difficulties experienced by the Government lies in the *lack of care* with which the case for a maximum 90 day detention period was promoted.[350] (emphases added)

The JCHR report on the Terrorism Bill 2005 concluded that, 'in our view the proportionality case for any increase from the current 14 day limit has not so far been made out on the evidence'.[351]

---

[345]   Fourth Report of Session 2005–06, HC 910–1.

[346]   Critics of such a proposal often observe that a 90-day detention period was one of the most notorious aspects of the apartheid regime in South Africa: see eg Lord Joffe, *Hansard*, HL Deb, vol 667, cols 1224–6 (25 January 2006). See also Justice Chaskalson, 'The Widening Gyre: Counter-terrorism, Human Rights and the Rule of Law', Seventh Sir David Williams Lecture, <http://www.icj.org/IMG/Speech_AC_May_2007.pdf>.

[347]   See P Wintour and T Branigan, 'Ministers Stay Firm on 90-day Detention Plan' *The Guardian* (UK), 8 October 2005.

[348]   HAC Report, n 345 above at para 148.

[349]   *Ibid* at para 29.

[350]   *Ibid* at paras 29, 31.

[351]   JCHR, Third Report of Session 2005–06, above n 338 at para 92.

It turned out that the government essentially relied on a police briefing for its case.[352] The proposal for extended detention had not even been the subject of a formal working party within the Association of Chief Police Officers (ACPO), but was 'the product of a lot of discussion and reflection by practitioners over a period of some two to three years'.[353] The written material submitted by ACPO or the Metropolitan Police Service in support of the proposal for 90-day detention of terrorism suspects before the government's decision to support that proposal was taken consisted of the briefing note, three ACPO press releases and two sides of A4 describing two operations. It appeared that the government simply did not ask for evidence or justification of the case for an extension of detention additional to that information. In addition, there was some concern that the police were being encouraged to lobby Parliament to vote for 90 days.[354]

The HAC's recommendation was that there needed to be a more careful, open presentation[355] and evidence-based justification of the government's case for legislation imposing significant human rights restrictions. In normal circumstances one would expect a government's proposals to be treated by the legislature and by the public with a sceptical and critical response. The burden of proof is on the government to make its case and support it with evidence. On the extended detention period the government did not do this. Even accepting that government and opposition parties have their own political agendas, the result is difficult to defend in rational terms. Indeed, in governance terms, the outcome is slightly perverse. There is an arguable case that 'there have been situations in which significant conspiracies to commit terrorist acts have gone unprosecuted as a result of the time limitations placed on the control authorities following arrest'.[356] The period agreed is shorter than the government or the police wanted. It seems probable that the legislature would have agreed to a longer period but not necessarily as long as the government wanted.[357] The HAC recommended that a committee

---

[352] *Ibid*, appendix.

[353] *Ibid* at para 23.

[354] The HAC was divided on a specific reference to this issue: see HAC Report, n 345 above at 60 (minutes).

[355] *Ibid* at para 35.

[356] This is the view of Lord Carlile of Berriew QC, the government-appointed independent reviewer of terrorism legislation, cited in *ibid* at para 33.

[357] Gordon Brown, the current Prime Minister, had signalled his support for the longer periods: see 'Securing Our Future', Speech by the Rt Hon Gordon Brown MP, Chancellor of the Exchequer, at the Royal United Services Institute (RUSI), London, 13 February 2006, <http://www.hm-treasury.gov.uk>.

independent of government be created to keep the maximum detention period under annual review and to recommend the introduction of new legislation as necessary:[358]

Many of the difficulties the Government experienced in the passage of the Terrorism Bill arose from the speed with which it was drafted and presented to Parliament: this inquiry did the job of examining the police arguments for extended detention which the Home Office should have done before introducing the Terrorism Bill. Any new legislation on terrorism should not in our view propose a longer period of detention than 28 days unless there is such compelling evidence as we have already referred to earlier. The new legislation on terrorism, including the promised consolidation of existing measures, should be extensively examined in draft, either by this Committee or by a joint committee of both Houses. The Government should ensure that it meets the commitment to build this into the timetable.[359]

These were damning recommendations. The government could not be trusted to use intelligence properly and adduce evidence in support of its case so the function had to be delegated to a committee independent of government.

The government's response to the HAC was that the case for the 90-day detention period was ultimately one of operational judgement and experience in light of the changing threat from terrorism.[360] On the detention period it stated that:

> If experience shows that 28 days is inadequate then Parliament will need to consider whether the legislation needs to be changed to provide for a longer period of pre-charge detention. In doing so it will need to take into account any advice received from the police arising from their operational experience. Given the role of the Independent Reviewer of Terrorism Legislation and the early stage we are at on the operation of the extended pre-charge detention period, we do not believe that an independent committee is required to review the detention period at this stage.[361]

It is fair to note that the government consulted much more widely and actively sought a wider political consensus with respect to the measures in the Counterterrorism Bill 2008.

---

[358]   HAC Report, n 345 above at para 148.

[359]   *Ibid* at para 151.

[360]   See *Government Reply to the Fourth Report from the Home Affairs Committee Session 2005–06*, HC 910, Cm 6906 (September 2006).

[361]   *Ibid* at 14–15.

D. The Use of Intelligence

There are other factors that are important to bear in mind in making an assessment of the executive's performance. First, when the government claims to rely on intelligence the public trust in those who have access to confidential information has been severely damaged by the Iraq War 2003.[362] There is a widespread perception that the government misused intelligence information and the intelligence services in support of its case for war.[363] Before the HAC the then Home Secretary conceded that a 'central task of government is to regain the trust of the country in the integrity of our assessments of this kind'.[364]

E. Preventive Detention; Judicial Oversight?

Second, the context and purpose of detention is now understood differently. The evidence from the police to the HAC made clear that the interviewing of suspects had become virtually irrelevant:

> In general it cannot be expected that interviews of suspects during extended detention will lead to significant additional information that can be used in court. While we can understand that there may be cases in which confrontation of a suspect with new evidence might lead to admissions, it appears that the case for extended detention rests on two arguments: first, the need to seek and analyse evidence from a complex range of sources and, second, the need to ensure the protection of the public. This latter point has been referred to in our evidence and the Parliamentary debates. It does not, however, form any part of the legal basis for an application for extended detention.[365]

The changed nature of terrorism means that arrests are used to disrupt conspiracies. As the HAC made clear, preventive detention is a significant new development but one that was *not made explicit during the passage of the Bill*, during which extended detention was primarily justified on the grounds of the time needed to collect and analyse evidence.[366] Again this seems a damning criticism in terms of a rational assessment of the necessary legislation. The HAC recommended that any legislation should recognise in terms this important new purpose of pre-charge detention. One important aspect of this was whether the nature and role

---

[362] In the *A (Belmarsh Detainees)* case, considered in Section VII above, Lord Hoffmann made a scathing reference to the 'widespread scepticism which has attached to intelligence assessments since the fiasco over Iraqi weapons of mass destruction' (para 94).

[363] See D McGoldrick, *From 9–11 to the Iraq War 2003 – International Law in an Age of Complexity* (Oxford, Hart Publishing, 2004) 96–116.

[364] HAC Report, n 345 above at para 33.

[365] *Ibid* at para 90.

[366] *Ibid* at para 94.

of judicial oversight needed to be modified. The HAC was uneasy at the prospect of the existing system being used to provide judicial oversight of even longer pre-charge detention.[367] It considered that the combination of pre-charge detention for up to four weeks with 'a vast amount' of arrests leading to detention intended to disrupt or prevent terrorist activity meant that new forms of judicial oversight were needed:

> In particular, there is no tradition in the United Kingdom of preventive detention at such an early stage. A new and different legal framework, in addition to existing post-arrest oversight, would therefore be needed to provide judicial oversight of such cases and of the police's exercise of the powers [of detention without charge under terrorist legislation].[368]

Lord Carlile had recommended a strengthened system of judicial oversight once a suspect has been arrested. Among his proposals were that:

> Where detention beyond 14 days is to be applied for, the introduction of one of a small group of security-cleared, designated senior circuit judges as examining judge and 'judicial authority' under the legislation; That judge to be provided with a full and continuing account of all matters involved in the investigation in question; The introduction of a security-cleared special advocate, also fully briefed as to the investigation, to make representations on the interests of the detained persons and to advise the judge; The judge to have the power to require specific investigations to be pursued if reasonably necessary for the proper exercise of his/her jurisdiction; Suitable opportunity for written and oral defence representations against extended detention, with oral hearings at the discretion of the judge; Weekly decisions with reasons if extended detention granted; The keeping of a written record (if necessary protected from disclosure for the purposes of any subsequent trial) of the judge's activities in a case; Appeal with permission to the High Court.[369]

The then Home Secretary was personally sympathetic to these ideas and considered that 'a supervisory system and investigating magistrates regime is very superior to the system that we have in this country'.[370] The HAC accepted the thrust of these proposals but believed that they should be extended:

> Firstly, we believe that supervision should provide for a continual reassessment of whether alternative methods, such as tagging and control orders, would be appropriate. Secondly, as we have argued in the section on disruption and prevention, we believe that there should be appropriate judicial oversight when arrests are made under the Terrorism Act. This would enable proper independent consideration to be given where an arrest is to be made for

---

[367]   *Ibid* at para 124.
[368]   *Ibid* at para 125.
[369]   Report by Lord Carlile, Independent Reviewer, *Proposals by Her Majesty's Government for changes to the laws against terrorism*, <http://security.homeoffice.gov.uk> at paras 65–7.
[370]   Cited in the HAC Report, n 345 above at para 127.

its disruptive and preventative value rather than primarily for its investigative purpose. It would also enable consideration from the outside of alternatives to arrest and detention. We recognise that this would bring some procedures more common in other jurisdictions into our criminal justice system.[371]

It considered that the 'principle of independent judicial oversight from the time that arrest is first considered should be adopted'.[372] This would also ensure that the police alone do not have to bear responsibility for arrests intended to protect the public.

The government's response to the HAC's proposals was lukewarm:

We believe that the idea that arrest and detention of some terrorist suspects is carried out solely as a 'preventative' measure, is misleading. While an arrest may have a preventative or disruptive effect on a terrorist or network of terrorists, and while this may be the impetus for executing arrests at any point during an investigation, the legislation does not allow continued detention on this basis. Once a person has been arrested, their continued detention can only be authorised on the grounds that it is necessary to obtain, examine or analyse evidence, or information with the aim of obtaining evidence. The purpose of the extended detention time is to secure sufficient admissible evidence for use in criminal proceedings ...

As mentioned in our response to the Committee's recommendations ... while an arrest may have a preventative effect, the legislation does not allow for continued detention on this basis. We are aware that a number of suggestions have been made concerning the role of the judiciary in issuing extension of detention warrants. At present, this process is thorough and detailed, and both the investigating team and the detainee's legal representative are able to make representations to the judicial authority about any application for an extension of detention. We will consider carefully the proposals of Lord Carlile and others concerning further judicial oversight, although as stated above, we do not feel it is appropriate for the current control order regime to be combined with the extension of detention process.[373]

XIV. POWERS OF STOP AND SEARCH

R (Gillan and Another) v Commissioner of Police for the Metropolis and Another[374] concerned the exercise of exceptional stop and search powers in sections 44–7 of the TA 2000. Section 44 required a prior authorisation by a senior police officer. The authorisation could only be given if the person giving it 'consider[ed] it *expedient* for the prevention of acts of terrorism' (section 44(3) – emphasis added). The authorisation had to be confirmed by the Secretary of State. Under section 45(1) the stop and

---

[371] *Ibid* at para 129.
[372] *Ibid* at para 131.
[373] *Government Reply to the Fourth Report*, n 360 above at 10, and 13–14.
[374] [2006] UKHL 12, [2006] UKHRR 740.

search power (a) may be exercised only for the purpose of searching for articles of a kind which could be used in connection with terrorism, and (b) may be exercised whether or not the constable has grounds for suspecting the presence of articles of that kind. As is clear, section 45(1) did not impose a condition of reasonable suspicion.

Mr Gillan, a PhD student studying in Sheffield, went to London in September 2003 to protest peacefully against an arms fair being held at the ExCel Centre, Docklands, in east London. He was riding his bicycle near the Centre when he was stopped by two male police officers. They searched him and his rucksack and found nothing incriminating. They gave him a copy of the Stop/Search Form 5090, which recorded that he was stopped and searched under section 44. The search was said to be for 'articles concerned in terrorism'. The whole incident lasted about 20 minutes. A second appellant, Ms Quinton, was an accredited freelance journalist who went the Centre to film the protests taking place against the arms fair. She was stopped by a female police officer near the Centre and asked to explain why she had appeared out of some bushes. Q was wearing a photographer's jacket and carrying a small bag and a video camera. She explained she was a journalist and produced her press passes. The officer searched her, found nothing incriminating, and gave her a copy of Form 5090. This recorded that the object and grounds of the search were 'P.O.T.A.' (intended to be a reference to the TA 2000). The form showed the length of the search as five minutes, but Q estimated that it lasted for 30 minutes. Each of the appellants had formed the view that he or she was stopped and searched for public order reasons not connected with terrorism but with protests and disturbances that the police apprehended might occur at the Docklands arms fair. However, the House of Lords did not deal with their individual cases. It only concerned itself with the generality of the legislation.

The House of Lords unanimously rejected the appeal.[375] First, the powers were exceptional but the expression 'expedient' in section 44(3) could not be interpreted to mean 'necessary'. The principle of legality had no application in this context because, even if the powers infringed a fundamental human right, they did not do so by general words but by provisions of a detailed, specific and unambiguous character.[376] Second, the court upheld the authorisation procedure. Under section 44 the authorisations lasted for 28 days. That might suggest that they were intended to be exceptional. In fact what had happened was that the authorisations had been made continually for successive periods since the 2000 Act came into force. The appellants attacked this and the fact

---

[375] So too had the Court of Appeal: see [2004] EWCA Civ 1067, [2005] QB 388.
[376] *Gillan* at para 15, per Lord Bingham.

that they covered the whole of the London Metropolitan Police District. Although these submissions were considered attractive they were rejected because the police and intelligence evidence was to the effect that the terrorist threats were London-wide. Thus,

> the House has before it what appear to be considered and informed evalua-
> tions of the terrorist threat on one side and effectively nothing save a measure
> of scepticism on the other. There is no basis on which the respondents'
> evidence can be rejected. This is not a question of deference but of what in *A v
> Secretary of State for the Home Department* [2004] UKHL 56, [2005] 2 AC 68, para
> 29, was called 'relative institutional competence'.[377]

Third, there had been no deprivation of liberty for the purposes of Article 5 ECHR. The House of Lords thought that there was no direct Strasbourg jurisprudence on this point. For them it was significant that the stop and searches were relatively brief. They thought that they were better considered as being kept waiting rather than being deprived of liberty.[378] Fourth, there was no interference with Article 8 ECHR rights. A superficial search of persons and the opening of their bags did not reach the necessary level of seriousness for Article 8 purposes.[379] Fifth, even if there had been an interference with Article 5, 8, 10 or 11 it had been prescribed by law for ECHR purposes. The powers and the Codes of Practice relating to them were accessible. It was not necessary for the individual authorisations to have been made public. The powers were not so insufficiently certain that they were not 'prescribed by law'.[380]

One of the criticisms of the section 44 powers has been that its use has been discriminatory. The Commission for Racial Equality reported a 36 per cent increase in the number of Asians stopped over the course of 2002/03 under section 44 compared to a 17 per cent increase for Whites.[381] Doubtless conscious of these concerns, three of the Law Lords specifically focused on whether there were sufficient safeguards against the discriminatory use of section 44. There was no actual need to do this on the facts of the case because there no discrimination was alleged (and neither of the appellants was Asian). Nonetheless, Lord Hope posed the difficult questions:

> How does the fact that it is likely to be difficult in practice to detect discrimi-
> natory use of the power square with the principle of legal certainty that
> requires that the use of such powers must be in accordance with the law if they

[377] *Ibid* at para 17, per Lord Bingham.
[378] *Ibid* at paras 21–5.
[379] *Ibid* at para 28. So too for Arts 10 and 11 ECHR.
[380] *Ibid* at paras 31–7.
[381] The report was cited by Lord Brown, in *ibid* at para 82. More generally see J Rehman, 'Islamophobia After 9–11: International Terrorism, *Sharia* and Muslim Minorities in Europe: The Case of the United Kingdom' (2003–04) 3 *European Yearbook of Minority Issues* 217–35.

are to be compatible with the Convention rights? And how in practice is discriminatory use of the power to be prevented, given the nature of the terrorist threats that it is designed for? ... the current wave of international terrorism is linked to groups that have an Islamic fundamentalist background. What then if it is found that the police are using the section 44 power more frequently to stop Asians than other racial groups in the community? Does this amount to direct discrimination contrary to domestic law ...?[382]

Lord Hope stressed that each person had to be treated as an individual and not assumed to be like other members of the group.[383] The mere fact that the person appeared to be of Asian origin was not a legitimate reason for exercise of the stop and search powers.[384] Their use against Asians would not necessarily be discriminatory; however, Lord Hope acknowledged that the risk that the power would be exercised in a discriminatory fashion could not be discounted. This raised the question of whether section 44 was, by its very nature, arbitrary, and therefore did not meet the ECHR standards for legal certainty. After close examination he concluded that structure of law within which the powers were to be exercised was 'sufficient in all the circumstances to meet the requirement of legality'.[385] For Lord Brown:

> It seems to me inevitable, however, that so long as the principal terrorist risk against which use of the section 44 power has been authorised is that from al Qaeda, a disproportionate number of those stopped and searched will be of Asian appearance (particularly if they happen to be carrying rucksacks or wearing apparently bulky clothing capable of containing terrorist-related items).[386]

He considered that this conclusion was neither inimical to Convention jurisprudence nor inconsistent with domestic discrimination law. Ethnic origin accordingly could and properly should be taken into account in deciding whether and whom to stop and search provided always that the power was used sensitively and the selection was made for reasons connected with the perceived terrorist threat and not on grounds of racial discrimination.[387] Bearing in mind the imperative of not imperilling good community relations, or exacerbating a minority's feelings of alienation and victimisation, the use of these supposed preventative powers could tend actually to promote rather than counter the present terrorist threat.

---

[382]   *Gillan* at paras 39, 42–3.
[383]   *Ibid* at paras 40–47, relying on *R (European Roma Rights Centre) v Immigration Officer at Prague Airport (United Nations High Commissioner for Refugees intervening)* [2005] 2 AC 1.
[384]   *Ibid* at para 91, per Lord Brown.
[385]   *Ibid* at paras 48–57, per Lord Hope.
[386]   *Ibid* at para 81.
[387]   *Ibid.*

Thus, the stop and search powers ought to be used only sparingly. If so used, they could not be impugned either as arbitrary or as inherently and systematically discriminatory.[388]

Lord Scott did not think that domestic discrimination law would invalidate what otherwise would be a lawful use of the section 44 powers:

> If and to the extent that a use of stop and search powers for the statutory purpose expressed in section 45(1) might require some degree of stereotyping in the selection of the persons to be stopped and searched and arguably, therefore, some discrimination, that use would, I think, be validated by the statutory authority of the 2000 Act (see s 41(1)(a) and s 42 of the Race Relations Act 1976, as amended).[389]

Given that the Race Relations Act was amended in 2000 to extend its provisions to cover the police, it would be unfortunate, to say the least, if statutory authority for discrimination was found in the 2000 Act. For completeness, Lord Scott accepted that the balance to be struck was between the degree of interference with ordinary liberties brought about by police exercising their section 44 stop and search powers and the degree of risk to the public posed by the terrorist threat as it appeared from the available intelligence material. However, he disagreed with the assertion that the balance struck in the giving of the authorisation could be judged to be a disproportionate response. First, the interference with the fundamental rights of individuals was not of overwhelming weight. Second, a challenge to the validity of a section 44 authorisation, based on the alleged disproportionate nature of that response to a perceived threat of terrorism, could not be expected to succeed without the court having had an opportunity to review the intelligence material that had been relied on. Prior to the Divisional Court hearing, the Home Secretary offered the appellants a procedure (involving the use of a Special Advocate) whereby the Divisional Court could review in closed session the underlying intelligence material on the basis of which the Home Secretary had confirmed the authorisation. But the offer had not been taken up. Neither the Divisional Court, the Court of Appeal nor the House of Lords had reviewed that material. In such a situation, no court could reasonably have concluded that the authorisation was a disproportionate response to the threat of terrorist activity in London appearing from the available intelligence material.[390]

The real issue in the *Gillan* case is perhaps not so much the decision of the House of Lords itself, but that the search powers are so widely drawn

---

[388]   *Ibid* at para 92.
[389]   *Ibid* at para 68, per Lord Scott.
[390]   *Ibid* at paras 61–5.

by the legislation. The usual protection of 'reasonable suspicion' is absent and, in practice, the result has been that the powers are statistically disproportionately applied to ethnic minorities. As Walker has observed, their Lordships' acceptance of the continuous, but effectively secret, reauthorisation of the powers across London since 2001 sits uneasily with the police view that community consultation in advance of section 44 authorisations is good practice.[391]

XV. THE JUDICIARY AND EVIDENCE LINKED TO FOREIGN TORTURE

In a follow-up to the first *A (Belmarsh Detainees)* case on detention came the issue of evidence linked to torture. This was considered by a seven-member House of Lords in *A (FC) and others (FC) v Secretary of State for the Home Department*[392] (hereinafter *Re A (Foreign Torture Evidence)*). It is important to identify closely the issues that were and those that were not before the courts.[393] The central issue was whether the SIAC, when hearing an appeal under section 25 ATCSA by a person certified and detained under sections 21 and 23 of that Act, could receive evidence which 'has or been or may have been procured by torture inflicted, in order to obtain evidence, by officials of a foreign state without the complicity of the British authorities'.[394] If the torture had been inflicted by or with the complicity of the British authorities it was accepted that they evidence could not be received. Moreover, the Home Secretary indicated that it was not his intention to rely on, or present to the SIAC or to the Administrative Court in relation to control orders, evidence which he knew or believed to have been obtained by a third country by torture. That intention was, however, based on policy and not on any acknowledged legal obligation. The policy could be altered by a successor in office or if circumstances changed. The SIAC held that the fact that evidence had, or might have been, procured by torture inflicted by foreign officials without the complicity of the British authorities was relevant to the weight of the evidence but did not render it legally inadmissible. A majority of the Court of Appeal upheld this decision.[395] A unanimous House of Lords allowed the appeal.

---

[391] See C Walker, Case comment (2006) *Criminal Law Review* 751–7.
[392] [2005] UKHL 71, [2006] 2 AC 221, [2006] HRLR 6.
[393] See also T Thienel, 'The Admissibility of Evidence Obtained By Torture Under International Law' (2006) 17(2) *European Journal of International Law* 349–67.
[394] *Re A (Foreign Torture Evidence)* at para 1.
[395] [2004] EWCA Civ 1123, [2005] 1 WLR 414, Pill and Laws LJJ, Neuberger LJ dissenting in part. On the Court of Appeal decision see R O'Keefe, 'Decisions of British Courts During 2004' (2004) 75 *British Yearbook of International Law* 468–83.

What is notable is that, although extensive reference was made to the ECHR and international prohibitions on torture, their Lordships' opinions were strongly located in the common law. For Lord Bingham, for example:

> The principles of the common law, standing alone, in my opinion compel the exclusion of third party torture evidence as unreliable, unfair, offensive to ordinary standards of humanity and decency and incompatible with the principles which should animate a tribunal seeking to administer justice. But the principles of the common law do not stand alone. Effect must be given to the European Convention, which itself takes account of the all but universal consensus embodied in the Torture Convention. The answer to the central question posed at the outset of this opinion is to be found not in a governmental policy, which may change, but in law.[396]

The House was split, however, on the application of the burden of proof. This was particularly important in practice because the position of the Secretary of State was that, although he did not as a matter of principle rely on information that he '*knows* has been obtained by torture', he was 'willing to accept and act upon information whose origin is obscure and undetectable, in the knowledge that it may have come from countries that use torture'.[397] For the majority (Lords Hope, Brown, Rodger and Carswell) the SIAC should refuse to admit the evidence if it concluded that the evidence *was* obtained by torture.[398] So the SIAC should not admit the evidence if it concluded on a balance of probabilities that it was obtained by torture. If the SIAC was left in doubt as to whether the evidence was obtained in this way, it should admit it. This test would involve fewer practical problems. For the minority (Lords Bingham, Nicholls and Hoffmann) the SIAC should refuse to admit the evidence if it was unable to conclude that there was not a real risk that the evidence had been obtained by torture.[399] They considered that the majority's test would largely nullify the principle that the courts would not admit evidence procured by torture.

A number of their Lordships emphasised that the position in judicial proceedings was not the same as executive action because the judiciary and the executive had different functions and different responsibilities. So decisions on investigation, arrest and detention could be based on information derived from torture, even if that information could not then be used as evidence in court proceedings (except to defend the legality of

---

[396] See *Re A (Foreign Torture Evidence)* at para 52. See also para 112, per Lord Hope; para 152, per Lord Carswell.
[397] *Ibid* at para 115.
[398] *Ibid* at para 118, per Lord Hope.
[399] *Ibid* at para 56, per Lord Bingham.

arrest or detention).[400] As Lord Brown stated, the 'question here is not the power of the executive but rather the integrity of the judicial process'.[401] He also suggested that if the ruling impeded the executive in its vitally important task of safeguarding the country so far as possible against terrorism, it did so only to a very limited extent.[402] But to whatever extent it did limit the executive, this was required by the rule of law.[403]

Re A (Foreign Torture Evidence) is another seminal decision that sends out the important message that the integrity of the judicial process will not be compromised in the war on terror.[404] As noted, their Lordships' opinions were strongly located in the common law principles and the rule of law, supported by human rights considerations.

XVI. THE PROTECTION OF NATIONALS AND RESIDENTS SUBJECT TO ANTI-TERRORIST MEASURES ABROAD

Two leading cases have raised the issue of the obligations on the government to protect nationals or non-nationals when they are abroad and subjected to anti-terrorist measures. The protection of nationals is a classic aspect of the prerogative powers relating to foreign affairs, and the UK courts have traditionally been cautious in exercising any degree of judicial supervision over them.[405]

A. The Protection of UK Nationals Detained at Guantanamo Bay

In *R on the Application of Abbasi & Anor v Secretary of State for Foreign and Commonwealth Affairs & Secretary of State for the Home Department*[406] it was submitted that Abbasi, a British national detained by the United States in

---

[400] *Ibid* eg at paras 70–75, per Lord Nicholls, at para 93, per Lord Hoffmann; at para 131, per Lord Rodger; at para 149, per Lord Carswell; and at paras 161–2, 169, per Lord Brown.

[401] *Ibid* at para 164, per Lord Brown.

[402] *Ibid* at para 166.

[403] *Ibid* at para 167.

[404] See S Shah, 'The UK's Anti-Terror Legislation and the House of Lords: The Battle Continues' (2006) 6(2) *Human Rights Law Review* 416–34. On the use of torture in the war on terror see A Linklater, 'Torture and Civilisation' (2006) 21 *International Relations* 111–18. See also the important Court of Appeal decision blocking deportation of foreign nationals to jurisdictions where there was a real risk that evidence derived from torture would be used in their trials, *Othman (Jordan) v Secretary of State for the Home Department* [2008] EWCA Civ 290 (9 April 2008), discussed in Section XVII.D below.

[405] See *Council for Civil Service Unions v Minister for the Civil Service* [1985] AC 374 (national security was *par excellence* a non-justiciable issue); *Secretary of State for Foreign and Commonwealth Affairs v Everett* [1989] 1 QB 811.

[406] [2002] EWCA Civ 1598, [2003] UKHRR 76. See R O'Keefe, 'Decisions of British Courts During 2002' (2002) 73 *British Yearbook of International Law* 414–28; C Kilroy, Case comment, [2003] *European Human Rights Law Review* 222–9.

Guantanamo Bay, was subject to a violation by the United States of one of his fundamental human rights and that, in those circumstances, the Foreign Secretary owed him a duty under English public law to take positive steps to redress the position, or at least to give a reasoned response to his request for assistance. It was accepted that no legal precedent established such a duty, but it was submitted that the increased regard paid to human rights in both international and domestic law required that such a duty should be recognised.[407] The Foreign Secretary's argument was that when faced with a request for assistance, Foreign and Commonwealth Ministers and Her Majesty's diplomatic and consular officers had to make an informed and considered judgement about the most appropriate way in which the interests of the British national may be protected, including the nature, manner and timing of any diplomatic representations to the country concerned. In particular,

> [a]ssessments of when and how to press another State require very fine judgements to be made, based on experience and detailed information gathered in the course of diplomatic business. In cases where a person is detained in connection with international terrorism, these judgements become particularly complex.[408]

The Secretary of State submitted that the authorities clearly established two principles that posed insuperable barriers to the relief claimed: (1) the English court would not examine the legitimacy of action taken by a foreign sovereign state; (2) the English court would not adjudicate upon actions taken by the executive in the conduct of foreign relations.[409] The court found that it was not possible to approach the claim for judicial review other than on the basis that, 'in apparent contravention of fundamental principles recognised by both jurisdictions and by international law, Mr Abbasi is at present arbitrarily detained in a "legal black-hole"'.[410] It was 'objectionable' that Mr Abbasi had no opportunity to challenge the legitimacy of his detention before any court or tribunal.[411] The facts of the case brought it within the class of exceptional cases where the court was willing make a judgment on the legality of the actions of a foreign state.

For the court there were three considerations which led it to reject the proposition that there is no scope for judicial review of a refusal to render diplomatic assistance to a British subject who was suffering violation of a

---

[407] *Abbasi* at para 25.
[408] *Ibid* at para 7.
[409] *Ibid* at para 26.
[410] *Ibid* at para 64.
[411] *Ibid* at para 66. On this point see *Rasul v Bush*, 542 US 466 (2004) (US courts have jurisdiction to consider challenges to the legality of the detention of foreign nationals captured abroad in connection with hostilities and incarcerated at Guantanamo Bay).

fundamental human right as a result of the conduct of the authorities of a foreign state.[412] The first consideration was the development of the law of judicial review in relation (i) to the doctrine of legitimate expectation and (ii) to the invasion of areas previously immune from review, such as the exercise of the prerogative. The issue of justiciability depended not on general principle, but on subject matter and suitability in the particular case. Second, to a degree, the Foreign and Commonwealth Office had promulgated a policy which was capable of giving rise to a legitimate expectation. The policy was that where there was evidence of miscarriage or denial of justice the 'UK Government would ... consider making direct representations to third governments on behalf of British citizens where [it believed] that they were in breach of their international obligations'.[413], in the light of the policy it must be a 'normal expectation of every citizen' that, if subjected abroad to a violation of a fundamental right, the British government would not simply wash their hands of the matter and abandon them to their fate.[414]

The court stressed that the British nationals' expectation was of a very limited nature. Where certain criteria were satisfied, the government would 'consider' making representations.[415] Whether to make any representations in a particular case, and if so in what form, was left entirely to the discretion of the Secretary of State. The Secretary of State must be free to give full weight to foreign policy considerations, which were not justiciable. Even where there had been a gross miscarriage of justice, there might be overriding reasons of foreign policy which may lead the Secretary of State to decline to intervene.[416] Foreign policy remained a 'forbidden area'.[417] However, that did not mean the whole process was immune from judicial scrutiny. The citizen's legitimate expectation was that his request would be 'considered', and that in that consideration all relevant factors would be thrown into the balance.[418] The court even went so far as to try and pinpoint a case where judicial review would lie in relation to diplomatic protection, namely,

> if the Foreign and Commonwealth Office were, contrary to its stated practice, to refuse even to consider whether to make diplomatic representations on behalf of a subject whose fundamental rights were being violated. In such,

---

[412] *Ibid* at para 80.
[413] *Ibid* at para 90.
[414] *Ibid* at para 98.
[415] *Ibid* at para 92.
[416] *Ibid* at para 100.
[417] *Ibid* at para 106.
[418] *Ibid* at para 99.

unlikely, circumstances we consider that it would be appropriate for the court to make a mandatory order to the Foreign Secretary to give due consideration to the applicant's case.[419]

The court would not go beyond this and make general propositions:

> In some cases it might be reasonable to expect the Secretary of State to state the result of considering a request for assistance, in others it might not. In some cases he might be expected to give reasons for his decision, in others he might not. In some cases such reasons might be open to attack, in others they would not.[420]

On the facts the court held that Abbasi was not entitled to relief.[421] First, the Foreign and Commonwealth Office had considered his request for assistance. The British detainees were the subject of discussions between the United Kingdom and the United States, both at Secretary of State and lower official levels. Abbasi could not reasonably have expected more than this. If the Foreign and Commonwealth Office were to make any statement as to its view of the legality of the detention of the British prisoners, or any statement as to the nature of discussions held with US officials, this might well undermine those discussions. Second, on no view would it be appropriate to order the Secretary of State to make any specific representations to the United States, even in the face of what appeared to be a clear breach of a fundamental human right, as it was obvious that this would have an impact on the conduct of foreign policy, and an impact on such policy at a particularly delicate time. Third, the position of detainees at Guantanamo Bay was to be considered further by the appellate courts in the United States. Fourth, the Inter-American Commission on Human Rights had taken up the case of the detainees and it was unclear what the result of the Commission's intervention would be.

What is particularly interesting about *Abbasi* was the length to which the court went to find a sliver of scope for justiciability to operate in an area which traditionally the courts had considered non-justiciable.[422] To even countenance a mandatory order against a Foreign Secretary is quite a step forward to take.

---

[419] *Ibid* at para 104.
[420] *Ibid* at para 105.
[421] *Ibid* at para 107.
[422] It rejected an enforceable duty to protect the citizen based on international law or on the ECHR, as incorporated by the HRA: *ibid* at 106. On *Abbasi*, see also S Palmer, 'Arbitrary Detention in Guantanamo Bay: Legal Limbo in the Land of the Free' (2003) 62 *Cambridge Law Journal* 6–9; S Wilkinson, 'Focus on Article 1 [ECHR]' (2004) 9 *Judicial Review* 243–9.

B. The Protection of UK Residents (Non-nationals) Detained at Guantanamo Bay

If the decision in *Abbasi* was interesting in terms of judicial scrutiny the detailed consideration in the High Court and the Court of Appeal is even more striking in *R. (on the application of Al Rawi and others) v Secretary of State for Foreign and Commonwealth Affairs*.[423] This case concerned the position of three individuals detained at Guantanamo Bay who were long-term residents in the United Kingdom, but not British nationals.

The detainees claimed that in addition to the underlying arbitrary nature of the detention, which in itself breached their fundamental human rights, the conditions of detention amounted to breaches of the Convention on Torture, and Article 3 of the ECHR, or at the very least gave rise to a real risk of their being exposed to such breaches.[424] Their first claim was that their connection with the United Kingdom was such that they had a legitimate expectation that the British government would make a formal and unequivocal request for their return to that country, in the same way as it did in relation to British nationals, who were returned after such requests in March 2004 and January 2005. The second and third applicants were refugees and it was argued that refugees should be afforded diplomatic protection by the state that has accepted that status. The government response was that the United Kingdom had no right to give consular protection to any of these claimants because they were not British nationals. The United Kingdom might make (and indeed had actually made) representations on human rights or humanitarian grounds but these would be directed towards encouraging the third state to bring its actions into conformity with international law. It would not, in the exercise of consular assistance or diplomatic protection, make a formal request for their return to the United Kingdom. Given the limited decision in *Abbasi* it might be thought that the application would be given short shrift. Yet when the case reached the Court of Appeal, that Court asked itself the question: What has been the engine of so painstaking a review in an area which in recent years was thought barely apt for judicial review at all?[425] answer was that it was the 'legal and ethical muscle of human rights and refugee status'.[426]

The High Court dismissed Al-Rawi's claim:

> the first defendant was entitled to conclude that it had no duty either in domestic or international law to accord the same rights to the three claimants

[423] [2006] EWHC 972, [2006] HRLR 30.
[424] *Ibid* at para 27.
[425] *R. (on the application of Al Rawi and others) v Secretary of State for Foreign and Commonwealth Affairs* [2006] EWCA 1279 at para 3.
[426] *Ibid* at para 4.

as non-nationals as to nationals such as Mr Abbasi. As we have said, the fact that that position may change, at least in relation to those who have refugee status in the future, does not affect that position. The first defendant has a discretion as to whether, and if so, how to make representations on behalf of these claimants but against the background that they do not have the same claim as nationals to any international law right of the State to make the representations on their behalf.[427]

The second line of argument for the applicants was that the

first defendant is under a duty to make representations in relation to the detained claimants because the evidence establishes that they have either been tortured, or are at risk of torture. This, it is said, imposes a positive obligation on the UK Government to take such steps as it can to forestall the risk of torture, and the appropriate step is to make a formal request for the claimants' return.[428]

This claim was also rejected:

Even if, therefore, torture or a real risk of torture were established on the evidence, that would impose no duty on the United Kingdom Government to do other than cooperate with other States to bring to an end through lawful means the circumstances giving rise to that situation. International law imposes no further duty on an individual State to intervene. The European Convention on Human Rights does not assist the claimants in this respect. The present predicament of the claimants is not under the control or authority of the United Kingdom. In our judgment the question which arises in relation to the allegations of torture or risk of torture is whether the first defendant's evaluation of the facts is a justifiable basis for his conclusion that the circumstances do not require him to exercise any discretion he may have to make requests or representations beyond those that have been and are already being made in relation to these claimants, and Guantanamo Bay generally.[429]

The court rejected a claim that the refusal to afford protection constituted racial discrimination because the difference in status was recognised in international law.[430] Finally, the court considered claims made by the family members of the detainees that the attitude and inaction of the UK government had subjected those family members to inhuman or degrading treatment, contrary to Article 3 ECHR, and amounted to an interference with the claimants' rights to respect for their private and family life under Article 8 ECHR, and was discriminatory, in breach of Article 14 ECHR. The Article 3 claim was rejected because there was no wrongful action of the United Kingdom that caused distress. The United Kingdom

---

[427] *Al Rawi and others v Secretary of State for Foreign and Commonwealth Affairs* [2006] EWHC 972, [2006] HRLR 30 at para 65.
[428] *Ibid* at para 67.
[429] *Ibid* at para 70.
[430] *Ibid* at para 72.

was not responsible for the claimants' continued detention in Guantanamo Bay.[431] There were similar causation problems in relation to the Article 8 claims as, on the evidence, any request for the detainees' return would probably not have been acceded to. Finally, in relation to whether the United Kingdom could justify the difference in treatment for Article 14 purposes, the court clearly had some sympathy for the 'powerful submissions' of the claimants and critically described the attitude of the Foreign Secretary as displaying 'undue, if not, supine, deference to the assurances given by the United States authorities, particularly bearing in mind the way the United States Authorities seek to confine the definition of torture'.[432] However, after emphasising that decisions affecting foreign policy was a context in which the courts had consistently trod cautiously,[433] it concluded that:

> whatever view the court were to take as to the stance so far taken by the first defendant, it could not require the first defendant to make a formal request. That would be an interference in the relationship between sovereign states which could only be justified if a clear duty in domestic or international law had been identified; for the reasons that we have already given, there is no such duty in the present case.[434]

The court accepted that the real problem was the UK's judgement that any formal request for the applicant's return as claimed would be ineffective and counterproductive. The court considered that: 'Prima facie these are judgments which are quintessentially judgments taken in the context of a foreign policy decision which the court simply does not have the tools to evaluate.'[435] Even then, however, the court put down a marker that the issue might be revisited in time and in certain circumstances:

---

[431]   *Ibid* at para 83. See A Frean, 'Wife Takes Guantanamo Detainee Battle To Court' *The Times* (UK), 16 June 2006.

[432]   *Ibid* at para 87, b.

[433]   Citing *Abbasi* and the decision in *R v Jones v Saudi Arabia* [2006] UKHL 16, [2006] 2 WLR 1424, upholding a claim for state immunity in the face of allegations of torture. See also *R v Jones (Margaret)* [2006] UKHL 16, [2006] 2 WLR 772, [2006] 2 All ER 741 (the crime against peace (or crime of aggression) was not capable of being a 'crime' within the meaning of s 3 of the Criminal Law Act 1967 or an 'offence' within the meaning of s 68(2) of the Criminal Justice and Public Order Act 1994, so there was no legal justification for what the defendants had allegedly done. There were no compelling reasons in the instant case for departing from the democratic principle that it was for Parliament, not the executive or judiciary, to determine what types of conduct attracted criminal penalties. The court would be very slow to review the exercise of prerogative powers in relation to the conduct of foreign affairs and the deployment of the armed services, and slow to adjudicate on rights arising out of transactions entered into between sovereign states on the plane of international law. The discretionary nature or non-justiciability of the power to wage war was one of the reasons why aggression was not a crime in domestic law).

[434]   *Al Rawi* at para 90.

[435]   *Ibid* at para 92.

We would, however, be prepared to interfere in order to require reconsideration of the decision if we thought that those views might have been affected by an approach to the question of status which manifestly failed to take into account the present proposals for assimilation of refugee status with that of nationals; and we would also be prepared to interfere to require reconsideration if the decision had been based upon a wholly unrealistic approach to the conditions of detainees in Guantanamo Bay.[436]

The court expressly acknowledged that the failure of the claims was perhaps uncomfortable and unsatisfactory.[437] The application ultimately failed because the court accepted that the United Kingdom had made it abundantly plain that it wished the Guantanamo Bay facility to close. It was in continuous dialogue with the US authorities with a view to securing a solution to the problems presented by Guantanamo Bay, which included the allegations of breaches of human rights, including torture:

> Those discussions, whilst not specific to the three detained claimants, affect them. It is impossible for this court, without knowledge of how those discussions have progressed to make a judgment about the way in which they can best be progressed in order to achieve the aims of United Kingdom foreign policy, which is clearly to secure closure of Guantanamo Bay.[438]

Subsequently it emerged that Bisher al Rawi had been accorded a separate status, and official calls had been made for his release, apparently because of his reported links to the intelligence services.[439] Indeed, by the time of the Court of Appeal hearing the Foreign Secretary had made a request for his release but this was expressly stated not to be on consular grounds or on humanitarian grounds. However, he was not released at that time because the United Kingdom could not provide the United States with the required assurances as to security arrangements in relation to him.[440] He was eventually released in March 2007 and returned to the United Kingdom.

In a letter published by *The Times* (UK) on 18 September 2006, 120 signatories from the medical profession called for an independent investigation to determine the medical needs of the detainees at Guantanamo, and criticised the 'shameful' refusal of the Foreign and Commonwealth Office to respond to a request by the British Medical Association to send

---

[436] *Ibid* at para 93.

[437] *Ibid* at para 96.

[438] *Ibid*. See also Lord Falconer of Thoroton, 'Finding the Balance Between Security and Liberty in the Modern World', 3 October 2006, <http://www.dca.gov.uk/speeches>.

[439] D Rose and R Beeston, 'Doctors demand an end to British "collusion" over Guantanamo Bay' *The Times* (UK), 18 September 2006.

[440] The United Kingdom considered that measures under non-derogating control orders would be insufficient to satisfy the United States.

a team of doctors to Cuba. It described the refusal to act for British residents, rather than just British citizens, as morally repugnant.

The Court of Appeal rejected the appeal.[441], the UK policy did not violate the Race Relations Act 1976. A person who was not a British national was not entitled to the protection of a state-to-state claim made by the Foreign Secretary. That was not an attribute of the non-British national. It was not a function of how he was likely to behave. It was simply a legal fact. The national and the non-national were in materially different cases one from the other for the purpose of the exercise of the right of diplomatic protection by means of state-to-state claims. Such a difference ought only to be disregarded if it assumed or implied a process of racial stereotyping, but it did not. The difference was therefore a proper and legitimate basis of distinction for the purposes of the Race Relations Act 1976. The non-nationals have been treated differently from the nationals not because of their race (nationality) but because one group was entitled to diplomatic protection and the other was not.[442] No different result could be arrived at for the purposes of Article 14 ECHR.[443] Second, there was no basis for a legitimate expectation equivalent to that enjoyed by nationals.[444] Third, as for the family claimants, there was no ECHR right that gave rise to an obligation on states parties to ensure that non-states parties (the United States in this case) respected the rights in the ECHR or in other international law treaties.[445] Fourth, it rejected the argument that it should discern an emerging principle of customary international law by which the status of refugees would be assimilated with that of nationals in the context of diplomatic protection, and that the first respondent should have recognised its force in deciding what, if any, action to take in relation to the detainee claimants.[446] The principle was at best proposed as a future law, and the United States had considered the proposals objectionable. In any event the point did not really confront the Foreign Secretary's central factual position, namely that any formal representations to the United States on behalf of the detainee claimants would be ineffective and counterproductive.[447] Fifth, the appellants' submissions in relation to material consideration under the *Wednesbury* case fell foul of two principles: (1) they invited the court

---

[441] *R. (on the application of Al Rawi and others) v Secretary of State for Foreign and Commonwealth Affairs* [2006] EWCA 1279.

[442] *Ibid* at para 78.

[443] *Ibid* at para 84.

[444] *Ibid* at paras 88–90.

[445] *Ibid* at paras 91–114.

[446] *Ibid* at paras 115–120.

[447] *Ibid* at para 120. The Court of Appeal considered that any possible violation of Art 16 of the Refugee Convention by the US carried 'no consequence that the Foreign Secretary should make representations of the kind sought by the appellants' (para 125).

to enter into what in *Abbasi* was described as a 'forbidden area', that is, the conduct of foreign relations; (2) what was and what was not a relevant consideration for a public decision-maker to have in mind was (absent a statutory code of compulsory considerations) for the decision-maker, not the court, to decide.[448] As for the latter point, it stressed that the court was a judge of the legality of the government's action. To think that it was making a judgment on the wisdom of the government's action was an elementary mistake.[449] In the area of the government's responsibility to make decisions touching the conduct of foreign relations, the class of factors which were neither compulsory nor forbidden, but which it is open to the decision-maker to treat as relevant or not, had to be particularly wide. The appellants' position had wholly failed to confront that dimension in the case. The claims of fundamental human rights and refugee status had not transformed the 'constitutional nature of judicial review of the government's conduct of foreign relations'.[450]

Having dismissed the appeal for all of these reasons, the Court of Appeal commented on what it described as 'two connected, overarching issues. (1) How does the law approach the balance of individual claims of right with the general public interest in a context as acute as this? (2) How big is the court's role as decision-maker?'[451] The Court of Appeal referred to the search for a 'principled means' of disentangling the functions of the executive and the judiciary:

> The reach of the executive's role has sometimes been described by reference to the 'deference' accorded to it by the courts, though the term was somewhat disapproved by Lord Hoffmann in *R (ProLife) v BBC* [2004] 1 AC 185 at paragraph 75. He said, 'In a society based upon the rule of law and the separation of powers, it is necessary to decide which branch of government has in any particular instance the decision-making power and what the legal limits of that power are. That is a question of law and must therefore be decided by the courts.'[452]

For the Court of Appeal the difficulty in deciding this question of law arose from the fact that, particularly since the HRA

> our conception of the rule of law has been increasingly substantive rather than merely formal or procedural. Thus the rule of law requires not only that a public decision should be authorised by the words of the enabling statute, but also that it be reasonable and (generally in human rights cases) proportionate to a legitimate aim. But reasonableness and proportionality are not formal legal

---

[448] *Ibid* at paras 131–41. See *Associated Provincial Picture Houses v. Wednesbury Corporation* [1948] 1 KB 223.
[449] *Ibid* at para 137.
[450] *Ibid* at para 140.
[451] *Ibid* at para 144.
[452] *Ibid* at para 146.

standards. They are substantive virtues, upon which, it may be thought, lawyers do not have the only voice: nor necessarily the wisest. Accordingly the ascertainment of the weight to be given to the primary decision-maker's view (very often that of central government) can be elusive and problematic.[453]

As for the issues in *Al Rawi* the Court of Appeal approached them on the basis that:

> The courts have a special responsibility in the field of human rights. It arises in part from the impetus of the HRA, in part from the common law's jealousy in seeing that intrusive State power is always strictly justified. The elected government has a special responsibility in what may be called strategic fields of policy, such as the conduct of foreign relations and matters of national security. It arises in part from considerations of competence, in part from the constitutional imperative of electoral accountability.[454]

In support of this approach it cited Lord Hoffmann's view in *Rehman* on the need for democratic legitimacy.[455] The Court of Appeal's concluding comment was that:

> This case has involved issues touching both the government's conduct of foreign relations, and national security: pre-eminently the former. In those areas the common law assigns the duty of decision upon the merits to the elected arm of government; all the more so if they combine in the same case. This is the law for constitutional as well as pragmatic reasons, as Lord Hoffmann has explained. The court's role is to see that the government strictly complies with all formal requirements, and rationally considers the matters it has to confront. Here, because of the subject-matter, the law accords to the executive an especially broad margin of discretion ... it is the court's duty to decide where lies the legal edge between the executive and judicial functions.[456]

XVII. ANTI-TERRORISM STRATEGY – THE POLICY OPTIONS

The United Kingdom's anti-terrorism policies are complex and interrelated. As the challenge faced evolves, particular policies have likewise evolved in the face of political and legal challenges. In 2007 the UK government announced proposals for new counterterrorism legislation, and a Counterterrorism Bill was published in 2008.[457] It is helpful to

---

[453] *Ibid.*

[454] *Ibid* at para 147.

[455] [2001] UKHL 47, [2003] 1 AC 153 at para 62.

[456] *Al Rawi* (CA) at para 148.

[457] The Secretary of State for the Home Department, 'Statement on counter-terrorism', *Hansard*, HC, vol 461, cols 421–3 (7 June 2007); Prime Minister, 'Statement on National Security', *Hansard*, HC, vol 463, cols 841–5 (25 July 2007); Queen's Speech, 6 November 2007.

outline the major policies and proposals and how they interrelate. None is cost-free in human rights terms.[458]

A. More Prosecutions

This is the government's preferred strategy. More lower-level terrorist-related offences have been created[459] and prosecuted.[460] The strategy is supported by the JCHR and some human rights organisations, for example Liberty. The UK police arrest statistics for offences of terrorism (excluding Northern Ireland) from 11 September 2001 to 31 March 2007 showed that 1,228 arrests were made: 1,165 arrests under the TA 2000 and 63 under legislation other than the TA 2000, where the investigation was conducted as a terrorist investigation.[461]

The charging threshold has effectively been lowered for terrorism and other serious cases by the introduction of a 'threshold test' for charging by the Crown Prosecution Service (CPS). Instead of requiring prosecutors to be satisfied that there is a realistic prospect of conviction before charging a suspect, the threshold test enables Crown prosecutors to charge a suspect where there is only a reasonable suspicion that the suspect has committed an offence, provided there is a reasonable likelihood of relevant evidence becoming available within a reasonable time which will enable the higher charging threshold to be applied. In 2008 the JCHR recommended that the threshold test for charging in terrorism cases be put on an explicit statutory footing; that there should be an explicit requirement that the CPS inform both the suspect and the court when the suspect has been charged on the basis of the threshold test; and that the timetable for the receipt of the additional evidence be set by the court, not the prosecutor.[462]

---

[458] The financial costs have also grown massively. By 2008, the UK government's annual spending on counter-terrorism, intelligence and resilience will reach £2.25bn, which is double what it was prior to 11 September 2001.

[459] Offences include committing acts preparatory to terrorism, possessing material for a terrorist purpose, being a member of a terrorist organisation, funding terrorism, attending a terror training camp, and inciting terrorism. See PTA 2005 and TA 2006 (notably the offence of encouragement of terrorism).

[460] 'During the debates on renewal four options were put forward by the opposition parties for increasing the number of successful prosecutions of suspected terrorists: introduction of the so-called "threshold test"; making greater use of plea-bargaining so that "supergrasses" may give evidence; the use of intercept as evidence; and extending the use of post-charge questioning. Two of these measures are already in place (plea-bargaining and the "threshold test")': *Government Response to JCHR's Eighth Report*, n 207 above at 6.

[461] See <http://www.homeoffice.gov.uk/security/terrorism-and-the-law>.

[462] JCHR, Ninth Report of Session 2007–08, n 253 above at para 4.

B. Use of Intercepted Intelligence in Courts

To obtain more convictions, one strategy would be the use of intercepted intelligence information in courts, particularly information derived from the tapping of phones. To date the government has not been entirely convinced. Under current legislation, the Regulation of Investigatory Powers Act 2000 (the RIPA), there is a statutory ban on the use of intercept as evidence.[463] The government's position has been that it would change the law to permit intercept evidence only if the necessary safeguards could be put in place to protect sensitive techniques and to ensure that the potential benefits outweigh the risks. A comprehensive review of intercept as evidence was conducted in 2003/04 following a request from the Prime Minister in 2003. Following the review's completion in 2004, the government concluded that it was not the right time to change the law and that the impact of new technology needed to be properly considered and factored into the decision-making process. The then Attorney-General, Lord Goldsmith, indicated that he favoured allowing intercept evidence to be used in court.[464] So has a former Head of MI5.[465] For its report, *Counter-terrorism Policy and Human Rights: 28 days, intercept and post-charge questioning*, the JCHR heard substantial evidence on the arguments for using intercept intelligence.[466] It welcomed in principle the government's review of the use of intercept as evidence. It remained convinced that the ability to use it would help bring more prosecutions against terrorists. It made recommendations on implementation and considered that the law of public interest immunity would protect the public interest in non-disclosure.[467] The government established an independent and cross-party Privy Council review into the use of this evidence in terrorist trials. It was cautious about such proposals and it instructed the Council to consider the exposure of interception capabilities and techniques.[468] The *Privy Council Review of intercept as evidence: Report to the Prime Minister and the Home Secretary* (the Chilcot Report), published in 2008, favoured the possibility of use but

---

[463]   The prohibition on the use of intercept material does not apply in the SIAC.

[464]   'Goldsmith for phone-tap evidence', 21 September 2006, <www.bbc.co.uk>.

[465]   See E Manningham-Buller, 'The International Terrorist Threat and the Dilemmas in Countering It' The Hague, 1 September 2005 <http://www.mi5.gov.uk/output/Page387.html>

[466]   JCHR, n 101 above at Ev 1–9. Among those who gave evidence was Sir Swinton Thomas, who has recently retired from his role as the Interception of Communications Commissioner. He believed that a change in the law was undesirable.

[467]   *Ibid* at paras 99–155.

[468]   See F Elliot, P Webster and R Ford, 'Wire-tap Evidence Will Alert Terrorists to Secret Methods, Minister Fears', *The Times* (UK), 5 November 2007.

with the security services having a veto.[469] The Report suggested nine tests to be passed before any such evidence would be admitted in a court. Any change will necessarily give rise to very difficult issues of disclosure.

C. Longer Pre-trial Detention and Post-charge Questioning

On 25 July 2007, the Prime Minister announced new anti-terrorism measures, including proposals to extend the maximum limit for pre-trial detention to a possible 56 days (as discussed above, under the TA 2000 the current limit is 28 days). The human rights organisation Liberty was strongly opposed to this.[470] JCHR was not convinced of the need for it and recommended thorough scrutiny of the evidence, stronger judicial safeguards and improved parliamentary oversight. It found a lack of direct evidence of necessity. The evidence was at best precautionary.[471] The JCHR considered that any extension to pre-charge detention was a serious interference with liberty that required a compelling, evidence-based case. It did not accept that the government had made such a case for extending pre-charge detention beyond the current limit of 28 days.[472] It also considered that there should be an upper limit on pre-charge detention and that Parliament, not the courts, should decide that limit after considering all the evidence.[473]

The Counterterrorism Bill 2008 does not provide for a permanent, automatic or immediate extension to pre-charge detention beyond the current maximum limit of 28 days. It does provide for a higher limit but that would only become available if there was a clear and exceptional operational need, supported by the police and the CPS, and approved by the Home Secretary. Second, even if brought into force, the higher limit could only remain available for a strictly limited period of time – up to 60 days, with no possibility of renewal. The bringing into force of the availability of the extended period would be subject to parliamentary

---

[469] Cm 7324 (4 February 2008), < http://www.official-documents.gov.uk/document/cm73/7324/7324.asp?>

[470] See 'Extending Pre-Charge Detention For Terror Suspects', <http://www.liberty-human-rights.org.uk/issues/2-terrorism/extension-of-pre-charge-detention/index.shtml>. It argued, inter alia, that emergency measures in the Civil Contingencies Act 2004 could be triggered in a genuine emergency in which the police are overwhelmed by multiple terror plots, allowing the government to temporarily extend pre-charge detention subject to parliamentary and judicial oversight. This was preferable to creating a permanent state of emergence by re-introducing internment. The 2004 Act contains a broad power to make emergency regulations subject to parliamentary and judicial oversight, including a power to extend pre-charge detention periods for up to 30 days at a time.

[471] JCHR, Nineteenth Report of Session 2006–07, n 101 above at para 51.

[472] JCHR, *Counter-Terrorism Policy and Human Rights: 42 days*, Second Report of Session 2007–08, HL 23/HC 156, 14 December 2007.

[473] *Ibid* at paras 14–57.

approval by both Houses. This would have to happen within 30 days. Whether any individual was held under that power would be a decision for a senior judge, who could approve periods of up to seven days. Even in the exceptional circumstances that could trigger the new power becoming available, no one could be held for more than 42 days at most. The normal limit of 28 days would continue to be subject to annual renewal by Parliament.[474] After the government introduced a number of additional safeguards, the 42 day limit was approved by the House of Commons on 11 June 2008 by 315 votes to 306.[474a]

The Counterterrorism Bill 2008 also provides that terrorist suspects may be questioned after they have been charged.[475] The questioning will be limited to the offence for which the person has been charged, and adverse inferences from the silence of the suspect may be drawn by a court.[476] This would allow for a charge to be replaced with a more appropriate offence at a later stage. As we have noted, the context and purpose of detention are now understood differently.[477] The interviewing of suspects has become virtually irrelevant and arrests are used to disrupt conspiracies.

Finally, the 2008 Bill ensures that the police and intelligence services can make full use of DNA evidence and that convicted terrorists provide police with personal information when they are released from prison. Convicted terrorists can be banned from travelling overseas. The courts will be able to consider a terrorist connection as an aggravating factor when considering sentence This will enable the courts to impose longer sentences for credit frauds or possessing false documents when there is evidence that the offences are linked to terrorism.[478]

---

[474] The JCHR has maintained its criticisms of the proposals on pre-trial detention: JCHR, Ninth Report of Session 2007–08, n 253 above at paras 10–21.

[474a] See Hansard, HC, Vol. 477, cols. 312–423. The JCHR had continued its opposition, see JCHR, *Counter-Terrorism Policy and Human Rights* (Tenth Report): *Counter-Terrorism Bill*, Twentieth Report, Session 2007–08, 14 May 2008, HL 108/HC 554; *Counter-Terrorism Policy and Human Rights*, (Eleventh Report): *42 Days and Public Emergencies*, Twenty-first Report, Session 2007–08, 5 June 2008 HL 116/HC 635.

[475] The JCHR has recommended amendments on the face of the Bill to include important safeguards against the power being used oppressively: *ibid*, paras 22–8. For criticism of the original proposals see F Gibb, 'Extra detention of terror suspects is compared to apartheid era', *The Times* (UK), 5 November 2007 (referring to speech at Bar Council by Sir Sydney Kentridge).

[476] JCHR, Nineteenth Report of Session 2006–07, n 101 above at paras 156–75 for discussion of the proposals.

[477] See Section XIII.E above.

[478] R Ford, 'Home Office relief over control orders, but other measures are in pipeline', *The Times* (UK), 31 October 2007.

D. Deportations

The government's preferred policy is to deport foreign nationals who are a security risk (of course, this strategy is not open to application with respect to UK nationals).[479] In some cases ECHR jurisprudence prevents this. One UK strategy has been to support an attempt to revise rather than reverse the ECHR jurisprudence stemming from the *Chahal* case.[480] The second has been to seek to deport on bases of memorandums of understanding (MOUs) or assurances from the foreign governments concerned, for example Libya and Algeria. The argument is that the assurances reduce the real risk of a violation of Article 3 ECHR or a flagrant violation of another Convention Article.[481] The argument has been accepted by the courts in principle.[482] Argument is now focused on the quality of the assurances.[483] The effectiveness of assurances is a question of fact to be decided by the SIAC.[484] The Court of Appeal can only deal with errors of law[485] but satisfying the ECHR standards has proved to be very challenging for the government. In *AS & DD (Libya) v Secretary of State for the Home Department & Anor*[486] the Court of Appeal

---

[479] On allegations of irregular renditions, see Report of the UK Intelligence and Security Committee, *Rendition*, Cm 7171, July 2007, p 67, concluding that there was no evidence that US rendition flights had used UK airspace (other than two 'Rendition to Justice' cases in 1998 which were approved by the UK government following US requests) and no evidence of such flights having landed at UK military airfields.

[480] *Chahal v United Kingdom* (1996) 23 EHRR 413.

[481] In *Othman (Jordan) v Secretary of State for the Home Department* [2008] EWCA Civ 290 (09 April 2008) the alleged risk of violations related to Arts 3, 5 and 6 ECHR. These were rejected by the SIAC but violation of one aspect of Art 6 was accepted by the Court of Appeal.

[482] *Omar Othman (aka Abu Qatada) v Secretary of State for the Home Department* [2007] UKSIAC 15/2005 (26 February 2007) (the memorandum of understanding (MOU) with Jordan would reduce the risk sufficiently for removal of the appellant not to breach the UK's obligations (para 516)). Affirmed by the Court of Appeal in *MT (Algeria), RB (Algeria) v Secretary of State for the Home Department* [2007] EWCA Civ 808, [2007] UKHRR 1267, and *Othman (Jordan) v Secretary of State for the Home Department* [2008] EWCA Civ 290 (09 April 2008) at paras 6–8.

[483] See eg *BB v Secretary of State for the Home Department* [2006] UKSIAC 39/2005 (05 December 2006); *Y v Secretary of State for the Home Department* [2006] UKSIAC 36/2004 (24 August 2006); *DD & Anor v Secretary of State for the Home Department* [2007] UKSIAC 42/2005 (27 April 2007) (MOU not sufficient to remove a real risk in light of the governmental system in Libya). Four Algerian citizens withdrew their appeals to the SIAC and were deported to Algeria: see the discussion in *U v Secretary of State for the Home Department* [2007] UKSIAC 32/2005 (14 May 2007).

[484] *MT (Algeria), RB (Algeria) v Secretary of State for the Home Department* [2007] EWCA Civ 808, [2007] UKHRR 1267.

[485] On the proper approach to appeals from such specialist tribunals see *AH (Sudan) v SSHD* [2007] EWHL 49, [2007] 3 WLR 832, especially per Baroness Hale at para 30.

[486] [2008] EWCA Civ 289 (9 April 2008).

could find no errors of law in the SIAC's decision that a MOU with Libya was not sufficient to remove a real risk of rights violations in light of the governmental system in Libya.

In *Othman (Jordan) v Secretary of State for the Home Department*[487] the Court of Appeal held that it was not open to the SIAC to conclude that the deportation of Mr Othman to Jordan would not breach his rights under the ECHR. The SIAC had understated or misunderstood the fundamental nature in Convention law of the prohibition against the use of evidence obtained by torture. Once the SIAC had found as a fact that there was a high probability that evidence that may very well have been obtained by torture or in respect of which there was a very real risk that it had been obtained by torture or other conduct breaching Article 3 would be admitted at the trial of Mr Othman, then the SIAC had to be satisfied that such evidence would be excluded or not acted on. The SIAC had erred in approaching the question of evidence obtained by torture as just one element in the overall issue of whether the trial as a whole would be fair; rather than as a separate question that raised fundamental Convention issues reaching beyond the boundaries of Article 6. The grounds relied on by the SIAC for not finding a threatened breach of Article 6 in that respect were insufficient.[488] The SIAC had made additional errors of law. It was wrong, in assessing the rules as to the admissibility of evidence in a foreign case, to give weight to the principle that admissibility is a matter for the domestic legal system. The effect of the speeches in the House of Lords in *A and others (No 2)* was wrongly stated, with the result that the SIAC wrongly relied on that case for support for its conclusions. Finally, the SIAC wrongly allowed itself to be influenced by the potential for derogation on the part of a signatory state.[489] Therefore the SIAC's decision dismissing Othman's appeal against that deportation order was quashed. The decision in *Othman* gives strong support to the fundamental status of the prohibition of the use of evidence obtained by torture.[490] Othman, otherwise known as Abu Qatada, was once described by a Spanish judge as Osama bin Laden's Right-hand man in Europe. In May 2008 he was granted bail by SIAC subject to stringent conditions.

E. Derogation from Article 5 of the ECHR/Denunciation of the ECHR

The possibility of this has been raised by the government. In March 2007 the relevant Minister's statement on control orders stated that: 'We will

---

[487] [2008] EWCA Civ 290 (9 April 2008).
[488] *Ibid* at paras 45–6.
[489] *Ibid* at para 47.
[490] See Section XV above discussing *Re A (Foreign Torture Evidence)*.

consider other options – including derogation – if we have exhausted ways of overturning previous judgments on this issue.'[491] A nuclear option would be to denounce the ECHR. That might mean that the United Kingdom would have to withdraw from the Council of Europe and potentially even the European Union, as membership of the latter is predicated on membership of the Council of Europe and being a party to the ECHR.

XVIII. THE ATTACK ON HUMAN RIGHTS: UNDERMINING THE SEPARATION OF POWERS?

A. The Attack on Human Rights

Since 2000, there have been five major pieces of terrorist legislation enacted in the United Kingdom (with the new Act in 2008). There is now an extensive range of new offences and new powers in the United Kingdom.[492] These reflect the use of criminal law and the justice system as the executive's preferred option.[493] Although there have been over 12 terrorism-related arrests, over 430 charges and more than 220 convictions in the period from 11 September 2001 to 31 March 2007, attention tends to focus on the cases at the extreme of the legal system – powers of indefinite detention without trial, a system of special hearings before the SIAC which has greatly restricted powers and procedures, extensive powers of detention and for extended periods, and widely defined criminal offences. In a sustained critique, Amnesty International has accused the UK government of 'undermining the proper separation of powers between the judiciary and the executive'.[494] As we have seen, some of the legislative provisions have now been interpreted by the courts and tested for their compatibility with the ECHR.[495] Some have

---

[491] 'Update on control orders', Written ministerial statement by the Secretary of State for the Home Department, 22 March 2007.

[492] The exceptional powers have in some cases been normalised and extended to other areas of serious crime. Anti-terrorism measures also impact on other human rights, eg freedom of expression. See I Cram, 'Regulating the Media: Some Neglected Freedom of Expression Issues in the United Kingdom's Counter-Terrorism Strategy' (2006) 18 *Terrorism and Political Violence* 335–55.

[493] See also L Zedner, 'Securing Liberty in the Face of Terror: Reflections from Criminal Justice' (2005) 32(4) *Journal of Law and Society* 507–33. Liberty's view is that prosecution is the proper policy even it means the use of intercept evidence.

[494] Amnesty International, 'UK – Human Rights: A Broken Promise', 23 February 2006, <http://web.amnesty.org /library/Index/ENGEUR450042006?open&of=ENG-GBR>.

[495] On offences of possessing articles for terrorist purposes see *Zafar and Others v R* [2008] EWCA Crim 50. There have also been important decisions on the burden of proof in prosecutions under particular terrorist offences. See eg *Attorney General's Reference (No 4 of 2002)* [2004] UKHL 44; *Sheldrake v DPP* [2004] UKHL 43, [2005] 1 AC 264 (burden of proof in

passed but others have failed. Some of those decisions have been subjected to strongly adverse comments from senior members of the government.[496] Both the current Labour government and the main Conservative opposition have raised the prospect of reforming, if not repealing, the HRA to ensure that the legislative and executive assessments of national security are given greater weight than individual human rights. The former Prime Minister, Tony Blair, has argued that 'We must put safety before liberty' and that the nation must recognise that 'no greater civil liberty' exists than to 'live free from terrorist attack'.[497] He described a decision preventing the deportation of nine Afghan refugees who hijacked a plane to Britain was described as 'abuse of common sense'.[498] More generally he has submitted that there needed to be proper, considered intellectual and political debate about the nature of liberty in the modern world, from first principles and preferably unrelated to the immediate convulsion of the moment.[499] There needed to be a radical change in political and legal culture:

> This is not an argument about whether we respect civil liberties or not; but whose take priority. It is not about choosing hard line policies over an individual's human rights. It's about which human rights prevail. In making that decision, there is a balance to be struck. I am saying it is time to rebalance the decision in favour of the decent, law-abiding majority who play by the rules and think others should too … These questions are fundamental, difficult and immensely controversial. Unsurprisingly, there is a strong desire to escape their fundamental nature by taking refuge in simple explanations and remedies. One is repeal of the Human Rights Act. There are issues to do with the way the Act is interpreted and its case law, which we are examining. But let me be very clear. These problems existed long before the Human Rights Act. Every modern democracy has human rights legislation: and in any event the British

TA 2000, s 11); *R v DPP ex parte Kebilene and Others* [2000] 2 AC 326. See D Tausz and A Ashworth, Case comments, (2005) *Criminal Law Review* 215–20.

[496] See eg P Naughton, 'Clarke Stands Firm Over Terror Detainees After Ruling', *The Times* (UK), 16 December 2004; AS Travis, 'Anti-terror Critics Just Don't Get It, says Reid', *The Guardian* (UK), 10 August 2006 (accusing the government's anti-terror critics of putting national security at risk by their failure to recognise the serious nature of the threat facing Britain); N Temko and J Doward, 'Revealed: Blair Attack On Human Rights Law', *The Observer* (UK), 14 May 2006.

[497] Quotation taken from 'We must put safety before liberty, says Blair', *News Telegraph* (UK), 24 February 2005, <http://news.telegraph.co.uk/news/main.jhtml?xml=news/2005/02/24/nterr24.xml>, accessed 9 March 2005).

[498] R Ford, 'Afghan hijackers win asylum after six-year struggle', *The Times* (UK), 11 May 2006. Sullivan J had held that the Home Office had failed to follow correct legal procedures and had 'deliberately delayed' giving effect to rulings by an immigration adjudication panel: see *S & Ors; R (on the application of) v Secretary of State for the Home Department* [2006] EWHC 1111 (Admin) (10 May 2006).

[499] T Blair, UK Prime Minister, 'Our Nation's Future — Criminal Justice System', *The Times* (UK), 23 June 2006.

Human Rights Act is merely the incorporation into British law of the provisions of the ECHR, to which we have been bound for over half a century.
Besides, in the ECHR, there are countervailing provisions to do with public
safety and national security which would permit precisely the more balanced
approach I advocate. In addition, of course, Parliament has the right expressly
to override the Human Rights Act. And it's not the existence of the Human
Rights Act or the ECHR that has made Parliament behave in the way it has ...
I am afraid the issue is far more profound: it is the culture of political and legal
decision-making that has to change, to take account of the way the world has
changed. It is not this or that judicial decision; this or that law. It is a complete
change of mindset, an avowed, articulated determination to make protection of
the law-abiding public the priority and to measure that not by the theory of the
textbook but by the reality of the street and community in which real people
live real lives.[500]

It has been suggested that 'the reflex now is to denigrate human rights'
and what one Minister described as the 'individualist legalism of the
rights culture'.[501] In July 2006 the former Home Secretary Charles Clarke
criticised Britain's most senior judges for repeatedly refusing to meet him
to discuss how to view human rights legislation in the light of new
pressures created by terrorism and the 7 July bombings.[502] Mr Clarke
echoed other cabinet ministers' claims that the legal establishment was
out of touch:

One of the consequences of the Human Rights Act is that our most senior
judiciary are taking decisions of deep concern to the security of our society
without any responsibility for that security ... One of my depressing experiences as home secretary was the outright refusal of any of the law lords to
discuss the principles behind these matters in any forum, private or public,
formal or informal. That attitude has to change. It fuels the dangerously
confused and ill-informed debate which challenges Britain's adherence to the
European Convention on Human Rights. It is now time for the senior judiciary
to engage in a serious and considered debate about how best legally to
confront terrorism in the modern circumstances that have changed so profoundly since 9/11 and 7/7.[503]

Speaking extra-judicially, Lord Bingham has observed that the convention had been that Ministers, however critical of a judicial decision, and

---

[500] *Ibid.*
[501] M Kettle, 'This dialogue of the deaf is corroding our human rights', *The Guardian*
(UK), 10 June 2006.
[502] See P Wintour and T Branigan, 'Clarke Blames Judges for Confusion on Rights', *The
Guardian* (UK), 4 July 2006).
[503] *Ibid.* See also his evidence before the House of Lords Constitution Committee: 'Short
Inquiry into relations between the executive, judiciary and Parliament' on 17 January 2007,
when he strongly criticised the Law Lords and advocated some form of prior legal review
of key measures: <http://www.publications.parliament.uk /pa/ld200607/ldselect/
ldconst/999/const170107.pdf>.

exercising their right to appeal against it or, in the last resort, legislating to reverse it retrospectively, forbore from public disparagement of it. However, the convention appeared to have 'worn a little thin in recent times'.[504] He considered this unfortunate since if Ministers made what were understood to be public attacks on judges, the judges might be provoked to make similar criticisms of Ministers, and the rule of law was not well served by public dispute between two arms of the state.

The Conservative leader, David Cameron, has stated that the Conservatives would consider getting rid of the HRA and replacing it with a British Bill of Rights that 'strikes a better balance between security and freedom'.[505] He argued that the Act 'hindered the fight on crime and terrorism' and 'stopped us responding properly in terms of terrorism, particularly in terms of deporting those who may do us harm in this country – and at the same time, it hasn't really protected our human rights'.[506] Superficially there may now be all-party support for a UK Bill of Rights and Responsibilities, and the beginnings of a national debate as part of a package of constitutional reforms,[507] but the context is not one of adding rights beyond the ECHR but of reversing rulings that the current government or any future Conservative government dislike.[508] In response to Conservative attacks the Labour government has been forced to defend the HRA and criticise the Conservatives' proposals. There have also been academic attacks on the HRA.[509]

[504]   Lord Bingham, n 56 above at 24.

[505]   The Rt Hon David Cameron MP, 'Balancing Freedom And Security – A Modern British Bill Of Rights', speaking at The Centre for Policy Studies, 26 June 2006, <http://www.cps.org.uk>.

[506]   'Cameron "could scrap" Rights Act', *BBC News*, 25 June 2006, <http://news.bbc.co.uk>. He made it clear that the UK would remain a party to the ECHR.

[507]   For an excellent discussion paper see *A British Bill of Rights: Informing the debate*, The final report of the JUSTICE Constitution Committee, – 19 November 2007 <http://www.justice.org.uk/images/pdfs/ABritishBillofRights.pdf>. See also J Straw, 'Towards a Bill of Rights and Responsibility', <http://www.justice.gov.uk/news/sp210108a.htm>, and the JCHR's inquiry in to a British Bill of Rights <http://www.parliament.uk>; Bill of Rights Forum (Northern Ireland) Final Report (31 March 2008) <http://www.billofrightsforum.org>.

[508]   See F Klug, 'Enshrine These Rights', *The Guardian* (UK), 27 June 2006; F Klug, 'A Bill of Rights: Do We Need One or Do We Already Have One?' (2007) *Public Law* 401–19. Cf B Goold, L Lazarus and G Swiney, *Public Protection, Proportionality, and the Search for Balance*, UK Ministry of Justice Research Series 10/07, <www.justice.gov.uk/docs/270907.pdf>, who submit that, on the evidence of comparative experience, a 'British Bill of Rights' would most likely result in stricter rights protections in British courts.

[509]   Most notably, K Ewing, 'The Futility of the HRA' [2004] *Public Law* 829, with an addendum in (2005) 37 *Bracton Law Journal* 41–7; J-C Tham and KD Ewing, 'Limitations of a Charter of Rights in the Age of Counter-terrorism' (2007) 31 *Melbourne University Law Review* 462–98. In defence of the HRA see C Gearty, *Principles of Human Rights Adjudication* (Oxford, Oxford University Press, 2004); A Lester, 'The Utility of the Human Rights Act: a reply to Keith Ewing' [2005] *PL* 249; Kettle, n 501 above (discussion of the real madness not being human rights, but the attack on human rights).

The HRA is routinely attacked in the media with little defence from the government. In May 2006, *The Sun* newspaper campaigned against 'human rights madness' after the Bridges Report into the murder committed on licence in 2005 by the life sentence prisoner Anthony Rice: 'The whole concept of "human rights" in Britain has become a travesty.'[510] In fact the report had made clear that Rice was wrongly released because of bad and bungled offender management procedures, not because of anything in the HRA. In June 2006 an alleged car thief in Gloucester climbed up onto a roof to try to escape the police. His pursuers surrounded the building and waited to talk him down. After 10 hours, he asked for food and drink, which were supplied. As the sun was setting, the wanted man came down and was arrested. The newspapers reported that, according to the Gloucester police, he had been given fried chicken and Pepsi because they still had to look after his well-being and human rights.[511] The human rights claim was ridiculed by the national tabloid newspapers.[512] In the event it appeared the police made no such statement and the food and drink were simply given as part of the negotiations that had successfully ended the incident without harm to anyone.

B. Defending Human Rights

In November 2006, following a number of controversial cases, the Joint Committee on Human Rights published a major report on reviews of the HRA as part of its inquiry into the case for the HRA.[513] In its view none of the three cases that had sparked controversy – the Afghani hijackers' judgment, the Anthony Rice case and the failure to consider foreign prisoners for deportation – demonstrated a clear need to consider amending the HRA. It noted that the Lord Chancellor agreed and confirmed that it was the view of the government as a whole that none of them justified amendment or repeal of the HRA. While welcoming the Lord Chancellor's assurance that there was now an unequivocal commitment to the HRA across the government, the committee commented that 'public misunderstandings will continue so long as very senior Ministers

[510] On 12 May 2007 *The Sun* newspaper launched a campaign to persuade the government to 'rip up the Human Rights Act'.

[511] See 'Human Rights Farce', *Daily Express* (UK), 7 June 2006, <http://www.express.co.uk>.

[512] See J Bartholomew, 'Kentucky Fried Farce that shows folly of the Human Rights Act', *Daily Express* (UK) 8 June 2006; S Glover, 'Why have our police lost all common sense?', *Daily Mail* (UK), 8 June 2006 (denounces the 'political correctness and weak-mindedness' of police chiefs who had evidently ingested wholesale the HRA).

[513] See JCHR, *The Human Rights Act: The Department for Constitutional Affairs and Home Office Reviews* Thirty-second Report of Session 2005–06, HL 278/HC 1716 (14 November 2006).

make unfounded assertions about the Act and use it as a scapegoat for administrative failings in their departments'.[514]

The JCHR's report on the HRA coincided with a Joseph Rowntree Report entitled *The Rules of the Game: Terrorism, Community and Human Rights*.[515] This argued that ministerial attacks on the judiciary for confounding their anti-terror legislation were, 'unfounded and constitutionally illiterate'.[516] Moreover, the government's counterterrorism campaign was often driven by party political and electoral motives that were 'submerging' its own 'sensible' counter terrorism strategy.[517] report's principal recommendation was that 'human rights provided the only appropriate framework for counter terrorism laws and practice'.[518] It also emphasised that compliance with human rights standards was essential if anti-terrorism strategies were to receive the necessary community support. Such compliance may also serve to reduce public support for, and recruitment to, terrorist organisations. Disregarding human rights standards may encourage other states to do the same and weaken the increased solidarity that 11 September 2001 and the war on terror has induced between states.

XIX. CONCLUDING COMMENTS

A. The Judicial Response After 11 September 2001

The principal focus of this chapter has been on the judicial response after 11 September 2001.[519] Unsurprisingly, perhaps, the picture is mixed in terms of individual decisions (or particular aspects of them), but the direction of a stronger judicial role in human rights protection appears clear and it has not been stopped in its tracks by the events on 11 September and their aftermath. It is possible that the contours of an evolving human rights paradigm in the United Kingdom are emerging. There have been strong assertions that judicial protection of human

---

[514]   *Ibid*, para 41.

[515]   A Blick, T Choudhury and S Weir, *The Rules of the Game: Terrorism, Community and Human Rights*, Joseph Rowntree Report, November 2006, <http://www.jrrt.org.uk/Terrorism_final.pdf>, in particular, ch 5, 'The Effects on Human Rights'.

[516]   *Ibid* at 66.

[517]   *Ibid* at ch 4.

[518]   *Ibid* at 67.

[519]   See Goold, Lazurus and Swiney, n 17 above, who conclude that UK courts are less consistent in their application of proportionality than countries with constitutional rights protections. The latter tend to be more rigorous in their protections of rights than are countries that rely instead on the ECHR (as the UK now does under the HRA). See generally H Fenwick, R Masterman and G Phillipson (eds), *Judicial Reasoning under the HRA* (Cambridge, CUP, 2007).

rights is both democratic and based on the rule of law (*A (Belmarsh Detainees) case; Al Rawi*).[520] These assertions were reinforced by the HRA and the Constitutional Reform Act 2005, but not based on them. The courts have a special responsibility in the field of human rights, and it was the court's duty to decide where lies the legal edge between the executive and judicial functions (*Al Rawi*). The judiciary continues to maintain that the common law contains a deep well of principles that offer protection equivalent to those in European human rights standards (*A (Foreign Torture Evidence)*). The scope of judicial review pushes further and further into what had hitherto been the largely non-justiciable interstices of prerogative powers (*Abbasi; Al Rawi*).[521] Standards of judicial review are becoming more refined (*Abbasi, Re MB*) and the proportionality analysis in determining ECHR compatibility can be demanding (*A (Belmarsh Detainees) case*).[522] To the extent that the courts doing quite a good job[523] (and better than in previous times of crisis), this is likely to be enhanced when the United Kingdom formally has a Supreme Court.[524] It could be that the judiciary is reconceptualising its 'position in the constitution'[525] and asserting its rightful relative institutional competence within the context of a democratic dialogue (*A (Belmarsh Detainees) case;*

---

[520]   See also J Steyn, 'Democracy, The Rule of Law and the Role of Judges' [2006] *European Human Rights Law Review* 243–53.

[521]   See *Campaign for Nuclear Disarmament v Prime Minister of the United Kingdom and Others* [2002] EWHC 2777 (QB), *The Times* (UK), 27 December 2002: the court had no jurisdiction to declare the true interpretation of an international instrument (Security Council Resolution 1441) that had not been incorporated into English domestic law and which it was unnecessary to interpret for the purposes of determining a person's rights or duties under domestic law. The government's decision to declare or to authorise the use of armed force against a third country was the classic example of a non-justiciable decision.

[522]   It has not been possible within the scope of this chapter to examine the extra-territorial application of the HRA. On this see D McGoldrick, 'Human Rights and Humanitarian Law in the UK Courts' (2007) 40(2) *Israel Law Review* 527–62. This examines in particular the decisions culminating in *R. (on the application of Al-Skeini) v Secretary of State for Defence* [2007] UKHL 26 (HL) on the application of the HRA to British forces operating in Iraq. That decision was applied in *R (Smith) v Assistant Deputy Coroner for Oxfordshire and Secretary of State for Defence* [2008] EWHC 694 (Admin) (member of UK armed forces serving in Iraq remained within jurisdiction of UK for purposes of HRA (1998)).

[523]   See B Dickson, 'Safe in Their Hands? Britain's Law Lords and Human Rights' (2006) 26(3) *Legal Studies* 329–46, who submits that the Law Lords are generally doing a good job. See also C Gearty, *Can Human Rights Survive?* (Cambridge, Cambridge University Press, 2006); S Sedley, 'The Rocks or the Open Sea: Where is the Human Rights Act Heading?' (2005) 32 *Journal of Law and Society* 3–17.

[524]   See A Barak, 'Foreword: A Judge on Judging: The Role of a Supreme Court in a Democracy' (2002) 116 *Harvard Law Review* 16–162.

[525]   D Feldman, 'Human Rights, Terrorism and Risk: The Roles of Politicians and Judges' [2006] *Public Law* 364–84 at 383. See also the strong assertion of the responsibility of courts to secure the rule of law in the *BAE* case, n 63a above.

Re JJ and Others; Gillan).[526] It could be that the United Kingdom is incrementally evolving towards a system of constitutional supremacy under which fundamental rights would not be subject to executive or parliamentary removal.[527]

B. A New Human Rights Paradigm?

The case for a new human rights paradigm is as follows: the combination of the HRA, a strong version of principle of legality, new statutory duties concerning the rule of law, statutory recognition of judicial independence, a new Supreme Court and a understanding of parliamentary sovereignty as a qualified, general principle has resulted and will continue to result in enhanced standards of judicial review of fundamental rights, minimal non-justiciability and limited judicial deference to the executive and the legislature.[528] The case against any new human rights paradigm is that the courts are simply following Parliament's own directions in the HRA and applying it to the narrow technical legal issues where courts feel they are institutionally more competent and traditionally feel that they have proper expertise, such as those of discrimination, equality, burden of proof, standards of judicial review and statutory interpretation.[529] The overall picture of judicial decisions is mixed in the face of the complexity and variety of government arguments on asserted risks that the courts have had to consider.[530] In some contexts it can be argued that the courts, for example the SIAC or the High Court, are in a better place than the executive or legislature to evaluate intelligence information in specific cases for the simple reason that they are the only

---

[526]   See D Nicol, 'Law and Politics After the Human Rights Act' [2006] *Public Law* 722; T Hickman, 'The Courts and Politics after the Human Rights Act: A Comment' [2008] *Public Law* 84–100.

[527]   See the discussion in *International Transport Roth GMBH and Others v Secretary of State for the Home Department* [2002] UKHRR 479; *R (on the application of Jackson) v Attorney-General*, on which see A Bradley, 'Note to Select Committee on the Constitution', <http://www.publications.parliament.uk/pa/ld200506/ldselect/ ldconst/141/14106.htm>.

[528]   For a striking recent example in a non-terrorism context, see *R. (on the application of Bancoult) v Secretary of State for Foreign and Commonwealth Affairs* [2007] EWCA Civ 498 (reviewability of Orders in Council). The decision has been appealed to the HL.

[529]   On the approach to the burden of proof in terrorist contexts see *Sheldrake v DPP; A-G's Reference (No 4 of 2002)* [2004] UKHL 43, [2005] 1 AC 264. D was charged with belonging to and professing to belong to a proscribed organisation contrary to s 11(1) of the TA 2000. D argued that, at the time when he became a member or professed to become a member of the organisation, it had not yet been proscribed (a defence provided by s 11(2)). In accordance with s 3(2) of the HRA, s 11(2) of the TA 2000 was read down to impose an evidential burden only.

[530]   See T Poole, *Courts and Conditions of Uncertainty in times of Crisis in 'Times of Crisis'*, LSE Law and Society Working Papers 7/2007, <www.lse.ac.uk/collections/law/wps/wps/htm>, [2008] *Public Law* 234–59, arguing that it is ultimately better for courts to confront these arguments directly in their judgments.

institutions which may have had access to that information.[531] In other contexts a greater degree of deference to the executive and the legislature is apparent (*Rehman; Gillan; Al Rawi*).[532]

C. Parliamentary and Executive Culture

In addition to stronger judicial protection of human rights there is also some positive evidence of the development of a parliamentary culture of human rights.[533] The parliamentary Joint Committee on Human Rights has been one of the strongest and most consistent critics of the government's anti-terrorism laws, and its reports have been central to many of the key parliamentary debates.[534] The establishment of an Equality and Human Rights Commission in October 2007 may in time strengthen the weak social and political culture of human rights.[535]

While the direction in the United Kingdom may be towards a stronger, more activist,[536] judicial role in human rights protection,[537] the political and academic forces against it should not be underestimated.[538] In introducing the HRA the Labour government claimed that it was seeking to develop not just the legal protection of human rights but also a culture

---

[531] See Feldman, n 525 above at 381–2.

[532] See also *R on the Application of Gentle and Clarke v The Prime Minister, The Secretary of State for Defence, The Attorney-General* [2006] EWCA Civ 1690 (12 December 2006), dismissing application for judicial review of the government's decision not to hold an independent inquiry into the circumstances which led to the invasion of Iraq. The central part of the argument was based on positive obligations under Art 2 ECHR. A nine-member House of Lords dismissed the appeal: *R (on the application of Gentle (FC) and another (FC)) (Appellants) v The Prime Minister and others (Respondents)* [2008] UKHL 20.

[533] See JL Hiebert, 'Parliamentary Review of Terrorism Measures' (2005) 68 *MLR* 676–80. For a methodological approach to evaluation see S Evans and S Evans, 'Evaluating The Human Rights Performance of Legislatures' (2006) 6 *Human Rights Law Review* 545–69.

[534] See JL Hiebert, 'Parliament and the Human Rights Act: Can the JCHR Help Facilitate a Culture of Rights?' (2006) 4(1) *International Journal of Constitutional Law* 1–38.

[535] * See Equality Act 2006, Part I; A Lester and K Beattie, 'The New Commission for Equality and Human Rights' [2006] *Public Law* 197–208. The first inquiry launched by the Commission in March 2008 was into human rights and British attitudes to them, <http://www.equalityhumanrights.com>.

[536] On the complexities of assessing judicial activism see M Cohn and M Kremnitzer, 'Judicial Activism: A Multidimensional Model' (2005) 28(2) *Canadian Journal of Jurisprudence* 333–56.

[537] Of course national courts have a greater awareness of comparative human rights and constitutional jurisprudence from other jurisdictions. In this sense, movements in a particular direction can get inspiration and support from other jurisdictions and from transnational and international human rights norms. For a comparative perspective see M Arden, 'Meeting the Challenge of Terrorism: The Experience of English and Other Courts' (2006) 80 *Australian Law Journal* 818–38. The author stresses the need to hold on to the fundamental values of a plural, democratic society subject to the rule of law.

[538] Compare Feldman, n 525 above; R Ekins, 'Constitutional Law, Judicial Supremacy and the Rule of Law' (2003) 119 *LQR* 127–52 (posits that judicial supremacy is profoundly undemocratic); P Craig, 'Constitutional Foundations, The Rule of Law and Supremacy'

of human rights.[539] This was necessarily a more sociological and long-term process.[540] Evidence of a positive executive culture of human rights is much more mixed. In the terrorist detention and deportation cases, in particular, there is deep frustration in government that human rights principles limit the options they consider necessary to protect the public.[541] It has been reported that the government is preparing a new anti-terror law that would sideline human rights legislation protecting suspects from torture if Ministers ruled that there were 'overriding considerations of national security'.[542] The HRA could be amended if British courts continue to block moves to deport terror suspects on the basis of 'memorandums of understanding' with foreign states that they would not be tortured.[543] In April 2008 the government suffered two major defeats on aspects of MOUs.[544] It was considering appealing the decision relating to the use of evidence derived from torture but it immediately announced that it would not appeal against the judgment in the Libyans' case. In February 2008, in *Saadi v Italy*,[545] the Grand Chamber of the European Court of Human Rights unanimously rejected all arguments that it should change its approach in the *Chahal* case so as to permit some balancing of threats to national security against the risk of violations of Article 3 ECHR rights relating to inhuman or degrading treatment:

> the Court cannot accept the argument of the United Kingdom Government, supported by the respondent Government, that a distinction must be drawn under Article 3 between treatment inflicted directly by a signatory State and

[2003] *Public Law* 92–111; C Gearty, *Are judges now out of their depth?*, JUSTICE Tom Sargant memorial annual lecture, 17 October 2007, <http://www.conorgearty.co.uk/pdfs/Justice_lecture2007.pdf>.

[539] See D McGoldrick, 'The HRA in Theory and Practice' (2001) 50 *ICLQ* 901–53.

[540] See L Clements and J Young (eds), 'Human Rights: Changing the Culture' (Special edition, 1999) 26 *Journal of Law and Society* 1.

[541] See P Riddell, 'Balancing Act of Rival Judges and Politicians Cannot Last', *The Times* (UK), 16 June 2006.

[542] See D Leppard, 'Reid Fights To End Torture Shield For Terror Suspects', *The Sunday Times* (UK), 1 October 2006.

[543] The critical legal issue in the MOU cases would be whether the MOUs reduced the risk of an Art 3 violation to below the level of a real risk. The first challenge to an MOU (between the UK and Jordan) failed before the SIAC in *Abu Qatada v Secretary of State for the Home Department* [2007] UKSIAC 15/2005 (26 February 2007), on which see C Walker, 'The Treatment of Foreign Terrorist Suspects' (2007) 70 *MLR* 441–50, but, as we have noted, succeeded on one issue before the Court of Appeal: see n 481 above. For a defence of deportations with assurances as compatible with human rights law see K Jones, 'Deportations With Assurances: Addressing Key Criticisms' (2008) 57 *International and Comparative Law Quarterly* 183–94.

[544] See nn 486 and 487 above.

[545] Application No. 37201/06 (unreported). The UK intervened as a third party in the case. The UK also put the arguments in *Ramzy v Netherlands*, n 121 above, but the *Saadi* case reached the European Court first. The authoritative guidance in *Saadi* was quickly relied upon in the UK courts: see n 486 above,

treatment that might be inflicted by the authorities of another State, and that protection against this latter form of ill-treatment should be weighed against the interests of the community as a whole ... Since protection against the treatment prohibited by Article 3 is absolute, that provision imposes an obligation not to extradite or expel any person who, in the receiving country, would run the real risk of being subjected to such treatment. As the Court has repeatedly held, there can be no derogation from that rule ... It must therefore reaffirm the principle stated in the *Chahal* judgment... that it is not possible to weigh the risk of ill-treatment against the reasons put forward for the expulsion in order to determine whether the responsibility of a State is engaged under Article 3, even where such treatment is inflicted by another State. In that connection, the conduct of the person concerned, however undesirable or dangerous, cannot be taken into account...

The Court considers that the argument based on the balancing of the risk of harm if the person is sent back against the dangerousness he or she represents to the community if not sent back is misconceived. The concepts of 'risk' and 'dangerousness' in this context do not lend themselves to a balancing test because they are notions that can only be assessed independently of each other. Either the evidence adduced before the Court reveals that there is a substantial risk if the person is sent back or it does not. The prospect that he may pose a serious threat to the community if not returned does not reduce in any way the degree of risk of ill treatment that the person may be subject to on return. For that reason it would be incorrect to require a higher standard of proof, as submitted by the intervener, where the person is considered to represent a serious danger to the community, since assessment of the level of risk is independent of such a test.

With regard to the second branch of the United Kingdom Government's arguments, to the effect that where an applicant presents a threat to national security, stronger evidence must be adduced to prove that there is a risk of ill-treatment ... the Court observes that such an approach is not compatible with the absolute nature of the protection afforded by Article 3 either. It amounts to asserting that, in the absence of evidence meeting a higher standard, protection of national security justifies accepting more readily a risk of ill-treatment for the individual. The Court therefore sees no reason to modify the relevant standard of proof, as suggested by the third-party intervener, by requiring in cases like the present that it be proved that subjection to ill-treatment is 'more likely than not. On the contrary, it reaffirms that for a planned forcible expulsion to be in breach of the Convention it is necessary – and sufficient – for substantial grounds to have been shown for believing that there is a real risk that the person concerned will be subjected in the receiving country to treatment prohibited by Article 3 ... [546]

As we have noted, further anti-terrorist measures have been proposed or mooted. These include extending the pre-charge period in terrorist cases

---

[546] *Ibid* at paras 138–40. For the UK's arguments see *ibid* at paras 117–23.

from 28 days upwards to 42 days; strengthening race hatred laws so as to catch people who insult Muslims; new laws covering what could be said and done at public demonstrations, including the banning of the burning of flags and effigies and preventing demonstrators covering their faces; post-charge questioning; the use of intercept evidence in court proceedings; faster and more open court proceedings in terrorist cases so that the public would gain a greater understanding of the real threat;[547] increased surveillance[548] and the deployment of increasingly sophisticated technology.[549] New measures will doubtless be subjected to human rights challenges. Some will pass muster; others will not. Perhaps more important than the individual measures is how the executive and the legislature responds to defeats grounded in human rights law under the emerging paradigm.

D. What If?

A recent phenomenon in the discipline of history is to consider how history might have been different if particular events had not occurred or the outcomes of particular conflicts or events had been different. The genre is sometimes described as 'What If' or 'Virtual History'.[550] In a similar vein, it is interesting to speculate as follows: *if 11 September 2001 had occurred before the HRA (1998), would the latter have been passed?* The meta-concept that the war on terror has become might suggest that the answer would be in the negative. In a domestic UK context, the greatest victory that the terrorists could achieve is the denigration of human

---

[547] Full details of a series of terror atrocities that would have killed thousands of people in the United Kingdom and the United States were outlined in court for the first time only in November 2006 in the trial of British-based Al Qaeda operative, Dhiren Barot: see A Fresco, '"Die Hard" – The Evidence Against Dhiren Barot', *The Times* (UK), 6 November 2006. Barot's case led to the seizure of some 270 computers, 2,000 computer discs and a total of 8,224 exhibits. There were seven co-conspirators and during the investigation police carried out enquiries in the United States, Pakistan, Malaysia, the Philippines, Indonesia, France, Spain and Sweden. In another recent case, 30 addresses were searched within two hours of the start of the arrest phase of the operation. Four hundred computers and 8,000 computer discs were seized, with a total of over 25,000 exhibits.

[548] See *A Report on the Surveillance Society for the Information Commissioner, Richard Thomas*, September 2006, <http://www.ico.gov.uk>. The report looked at surveillance in 2006 and projected forward 10 years to 2016. It described a surveillance society as one where technology is extensively and routinely used to track and record the activities and movements of individuals. This included systematic tracking and recording of travel and use of public services, automated use of CCTV, analysis of buying habits and financial transactions, and the workplace monitoring of telephone calls, email and internet use.

[549] See L Bannerman, 'Police Target Dangerous Suspects Before They Can Offend', *The Times* (UK), 27 November 2006.

[550] See eg R Crowley, *What If? Military Historians Imagine What Might Have Been* (New York, GP Putnam's Sons, 1999); N Ferguson (ed), *Virtual History: Alternatives and Counterfactuals* (London, Papermac, 2003).

rights as a matter of legal and political culture. The obligation to prevent that from happening rests on us all. As the Chief Justice of South Africa has recently observed: 'In a democracy parliament and civil society are also defenders of the rule of law and it is essential that they should play their part in its protection.'[551]

---

[551] Cf Justice Chaskalson, 'The Widening Gyre: Counter-terrorism, Human Rights and the Rule of Law', Seventh Sir David Williams Lecture, <http://www.icj.org/IMG/Speech_AC_May_2007.pdf>, 67 CLJ (2008) 69–91. See also D Kostakopoulou, 'How to do Things with Security Post 9/11' (2008) 28 *Oxford Journal of Legal Studies* 317–342 (on how a 'siege mode of democracy' has shaped counter-terrorist legislation in the UK post 9/11).

6

Terror Financing, Guilt by Association and the Paradigm of Prevention in the 'War on Terror'

DAVID COLE

I. INTRODUCTION

GUILT BY ASSOCIATION is an attractive principle to law enforcement officials concerned about preventing future harms. Without the concept of guilt by association, government officials must carry out costly investigations to catch individuals in the act of either committing a crime, or conspiring to commit one. Guilt by association, by contrast, permits the government to incarcerate persons based not on their involvement in past illegal conduct, and not even on their involvement in planning future crimes, but on the basis of their affiliation or association with others who have engaged in illegal conduct.

The United States' formative experience with guilt by association came during the Cold War. Fearing a communist takeover, Congress made membership in the Communist Party a criminal offense, in a statute known as the Smith Act. In 1961, in *Scales v United States*, the Supreme Court considered the validity of this law.[1] The Court interpreted the statute narrowly in order to avoid the grave constitutional concerns that it said the statute would otherwise present. As the Court explained, the First Amendment right of association includes the right to associate with groups that have both legal and illegal aims, so long as the individual does not seek to further the group's illegal aims. In addition, the Fifth Amendment requires proof of 'personal guilt', and therefore precludes holding an individual criminally liable for the acts of another (group or individual) absent proof that the individual sought to further the other's illegal conduct.[2] In the interest of avoiding the constitutional problems

---

[1] 367 US 203 (1961).
[2] *Ibid*, at 224–7.

presented by a broad ban on membership, the Court in *Scales* interpreted the Smith Act to require proof that the defendant specifically intended to further the Communist Party's illegal ends. Mere association, or association in furtherance of the Party's legal ends (such as its civil rights advocacy or labour union organising), were insufficient to violate the statute. Only a showing of specific intent, the Court said, would distinguish those who seek to further illegal ends from those who associate for legal purposes. While the Court's decision in *Scales* was technically an interpretation of the statute, it was driven by its constitutional analysis, and subsequent cases treated *Scales* as establishing a constitutional principle, not just a reading of a specific statute.[3]

There the law essentially stood – until 11 September 2001. In the wake of the terrorist attacks of that day, the Bush administration aggressively pursued a theory of collective guilt that for all practical purposes revived the tactics of the Cold War. In the name of cutting off support for terrorist organisations, US law now makes it a crime to provide anything of support – from dues to volunteer services – to any organisation or individual that the government has label;ed 'terrorist'.[4] The prohibition is not limited to those who intend to support the illegal or terrorist acts of so-called terrorist organisations. It criminalises any and all support – including support that is otherwise entirely lawful, peaceful and non-violent. Indeed, the criminal bar applies even to aid that is designed to *reduce* a group's reliance on violence, and even where the aid can be shown to have had precisely that beneficial effect.[5] Thus, the government has argued that the material support law prohibits a human rights group from providing human rights training to the Kurdistan Workers' Party in Turkey, even though the undisputed purpose of the training is to encourage that group to resolve its differences with the Turkish government through peaceful, non-violent, legal means.[6]

The government insists that these laws do not impose guilt by association, because the laws target not association per se, but 'material support', and several courts have accepted that distinction.[7] But in the end, it is largely a distinction without a difference, for what good is it to have a right to join or associate with a group if the government can make it a

---

[3]   See, eg, *NAACP v Claiborne Hardware*, 458 US 886, 932 (1982) (guilt by association violates the First Amendment).

[4]   See Section II below.

[5]   *Ibid.*

[6]   See *Humanitarian Law Project v Reno*, 205 F.3d 1130 (9th Cir 2000) (declaring prohibition on providing 'training' and 'personnel' to designated terrorist organisations unconstitutional because it could make it a crime to, for example, teach international law); *Humanitarian Law Project v US Dept of Treasury*, 473 F Supp 2d 1049, 1059–63 (CD Cal 2006) (upholding criminal ban on providing all 'services' to designated terrorist groups, where regulation defined services to include 'educational' and 'legal' services, among others).

[7]   See, eg, *Humanitarian Law Project v Reno*, 205 F.3d 1130.

crime to do anything whatsoever on the group's behalf? No association can survive without the support of its members.

Just as the fear of future threats from communism in the Cold War spawned a sweeping approach that failed to distinguish between the culpable and the innocent, so too the fear of future terrorist attacks in the wake of 11 September 2001 has created a similar initiative. Moreover, through the United Nations, the United States has sought to encourage other nations to adopt a similar approach, with some success.

This chapter argues that the 'material support' principle is 'guilt by association' in twenty-first-century garb, and presents all of the same problems that criminalising membership and association did during the Cold War. I will first outline the ways in which guilt by association has been revived through the concept of penalising 'material support' for organisations labelled terrorist. I will then discuss the constitutional questions that these laws present, and sketch how the courts have, at least thus far, resolved those questions. In short, the courts have sought to trim the worst excesses of the laws, but have been largely unwilling to confront head on their fundamental infirmity – the imposition of guilt by association without any proof of intent to further any terrorist acts.

Finally, I will conclude by explaining how the material support laws fit into the United States' broader 'paradigm of prevention' in confronting the threat of terrorism. That term, coined by former Attorney General John Ashcroft, describes an amalgam of tactics in which the government employs highly coercive and intrusive measures against groups and individuals based not on proof of past wrongdoing, but on necessarily speculative fears about what they might do in the future.[8] The material support laws further this goal by expanding the definition of what constitutes a past crime, just as the Smith Act membership provision of the Cold War era did. These laws are not purely preventive, in that they

---

[8] Attorney General Ashcroft first announced this preventive policy in a speech to the US Conference of Mayors in October 2001. As he put it: 'Let the terrorists among us be warned: If you overstay your visa – even by one day – we will arrest you. If you violate a local law, you will be put in jail and kept in custody as long as possible. We will use every available statute. We will seek every prosecutorial advantage. We will use all our weapons within the law and under the Constitution to protect life and enhance security for America. In the war on terror, this Department of Justice will arrest and detain any suspected terrorist who has violated the law. Our single objective is to prevent terrorist attacks by taking suspected terrorists off the street': Prepared Remarks of Attorney General John Ashcroft for the US Mayors Conference, 25 October 2001, available at <http://www.usdoj.gov/archive/ag/speeches/2001/agcrisisremarks10_25.htm>. See also Prepared Remarks of Attorney General John Ashcroft, Council on Foreign Relations, 10 February 2003 ('In order to fight and to defeat terrorism, the Department of Justice has added a new paradigm to that of prosecution – a paradigm of prevention.'), available at <http://www.usdoj.gov/archive/ag/speeches/2003 /021003agcouncilonforeignrelation.htm>.

do require proof of some past 'wrongdoing'. But their expansive definitions of wrongdoing stretch that concept beyond its limits in the name of preventing future harm.

The same preventive justification that underlies the material support laws has also led the United States to embark on indiscriminate preventive detention schemes; to use highly coercive interrogation techniques amounting, at least in some circumstances, to torture; and to wage war 'preventively' against Iraq, a country that neither attacked the United States nor posed a threat of imminent attack. The centrality of the 'preventive paradigm' to the rationale for the material support laws suggests strong reason for scepticism about their fairness, and underscores the need for careful scrutiny of their application.

II. THE LEGAL REGIME

Three different federal laws authorise US officials to designate groups or individuals as 'terrorist' and then punish 'material support' provided to them. All three statutes share a common attribute – they penalise support of designated groups or persons without regard to the character or intent of the support provided, and without regard to the effect of the support in question. Thus, aid having nothing to do with terrorism, and even aid designed to *discourage* terrorism, is treated identically to aid designed to further terrorism. In addition, all three statutes afford federal officials wide discretion – a virtual 'blank cheque' – in selecting disfavoured groups or persons for designation. And all three statutes provide inadequate procedures for challenging designations.

A. The Criminal 'Material Support' Statute – 18 USC §2339B and 8 USC §1189

The Antiterrorism and Effective Death Penalty Act (AEDPA) of 1996, amended by the USA Patriot Act in 2001, and again in 2004, authorises the Secretary of State to designate 'foreign terrorist organizations', and makes it a crime for anyone to support even the wholly lawful, nonviolent activities of those designated organisations.[9]

The law works in two steps: designation and prohibition. As an initial matter, the Secretary of State

> is authorized to designate an organization as a foreign terrorist organization ... if the Secretary finds that –

---

[9] See 8 USC § 1189 and 18 USC § 2339B.

(a) the organization is a foreign organization;

(b) the organization engages in terrorist activity; and

(c) the terrorist activity of the organization threatens the security of United States nationals or the national security of the United States.[10]

The term 'terrorist activity' is broadly defined far beyond its commonly understood meaning to include virtually any unlawful use of, or threat to use, a weapon against person or property, unless for mere personal monetary gain. 'National security' is also broadly defined to mean 'national defense, foreign relations, or economic interests of the United States'. The Secretary's determination that a group's activities threaten US 'national security' under the statute is judicially unreviewable.[11] Thus, this statute is not limited to terrorist organisations as they are commonly understood, or to national security as it is commonly understood, but broadly empowers the Secretary to designate any foreign group that has used or threatened to use a weapon and whose activities are deemed contrary to the United States' *economic* interest.

The second step is the prohibition of support. Once the Secretary designates an organisation and publishes the designation in the Federal Register, it becomes a crime, punishable by up to 15 years of imprisonment (or life imprisonment if death results) and a substantial fine, to 'knowingly provide[] material support or resources to a foreign terrorist organization, or [to] attempt[] or conspire[] to do so'.[12] 'Material support or resources' is defined as:

> any property, tangible or intangible, or service, including currency or monetary instruments or financial securities, financial services, lodging, training, expert advice or assistance, safehouses, false documentation or identification, communications equipment, facilities, weapons, lethal substances, explosives, personnel (1 or more individuals who may be or include oneself), and transportation, except medicine or religious materials.[13]

The statute does not on its face require any showing that the defendant intended that his donation be used for any illicit purpose. The United States maintains that Congress in effect adopted an irrebuttable presumption that *all* support to such organisations furthers their terrorist ends.[14] In fact, Congress heard no testimony about any particular terrorist organisations that would support such a presumption even as to that

---

[10]   8 USC § 1189(a)(1).

[11]   *People's Mojahedin Org of Iran v US Sec of State*, 182 F.3d 17, 23 (DC Cir 1999), cert denied, 529 US 1104 (2000).

[12]   18 USC § 2339B(a).

[13]   18 USC § 2339A(b).

[14]   Antiterrorism and Effective Death Penalty Act, Pub L No 104–132, § 301(a)(7), 110 Stat 1214, 1247 (24 April 1996).

group, much less as to all groups that might henceforth be labelled 'foreign terrorist organisations'. At the same time, and directly contrary to this presumption, the statute permits the donation of unlimited amounts of medicine and religious materials to designated organisations. And a provision added in 2005 permits the Secretary of State and Attorney General to grant advance approval for aid in the form of 'training', 'personnel,' and 'expert advice or assistance' where the Secretary determines that the aid may not be used to carry out terrorist activity.[15] Thus, the statute expressly discriminates between religious and political aid, permitting unlimited amounts of religious aid (even if it is intended to further terrorist activity),[16] while barring all political aid, even if it counters terrorism and promotes peace.

Procedures for challenging designation are largely a sham. Once the Secretary of State designates a group and publishes that fact in the Federal Register, the designated group has 30 days to file a legal challenge in the federal court of appeals in Washington, DC. Even if it manages to learn of the designation, find a lawyer, and file the challenge in time, the review process is one-sided. The court does not consider any new evidence, but merely reviews the evidence the State Department developed unilaterally. The State Department is able to present the record in secret and behind closed doors, so the designated group in many instances will not even be able to see the evidence used against it. And as noted above, the critical criterion – that the group's activities threaten 'national security',— has been deemed unreviewable by the courts.[17] Not surprisingly, no group has succeeded in challenging its designation under this law.

B. Immigration Consequences of 'Material Support' under 8 USC §1182

Immigration law also penalises 'material support', but does so even more expansively than the criminal law. Foreign nationals can be denied entry or deported for having provided material support not only to organisations designated as 'terrorist', but even to organisations that have never been designated terrorist, but merely have at some point threatened to use a weapon against person or property. In one case, for example, a

[15]   18 USC § 2339B(j).

[16]   18 USC § 2339A prohibits the provision of 'material support or resources' for the purpose of furthering specified terrorist activities, but then exempts the provision of 'medicine and religious articles' from the definition of 'material support'. Accordingly, even if an individual donated medicine *for the purpose of furthering terrorist activity*, his action would not be prohibited by the 'material support' provisions: 18 USC §§ 2339A and 2339B.

[17]   See n 11 above.

national of India was deported for having set up a tent for religious services that were then attended by, among others, some members of an Indian guerrilla organisation.[18] Moreover, the Department of Homeland Security, which enforces immigration law, interprets this provision to apply even to those who are coerced into providing material support to such a group. Thus, if guerrillas ransack a village and demand food at gunpoint, anyone who relents and gives them food will, absent a waiver, be deemed inadmissible to the United States for having materially supported a terrorist group.[19]

In another case the government invoked these immigration provisions to seek the deportation of two long-time lawful permanent residents, Khader Hamide and Michel Shehadeh, for having provided 'material support' to a 'terrorist organization' by distributing PLO magazines in Los Angeles in the 1980s, when it was fully lawful to do so (the magazines were then and are still available in libraries across the nation). The government never alleged that Hamide or Shehadeh sought to further any illegal activities of the PLO group they were alleged to have supported. But under the government's view of the immigration law, that fact was irrelevant. (In October 2007, after a 21-year legal battle, and after an immigration judge dismissed the case for prosecutorial misconduct, the government abandoned its efforts to deport Hamide and Shehadeh).

C. Embargoing Individuals and Groups under the International Emergency Economic Powers Act

The third statute that the government relies upon to penalise support of 'terrorists' is the International Emergency Economic Powers Act (IEEPA).[20] This statute was originally enacted to empower the President during emergencies to impose economic embargoes on foreign nations. It was used exclusively for that purpose until 1995, when President Bill Clinton first used it not to target nations as a matter of nation-to-nation diplomacy but to target disfavoured political groups. Clinton named ten Palestinian organisations and two Jewish groups as 'specially designated terrorists'.[21] Designation under IEEPA has the effect of freezing the entity's assets in the United States and making it a crime for anyone in

---

[18] *Singh-Kaur v Ashcroft*, 385 F.3d 293 (3rd Cir, 2004).
[19] Human Rights First, 'Abandoning the Persecuted: Victims of Terrorism and Oppression Barred From Asylum' (2006); Refugee Council USA, 'The Material Support Problem: Punishing Refugee Victims of Terror: March 8, 2007', available at <http://www.rcusa.org/uploads/pdfs/ms-backgrd-info3–8-07.pdf>.
[20] 50 USC §§1701–06 (2000).
[21] Executive Order 12947 (1995).

the United States to engage in any transactions with the groups, again regardless of the purpose and effect of the support in question.[22] After the attacks of 11 September 2001, President Bush invoked the same authority to name 27 'specially designated global terrorists'.[23] He offered no explanation for why any of them were designated, or any criteria used for the determination. At the same time, he authorised the Secretary of the Treasury to designate still others using extremely broad criteria. Until recently, the Treasury Secretary could designate an individual or entity based solely on a finding that he or it was merely 'otherwise associated with' someone else on the list.[24]

Hundreds of individuals and groups have been placed on this 'terrorist' list since 2001. Remarkably, there is no definition in federal statutes of a 'specially designated terrorist' or a 'specially designated global terrorist'. Thus, the President and the Secretary of Treasury can apply these labels to literally anyone or any group that can conceivably be reached under IEEPA. The only limitation IEEPA places is that there must be some 'foreign interest' in the entity or person designated, but that term has been applied very loosely. Indeed, IEEPA has been used to designate a US citizen, Mohammed Salah, a resident of Chicago.[25] Under the terms of IEEPA, it is a crime to provide Mr Salah with anything of value, or even to make a donation to him. Literally applied and enforced, the designation would lead to Mr Salah starving to death, since it would be a crime for anyone even to sell or give him a loaf of bread. Yet this penalty was imposed without any jury, without any notice, without any hearing, and without any statutory definition of the label imposed.

Groups or individuals designated under this authority may challenge their designation in federal courts, but as with the State Department list described above, the court will not take any new evidence. The court reviews the designation entirely on the administrative record created by the Treasury Department, in most instances without any input from the designated entity.[26] Here, too, the government can defend its designation

---

[22] 50 USC §§1701–06.

[23] Executive Order 13224 (18 September 2001).

[24] In 2006, a federal court declared that provision unconstitutional: *Humanitarian Law Project v US Dept of Treasury*, 463 F Supp 2d 1049 (CD Cal, 2006). The Treasury Department then amended its regulations to define 'otherwise associated' more narrowly, to mean those entities or individuals that 'own or control; or (b) ... attempt, or ... conspire with one or more persons, to act for or on behalf of or to provide financial, material, or technological support, or financial or other services, to a designated entity': 31 CFR § 594.316 (2007). The district court upheld the term as narrowed: *Humanitarian Law Project v US Dept of Treasury*, 484 FSupp2d 1099, 1105–07 (CD Cal, 2007).

[25] See D Cole, *Enemy Aliens: Double Standards and Constitutional Freedoms in the War on Terrorism*, revised edn (New York, NY, New Press, 2005) 78.

[26] See, eg, *Holy Land Foundation v Ashcroft*, 333 F.3d 156 (DC Cir, 2003), cert denied, 540 US 1218 (2004); *National Council of Resistance of Iran v. Department of State*, 251 F.3d 192, 207 (DC Cir, 2001).

by submitting secret evidence that the court examines outside the presence of the challenger. Here, too, the decks are stacked; no one has yet succeeded in challenging their designation in court.[27]

III. CONSTITUTIONAL CONCERNS

The statutes described above prohibit virtually all associational support to selected political organisations, while granting executive branch officials effectively unreviewable discretion to target disfavoured groups. These laws make it a crime to write an opinion piece for a newspaper, provide legal advice, volunteer one's time, or distribute a magazine for any 'designated' group, even if there is no connection whatsoever between the individual's support and any illegal activity of the proscribed group.

Under these statutes, a US citizen who sends a treatise on non-violence to the Kurdistan Workers' Party to encourage it to forgo violence for peace can be sent to prison for 15 years. This is so even if he proves that he intended the treatise to be used only for peaceful ends, and that it was in fact used solely for that purpose. Such a moral innocent can be said to be 'guilty' only by association.

The Supreme Court has declared guilt by association 'alien to the traditions of a free society and the First Amendment itself'.[28] It violates both the Fifth Amendment, which requires that guilt must be personal, and the First Amendment, which guarantees the right of association.

The statutes are analytically indistinguishable from the McCarthy era laws that penalised association with the Communist Party. Congress specifically found that the Communist Party was a foreign-dominated group engaged in terrorism for the purpose of overthrowing the United States.[29] The Supreme Court did not question that finding, but nonetheless ruled that even with respect to such a group, individuals could not be penalised for their associations absent proof of 'specific intent' to further the group's illegal ends.[30] The material support statutes require no 'specific intent', and punish people solely for their associational support of specified groups.

---

[27] See, eg, *Islamic American Relief Agency v Gonzales*, 477 F.3d 728 (DC Cir, 2007); *Global Relief Foundation, Inc v O'Neil (GRF)*, 315 F.3d 748 (7th Cir, 2002); *Holy Land Foundation v. Ashcroft*, 333 F.3d 156 (D.C.Cir. 2003).

[28] *NAACP v Claiborne Hardware*, 458 US 886, 932 (1982).

[29] 50 USC § 781 (West, 1991) (repealed 1993).

[30] See, eg, *United States v Robel*, 389 US 258, 262 (1967) (government could not ban Communist Party members from working in defence facilities absent proof that they had specific intent to further the Party's unlawful ends; *Keyishian v Board of Regents*, 385 US 589, 606 (1967) ('[m]ere knowing membership without a specific intent to further the unlawful

The courts have nonetheless largely approved of these laws. In the leading case, *Humanitarian Law Project v Reno*, the US Court of Appeals for the Ninth Circuit concluded that the criminal material support statute is valid because it does not penalise membership as such, but only 'material support'.[31] Several other courts have adopted that reasoning.[32] But that distinction makes the prohibition on guilt by association a meaningless formality; instead of criminalising membership of disfavoured groups, legislatures may simply criminalise the payment of dues or volunteering of services to those groups. Since associations cannot exist without the material support of their members, the court's reasoning eviscerates the right of association.[33]

The notion that material support can be penalised even if membership cannot is directly contrary to Supreme Court precedent. In *NAACP v Claiborne Hardware*, for example, the Supreme Court unanimously held that the leaders and members of the National Association for the Advancement of Colored People (NAACP), a prominent civil rights group, could not be held liable for injuries sustained during an NAACP-led boycott that grew violent absent proof that 'the individual[s] held a specific intent to further [the boycott's] illegal aims'.[34] But if material support is constitutionally distinct from association, the NAACP's thousands of individual *donors* could have been held liable without any showing of specific intent, even if its leaders could not be.

---

aims of an organization is not a constitutionally adequate basis' for barring employment in the state university system to Communist Party members); *Elfbrandt v Russell*, 384 US 11, 19 (1966) ('a law which applies to membership without the "specific intent" to further the illegal aims of the organization infringes unnecessarily on protected freedoms'); *Noto v United States*, 367 US 290, 299–300 (1961) (First Amendment bars punishment of 'one in sympathy with the legitimate aims of [the Communist Party], but not specifically intending to accomplish them by resort to violence').

[31]   205 F.3d 1130 (9th Cir, 2000), cert denied, 532 US 904 (2001).

[32]   *United States v Hammoud*, 381 F.3d 316 (4th Cir, 2004); *United States v Assi*, 414 F. Supp. 2d 707 (ED Mich, 2006); *United States v Paracha*, 2006 US Dist LEXIS 1 (SDNY, 2006); *Holy Land Foundation for Relief and Development v Ashcroft*, 333 F.3d 156 (DC Cir, 2003).

[33]   As the Supreme Court has said, 'The right to join together "for the advancement of beliefs and ideas" … is diluted if it does not include the right to pool money through contributions, for funds are often essential if "advocacy" is to be truly or optimally "effective"': *Buckley v Valeo*, 424 US 1, 65–6 (1976) (quoting *NAACP v Alabama*, 357 US 449, 460 (1958)). Monetary contributions to political organisations are a protected form of association and expression: *ibid*, at 16–17, 24–5; *Roberts v United States Jaycees*, 468 US 609 (1984) (First Amendment protects non-profit group's right to solicit funds); *Citizens Against Rent Control v Berkeley*, 454 US 290, 295–6 (1981) (monetary contributions to a group are a form of 'collective expression' protected by the right of association); *Service Employees Int'l Union v Fair Political Practices Comm'n*, 955 F.2d 1312, 1316 (9th Cir) ('contributing money is an act of political association that is protected by the First Amendment'), cert denied, 505 US 1230 (1992); *In re Asbestos Litig*, 46 F.3d 1284, 1290 (3rd Cir, 1994) (contributions to political organisation are constitutionally protected absent specific intent to further the group's illegal ends).

[34]   458 US 886, 920 (1982).

The asserted distinction between support and membership also cannot be squared with the Fifth Amendment requirement that the government prove *personal* guilt. In *Scales v United States*,[35] discussed in the Introduction, the Supreme Court stated:

> In our jurisprudence guilt is personal, and when the imposition of punishment on a status *or on conduct* can only be justified by reference to the relationship of that status *or conduct* to other concededly criminal activity, … that relationship must be sufficiently substantial to satisfy the concept of personal guilt in order to withstand attack under the Due Process Clause of the Fifth Amendment.[36] (emphasis added)

In other words, the Fifth Amendment forbids holding a moral innocent culpable for the acts of others. The principle is not limited to penalties based on membership alone: it encompasses any punishment of 'status *or conduct*' that 'can only be justified by reference to the relationship of that status *or conduct* to other concededly criminal activity'. The prohibition on material support to specified groups is explicitly 'justified by reference to the relationship of that . . . conduct to other concededly criminal activity', namely the group's 'terrorist activity'.

The asserted distinction between support and membership makes even less sense under the Fifth Amendment principle of personal guilt than under the First Amendment. Surely it seems more reasonable to attribute criminal liability for a gang crime to a member of a violent gang than it would to attribute liability to a social worker who provided the gang with vocational training or counselling services. Yet under the courts' analysis of the 'material support' laws, the gang member could not be held liable absent proof of specific intent to further the gang's illegal ends, but the social worker could be.

The government has argued that broadly criminalising support even of groups' otherwise lawful activities is necessary because money is fungible, and therefore any support, even to legitimate activities, frees up resources that can be used to support a group's illegal activities. That argument proves too much, for it would render nugatory the constitutional ban on guilt by association. The fact that a group engages in illegal activities – even illegal activities that threaten national security – does not permit the government to prohibit association with the group's legal activities. Yet on the government's view, because all support of a group frees up resources that could be used for illegal activities, *all* support to any group that engages in illegal activities could be criminalised. On this theory, the fact that the Democratic and Republican Parties violate campaign finance laws would authorise a prohibition on all support of

---

[35] 367 US 203 (1961).
[36] *Ibid*, at 224–5.

those parties. The United States made just such a broad 'freeing-up' argument to the Supreme Court in *Scales v United States* as a reason for rejecting the specific intent test, without success.[37]

In addition, neither these statutes nor the United States' enforcement of them is consistent with the freeing-up theory. As noted above, the criminal material support statute itself permits unlimited donations of 'medicine and religious articles' to terrorist groups.[38] Yet donations of medicine and religious articles are just as capable of freeing up resources as the prohibited donations. And the statute contemplates approval of certain forms of training, expert advice or assistance, and personnel, where the support may not be used to carry out terrorist activity. But under the government's theory, it should not matter if the support itself may be used to pursue terrorism, because even if it cannot, it theoretically frees up other resources that can be so employed.

The courts have recognised that the breadth of the material support statutes is troubling, and have invalidated the laws at their furthest reaches. Thus, several courts have ruled that the definition of 'material support' is too broad, and have struck down as unconstitutionally vague the prohibitions on providing 'training', 'expert advice or assistance' and 'services' to terrorist groups.[39] In addition, a federal court ruled unconstitutional the President's authorisation to the Secretary of the Treasury to designate 'specially designated global terrorists' on the basis of mere association and, as noted above, in the wake of that decision, the government narrowed the 'association' ground considerably.[40] These decisions have been important in reining in the worst excesses of the material support regime. But they leave in place its fundamental infirmity – the imposition of guilt by association.

Similarly, the courts have generally upheld the procedures employed for designated entities to challenge their designation – while rejecting all challenges that have come before them. The courts have to date permitted the government to defend its designations using secret evidence not

[37] Brief for the United States on Reargument at 8, *Scales v United States*, 367 US 203 (arguing that showing 'specific intent' is unnecessary 'on the principle that knowingly joining an organization with illegal objectives contributes to the attainment of those objectives because of the support given by membership itself').
[38] 18 USC § 2339A(b).
[39] See *Humanitarian Law Project v Reno*, 205 F.3d 1130 (9th Cir, 2000) (declaring 'training' and 'personnel' unconstitutionally vague); *Humanitarian Law Project v Gonzales*, 380 F.Supp.2d 1134 (CD Cal, 2005) (declaring 'training'. 'expert advice or assistance', and 'services' unconstitutionally vague); *United States v Sattar*, 272 F.Supp.2d 348 (SDNY, 2003) (declaring 'personnel' and 'communications' unconstitutionally vague).
[40] See n 24 above.

disclosed to the challenger, and have declined to accept evidence proffered by the designated entities, limiting their decisions to the administrative record.[41] The courts have required that where a designated entity has a presence within the United States, due process requires that it be afforded an opportunity to make a presentation in writing, to be included as part of the administrative record. But that is the extent of the entity's opportunity to defend itself. No hearing is required, and accordingly there is no opportunity to present witnesses or to confront the government's witnesses.[42]

To adhere to the constitutional prohibition on guilt by association and bar criminalisation of material support without a showing of intent would not leave the nation defenceless against terrorist plots. There are many more precisely calibrated ways to stem the flow of funds for terrorist activity. Congress can make and has made it a crime to provide material support to a wide range of terrorist crimes.[43] Conspiracy and 'aiding and abetting' statutes penalise not only those who actually commit acts of violence, but also those who engage in overt acts in furtherance of such conduct, even if the ultimate wrongdoing never comes to fruition.[44] Money laundering statutes expressly prohibit the transmission of money or funds with the intent of promoting terrorist activity.[45] And the Racketeering Influenced and Corrupt Organizations Act (RICO), permits the government to target ostensibly legitimate activities when they are a front for illegal conduct.[46] Thus, the constitutional prohibition on guilt by association permits the government to criminalise the financing of terrorism. It simply requires it to target terrorism rather than political association.

The international approach to terrorist financing illustrates a greater sensitivity to concerns about guilt by association than is reflected by the US regime. The United States has actively encouraged other nations to

---

[41] See, eg, *Holy Land Foundation v Aschroft*, 333 F.3d 156.

[42] *National Council of Resistance to Iran v Department of State*, 251 F.3d 192 (DC Cir, 2001).

[43] 18 USC §2339A(a) (criminalising aid to a long list of specific terrorist acts).

[44] Sheikh Omar Abdel Rahman, for example, was convicted of seditious conspiracy for his part in encouraging a plan to bomb various tunnels and bridges in New York City, even though he did not undertake any violent act himself: *United States v Rahman*, 189 F.3d 88 (2nd Cir, 1999), cert denied, 528 US 1094 (2000).

[45] The Money Laundering Control Act makes it a crime, among other things, to transmit funds 'with the intent to promote the carrying on of specified unlawful activity', including terrorism: 18 USC §1956(a)(2)(A). The USA PATRIOT Act added extensive new money laundering provisions designed to facilitate the investigation, prevention, and prosecution of money laundering related to terrorism: USA PATRIOT Act, §§ 301–76.

[46] 18 USC §§ 1961–8. RICO prohibits the acquisition or maintenance of any enterprise through a pattern of racketeering, or with income derived from a pattern of racketeering: 18 USC § 1962. A wide range of terrorist activity and fundraising for terrorist activity is included within the definition of racketeering activity: see 18 USC § 1961(1) and 18 USC § 2332b(g)(5).

crack down on 'terrorist financing', and shortly after 11 September 2001 convinced the UN Security Council to issue Resolution 1373. That resolution, however, calls on all UN member states to enact laws criminalising the willful provision or collection of funds with the knowledge or intention that they will be used to carry out terrorist acts, and thus is in keeping with a requirement of individualised intent.[47] States are required to freeze the assets of persons who facilitate terrorist acts.[48]

Many nations have responded, but generally by penalising only those who provide material support with the intent of furthering terrorist acts, not those who merely support a group without any intent to further its criminal ends. The European Union, for example, maintains a list of terrorist groups and supporters.[49] Funds of those listed are frozen, and the European Community is required to ensure that assets will not be made available to the parties on the list.[50] A European Council Framework Decision of June 2002 on combating terrorism requires member states to make it a crime to 'participate in the activities of a terrorist group, including by supplying information or material resources, or by funding its activities in any way, *with knowledge of the fact that such participation will contribute to the criminal activities of the terrorist group*' (emphasis added).[51] That formulation respects the principle of individual culpability that the United States has abandoned.

These laws illustrate that it is possible to target terror financing while being attentive to the distinction between *intentional* support of terrorist *acts*, and aid to terrorist *groups* that is intended to further only lawful ends. The European courts have also demanded greater procedural protections for those who challenge their inclusion on the list, requiring, for example, a statement of reasons and the right to a fair hearing.[52]

In short, the United States' approach to material support for terrorist organisations contravenes basic constitutional principles of fairness, due process and the right of association. There are more narrowly tailored alternatives available, as illustrated by the other US laws discussed above, and by the responses of other nations to the same problem. Here, as elsewhere in the 'war on terror', the United States has gone out on a limb.

---

[47]   UN Security Council Resolution 1373, Art 1(b).

[48]   *Ibid*, Art 1(c).

[49]   The latest complete version of this list is at Council Common Position 2006/380/CFSP of 29 May 2006, OJ L 144 p 25. (DOC 9).

[50]   2001/931/CFSP, Council Common Position of 27 December 2001 on the application of specific measures to combat terrorism, OJ 2001 L344/93, at Arts 2 and 3. (DOC 10).

[51]   EC Council Framework Decision of 13 June 2002 on Combating Terrorism, Art 2.2(b).

[52]   *Organisation des Modjahedines du people d'Iran v Council of the European Unio*, Court of First Instance of the European Communities (Second Chamber) (12 December 2006).

IV. THE BROADER CONTEXT – THE PREVENTIVE PARADIGM

The material support regime is just one part of a much broader initiative launched by the Bush administration in the wake of 11 September 2001. The administration insisted that 'everything changed' after that date, and that it must operate within a new paradigm of prevention. When suicide bombers attack, prosecution after the fact is a patently insufficient response – it is far better to stop them before they act. Citing the need to prevent terrorist attacks, the administration has invoked the 'preventive paradigm' at home and abroad as a justification for abandoning traditional limits on the use of coercive state power, and thereby freeing the state to use force not merely reactively, to defend against attacks or to punish wrongdoers, but proactively, to prevent terrorist attacks before they are launched.[53]

The preventive rationale is what the United States used to justify its decision to launch a war against Iraq. The Pentagon's 2002 National Security Strategy advanced a new and controversial 'preventive' justification for going to war, arguing that in light of the threats now posed by weapons of mass destruction, war is justified not only when the nation is under attack or the threat of imminent attack – the only justifications recognised by international law – but also when it faces a more speculative but potentially catastrophic future threat.[54] No one argued that an attack by Iraq on the United States was imminent. Instead, the administration contended that the potential for attack with weapons of mass destruction at some undetermined time in the future and by some undetermined terrorist group that might obtain the weapons from Saddam Hussein was sufficient to justify war as a preventative measure.

The administration has similarly defended the use of cruel, inhuman, and degrading treatment to interrogate al Qaeda suspects on the ground that the information so obtained may help prevent future attacks. No one defends torture or coercive interrogation as a way of solving past crimes or punishing perpetrators – the only justification offered is the forward-looking one of preventing future harms. And the administration has also cited a 'new paradigm' to argue that the Geneva Conventions and other rules of war do not apply to the conflict with al Qaeda. It claimed that the Geneva Conventions apply only to wars between nations and internal civil wars, and that therefore traditionally recognised rules of war, including the obligation to treat detainees humanely, are inapplicable at

---

[53] For a more complete discussion and critique of the 'paradigm of prevention' discussed here, see D Cole and J Lobel, *Less Safe, Less Free: Why America is Losing the War on Terror* (New York, NY, The New Press, 2007).

[54] The White House, National Security Strategy of the United States of America, 17 September 2002, available at <http://www.whitehouse.gov/nsc/nss.all.html>.

Guantanamo and at secret CIA 'black sites' where al Qaeda detainees are held.[55] Here, too, the motive for denying Geneva Conventions protection was precisely to allow interrogators to use coercive means to extract intelligence from suspects.

At home, Attorney General John Ashcroft repeatedly trumpeted a parallel new 'paradigm of prevention' in law enforcement and intelligence gathering.[56] Asserting that it would help prevent the next attack, the administration subjected 82,000 Arab and Muslim immigrant men to fingerprinting and registration, subjected 8,000 Arab and Muslim men to FBI interviews, and preventively detained over 5,000 foreign nationals, also nearly all Arabs and Muslims.[57] As part of its preventive paradigm, the government adopted an aggressive strategy of arrest and prosecution on 'pretextual' minor charges – such as immigration violations, credit card fraud or false statements – or on no charges at all, as 'material witnesses', when it suspected them of terrorist ties but lacked the evidence to try them for terrorism. On a similar preventive rationale, the administration pushed for expansive new powers in the USA Patriot Act, and since then the FBI has used that Act to issue annually tens of thousands of 'national security letters' – administrative subpoenas that demand the secret production of information on customers from telephone and internet companies and financial institutions without any court review.[58] And most recently, the preventive rationale has been advanced to justify the National Security Agency's (NSA's) warrantless wiretapping of countless persons in the United States, without congressional or judicial approval, pursuant to an executive order adopted in secret and in contravention of a criminal prohibition on such surveillance.[59]

The same preventive rationale underlies the material support laws. The justification for criminalising human rights advocacy training or humanitarian aid is not that such support is itself somehow morally wrong, or harmful. The argument is that if we cut off all support to

---

[55] The White House, Fact Sheet on Status of Detainees, 7 February 2002, available at <http://www.whitehouse.gov/news/releases/2002/02/20020207–13.html>.

[56] See n 8 above.

[57] See Cole, n 25 above, at 25–35.

[58] US Dept of Justice, Inspector General, A Review of the Federal Bureau of Investigation's Use of National Security Letters (March 2007), available at <http://www.usdoj.gov/oig/special/s0703b/final.pdf>; D Eggen, 'FBI Sought Data on Thousands in '05' *The Washington Post*, 2 May 2006, A4.

[59] In a radio address following disclosure of the NSA warrantless wiretapping program, President Bush argued that 'the activities conducted under this authorization have helped detect and prevent possible terrorist attacks in the United States and abroad': GW Bush, 'The President's Radio Address' 17 December 2005, available at <http://www.whitehouse.gov/news/releases/2005/12/20051217.html>; see also R Stevenson and A Liptak, 'Cheney Defends Eavesdropping Without Warrants', *New York Times*, 21 December 2005, A36.

entities and individuals we label as 'terrorists', we will make it more difficult for these entities and individuals to carry out terrorist activity in the future. Thus, while material support laws as a formal matter punish past acts, not future predictions, the justification for punishing the past acts is the speculation that they might facilitate bad acts in the future.

Whether in the context of material support, interrogation, detention or war-making, the preventive paradigm puts tremendous pressure on the values we associate with the rule of law. Designed to place enforceable constraints on state power, the rule of law generally reserves detention, punishment and military force for those who have been shown, on the basis of sound evidence and fair procedures, to have committed some wrongful act in the past that warrants the government's response. The administration's 'preventive paradigm', by contrast, justifies coercive action – from detention to torture to bombing – on the basis of speculation about future contingencies, without either the evidence or the fair processes that have generally been considered necessary before the state imposes coercive measures on human beings.

When the state begins to direct highly coercive measures at individuals and other states based on necessarily speculative predictions about future behaviour, it inevitably leads to substantial compromises on the values associated with the rule of law – such as equality, transparency, individual culpability, fair procedures and checks and balances. We have seen just those compromises in the context of the material support laws. Groups are selected for designation in a necessarily subjective and secretive process, and denied a meaningful opportunity to challenge their designations. Individuals are then held responsible not for their own acts, but for their associational support of others, without regard to whether the individual being punished has ever done anything to facilitate violence. And the material support laws frustrate checks and balances by granting the executive branch wide leeway in designation decisions, and by providing for only a charade of judicial review.

V. CONCLUSION

Many of the United States' initiatives in the 'paradigm of prevention' have come back to haunt it. Guantanamo and Abu Ghraib have done incalculable damage to the United States' image abroad. The round-up and preventive detention of thousands of Arab and Muslim immigrants within the United States after 11 September 2001, none of whom had any connection to terrorism, has alienated Arab and Muslim communities both at home and abroad, and the war in Iraq has been an unmitigated disaster.

The reason these measures have backfired is because they are so inimical to the core values of the rule of law. So, too, the punishment of material support, a twenty-first century version of guilt by association, is contrary to fundamental principles, not only of US constitutional law, but of international human rights law. In the long run, like other preventive paradigm initiatives, it is likely to alienate potential allies, fuel the propaganda of enemies, and inflict unnecessary harm on both the moral innocents targeted, and on the reputation of the United States world-wide. A lot may have changed after 11 September 2001, but not the need to respond to wrongdoers within the framework of the rule of law.

7

United We Stand:

National Courts Reviewing Counterterrorism Measures[*]

EYAL BENVENISTI

I. INTRODUCTION

T HE 'WAR ON terrorism' is far from over, if it will ever be. However, more than five years into the coordinated global effort against Al Qaeda and its associated groups, we can hesitantly point to one possible victor: the national courts. The persistent attempts of the executive and legislative branches of several democracies to curtail the authority of courts to review counterterrorism policies have, by and large, failed. They have not convinced the courts to defer judgment and, in fact, have generated a counter-reaction on the part of the judiciary. Hesitant at first, the courts regained their confidence and asserted novel claims that bolster their judicial authority, claims that may well resonate beyond the context of terrorism and counterterrorism. The aim of this chapter is to describe and explain this reaction.

In the wake of the 11 September 2001 terrorist attacks, national courts faced a major challenge to their authority. Concerned with the potentially devastating effects of global terrorism, national bureaucracies sought to intensify restrictions on rights and liberties perceived as facilitating terrorist acts or impeding counterterrorism efforts. They insisted on their exclusive discretion in shaping and implementing these restrictions as they deemed fit. The executive's demand for broad, sole discretion rested on its claim of a relative advantage over the other branches of government in assessing the risks of terrorism and in managing those risks.

* This chapter is based on research conducted since 11 September 2001, on the ways in which national courts cope with international terrorism, funded by the Israel Science Foundation and the Minerva Center for Human Rights at Tel Aviv University. The author is grateful to Tomer Amar, Renana Keidar, Yifat Pagis and Yoav Szutan for their excellent research assistance.

Most legislatures complied without demur. Far-reaching legislative changes, hurriedly introduced in most democracies in the weeks and months following the Al Qaeda attacks, sailed through legislatures with little public debate or scrutiny.[1] The threat of suicide terrorists intent on using weapons of mass destruction to kill scores of innocents – a threat promulgated by government officials – was sufficient for legislators to support wide-scale curtailment of basic rights, particularly when minorities and immigrants were regarded as one possible source of the threat and, hence, were the targets of the restrictive measures. The demand for enhanced security in many countries seemed to justify far-reaching limitations on individual liberties, without providing the traditional guarantees of judicial review. The immediate shock of 11 September 2001 led many to view basic principles of due process, shaped by democratic societies' preference to err in favour of liberty, as entailing unacceptable risks. To allow nine criminals to walk free rather than put one innocent person behind bars, the risk-management rule informing the rights of the accused, was now deemed intolerable when some of those nine could be capable of wreaking horrendous injury and suffering.

The wave of acquiescence to the demands of the national political leaders for absolute discretion in acting to guarantee national security swept the courts as well. In fact, conformity of this nature had been the hallmark of judicial practice in previous wars and national crises.[2] Suffice it to recall the decisions of the UK and US courts during the two World Wars and the early Cold War era, in which they deferred to the executive's discretion, based on the courts' limited authority and institutional capacity to assess and manage the risks of war.[3] And thus, indeed, in the weeks following 11 September, the familiar rhetoric of judicial deference by frightened judges was repeated. Lord Hoffmann of the British House of Lords explained in *Rehman* his approval of the Secretary of State's

---

[1] In some countries, the legislative process was brief and did not come up against any significant opposition. Bills were passed within a few weeks or days (even hours in the case of Germany) of the events of 11 September. On the legislative changes in the various democratic countries, see the country reports in C Walter, S Vöneky, V Röben and F Schorkopf (eds), *Terrorism as a Challenge for National and International Law: Security versus Liberty?* (Berlin/Heidelberg, Springer, 2004); Kent Roach, 'Sources and Trends in Post 9/11 Anti-Terrorism Laws' (2006), available at <http://ssrn.com/abstract=899291>.

[2] On wartime jurisprudence, see E Benvenisti, 'National Courts and the "War on Terrorism"' in A Bianchi (ed), *Enforcing International Law Norms Against Terrorism* (Oxford/Portland, OR, Hart Publishing, 2004) 309–15 at 307.

[3] Recall Justice Jackson's opinion in *Korematsu v US*, 65 S Ct 193, 245 (1944): 'In the nature of things, military decisions are not susceptible of intelligent judicial appraisal. They do not pretend to rest on evidence, but are made on information that often would not be admissible and on assumptions that could not be proved … Hence courts can never have real alternative to accepting the mere declaration of the authorities that issued the order that it was reasonably necessary from a military viewpoint.'

decision to deport a Pakistani national based on (disputed) evidence linking him to Islamic terrorist groups operating on the Indian subcontinent:

> [T]he question of whether something is 'in the interests' of national security is not a question of law. It is a matter of judgment and policy. Under the constitution of the United Kingdom and most other countries, decisions as to whether something is or is not in the interests of national security are not a matter for judicial decision. They are entrusted to the executive.[4]

In Lord Hoffmann's view, not only are the courts unable to assess what national security requires, they also lack the authority to balance security interests against interests in liberty. In other words, the courts possess neither the tools nor the legitimacy to make an independent judgment in such matters. Lord Hoffmann continued:

> It is not only that the executive has access to special information and expertise in these matters. It is also that such decisions, with serious potential results for the community, require a legitimacy which can be conferred only by entrusting them to persons responsible to the community through the democratic process. If the people are to accept the consequences of such decisions, they must be made by persons whom the people have elected and whom they can remove.[5]

The 11 September attack, in some inexplicable way, 'proved' more clearly than ever the case for judicial silence.[6] As Lord Steyn added, in the same judgment, 'the tragic events of 11 September 2001 in New York reinforce compellingly that no other approach is possible'.[7], the Law Lords were following the traditional explanation for their abdicating responsibility during wartime.[8]

Three years into this new era, however, the Lords transformed themselves into the guardians of the constitution and the champions of individual rights, even as the war on terror continued with only modest success. The 8-to-1 majority in the so-called *A (Belmarsh Detainees)* case,[9]

---

[4] *Secretary of State for the Home Department v. Rehman* [2001] 3 WLR 877.

[5] *Ibid* at para 62.

[6] Lord Slynn and Lord Steyn offered a similar, although more refined take on the role of the courts. Lord Slynn (*Rehman, ibid* at para 26) stated that 'the Commission must give due weight to the assessment and conclusions of the Secretary of State in the light at any particular time of his responsibilities, or of Government policy and the means at his disposal of being informed of and understanding the problems involved. He is undoubtedly in the best position to judge what national security requires even if his decision is open to review. The assessment of what is needed in the light of changing circumstances is primarily for him.' Lord Steyn (at para 29), in turn, asserted: 'The dynamics of the role of the Secretary of State, charged with the power and duty to consider deportation on grounds of national security, irresistibly supports this analysis.'

[7] *Ibid*, para 29.

[8] See n 2 above and accompanying text.

[9] *A (FC) and Others (FC) (Appellants) v Secretary of State for the Home Department (Respondent)* [2004] UKHL 56.

asserting judicial competence and legitimacy to review security measures against non-British suspected terrorists, was a stunning departure from the Anglo-American tradition of judicial deference. In a public lecture on 10 June 2005, Lord Steyn, who was not on the panel in *Belmarsh Detainees*, commended the House of Lords for its landmark decision, affirming the stance that courts are fully authorised and competent to make 'exceedingly difficult choices as to when they should defer to the other branches of government and when not'.[10] He made another reference to 11 September 2001, but focused rather on the reactions of the UK and US governments to the attack:

> Nobody doubts in any way the very real risk of international terrorism. But the *Belmarsh* decision came against the public fear whipped up by the governments of the United States and the United Kingdom since 11 September 2001 and their determination to bend established international law to their will and to undermine its essential structures. It was a great day for the law – for calm and reasoned judgment, analysis without varnish, and for principled democratic decision making by our highest court.[11]

Lord Hoffmann joined the majority in the *A (Belmarsh Detainees)* opinion. He made no reference to his earlier position, in *Rehman*, even though that stance was indirectly criticised in the other majority opinions in *Belmarsh Detainees* and endorsed only by the minority. Instead, he took the most extreme assertion any judge has ever made in this context. In his view, the court was entitled not only to assess the proportionality of certain measures deemed necessary by the executive to contend with grave risks to society, it was perfectly capable of examining, and was in fact required to examine, the executive's determination of those risks. And preferring his own determination, he dismissed the latter's assessment of the risk at hand: 'Terrorist violence, serious as it is, does not threaten our institutions of government or our existence as a civil community.'[12]

The transformation manifested in the *A (Belmarsh Detainees)* decision is not limited to the UK context. In light of the similar, if not as dramatic, changes in the ways in which national courts have reacted to their executive's security-related claims since 11 September 2001,[13] it is possible to now speak of a new phase in the way democracies are addressing the threat of terrorism: executive unilateralism is being challenged by national courts in what could perhaps be a globally coordinated move.

---

[10] Lord Steyn, '2000–2005: Laying the Foundations of Human Rights Law in the United Kingdom' (2005) 4 *European Human Rights Law Review* 349 at 361.

[11] *Ibid* at 350: 'I feel free, however, to say that the *Belmarsh* decision, and in particular Lord Bingham's opinion, was a vindication of the rule of law, ranking with historic judgments of our courts.'

[12] *A (Belmarsh Detainees)* [2004] UKHL 56, para 96, per Lord Hoffmann.

[13] These cases will be discussed in Section II.

Courts have embarked on this challenge by relying on a number of techniques that allow them to ratchet up or down their level of intervention in the political branches' exercise of power. They prefer to affect outcomes by using the least restrictive, lowest-profile methods possible and thereby engage the executive and the legislature in ongoing institutional negotiations that encourage the political branches to reconsider their policies. This chapter describes these techniques and demonstrates the measured use that has been made of them. Amongst these techniques, the use of international law is particularly intriguing, given the traditional judicial hesitation to resort to international law and the reluctance of some societies to accept international law as a legitimate set of norms that ought to constrain the domestic political process.[14] Section II outlines the different judicial responses to the executive's claim to autonomous discretion. These techniques reveal an emerging judicial theory on the role of courts in a democracy, which goes beyond the context of terrorism. Section III explores this theory and assesses its origins. Section IV attempts to explain the use of the different techniques and to suggest a theory for the evolving judicial approach that could be viewed as a coordinated response on the part of a group of national courts to the coordinated counterterrorism policies of their national governments, and Section V concludes.

II. POST-11 SEPTEMBER 2001 JUDICIAL RESPONSES: CLIMBING UP THE LADDER OF JUDICIAL REVIEW

To elucidate the ability of courts to engage the political branches in a dialogue over the fine-tuning of counterterrorism measures, this Section describes the medley of tools that courts employ when reviewing security measures. Leaving aside possible claims of non-justiciability, acts of state and similar avoidance doctrines,[15] the judicial review of executive action is a two-tiered process. The first tier is institutional: the courts inquire into whether the executive has been given the authority to act. In the framework of this inquiry, courts track the line of possible sources of authorisation for executive power/action, starting with the constitution, through the authorising statute, down to the administrative regulation. The second tier focuses on substance: the courts examine whether the executive has exercised its authority in line with the restrictions set by the authorising law, as interpreted and constrained by constitutional law

---

[14] E Benvenisti, 'Judicial Misgivings Regarding the Application of International Norms: An Analysis of Attitudes of National Courts' (1993) 4 *European Journal of International Law* 159.

[15] For an analysis of the various avoidance doctrines, see *ibid* at 169–73.

(and international law, if domestic law refers to it). In this process, the courts examine not only the relevant constraints imposed by the law but also the way they were applied by the executive to the facts of the specific case. This inquiry requires that the courts either weigh up the conflicting risks and interests or review how the executive performed this delicate balancing act.

Courts that operate in a legal and political environment that views judicial intervention with suspicion will tend to avoid as much as possible making a determination of illegal executive action based on second-tier considerations. They will, rather, rule on the question of institutional authority to act, a question that is without doubt the domain of the courts and, in so doing, will prefer to leave room for the legislature to weigh-in on the matter. Their hope would be that the legislature will cooperate by imposing effective constraints on the executive. But before referring the matter to the legislature, a court might clarify the considerations that the executive must take into account in exercising its discretion and then try to induce the executive to reconsider its original decision in light of this determination. After pleading with the executive to rethink its action, the least controversial judicial intervention would be to declare the action unauthorised by law or read into the existing source of authorisation stringent standards that the executive has to comply with, thereby inviting the legislature to clarify the limits of executive authority in the particular matter. While focusing on the institutional level, the courts can set higher barriers for legislative authorisation by invoking international law and, ultimately, the constitution as precluding certain authorising legislation. The latter two possibilities, which limit or even pre-empt the regular democratic process, will prove difficult for courts whose political sphere is apprehensive about such judicial intervention.

Through the prisms of these two tiers of review, we can identify five possible positive judicial responses to requests for judicial review of executive actions. As the Canada Supreme Court 2002 decision in *Suresh v Canada*[16] demonstrated, referring an action back to the executive for reconsideration constitutes the least controversial, but often a quite effective, response. The next step up the ladder would be to refer the matter to the legislature to clarify the scope of authorisation granted to the executive. By rejecting open-ended and vague authorisations and insisting on legislative involvement[17] or by reading into existing authorisations strict requirements that constrain the executive's discretion,

---

[16] *Suresh v Canada (Minister of Citizenship and Immigration)* (2002) 1 SCR 3, 2002 SCC 1, available at <http://scc.lexum.umontreal.ca/en/2002/2002scc1/2002scc1.html>.

[17] See, eg, *Leung Kwok Hung v HKSAR* Hong Kong Court of First Instance HCAL 107/2005 (9 February 2006) (Hong Kong Unreported Judgments, available at Lexis as [2006] HKCU 230) (legislation authorising covert surveillance, including the secret interception of

thereby giving the legislature the opportunity to intervene,[18] the courts position themselves as guardians of the democratic process. It is when they restrict democratically accepted outcomes that their competence becomes more controversial. Thus, a third type of referral would require the legislature to depart from its international treaty obligations and would impose significant limits on the legislature's discretion (unless the executive and legislature assign little value to how their courts interpret their international obligations). Beyond these three types of judicial responses is the realm of constitutional review. Judicial determinations as to the incompatibility of specific measures with the national constitution constitute the most extreme form of judicial intervention. In the framework of this fourth manner of response, the court would declare a certain piece of legislation unconstitutional, but allow the legislature to re-legislate it in a more circumscribed fashion so as to conform to constitutional standards. Finally, and ultimately, the fifth response would be to declare a certain measure as utterly infringing constitutional limitations and therefore beyond the legislature's scope of authority. Such a response could be in the form of an explicit declaration of the unconstitutionality of the enabling statute, or it could be implicit, in the form of reading into the relevant statute strict standards that would make it, in the eyes of the court, compatible with the constitution.

These five types of responses can be depicted as five steps up the ladder of judicial review. Relative to any prevailing political resistance to judicial intervention, we can anticipate that courts will climb up or down that ladder, summoning the political branches to enter into a dialogue and thereby also seeking to share with them responsibility for the outcome. The remainder of this Section considers the different steps on which different national courts have perched, while Section III examines the justifications provided by those courts for climbing up the ladder beyond the initial and obvious first step of review.

On 11 January 2002, a few months into the new counterterrorism era, the Supreme Court of Canada came to a unanimous decision in the matter of Suresh, a member of the LTTE ('Liberation Tigers of Tamil

---

private communications, infringes the right to privacy and is therefore incompatible with the Basic Law due to wide discretionary powers it allows to the executive).

[18] See the New Zealand Supreme Court decision concerning the deportation of refugees who face the risk of torture in their home countries (the *Suresh* scenario), *Zaoui v Attorney-General (No 2)* [2006] 1 NZLR 289, para 93: 'the Minister, in deciding whether to certify under s 72 of the Immigration Act 1987 that the continued presence of a person constitutes a threat to national security, and members of the Executive Council, in deciding whether to advise the Governor-General to order deportation under s 72, are not to so decide or advise if they are satisfied that there are substantial grounds for believing that, as a result of the deportation, the person would be in danger of being arbitrarily deprived of life or of being subjected to torture or to cruel, inhuman or degrading treatment or punishment'.

Eelam'), the Tamil Tigers organisation struggling against the Sri Lankan government. The judgment approved in principle the decision of the Minister of Citizenship and Immigration to deport Suresh to Sri Lanka, despite the possibility that he would be tortured there. This decision reiterated the *Rehman* line of reasoning, that the authority to balance the conflicting interests rests with the Minister rather than the Court[19] and that, in principle, there is no prohibition on deportation to a country that may inflict torture on the deportee.[20] The *Suresh* decision did, however, set forth the required decision-making process in cases where there is a prima facie risk of torture and remanded the case back to the Minister for reconsideration in line with the guidelines set by the Court. Thus, the Minister was required to explain in writing the reasons for deporting a person to a country that is likely to torture him or her. No doubt, the Court anticipated that this procedural requirement would prove a sufficiently high threshold to preclude such deportations. As it has indeed since turned out, no Canadian Minister has been willing to issue such a statement, and therefore no deportee from Canada has subsequently been exposed to the threat of torture.[21]

---

[19] *Suresh*, n 16 above, para 38: 'The court's task, if called upon to review the Minister's decision, is to determine whether the Minister has exercised her decision-making power within the constraints imposed by Parliament's legislation and the Constitution. If the Minister has considered the appropriate factors in conformity with these constraints, the court must uphold his decision. It cannot set it aside even if it would have weighed the factors differently and arrived at a different conclusion.'

[20] *Ibid* at para 76: '*barring extraordinary circumstances*, deportation to torture will *generally* violate the principles of fundamental justice' (emphasis added).

[21] See also the recent order of Deputy Judge MacKay of the Federal Court of Canada in the *Jaballah* case, rendered on 16 October 2006, at <http://www.fct-cf.gc.ca/bulletins/whatsnew/DES-04–01_determinations.pdf>, ruling that an Egyptian national who has resided in Canada since May 1996 can be deported from Canada but not to countries where he would face a serious risk of being tortured; the allegations that Mr Jaballah poses a security threat in Canada are not of such an 'exceptional' nature as to justify exposing him to torture. This follows an earlier decision of MacKay's in the same matter, where he referred to the exercise of discretion in such cases as follows: 'In assessing "exceptional circumstances" that would justify Mr Jaballah's deportation to face torture, the Minister's delegate made no reference to circumstances facing Canada or its security, other than the conclusion that it is endangered by Mr Jaballah's presence in Canada. In *Suresh v Canada (Minister of Citizenship and Immigration)*, the SCC referred to "exceptional circumstances" in terms of "natural disasters, the outbreak of war, epidemics and the like", and to cases where the exceptional circumstances referred to appear to concern those facing Canada as a nation. In the present case, the Minister's delegate made no reference to such circumstances that would warrant exception from the protection of section 7 of the Canadian Charter of Rights and Freedoms, either in the balancing of fundamental rights or in the examination of evidence to support an exception based on section 1 of the Charter. The delegate's assessment of the danger posed by Mr Jaballah also failed to consider the limits on his freedom should he remain in Canada. The delegate thus erred in law': *In the Matter of Mahmoud Jaballah* 2005 FC 399, available at <http://reports.fja.gc.ca/en/2005/2005fc399/2005fc399.html>.

A good example of climbing up the first, second and third steps of the judicial review ladder can be found in the US Supreme Court jurisprudence regarding the treatment of post-11 September 2001 detainees in Guantanamo and elsewhere. Referral back to the executive or legislature is the first stage of the Court's involvement in this matter. The *Rasul*[22] and *Hamdi*[23] decisions, rendered on the same day, asserted the Court's jurisdiction to review executive action with respect to unlawful combatants held on US territory or territory under US administration, including Guantanamo, and that neither Congress nor the Constitution grants the executive a blank cheque to act as it pleases. In these decisions, the Court referred the policies back to the government to assert its authority to act. The second round came two years later with the *Hamdan* decision,[24] which rejected the government's response to the earlier decisions. In *Hamdan*, the majority relied on international law as the standard for assessing the legality of the military commissions established by the President to determine the status of Guantanamo detainees. In its judgment, the Court diverged from the executive's position in two important aspects: first, that Common Article 3 of the 1949 Geneva Conventions applies to the conflict with Al Qaeda and, second, that the standards set by that Article are not met by the commissions.[25] The justices still resorted to the referral technique when they emphasised that the executive can seek Congress's approval for derogating from the requirements of international law, without acknowledging that such derogations may be costly to the United States in the international sphere.[26] It is noteworthy that the justices refrained from directly invoking the constitutional guarantees of due process, but Justice Kennedy, joined by Justices Souter,

---

[22] *Rasul v Bush*, 542 US 466 (2004).

[23] *Hamdi v Rumsfeld*, 542 US 507 (2004).

[24] *Hamdan v Rumsfeld*, 126 SCt 2749 (2006).

[25] Justice Stevens, *ibid* at 126: 'Common Article 3, by contrast, affords some minimal protection. ... While Common Article 3 does not define its "regularly constituted court" phrase, other sources define the words to mean an "ordinary military court" that is "established and organized in accordance with the laws and procedures already in force in a country." At a minimum, a military commission can be "regularly constituted" only if some practical need explains deviations from court-martial practice. No such need has been demonstrated here. Common Article 3's requirements are general, crafted to accommodate a wide variety of legal systems, but they are *requirements* nonetheless. The commission convened to try Hamdan does not meet those requirements.'

[26] As Justice Breyer said in *Hamdan* at 135–6, 'The Court's conclusion ultimately rests upon a single ground: Congress has not issued the Executive a "blank check" ... Indeed, Congress has denied the President the legislative authority to create military commissions of the kind at issue here. Nothing prevents the President from returning to Congress to seek the authority he believes necessary. Where, as here, no emergency prevents consultation with Congress, judicial insistence upon that consultation does not weaken our Nation's ability to deal with danger. To the contrary, that insistence strengthens the Nation's ability to determine – through democratic means – how best to do so. The Constitution places its faith in those democratic means. Our Court today simply does the same.'

Ginsburg and Breyer, added an important warning: the Court may eventually resort to the third and ultimate response, namely, the examination of the constitutionality of the military commissions once they are established by Congress:

> Because Congress has prescribed these limits, Congress can change them, requiring a new analysis *consistent with the Constitution* and other governing laws. At this time, however, we must apply the standards Congress has provided. By those standards the military commission is deficient.[27] (emphasis added)

This muffled threat did not deter Congress when it enacted the Military Commissions Act of 2006.[28] The Act sent a strong and unequivocal message to the Court. It aimed at stripping the courts of habeas corpus jurisdiction with respect to non-US citizens ('aliens') determined by the executive to be enemy combatants;[29] it declared that the Act conformed with the standards set by the 1949 Geneva Conventions[30] and, at the same time, provided that the Conventions could not be invoked by any 'alien unlawful enemy combatant subject to trial' under the Act[31] and nor could the definition of Common Article 3 violations be interpreted by the courts using 'foreign or international source[s] of law'.[32] In the wake of this Act, Professor John Yoo suggested, 'in the struggle for power between the three branches of government, it is not the presidency that "won". Instead, it is the judiciary that lost. The new law is, above all, a stinging rebuke to the Supreme Court'.[33] At the time of writing, it is not

---

[27] *Ibid* at 164.

[28] S 3930, passed by the US Senate on 28 September 2006, and by the US House of Representatives on 29 September 2006.

[29] *Ibid*, s 950j(b): 'No court, justice, or judge shall have jurisdiction to hear or consider an application for a writ of habeas corpus filed by or on behalf of an alien detained by the United States who has been determined by the United States to have been properly detained as an enemy combatant or is awaiting such determination.'

[30] *Ibid*, s 948b(f): 'A military commission established under this chapter is a regularly constituted court, affording all the necessary "judicial guarantees which are recognized as indispensable by civilized peoples" for purposes of common Article 3 of the Geneva Conventions.'

[31] *Ibid*, s 948b(g): 'No alien unlawful enemy combatant subject to trial by military commission under this chapter may invoke the Geneva Conventions as a source of rights.' The Act also prohibits any reliance on foreign and international sources.

[32] *Ibid*, s 6(a)(2): 'No foreign or international source of law shall supply a basis for a rule of decision in the courts of the United States in interpreting the prohibitions enumerated in [Common Art 3].'

[33] John Yoo, Op-Ed, 'Sending a Message: Congress to Courts: Get out of the War on Terror', *Wall St Journal* (US), 19 October 2006, <http://www.opinionjournal.com/editorial/feature.html?id=110009113>. Yoo further states: '*Hamdan* was an unprecedented attempt by the court to rewrite the law of war and intrude into war policy. The court must have thought its stunning power grab would go unchallenged.'

clear whether the Court will respond to this challenge by climbing one of the two final, constitutional, rungs of the judicial review ladder.[34]

It should be noted that, in some specific instances, the second step may effectively be the ultimate one. In the *A (Belmarsh Detainees)* decision, the House of Lords mentioned that, under the 1998 Human Rights Act, the ultimate determination lies with Parliament, since the court has the authority only to declare a legislative act as incompatible with the European Convention on Human Rights (ECHR) and not to declare a law invalid. Formally, Parliament can disregard the House of Lords' declaration. But in a political and social atmosphere where international law in general and the ECHR in particular weigh heavily, such a step would seem politically unlikely (especially in view of a possible vindication of the House of Lords' position by the European Court on Human Rights).[35]

In a different legal setting, the reliance of the Israeli High Court of Justice on international law effectively constitutes the final word with respect to the legality of Israeli measures in the territories occupied by Israel. Under the legal regime in those territories, it is the Israeli Army that wields authority there in accordance with international law, whereas the Israeli legislature is not directly involved. The Israeli Parliament (*Knesset*) cannot modify judicial limitations of the occupying power's authority without shattering the formal legal wall that separates the Israeli legal system from the legal system in the Occupied Territories. Hence, judicial determinations that certain measures violate the law of occupation or the laws of armed conflict effectively bind the Israeli political branches.[36]

The French *Conseil constitutionnel* and the German *Bundesverfassungsgericht* (the German Constitutional Court) have, for their part, climbed the final two steps of the ladder to explicitly reject as unconstitutional certain legislative Acts related to terrorism. In 1996, the *Conseil constitutionnel* found unconstitutional provisions of the Act to Strengthen Enforcement Measures to Combat Terrorism and Violence against Holders of Public Office or Public Service Functions and to Enact Measures relating to the Criminal Investigation Police.[37] In this decision, some of the measures (classifying assistance to illegal entry of foreign nationals as terrorism related and authorising the conduct of searches without judicial warrant) were declared disproportionate or excessive (the fourth step), while the Act's retroactive force in overseas territories was declared

---

[34] For more on the use of international law and its significance, see Section IV below.

[35] On the 'margin of appreciation' granted by the European Court to the member states, see n 77 below and accompanying text.

[36] For examples of such decisions, see nn 44, 55 and 57.

[37] Decision 96–377 DC of 16 July 1996, English translation at <http://www.conseil-constitutionnel.fr/langues /anglais/essential.htm>.

unconstitutional based on the principle that criminal legislation cannot have retroactive effect (the fifth step).

In 2005, the *Bundesverfassungsgericht* took the fourth step in the *European Arrest Warrant* case.[38] In this case, the court examined the European Arrest Warrant Act passed by the German *Bundestag* to implement the Framework Decision on the European Arrest Warrant, which had been promulgated in view of facilitating inter-European cooperation in combating crime and terrorism. The court found the Act to infringe on constitutional rights in a manner beyond what was necessary to meet the goals of the European policy. It thereby referred the matter back to the legislature to re-enact the Act so that the restriction of the fundamental right to freedom from extradition would be rendered proportionate.[39] But when it found the Air Security Act of 2005 unconstitutional, the German Court took the fifth and final step. This Act, which authorised federal authorities to order the downing of any civilian aircraft carrying hostages whose hijackers intend to crash the plane on a populated target (the 11 September scenario), was deemed to violate, inter alia, the principle of human dignity.[40]

In 2004, the Indian Supreme Court resorted to implicit constitutional review when it read into the 2002 Prevention of Terrorism Act (POTA) several additional conditions to a number of key provisions in the Act. The Court deemed such conditions to be mandated under the Indian Constitution[41] and authorised lower courts in administrative and criminal matters to further expound the constitutional requirements identified by the Court.

Most recently, in February 2007, a unanimous decision by the Canada Supreme Court declared the procedures allowing for the deportation of non-citizens suspected of terrorist activities on the basis of confidential information, as well as denying prompt hearing to foreign nationals, to

[38] Judgment of 18 July 2005, 2 BvR 2236/04, available at <http://www.bverfg.de/entscheidungen /rs20050718_2bvr223604en.html>.

[39] In an earlier decision that also related to counterterrorism, the Court emphasised the principle of 'informational self-determination', based on human dignity and privacy rights, which protects individuals from the gathering of information by state authorities. The Court did not find the use of GPS tracking systems, in addition to other surveillance devices, against suspected terrorists to be unauthorised, but did caution the *Bundestag* (German Federal Parliament) to monitor advances in surveillance technology and to develop new statutory safeguards to protect personal data by limiting the use of more powerful innovations: Judgment of 12 April 2005, 2 BvR 581/01, available at <www.bverfg.de/entscheidungen/rs20050412_2bvr058101.html> (in German). See Jacqueline Ross, 'Germany's Federal Constitutional Court and the Regulation of GPS Surveillance' (2005) 6(12) *German Law Journal*, <http://www.germanlawjournal.com/print.php?id=678>.

[40] BVerfG, 1 BvR 357/05 vom 15.2.2006, <http://www.bverfg.de/entscheidungen/rs20060215_1bvr035705.html>. See Nina Naske and Georg Nolte, 'Aerial Security Law' (case note) (2007) 101 *American Journal of International Law* 466.

[41] *People's Union for Civil Liberties v Union of India* [2004] 1 LRI 1.

be incompatible with the Canadian Charter of Rights and Freedoms.[42] This decision – a rather bold one for a court that belongs to the Anglo-American tradition – invited the legislature to respond by reshaping the hearing procedures: the declaration concerning the illegality of these procedures was suspended for a period of one year from the day of the judgment's rendering, 'to give Parliament time to amend the law' in light of the Court's suggestions.[43]

III. THE EMERGING JUDICIAL PHILOSOPHY CONCERNING THE REVIEW OF COUNTERTERRORISM MEASURES

In principle, one would expect that the more invasive the judicial intervention into the executive's and legislature's spheres of action, the stronger the reasoning presented by the court for such intervention. But courts do not necessarily engage in an open discussion of their justifications, often masking their decisions behind formal reasoning that does not acknowledge their activism. The *Conseil constitutionnel* and the *Bundesverfassungsgericht* do not waste words on explaining the source of their authority, as judicial institutions, to constrain the legislature. To them, their authority to interpret the constitution and assess the proportionality of limitations on individual liberties is self-evident, entrenched in the legal and political environment of the two countries. This may also explain the willingness of these courts to so closely scrutinise their legislatures. Such a role is apparently less acceptable in countries from the Anglo-American tradition, and it is thus here that the judiciary goes to such great lengths to present reasons for its growing assertiveness. At times, however, the judiciary's insecurity in its reviewing role is what leads it to underplay its exercise of discretion, resorting to formal reliance on 'clear' text that governs the case and leaves the judges no discretion in the interpretative exercise, but only to announce its outcome.

Since the interpretation of legal texts is the quintessential domain of the courts, they can present themselves as passively accepting the necessary inference of the constitutional or international text. Such interpretations do not require that the court address directly the government's assertions related to the war on terrorism when the text provides 'clear' rules that are not subject to a balancing of conflicting interests. This is the formal approach discernible in a number of Israeli High Court of Justice decisions. By interpreting international treaty obligations as prescribing

---

[42] *Charkaoui v Canada (Citizenship and Immigration)*, 2007 SCC 9 (23 February 2007).
[43] *Ibid* at para 140.

clear prohibitions under the law of armed conflict or the law of occupa-tion,[44] the Court has placed limits on the operations of the Israeli Army without any need to reason its authority to intervene. The US Supreme Court ruling that Common Article 3 of the Geneva Conventions applies to the conflict with Al Qaeda was based on a cursory examination of the text and on foreign sources,[45] with no discussion of the Court's authority to interpret such international texts. Moreover, the Court's assertion that the Geneva Conventions set a higher standard of due process than the standard followed by the military tribunals set up by Military Commis-sion Order No 1 was presented as an almost logical conclusion from a treaty text that leaves no room for doubt or for judicial discretion.[46]

The reason a court gives for its role as reviewer of the other branches of government in the context of the war on terrorism is contingent on which steps it climbs on the scale of review: on whether the outcome of the decision is referral of the matter to (or back to) the executive or the legislature or whether the decision significantly constrains the legisla-ture. Referral to the legislature requires only that the court state that it is protecting the political process against attempts on the part of the executive to short-circuit that process (and, of course, that ensuring the smooth operation of the political process is important also during times of crisis). As Justice Breyer stated in *Hamdan*:

> Nothing prevents the President from returning to Congress to seek the author-ity he believes necessary. Where, as here, no emergency prevents consultation with Congress, judicial insistence upon that consultation does not weaken our

---

[44]   As it did, for instance, in its decisions prohibiting torture of suspected terrorists (HCJ 5100/94, *Public Committee Against Torture in Israel v State of Israel*, 53(4) PD 817 (1999), transcript available at <http://elyon1.court.gov.il/files_eng/94/000/051/a09/94051000. a09.pdf>), the use of civilians as 'bargaining chips' for the release of soldiers held as POWs (Crim FH 7048/97, *Anonymous v Minister of Defense*, 54(1) PD 721 (1998)), and using civilians as intermediaries when trying to convince terrorists to lay down their weapons and surrender (HCJ 3799/02, *Adalah v GOC Central Command*, IDF (2005), English translation available at <http://elyon1.court.gov.il/files_eng/02/990/037/a32/02037990.a32.pdf>). On the jurisprudence of the Israeli courts related to counterterrorism, see Yigal Mersel, 'Judicial Review of Counter-Terrorism Measures: The Israeli Model for the Role of the Judiciary During the Terror Era' (2005) 38 *New York University Journal of International Law & Policy* 67; Daphne Barak-Erez, 'The International Law of Human Rights and Constitutional Law: A Case Study of an Expanding Dialogue' (2004) 2 *International. Journal of Constitutional Law* 611.

[45]   On the applicability of Common Art 3, see Justice Stevens' opinion in *Hamdan*, n 24 above at 126: 'In context, then, the phrase "not of an international character" bears its literal meaning.' On the interpretation of Common Article 3, see Justice Stevens' opinion, at 129: 'While the term "regularly constituted court" is not specifically defined in either Common Article 3 or its accompanying commentary, other sources disclose its core meaning.'

[46]   On the standard set by the Convention, see Justice Stevens' opinion, *ibid* at 131: '[The phrase "all the judicial guarantees which are recognized as indispensable by civilized peoples"] is not defined in the text of the Geneva Conventions. *But it must be understood* to incorporate at least the barest of those trial protections that have been recognized by customary international law' (emphasis added).

Nation's ability to deal with danger. To the contrary, that insistence strengthens the Nation's ability to determine – through democratic means – how best to do so. The Constitution places its faith in those democratic means. Our Court today simply does the same.[47]

Justice Kennedy added that the democratic process, given the stability that it provides, is in itself no less an important asset in national crisis:

Respect for laws derived from the customary operation of the executive and legislative branches gives some assurance of stability in time of crisis. The Constitution is best preserved by reliance on standards tested over time and insulated from the pressures of the moment.[48]

It is when they restrict the legislature's margin of discretion that the Anglo-American courts are most challenged to justify their action. Thus, when they choose to address this challenge openly, rather than present themselves as passive interpreters, they must contend with the criticism regarding their institutional deficiency vis-à-vis the political branches. It is in this context that the new philosophy of the courts has recently emerged. Three explanations have been put forth by judges in response to this challenge to the courts' authority to intervene. The first is a formal explanation, namely, that the courts implement a constitutional – and, hence, fully democratic – mandate.[49] The second explanation asserts a special role for the courts to correct the flaws of the democratic process that may work against minorities.[50] Finally, the third and most far-reaching explanation maintains that the courts, as expert balancers, are better equipped than the political branches to resolve conflicts between liberty and security.

---

[47] See *Hamdan*, n 24 above at 135–6.

[48] See *ibid* at 136. His opinion continues at 136–7: 'This is ... a case where Congress, in the proper exercise of its powers as an independent branch of government, and as part of a long tradition of legislative involvement in matters of military justice, has considered the subject of military tribunals and set limits on the President's authority. Where a statute provides the conditions for the exercise of governmental power, its requirements are the result of a deliberative and reflective process engaging both of the political branches. Respect for laws derived from the customary operation of the Executive and Legislative Branches gives some assurance of stability in time of crisis. The Constitution is best preserved by reliance on standards tested over time and insulated from the pressures of the moment.'

[49] Lord Bingham of Cornhill, in the *A (Belmarsh Detainees)* decision, n 9 above at para 42, stated: 'The [Human Rights Act 1998] gives the courts a very specific, wholly democratic, mandate.' See also *Hamdi*, n 23 above: 'Whatever power the United States Constitution envisions for the Executive in its exchanges with other nations or with enemy organizations in times of conflict, it most assuredly envisions a role for all three branches when individual liberties are at stake.' The Indian Supreme Court asserts a similar ground for constitutional review: 'Our Constitution laid down clear limitations on the state actions within the context of the fight against terrorism. To maintain this delicate balance by protecting "core" human rights is the responsibility of court in a matter like this': *People's Union for Civil Liberties v Union of India*, n 39 above at para 15.

[50] This is the process-based justification for judicial review, expounded by John Hart Ely in *Democracy and Distrust* (1980) and resorted to in the context of counterterrorism measures

The final claim is novel and has extensive consequences and thus warrants an exploration of both its foundation and ramifications. It constitutes an unabashed refutation of the rhetoric that emanates from the 'countermajoritarian difficulty', which has proved to be the 'obsession' or 'fixation'[51] of US constitutional theory since 1962, when Alexander Bickel published his influential treatise *The Last Dangerous Branch*.[52] Casting-off the position of the less capable institution – the 'inferiority complex' status that accompanied the characterisation of 'countermajoritarian' – the newly asserted argument celebrates the courts' institutional superiority to the political branches: the executive may have the expertise for weighing security needs; the legislature may be the most qualified to set general national priorities, but the courts have the necessary expertise for balancing those interests against individual rights. Therefore, in democracies, the courts must be the ultimate decision-makers in matters related to restrictions on human rights, for there is no better institution to entrust with such a task. More than any other branch of government, the courts are 'the guardians of human rights'[53] 'The courts are charged by Parliament with delineating the boundaries of a rights-based democracy', argues Professor Jeffrey Jowell,[54] cited with approval in the *Belmarsh Detainees* decision[55] and presented more clearly by President Barak of the

by two Law Lords in the *A (Belmarsh Detainees)* decision, n 9 above. Lord Hope of Craighead, at para 108, noted: 'We are dealing with actions taken on behalf of society as a whole which affect the rights and freedoms of the individual. This is where the courts may legitimately intervene, to ensure that the actions taken are proportionate. It is an essential safeguard, if individual rights and freedoms are to be protected in a democratic society which respects the principle that minorities, however unpopular, have the same rights as the majority.' Baroness Hale of Richmond, at para 237, added, 'Democracy values each person equally. In most respects, this means that the will of the majority must prevail. But valuing each person equally also means that the will of the majority cannot prevail if it is inconsistent with the equal rights of minorities.' Note that these minorities may also be non-citizens who cannot participate in the political process. Nonetheless, the common perception under both international human rights law and domestic constitutional norms is that non-citizens are entitled to the protection guaranteed by these norms.

[51] These terms are aptly used by Barry Friedman, 'The Birth of an Academic Obsession: The History of the Countermajoritarian Difficulty, Part Five' (2002) 112 *Yale Law Journal* 153.

[52] Alexander Bickel, *The Last Dangerous Branch* (Indianapolis, Bobbs-Merrill, 1962).

[53] Lord Steyn, n 10 above at 349, states: 'By the [Human Rights Act 1998] Parliament made the judiciary the guardians of the ethical values of our bill of rights.' He refers also to Simon Brown LJ, who said, 'The court's role under the Human Rights Act is as the guardian of human rights. It cannot abdicate this responsibility': *International Transport Roth GmbH v Secretary of State for the Home Deartment* [2003] QB 728 at para 78.

[54] Jeffrey Jowell, 'Judicial Deference: Servility, Civility or Institutional Capacity?' (2003) PL 592 at 597.

[55] See n 9 above at para 42.

Israeli Supreme Court in his *Beit Sourik* opinion concerning the proportionality of the route set for the 'Wall' or 'separation fence' built by Israel on West Bank territory.[56] According to Barak:

> The question is whether the route of the separation fence, according to the approach of the military commander, is proportionate. The standard for this question is not the subjective standard of the military commander. The question is not whether the military commander believed, in good faith, that the injury is proportionate. The standard is objective. The question is whether, by legal standards, the route of the separation fence passes the tests of proportionality. This is a legal question, the expertise for which is held by the Court.[57]

Justice Barak continued this argument, citing an earlier decision of his:

> Judicial review does not examine the wisdom of the decision to engage in military activity. In exercising judicial review, we examine the legality of the military activity. Therefore, we assume that the military activity that took place in Rafah was necessary from a military standpoint. The question before us is whether this military activity satisfies the national and international standards that determine the legality of that activity. The fact that the activity is necessary on the military plane does not mean that it is lawful on the legal plane. Indeed, we do not substitute our discretion for that of the military commander's, as far as it concerns military considerations. That is his expertise. We examine the results on the plane of the humanitarian law. That is our expertise.[58]

These assertions can be understood in two different but compatible ways. The first sense emphasises the characterisation of determining proportionality as a legal task ('This is a legal question.'). By defining this task as belonging to the legal sphere, Barak implied that the ultimate arbiter of legal questions is the court – at the apex of the judicial branch. In other words, proportionality analysis, just like interpretation of texts, is the domain of courts. This assertion is similar to that made in *Marbury v Madison*,[59] where the US Supreme Court claimed exclusive authority to interpret the Constitution since interpretation is a matter of legal reasoning. Barak's claim is therefore susceptible to the same criticism directed at *Marbury*: the fact that a question is one of law does not in and of itself necessitate that the courts have exclusive authority to interpret it.[60]

---

[56] HCJ 2056/04, *Beit Sourik Village Council v Government of Israel* (2004), English translation available at <http://elyon1.court.gov.il/files_eng/04/560/020/a28/04020560.a28.pdf>.

[57] *Ibid* at para 48.

[58] HCJ 4764/04, *Physicians for Human Rights v Commander of the IDF Forces in the Gaza Strip*, at para 9, (2004), English translation available at <http://elyon1.court.gov.il/files_eng/04/640/047/a03/04047640.a03.pdf>.

[59] 5 US 137 (1803).

[60] On this point, see Michel Troper, 'The Logic of Justification of Judicial Review' (2003) 1 *International. Journal of Constitutional Law* 99 at 103–5.

The second sense of Barak's assertions goes beyond mere formality: the courts are experts at balancing just as the security services are experts at assessing threats ('We examine the results on the plane of the humanitarian law. That is our expertise.').[61] Proportionality is what courts are designed to assess; this is what they do better than other branches of government; this is why they have the ultimate word in such matters. This novel claim redefines the judicial role, the role of guardians of human rights. Such an assertion may seem trivial to constitutional lawyers and to politicians on the Continent,[62] but for those intrigued by the justifications for the activism of this countermajoritarian institution, this argument must be viewed as far-reaching. Critics of the human rights 'movement' have often derided what they maintain to be the inflated claims of its visionaries: the concept of human rights will be empty as long as different societal interests can be dressed up as human rights. If, for example, national security can be reconceptualised as the right to life of all or some citizens (or their right to property), then the protection granted by the rights rhetoric to individuals against the collective interest becomes bereft of any real significance. Rights no longer trump social interests. While this criticism is valid, the emerging discourse in the House of Lords and the Israeli High Court suggests that the 'human rights revolution' did ultimately matter. Its real impact was, however, institutional rather than substantive: although the pull of the rights rhetoric elevated also societal interests to the status of individual rights and therefore essentially levelled the playing field between the competing rights, it also reallocated the authority to weigh these interests by transferring them from the political branches to the courts. The human rights paradigm provides a platform for the courts to assert their institutional supremacy over the political branches and determine the balance between conflicting rights. The challenge to the political branches has never been clearer.

---

[61] In an article published in 2002, Justice Barak referred to an earlier case, in which the Court intervened to order the equal distribution of gas masks in the West Bank during the 1991 Gulf War: 'We did not intervene in military considerations, for which the expertise and responsibility lie with the executive. Rather, we intervened in considerations of equality, for which the expertise and responsibility rest with the judiciary': A Barak, 'Foreword: A Judge on Judging: The Role of a Supreme Court in a Democracy' (2002) 116 *Harvard Law Review* 16, 152.

[62] For the approaches in France and Germany, see nn 35–8 above and accompanying text.

IV. THE EMERGING INTERNATIONAL COALITION OF NATIONAL COURTS

From the discussion thus far, an evolving practice on the part of national courts has emerged, characterised by a number of striking features in contrast to previous trends and initial expectations. First, national courts are refusing simply to rubber-stamp the actions of the political branches. They respect the executive and legislature and seek to engage in meaningful dialogue with them, as well as, no doubt, to share responsibility with them for outcomes; but they also have clearly signalled their intention to set limits to counterterrorism measures they deem excessive. Second, courts of the Anglo-American tradition alternate between couching their activism in formal language and asserting themselves as the better-equipped institution to balance security and liberty. Third, they do not hesitate to invoke international law and engage in serious analysis of the international norms they apply.

I will not dwell here on the first feature, the least surprising of the three. Judicial silence could be tolerated during crises that are both overwhelming and limited in duration. During a major war, there would be judges who would subscribe to Chief Justice Rehnquist's suggestion to defer judgment until after the conflict has been resolved. Some human rights activists might even agree with this proposition, for 'if, in fact, courts are more prone to uphold wartime claims of civil liberties after the war is over, may it not actually be desirable to avoid decision on such claims during the war?'[63] But the current so-called war on terror is emerging as a protracted and, thus far, not overwhelming one. And as I have suggested elsewhere, under such conditions, the need for judicial intervention in legislative and executive action is compelling. The prolongation of low-key war brings back the institutional necessity of any administration to rely on the court as a legitimising agent. At the same time, it demonstrates the court's resolve to maintaining a reputation as an independent institution. These two factors may take the back seat during short and well-defined emergency situations, but as emergency becomes a way of life, the public's – and hence also the government's – interest in and reliance on an independently minded court resume.[64]

In this final section, I will focus on the two other features of the emerging jurisprudence. I will argue that the underlying logic of these features is the desire to coordinate a transnational coalition of national courts. Both the assertiveness of the courts and their use of international law have facilitated the evolution of such cooperation. To explain the reasons for the emergence of this alliance, it is necessary to return to the

---

[63] W Rehnquist, *All the Laws but One* (New York, Knopf, 1998) 222.
[64] See n 2 above at 318.

early 1990s, when national courts exhibited little interest in such cooperation and, in fact, ensured their respective governments a free hand in
handling international affairs.

Almost 15 years ago, I presented a comparative analysis of the
approaches taken by national courts to the implementation of international law.[65] The article focused on the use of international law in general
but, in particular, in security matters and described a consistent policy on
the part of national courts of avoiding applying international law against
the will of the executive branch. Through an assortment of avoidance
doctrines (such as 'standing', the 'political question', non-justiciability
and other doctrines), the identification or misidentification of customary
international law, or the interpretation of treaties, national courts had
managed to align their findings and judgments with the preferences of
their governments. Some courts acknowledged their reticence and
explained their deference as a tribute to the executive's expertise in
negotiating international relations and referred to the necessity for the
state 'to speak in one voice'.[66] The article also identified a judicial policy
of guaranteeing complete leeway to the executive in external affairs,
intertwined with a sense of very limited recognition of international law
as a legitimate constraint on the domestic political process. Ultimately, I
argued:

> National courts are the prisoners in the classic prisoner's dilemma. If they
> could have been assured that courts in other jurisdictions would similarly
> enforce international law, they would have been more willing to cooperate.
> They might have been ready to restrict their government's free hand, had they
> been reassured that other governments would be likewise restrained. But in
> the current status of international politics, such cooperation is difficult to
> achieve, and rational judges act like the prisoner who cannot be sure that his or
> her fellow prisoner will cooperate.[67]

The ways governments interact have changed considerably over the last
15 years. In a globalised environment, the regulation of human activity is
subject to a mesh of formal and informal international commitments. The
contemporary ease of communication, on the one hand, and global
interdependency, on the other, have resulted in a significant increase and
deepening of coordinated efforts amongst national bureaucracies. The
availability of means of communication and the need to make use of
them bring diverse parts of national bureaucracies into direct contact,
sometimes on a daily basis, with their foreign counterparts. This is
particularly true for the post-11 September 2001 global counterterrorism

---

[65] See Benvenisti, n 14 above.
[66] *Ibid* at 173–4.
[67] *Ibid* at 175.

effort, which effectively united national security agencies in a concerted effort for a common cause, acting both directly and through a web of international institutions (formal and informal),[68] openly and clandestinely, legally and also illegally (for example, the practices of 'extraordinary renditions' and 'secret prisons'). This novel, multi-faceted activity has set a new challenge for the national courts that is unique in two aspects. First, the issue is no longer one of ensuring the executive a free hand in conducting international affairs, because the intensive external peer pressure faced by most governments leaves them little room to manoeuvre. Second, the issue is no longer one of international affairs, because the spheres of the coordinated counterterrorism policies cut deeply across the fabric of the domestic regulation of daily lives, and the timeframe for such measures is indefinite.

In light of the web of international commitments, it makes little sense to maintain that governments enjoy complete leeway in conducting international affairs and that, therefore, national courts should refrain from influencing their government's policy choices. In fact, quite the contrary is often the case: opposing pressure from a disapproving court may in fact result in a government enjoying *more* latitude in its relations with its foreign counterparts, because it can use the constraining court decision to explain why it is prevented from bowing to the external pressure to limit its citizens' rights.[69] Moreover, due to their pervasive effects and indefinite duration, counterterrorism measures do not stop at a state borders. Measures impinging on human rights can entail also far-reaching limitations on the political freedoms and privacy within the country and impinge severely on the rights of the citizens. Thus, acquiescing to the executive's demand for judicial deference threatens the courts' very authority as the so-called guardians of human rights and democracy.

An assertive judiciary gives rise to a number of primary as well as secondary concerns. The primary concerns relate to the direct and

---

[68] The main UN body set up to curb terrorism is the Counter-Terrorism Committee (CTC) (for its mandate and activities, see <http://www.un.org/sc/ctc/>). Post-11 September informal institutions devoted to counter-terrorism include the Financial Action Task Force's (FATF) so-called Nine Special Recommendations (concerning the financing of terrorism) (available at <http://www.fatf-gafi.org/document/9/0,2340,en_32250379_ 32236920_34032073_1_1_1_1,00.html>) and the Proliferation Security Initiative (PSI), initiated by the US government in 2003 (available at <http://www.state.gov/t/np/ c10390.htm>).

[69] This is the logic of the so-called two-level game, which depicts governments' need to negotiate treaties both at the international level and at the domestic level (to obtain domestic ratification for the treaties). The weaker a government is domestically, the more valid claims it can make for concessions from the other governments. See R Putnam, 'Diplomacy and Domestic Politics: The Logic of Two-Level Games' (1988) 42 *International Organization* 427.

tangible consequences of judicial activism: greater risk of terrorist attacks and greater risk of politicians attempting to curtail the power of the courts. There is no way to diminish the first concern other than to manage it through the balancing process, which is essentially an act of risk management. To ameliorate the second primary concern, the courts, as I have shown, employ an array of techniques to ratchet up and down the extent of their intervention, inviting the politicians to enter into a dialogue with them.

The secondary concerns are related to the interaction between the different countries. Constraints imposed by a court in one state but not by courts in other states may expose the citizens of the former state to an increased risk of terrorist attack. A state that does not deport refugees due to concerns regarding torture or a country in which privacy rights are strictly respected could become (or could be seen as potentially becoming) a haven for terrorist cells if other countries were to opt for more stringent limitations of those same rights. Another secondary concern is the international pressure that could be brought to bear on a government not to comply with its courts' decisions or else risk the loss of peer protection for failing to conform to the group's demands. The optimal response to these secondary concerns is coordination amongst courts. A transnational united front amongst the highest national courts ensures that no country becomes more terrorist-friendly than its neighbours, and little peer pressure is exerted on the different governments to ignore their courts' judgments. The court decisions described above function as signals to other courts, emboldening them or weakening their resolve in the face of the same dilemmas.

It is in this context that comparative analysis takes centre stage. Extensive cross-reference amongst courts[70] indicates attention to one another's approaches and an openness to coordinated stances. Courts compare statutory arrangements in different countries as a way to determine the measures that minimally impair constitutional rights.[71]

---

[70] See, eg, Lord Carswell in the *A (Belmarsh Detainees)* decision, n 9 above at para 150 (citing the statement of President Barak of the Israel High Court of Justice in *Public Committee Against Torture in Israel v State of Israel*, n 40 above, concerning the need to follow the rule of law in combating terrorism). In *A (FC) and Others (FC) v Secretary of State for the Home Department* [2005] UKHL 71, concerning the admissibility of evidence obtained through torture by foreign officials, the Law Lords engaged in a comparative analysis of the jurisprudence of foreign courts, including Canadian, Dutch, French, German, and US courts, and, in particular, explored the decision of the Higher Regional Court of Hamburg in the *El Motassadeq* decision of 14 June 2005 (see *ibid* at para 37).

[71] In the recent *Charkaoui* decision (n 42 above), the Canadian Supreme Court presented the procedure adopted in the United Kingdom as a model for the Canadian Parliament to consider when it re-enacts the statute found by the Court to be incompatible with the Canadian Charter of Rights and Freedoms (see especially para 86: 'Why the drafters of the legislation did not provide for special counsel to objectively review the material with a view

Even more importantly, international law, as the source of collective standards, becomes a most valuable coordination tool. The fact that national courts can rely on the same or similar legal norms (international treaties such as the 1949 Geneva Conventions and human rights law) facilitates harmonisation among the courts.[72] International norms perform another important task, mentioned above:[73] they allow courts to take a step up the ladder of judicial review and impose a significant, if not fatal, burden on the legislature. These two features may explain why national courts in the post-11 September 2001 era have departed from their tradition of deference and have begun to assert their authority to interpret and apply international law.[74]

Note that my analysis thus far has omitted any discussion of the potential influence of the various international tribunals on the stances of national courts. No doubt, the emerging transnational litigation on matters concerning violations of human rights and the laws of war (international criminal tribunals, foreign courts exercising universal jurisdiction for war crimes, foreign courts adjudicating civil suits for damages for violations of international law) is having a significant impact on the jurisprudence of national courts. It makes sense to argue, as Amichai Cohen does,[75] that the potential for rebuke from a foreign court helps convince certain bureaucrats that it is best that their own national courts pass judgment on their acts, thereby strengthening the courts' confidence to engage in such analysis. Indeed, just such an impact on perceptions of this matter can be discerned in the Israeli context.[76]

---

to protecting the named person's interest, as was formerly done for the review of security certificates by SIRC *and is presently done in the United Kingdom,* has not been explained' (emphasis added)).

[72] See A Slaughter, *A New World Order* (Princeton, NJ, Princeton University Press, 2004) ch 2.

[73] See discussion in nn 35–6 above and accompanying text.

[74] Nowhere is this departure more pronounced than in the jurisprudence of the US Supreme Court. Until the *Hamdan* decision, n 24 above, deference to executive treaty interpretation was near absolute, based on the theory that the President has both the constitutional responsibility for, and special competency in, foreign affairs. See Justice Thomas's dissenting opinion, *ibid* at 169: 'Our duty to defer to the President's understanding of the provision at issue here is only heightened by the fact that he is acting pursuant to his constitutional authority as Commander in Chief and by the fact that the subject matter of Common Article 3 calls for a judgment about the nature and character of an armed conflict.' On the doctrine of deference, see also R Chesney, *Disaggregating Deference: The Judicial Power and Executive Treaty Interpretations,* available at <http://papers.ssrn.com/sol3/papers.cfm?abstract_id=931997>; D Bederman, 'Revivalist Canons and Treaty Interpretation' (1994) 41 *UCLA Law Review* 953.

[75] Amichai Cohen, 'Domestic Courts and Sovereignty', International Law Forum of the Hebrew University of Jerusalem Law Faculty, Research Paper No 7, 6 July 2006, <www.ssrn.com/abstractid =917048>.

[76] *Ibid.* See also E Benvenisti, 'Case Review: *Ajuri et al v IDF Commander in the West Bank et al'* (2003) 9 *European Public Law* 481 at 491: 'One explanation for the decisive change may be the growing demand from Israeli officials for a more assertive judiciary, one that both

But there are reasons to doubt the proposition that national courts are motivated to conform to the jurisprudence emerging from the new judicial forums, at least as an autonomous explanation for their new assertiveness. Some courts – notably the US Supreme Court – are less troubled by international or foreign supervision. The Canadian Supreme Court may be rebuked by the Human Rights Committee or the Committee Against Torture, but this would not terribly damage the Court's reputation. The decisions of European courts may be reviewed by the European Court of Human Rights (ECtHR), but the latter assigns a wide margin of appreciation to the balancing processes of national courts.[77] That the different European national courts are not motivated by a desire to please the ECtHR is highlighted by the fact that they do not adopt the rhetoric of margin of appreciation that the ECtHR eventually uses in reviewing national courts' decisions. Instead, they insist on conducting the proper balancing themselves. In fact, the House of Lords in the *A (Belmarsh Detainees)* case emphatically rejected the government's claim that it should be allowed the same margin of discretion that the ECtHR allows member states,[78] with Lord Hoffmann explicitly suggesting that the margin of appreciation doctrine 'means ... that we, as a United Kingdom court, have to decide the matter for ourselves'.[79]

Even more profoundly, there may be grounds to argue that the newly created venues of international adjudication are prompting national courts to act collectively *against* the evolving and expected jurisprudence of these tribunals. National governments have good reason to be wary of the activism of international tribunals such as the ICTY and the ICTR, which have departed from agreed texts and transformed the laws of

---

legitimizes Israeli policies in the face of the widespread foreign criticism and protects those same officials from being subject to international criminal liability. The evolving possibilities of international criminal adjudication (highlighted by, amongst other things, the criminal charges brought against Prime Minister Sharon in Belgium and the entry into force of the ICC Statute) have increased public awareness in Israel regarding the potential consequences of violating international law. The Court's recent interventionist decisions have offered Israeli officials legal backing for their policies, and if they have been denied such backing – an explanation to the Israeli public as to why harsher measures cannot be adopted.'

[77]   P de Hert suggests that the ECtHR does not seem ready to scrutinise surveillance and other law enforcement countermeasures adopted post-11 September 2001: P de Hert, 'Balancing Security and Liberty within the European Human Rights Framework' (2005) 1 *Utrecht Law Review* 68, <http://www.utrechtlawreview.org/>.

[78]   See the *A (Belmarsh Detainees)* decision, n 9 above at para 37, per Lord Bingham, citing the Attorney-General's argument: 'Just as the European Court allowed a generous margin of appreciation to member states, recognising that they were better placed to understand and address local problems, so should national courts recognise, for the same reason, that matters of the kind in issue here fall within the discretionary area of judgment properly belonging to the democratic organs of the state. It was not for the courts to usurp authority properly belonging elsewhere.'

[79]   *Ibid* at para 91.

war.[80] National courts have their own concerns about potential tension between their own interpretations of the law (given their own legal and institutional constraints) and those of international tribunals, whose only allegiance is to their understandings of international law. In other words, the international tribunals pose a common threat to national courts. The latter must respond collectively to this threat. This chapter has sought to show that this is precisely what they are doing: united, they can deter both domestic and international sources of threat.

V. CONCLUSION

Following the initial shock that ensued after 11 September 2001, this chapter has suggested, national courts began to assert their authority to limit what they deem to be excesses of executive power, in the context of internationally coordinated counterterrorism measures impinging considerably on individual rights. They have preferred to engage the legislature as a potential ally in this task, but in the face of reluctance on the part of the latter to share the burden, the courts have acted alone. In this intensifying process of review, the national courts climb up a ladder whose rungs represent different techniques that enable them to tailor their intervention in legislative and executive acts to the political circumstances, inviting the political branches to share in the deliberative process. The chapter has raised possible reasons for this assertiveness on the part of the judiciary, which may actually amount also to an emerging trend of coordination amongst the highest national courts of several democratic states. Counterterrorism measures in the wake of 11 September 2001 included far-reaching restrictions on the political freedoms and privacy of individuals. Acceding to the executive's demand for deference to its discretion in security matters would entail that the courts abdicate their competence in areas that are significant to many, if not most, citizens. The courts have reacted consistently to the extensive restrictions placed on political freedoms, privacy and other rights by the executive's counterterrorism measures, which have threatened not only individual freedoms but also the courts' very authority to protect those freedoms. To prevent their jurisdictions from becoming a haven for terrorists and to thwart international pressure on their governments not to comply with the courts' rulings, it has been necessary for the courts to coordinate outcomes across national jurisdictions – hence the endeavour towards

---

[80] A Marston Danner, 'When Courts Make Law: How the International Criminal Tribunals Recast the Laws of War' (2006) 59 *Vanderbilt Law Review* 1 (analysing how the criminal tribunals created by the UN in the mid-1990s have transformed the laws of war through their interpretation and application of treaty law).

inter-judicial coordination. The availability of identical or similar norms (grounded in international law and human rights law) has facilitated this coordination effort. It remains to be seen whether this unity will persist and to what extent the courts' self-perception as guardians of human rights will extend beyond the context of counterterrorism.

The analysis of the different techniques that national courts apply in their review process, particularly their use of international standards to encumber legislatures and strengthen inter-judicial coordination, should be taken into account by the drafters of international agreements. Specifically, those seeking to strengthen courts vis-à-vis their political branches and promote judicial cooperation should be attentive to the distinction between rules and standards. Clear rules, like the rules against torture and hostage-taking, make the judicial task of reviewing national policies less politically contested than do vague standards.[81] Standards invite courts to exercise their discretion and thereby open up the possibility of different judicial outcomes and greater tension with the political branches whose discretion the courts might challenge. Albeit only one factor amongst several that should shape the way treaties are drafted, this factor is nevertheless a significant one, as emphasised in this chapter.

---

[81] On the importance of reliance on clear rules in the context of the international prohibition on torture, see E Benvenisti, 'The Role of National Courts in Preventing Torture of Suspected Terrorists' (1997) 8 *European Journal of International Law* 596.

8

'The Last Refuge of the Tyrant'?

Judicial Deference to Executive Actions in Time of 'Terror'*

IAIN SCOBBIE

I. JUDICIAL DEFERENCE REDUX?

A CASE THAT has attracted the attention of the US judiciary in recent proceedings which deal with aspects of the 'war on terror' is *Ex parte Quirin*,[1] decided by the US Supreme Court at the height of World War Two. As recent historiography makes clear, this is a prime example of judicial deference to executive desire.[2] The case dealt with the fate of eight German saboteurs, landed by submarine on the east coast of the United States in June 1942, who were arrested almost immediately and charged with various counts of attempted sabotage and espionage. On 2 July 1942, President Roosevelt issued Proclamation 2561, entitled *Denying certain enemies access to the courts of the United States*, which created a military tribunal to try the saboteurs. The initial paragraph of this Proclamation asserted that the:

> safety of the United States demands that all enemies who have entered upon the territory of the United States as part of an invasion or predatory incursion, or who have entered in order to commit sabotage, espionage, or other hostile or warlike acts, should be promptly tried in accordance with the law of war.[3]

Promptly tried they were: the trial started on 8 July and concluded on 1 August. After deliberation, two days later the members of the tribunal

---

* *In memorium* John Saul Marco LLB (Hons) (Glasgow), LLM (NYU). With thanks to Sorcha MacLeod for her thoughts on structure.
[1] 317 US 1 (1942).
[2] See, eg, M Dobbs, *Saboteurs: the Nazi Raid on America* (New York, Knopf, 2004), and L Fisher, *Nazi Saboteurs on Trial: A Military Tribunal and American Law* (Kansas, University Press of Kansas, 2003).
[3] Available at <http://www.presidency.ucsb.edu/ws/index.php?pid=16281>; also quoted in Fisher, n 2 above at 50 (see 50–53 generally); and Dobbs, n 2 above at 204–5.

decided that all eight accused were guilty and sentenced them to death, submitting their verdict to President Roosevelt for review in accordance with the terms of Proclamation 2561. On 4 August, the custodial officer in charge of the prisoners was informed that President Roosevelt had decided that six were to be executed, with the sentences of the remaining two commuted to life imprisonment because they had assisted the US authorities in the apprehension and conviction of the others. The executions took place on 8 August, but the prisoners' defence counsel were not officially informed of the verdicts and only learnt of the executions through press reports.[4]

During the 19 days from 8 July to 1 August, proceedings had not only taken place before the military tribunal. On 28 July, a federal district court in the District Court of Columbia dismissed a request which sought permission to file a petition for a writ of habeas corpus on behalf of seven of the accused which was aimed at challenging the constitutionality of Proclamation 2561. The judge ruled that the accused fell within the category of subjects, citizens or residents of a nation at war with the United States which, under the terms of the Proclamation, was 'not privileged to seek any remedy or maintain any proceeding directly or indirectly, or to have any such remedy or proceeding sought on their behalf, in the courts of the United States'. This was a pre-arranged formality aimed at granting the Supreme Court jurisdiction to hear the petition.[5] It heard oral argument on 29 and 30 July, issuing a *per curiam* (unreasoned) decision on 31 July that upheld the jurisdiction of the military tribunal on the ground that President Roosevelt had authority to create the commission. The Court, accordingly, denied the motions for leave to file for writs of habeas corpus. The Supreme Court did not deliver its reasoned decision until 29 October 1942.[6] As one commentator observes:

> There was never a likelihood that the [Supreme] Court would exercise judicial review in any but the most limited sense. It would not scrutinize the record of the tribunal, attempt to take the case away and transfer it to a civil court, or reverse President Roosevelt. Still, the Court wanted to indicate that the judiciary is not irrelevant in time of war, even if during World War II the Court largely acquiesced to the political branches ... Instead of functioning as an independent institution, it served more as a wing of the White House. No one looking at the record of the Court during World War II could take seriously its claim that the courts, 'in time of war as well as in time of peace' would 'preserve unimpaired the constitutional safeguards of civil liberty'.[7]

---

[4] See Dobbs, n 2 above at 253–65; and Fisher, n 2 above at 77–9.
[5] On the proceedings before the District Court as a prelude to those before the Supreme Court, see Dobbs, n 2 above at 233–7; and Fisher, n 2 above at 64–9.
[6] See Dobbs, n 2 above at 238–47 and 268–9; Fisher, n 2 above at 87–125.
[7] Fisher, n 2 above at 121–2 (paragraph break suppressed).

Nevertheless, in *Hamdi et al v Rumsfeld, Secretary of Defense et al*,[8] the Supreme Court repeatedly referred to *Quirin*, and expressly reaffirmed its ruling that the military has the authority to try US citizens accused of espionage during wartime in the following terms:

> *Quirin* was a unanimous opinion. It both postdates and clarifies *Mulligan*, providing us with the most apposite precedent we have on the question of whether citizens may be detained in such circumstances. Brushing aside such precedent – particularly when doing so gives rise to a host of new questions never dealt with by this Court – is unjustified and unwise.[9]

Does this indicate that we should expect a judiciary supine to the desires of the executive in the context of the current so-called 'war on terror'? Is judicial deference inevitable? Should we 'accept the proposition that, though the laws are not silent in wartime, they speak with a muted voice'?[10]

---

[8] 542 US 507 (2004), decided 28 June 2004: available at <www.supremecourtus.gov/opinions/03pdf/03–6696.pdf>, and reprinted 43 ILM 1166 (2004). All subsequent references are first to the pdf version, followed by the ILM version in parentheses. The plurality opinion of the Court was delivered by Justice O'Connor (43 ILM 1166), in which Chief Justice Rehnquist and Justices Kennedy and Breyer joined. Justice Souter, concurring with the plurality, delivered a separate opinion (43 ILM 1179), in which Justice Ginsberg partially joined. She also concurred in the judgment of the Court. Justice Scalia delivered a dissenting opinion (43 ILM 1186), in which Justice Stevens joined. Justice Thomas also delivered a dissenting opinion (43 ILM 1197).

[9] *Hamdi v Rumsfeld*, opinion of Justice O'Connor, 15 (43 ILM 1172): compare Justice Scalia, dissenting, at 17 (43 ILM 1193): 'The case was not this Court's finest hour.' See also *Hamdan v Rumsfeld, Secretary of Defense et al*, decided 29 June 2006, <http://www.supremecourtus.gov/opinions/05pdf/05–184.pdf> (reprinted 45 ILM 1130 (2006)), opinion of the Court delivered by Justice Stevens at, eg, 23–5 (45 ILM 1142), 28–9 (45 ILM 1143), and 33 (45 ILM 1144), 'Quirin represents the high-water mark of military power to try enemy combatants for war crimes'. In *Hamdan*, Judge Stevens delivered the judgment of the Court, in which Justices Souter, Ginsberg and Breyer joined, apart from Parts V and VI-D-iv which represented Justice Stevens' views alone. Justice Breyer, concurring in the Court's judgment, delivered a separate opinion (45 ILM 1163), in which Justices Kennedy, Souter and Ginsberg joined. Justice Kennedy, concurring in the Court's judgment in part, delivered a separate opinion (45 ILM 1163), in which Justices Souter, Ginsberg and Breyer joined in relation to Parts I and II. Justice Scalia delivered a dissenting opinion (45 ILM 1181), in which Justices Thomas and Alito joined. Justice Thomas also delivered a dissenting opinion (45 ILM 1181), in which Justice Scalia joined, and also Justice Alito with the exception of Parts I, II-C-1 and III-B-2. Not to be outdone, Justice Alito delivered a dissenting opinion (45 ILM 1199), in which Justices Scalia and Thomas joined in regard to Parts I–III. Chief Justice Roberts took no part in this case.

[10] United States Supreme Court Chief Justice Rehnquist, Speech to Dickinson College of Law, Pennsylvania State University, 12 November 1999, as quoted in Dobbs, n 2 above at 270; see also WH Rehnquist, *All the Laws but One: Civil Liberties in Wartime* (New York, Knopf, 1998).

II. THE CONCEPTUAL FRAMEWORK FOR DECISION

Chaïm Perelman's notion of judicial ontology provides a useful framework within which to explore the broad issue of judicial deference to the executive in time of terror.[11] His theory of legal reasoning, which is a specific application of the general theory of practical reasoning he developed in collaboration with Lucie Olbrechts-Tyteca,[12] starts from the proposition that the activity of any court depends on the political and legal structure supporting it. The influence of this structure – or ontology – is system-specific as the administration of justice, and thus the nature of the judicial function, depends on the constitutional allocation of powers within the given system. Perelman's concept of judicial ontology, however, goes further than legal formalities. It is aimed not simply at locating a court within its underlying constitutional structure, but also attempts to take into account influences on the performance of the judicial function which are not dependent on the classical tripartite separation of powers thesis derived from Montesquieu.[13] It aims to encapsulate the philosophical basis of a given legal system.

Perelman demonstrates this concept by reference to the French judiciary. Taking the starting point of 1804 – the date of the promulgation of the *Code civil* – he argues that judicial reasoning in France has demonstrated three major ontological periods: the exegetical school (1804–80); the functional and sociological school (1880–1945); and the post-World War II topical school. This trichotomy is a schematic simplification, because the reasoning techniques characteristic of the ideology of one period were sometimes used in others.[14] Whether or not Perelman's analysis is historically correct, the notion of ontology is useful because it emphasises that the relationship between the different branches of government is not fixed but subject to change over time, and that judicial ideology, the way

---

[11] Perelman espoused a significant, if flawed, rhetorical theory of legal reasoning which has been unduly disregarded in anglophone legal circles, perhaps principally because his major legal work *Logique juridique: nouvelle rhétorique* (Paris, Dalloz, 1976) remains untranslated.

[12] The most extensive statement of this theory is C Perelman and L Olbrechts-Tyteca, *The New Rhetoric: A Treatise on Argumentation* (London, University of Notre Dame Press, 1969), originally published as *La nouvelle rhétorique: traité de l'argumentation* (Paris, Presses Universitaires de France, 1958). For the idea that Perelman's *logique juridique* is but an application of this *nouvelle rhétorique*, see his *Logique juridique*, n 11 above at 114, para 56.

[13] See Montesquieu, *L'esprit des lois*, Book 11, ch 6, *De la constitution d'Angleterre* (1748) at Vol I, 294–304 in the Goldschmidt edition (Paris, Garnier-Flammarion 1979). *L'esprit des lois* has been translated as *The spirit of the laws* (Cambridge, Cambridge University Press, 1989) by A Cohler, B Miller and H Stone: *De la constitution d'Angleterre* is at 156–66.

[14] Perelman, *Logique juridique*, n 11 above at 23 *et seq*: compare T Sauvel, 'Histoire du jugement motivé', (1955) 71 *Revue du droit public et de la science politique* 5.

that judges perceive their own role, is crucial in formulating this balance.[15] Judging is a self-reflecting process and, to an extent, judges formulate the parameters of the proper discharge of their role. Paterson refers to this as role negotiation and argues that because of their position in the legal hierarchy, UK Law Lords have a larger degree of autonomy in the definition of their role than lower-status actors.[16] For instance, a former Law Lord, Lord Steyn of Swafield, has observed that as the power of the executive has grown, so the role of the judiciary has changed:

> there has been a general expansion of the power and influence of the judiciary in Britain as discontent with the working of our democracy increased . . . judges nowadays accept more readily than before that it is their democratic and constitutional duty to stand up where necessary for individuals against the government. The greater the arrogation of power by a seemingly all-powerful executive which dominates the House of Commons the greater the incentive and need for judges to protect the rule of law.[17]

In a recent monograph, Richard Posner sets out his views on the methods of US constitutional interpretation apposite to the 'war on terror'.[18] This is a clear example of an ontological statement by a practising judge. Posner argues that when a case involves a conflict between civil liberties and national security, decision-making must involve standards rather than rules because competing values must be balanced: 'One is not to ask whether liberty is more or less important than safety. One is to ask whether a particular security measure harms liberty more or less than it promotes safety.'[19] He claims that judges are ill equipped to do this because they lack the relevant expertise in security matters. Thus he is:

> against an aggressive role for the courts in policing the boundary between national security and civil liberties in the name of the Constitution. Most judges know little about national security; the danger of catastrophic terrorism is real; and a constitutional decision forbidding a counterterrorist measure is

---

[15] Perelman, *Logique juridique*, n 11 above at 21, para 15; 135–7, para 71; and 153–4, para 81.

[16] See AA Paterson, *The Law Lords* (London, MacMillan, 1982) 204: see generally 9–34 on the influence of reference groups in determining the performance and content of the judicial role of members of the Judicial Committee of the House of Lords.

[17] Lord Steyn of Swafield, *Democracy, the Rule of Law and the Role of Judges*, The Attlee Foundation Lecture: 11 April 2006, available at <www.attlee.org.uk/Transcript-Steyn.doc>, text surrounding n 6.

[18] R Posner, *Not a Suicide Pact: The Constitution in a Time of National Emergency* (Oxford, Oxford University Press, 2006): for critical commentary, see D Cole, 'How to Skip the Constitution' (2006) 53(18) *New York Review of Books*, available at <www.nybooks.com/articles/19595>. This gave rise to a subsequent exchange of views between Posner and Cole in 'How to Skip the Constitution: An Exchange' (2007) 54(1) *New York Review of Books* 63, available at <www.nybooks.com/articles/19800>. It should be noted that Posner rejects 'the metaphor of a "war on terror"', *ibid*; see also *Not a Suicide Pact* at 11.

[19] Posner, *Not a Suicide Pact*, n 18 above at 31–2: on balancing, see 31–4 generally, and also 40, 148–9, 152–3.

almost impossible to change. It is better to leave these matters to be sorted out by the executive and legislative branches of government, where the relevant expertise resides.[20]

Posner asserts that when there is a perceived clash between civil liberties and national security, it is not clear why the judiciary should have the decisive voice, particularly because constitutional decisions are difficult to amend or overturn.[21] Supreme Court justices are not democratically accountable and largely unconstrained by authority: they thus possess wide discretion in their decision-making which results in judgments that essentially rest on policy choices.[22] Unlike parliamentary systems where the legislature and executive are fused, in the US constitutional system they are in competition with one another and thus Congress is available as a mechanism to prevent executive over-reach.[23] In addition, because Posner thinks that Congressional expertise in national security issues is much greater than that of the judiciary, he takes the view that where these are implicated in proceedings, the judiciary should defer to both Congress and the President.[24] This is clearly an ontological argument but there is a contradiction at its heart. Posner criticises judicial discretion because judges are not democratically accountable. It would be more consonant with his views on accountability if judges employed predetermined rules, whether constitutional or statutory, rather than the discretionary standards he prefers. Further, as his thesis is hardly candid on the methodology judges should use to balance values, this can only augment unfettered judicial discretion.

The aim of this chapter is to attempt to identify ontological factors relevant to the decision-making in various domestic superior courts in cases involving executive action taken as part of the 'war on terror'. Should these courts be expected to act as Posner counsels, and as the US Supreme Court did in *Quirin*, and simply defer to executive wishes, or is there reason to argue that they should take a more critical view of executive action? Also, some cases appear to demonstrate a growing awareness of international law by superior courts, particularly of human rights and humanitarian law norms. These are normative factors which would not have been available to the US Supreme Court in *Quirin*, as

---

[20] Posner, 'How to Skip the Constitution: An Exchange', n 18 above.

[21] Posner, *Not a Suicide Pact*, n 18 above at 18–19, 150. Posner's monograph deals only with constitutional interpretation, and this point should be not generalised. Judicial decisions upon executive responses to terrorism need not implicate constitutional provisions, and thus may be reversed by legislation or circumvented by new executive measures which are not impugned by the judgment – see below on the Congressional response to *Hamdan v Rumsfeld*.

[22] Posner, *Not a Suicide Pact*, n 18 above at 18–25.

[23] *Ibid* at 36–7.

[24] *Ibid* at 35–6.

international human rights law only emerged after World War II, while international humanitarian law has become increasingly sophisticated and elaborate since then. Perception of the relevance of international law has arguably caused an ontological shift in national judicial circles,[25] causing the judges of (some) superior courts to cast themselves into the role of ensuring that the executive observes the requirements of international law. Nevertheless, a court's attitude to the executive and its recourse to arguments drawn from international law are conceptually two distinct issues although, on occasion, international law may be used as a justification for a refusal to defer to executive wishes.

III. THE POLITY OF THE ISRAELI JUDICIARY

An illustration that ontology goes beyond the classic formal separation of powers but may extend into more ideological concerns is provided by Israel's Supreme Court.[26] Some commentators have argued that the Court subscribes to or identifies with 'the official version of national history', and hence it supports 'the Zionist vision, [which] apparently contribute[s] to the legitimacy of its rulings in the public eye. This legitimacy leads to passive acceptance of the Court's decisions, even when unpleasant or uncomfortable'.[27] Further, it has been claimed that the Court occupies a 'unique role' in the Israeli political system:

> Its judges enjoy enormous prestige and respect, especially among the political and legal elites. The judges are regarded not only as experts in matters of law, but also as guardians of society's moral fabric.[28]

[25] See, eg, A Barak, 'Foreword: A Judge on Judging: the Role of a Supreme Court in a Democracy' (2002) 116 *Harvard Law Review* 16, 110–14; C McCrudden, 'A Common Law of Human Rights? Transnational Judicial Conversations on Constitutional Rights' (2000) 20 *Oxford Journal of Legal Studies* 499; and AM Slaughter, *A New World Order* (Princeton, NJ, Princeton University Press, 2004) ch 2.

[26] Israel's Supreme Court fulfils two broad functions. As the Supreme Court it serves as a court of appeal from the decisions of lower courts, and as the High Court of Justice it acts as a court of first and last instance in petitions for the review of governmental actions, including actions taken in the Occupied Territories: see D Kretzmer, *The Occupation of Justice: The Supreme Court of Israel and the Occupied Territories* (Albany, NY, SUNY Press, 2002) 10–11. See also E Benvenisti, *The International Law of Occupation* (Princeton, NJ, Princeton University Press, 1993) 118–23; and Y Dotan, 'Judicial Rhetoric, Government Lawyers, and Human Rights: The Case of the Israeli High Court of Justice During the Intifada' (1999) 33 *Law and Society Review* 319, 322–4.

[27] D Barak-Erez, 'Collective Memory and Judicial Legitimacy: The Historical Narrative of the Israeli Supreme Court' (2001) 16 *Canadian Journal of Law and Society* 93, 111. For further argument that Israeli courts have played a role in the construction of Israeli national identity, see O Ben-Naftali and Y Tuval, 'Punishing International Crimes Committed by the Persecuted: the Kapo Trials in Israel (1950s–1960s)' (2006) 4 *Journal of International Criminal Justice* 128.

[28] Kretzmer, n 26 above at 190: see also Dotan, n 26 above at 345–50.

This view resonates with the philosophy expounded by the recently retired President of Israel's Supreme Court, Aharon Barak in his extra-judicial writing[29] which, he affirmed, 'is the most important tool with which I realise my judicial role'.[30] When exercising powers of judicial review over the actions of the executive and legislature, Barak argues that the role of the judiciary is to ensure that the values of substantive, as opposed to merely formal, democracy are observed.[31] While the latter rests simply on the representation of the people within government, substantive democracy requires the realisation of values based on human dignity, equality and tolerance – namely the protection of individual human rights that cannot be removed by the fiat of the majority.[32] Unlike members of the other branches of government, judges are not representa-tives of the people[33] and are thus possessed of an independence which detaches them from the exigencies of public opinion.[34] This conception of the judges' role in a democracy stands in sharp contrast to Posner's antipathy to judicial intervention in the political process. In particular, when reviewing executive action, Barak argues that any claim that the judiciary may be thwarting the views of the majority is irrelevant because, if no constitutional provisions are implicated, the legislature may overrule the judiciary's views by changing the law.[35] While Barak acknowledges that the judge must understand the preferences of the community – 'the deep consensus and shared values of the society'[36] – the task of the judiciary is 'to formulate properly the fundamental principles of his period'[37] and to implement these in order to protect democracy and the constitution.

This duty to protect democracy and individual rights is acutely tested in time of strife, but judicial rulings will remain embedded in national jurisprudence and thus be the basis for further judicial development.

---

[29]   See in particular A Barak, 'The Role of the Supreme Court in a Democracy' (1999) 33 *Israel Law Review* 1; 'The Role of a Supreme Court in a Democracy' (2001–2002) 53 *Hastings Law Journal* 1205; 'The Role of a Supreme Court in a Democracy, and the Fight Against Terrorism' (2003) 58 *University of Miami Law Review* 125 (hereinafter 'Terrorism'); and, at greater length, his 'Foreword' (n 25 above). Admirers of Barak's judicial philosophy include Lord Falconer of Thoroton, the former UK Lord Chancellor: see his 'The Role of Judges in a Modern Democracy', Magna Carta Lecture, Sydney, 13 September 2006), <www.dca. gov.uk/speeches/2006/sp060913.htm>; and Justice Richard Goldstone: see his 'The Juris-prudential Legacy of Justice Aharon Barak' (2007) 48 *Harvard International Law Journal Online* 54, <www.harvardilj.org/online/108>.

[30]   Barak, 'Foreword', n 25 above at 116.

[31]   *Ibid* at 120–24.

[32]   *Ibid* at 125; and Barak, 'Terrorism', n 29 above at 127.

[33]   Barak, 'Foreword', n 25 above at 161.

[34]   Barak, 'Terrorism', n 29 above at 129.

[35]   Barak, 'Foreword', n 25 above at 139.

[36]   Barak, 'Role of the Supreme Court' (1999), n 29 above at 7.

[37]   *Ibid* at 8.

Accordingly, mistakes made by the judiciary in the face of a perceived threat are more serious than any made by the executive or legislature as the latter can always subsequently erase their actions. Consequently, Barak claims that no 'sharp distinction' can be drawn between 'the status of human rights' depending on whether the state is at peace, at war or threatened by terrorism.[38] Nevertheless, democracies threatened by terrorism must balance human rights and national security:

> Human rights are not a stage for national destruction; they cannot justify undermining national security in every case and in all circumstances... a constitution is not a prescription for national suicide. But on the other hand... [n]ational security cannot justify undermining human rights in every case and in all circumstances. National security does not grant an unlimited licence to harm the individual.[39]

A compromise must be drawn between the two, but the point of balance between conflicting values is not fixed but differs from case to case and issue to issue.[40] Barak rejects the view that a simple affirmation by the executive that the impugned action is required for security reasons is conclusive. The court should not simply defer to this assertion but require that these reasons be presented to the court in order that it may determine whether they were the operative reasons for the measure and not simply a pretext, and that the measure adopted was the one least damaging to human rights.[41]

When reviewing executive action to determine their legality, the governing test is that the action in question must be reasonable. Barak concedes that this is 'notoriously vague':

> Put simply, the executive must act reasonably, for an unreasonable act is an unlawful act. In many cases, the test of reasonableness allows for only one possibility, which the executive must choose. Sometimes, however, the reasonableness test allows for several possibilities, thereby creating a 'zone of reasonableness'. The executive has freedom of choice within this zone. The principle of the separation of powers requires the executive, rather than the judiciary, to choose one possibility within this zone. But the principle of the separation of powers requires the court, rather than the executive, to determine the limits of the zone of reasonableness.[42]

The role of the court is simply to determine whether a reasonable person responsible for security would adopt the measures under scrutiny,[43] but

---

[38] Barak, 'Foreword', n 25 above at 149; and 'Terrorism', n 29 above at 129.
[39] Barak, 'Foreword', n 25 above at 153, note omitted; see also 'Terrorism', n 29 above at 132.
[40] Barak, 'Foreword', n 25 above at 135.
[41] Ibid at 157–8; and Barak, 'Terrorism', n 29 above at 138–9.
[42] Barak, 'Foreword', n 25 above at 145; see also 'Terrorism', n 29 above at 138.
[43] Barak, 'Foreword', n 25 above at 147 and 159; and 'Terrorism', n 29 above at 140.

the judiciary must not substitute its own judgment of the measures that should be adopted, as 'the efficiency of the security measures is a matter that is in the proper jurisdiction of the other branches of government'.[44] In assessing reasonableness, the concept of proportionality may be employed. This involves three cumulative sub-tests: that the measure is appropriate to achieve its aim; that there are no other appropriate means which would cause lesser damage to values that should be protected (such as human rights); and that the damage caused is not disproportionate to the benefits obtained.[45] Accordingly, although Barak's views – which expound both a judicial ontology and a judicial role statement – may be seen to have affinities to those of Posner, whose work Barak admires,[46] he sets out a much more articulate account of the methodology judges should employ to balance values, particularly when security concerns clash with human rights.

IV. FROM THEORY TO PRACTICE

Given Barak's extensive exposition of his judicial ideology, it is apposite to examine some cases decided by Israel's Supreme Court involving security concerns arising in the Occupied Palestinian Territories. The cases selected have been decided by the Supreme Court when it has been sitting as the High Court exercising judicial review over executive action taken in the Territories since the start of the Second, or al-Aqsa, Intifada in September 2000. In these cases, because of the status of the Territories, the High Court invariably has had recourse to international legal materials, principally the relevant rules of international humanitarian law. The focus in this analysis is not on the substance of the Court's decisions, but rather its methodology and the structure of its reasoning and, consequently, the judiciary's understanding of its role in relation to the executive.

In recent cases involving security concerns, Israel's High Court appears to have taken the notions of balancing values and seeking proportionality almost to the status of a fetish. For instance, in *Adalah v Israel Defense Forces*,[47] one issue before the Court was whether an inhabitant of the Occupied Territories could consent to be used by the Israel Defence Forces (IDF) to relay a warning to a suspected terrorist of

[44]   Barak, 'Terrorism', n 29 above at 138; see also 'Foreword', n 25 above at 151 and 157.
[45]   Barak, 'Foreword', n 25 above at 147–8.
[46]   *Ibid* at 115 – although at 116, he states that Dworkin's theory of judicial reasoning is 'the closest to the judicial philosophy that should guide a judge'. This is apparent in Barak's claim that the task of the judge is to formulate fundamental societal principles.
[47]   HCJ 37799/02 (6 October 2005), available at <http://elyon1.court.gov.il/files_eng/02/990/037/a32/02037990.a32.pdf> and at 45 ILM 491 (2006).

possible injury to himself or others present during an impending arrest. The Court proceeded on the basis that its decision on this point required 'a balancing between conflicting considerations', namely the avoidance of the need to use force in the arrest and thus safeguard the lives of the civilian population as against the occupying army's duty to safeguard the life and dignity of the civilian sent to issue the warning. President Barak solved this equation easily. He cited no considerations in favour of the first proposition, but four in favour of the latter: namely, the prohibition of the use of protected persons in furtherance of the military needs of the occupying army (from which he derived the specific prohibition of the use of them as 'human shields'); the principle of distinction between combatants and civilians which entailed that local residents should not be brought into the combat zone even if they consent; the lack of real consent on the part of the resident given the power imbalance between the civilian population and occupying army; and the impossibility of knowing whether the civilian will be exposed to danger, including possible subsequent danger if the individual is seen as a collaborator:

> The ability to properly estimate the existence of danger is difficult in combat conditions, and a procedure should not be based on the need to assume a lack of danger, when such an assumption is at times unfounded.[48]

Given the one-sided nature of this analysis, it is difficult to see how this should be seen as the application of proportionality, as opposed to a mere preponderant cumulation of argument.

On the other hand, a more discursive analysis of proportionality took place in President (Emeritus) Barak's opinion in *The Public Committee against Torture in Israel v The Government of Israel* (the *Targeted Killings* case).[49] This is consonant with the views expressed in his extra-judicial writings. The case concerned the legality of Israel's policy of 'preventative strikes' which are aimed at killing specific alleged terrorists in the Occupied Territories and which sometimes also harm innocent civilians. The petitioners argued that this policy was:

> totally illegal, and contrary to international law, Israeli law, and basic principles of human morality. It violates the human rights recognized in Israeli and international law, both the rights of those targeted, and the rights of innocent passersby caught in the targeted killing zone.[50]

The respondents raised an initial plea that the case was non-justiciable because the dominant aspect of the case was not legal as it dealt with IDF combat activity. Accordingly, they argued that the Court should exercise

---

[48] *Adalah v Israel Defense Forces*, opinion of President Barak, paras 23–4 (45 ILM 498–9).

[49] HCJ 769/02, (13 December 2006), <http://elyon1.court.gov.il/Files_ENG/02/690/007/a34/02007690.a34.pdf>. All subsequent references are to this pdf version.

[50] *Ibid*, opinion of President (Emeritus) Barak at para 3.

judicial restraint and refrain from entertaining the case, noting that supervision and control of these actions were undertaken by the executive. President Barak decisively rejected this plea, ruling that there was always a legal norm available to decide a case. Further, he ruled that a plea of institutional non-justiciability – that the Court was not the appropriate forum for decision – could not be accepted in order to prevent the examination of an alleged infringement of human rights: in the instant case, the right to life.[51]

In addition to Israeli law, the substance of President Barak's opinion contains an extensive examination of international legal materials aimed at elucidating the operative legal categories to be applied to individuals in time of an international armed conflict. The necessity for this analysis arose as a result of the balancing test which formed President Barak's fundamental predicate in the case:

> human rights are protected by the law of armed conflict, but not to their full scope. The same is so regarding the military needs. They are given an opportunity to be fulfilled, but not to their full scope. This balancing reflects the relativity of human rights, and the limits of military needs. The balancing point is not constant. 'In certain issues the accent is upon the military need, and in others the accent is upon the needs of the civilian population'.[52]

A key issue in determining the location of the balancing point was the classification of the individual harmed, namely whether he was a civilian or combatant in accordance with the principle of distinction operative in international humanitarian law.[53] In doing so, President Barak rejected the state's claim that a third category should be recognised. It had argued that members of terrorist organisations were unlawful combatants;[54] in its stead, President Barak utilised the category, recognised in customary international law, of civilians who take a direct part in hostilities, ruling that they were legitimate targets for military action during the period of that participation.[55] Nevertheless, a proportionality test, reflecting his core balancing test, was relevant here: during the period a civilian was taking a direct part in hostilities, he should not be attacked if a less harmful measure, such as arrest, could be employed to neutralise him.[56] Further, President Barak held that proportionality is a general principle of law, forming part of Israel's 'legal conceptualization of human

---

[51]   *Ibid* at paras 9, and 47–54.

[52]   *Ibid* at para 22, citing Israel High Court judgment, HCJ 393/82, *Jami'at Ascan el-Malmun el-Mahdudeh el-Masauliyeh, Communal Society registered at the Judea and Samaria Area Headquarters v The Commander of IDF Forces in the Judea and Samaria Area* 37(4) PD 785 at 794.

[53]   See *ibid* at paras 23–8 for Barak's initial analysis of the principle of distinction.

[54]   *Ibid* at paras 27–8.

[55]   *Ibid* at paras 29–40.

[56]   See *ibid* at paras 40 and 62.

rights . . . [as well as] an important component of customary international law'.[57] He noted that it is, for instance, a substantive element in assessing permissible collateral damage to civilians during military operations, although this can only be done on a case-by-case basis using an iterative methodology.[58]

Moreover, President Barak stated that in exercising judicial review over executive action in the Occupied Territories, the function of the High Court was to review the legality of the executive's use of discretion. The scope of its review varied according to the nature of the question posed. At one extreme, it could focus on the determination of the applicable law where:

> The question which the Court must ask itself is not whether the executive branch's understanding of the law is a reasonable understanding; the question which the Court must ask itself is whether it is the correct understanding . . . and whether the understanding of the military commander is in line with that law.

At the other extreme is a decision made using military knowledge. President Barak ruled that the executive had the expertise to make that decision, and the Court should determine whether a reasonable military commander could have made that decision. If so, the Court would not substitute its own assessment of security for that of the relevant military commander.[59] Where a question lies between these two extremes, in exercising judicial review, the Court assumes that the action in question was necessary from the military point of view, and then determines whether it adhered to the governing legal standards. In the instant case, the application of proportionality took a similar approach. Whether the benefit from a targeted killing outweighed any collateral damage was a legal question to be decided by the judiciary. Proportionality is, however, not precise and can be fulfilled in various ways: the executive has a margin of appreciation – the zone of proportionality – within which to operate.[60]

President Barak's analysis of proportionality in this case was abstract and detached. It was not made operative in terms of the question posed for decision as he offered no definitive ruling on the legality or otherwise of the targeted killings policy. The legality of each act depended on its unique circumstances,[61] and little practical guidance was given – apart from an implicit ruling that the use, in July 2002, of a 1,000 kg bomb in

---

[57] Ibid at para 41.
[58] See ibid at para 46.
[59] Ibid at paras 56–7: quotation at para 56.
[60] Ibid at para 58.
[61] See, in particular, ibid at para 60.

order to kill one individual in a densely populated area of Gaza, but which also killed several civilians and injured scores, was disproportionate.[62]

Nevertheless, he offered a reasonably sophisticated analysis which did not blindly endorse the wishes of the executive. This is in contrast to other decisions of the Court, such as those delivered in two cases involving the freedom to worship, namely *Hass v IDF Commander in the West Bank* (the *Machpela Cave* case)[63] and *Bethlehem Municipality v the State of Israel* (*Rachel's Tomb* case).[64] Both involved the requisition of privately owned land in the West Bank to ensure the security of Jewish worshippers at religious sites. Further, in both, the background to the application of a proportionality test to decide whether the executive had properly balanced freedom of religion and worship against property rights was that the High Court had already performed a mediative function between the parties which had resulted in the amendment and curtailment of the initial land requisition orders.[65] In these circumstances, the balancing of values appeared almost automatic: as the executive had averred that the amended requisition orders constituted the minimum infringement of property rights required to ensure the security of Jewish worshippers at these sites, the orders could not be disproportionate. One is, however, left with the impression that the balancing employed in these cases was not so much between the rights of religion and property but was merely an iterative comparison of the extent of the successive requisition orders. This seems rather a schematic method of determining whether the measure finally adopted was that least damaging to human rights.[66]

A striking feature of President Barak's opinion in the *Targeted Killings* case is his extensive reference to international norms and their doctrinal elaboration. For instance, he makes repeated citations to the International Committee of the Red Cross's study on customary international humanitarian law.[67] Again, this is in contrast to some other judgments where the

---

[62]   *Ibid*; cf paras 8 and 46.

[63]   HCJ 10356/02 (4 March 2004), [2004] *Israel Law Reports* 53. This case was joined with HCJ 10497/02, *Hebron Municipality v IDF Commander in Judaea and Samaria*. The leading judgment was delivered by Justice Procaccia, in which President Barak and Justice Cheshin concurred.

[64]   HCJ 1890/03 (3 February 2005), <http://elyon1.court.gov.il/files_eng/03/900/018/n24/03018900.n24.pdf>. The leading judgment was delivered by Justice Beinisch, in which Justices Rivlin and Chayut concurred.

[65]   See *Machpela Cave*, opinion of Justice Procaccia, at para 5, and *Rachel's Tomb*, opinion of Justice Beinisch at paras 4–6. On the mediative function of the High Court, see Dotan, n 26 above at 331–6 and 342–50; and Kretzmer, n 26 above at 189–90.

[66]   See Barak, 'Foreword', n 25 above at 157–8; and 'Terrorism', n 29 above at 138–9.

[67]   J-M Henckaerts and L Doswald-Beck, *Customary International Humanitarian Law* (Cambridge, Cambridge University Press, 2005, 3 vols); see, eg, *Targeted Killings* case, opinion of President (Emeritus) Barak, n 49 above at paras 23, 29, 30, 33, 34, 40, 41 and 46.

High Court has referred to international law only to have recourse to these norms as they have been interpreted by Israeli courts. This does not always correspond to the international interpretative consensus. For instance, in the *Machpela Cave* case, Justice Procaccia observed:

> Article 52 of the [1907] Hague [Regulations] provides that no requisition of land shall be made in an occupied area, except for military purposes. This article has been interpreted broadly in case law as applying also to the need to requisition land in order to establish military positions and outposts, and also in order to pave roads for the purpose of protecting Israeli inhabitants living in [occupied territory] (HCJ 24/91 *Timraz v IDF Commander in Gaza Strip* [[1991] IsrSC 45(2) 767]; *Wafa v Minister of Defence* [[1996] IsrSC 50(2) 848], at p.856; HCJ 401/88 *Abu Rian v IDF Commander in Judaea and Samaria* [[1988] IsrSC 42(2) 767]).[68]

This interpretation cannot be supported even by the text of Article 52, which provides in part:

> Requisitions in kind and services shall not be demanded from municipalities or inhabitants except for the needs of the army of occupation

Leaving to one side the question of whether land can fall into the category of 'requisitions in kind and services', civilian Israeli inhabitants do not form part of the 'army of occupation'.[69]

Dotan has argued that to forestall any governmental interference that would circumscribe its autonomy, the Court must maintain a favourable public perception;[70] consequently, 'in cases of petitions by Palestinians ... the Court's willingness to quash governmental actions is minimal'.[71] Accordingly, as various studies have concluded, the Court's 'rhetoric of judicial activism' has not been implemented in challenges to decisions of the military authorities which prejudice the rights of Palestinians in the Occupied Territories, particularly when these rights conflict with alleged Israeli security concerns.[72] The Court's 'rights-minded

---

[68] *Machpela Cave* case, opinion of Justice Procaccia at para 9.

[69] See further N Keidar, 'An Examination of the Authority of the Military Commander to Requisition Privately Owned Land for the Construction of the Separation Barrier' (2005) 38 *Israel Law Review* 247.

[70] Dotan, n 26 above at 345–50: cf Paterson, n 16 above at 9–34 on the influence of reference groups in determining the performance and content of the judicial role of members of the Judicial Committee of the House of Lords.

[71] Dotan, n 26 above at 342.

[72] *Ibid* at 329. Dotan gives as an example the High Court's refusal, on grounds of national security, to issue an injunction against the deportation of 415 members of Hamas in 1992 (see 347–8); on this case, see also Kretzmer, n 26 above at 184–6. See also Benvenisti, n 26 above at 120–21; AM Gross, 'The Construction of a Wall Between the Hague and Jerusalem: The Enforcement and Limits of Humanitarian Law and the Structure of Occupation' (2006) 19 *Leiden Journal of International Law* 393 at 411; and M Sfard, 'The Human Rights Lawyer's Existential Dilemma' (2005) 38 *Israel Law Review* 154 at 160–64.

approach is generally conspicuous by its absence in decisions relating to the Occupied Territories. The jurisprudence of these decisions is blatantly government-minded'.[73]

It has been argued that these cases are not 'normal'. They are not disputes between a governmental agency and an individual but rather disputes which challenge the authority and security of the state in a time of perceived crisis:

> most of the Jewish public in Israel regard challenges to the authority of the IDF in the Territories as acts of war that threaten the very security of the state itself, rather than expressions of the desires of a people subject to military occupation to be free of the occupying army. Since continued domination of the Occupied Territories is regarded as essential to the security of the state, attempts to force Israel to relinquish control are perceived as being directed against state security.[74]

Kretzmer further argues that these cases threaten Israel's construction of itself – 'the Zionist narrative of its conflict with the Palestinians' – and are perceived as contrary to its very right to existence. Consequently, when the High Court reviews security measures taken against Palestinians in the Occupied Territories, 'it has rarely been prepared to rule that insufficient weight has been given to basic individual rights'.[75] It is possible that the Court's frequent reliance on proportionality as the fulcrum of its decisions may contribute to this result. The legitimacy of the executive action under consideration is assumed at the outset: 'The action of the military commander in making the requisition order has the presumption of administrative propriety as long as no factual basis has been established to the contrary.'[76] If the petitioners fail to demonstrate that the impugned action lacks propriety, then only if it can be shown to be disproportionate will the measure be struck down. This essentially leaves the matter at the discretion of the Court in balancing values rather than applying rules to vindicate rights.

On the other hand, as Gross has observed, the High Court has been more accommodating to Palestinian rights when cases have gained international attention. When it ruled that some interrogation techniques employed by Israel's security services were illegal, it had been alleged that these techniques amounted to torture and the attention of both the international media and legal community had been engaged:

[73] Kretzmer, n 26 above at 188.
[74] *Ibid* at 194–5: see 191–5 generally; and also Dotan, n 26 above at 335.
[75] Kretzmer, n 26 above at 193–4.
[76] *Machpela Cave* case, opinion of Justice Procaccia at para 12.

The [High Court] views itself as part of a cosmopolitan, human-rights community of jurists, and making the issue a matter of international law would not allow it to dismiss the petition outright, as it had done in similar cases previously.[77]

The focus of Gross's analysis in reaching this observation was the High Court's principal judgments concerning the barrier wall Israel is building in the West Bank, namely *Beit Sourik Village Council v Government of Israel and Commander of the IDF Forces in the West Bank* and *Mara'abe and others v The Prime Minister of Israel and others*.[78] In both, the executive was ordered to change the route of the barrier wall in specific localities.

A subsequent case – *Head of the 'Azzum Municipal Council v State of Israel*[79]– dealt with the route of the barrier wall in the neighbourhood of the Palestinian villages of Jayus, 'Azzum and Nabi Elias, and an Israeli settlement, Tzofin. The section of the barrier wall under consideration in *'Azzum Municipal Council* had been challenged before the High Court in two joined unpublished cases in 2002. In its argument in these cases, the executive had stated that the route in this sector was determined only by operational security reasons. The High Court had denied the petitions because 'in view of the security considerations underlying the decisions on the route of the fence, its injury to the petitioners was proportionate'.[80] The petition in issue in *'Azzum Municipal Council* argued that, contrary to the claims made by the executive in the earlier cases, the route had not been determined as a result of security considerations but had intended to encompass areas designated for the expansion of the Tzofin settlement on the Israeli side of the barrier wall.[81]

During the proceedings, the executive conceded that expansion of the settlement, as well as security reasons, had determined the route of the barrier in this sector and subsequently announced that it would change

---

[77] Gross, n 72 above at 431.

[78] HCJ 2056/04, judgment delivered 30 June 2004, 43 ILM 1099 (2004), and HCJ 7857/04, judgment delivered 15 September 2005, 45 ILM 202 (2006), respectively. Both are available in English on the website of the Israeli Supreme Court, <http://elyon1.court.gov.il/eng/home/index.html>. As I have discussed these cases and the associated ICJ advisory opinion elsewhere, I shall not repeat that analysis here: see, eg, I Scobbie, 'Smoke, Mirrors and Killer Whales: The International Court's Advisory Opinion on the Israeli Barrier Wall' (2004) 5 *German Law Journal* 1107, available at <www.germanlawjournal.com/pdf/Vol05No09/PDF_Vol_05_No_09 _1107–1131_EU_Scobbie.pdf>, and 'Regarding/Disregarding: The Judicial Rhetoric of President Barak and the International Court of Justice's Wall Advisory Opinion', (2006) 5 *Chinese Journal of International Law* 269.

[79] HCJ 2732/05, judgment delivered 15 June 2006, unpublished: I am grateful to Michael Sfard, who represented the petitioners in this case, for supplying me with a copy of the judgment.

[80] *'Azzum Municipal Council*, opinion of President Barak at para 3: the earlier cases were *Ibtiassem Muhammed Ibrahim v the Military Commander*, HCJ 8172/02, and *Rashid Salameh v the Commander of the IDF*, HCJ 8532/02.

[81] *'Azzum Municipal Council*, opinion of President Barak at para 4.

the route in favour of the Palestinian petitioners. Consequently, the High Court upheld the petition, declared the route unlawful but expressed no view on the lawfulness of the amended route under consideration by the executive. It did, however, rebuke the executive:

> In the petition before us, a grave phenomenon was revealed. In the first petition presented to the Supreme Court, a complete picture was not presented. The court denied the first petition on the basis of information that was only partially grounded . . . the petition before us indicates an incident that must not be dismissed lightly, in which information provided to the court did not fully reflect the considerations borne in mind by the decision-makers. As a result, a petition was denied that even the Respondents agree should have been accepted . . . We hope that it will not be repeated.[82]

This case perhaps demonstrates the limits to Barak's affirmation in his extra-judicial writings that courts should not merely defer to executive claims that a measure is necessary for security reasons but require that these be presented so the court may decide whether they were the operative reasons and not simply a pretext.[83] If a court starts from the assumption that executive action is legitimate until proved otherwise, and then accepts the executive's justification at face value, can it be said to subject that action to thorough scrutiny?[84]

Moreover, given the presumption that executive action is proportionate until demonstrated otherwise, an iterative use of proportionality, such as that employed in the *Machpela Cave* and *Rachel's Tomb* cases, could encourage a strategy on the part of the executive initially to make an inflated claim. As this might subsequently be reduced by virtue of the mediative function of the Court, it is conceivable that the Court could mechanically privilege the executive's final position as reasonable, simply because it has been reduced to an ostensible declared minimum. Axiomatically, this strategy is not available for the protection of Palestinian interests as the starting point for judicial review is impugned executive action. Thus the methodology employed by the Court may itself create an additional barrier to the vindication of individual rights in the face of prejudicial public action.

One may also wonder whether petitions which challenged executive action in the Occupied Territories pushed former President Barak's judicial philosophy to its limits, perhaps demonstrating a deficiency in its underlying Dworkinian roots. President Barak has argued that the task of the judge is to formulate properly fundamental societal principles in

---

[82] *Ibid* at para 7.

[83] See Barak, 'Foreword', n 25 above at 157–8; and 'Terrorism', n 29 above at 138–9.

[84] Cf *Beit Sourik*, opinion of President Barak at para 45 (43 ILM 1116): see also his opinion in *Mara'abe* at paras 31–2 (45 ILM 216–17).

order to protect democracy and the constitution, but which value preferences should a judge favour when his decision concerns two different societies? Even if it is assumed that the fundamental values of Israeli and Palestinian society do not differ radically, it is apparent that petitions against executive action expose divergences on immediate aspirations. Could any judge synthesise these differences? Israeli commentators conclude that the High Court is government minded when dealing with petitions concerning the Occupied Territories, thus indicating that the values consistently privileged in these cases are those of Israeli society, but this also points to a schism in the Court's ontology. While perceived as activist when sitting as the Supreme Court in Israeli cases, there is a record of deference when it sits as the High Court hearing Palestinian petitions. This suggests that the Court adopts different perceptions of its proper role and relationship to the government in the two classes of case.

V. THE VIEW ELSEWHERE – JUDICIAL RESISTANCE TO EXECUTIVE ACTION

Following the 11 September 2001 attacks, Lepsius comments that:

> Freedom in general, democracy in general and the 'consciousness of the Western world' were seen as threatened. The lawmakers reacted less to the actual dangers to life as to the symbolic threat to the value system of the entire Western world.[85]

This is also true of executive actions taken in response to the perception of the threat posed by international terrorism. How have Western supreme courts reacted?

A. The United States Supreme Court

Considerations of both judicial ontology and role negotiation may be seen to be in play in the recent US Supreme Court cases of *Hamdi v Rumsfeld* and *Hamdan v Rumsfeld*. To a great extent, the key issue in both was not the substantive legal issues at stake, but rather the role of the judiciary in relation to executive action.

Hamdi arose because, after the 11 September 2001 attacks, the US Congress adopted a resolution, entitled 'Authorization for Use of Military Force', which empowered the President to 'use all necessary and

---

[85] O Lepsius, 'Liberty, Security, and Terrorism: The Legal Position in Germany' (2004) 5 *German Law Journal* 435, 438, available at <www.germanlawjournal.com/pdf/Vol05No05/PDF_Vol_05_No_05_435460_special_issue_Lepsius.pdf>.

appropriate force against those nations, organizations or persons he determines planned, authorized, committed or aided the terrorist attacks' or 'harbored such organizations or persons, in order to prevent any future acts of international terrorism against the United States by such nations, organizations or persons'.[86] Pursuant to this, President Bush ordered the invasion of Afghanistan where Hamdi, allegedly a member of the Taliban, was detained. He was transferred to Guantanamo Bay, but when it was found out that he is a US citizen, he was transferred to naval prison. Hamdi's father then brought a petition for habeas corpus. In the resultant proceedings, the US government argued that Hamdi was an enemy combatant and that this in itself justified his indefinite detention, without formal charges or proceedings being brought against him. The sole evidence the US government provided to the Court to justify Hamdi's detention was a declaration by Michael Mobbs, who was a Special Advisor to the Under Secretary of Defence for Policy.[87]

One of the key arguments raised by the US government to justify the continued detention of Hamdi was, essentially, that in determining the lawfulness of the detention, the courts should simply defer to the evidence it had produced. Justice O'Connor, writing the Court's plurality opinion, summarised this as:

> the argument that further factual exploration is unwarranted and inappropriate in light of the extraordinary constitutional interests at stake. Under the Government's most extreme rendition of this argument, '[r]espect for separation of powers and the limited institutional capabilities of courts in matters of military decision-making in connection with an ongoing conflict' ought to eliminate entirely an individual process, restricting the courts to investigating only whether legal authorization exists for the broader detention scheme ... At most, the Government argues, courts should review its determination that a citizen is an enemy combatant under a very deferential 'some evidence' standard ... Under this review, a court would assume the accuracy of the Government's articulated basis for Hamdi's detention, as set out in the Mobbs Declaration, and assess only whether that articulated basis was a legitimate one.[88]

The Court rejected this argument on constitutional grounds which it called separation of powers, and which I prefer to call ontological:

> we necessarily reject the Government's assertion that separation of powers principles mandate a heavily circumscribed role for the courts in such circumstances. Indeed, the position that the courts must forgo any examination of the individual case and focus exclusively on the legality of the broader detention scheme cannot be mandated by any reasonable view of separation of powers

---

[86] *Hamdi v Rumsfeld*, opinion of O'Connor J at 2 (43 ILM 1166).
[87] *Ibid* at 4–5 (43 ILM 1167–8).
[88] *Ibid* at 20 (43 ILM 1173–4).

as this approach serves only to *condense* power into a single branch of government. We have long since made clear that a state of war is not a blank check for the President when it comes to the rights of the Nation's citizens . . . Whatever power the United States Constitution envisions for the Executive in its exchanges with other nations or with enemy organizations in times of conflict, it must assuredly envision a role for all three branches when individual liberties are at stake.[89]

In contrast, in his dissenting opinion, Justice Scalia started from the premise that '[t]he very core of liberty secured by our Anglo-Saxon system of separated powers has been freedom from indefinite imprisonment at the will of the Executive'.[90] Accordingly, if Hamdi were imprisoned in violation of the Constitution, then the writ of habeas corpus should have been granted, forcing the executive either to hand him over to the criminal authorities or else to release him. On the contrary, the Court had disposed of the petition by remanding it to the District Court for reconsideration of the fact-finding process. This Scalia excoriated, remarking: 'This judicial remediation of executive default is unheard of. The role of habeas corpus is to determine the legality of executive detention, not to supply the omitted process necessary to make it legal.'[91] He accordingly dissociated himself from the Supreme Court's assertion of powers of review over executive action, and commented: 'As usual, the major effect of [the Court's] constitutional improvisation is to increase the power of the Court.'[92] He continued:

If civil rights are to be curtailed during wartime, it must be done openly and democratically, as the Constitution requires, rather than by silent erosion through an opinion of this Court.[93]

A similar judicial exchange of views on the proper role of the Supreme Court in reviewing executive action came to the fore in *Hamdan v Rumsfeld*. Unlike Hamdi, Hamdan is not a US citizen. In November 2001, he was captured by militia forces in Afghanistan who turned him over to US military forces. He has been held since June 2002 at Guantanamo Bay. In July 2004, he was charged with conspiracy to commit terrorism, and arrangements were made to try him before a military commission created pursuant to Presidential Military Order of 13 November 2001, 'Detention, treatment, and trial of certain non-citizens in the war against terrorism'.[94]

---

[89] *Ibid* at 29 (43 ILM 1177).
[90] *Hamdi v Rumsfeld*, dissenting opinion of Scalia J at 2 (43 ILM 1186).
[91] *Ibid* at 24 (43 ILM 1195).
[92] *Ibid* at 23 (43 ILM 1194).
[93] *Ibid* at 26 (43 ILM 1196).
[94] 66 Fed Reg 57833, available at <www.cnss.org/milorder.pdf>. As the legal basis for this Order, in the preambular paragraph, President Bush relied upon 'the authority vested in me as President and as Commander in Chief of the Armed Forces of the United States by

The procedures to be followed by the commission so created were set out in Department of Defense Military Commission Order No 1 of 21 March 2002.[95] Hamdan filed a petition for writs of habeas corpus and mandamus claiming, inter alia, that the commission convened for his trial lacked lawful authority and the protections required by the Geneva Conventions and the US Uniform Code of Military Justice.[96] He complained, in particular, of the commission's ability to proceed with the trial in his absence.[97] The US Court of Appeals for the District of Columbia Circuit ruled, inter alia, that the commission had jurisdiction to try Hamdan because Congress had authorised its creation.[98] The Supreme Court reversed this decision, ruling that the military commission had not expressly been authorised by any Congressional Act, thus denying that President Bush had the competence to create it.

Further, Hamdan argued that Military Commission Order No 1 violated Article 36 of the Uniform Code of Military Justice, which empowered the President to promulgate rules of procedure for both courts martial and military commissions. This, however, required that these rules 'so far as practicable' conform to those employed in criminal trials in US district codes and not be inconsistent with the Uniform Code itself. Further, the rules promulgated for the different tribunals must be 'uniform insofar as practicable'. Hamdan alleged that the Order dispensed with 'virtually all evidentiary rules applicable in courts-martial'.[99] The US government countered that the military commissions would be of no practical use if the President had to comply with the Uniform Code of Military Justice provisions governing courts martial. It also noted the President's decision that the danger posed to the United States given the nature of international terrorism made it impractical to apply to the commissions the principles and rules of evidence generally recognised in civilian criminal trials in the United States.[100]

Justice Stevens rejected the government's arguments out of hand. While he conceded that the Order was a determination that it would be

---

the Constitution and the laws of the United States of America, including the Authorization for Use of Military Force Joint Resolution (Public Law 107–40, 115 Stat. 224) and sections 821 and 836 of title 10, United States Code'.

[95]   Available at <www.defenselink.mil/news/Mar2002/d20020321ord.pdf>.

[96]   *Hamdan v Rumsfeld*, opinion of Justice Stevens (opinion of the Court) at 1–4 (45 ILM 1135–6). Hamdan also claimed that the charge of conspiracy was not an offence recognised as a violation of the laws of war. This plea was upheld by four Justices – Stevens, Souter, Ginsberg and Breyer: see Part V of Stevens' opinion at 31–49 (45 ILM 1144–8).

[97]   See *ibid* at 57–8 (45 ILM 1151).

[98]   Decided 15 July 2005: <http://pacer.cadc.uscourts.gov/docs/common/opinions/200507/04–5393a.pdf> at 7–9.

[99]   See *Hamdan v Rumsfeld*, opinion of Stevens J (opinion of the Court) at 56–8 (45 ILM 1151).

[100]   *Ibid* at 58 (45 ILM 1151).

impracticable to apply civilian criminal rules to military commissions, and that the Court assumed 'that complete deference is owed to that determination', no similar determination had been made for courts martial.[101] Justice Stevens noted that no evidence had been led to demonstrate why it would be impractical to apply the rules governing courts martial to the military commissions. Further, even if this were the case, the only apparent reason for this claim seemed to be the danger posed by international terrorism, but it was not clear why this would justify a departure from the courts martial rules. In relation to the accused's right to be present at his trial, Stevens stated that 'the jettisoning of so basic a right cannot lightly be excused as "practicable"'.[102] He buttressed his conclusions by arguing that the arrangements made for trial before the military commissions breached common Article 3 of the 1949 Geneva Conventions. This required that Hamdan be tried by 'a regularly constituted court, affording all the judicial guarantees which are recognised as indispensable by civilised peoples'. The Court ruled that regularly constituted courts in this context meant courts martial, and that military commissions could only be substituted for courts martial if there were some practical need to do so, which the government had failed to demonstrate.[103] Further, Justice Stevens observed that the procedures governing the military commissions were as relevant as the question of their regular constitution to determine whether they fulfilled recognised judicial guarantees. He argued that these encompassed elements found in customary international law and embodied in Article 75 of 1977 Protocol I Addition to the Geneva Conventions, despite the fact that the United States is not party to Additional Protocol I.[104] Justice Stevens' reliance on Common Article 3 and Article 75 was strictly unnecessary, as the arguments he marshalled under US law were sufficient to decide the case. Justice Kennedy made this clear in his opinion, emphasising that he was reluctant to conclude that Article 75 was binding in the light of the United States' decision not to ratify Additional Protocol I.[105]

In *Hamdan*, the ontological discussion regarding the proper function of the Supreme Court effectively took place in some of the other opinions. For instance, Justice Breyer issued a one-page opinion which solely addressed separation of powers issues, rejecting the dissenters' view that the judgment hampered the President's ability to deal with 'a new and

---

[101] *Ibid* at 59–60 (45 ILM 1152).
[102] *Ibid* at 60–61; quotation at 61 (45 ILM 1152).
[103] *Ibid* at 69–70 (45 ILM 1154), and also at 72 (45 ILM 1155).
[104] *Ibid* at 70–72 (45 ILM 1155); in his invocation of Article 75, Justice Stevens was not expressing the opinion of the Court, as only Justices Breyer, Ginsberg and Souter concurred in this part of his opinion (Part VI-D-iv).
[105] *Hamdan v Rumsfeld*, opinion of Justice Kennedy at 18–20 (45 ILM 1170).

deadly enemy'. Congress had denied the executive the legislative authority to create the military commissions, but the President could seek that authority:

> Where, as here, no emergency prevents consultation with Congress, judicial insistence upon that consultation does not weaken our Nation's ability to deal with danger. To the contrary, that insistence strengthens the Nation's ability to determine – through democratic means – how best to do so. The Constitution places its faith in those democratic means. Our Court today simply does the same.[106]

Justice Kennedy, like Justice O'Connor in *Hamdi*, underlined separation of powers concerns by observing that, as military commissions were located within a single branch of government, this ran the risk that offences would be defined, prosecuted and adjudicated by executive officials without the opportunity for independent review.[107] He concluded his opinion by inviting Congress to provide further guidance on military commissions as it, rather than the Supreme Court, was the branch of government better positioned to establish principles which were not inconsistent with the national interest and international justice.[108]

In contrast, in their dissenting opinions, Justices Scalia and Thomas took a more Posnerian view of the Supreme Court's judicial function. Justice Scalia wondered where the Supreme Court had found the authority to disagree with the political branches of government, and noted that the judiciary had placed itself in direct conflict with the executive on a matter where the executive's competence was at a maximum and the

---

[106] *Hamdan v Rumsfeld*, opinion of Justice Breyer at 1 (45 ILM 1163).

[107] *Hamdan v Rumsfeld*, opinion of Justice Kennedy at 2 (45 ILM 1164).

[108] *Ibid* at 20 (45 ILM 1171); see also opinion of Justice Breyer at 1 (45 ILM 1163). In response to the decision in *Hamdan* that military commissions created to try aliens designated as 'unlawful enemy combatants' lacked proper legal authorisation, Congress, at the request of President Bush, enacted the 2006 Military Commissions Act (reproduced at 45 ILM 1241 (2006)). Section 3.a of this Act expressly authorises the President to establish such tribunals (45 ILM 1248). Moreover, the Act prevents those accused from invoking the 1949 Geneva Conventions as a source of rights during commission proceedings (section 5.a, 45 ILM 1274), and retrospectively deprives them of the right to file habeas corpus petitions (section 7, 45 ILM 1277–8). *Hamdan* has subsequently challenged the Military Commissions Act, inter alia, on the ground that it is unconstitutional: see *Hamdan v Rumsfeld, Petitioner's opposition to motion to dismiss for lack of subject matter jurisdiction*, 45 ILM 1291 (2006) and *Respondent's reply in support of motion to dismiss for lack of subject matter jurisdiction*, 45 ILM 1323 (2006). The US Court of Appeals for the DC Circuit has, nevertheless, dismissed a number of habeas corpus petitions on the ground that the Military Commissions Act deprived federal courts of jurisdiction over habeas proceedings: see *Boumediene et al v Bush et al* and *Al Odah et al v United States et al* (20 February 2007), <www.opiniojuris.org/files/DCcir2–20–07.8.pdf>, judgment of the Court delivered by Justice Randolph at 9–13. The Court further held that the Act's suspension of habeas corpus was not unconstitutional because it dealt with aliens held outside US territory (namely, at Guantanamo Bay) – see opinion of Justice Randolph at 13–24.

judiciary's virtually non-existent.[109] Unlike his critical comments in *Hamdi*, he did not even mention the 'judicial remediation' provided by Justices Breyer and Kennedy; namely, that legislative action could cure the defect in the creation of the commissions.

Justice Thomas was more outspoken. Starting from the premise that 'it is important to take measure of the respective roles the Constitution assigns to the three branches of our Government in the conduct of war',[110] he affirmed that the Court's duty was to defer to the executive's military and foreign policy judgement: 'It is within this framework that the lawfulness of Hamdan's commission should be examined.'[111] In particular, Justice Thomas argued that Hamdan's claim to benefit from the provisions of common Article 3 was 'meritless' because President Bush had accepted the view of the Department of Justice that it did not apply to Al Qaeda detainees. The Court was bound to defer to this as he was 'acting pursuant to his constitutional authority as Commander in Chief'.[112] Furthermore, even if common Article 3 were applicable, Hamdan could not rely upon it for relief, as the military commissions had been regularly constituted.[113]

B. The House of Lords

Like the Supreme Court, the House of Lords in some recent cases has adopted a critical attitude to executive action, although its members have been more united, and more robust, in their approach. Further, the House of Lords has been more willing to employ international and comparative law when engaged in its review of executive action. One reason for this is undoubtedly structural, namely the incorporation of certain rights contained in the European Convention on Human Rights into domestic law by the Human Rights Act 1998. Section 2.1 of the 1998 Act requires courts to take into account when deciding issues which implicate Convention rights, inter alia, any relevant jurisprudence of the European Court of

---

[109] *Hamdan v Rumsfeld*, dissenting opinion of Justice Scalia at 21 and 23 (45 ILM 1178).

[110] *Hamdan v Rumsfeld*, dissenting opinion of Justice Thomas at 1 (45 ILM 1181).

[111] *Ibid* at 5–6; quotation at 6 (45 ILM 1182–3; quotation at 1183). While Justice Scalia joined with Justice Thomas in this part of his opinion (Part I), Justice Alito did not.

[112] See *ibid* at 42–4; quotation at 43 (45 ILM 1193–4; quotation at 1193). Once again, while Justice Scalia joined with Justice Thomas in this part of his opinion (Part III-B-2), Justice Alito did not.

[113] *Ibid* at 44–8 (45 ILM 1194–5); Justice Alito did concur in this part of Justice Thomas's opinion (Part III-B-3), and, indeed, the burden of his own opinion is that the military commissions conformed to the requirements of common Art 3 (see 45 ILM 1199–203).

Human Rights, and opinions and decisions of the Commission. Nevertheless, in interpreting some Convention rights, the House of Lords has cast its net more widely to examine international legal materials unconnected with the Convention.

These elements are apparent in the House of Lords' decision in the *A (Belmarsh Detainees)* case.[114] This case concerned the lawfulness of the indefinite detention of aliens, certified as suspected international terrorists by the Home Secretary under section 21 of the Anti-Terrorism, Crime and Security Act 2001. Section 23 of that Act allowed for the detention of persons certified under section 21 pending deportation, even if physical removal from the United Kingdom would be delayed temporarily or indefinitely by virtue of the operation of law or for some practical consideration. As the European Court has held that Article 3 of the European Convention prevents the deportation of aliens to states where they face a real risk of torture or inhumane or degrading treatment or punishment, in order to implement section 23 of the 2001 Act, on 11 November 2001, the Home Secretary made a formal derogation under Article 15 of the European Convention regarding Article 5.1 (the right to liberty) on the basis that the threat of terrorism posed a public emergency threatening the life of the nation.[115] The derogation was made in relation to Part 4 ('Immigration and asylum') of the 2001 Act, which contains section 23. A corresponding derogation was made in relation to Article 9 of the International Covenant on Civil and Political Rights.[116] The case focused on the legality of the derogation order.

On behalf of the UK government, the Attorney-General had argued that the government was responsible for public safety and that any 'judgment on this question was pre-eminently one within the discretionary area of judgment reserved to the Secretary of State and his colleagues, exercising their judgment with the benefit of official advice'.[117] Lord Bingham, in the leading opinion, set out the parameters of judicial deference to executive actions:

> It is perhaps preferable to approach this question as one of demarcation of functions . . . The more purely political (in a broad or narrow sense) a question is, the more appropriate it will be for political resolution and the less likely it is to be an appropriate matter for judicial decision. The smaller, therefore, will be the potential role of the court. It is the function of political and not judicial bodies to resolve political questions. Conversely, the greater the legal content

---

[114] *A (FC) and others (FC) v Secretary of State for the Home Department* [2004] UKHL 56, available at <www.parliament.the-stationery-office.co.uk/pa/ld200405/ldjudgmt/jd041216/a&others.pdf>. All references are to the pdf version.

[115] The Human Rights Act 1998 (Designated Derogation) Order 2001, SI 2001/3644, available at <www.opsi.gov.uk/si/si2001/20013644.htm>.

[116] See *A (Belmarsh Detainees)* case, opinion of Lord Bingham of Cornhill at paras 5–15.

[117] *Ibid* at para 25.

of any issue, the greater the potential role of the court, because under our constitution and subject to the sovereign power of Parliament it is the function of the courts and not of political bodies to resolve legal questions. The present question seems to me to be very much at the political end of the spectrum . . . I conclude that the appellants have shown no ground strong enough to warrant displacing the Secretary of State's decision on this important threshold question.[118]

The view that the assessment of a national security threat was properly one which lay pre-eminently within the purview of the executive and Parliament, rather than the courts, was shared by the other members of the House of Lords.[119] Nevertheless all – including the sole dissenter, Lord Walker – saw the assessment of national security interests as only a preliminary question and that, in contrast, the courts were empowered to assess the legality of the specific measures adopted to meet any potential threat. Where these measures resulted in indefinite detention, they 'plainly invite judicial scrutiny of considerable intensity'.[120] Article 15 of the European Convention required that any derogations undertaken by a party must be 'strictly required by the exigencies of the situation', that is, the measures taken must be proportionate. Accordingly, deference to the government's views on derogation:

cannot be taken too far. Due deference does not mean abasement before those views, even in matters relating to national security . . . Indeed the considerable deference which the European Court of Human Rights shows to the views of the national authorities in such matters really presupposes that the national courts will police those limits.[121]

This supervisory role of domestic courts, because it affects the competence of the judiciary in relation to other branches of government, may be seen as an ontological factor. Moreover, it is firmly rooted in international law.

The test employed by the House of Lords to determine proportionality, which it expressly noted was similar to that employed by the Supreme Court of Canada (and indeed that propounded by President Barak), provided:

whether: (i) the legislative objective is sufficiently important to justify limiting a fundamental right; (ii) the measures designed to meet the legislative objective

---

[118] *Ibid* at para 29.
[119] *A (Belmarsh Detainees)* case, opinions of Lord Nicholls of Birkenhead at para 79; Lord Hope of Craighead at paras 107 and 116; and Lord Walker of Gestingthorpe at para 192.
[120] *Ibid*, opinion of Lord Walker of Gestingthorpe at para 192.
[121] *Ibid*, opinion of Lord Rodger of Earlsferry at para 176.

are rationally connected to it; and (iii) the means used to impair the right or freedom are no more than is necessary to accomplish the objective.[122]

In arguing that indefinite detention was a proportionate response to the threat posed by terrorism, the Attorney-General had claimed that as Parliament and the executive were alone competent to assess that threat, it was equally for them and not the courts to judge the measures necessary to meet this:

> These were matters of a political character calling for an exercise of political and not judicial judgment . . . [which] fall within the discretionary area of judgment properly belonging to the democratic organs of the state. It is not for the courts to usurp authority properly belonging elsewhere.[123]

As Lord Hope emphasised, this submission was based in part on the claim that these branches of government possessed 'democratic legitimacy', but he countered that courts had the responsibility 'to minimise the risk of arbitrariness and to ensure the rule of law'.[124] Thus 'the courts may legitimately intervene, to ensure that the actions taken are proportionate'.[125]

Drawing on the jurisprudence of the European Court and the Supreme Courts of Canada and the United States, Lord Bingham also rejected the Attorney-General's claim, holding that considerations of deference did not preclude the courts from reviewing the proportionality of the derogation order or the compatibility of section 23 of the 2001 Act with the European Convention. Moreover he rejected:

> the distinction which [the Attorney-General] drew between democratic institutions and the courts. It is of course true that the judges in this country are not elected and are not answerable to Parliament . . . But the function of independent judges charged to interpret and apply the law is universally recognised as a cardinal feature of the modern democratic state, a cornerstone of the rule of

---

[122]   *Ibid*, opinion of Lord Bingham of Cornhill at para 30. Lord Bingham made express reference to the proportionality test laid down by the Canadian Supreme Court in *R v Oakes* [1986] 1 SCR 103. In *Charkaoui v Canada (Citizenship and Immigration)* 2007 SCC 9 (23 February 2007), available at <http://scc.lexum.umontreal.ca/en/2007/2007scc9/ 2007scc9.pdf>, the Supreme Court used the *Oakes* test (see para 67) to determine that provisions of the Immigration and Refugee Protection Act 2001 were inconsistent with the Canadian Charter of Rights and Freedoms. In particular, it ruled that 'Mechanisms developed in Canada and abroad illustrate that the government can do more to protect the individual while keeping critical information confidential than it has done in the *IRPA*. Precisely what more should be done is a matter for Parliament to decide. But it is clear that more must be done to meet the requirements of a free and democratic society' (para 87). One of the mechanisms the Court reviewed was the Special Advocate system utilised by the UK Special Immigration Appeals Tribunal (see paras 80–84).

[123]   *A (Belmarsh Detainees)* case, opinion of Lord Bingham of Cornhill at para 37.

[124]   *A (Belmarsh Detainees)* case, opinion of Lord Hope of Craighead at para 107.

[125]   *Ibid* at para 108.

law itself. The Attorney General is fully entitled to insist on the proper limits of judicial authority, but he is wrong to stigmatise judicial decision-making as in some way undemocratic.[126]

The detainees thus had a right to challenge the derogation order which, to be meaningful, meant that 'the judges must be intended to do more than simply rubber-stamp the decisions taken by ministers and Parliament'.[127] In the event, the House of Lords held that the detention order was disproportionate because it discriminated against the detainees on the grounds of their nationality, as suspected international terrorists who were UK nationals would not have been subject to a similar deprivation of liberty. It thus rejected the Secretary of State's choice of immigration control as a means to address a national security problem and quashed the order.[128] The House of Lords thus reconceptualised the government's classification of the issue to determine its true import.

The Belmarsh detainees were involved in further litigation – the *A (Foreign Torture Evidence)* case[129] – to determine whether, in hearing an appeal against detention under the Anti-Terrorism Crime and Security Act 2001 brought by a person who had been detained under that Act, the Special Immigration Appeals Commission could receive evidence which had, or may have been, obtained by torture in another country which had been committed without the complicity of the UK authorities. It was agreed by the litigants that if the UK authorities had themselves inflicted or been complicit in the acts of torture, then any evidence so gained was inadmissible.[130] The impugned executive action in question was the rules promulgated for the Special Immigration Appeals Commission which provided that it could receive evidence which would not be admissible in a court of law. The House of Lords unanimously held that the Commission could not hear evidence thought to have been obtained through the use of torture, although the individual judges differed on the standard to be used to establish whether evidence had been so obtained.

Lord Bingham again delivered the leading judgment in the case.[131] He initially classified the matter not as a technical rule of evidence but rather

---

[126] *Ibid*, opinion of Lord Bingham of Cornhill, para 42; see paras 38–44 generally.
[127] *Ibid*, opinion of Lord Rodger of Earlsferry at para 164: see also opinion of Baroness Hale of Richmond at para 226.
[128] See *ibid*, eg, opinion of Lord Bingham of Cornhill at paras 45, 53–4 and 73.
[129] *A (FC) and others (FC) v Secretary of State for the Home Department* [2005] UKHL 71, available at <www.publications.parliament.uk/pa/ld200506/ldjudgmt/jd051208/aand. pdf>. All subsequent references are to the pdf version.
[130] *Ibid*, opinion of Lord Bingham of Cornhill at para 1.
[131] Lord Bingham's opinion contained the most extensive discussion of the legal nature and implications of the prohibition on torture. On the whole, the other Law Lords regarded the prohibition as absolute, often expressly affirming Lord Bingham's analysis, and concentrated on the requisite standard to be used to determine whether evidence had been obtained by torture.

as a constitutional principle under English law.[132] He then drew on the jurisprudence of the European Court of Human Rights, emphasising that in the *Soering* case[133] that Court had identified the prohibition on torture and inhuman or degrading treatment contained in Article 3 of the European Convention on Human Rights as a fundamental value of the democratic states which constituted the Council of Europe.[134] He buttressed his argument by affirming that, under general international law, the prohibition on torture has *ius cogens* status, which consequently generates obligations *erga omnes* for other states.[135] The *ius cogens* status of the prohibition on torture was accepted as common ground by the parties and, moreover, had already been recognised in English law in the *Pinochet No 3* case.[136] Drawing on materials as diverse as the Human Rights Committee General Comment 20 (1992) on Article 7 of the International Covenant on Civil and Political Rights, Article 41 of the International Law Commission's 2001 Articles on State responsibility, and para 159 of the *Legal consequences of the construction of a wall in Occupied Palestinian Territory* advisory opinion,[137] Lord Bingham ruled: 'There is reason to regard it as a duty of states . . . to reject the fruits of torture inflicted in breach of international law.'[138]

The UK government had argued that, in cases involving terrorism, there was a practical need to obtain intelligence and evidence from official foreign sources, and that this cooperation might cease were enquiries to be made regarding how that information had been obtained.[139] Lord Bingham rejected this claim based on practicality. He observed that:

> The House has not been referred to any decision, resolution, agreement or advisory opinion suggesting that a confession or statement obtained by torture is admissible in legal proceedings if the torture was inflicted without the participation of the state in whose jurisdiction the proceedings are held, or that such evidence is admissible in proceedings related to terrorism.[140]

Further, he held that the domestic prohibition on the use of torture, as well as that established under international law, could not be overruled

---

[132] *A (Foreign Torture Evidence)* case, opinion of Lord Bingham of Cornhill at para 12. Lord Hoffmann also expressly affirmed the constitutional status of the prohibition on torture: see para 83.

[133] *Soering v UK* (1989) EHRR 439.

[134] See *A (Foreign Torture Evidence)* case, opinion of Lord Bingham of Cornhill at para 29.

[135] *Ibid* at paras 33 and 34.

[136] *Ibid* at para 33 (the earlier case was *R v Bow Street Metropolitan Stipendiary Magistrate, ex parte Pinochet Ugarte (No 3)* [2000] 1 AC 147 at 197–9).

[137] Reproduced in (2004) 43 *International Legal Materials* 1009.

[138] *A (Foreign Torture Evidence)* case, opinion of Lord Bingham of Cornhill at para 34.

[139] See *ibid* at para 46.

[140] *Ibid* at paras 45 and 50.

by a statute and procedural rule which did not expressly mention torture. This, he argued, engaged another core principle – the principle of legality. This entails that although Parliament may legislate in breach of fundamental human rights, to have legal effect this must be done openly and expressly in order that the government may accept the political cost of doing so.[141] As in *Hamdan*, the reliance on international law in the *A (Foreign Torture Evidence)* case was superfluous: the decision was effectively based on principles of English law and the court's reasoning need have gone no further. As Lord Bingham observed:

> The principles of the common law, standing alone, in my opinion compel the exclusion of third party torture evidence as unreliable, unfair, offensive to ordinary standards of humanity and decency and incompatible with the principles which should animate a tribunal seeking to administer justice. But the principles of the common law do not stand alone.[142]

C. German Federal Constitutional Court

The German Federal Constitutional Court has adopted an equally vigorous approach based on human rights, albeit in relation to legislative rather than executive action. In early 2006 it struck down as unconstitutional a provision in federal anti-terrorist legislation (the Air Transport Security Act) which empowered the Minister of Defence to order a civilian passenger airline to be shot down by the military if it could be assumed that the aircraft would be used to kill others, and if this could only be prevented by shooting it down.[143] This Act was only one of a series of measures which had been adopted in Germany after September 2001.[144] Lepsius argues that in promulgating these measures, infringements of civil rights were of little concern for the political branches of government, as security issues always trumped individual freedom: 'One

---

[141] *Ibid* at para 51; see also the opinions of Lord Hoffmann at para 96; Lord Hope of Craighead at para 114; and Lord Rodgers of Earlsferry at para 137.

[142] *Ibid*, opinion of Lord Bingham of Cornhill at para 52.

[143] See O Lepsius, 'Human Dignity and the Downing of Aircraft: The German Federal Constitutional Court Strikes Down a Prominent Anti-terrorism Provision in the New Air-transport Security Act' (2006) 7 *German Law Journal* 761, available at <www.germanlawjournal.com/pdf/Vol07No09/PDF_Vol_07_No_09_761–776_Developments_Lepsius.pdf>: compare M Ladiges, 'Comment – Oliver Lepsius's Human Dignity and the Downing of Aircraft: The German Federal Constitutional Court Strikes Down a Prominent Anti-terrorism Provision in the New Air-transport Security Act' (2007) 8 *German Law Journal* 307, <www.germanlawjournal.com/pdf/Vol08No03/PDF_Vol_08_No_03_307–310_Developments_Ladiges.pdf>. Subsequently the German Interior Minister has proposed that the Constitution should be amended to reverse the Court's decision, see <http://jurist.law.pitt.edu/paperchase/2007/01/german-justice-minister-balks-at-draft.php>.

[144] For an overview of the measures in general, see Lepsius, 'Liberty, Security, and Terrorism', n 85 above.

could even say that the executive and legislative branches lost an appropriate understanding of individual liberty.'[145]

The Constitutional Court relied on German constitutional law to reach its decision. Although it could simply have based its ruling on a separation of powers issue – that, under the Constitution, the federal government was not granted the power to deploy the armed forces domestically except for defensive purposes against military attacks per se[146] – it proceeded to rule that the legislation also violated the fundamental right to life and human dignity guaranteed by the Basic Law:[147]

> A far-reaching implication of the decision also signals to the authorities that collective goods may not, under any circumstances, outstrip individual rights. The collective right to safety at least is not in a constitutionally privileged position in contrast to individual rights. Therefore, the Court has readjusted the balancing of liberty and security and has given individual liberty a higher stake than collective security ... The Court, hence, has become the most reliable safeguard against the silent erosion of individual rights in the aftermath of 11 September 2001.[148]

Moreover, the Constitutional Court implicitly employed a test of proportionality which requires that the measure under scrutiny must be shown to be pursuing some legitimate end, and the means used to do so must be suitable, necessary and appropriate or fair. The Court found the statutory provision before it also to be disproportionate because it could not achieve the end it claimed to pursue: the information that a passenger aircraft was to be used as a weapon could never be definitive at the time when the Minister of Defence ordered its destruction. This order could only be given on the basis of a presumption, not a certainty, and this could not justify depriving the passengers of their human rights.[149]

VI. CONCLUDING THOUGHTS

The *Downing of aircraft* case throws into relief one aspect of cases that involve governmental action in response to threats to national security and of terrorism: whether, and the extent to which, these threats exist is essentially a factual and not a normative question. When courts attempt to balance issues of security against the values embedded in human rights norms, one may legitimately wonder if judges are attempting the impossible by trying to weigh incommensurables:

---

[145]   Lepsius, 'Downing of Aircraft', n 143 above at 762.
[146]   *Ibid* at 764–6.
[147]   See *ibid* at 766–71.
[148]   See *ibid* at 772.
[149]   See *ibid* at 774–5.

Security seems to have become a self-evident public interest that does not need a normative, constitutionally rooted justification. Its legitimacy is presupposed and security is presented as a legitimate purpose. The justifying purpose is supported by a factual understanding only . . . One can no longer speak of the 'weighing' of two legally protected rights. The relationship between freedom and security now represents a disproportionality of normative and empirical (factual) aspects . . . By not even attempting to put forward normative arguments, 'security' cannot be understood in a normative sense and thus becomes (normatively) untouchable. Security purposes . . . enter into the weighing process as self evident fact; this no longer allows for the common constitutional 'balancing-principles' to function . . . A particular problem associated with the balancing of security and freedom lies in the fact that in contrast to the quite precisely defined civil liberties, the public good of security is rather diffuse and non-determined. Thus, security does not constitute a weighable position. Security cannot be positively, but only negatively defined in the sense of defense against dangers.[150]

There is a clear trend, even unanimity, in the jurisprudence of superior courts that the assessment of threats to national security is a matter best left to the executive branches but that the judiciary can intervene to police the measures adopted in response. Nevertheless, there are difficulties in judicial scrutiny of national security claims. The dilemmas faced by judges in attempting to determine conflicts between security claims and human rights are:

heightened by the secrecy which necessarily attends most issues of national security . . . a portentous but non-specific appeal to the interests of national security can be used as a cloak for arbitrary and oppressive action on the part of government. Whether or not patriotism is the last refuge of the scoundrel, national security can be the last refuge of the tyrant.[151]

One way by which judges may escape from the horns of this dilemma is by employing the second part of the proportionality test, by assessing whether the means chosen adequately fit the end pursued. This can stand the impugned executive action on its head. As the *Downing of aircraft* judgment demonstrated, reliance on factual considerations in assessing the efficacy of an executive measure evaluates it on the basis of its own assumptions and can avoid or negate a conflict between fact and value.

Some would counsel against this: Posner, for instance, would argue that judges have no expertise in national security matters and therefore should automatically defer to the desires of the executive and legislative

---

[150] Lepsius, 'Liberty, Security and Terrorism', n 85 above at 458–9: see also V Zoller, 'Liberty dies by inches' (2004) 5 *German Law Journal* 469 at 474: available at <www.germanlawjournal.com/pdf/Vol05No05/PDF_Vol_05_No_05_469–494_special_issue_Zoeller.pdf>.
[151] *A (Belmarsh Detainees)* case, opinion of Lord Walker of Gestingthorpe at para 193.

branches. A similar view was expressed by Justices Scalia and Thomas in *Hamdan*. Amongst the senior judiciary, however, this is not an argument which has found favour, being clearly rejected by the Israeli and US Supreme Courts and the House of Lords : 'The argument that the impingement' upon human rights is due to security considerations does not rule out judicial review. "Security considerations" or "military necessity" are not magic words.'[152] There are, however, two strands to claims that the judiciary should defer to the executive. Posner (as well as Scalia and Thomas) appear to argue in favour of a complete deference, which amounts to what Barak would term institutional non-justiciability. This is deference at a macro level, which insulates national security considerations from any judicial scrutiny. Deference at a micro level, in the assessment of the legality of specific measures, nevertheless appears to be accepted as legitimate by Israel's High Court. Thus, for instance, in its examination of the legality of the route of the barrier wall in *Beit Sourik*, President Barak opined that this:

> raises problems within the realm of military expertise. We, Justices of the Supreme Court, are not experts in military affairs. We shall not examine whether the military commander's military opinion corresponds to ours – to the extent that we have an opinion regarding the military character of the route ... All we can determine is whether a reasonable military commander would have set out the route as this military commander did.[153]

Other courts, such as the House of Lords in the *A (Belmarsh Detainees)* case, appear to be much more critical and searching in their scrutiny of executive action.

Similarly, Posner's argument that judges should defer to the executive (and legislature) because the judiciary is not democratically accountable has found little support from the judges of superior courts. For them, democracy is more than the periodic resort of the population to ballot boxes but rather resides in the underpinning public values of the polity and the defence of the rule of law against encroachment by the elected branches of government. Thus in *Hamdi*, in delivering the opinion of the plurality, Justice O'Connor resisted the attempt 'to *condense* power into a single branch of government';[154] while in *A (Belmarsh Detainees)*, Lord Hope affirmed 'the responsibility that rests on the courts to give effect to the guarantee to minimise the risk of arbitrariness and to ensure the rule of law';[155] and President Barak exults in the fact that as judges are not the representatives of the people, they have the independence to express the

---

[152] *Mara'abe v Prime Minister of Israel*, opinion of President Barak at para 31 (45 ILM 216).
[153] *Beit Sourik*, opinion of President Barak at para 46 (43 ILM 1116): see also his opinion in *Mara'abe* at paras 31–32 (45 ILM 216–17).
[154] *Hamdi v Rumsfeld*, opinion of Justice O'Connor at 29 (43 ILM 1177).
[155] *A (Belmarsh Detainees)* case, opinion of Lord Hope of Craighead at para 107.

fundamental principles of their society. These examples enunciate views of the proper relationship and division of constitutional powers and responsibilities between the different branches of government. In contrast, Posner's argument essentially seems retrogressive inasmuch as it seems to demand that judges conform to an unreconstructed *'bouche de la loi'* doctrine in relation to executive acts akin to that which Montesquieu argued they should adopt in relation to legislation:

> *les juges de la nation ne sont, comme nous avons dit, que la bouche qui pronounce les paroles de la loi; des êtres inanimés qui n'en peuvent modérer ni la force, ni la rigueur.*[156]

Judicial ontology, and conceptions of the proper functions of the different branches of government, no longer correspond to the schematic vision of Montesquieu.

It is clear that one factor in this changed ontology may be institutional, such as the influence of the provisions of the European Convention on Human Rights and the jurisprudence of the European Court of Human Rights on the decision-making of European courts. More broadly, international law is increasingly a factor which domestic courts employ to constrain the executive. In *Hamdan*, and in the *A (Belmarsh Detainees)* and *A (Foreign Torture Evidence)* cases, the US Supreme Court and the House of Lords both had recourse to international legal norms, which was technically superfluous as these decisions could have been based solely on the domestic law. Section 6.a.2 of the Military Commissions Act, however, ostensibly forecloses this strategy for US federal courts in some cases. It prohibits recourse to foreign or international law sources in the interpretation of violations of common Article 3 of the Geneva Conventions as these are defined in the Act.[157] In contrast, a striking feature of the *A (Belmarsh Detainees)* case was the impact of international law, both structurally as an ontological factor due to the impact of the European Convention on Human Rights, and substantively as a basis of argument which is at its most extensive in the leading opinion delivered by Lord Bingham,[158] features replicated in the *A (Foreign Torture Evidence)* case.

---

[156] See Montesquieu, n 13 above (Book 11, ch 6, *De la constitution d'Angleterre*) at Vol I, 301 in the Goldschmidt edition ['a nation's judges are, as we have said, only the mouth that utters the words of the law; inanimate beings who cannot curb [or limit] either its strength or its vigour'; author's translation].

[157] For the text of s 6.a.2, see 45 ILM 1275 (2006): in his introductory note to the Act, Scheffer predicts that this prohibition will be tested in future litigation: *ibid* at 1242.

[158] See *A (Belmarsh Detainees)* case, opinion of Lord Bingham of Cornhill at, eg, paras 58–63, 68–9. In contrast, Lord Hoffmann restricted his grounds of decision to considerations peculiar to the United Kingdom, starting from the proposition that 'I would not like anyone to think that we are concerned with some special doctrine of European law. Freedom from arbitrary arrest and detention is a quintessentially British liberty, enjoyed by the inhabitants of this country when most of the population of Europe could be thrown into prison at the

Israel's High Court has a mixed record on the use of international law: at times, its substantive interpretation is idiosyncratic, serving to justify governmental acts which are not warranted under the applicable instruments. In other cases, however, that Court embraces the mainstream as is apparent in President Barak's opinion in the *Targeted Killings* case. Nevertheless, it is significant that the High Court at least uses the rhetoric of international law. Any account of why domestic courts employ international law, especially when they need not do so, can only be speculative, but Lord Bingham's observation that 'the principles of the common law do not stand alone'[159] is at least suggestive. Recourse to international law may be used to strengthen the legitimacy of the decision: it demonstrates that the judgment is based not simply on local interests[160] but transcends the state and its peculiar concerns. It is a claim to the universalisation of the decision reached: the claim that all states, all courts, would reach the same decision. This claim, or emerging trend, of universalisation constitutes another ontological shift: justice must no longer be local to be legitimate.

whim of their rulers. It was incorporated into the European Convention in order to entrench the same liberty in countries which had recently been under Nazi occupation' (para 88). For a commentary on Lord Hoffmann's judicial strategy, see T Poole, 'Harnessing the Power of the Past? Lord Hoffmann and the Belmarsh Detainees Case' (2005) 32 *Journal of Law and Society* 534.

[159] *A (Foreign Torture Evidence)* case, opinion of Lord Bingham of Cornhill at para 52.
[160] See, however, McCrudden, n 26 above.

9

The Abuse of Executive Powers:

What Remedies?

CHRISTIAN J TAMS

I. INTRODUCTION

WRITING IN 1961, Justice Guha Roy of India noted:

That a wrong done to an individual must be redressed by the offender himself or by someone else against whom the sanction of the community must be applied is one of the timeless axioms of justice without which social justice is unthinkable'.[1]

The statement underlines the essential importance of remedies, also encapsulated in maxims such as *ubi ius ibi remedium*. Yet experience during the recent and ongoing fight against terrorism suggests that the availability of a remedy may not be as axiomatic as Justice Roy claimed. To certain groups of individuals, his statement is likely to ring hollow. They notably include those held incommunicado in notorious or unknown detention facilities, those tortured or treated inhumanely by police forces or secret service agents, those kidnapped and deported in instances of so-called 'extraordinary renditions', or those delivered to foreign police forces known for their effective interrogation methods. Other chapters in this volume analyse whether the respective forms of conduct can, if only exceptionally, be brought in line with international law, or justified under concepts such as 'necessity' or 'state of emergency'. The present chapter assesses possible means of redress. The focus therefore is on the international regime of remedies – remedies being understood as a 'secondary' set of rules aimed at establishing justice and

---

[1] Guha Roy, 'Is the Law of Responsibility of States for Injuries to Aliens a Part of Universal International Law?' (1961) 55 *American Journal of International Law* 863.

redressing wrongs committed[2] ('secondary', of course, not in terms of relevance, but only in that they presuppose a wrong).[3] In contrast, the substantive (or if one prefers, 'primary') rules determining what types of government conduct constitute a wrong are treated only in passing.

Notwithstanding this caveat, the ground to be covered is broad, and this chapter adopts a fairly general approach which will hint at, rather than explore, many of the issues. The reason for this lies in the general nature of the notion of 'remedy', and the diversity of fora from which remedies may be sought. As regards the former aspect, a standard law dictionary defines remedies as 'means by which a right is enforced or the violation of right is prevented, redressed or compensated'.[4] But that definition is extremely general, and would cover many different forms of conduct, ranging from public protests against government policies to Amnesty International petitions for the release of a prisoner held captive in a military camp. The present chapter will focus on a more restrictive range of remedies. First, it proceeds from the perspective of victims of abusive executive conduct, and queries whether these victims have a right to obtain redress for the wrongs committed. Second, the focus will be on judicial or quasi-judicial proceedings, while other, less formalised methods of obtaining redress (such as naming perpetrators, or the blaming and shaming of governments) will not be addressed. And third, given the title of this Part of the book ('Balancing Security Concerns and Individual Freedoms'), it will only deal with remedies aimed at redressing wrongful conduct that affects rights of individuals under human rights or humanitarian law, thus notably leaving out violations of the rights of other states.[5]

Of course, the range of remedies to be looked at is still relatively heterogeneous. Depending on the type of violation, redress may take different forms, ranging from declarations that a certain executive conduct was illegal to the prosecution of individual perpetrators. What is more, when seeking to clarify the international legal framework, one has to take account of the different avenues which victims may pursue. Experience with human rights litigation post-11 September 2001 shows that executive conduct has been challenged in different fora. Courts of

---

[2] For comment on this dual nature of the remedies see D Shelton, *Remedies in International Human Rights Law*, 2nd edn (Oxford, Oxford University Press, 2006) 7 *et seq*.

[3] It is readily admitted that the notion of 'secondary rules' may be misleading. It has been used before to describe different types of rules, notably in HLA Hart's 'Concept of Law' and (probably independently of Hart, although this is still being debated) by the International Law Commission (ILC) in its work on state responsibility. Both the ILC's and Hart's use of the term is broader, but comprises rules of remedies.

[4] *Black's Law Dictionary*, 6th edn (St Paul, Minnesota, West Publishing, 1990) 1294.

[5] These may notably be affected by extra-territorial conduct of state organs acting without the consent of the territorial state, or by violations of rights of foreign nationals (triggering a right of other states to bring claims of diplomatic protection).

the state allegedly responsible for the abuse of executive powers (the 'perpetrator state') naturally have been the first to be confronted with claims for redress – hence the many Guantanamo-related proceedings before US courts, or challenges of British conduct within the UK. However, remedies may also be sought outside the domestic legal system of the perpetrator state, in particular from courts of other states and international institutions competent to monitor compliance with human rights. While these forms of proceedings have been far less numerous, they cannot be ignored. Quite to the contrary, there is an increasing reliance on foreign courts and international institutions, which underlines the transnational character of modern human rights litigation. Yet, clearly, remedies sought from foreign courts or international institutions raise questions and involve legal concepts that are entirely different from those applicable to proceedings before courts of the perpetrator state. A distinction will thus be drawn between attempts to obtain redress within the perpetrator state, within other states, and before international institutions. The third, fourth and fifth sections of this chapter outline the respective legal regimes, focusing throughout on the applicable rules of international law, while Section VI offers some tentative conclusions on the current state of the international regime of remedies. Before dealing with remedies, however, it is necessary to briefly clarify two preconditions for their availability, which have been much discussed recently: the application of human rights to extra-territorial conduct of states, and the distinction between perpetrator states and other third states.

II. TWO PRELIMINARY ISSUES

A. Standards Applicable to Extra-territorial Conduct

The first question concerns the yardstick against which state conduct is to be measured. As has been noted at the outset, the present chapter will focus on standards prescribed by human rights law and humanitarian law. While states often adopt widely divergent interpretations as to the content of the relevant obligations, it is not contested that both act as constraints on their conduct. However, there is some debate about the scope of application of human rights norms, which needs to be addressed at least briefly. A number of statements suggest a restrictive analysis of human rights,[6] which are said to apply only to conduct on the territory of states – hence many detention facilities are curiously located on foreign

---

[6] See in particular the statements in the US country report under Art 40 of ICCPR (UN Doc CCPR/C/USA/3, para 469 and Annex I).

territory (the most famous being Camp Delta, formally on Cuban soil). It is not necessary here to assess whether there is a moral or political justification for locking people up in faraway places (a method that certainly has a long tradition) or to assess how the applicable domestic legal systems treat questions of extra-territoriality. For present purposes, it is sufficient to note that even if it takes place outside the state's borders, the abuse of executive powers can regularly be measured against international human rights law. It has long been recognised that a state is bound by human rights law (whether treaty or customary) wherever it exercises stable authority and effective control. Human rights supervisory bodies thus have held states responsible for human rights abuses committed abroad, be it in occupied territory[7] or in less formalised extra-territorial settings.[8] Human rights treaties in fact require them to do so since they typically oblige states to observe human rights of all persons within their territory *and* (or even exclusively) under their jurisdiction. The disjunctive territory/jurisdiction test, however, implies that human rights are not territorially limited. In fact, in the *Lopez Burgos* case, the Human Rights Committee has described it as 'unconscionable' to 'interpret the ... Covenant [International Covenant on Civil and Political Rights (ICCPR)] as to permit a state party to perpetrate violations ... on the territory of another state, which violations it could not perpetrate on its own territory'.[9] Admittedly, the extra-territorial application of human rights may find its limits. For example, states may (following a recent decision by the European Court of Human Rights) not be responsible under human rights law for violations committed through aerial bombardments.[10] However, this may also be read to reinforce that the real test is whether the state concerned exercises stable authority and effective control on the ground. This, however, is what states usually do in situations that might induce them to violate individual rights in the war on terror. Even if committed abroad, these violations typically occur in their prisons, in territory controlled by them, or under their stable authority. There is, in short, no reason not to measure their conduct against the yardstick of

[7] See eg the Human Rights Committee's observations with respect to Israel (UN Docs CCPR/CO/78/ISR [2003]; ICCPR/C/79/Add 93 [1998]), or the European Court of Human Rights decision in the Northern Cyprus cases (*Loizidou v Turkey*, 23 EHRR 513 [1996]; *Cyprus v Turkey*, ECtHR Reports 2001 IV, 1).

[8] See eg Human Rights Committee, *Lopez Burgos v Uruguay*, UN Docs CCPR/C/13/D/52/1979, and more generally, General Comment No 31, UN Doc CCPR/C/79/Add.50 (1995), para 19.

[9] Human Rights Committee, *Lopez Burgos v Uruguay*, UN Docs CCPR/C/13/D/52/1979, para 12.

[10] *Bankovic v Belgium et al*, ECtHR Reports 2001 XII, 333.

human rights law, and human rights bodies asked to comment on, for example, allegations of human rights abuses in extra-territorial prison camps have regularly done so.[11]

B. Principal and Other Forms of Responsibility

The second question concerns the identification of the perpetrator state. Very often, that identification may be a relatively easy process. Each state is principally responsible for the abuse of *its own* executive powers.[12] In other words, principal responsibility lies with the state whose organs have committed (or are alleged to have committed) the human rights abuse for which a remedy is sought: the United Kingdom with respect to detainees held in Belmarsh prison, or the United States with respect to human rights violations by US military personnel, whether committed within the United States or – as has just been shown – elsewhere under their effective control. But not all cases are based on simple fact-patterns like these. Especially given the (acknowledged and unacknowledged) cooperation of states in the fight against terrorism, many human rights abuses involve organs of more than one state. Examples in point are allegations against German military forces to have witnessed, or participated in, the degrading treatment of German resident Murat Kurnaz by US forces in Kandahar,[13] or European states tacitly accepting the use of their territory for the practice of abduction and illegal detention referred to as 'extraordinary rendition'.[14] In this case, one might still agree that the state whose organs have committed the eventual human rights violation is principally responsible. But how about states aiding and abetting in its conduct, or instigating or tolerating it? The question eschews a general answer, but at least a general tendency can be discerned: under human rights law, states can be responsible for human rights violations they do not commit themselves.

There are different strands to this general trend. One is the recognition, in the law of state responsibility, of responsibility for complicity in the

---

[11] See eg Inter-American Commission on Human Rights, in *Precautionary Measures in Guantanamo Bay*; as well as the recent observations (referred to below), by the Committee against Torture (CAT) and the Human Rights Committee (HRC), on the US country reports.

[12] See Art 4 of the ILC's Articles on State Responsibility.

[13] Cf 'Ex-Guantanamo inmate says German soldiers abused him', *Reuters*, 4 October 2006, <www.reuters.com>.

[14] For a detailed assessment see the report, 'Alleged secret detentions and unlawful inter-state transfers involving Council of Europe member states', prepared by Dick Marty and submitted to the Parliamentary Assembly of the Council of Europe, available at <http://assembly.coe.int/CommitteeDocs/2006/20060606_Ejdoc162006PartII-FINAL.pdf> (hereinafter 'Marty Report').

wrongful conduct of another state. The basic principle has been formulated in Article 16 of the International Law Commission's Articles on
State Responsibility, according to which:

> A State which aids or assists another State in the commission of an internation-
> ally wrongful act by the latter is internationally responsible for doing so if:
>
> (*a*) That State does so with knowledge of the circumstances of the internation-
> ally wrongful act; and
>
> (*b*) The act would be internationally wrongful if committed by that State.[15]

With respect more particularly to extraordinary renditions, the Venice
Commission's legal opinion, required by the Council of Europe, recently
observed that: 'Active and passive co-operation by a Council of Europe
member State in imposing and executing secret detentions engages its
responsibility under the European Convention on Human Rights.'[16] This
suggests that one state's collaboration in another state's human rights
abuse can violate human rights in itself.

Second, in the field of human rights and humanitarian law, the
prohibition against complicity in wrongful conduct has, at least for
certain important rights, been recognised as an autonomous, independent obligation pursuant to which states must refrain from exposing
individuals to human rights abuses by other states. The Torture Convention expressly prohibits parties from 'expelling, returning ("refouler") or
extraditing a person to another State where there are substantial grounds
for believing that he would be in danger of being subjected to torture'.[17]
Other human rights treaties such as the European Convention on Human
Rights (ECHR) or the ICCPR do not contain express provisions to this
effect, but have at times been interpreted similarly. Under the European
Court of Human Rights' jurisprudence, ECHR member states are obliged
not to extradite, deport or expel individuals to other states (including
states not bound by the ECHR) where they face a real risk for their life,

---

[15] For comment on responsibility for complicity see eg Klein, 'Beihilfe zum Völkerrech-
tsdelikt' in von Münch (ed), *Staatsrecht – Europarecht – Völkerrecht. Festschrift Schlochauer*
(Berlin/New York, de Gruyter, 1981) 425; Graefrath, 'Complicity in the Law of International
Responsibility' (1996) 29 *Revue Belge de Droit International* 370. In its judgment, of 26
February 2007, in the *Bosnian Genocide* case, available at <www.icj-cij.org>, the International
Court of Justice affirmed the customary nature of the prohibition against complicity in
international wrongs (at para 420).
[16] Venice Commission, 'Draft Opinion on the International Legal Obligations of Council
of Europe Member States in respect of Secret Detention Facilities and Inter-State Transport
of Detainees', available at <http://www.venice.coe.int/docs/2006/CDL-DI(2006)001rev-
e.asp>, para 126.
[17] Art 3 CAT. For similar provisions see eg Art 16 of the 2005 Convention for the
Protection of All Persons from Enforced Disappearance (hereinafter 'the Forced Disappearances Convention').

their right to be free from torture or basic fair trial rights.[18] This obligation comes into play not only if the deporting/extraditing state has precise knowledge about the other state's intentions. Rather, ECHR member states must ascertain the relevant facts and – if there are indications of a real risk, such as a widespread practice of human rights abuses within the other state[19] – they must secure reliable diplomatic assurances or refuse extradition/deportation. To underline the practical relevance of this obligation, it may be sufficient to refer to the recent *Agiza* case, in which the Committee Against Torture (CAT) found that Sweden had violated the Torture Convention by deporting the complainant to Egypt.[20] In the Committee's view, Sweden should have been aware of reports about the widespread use of torture in Egyptian prisons, and could not merely rely on diplomatic assurances.[21] This in turn means that states parties to human rights treaties such as the ECHR, the CAT and the ICCPR cannot pretend to be unconcerned by other states' conduct. By exposing individuals to the risk of severe abuses, they themselves violate their human rights obligations.

Taken together, both developments mean that the circle of perpetrator states may be broader than initially expected. It comprises principally responsible states as well as their accomplices and states breaching their obligation not to expose individuals to other states' human rights abuses. On that basis, it is now possible to analyse remedies available before national courts within the perpetrator state.

III. OBTAINING REDRESS BEFORE NATIONAL COURTS WITHIN THE PERPETRATOR STATE

In most cases, a person alleging a human rights violation is likely to seek redress before the national courts of the perpetrator state. The availability of redress in these proceedings first and foremost depends on the state's municipal law, and typically, arguments are framed in terms of national constitutional, criminal, administrative or police law. Yet international law does have a role to play. For present purposes, it is necessary to determine whether international law requires states to grant victims of

---

[18] See *Soering v United Kingdom* (ECHR, Ser A/161) [1989] ECHR 14; *Chahal v United Kingdom* [1996] ECHR 54 and subsequent jurisprudence.

[19] See eg the CAT decision in *Agiza v Sweden*, 24 May 2005, Doc CAT/C/34/D/233/2003 (§ 13.4). The same is now expressly provided for in Art 16(2) of the Forced Disappearances Convention.

[20] *Agiza v Sweden* §§ 13.2 *et seq.* For similar proceedings before the ECHR see *Ramzy v The Netherlands* (Application No 25424/05, pending).

[21] *Agiza v Sweden*, § 13.4. Similarly, in their recent observations, the HRC and the CAT criticised the United States for not requiring sufficient guarantees before expelling or deporting terror suspects to countries with notorious human rights records.

human rights abuses specific remedies (and if so, which).[22] Depending on the type of human rights abuse, victims may seek different types of remedies, three of which seem particularly relevant:

(1)   Persons detained because of their alleged involvement with terrorist organisations typically seek a judicial review of their detention.
(2)   Persons claiming to have been tortured or treated inhumanely typically want to see their cases investigated; similarly, in cases of suspicious deaths, family or relatives want to learn the truth about what has happened.
(3)   Victims of human rights abuses often seek compensatory justice for harm suffered, typically in the form of damages, and may also look for retributive justice aimed at punishing those responsible for the abusive conduct.

It therefore needs to be assessed whether international law requires states to provide any of these remedies.

A. Judicial Review of Detentions

First, does international law require states to permit the judicial review of detentions, and if so, what are the requirements for such a review? On the face of it, at least the first question can be answered relatively clearly. All major human rights treaties recognise the right to be free from arbitrary detention, which also forms part of customary law. Of course, this right is not absolute, but only requires states not to detain persons arbitrarily. However, it is supplemented by a specific procedural guarantee designed to ensure the cessation of illegal detentions: when a person is detained by a state, human rights law requires the availability of judicial review in habeas corpus proceedings. For example, the ICCPR provides in Article 9(4) that:

> Anyone who is deprived of his liberty by arrest or detention shall be entitled to take proceedings before a court, in order that the court may decide without delay on the lawfulness of his detention and order his release if the detention is not lawful.

Contrary to views expressed by the US government, most recently in its reports to UN treaty monitoring bodies, this provision applies to measures adopted as part of the 'war on terror' and is not simply superseded

---

[22] Of course, this is not the only type of interaction. In addition, it is worth noting that, depending on the openness of the state's domestic legal system vis-à-vis international law, individuals can at times invoke international law directly. More frequently, national courts and authorities are at least required to construe municipal law in the light of the state's obligations under international law.

by international humanitarian law.[23] That said, even international humanitarian law does not give states complete discretion in interning and detaining individuals. The Third and Fourth Geneva Conventions permit parties to an armed conflict to detain combatants as prisoners of war and to intern civilians because they constitute a threat to the security of the party or intend to harm it or for the purposes of prosecution on war crimes charges.[24] However, these special entitlements apply only to states involved in an international armed conflict, and for the duration of such an armed conflict. Notwithstanding the language used, the 'war on terror' does not per se qualify as an international armed conflict, and most combat situations that might have qualified as such seem to have ceased.[25]

As regards the content of international habeas corpus rights, Article 9 ICCPR and equivalent provisions require a review by a judicial body that is independent from the detaining authorities, and whose eventual rulings are binding and effective.[26] What is more, in habeas proceedings, states have to ensure impartiality and equality of arms and allow detainees to bring forward exculpatory evidence. International law (incidentally, heavily influenced by Anglo-American constitutional tradition) thus requires states to provide for specific safeguards against detention.

B. Investigation of Human Rights Abuses

Second, it may be asked whether international law obliges states to investigate allegations of human rights abuses. In this respect, human rights treaties are usually not as clear as with respect to habeas corpus rights. The Torture Convention forms an exception:[27] its Article 12 requires states to conduct a 'prompt and impartial investigation, wherever there is reasonable ground to believe that an act of torture has been committed in any territory under its jurisdiction'. General human rights treaties do not contain any equivalent clauses. But in more general terms,

[23] For a detailed treatment see H Duffy, *The 'War on Terror' and the Framework of International Law* (New York, Cambridge University Press, 2005) 298 *et seq*; and more generally J Wieczoreck, *Unlawful Combatants und das Völkerrecht* (Berlin, Duncker & Humblot, 2005) *passim*.

[24] Arts 68/70/78/79 Geneva Conventions I–IV.

[25] For a discussion see Duffy, n 23 above at 298 *et seq* and 392 *et seq*; Report to the UN Human Rights Commission, 'Situation of Detainees at Guantánamo Bay', UN Doc E/CN.4/2006/120.

[26] See eg Human Rights Committee, *A v Australia*, (560/93), para 9.5; *Torres v Finland* (291/88), para 7.2.

[27] The same applies to Art 3 of the Forced Disappearances Convention.

they at least require states to grant victims effective remedies.[28] In their jurisprudence, human rights monitoring bodies have concretised the scope and content of this general obligation.[29] Their case-law, as well as the UN General Assembly's resolution on reparation for gross and systematic human rights abuses,[30] establishes that at least where there are credible allegations of serious violations, states parties must investigate the complaints. In *Rodriguez v Uruguay*, the Human Rights Committee noted that 'In light of the gravity of the allegations [in a case involving claims of torture and ill-treatment], it was the State party's obligation to carry out investigations', and that this duty fell 'under the ... obligation to grant an effective remedy'.[31] In very similar terms, the European Court of Human Rights has required states to investigate allegations based on torture or inhumane treatment, and has stated that the required investigation must be effective (potentially involving criminal sanctions[32]), prompt and impartial.[33] Both institutions, as well as the Inter-American monitoring bodies, have clarified that the same obligation is triggered by suspicious deaths. This does not mean that modern international law requires states to follow up each and every far-fetched claim that a certain right has been infringed. However, the settled jurisprudence of human rights bodies establishes a duty to investigate at least allegations of torture or inhumane treatment, or suspicious deaths in custody.

C. The Duty to Make Compensation and to Prosecute Perpetrators

Third, does international law require states to identify and punish individuals responsible for human rights abuses, and/or to provide compensation for victims? Some treaties address these questions directly.

---

[28] See eg Art 2(3)(a) ICCPR; Art 13 ECHR; Art 25 (and Art 63) American Convention on Human Rights (ACHR).

[29] For a general assessment see C Tomuschat, 'The Duty to Prosecute International Crimes Committed by Individuals' in Cremer *et al* (eds), *Tradition und Weltoffenheit des Rechts. Festschrift für Helmut Steinberger* (Berlin et al, Springer, 2002) 315 *et seq*; I Bottigliero, *Redress for Victims of Crimes under International Law* (Leiden, Brill Academic Publishers, 2004) 111 *et seq*.

[30] UN GA Res 60/147 of 16 December 2005.

[31] UN Doc CCPR/C/51/D/322/1988.

[32] See Section III.C below.

[33] See eg *Caloc v France* [2000] ECHR 380; *Aksoy v Turkey* [1996] ECHR 68; *Aydin v Turkey* [1997] ECHR 75.

Article 9(5) ICCPR, for example, provides for a specific right to compensation for victims of unlawful arrest or detention,[34] whereas other provisions require states to prosecute and punish offenders.[35] The Geneva Conventions, requiring states parties to prosecute individuals responsible for grave breaches of the laws of war,[36] set an early precedent, which was followed in the Torture Convention.[37] The Torture Convention also contains a more broadly phrased remedies clause, Article 14, which obliges states to

> ensure in [their] legal system[s] that the victim of an act of torture obtains redress and has an enforceable right to fair and adequate compensation, including the means for as full rehabilitation as possible.

General human rights treaties lack express provisions, but again, their generally phrased obligations to provide for an 'effective remedy'[38] have been interpreted rather broadly. The Inter-American Court of Human Rights as well as the Human Rights Committee have been particularly clear in this regard.[39] According to the former, serious human rights violations affecting life, freedom or physical integrity are required to be met with criminal sanctions. Hence the routine rulings like the following (in a case involving forced disappearance and extrajudicial killing), 'the State must order an investigation to find the individuals responsible ... as well as to disclose the results from said investigation and punish the liable parties'.[40] The Human Rights Committee has been equally clear that serious violations of human rights trigger an obligation of the responsible state to investigate the matter and to prosecute and punish perpetrators.[41] As regards the content of this obligation, all human rights bodies have stressed the need for an effective and impartial prosecution

---

[34] Cf N Jayawickrama, *The Judicial Application of Human Rights Law* (Cambridge, Cambridge University Press, 2002) 423.

[35] For detailed assessments see eg D Orentlicher, 'Settling Accounts. The Duty to Prosecute Human Rights Violations of a Prior Regime' (1991) 100 *Yale Law Journal* 2537; Edelenbos, 'Human Rights Violations: A Duty to Prosecute?' (1994) 7 *Leiden Journal of International Law* 5; K Ambos, 'Völkerrechtliche Bestrafungspflichten bei schweren Menschenrechtsverletzungen' (1998) 36 *Archiv des Völkerrechts* 318.

[36] See Arts 51/52/131/148 Geneva Conventions I–IV, and Art 85 Additional Protocol I (1977).

[37] Cf Arts 5 and 7 CAT.

[38] See n 28 above.

[39] In contrast, the European Court of Human Rights has so far been more reluctant, but seems to be changing its approach: cf Tomuschat, n 29 above at 319.

[40] *Bámaca Velásquez v Guatemala*, Judgment of 25 November 2000, para 8 of the *dispositif*. For references to similar pronouncements see Tomuschat, n 29 above at 321 *et seq*.

[41] See eg *Muteba v Zaire* (concerning torture); *Arhuacos v Colombia* (right to life, forced disappearances).

which could not be undermined by blanket amnesties, executive interference or invocation of state secret privileges.[42]

The general obligation of states to ensure respect for human rights (and to provide for remedies) has also been used as a stepping stone for establishing a duty to provide compensation in cases of severe human rights violations.[43] Again, this obligation is typically restricted to serious violations of fundamental rights such as the right to life, or the right to be free from torture, inhumane treatment or prolonged detention. With respect to these, however, human rights bodies and modern codification attempts have been unequivocal that victims of abuses are entitled to monetary compensation. To give but one example of a fairly specific direction, in the *Trujillo Oraza* case (involving the torture and forced disappearance of a student), the Inter-American Commission required Bolivia to ensure that

> the victim's next-of-kin receive an adequate and timely reparation that includes full satisfaction for the corresponding human rights violations, and also payment of a fair compensation for patrimonial and extra-patrimonial damages, including moral damages.[44]

In short, there seems to be general agreement today that if a human rights violation reaches a certain gravity, it triggers an ancillary obligation of the state to investigate and punish, and to award compensation to the victim. In cases of grave violations, the generally flexible provisions on remedies thus are restricted and require particular forms of redress.

D. State Compliance with these Obligations

A brief look at domestic case-law suggests that, relatively frequently, states have not been in compliance with the international rules governing remedies. This clearly applies to states well renowned for their bad human rights record, in which detention without trial or torture is systematic and widespread. But the previous interpretation of human rights obligations also suggests that states generally proud of their

---

[42] For comment on amnesties see notably MP Scharf, 'Swapping Amnesty for Peace . . .' (1996) 31 *Texas International Law Journal* 1 *et seq*; A Boed, 'The Effect of a Domestic Amnesty . . .' (2000) 33 *Cornell International Law Journal* 297 *et seq*.

[43] For a detailed assessment see M Nowak, 'The Right of Victims of Gross Human Rights Violations to Reparation' in F Coomans *et al* (eds), *Rendering Justice to the Vulnerable: Liber Amicorum in Honour of Theo van Boven* (The Hague/Boston/London, Kluwer Law International, 2003) 203.

[44] Inter-American Court of Human Rights, Ser C No 64 (26 January 2000). See also Principle 3 of the Basic Principles and Guidelines on the Right to a Remedy and Reparation for Victims of Gross Violations of International Human Rights Law and Serious Violations of International Humanitarian Law (n 30 above).

human rights record have violated their obligation to grant effective remedies. In fact, breaches of all three remedies distinguished above seem to have been relatively common:

i. Lack of Habeas Corpus Proceedings

It is relatively evident, and widely acknowledged,[45] that the practice of secretly detaining terror suspects at unknown locations violates their habeas corpus rights recognised under international law. The same applies to the acknowledged detention of terror suspects at Guantanamo. In their concluding observations on the US country reports submitted in 2005, both the Human Rights Committee and the CAT have re-iterated these criticisms voiced since the beginning of the 'war on terror'. In particular, they have noted that the detentions 'cannot be justified by the stated need to remove [terror suspects] from the battlefield'[46] and have called on the United States to amend section 1005 of the Detainee Act which bars detainees from seeking review in case of allegations of ill treatment or poor conditions of detention.[47] As regards the review procedures established following the 2004 Supreme Court decision in *Rasul v Bush*,[48] it seems that neither Combatant Status Review Tribunals nor the Administrative Review Boards qualify as 'courts' within the meaning of international habeas corpus guarantees, and that the procedure before them (involving restrictions of the right to be present at the hearing and of the right to be represented by counsel as well as on the means of evidence permitted) do not satisfy the requirements of an impartial process.[49] In fact, it is telling that by the end of 2006, that is, five years after detention at Guantánamo Bay began, US federal courts had not decided a single habeas corpus petition on the merits.

ii. Failure to Investigate Serious Human Rights Abuses

The second breach concerns the unwillingness of states to investigate allegations of serious human rights abuses. Again, it is no surprise that countries with a culture of human rights neglect fail to abide by their obligations. However, in their observations on the most recent country

[45] For a detailed assessment see 'Situation of Detainees at Guantánamo Bay', n 25 above.

[46] See the 'Concluding observations of the Human Rights Committee' on the State Report submitted by the United States (UN Doc CCPR/C/USA/CO/3/Rev.1; hereinafter 'HRC Observations') at para 12; similarly the 'Conclusions and recommendations of the Committee against Torture' on the United States Report (UN Doc CAT/C/USA/CO/2; hereinafter 'CAT Conclusions') at paras 22 *et seq*.

[47] HRC Observations, n 46 above at para 15.

[48] 542 US 466 (2004).

[49] See 'Situation of Detainees at Guantánamo Bay', n 25 above) at paras 28–9.

report, the Human Rights Committee and the CAT have also identified serious shortcomings within the US legal system, while the Marty Report on Extraordinary Renditions suggests that similar problems exist within many European states. The Human Rights Committee in particular

> note[d] with concern shortcomings concerning the independence, impartiality and effectiveness of investigations into allegations of torture and cruel, inhuman or degrading treatment or ... alleged cases of suspicious death in custody in any of these locations

and reminded the United States to 'conduct prompt and independent investigations into all allegations concerning suspicious deaths, torture or cruel, inhuman or degrading treatment or punishment'.[50] The Marty Report suggests that many European states have been equally unconcerned about allegations of serious human rights abuses. While prosecutors in Italy or Spain as well as some parliamentary committees have begun to investigate allegations of torture or degrading treatment and the extent of government involvement therein,[51] European states on balance have not been particularly determined to investigate allegations. In the words of Dick Marty, 'most governments did not seem particularly eager to establish the facts'.[52] What is more, the Marty Report also noted that before parliamentary committees, 'government replies were almost without exception vague and inconclusive'.[53]

iii. Failure to Provide for Retributory or Compensatory Justice

Finally, many states seem to have disregarded their obligations to provide for retributory or compensatory justice. There have, of course, been criminal or disciplinary cases against soldiers accused of criminal conduct such as Lindsay England or others. However, these have been few and far between. Commenting in 2006, the Human Rights Committee criticised that within the United States,

> no sentence ha[d] been pronounced against an officer employee, member of the Armed Forces, or other agent of the United States Government for using harsh interrogation techniques that had been approved [by the government].

Where sentences had been passed, these 'appeared excessively light for offences of such gravity [torture or inhumane treatment, death in custody]'.[54] Along similar lines, the CAT was

---

[50]   HRC Observations, n 46 above at para 14.
[51]   For references see the Marty Report, n 14 above at paras 237 *et seq.*
[52]   *Ibid* at para 230.
[53]   *Ibid* at para 246.
[54]   HRC Observations, n 46 above at paras 13, 14.

concerned that the investigation and prosecution of many of these cases, including some resulting in the death of detainees, have led to lenient sentences, including of an administrative nature or less than one year's imprisonment.[55]

Also, there do not seem to have been any significant number of cases in which victims of wrongful conduct have been compensated. Information is sketchy, but for example suggests that none of the German terror suspects held for years in Guantanamo has officially received any monetary compensation after his release. The CAT took up the issue and showed itself

> concerned by the difficulties certain victims of abuses have faced in obtaining redress and adequate compensation, and that only a limited number of detainees have filed claims for compensation for alleged abuse and maltreatment.[56]

In short, a relatively large number of states, including states generally complying with human rights standards, do not seem to have fulfilled their obligations to provide effective remedies for human rights abuses. If one thinks of the law of remedies as a secondary set of human rights obligations, one might say that by denying remedies such as investigation or compensation, states have violated individual rights for a second time. In other circumstances, and faced with violations of an entirely different scope and intensity, German commentators have coined the term 'second guilt' in order to describe German society's failure to accept responsibility for wrongs committed between 1933 and 1945.[57] While the degree of guilt is manifestly different, the same term seems appropriate here.

IV. OBTAINING REDRESS BEFORE NATIONAL COURTS OF OTHER STATES

Given the relative difficulties of obtaining redress within the perpetrator state, victims may prefer to look for protection before foreign (national) courts. There have not been many cases of this kind so far, but that may be a matter of time. Examples of previous attempts to use foreign courts

---

[55] CAT Conclusions, n 46 above at para 28. For similar comments see 'Situation of Detainees at Guantánamo Bay', n 25 above at para 56.

[56] CAT Conclusions, n 46 above at para 27. See also HRC Observations, n 46 above at para 13: 'the State party should ensure that the right to reparation of the victims of such practices is respected'.

[57] Cf R Giordano, *Die zweite Schuld oder: Von der Last Deutscher zu sein* (Hamburg, Rasch & Röhring, 1987) (condemning West Germany's 'second guilt', ie its failure to have confronted past atrocities after 1945).

include criminal charges against US officials (including Donald Rumsfeld) before German courts.[58] If one looks at human rights litigation more generally, it seems that victims increasingly rely on foreign state courts to obtain retributory or compensatory justice against a foreign state or its organs, at least in high profile cases involving gross abuses. There may be a number of reasons for this trend towards transnational human rights litigation: if they do not have the nationality of the perpetrator state, victims may be more at ease when suing in their own state of nationality or residence. But even if they do not, they may consider the foreign legal system more open than the perpetrator state's system to recognise remedies, or foreign courts more inclined to award them. Whatever the reasons, it is clear that proceedings before foreign national courts raise issues of an entirely different nature from those addressed so far. In particular, foreign courts have to have jurisdiction over the alleged human rights abuse, and they must be entitled to exercise that jurisdiction over foreign states or state organs. The answers to both questions depend on the international regime governing jurisdiction and immunities.

A. Jurisdiction

Under the international regime of jurisdiction, foreign courts must first of all be competent to hear a case involving human rights abuses committed abroad. Whether this is so largely depends on the applicable domestic law, which regulates matters of jurisdiction. At a very general level, it is often said that jurisdiction presupposes a legitimate interest of the state concerned. However, that test is very vague. It is clearly met if the victim brings a case before courts of his home state; in this case, jurisdiction is founded on the passive personality principle.[59] But even if there is no personal (or similar) link, states (subject to the immunity rules described below) can stipulate that their courts have universal jurisdiction over serious human rights abuses committed elsewhere, by foreigners against foreigners.[60] A number of human rights treaties even require them to establish at least criminal jurisdiction over certain abuses. This obligation is notably inferred from the duty to prosecute as established by the

---

[58] Complaint of 30 November 2004 by the Center for Constitutional Rights and four Iraqi citizens; dismissed by German Federal Prosecutor Kay Nehm on 10 February 2005. The text of the complaint and decision are available at <www.ccr-ny.org>; for brief information see Hessbruegge, 'An Attempt to Have Secretary Rumsfeld and Others Indicted for War Crimes under the German Völkerstrafgesetzbuch' (Dec 2004) ASIL insight, available at <www.asil.org>.
[59] R Higgins, *Problems and Process* (Oxford, Oxford University Press, 1994) at 65.
[60] *Ibid* at 56–7.

Geneva Conventions.[61] In the Torture Convention it is formulated as an obligation of a state party to establish jurisdiction over perpetrators present in its territory.[62] Yet in the application of these obligations, states enjoy a considerable margin of appreciation. They may qualify universal jurisdiction to be subsidiary only, that is, accept the priority of other states' jurisdiction based on the territoriality or personality principles,[63] and they may also restrict it to cases in which the accused/defendant is present on their territory. Bearing in mind these factors, the decision by the German Federal Prosecutor not to investigate criminal charges against Donald Rumsfeld and others therefore was certainly defensible under international law.[64]

The brief assessment shows that, from a victim's perspective, it may be very difficult to establish an enforceable right that foreign states exercise universal jurisdiction, as this jurisdiction is usually not mandatory. On the other hand, states enjoy a probably even greater margin in extending their jurisdiction to cases in which there is no obligation to do so, notably by broadening the circle of human rights abuses covered. In short, the international regime of jurisdiction is relatively flexible: it allows states to enact laws which open up their courts to human rights abuses committed abroad, but does not usually force them do so (and if so, permits the flexible implementation of the obligation). All this means that victims of human rights abuses largely have to rely on national laws of the forum state when seeking redress before foreign courts.

B. Immunity

Even if they have jurisdiction, foreign state courts may, however, be precluded from exercising it under the rules of sovereign immunity. These derive from the principle of sovereign equality, and are often traced back to the maxim *par in parem non habet imperium*. However, there is increasing debate about immunity exceptions, especially in cases of human rights violations where the interest in bringing about justice through judicial decisions has to be balanced against the need for stable

---

[61] Arts 51/52/131/148 Geneva Conventions I–IV and Art 85 Additional Protocol I.

[62] Arts 7(1) and 5(2) CAT (but see below for restrictions on that obligation). As regards civil remedies see also Art 14 CAT which obliges a state to 'ensure in its legal system that the victim of an act of torture obtains redress and has an enforceable right to fair and adequate compensation'.

[63] See Art 5(2) CAT or Art 146(2) Geneva Convention IV (and similar provisions contained in the other Geneva Conventions), which allow states to extradite instead of prosecuting individual perpetrators.

[64] Decision of 10 February 2005, available at <www.ccr-ny.org>.

and reliable inter-state relations not disturbed by regular court proceedings involving foreign state conduct.[65] Moreover, especially with respect to human rights violations, the law seems to be evolving rather rapidly. At the risk of oversimplification, the following general observations can be made:

(1)   International law requires states to recognise the personal immunity of other states' sitting heads of state or government and foreign ministers. As the International Court of Justice confirmed in the 2002 *Arrest Warrant* case, these cannot be sued in foreign courts for human rights violations, whatever their gravity.[66]

(2)   Apart from that, the international regime is largely permissive. It allows states to restrict the immunity of foreign states or their organs (other than sitting heads of state or government and foreign ministers) for serious human rights violations. Whether they do so is, however, a matter for them to decide. By and large, few states have been inclined to do so, and some of those that have subsequently watered down their domestic law, the most famous examples being Belgium's 1993 Anti-Atrocity Law and Spain's 1985 Organic Law.[67] If their national laws allow victims to sue foreign states and/or their organs, it may yet be another question whether an eventual award can be enforced; at least with respect to monetary awards, the rules on immunity from execution will often prevent this from happening.[68]

(3)   It is more difficult to assess (but crucial from a victim's perspective) whether states are *obliged* to restrict immunity from prosecution in cases of human rights abuses. With respect to certain human rights abuses, some treaty provisions seem to point in that direction. For example, the Torture Convention's duty to prosecute[69] has rightly been read to imply a duty not to recognise immunity in criminal proceedings – as otherwise very little would remain of it.[70] However, in the absence of such treaty provisions, states are at present

---

[65] Literature on this topic is abundant: see eg A Bianchi, 'Immunity versus Human Rights: The Pinochet Case' (1999) 10 *European Journal of International Law* 237; Adams, 'In Search of a Defence of the Transnational Human Rights Paradigm: May *Jus Cogens* Norms Be Invoked to Create Implied Exceptions in Domestic State Immunity Statutes?' in C Scott (ed), *Torture as Tort* (Oxford/Portland, OR, Hart Publishing, 2001) 247.

[66] Case Concerning the Arrest Warrant of 11 April 2000 (*Democratic Republic of the Congo v Belgium*), ICJ Reports 2002, 3.

[67] For comment see S Ratner, 'Belgium's War Crimes Statute: A Postmortem', (2003) 97 *American Journal of International Law* 888.

[68] On immunity from execution see H Fox, *The Law of State Immunity* (Oxford, Oxford University Press, 2002) 368 *et seq.*

[69] *Ibid.*

[70] *R. v Bow Street Metropolitan Stipendiary Magistrate, ex parte Pinochet Ugarte (No 1)*, [1998] 3 WLR 1456; ILM 37 (1998) 1302; *R. v. Bow Street Metropolitan Stipendiary Magistrate, ex parte*

not obliged to withhold immunity in cases of human rights abuses. In particular (although this is controversial[71]) the *jus cogens* concept does not oblige them to withhold immunity for breaches of obligations under peremptory norms of international law,[72] that is, fundamental rules accepted by the international community in its entirety (such as the prohibitions against genocide, slavery, torture, war crimes, or crimes against humanity). Similarly, human rights guarantees providing for access to courts do not preclude courts from applying immunity rules and thus effectively closing proceedings.[73] From the perspective of international law, there was thus nothing wrong with English or Canadian courts denying damages claims against foreign states or their organs, even when these claims were based on alleged violations of peremptory rules and even if the victim could claim a right of access to court. By the same token, national courts would be justified under international law if they rejected claims based on allegations of torture or degrading treatment committed by foreign secret service agents in the fight against terror.

These factors severely limit the prospects of remedying human rights abuses before foreign national courts. International law imposes upon states very few strict and enforceable obligations of which victims may avail themselves. By and large, they depend on the willingness of states to enact laws that approach the question of jurisdiction liberally, and that provide for immunity exceptions in the case of human rights violations. On the other hand, victims that energetically pursue remedies before national courts remain free to choose a legal system of their liking. Forum shopping (or, rather, conscious forum choosing) thus may be one means of circumventing the relative weakness of international law in this area. On balance, however, for the time being, obtaining redress before foreign courts is likely to remain the exception rather than the rule.

Pinochet Ugarte (No 3),[1999] 2 All ER 97, [1999] 2 WLR 825. For comment see C Chinkin, 'Case Note: Pinochet III', (1999) 93 *American Journal of International Law* 703; A Paulus, *Die Internationale Gemeinschaft im Völkerrecht* (München, Beck, 2001) 270–84; Bianchi, n 65 above.

[71] Contrast eg A Orakhelashvili, *Peremptory Norms in International Law* (Oxford, Oxford University Press, 2006), with many further references.

[72] See, inter alia, the recent decisions in *Al-Adsani v United Kingdom* No 35763/97, [2001] ECHR 761 (ECtHR); *Bouzari v Iran* 128 *International Law Reports* 586 (2006) (Ontario CA); *Jones v Saudi-Arabia* [2006] UKHL 26 (HL). For discussion see eg T Giegerich, 'Do Damages Claims Arising from *Jus Cogens* Violations Override State Immunity from the Jurisdiction of Foreign Courts?' in C Tomuschat and JM Thouvenin (eds), *The Fundamental Rules of the International Legal Order* (Leiden, Martinus Nijhoff, 2005) 203; and A Bianchi, 'Serious Violations of Human Rights and Foreign States' Accountability Before Municipal Courts' in Lal Chand Vorah *et al* (eds), *Man's Inhumanity to Man. Essays on International Law in Honour of Antonio Cassese* (The Hague, Kluwer Law International, 2003) 149.

[73] *Al-Adsani v United Kingdom* (ECtHR), n 72 above.

V. OBTAINING REDRESS BEFORE INTERNATIONAL INSTITUTIONS

In addition to national courts, victims of human rights abuses can look to international institutions for redress. Nearly all human rights treaties not only set out substantive normative standards but also establish some sort of monitoring procedure. Frequently, this also includes a judicial or quasi-judicial complaints procedure open to individuals. From a victim's perspective, seeking remedies before international bodies can have distinct advantages: the proceedings are governed exclusively by international law; there is little risk of national bias; the institution consists of members with expertise in the field of human rights; and the case may also arouse a considerable degree of public attention (which may in itself be a form of satisfaction or at least a condition conducive to an acceptable settlement). In terms of the law, there is no problem of immunity, as sovereign immunity only applies in inter-state relations, but not before international human rights monitoring bodies.

Yet in a number of respects, international proceedings have serious drawbacks, which include the following:

(1)   For one, they are often simply unavailable. As treaty-specific forms of human rights monitoring, they depend first and foremost on the perpetrator's participation in the relevant treaty regime. Treaty participation in the field of human rights is extensive, but by no means universal. To give but three examples of potential relevance,[74] Pakistan cannot be held responsible for violations of the ICCPR, just as the United States is not bound by the provisions of American Convention on Human Rights or Iran by the CAT. Whereas the substantive provisions of human rights treaties often mirror parallel customary international law,[75] the same does not apply to monitoring procedures, which are treaty-specific.

(2)   More importantly, most of the treaties do not contain compulsory procedures for individual complaints. Instead, as a rule, these are optional.[76] Crucially, while human rights treaties regularly attract large numbers of ratifications, states have proved far more reluctant to submit to individual complaints procedures: For example, none of the following treaty parties has accepted the individual complaints procedure under the ICCPR: Lebanon, Egypt, Saudi Arabia, Turkey, Israel, the United Kingdom, the United States.[77] Similar lists can be drawn up for the ACHR or CAT; taken together, they show

---

[74] For detailed information see <http://www.ohchr.org/english/bodies/docs/status.pdf> and the information available at <http://www.bayefsky.com>.

[75] *Ibid.*

[76] See eg OP 1 to the ICCPR; Art 21 CAT; Art 62 ACHR.

[77] See sources cited in n 74.

that at least at the universal level, the system of human rights protection through individual petitions still has considerable gaps.

(3) If victims can avail themselves of an individual complaint procedure, procedural requirements often reduce its impact. Most importantly, complaints may only be lodged once domestic remedies have been exhausted.[78] While human rights monitoring bodies have, or at least have arrogated, the power to issue interim orders, decisions on the merits usually are rendered years after the violation.

(4) Finally, as regards their outcome, findings by human rights monitoring bodies, as a rule, are not formally binding, hence the designations such as 'views' or 'reports'. This does not mean that are meaningless. Contrary to popular perception, instances of states refusing to comply are few and far between. However, even victims obtaining findings in their favour will often find it difficult to secure their implementation. Few domestic systems provide for a re-opening of proceedings following adverse decisions by human rights monitoring bodies.

All this means that just as proceedings before foreign courts, complaints to international human rights institutions are likely to remain exceptional. Of course, findings by human rights monitoring bodies may lead states to change their policies, and thus prevent future violations. However, when it comes to securing retributory or compensatory justice for individual victims, their effect is limited to a few cases.

VI. CONCLUDING OBSERVATIONS

The previous sections show that while international law provides victims with many routes towards justice, none of them is straightforward, well paved or easy to travel. Proceedings before foreign courts or international institutions can rather be envisaged as long and rocky paths, involving many detours. Embarking on them may be an option, but whether the path leads anywhere is at best uncertain: the road to international institutions takes years of travelling, while in foreign courts, the path to justice may be blocked by barriers inscribed 'lack of jurisdiction' or 'immunity'.

There is, of course, the direct way to national courts within the perpetrator state. Unlike the other options, this should be a well-paved motorway. However, states facing or perceiving terrorist threats (even states with generally good human rights records) have frequently closed that motorway down. In terms of the law, it is astonishing (to put it

---

[78] See eg Art 22(5) CAT; Art 5(2)(b) OP to the ICCPR; Art 35(1) ECHR.

mildly) how lightly many of them seem to take their duty to provide for domestic remedies. In practice, this means that most victims of human rights abuses have found the road towards justice to be long and winding, and more often than not, blocked. Most victims of human rights abuses occurring during the fight against terrorism therefore would have only one answer to the question posed, 'what remedies?' – and this would be: none at all.

When inquiring into the reasons for this rather negative account, a number of different considerations come to mind. The most obvious explanation may be that the 'war on terror' simply brings about a new paradigm of reduced human rights compliance, affecting 'primary' and 'secondary' sets of rules alike. As states facing or perceiving a terrorist threat have been more willing than usual to bend or violate the substantive (primary) rules of international human rights or humanitarian law, bad compliance with secondary rules on remedies may simply be the natural second step. While this is certainly one explanation, there seem to be at least two other aspects.

One is that the secondary rules of remedies require states to confront their own wrongs, and to concede and make good past mistakes. As is well known, conceding mistakes is difficult, and states or state organs, adhering to that general pattern, may simply be unwilling to do so, at least as long as the terrorist threat is still being perceived.

The second aspect concerns the character of the law of remedies. Throughout, it has been presented here as part and parcel of international human rights and humanitarian law, and cases have been cited which support its recognition. However, it should not be ignored that the secondary rules on remedies have only entered the human rights debate relatively recently. General human rights treaties contain whole lists of substantive rights, but treat remedies much more cautiously. While human rights jurisprudence has begun to address them, it may simply be that the existence of a right to a remedy has not become as accepted as the existence of substantive human rights guarantees. This may be more a feeling than an ascertainable fact. Yet, it seems to be supported by the lack of protests, by other states, against the systematic and widespread denial of effective remedies. It is only in the special cases of habeas corpus rights that this denial has been widely denounced. In contrast, few states, and comparatively few other actors, have spoken out forcefully against the 'second guilt' of many states: their failure to grant effective remedies. If that observation is correct, then the fight against terrorism, even within states with generally good human rights records, may produce precisely the same 'culture of impunity' that the international community had begun to denounce in its dealings with dictatorial regimes.

10

The UN Security Council, Counterterrorism and Human Rights*

IAN JOHNSTONE

I. INTRODUCTION

THE FIGHT AGAINST terrorism has transformed the UN Security Council (SC). In the immediate aftermath of 11 September 2001, the five permanent members were more unified than at any time in the 60-year history of the Council,[1] enabling it to go beyond its crisis management role to take on quasi-legislative and quasi-judicial functions on an unprecedented scale. The promise inherent in that development has been offset by unease about an unrepresentative body writing general rules and making legal determinations that directly impact on the rights of individuals and non-governmental entities. This chapter does not question the competence of the SC to innovate in this way, or to act directly against individuals. However, I do argue that such action must respect basic human rights, both as a matter of law, based on Article 24(2) of the UN Charter, which requires the SC to act in accordance with the purposes and principles of the United Nations, and as a matter of good policy, which requires that the Council action be seen as legitimate.

In this chapter, I examine the impact of recent SC counterterrorism practice on human rights. The next section reviews Resolution 1373 on the suppression of terrorism, the Council's first truly legislative act. Section III then considers the quasi-judicial sanctions regime spawned by Resolution 1267. In Section IV, I draw on the concept of accountability as a frame of reference for assessing SC practice in this field, and conclude

---

* A similar version of this chapter appeared as part of 'Legislation and Adjudication in the UN Security Council: Bringing Down the Deliberative Deficit' (2008) 102(2) *American Journal of International Law*, April.

[1] Consensus among the five permanent members has typically translated into unanimity among the 15 members of the Council. Between 11 September 2001 and the end of 2006, 23 of 24 SC resolutions on terrorism were adopted unanimously; the lone exception being Resolution 1456, on which Syria abstained.

with a set of reforms based on three accountability principles: participation, reason-giving and independent review.

II. SUPPRESSION OF FINANCING OF TERRORISM

The SC was not set up as a legislative body, with powers analogous to those of a parliament. It does have a law-making function, of course: Article 25 of the UN Charter stipulates that all member states are bound by its decisions. But those 'laws' are typically directed at states and in respect of specific crises. Even sanctions resolutions that impose legal obligations on *all* states are designed to change the behaviour of a *particular* state. And although the SC has gone so far as to create international criminal tribunals that target individuals, which Martti Koskenniemi has characterised as 'precariously close to international legislation',[2] these were explicitly ad hoc arrangements set up to bring lasting peace to conflicts in former Yugoslavia and Rwanda.[3] They are not, therefore, truly legislative acts.

With Resolution 1373 (2001), the SC took its law-making role to a new level.[4] Adopted a few weeks after 11 September 2001, the resolution imposes binding obligations on all states, and yet is not directly related to a particular crisis or limited in time. It is not designed to resolve a specific dispute or bring about an end to a conflict, nor to compel a state to act or refrain from acting in a certain way. Instead, it imposes general obligations in a broad issue area for an indefinite period. Qualitatively different from the Council's normal crisis management role, in adopting Resolution 1373, the SC acted like a legislature.[5]

Under the resolution, states are obliged inter alia to 'prevent and suppress the financing of terrorist acts', 'freeze financial assets of persons who commit terrorists acts', 'take the necessary steps to prevent the

---

[2] M Koskenniemi, 'The Police in the Temple: Order, Justice and the UN – A Dialectical View' (1995) 6 *European Journal of International Law* 325 at 326.

[3] M Happold, 'Security Council Resolution 1373 and the Constitution of the United Nations' (2003) 16 *Leiden Journal of International Law* 593 at 601–5. Happold analyses the report of the UN Secretary-General in recommending the establishment of the Yugoslav Tribunal (ICTY), ICTY's own judgment on the Council's competence in creating the tribunal and debates around the creation of the International Criminal Court in concluding that the Council did not act as a legislator in that instance.

[4] For a comprehensive overview of law-making by the UN, see J Alvarez, *International Organizations as Law-makers* (New York, Oxford University Press, 2006).

[5] P Szasz, 'The Security Council starts legislating' (2002) 96 *American Journal of International Law* 901 at 902. Others who have characterised Resolution 1373 as international legislation are J Alvarez, 'Hegemonic International Law Revisited' (2003) 97 *American Journal of International Law* 873; J Stromseth, 'The Security Council's Counter-Terrorism Role: Continuity and Innovation', *ASIL Proceedings 2003*, 41–5 at 41; and M Happold, n 3 above at 593–610. The Council did it again in April 2004, when it adopted Resolution 1540.

commission of terrorists acts' and 'deny safe haven to those who finance, plan, support or commit terrorist acts'.[6] Most of the substantive content of the resolution comes from Conventions on the Suppression of Financing of Terrorism and the Suppression of Terrorist Bombings. Precisely what states must do to fulfil their obligations was left to be worked out in the Counter-Terrorism Committee (CTC), set up to oversee implementation of Resolution 1373.

Established as a subsidiary organ of the Security Council under Article 29, the composition of the CTC is the same as that of the Council: five permanent members plus 10 non-permanent members, who rotate as the Council rotates. It oversees implementation of the resolution, initially by reviewing reports submitted by states on steps they have taken to fulfil their obligations. It functions primarily as a capacity-building body, designed to raise the level of government performance against terrorism by requiring states to upgrade their legislative and executive machinery.[7] Thus the CTC was set up to engage states in an open-ended dialogue – it does not even declare them to be in non-compliance when that is the case.[8] In its capacity-building function, the Committee acts as a 'switch-board', brokering deals between states that need technical assistance and those that can provide it.[9]

Initially, the approach worked well, both in terms of compliance with the CTC's reporting requirement and the rate of ratification of counterterrorism Conventions.[10] But by late 2003, the dialogic approach of the CTC began to run out of steam, as reflected in a report of its new Chairman, Ambassador Arias of Spain, on problems of implementation.[11] This prompted the Committee to propose a set of reforms to 'revitalise' its work, the most important of which was creation of a Counter-terrorism Executive Directorate (CTED). Created in March 2004, but not fully staffed until September 2005 and not declared operational until December of that year, the CTED is a body of 20 experts, who advise the CTC and carry out its strategic and policy decisions in a more proactive manner, including by conducting field visits to assess the efforts of states in the implementation of Resolution 1373. After some wrangling among

---

[6] S/RES/1373 (2001), paras 1 and 2.

[7] E Rosand, 'Security Council Resolution 1373, the Counter-Terrorism Committee and the Fight Against Terrorism' (2004) 97 *American Journal of International Law* 333 at 334.

[8] *Ibid* at 336; also see Stromseth, n 5 above, at 44.

[9] Report by Chair of the Counter-Terrorism Committee on the problems encountered in the implementation of resolution 1373 (2001), S/2004/70, 26 January 2004, at 8.

[10] By September 2005, the Committee had received 613 reports, including first reports from all 191 states, and 169 second reports: A Millar and E Rosand, *Allied Against Terrorism* (New York, Century Foundation Press, 2007) at 107. It had also reached out to some 60 other international organisations to encourage them to become more involved in counterterrorism.

[11] Chairman's report, S/2004/70, n 9 above.

members and between members and the Secretariat, it was agreed that the CTED would operate under the 'policy guidance' of the CTC, but the Executive Director would be appointed by and report through the Secretary-General.[12]

One of the challenges the CTC faced was how to measure compliance with Resolution 1373. Given that the resolution does not provide a definition of terrorism, developing precise standards by which states would be judged was seen as important. Other international bodies, like the Financial Action Task Force (FATF), began disseminating a set of best practices.[13] FATF had developed 40 recommendations on money-laundering before 11 September 2001, and produced nine 'special recommendations' on terrorist financing afterwards. These go beyond the general terms of Resolution 1373 to include measures like seizing property used in the financing of terrorism and requiring financial institutions to report suspicious activities. FATF also published Special Interpretative Notes and papers on more technical issues like wire transfers by non-profit organisations.

In an attempt to institutionalise these standards, Resolution 1566 (2004) asked the CTC to develop a set of best practices in implementing Resolution 1373. The idea was picked up in Resolution 1617, which 'strongly urged' all member states to implement the 40 FATF recommendations on money-laundering and the nine on terrorist financing. In December 2006, the CTC welcomed the directory of best practices compiled by the CTED, which it described as 'an extremely useful practical tool for States'.[14] Thus, while the CTC has not yet formally endorsed the recommendations, a body of 'soft law' exists that is impacting on the work of the committee.[15]

Although the obligations imposed are on states, Resolution 1373 is unique both for its legislative character and the fact that the ultimate target is individual terrorists as well as states that support them. It is designed both to change the behaviour of states and to prevent individuals from engaging in terrorism. By in effect criminalising a wide range of

---

[12] That concerns about the Secretary-General's authority have persisted is reflected in the felt need of the Security Council to clarify reporting lines between the CTED, Secretariat and CTC: S/PRST/2006/56 (20 December 2006). Specifically, the Council decided that the CTED should present its draft work programme and semi-annual reports directly to the CTC rather than through the Secretary-General. This was based on a recommendation by the Secretary-General himself. See his letter to the President of the Security Council. S/2006/1002, 19 December 2006.

[13] Center on Global Counter-Terrorism Cooperation, *Report on Standards and Best Practices for Improving States Implementation of UN SC Counter-Terrorism Mandates* at 6.

[14] S/2000/989 (18 December 2006), paras 18 and 19.

[15] The Asia–Pacific Economic Cooperation (APEC) and the Organization for Security and Cooperation in Europe have adopted the FATF standards, so at least those countries take them into account in assessing their own practices.

acts, it is an innovative step by the SC and an important tool in the fight against terrorism. But the impact of the resolution on human rights is troubling to some: would the SC-mandated fight against terrorism lead to an erosion of civil liberties? These concerns prompted calls from the earliest days of the CTC to include human rights experts in its work. The Committee initially took the position that it was not a human rights body and therefore human rights considerations should be dealt with elsewhere in the UN system. But in January 2003, the SC adopted a resolution declaring, inter alia, that states 'must ensure that any measures taken to combat terrorism comply with ... international human rights, refugee and humanitarian law' (Resolution 1456). The CTC included a human rights expert on its staff and formalised a relationship with the Office of the High Commissioner for Human Rights by establishing a liaison office between the two. This alleviated some of the concerns raised by member states, international officials and human rights activists,[16] but as late as December 2005, a Special Rapporteur on human rights and counterterrorism complained that the CTC was not sending a strong enough message to states 'concerning their duty to respect human rights while countering terrorism'.[17]

The issue remained potent enough that in April 2006 the Secretary-General felt compelled to include an entire chapter on defending human rights in his report on a global counterterrorism strategy, which was endorsed by the General Assembly in September 2006.[18] Meanwhile, there have been indirect challenges to some of the implementing legislation in national courts.[19] In May 2006, the CTC gave 'policy guidance' to the CTED, and at the end of December encouraged the directorate to

---

[16] See statements of Brazil at 10; Germany at 15; Chile at 16; Ireland for the EU at 19; Liechtenstein at 3 (Resumption 1); Argentina for the Rio Group at 4 (Resumption 1); Mexico at 5 (Resumption 1); Costa Rica at 10 (Resumption 1); Canada at 12 (Resumption 1). The Secretary-General first expressed his concern that action against terrorism should not undermine human rights to the SC in January 2002: UN doc S/PV.4453 at 3. On the relationship between the CTC, the High Commissioner for Human Rights and other human rights actors in the UN system, see Curtis Ward, 'Building Capacity to Combat International Terrorism: The Role of the UN Security Council' (2003) 8 *Journal of Conflict and Security Law* 289 at 297–8.

[17] United Nations Economic and Social Council, 'Promotion and Protection of Human Rights', E/CN.4/2006/98, 28 December 2005.

[18] Report of the Secretary-General, 'Uniting against terrorism: recommendations for a global counter-terrorism strategy', A/60/285 (27 April 2006), Part VI. The General Assembly adopted a comprehensive counterterrorism strategy, based in part on the Secretary-General's report, on 8 September 2006: A/RES/60/280 (20 September 2006).

[19] D Dyzenhaus discusses a Canadian court case challenging an extradition claim by the United States based on Canada's United Nations Suppression of Terrorism Regulations, which were enacted pursuant to Resolution 1373: D Dyzenhaus, 'The Rule of (Administrative) Law in International Law', (Summer/Autumn 2005) 68(3&4) *Law and Contemporary Problems* 127 at 142–5.

continue to implement that policy, but the guidance is rather non-specific, simply encouraging the CTED to provide advice to the CTC on how to ensure human rights are respected as Resolution 1373 is implemented.[20]

III. TARGETED SANCTIONS REGIMES: 'LISTING' COMMITTEES AND DUE PROCESS

The SC has long been involved in dispute settlement, one of its enumerated functions in Chapter VI of the Charter, but it normally does this in a non-binding way – for example by calling on parties to settle their disputes by one of the means listed in Article 33. It went further in responding to Iraq's invasion of Kuwait. In Resolution 687 – the so-called Gulf War ceasefire resolution – the Council found that Iraq was financially liable for losses resulting from its invasion and occupation of Kuwait, and it declared that Iraq must respect the border set out in Agreed Minutes of 1963.[21] Similarly, in the wake of the bombing of Pan Am flight 103 over Lockerbie, Scotland, and UTA flight 772 over the Sahara, the SC adopted Resolution 748 demanding that Libya hand over two suspects for trial and pay compensation to families of the victims. These pronouncements are in effect judicial determinations – decisions that would normally be left to a court, better suited than the Council to hear pleadings, assess evidence and weigh legal claims.

The Security also plays a quasi-judicial role when it determines what constitutes a threat to the peace within the meaning of Article 39 of the UN Charter. In the normal course, this would not be controversial, as the Council must make such determinations in order to act under Chapter VII in respect of a particular crisis. However, the Council has also acquired the habit of adopting declarations that seem to enunciate legal principles without reference to a particular case. For example, at the conclusion of the Summit meeting in January 1992, the SC announced that 'the proliferation of all weapons of mass destruction constitutes a threat to international peace and security'. Although not binding in a formal sense, this declaration was designed to guide Council deliberations and actions in the future. But again, this amounts to the Council's interpretation of its own mandate and therefore is not seen as problematic.

[20] S/2006/989 (18 December 2006), paras 8, 26 and 27. The SC endorsed the CTC recommendations in S/PRST/2006/56 (20 December 2006).
[21] I Johnstone, *Aftermath of the Gulf War* (London, Lynn Rienner Publications, 1994); Alvarez, n 4 above at 419–24; K Harper, 'Does the United Nations Security Council have the Competence to Act as Court and Legislature?' (1994) 27 *International Law and Politics* 103 at 110–21.

Sanctions regimes that target individuals are more controversial than these other quasi-judicial acts. The origins of the Resolution 1267 regime is in a resolution adopted after the bombing of US embassies in Kenya and Tanzania, for which Osama bin Laden was deemed to be responsible. Resolution 1267 demanded that the Taliban end its support for terrorism and extradite bin Laden, and called for the setting up of a committee to monitor compliance with an asset freeze and travel ban on the Taliban. The sanctions were expanded by Resolution 1333 (2000) to include an arms embargo, diplomatic restrictions, a broadened aviation ban and an asset freeze on bin Laden and individuals associated with him. In that resolution, the Council called on the 1267 Committee to keep a list of targeted individuals.

The Committee later recommended establishing a sanctions monitoring and coordination team, which was approved by the SC in Resolution 1363. Just as the team was being set up, however, the 11 September terrorist attacks occurred.[22] After the overthrow of the Taliban, the SC lifted the broader aviation sanctions but continued the targeted travel and financial sanctions, as well as the arms embargo, on the Taliban and Al Qaeda (Resolution 1390). The Council established an Analytical Support and Sanctions Monitoring Team, composed of eight experts, to 'collate, assess, monitor and report on' steps being taken to implement the sanctions. Member states report on the actions they have taken and, like the CTC, the 1267 Committee engages in dialogue with the states through country visits and meetings with representatives in New York.

This is not the first time the SC has targeted sanctions on individuals – it did so in 1994 against the military junta in Haiti (Resolution 917) and again in 1998 against senior UNITA officials and their family members in Angola (Resolution 1127). In addition to the 1267 Committee, nine resolutions create committees that currently have some role in listing individuals and entities who are the target of sanctions: Sierra Leone (Resolution 1132), Iraq (Resolution 1518), Liberia (Resolution 1521), the Democratic Republic of the Congo (Resolution 1533), Côte d'Ivoire (Resolution 1572), Lebanon/Syria (Resolution 1636), Sudan (Resolution 1591), North Korea (Resolution 1718) and Iran (Resolution 1737).

These committees have given rise to concerns about procedural fairness. Whether viewed as criminal or non-criminal sanctions, they are seen by critics as imposing a penalty without due process of law.[23] The

---

[22] D Cortright and G Lopez, *Sanctions and the Search for Security* (Boulder, Colorado, Lynne Rienner, 2002) at 53.

[23] B Fassbender, *Targeted Sanctions and Due Process,* Study Commissioned by UN Office of Legal Affairs (2006) at 29–30; Thomas Watson Institute of International Studies, *Strengthening Targeted Sanctions Through Fair and Clear Procedures* (2006); Alvarez, n 4 above at 176; P Gutherie, 'Security Council Sanctions and the Protection of Individual Rights' (2004) 60 *New York University Annual Survey of American Law* 491 at 503–6; E de Wet and A Noellkaemper

due process concerns range from the adequacy of the presentation of the case against an individual prior to listing, the time period for making decisions, the lack of notification, the process of requesting exemptions, and the way de-listing petitions are submitted and decisions made. The Resolution 1267 regime has been the subject of most criticism, for a number of reasons. First, its scope is the widest. Almost half of the currently listed individuals and entities are under that regime and, given its global reach, there is no limit to the number of people who could be targeted in the future. Second, it is more directly focused on non-state actors than the other regimes (even the sanctions against UNITA were against a state-like entity that had control of a defined territory).[24] Third, as pointed out in the preamble to Resolution 1735, it is preventative in character, imposing restraints on people and corporations not for what they have done in the past, but for what they may do in the future. Fourth, and most important for the purposes of this chapter, other than the Lebanon/Syria regime which relates to a specific incident (the assassination of Rafik Hariri), it is the only regime clearly directed at terrorism. That makes it a special case because of the reluctance of many states to assert the primacy of human rights concerns in the context of counterterrorism.[25]

The 1267 Committee has placed some 500 names on its consolidated list. Most were designated by the United States after 11 September 2001, either alone or in conjunction with allies. A no-objection procedure is used: a name is submitted by any Council member and, unless there is an objection or hold placed within five days (originally it was 48 hours), all states must freeze the assets of the designated person and ban his or her travel. According to a US diplomat working with the Committee, in the early stages the listing was based largely on political trust, with the Committee having no formal guidelines or evidentiary standards for states to follow in proposing names.[26] Nor was there any provision for removing names from the list.

Over the years, some important procedural changes were made.[27] In August 2002, the Committee announced 'de-listing' procedures and, in

---

(eds), *Review of the Security Council by Member States* (Antwerp, Intersentia, 2003). For an interesting application of administrative law standards of procedural fairness to global governance, see B Kingsbury, N Krisch and R Stewart, 'The Emergence of Global Administrative Law' (Summer/Autumn 2005) 68 *Duke University School of Law* 15 at 32, 34, 38 and 39; D Dyzenhaus, n 19 above at 140–52.

[24]   I would like to thank Ulrik Ahnfeldt-Mollerup for drawing my attention to this point.
[25]   Watson Institute report, n 23 above at 7. See also Gutherie, 'Security Council Sanctions', n 23 above at 495; Fassbender Study, n 23 above.
[26]   Millar and Rosand, n 10 above at 20.
[27]   See Guidelines of the Security Council Committee Established Pursuant to Resolution 1267 (1999) for the Conduct of Its Work, November 2002 as amended 10 April 2003, revised

November, adopted written guidelines both for listing and de-listing. In December 2002, the SC carved out a set of humanitarian exemptions to the financial ban, allowing the release of funds for 'extraordinary expenses' relating to basic needs (Resolution 1452). Resolution 1526 of January 2004 calls on states proposing names to include information that demonstrates the individual's connection with bin Laden, Al Qaeda or the Taliban. And Resolution 1617 of July 2005 decides that states must provide the Committee with a detailed 'statement of the case describing the basis of the proposal'. The resolution also clarified what activities would constitute 'association' with Al Qaeda and the Taliban.

Nevertheless, by mid-2005, support for the regime was still eroding and pressure building for further reforms. The Secretary-General's High Level Panel on Threats Challenges and Change recommended a process for review of cases. The 2005 World Summit called for 'fair and clear procedures' for listing and de-listing individuals by all sanctions committees. The Office of Legal Affairs commissioned a study by Bardo Fassbender, which was meant to be reviewed by the UN Secretariat Policy Committee prior to submitting recommendations to the 1267 Committee. But the 1267 Committee decided it would only consider proposals from its members, so the Fassbender study was shelved.[28] Meanwhile, a number of governments commissioned a study by the Thomas Watson Institute at Brown University, also published in March 2006.[29] Despite the 1267 Committee's decision to all but ignore these academic studies, the Secretary-General and his Legal Counsel put their views on the table. The Secretary-General sent a letter to the President of the SC in mid-2006, which was never published, but at a public meeting on 22 June, the Legal Counsel Nicolas Michel read the contents of the letter into the record. In it, the Secretary-General set out what he thought were the minimum standards required to ensure fair and transparent procedures for listing and de-listing: the right of targeted individuals to be informed of measures taken against them and why; the right of such individuals to make written submissions and to be represented by counsel; the right to review by an impartial, independent mechanism able to provide a remedy; and periodic review of the lists by the SC itself.[30] These largely

on 21 December 2005 and amended on 29 November 2006, available at <http://www.un.org/Docs/sc/committees/1267/1267_guidelines.pdf>.

[28] Security Council Reports, January 2007, available at <www.securitycouncilreports.org> at 19.

[29] A month earlier, the Council of Europe-sponsored study by Professor Cameron came to similar conclusions: I Cameron, 'The European Convention on Human Rights, Due Process and United Nations Security Council Counter-terrorism Sanctions', Report commissioned by the Council of Europe, 6 February 2006.

[30] SPV 5474, 22 June 2006, at 7–8.

mirrored the Fassbender recommendations and constitute a much fuller set of procedural rights than the Council as a whole was prepared to guarantee.

However, the Committee and Council did ultimately revise the procedures again. In January 2006, the Monitoring Team submitted 38 recommendations on how to strengthen the work of the 1267 Committee, including improvements to the consolidated lists.[31] The Committee finally acted on these recommendations on 29 November 2006, endorsed by the SC in Resolution 1735 of 22 December 2006. The most important changes relate to the listing of names: a fuller statement of the case is now required, including specific information and supporting documentation to show that the individual deserves to be on the list; a request that designating states identify which parts of the statement can be publicly released; the submission of additional information as it becomes available; a requirement that the country of residence or nationality of the individual or entity be notified of the listing decision within two weeks, and an appeal to those states to endeavour to notify the individual of the decision and case against him or her. Resolution 1735 also extends the period for considering humanitarian exemptions from two to three working days.

Resolution 1735 does not add much to the de-listing procedures, other than to call on the Committee to keep working on guidelines. However, a few days earlier the SC had adopted a resolution establishing a 'focal point' for all sanctions regimes that target individuals (Resolution 1730). The focal point is in effect a mailbox, established to receive de-listing requests and forward them to the various governments concerned for possible consideration by the Committee. Individuals can send petitions directly to the focal point – a significant step – but that is no guarantee the Committee will consider the request. Some government must take up the cause – initially, either the designating government, or the governments of citizenship or residency. If none of them take action within three months, then any member of the committee can recommend de-listing. But at the end of the day, if no government acts, then the de-listing request is not considered by the Committee, and the individual is so-informed.

Despite the steps taken to address due process concerns, the regime remains contested. Over the years, at least 50 states have expressed such concerns.[32] A report issued by the Council of Europe in 2006 stated that the process does not comply with the European Convention on Human

---

[31]   S/2006/154, 10 March 2006.

[32]   Watson Institute, n 23 above at 6, and Chairman's report, S/2004/70, n 9 above. See also the open Security Council debate on 'Strengthening international law: the rule of law and maintenance of international peace and security', S/PV 5474, 22 June 2006.

Rights because it provides no protection against arbitrary decisions and has no mechanism for reviewing the accuracy of allegations made.[33] The Committee's decisions have also been challenged indirectly in regional and national courts.[34] Three Swedish citizens of Somali descent brought action in the European Court of First Instance (CFI) challenging the EU regulations that put them on the list pursuant to the SC's action.[35] The CFI initially reserved judgment on the merits and, soon thereafter, the SC sanctions committee de-listed two of the individuals.[36] In its ruling it decided it did have the authority to check whether SC resolutions were consonant with norms of *jus cogens*, since these were non-derogable (meaning that not even the SC can override them). It suggested, although did not make a firm determination, that the rights to property, a fair trial and an effective remedy were all *jus cogens* norms. The CFI did not consider – although the European Court of Justice may on appeal – whether the Resolution 1267 sanctions regime is inconsistent with the purposes and principles of the UN Charter (Article 24), and therefore ultra vires.[37]

The latest innovations may relieve some of the pressure on the 1267 Committee and other listing committees, but it is clear that due process concerns have not been fully met. Detailed criteria for adding names to the list have still not been specified. There is little advance consultation with affected states prior to listing decisions. The time limit for objecting to names being put on a list is only five days, making it hard for some representatives in New York to consult their capitals and make the necessary inquiries before a decision is made. Targeted individuals have no right to make their case to the Committee before being placed on the list, nor are they even informed that a decision is about to be taken

---

[33] I Cameron, 'The European Convention on Human Rights, Due Process and United Nations Security Council Counter-terrorism Sanctions', Report commissioned by the Council of Europe, 6 February 2006; D Crawford, 'UN Program Generates Blacklist', *The Wall Street Journal* (US), 2 October 2006, 9.

[34] As of March 2006, there were 15 known cases of targeted individuals and organisations who had initiated legal proceedings before national and regional courts: in Belgium, Italy, Switzerland, the Netherlands, Pakistan, Turkey, the US and European Regional Courts: Watson Institute, n 23 above at 10. Although the cases brought in the United States did not challenge the UN sanctions directly, two entities listed by the 1267 Committee challenged asset freezes made under US law: Gutherie, 'Security Council Sanctions', n 23 above at 518. Also, the Canadian case described by Dyzenhaus in n 19 above involved issues that arose under Resolution 1267 as well as Resolution 1373. See generally, E de Wet and A Knoellkamper (eds), *Review of the Security Council by Member States* (Antwerp, Intersentia, 2003).

[35] *Ahmed Ali Yusuf and Al Barakaat International Foundation v Council and Commission*, Case T-306/01 21 September 2005. A similar case brought at the same time involved a Saudi citizen: *Abdullay Kadi v Council and Commission*, Case T315/01, 21 September 2005. See also, *R Aden v Council of European Union*, 2002 ECR II-02387.

[36] Kingsbury *et al*, n 23 above at 32.

[37] Watson Institute, n 23 above at 22.

(because doing so would enable them to hide their assets). They may be informed afterwards by the state of residence and/or citizenship, but the notification requirement is qualified by the words 'to the extent possible'. Moreover, the individual is only notified of the decision and the public portion of the statement of the case: as of January 2007, no designating state had agreed to release any portion of the case. It is entirely up to the discretion of the Committee to grant a de-listing request, regardless of the evidence, and decisions are by consensus, meaning each member has a veto. The 1267 Committee is not required to give reasons for its decisions either to list, or not to de-list. Individuals must rely on states to take up their cause for the Committee to consider a delisting request. There is no independent review mechanism for challenging decisions of the Committee.

A further sign of the concern about the process is the reluctance to create a larger terrorism list pursuant to Resolution 1566. The resolution was adopted and a Working Group was established mainly in response to the seizure of some 1,200 hostages and the deaths of hundreds of children at a school in Beslan, Russia. The SC strongly condemned all acts of terrorism in Resolution 1566, and came close to adopting a definition of terrorism, but ultimately fell back on a reference to acts that constitute offences within the scope of existing international conventions and protocols.[38] The Working Group was mandated to consider measures to be imposed on individuals and entities involved in or associated with terrorism, in addition to those on the Al Qaeda/Taliban list. Lack of consensus in the Working Group has made it impossible to agree on an expanded list.[39]

IV. REFORM OF THE COUNTERTERRORISM REGIMES

Thus, while the SC's achievements in the field of counterterrorism are impressive and steps have been taken to address human rights concerns, problems remain. Many states wonder whether the Council has the legitimacy to act as global legislature and court, given its limited membership, dominance by five permanent members and closed decision-making processes. These questions are especially pointed in the field of counterterrorism, in part because the lack of a definition of terrorism opens the door to arbitrariness. When Resolution 1373 was adopted, the SC deliberately avoided any discussion of the definition of terrorism, aware of the impasse over the issue in the General Assembly. The idea was to move ahead on a pragmatic basis, trying to avoid political

---

[38]   Millar and Rosand, n 10 above at 21.
[39]   S/2005/789, 16 December 2005. The situation had not changed by March 2008.

disputes. But without an agreed definition, some states worry that the SC and its committees and expert bodies will not act in an even-handed way, targeting some states more aggressively than others (a complaint levelled by the ambassador of Qatar when Resolution 1735 was adopted[40]). More generally, it means there is no objective basis on which to assess compliance with the resolutions. Standards and 'best practices' have been developed, but none have yet been formally adopted.

Moreover, in their collective zeal for action against terrorism, the five permanent members of the Council may be too quick to agree on (or tolerate) measures that impinge on civil liberties. This is why the listing and de-listing process of the 1267 Committee has been subject to the closest scrutiny by outsiders, even though eight other committees have similar authority. And rather vague calls to combat terrorism leave considerable discretion to each state to decide how to go about doing that, carrying the potential for human rights abuses in the name of fulfilling SC-imposed obligations.[41]

The Secretary-General touched on some of these concerns in his report on a global counterterrorism strategy, as did the General Assembly in the strategy it adopted in September 2006.[42] Extensive debate and discussion has also occurred in and around the SC itself. What is missing from these discussions is a conceptual framework for assessing the legitimacy of SC action. In the remainder of this chapter, I propose a set of reforms designed to bring down the 'democratic deficit' in the SC, not by changing its composition but by enhancing its accountability.[43] The reforms are grouped in three categories: participation, reason-giving and independent review.[44]

---

[40] In explaining his vote on Resolution 1735 of 22 December 2006, the Permanent Representative of Qatar said he was 'extremely concerned' about some aspects of it, particularly the manner in which members of the Resolution 1267 monitoring team were appointed: see UN Press Release SC/8925, 22 December 2006.

[41] Special Rapporteur on the promotion and protection of human rights and fundamental freedoms while countering terrorism, *Report on Promotion and Protection of Human Rights*, E/CN.4/2006/98 (28 December 2005).

[42] Report of the Secretary-General, *Uniting Against Terrorism: Recommendations for a global counter-terrorism strategy*, A/60/825, 27 April 2006; United Nations General Assembly Resolution 60/288, 8 September 2006.

[43] On the concept of accountability in international institutions, see R Grant and R Keohane, 'Accountability and Abuses of Power in World Politics' (2005) 99(1) *American Political Science Review*, 1 February.

[44] My analysis and application of these principles draws on the work of Robert Keohane and various co-authors. See *ibid*; A Buchanan and R Keohane, 'The Preventive Use of Force: A Cosmopolitan Institutional Proposal' (Winter 2004) 18 *Ethics and International Affairs* 1–22; and R Keohane and J Nye, 'Redefining Accountability for Global Govenance', in M Kahler and D Lake (eds) *Governance in a Global Economy: Political Authority in Transition* (Princeton, NJ, Princeton University Press, 2003). I also draw on nascent global administrative law principles as identified in Kingsbury *et al*, n 23 above, and applications of the theory of deliberative democracy to international relations in the work of J Bohman, 'International

A. Participation

In democratic theory, the legitimacy of public policy decision-making depends on the participation of those affected.[45] Direct participation by all individuals who are affected by an SC decision is, of course, impossible. But it is not hard to imagine less direct ways for individuals to have some input. Governments that are most directly affected could be consulted when rules like those embodied in Resolutions 1267 and 1373 are made, and could be included on the SC committees established to oversee their implementation. Moreover, if the resolutions are framed in general terms (like Resolution 1373), then the principle of subsidiarity comes into play, which holds that only what needs to be decided at the highest level should be decided at that level. Leaving the specifics of how to implement the broad (though binding) goals set by the Council creates the possibility of citizen participation in law-making at the national level, through elected representatives (at least in democratic countries).

Non-state actors, such as non-governmental organisations (NGOs) and business associations, could be given greater access to the inter-governmental deliberations.[46] These actors would not have voting rights, nor even necessarily the right to speak, but the ability to present written proposals, evidence and argumentation in drafting resolutions and committee guidelines is a form of participation. The incremental incorporation of 'best practices' in respect of Resolution 1373 is an illustration of this, many of which originated in the private sector and are disseminated through FATF and other groups.[47]

A more important form of participation concerns the procedural rights of individuals who are targeted by SC sanctions. In domestic legal systems, the scope of due process varies with the nature of the penalty: those who are subject to criminal sanctions are typically granted more

regimes and democratic governance: political equality and influence in global institutions' (1999) 75(3) *International Affairs* 499–513; J Dryzek, *Deliberative Democracy and Beyond* (New York, Oxford University Press, 2000); D Thompson, 'Democratic Theory and Global Society' (1999) *Journal of Political Philosophy* 7 at 111–25; and T Zweifil, *International Organizations and Democracy* (London, Lynne Rienner Publishers, 2005) at 2.

[45] See Grant and Keohane, n 43 above, at 3.

[46] Over the years, NGOs have been granted some access to the SC. The President of the SC meets with the President of the International Committee of the Red Cross periodically. The SC has, on occasion, invited human rights NGOs to so-called 'Arria formula meetings', which are held in private chambers with no official records or Secretariat presence: I Johnstone, 'Security Council Deliberations: The Power of the Better Argument' (2003) 14 *EJIL* 437 at 461–2.

[47] See *Report on Standards and Best Practices*, n 13 above. There was little non-governmental input into the negotiation of Resolution 1373, but there was such an input into Resolution 1540 (2004), the SC's second truly 'legislative' act: M Datan, 'Security Council resolution 1540: Weapons of Mass Destruction and Non-State Trafficking' (April/May 2005) 79 *Disarmament Diplomacy*.

procedural protection than those who are deprived of entitlements through an administrative process. The SC and its committees cannot grant full due process without badly compromising its ability to discharge its primary function, which is the maintenance of international peace and security.[48] But the trade-off between due process and Council effectiveness is not zero-sum: inattention to procedural fairness can hurt the efficacy of targeted sanctions, through a combination of foot-dragging by member states and court challenges by individuals and NGOs.[49]

In addition to the steps already taken by the SC and its committees, including the appointment of a focal point for de-listing petitions, the following measures would help to meet the World Summit's appeal for 'fair and clear procedures':

- Inform individuals of listing decisions as soon after the fact as circumstances allow. Targeted individuals find out soon enough when their assets are frozen, of course, but they should also be informed officially by the committee or member state, along with the reasons for the decision (see below).
- Give individuals the opportunity to submit de-listing petitions directly to the committees, rather than having to rely on a member state to take up the cause. There is a precedent: 'in exceptional cases', the Liberia sanctions committee allows de-listing requests by the individual concerned.[50]
- The 'right to be heard' could be guaranteed through written submissions.
- Those targeted should have the right to be represented by a lawyer, relative or NGO, both in filing a petition and in making written submissions. This would also solve the problem of what to do about deceased persons on the lists.

B. Reason-giving

Closely associated with participation is the requirement that reasons be given for public policy decisions, a tenet of deliberative democracy.[51] The reason-giving requirement is also a fundamental administrative law

---

[48] Fassbender study, n 23 above at para 11 of part C. The Fassbender, Watson and Cameron studies all analyse and set out a number of due process rights recognised in international law.

[49] Watson Institute, n 23 above, Executive Summary.

[50] *Ibid* at 35. But the Committee must first decide by consensus whether a case is 'exceptional'. By March 2006, two attempts had been made to petition the committee directly, both unsuccessful.

[51] See the various contributions to J Elster (ed), *Deliberative Democracy* (Cambridge, Cambridge University Press, 1998); and J Bohman and W Rehg (eds), *Essays on Reason and*

principle.[52] Public reason-giving is a way for non-state actors to influence decision-making without participating directly in the work of the Council and committees, through the 'audience effect' – the felt need on the part of speakers to justify their actions in terms that all who have a stake in the outcome can understand. NGOs and the media are the eyes and ears of global civil society; the cooperation of business associations is needed to implement many of the counterterrorism resolutions. The more transparent and public the processes are, the greater the 'audience effect'. Transparency, the wide dissemination of information and the requirement of reason-giving combine to enhance the buy-in of those affected by the decision, even if they do not lead to better decisions all the time.

As for 'listing' decisions, the SC has taken steps in the direction of reason-giving by requiring states to provide the 1267 Committee with a statement of the case and 'as much detail as possible on the basis(es) for the listing of individuals', including evidentiary information to support the determination of an association with the Taliban, Al Qaeda or Osama bin Laden (Resolution 1735). The Council also requests states to try to inform individuals of the case against them. Other steps that could be taken without sacrificing efficiency unduly include:

- the adoption of more detailed criteria for how listing and de-listing decisions are made, with explicit standards on what constitutes an adequate statement of the case, what sort of evidence can be kept confidential and what should released;
- the public release of at least some portion of the statement of the case, for the benefit of both those directly affected (individuals, banks and so on) as well as others who may find themselves in similar circumstances;
- requiring the Committee to provide *written* reasons for listing and de-listing decisions. Member states recommend listing or de-listing, but it is the committee as a whole that decides and so the Committee should be required to explain the decision.

Politics: Deliberative Democracy (Cambridge, MA, The MIT Press, 1997). See also A Gutmann and D Thompson, *Democracy and Disagreement* (Cambridge, MA, Harvard University Press, 1996); and A Guttman and D Thompson, *Why Deliberative Democracy?* (Princeton, NJ, Princeton University Press, 2004).
[52] On administrative law principles, see Kingsbury *et al*, n 23 above at 28–9.

C. Independent Review

Accountability requires that decision-makers be held to a set of standards for decisions they make.[53] In democratic societies, politicians are held accountable through periodic elections and, in many societies, legal processes. The decisions of administrators and judges (other than those in the highest court) are reviewed through appeal processes. Review of decisions by the SC and its committees is rare. The 1267 Committee guidelines stipulate that names on the list that have not been 'updated' in four or more years should be reviewed. Not only is this time period rather long, but 'updating' occurs whenever new supporting information is added to the file, so many years can go by before a name is reviewed by the Committee as a whole. The SC also engages in periodic review of the bodies it creates, for example when the mandates of CTED and 1267 monitoring team are up for renewal. The 1267 Committee guidelines also provide for the possibility of referring de-listing decisions to the SC when committee members cannot reach a consensus. This gets around the problem of every committee member having a veto, but transferring the decision to the Council means five members have veto rights and the rest do not – a way of enhancing efficiency, but not legitimacy.

None of these forms of review are independent: the bodies making the decisions are their own court of appeal. Independent judicial review of Council action is not unheard of. In a number of cases the International Court of Justice has hinted at the possibility of judicial review.[54] It seems unlikely that the Council will ever declare the SC to have acted ultra vires. But it can engage, and has engaged, in 'expressive modes of review', signalling that the Council ought to take care to act in a manner that accords with the purposes and principles of the UN Charter as generally understood.[55] Review of Council counterterrorism action in

---

[53] Grant and Keohane, n 43 above.

[54] See Question of Interpretation and Application of the 1971 Montreal Convention arising from the Aerial Incident at Lockerbie (Libyan Arab Jamahiriya v USA), Order on Provisional Measures, 1992 ICJ Reports 17; Application of the Convention on the Prevention and Punishment of the Crime of Genocide (Bosnia and Herzegovina v Yugoslavia) 1993 ICJ 325 (13 September) The literature on the two cases is extensive. See eg, T Franck, 'The "Powers of Appreciation": Who is the Ultimate Guardian of UN Legality?' (1992) 86 *American Journal of International Law* 519 at 520; M Koskenniemi, 'The Place of Law in Collective Security' (1996) 17 *Michigan Journal of International Law* 455 at 460–61; V Gowlland-Debbas, 'The Relationship Between the International Court of Justice and the Security Council in Light of the Lockerbie Cases' (1994) 88 *American Journal of International Law* 643; J Alvarez, 'Judging the Security Council' (1996) 90 *American Journal of International Law* 1 at 22–3; J Gardam, 'Legal Restraints on Security Council Military Enforcement Action' (1996) 17 *Michigan Journal of International Law* 285 at 290; WM Reisman, 'The Constitutional Crisis in the United Nations' (1993) 87 *American Journal of International Law* 83.

[55] Alvarez, n 54 above.

regional and national courts has also occurred, in at least 15 cases.[56] So far, no court has declared the Council to have acted ultra vires and it is far from clear what the legal or practical impact of such a declaration would be. But there is little to stop individuals from trying their luck in courts, which is bound to complicate the Council's work. In fact the procedural reforms already made were motivated in part by a desire to pre-empt legal challenges. At a minimum, the prospect of embarrassing litigation will give some members of the Council pause for thought before acting in a manner that is likely to be seen as violating fundamental rights. Peter Gutherie argues that the best way of protecting individual rights from arbitrary Council action is by strengthening state mechanisms for review, through greater inter-governmental and inter-judicial cooperation.[57]

In addition to judicial review, a range of non-judicial review mechanisms have been proposed for listing decisions by the 1267 Committee and other committees. It was suggested that the 'focal point' being established in the Secretariat pursuant to Resolution 1730 be given review functions. An alternative proposal from the government of Qatar is a body of 'independent experts' to receive and review de-listing requests.[58] Denmark proposed something similar, in the form of an ombudsman. The Fassbender and Watson studies consider these and other options, a common feature of which is the notion of 'external' review by an impartial body. If an ombudsman were established, confidentiality issues would surely arise as states would be reluctant to provide him or her with intelligence information. But if evidentiary criteria for listing and de-listing are adopted and provisions for confidentiality are put in place (that is, only the ombudsman sees the confidential information), then independent review along these lines is conceivable.[59]

Finally, even without formal review mechanisms, concerns about reputation are a form of accountability. The Council and its members have to be concerned about their reputation for acting in an even-handed manner that respects basic rights. There is no sanction for failing to do so, but if they venture too far beyond what is generally acceptable, then those who must carry out the decisions will simply not comply. The effectiveness of these quasi-legislative and quasi-judicial acts depends on broad global cooperation, and that cooperation depends on perceived legitimacy.

---

[56] See fourth and fifth reports of the Monitoring Team, S/2006/154, 10 March 2006; S/2006/750, 20 September 2006; see also Gutherie, n 23 above.

[57] Gutherie, n 23 above at 535–40.

[58] Security Council Reports, n 28 above.

[59] See S Chesterman, *Intelligence and Collective Security* (Sydney, Lowy Institute for International Policy, 2007).

V. CONCLUSION

The SC's innovative and proactive approach to counterterrorism is, on balance, a positive development. The Council has the competence and, arguably, the responsibility to play a quasi-legislative and quasi-judicial role in this field. Moreover, sanctions targeted at individuals are widely seen as preferable to comprehensive economic sanctions, which tend to hurt innocent civilians more than those responsible for the threat the Council is trying to counter. But difficulty in implementing the SC's counterterrorism resolutions and the chorus of criticism directed at the committees suggests that further fine-tuning is needed. In this chapter, I have proposed a set of measures designed to enhance the accountability of the SC when it acts against individuals. If carefully designed, these modest and politically achievable reforms would enhance the legitimacy of Council counterterrorism practice. They would make the Council's actions more effective, while bringing them into line with the democratic principles that most states preach but often do not practice – especially in their foreign affairs.

Part Three

Is There a Need for New Legal Paradigms?

11

Judicial Balancing in Times of Stress:

A Comparative Constitutional Perspective

MICHEL ROSENFELD

I. INTRODUCTION

IN 2004, THE HIGHEST courts in three different countries, the United States, Israel and the United Kingdom, handed down major decisions regarding the war on terror.[1] All these involved conflicts between liberty and security in combating terrorism, and in all three countries the decisions were the product of judicial balancing.[2] The factual settings of the cases and the respective experiences with terrorism varied significantly from one country to the next, but all three countries have faced the war on terror under *conditions of stress* rather than under *conditions of crisis* or emergency. As will be discussed in Section II below, conditions of stress fall somewhere between ordinary conditions and conditions of crisis.

In ordinary times, judicial balancing or proportionality analysis is common and widespread in dealing with conflicts between liberty and

---

[1] The US cases are *Rasul v Bush*, 542 US 466 (2004); *Hamdi v Rumsfeld*, 542 US 507 (2004); and *Rumsfeld v Padilla*, 542 US 426 (2004). The Israeli cases are HCJ 2056/04 *Beit Sourik Village Council v The Government of Israel* [2004], available at <http://elyon1.court.gov.il/files_eng/04/560/020/ a28/04020560.a28.pdf> [hereinafter *Beit Sourik*], and HCJ 4764/04 *Physicians for Human Rights v Commander of the IDF Forces in the Gaza Strip* [2004], available at <http://elyon1.court.gov.il/ files_eng/04/640/047/a03/04047640.a03.htm> [hereinafter *Physicians for Human Rights*]. The UK case is *A (FC) v Secretary of State for the Home Department* [2004] UKHL 56, [2005] 2 AC 68 [hereinafter *A (Belmarsh Detainees)*].

[2] Consistent with the terminology used by many courts outside the United States – see, for example, *The Queen v Oakes* [1986] 1 SCR 103 (Can); *Pharmacy Case*, Bundesverfassungsgericht [BverfG] [Federal Constitutional Court] 11 June 1958, 7 Entscheidungen des Bundesverfassungsgerichts [BVerfGE] 379 (FRG) (Germany); *Hauer v Land Rheinland-Pfalz*, 1979 ECR 3727 (ECJ) – the Israeli Supreme Court referred to the test it used in its two decisions mentioned in n 1 above as a 'proportionality test'. For their part, the UK Law Lords used both a 'proportionality' test and 'balancing'. As will be discussed below in Section II.C, the US and UK 'balancing' approach and the Israeli and UK 'proportionality' analysis are not completely equivalent, but they largely overlap.

security, and more generally, between individual rights and important societal goals.[3] In times of crisis, however, balancing becomes problematic and highly contested. In some countries the Constitution provides for invocation of a state of emergency that allows for suspension or derogation of fundamental rights.[4] Even in the United States, where the Constitution does not provide for emergency powers, the right of habeas corpus can be suspended in a crisis,[5] and Presidents have de facto increased their powers in times of war or emergency.[6] Although the decisions in all three countries relied on judicial balancing, some of them yielded concurring and dissenting opinions relying on categorical approaches. Furthermore, some of the judges involved regarded the relevant controversies as arising under conditions of crisis, others regarded them as arising under conditions of stress, and yet others regarded them as arising under close to ordinary conditions.

To compound these difficulties, collectively these decisions make use of three different legal paradigms to deal with the various conflicts between liberty and security presented for adjudication. These paradigms are: (1) the 'law of war paradigm'; (2) the 'criminal law paradigm'; and (3) the 'police power law paradigm'. No straightforward correlation ties the three conditions described above to these three legal paradigms. Nevertheless, the law of war paradigm seems most compatible with conditions of crisis, whereas the other two paradigms seem best suited for ordinary times.

The thesis I defend here is that none of the decisions involved deals with the conflict between liberty and security in the context of the war on terror in the best possible way, and that it is necessary to treat the war on terror, absent extraordinary circumstances, as occurring under conditions of stress.

To elaborate this thesis, Section II sets the theoretical framework by focusing primarily on three issues: the distinctions between conditions of stress, ordinary conditions and conditions of crisis; the distinctions between the three existing paradigms of law that figure in the decisions under consideration; and the relationship between proportionality and judicial balancing. Section III examines the US cases, Section IV the Israeli cases, and Section V the UK case. Section VI compares US balancing,

---

[3] See cases cited in n 2 above.

[4] See cases cited in n 2 above; see also, eg, 1958 French Constitution, Art 16.

[5] See US Constitution, Art I, § 9, cl 2 (permitting suspension of habeas corpus in cases of invasion or insurrection).

[6] See C Rossiter, *The Supreme Court and the Commander and Chief* (expanded edition) (Ithaca, NY, Cornell University Press, 1976) 11–132.

Israeli proportionality analysis and their UK counterparts. Finally, Section VII explores the optimal role for judicial balancing consistent with the thesis that links times of stress and the war on terror law paradigm.

II. THE THEORETICAL FRAMEWORK

How to handle the conflict between liberty and security in the war on terror and how to do it through judicial balancing depend on the characterisation of the prevailing conditions, and on whether terrorists are conceived as criminals who must be prosecuted or as enemy warriors who must be killed or captured and detained until the end of hostilities. As will be demonstrated below, the decisions that will be examined are not consistent in their dealings with these issues.

A. Times of Stress versus Ordinary Times and Times of Crisis

Times of stress are neither ordinary times nor times of crisis. In the context of a crisis, be it military, economic, social or natural, the head of government may be entitled to proclaim exceptional powers and to suspend constitutional rights, including political rights. In an acute crisis, the polity is singularly focused on survival, and all other political concerns and objectives recede into the background.[7] In contrast, in ordinary times, the polity can readily absorb the full impact of the give and take of everyday politics, and constitutional rights ought to be protected to their fullest possible extent.

Times of stress differ from those of crisis primarily in terms of the severity, intensity and duration of the respective threats involved. The line between the two may be difficult to draw, but a less severe, less intense and more durable threat is likely to give rise to times of stress whereas a severe, intense, concentrated threat, of relatively shorter duration, is likely to provoke a crisis. For example, a foreign military invasion or a widespread domestic insurrection is likely to provoke a crisis. On the other hand, the aftermath of the terrorist attacks against New York City on 11 September 2001 – which involved threats, perceived threats, launching a 'war on terror' fought mainly in faraway countries, arrest

---

[7] The grant and duration of exceptional emergency powers are problematic not in relation to their proper use as means to combat threats to the life of the polity, but in relation to the potential for abuse in the invocation or prolongation of such powers. See B Ackerman, 'The Emergency Constitution' (2004) 113 *Yale Law Journal* 1029 at 1040.

and detention of potential terrorists, but no further terrorist attack on the United States as at the time of writing – has produced times of stress rather than times of crisis.[8]

The distinction between ordinary times, times of crisis and times of stress can be further elaborated consistent with a pluralist conception of the polity where politics looms as the ongoing confrontation between self and other. In a pluralist polity, different groups – ethnic, religious or ideological – and different interests compete for power and scarce political goods. Such competition, moreover, can be characterised as struggles between self and other. In ordinary times, conflicts between self and other do not threaten the unity of the polity and find resolution, or at least confinement, within the existing constitutional, institutional and political framework. Thus, in spite of the fact that a number of struggles relating to individual or group identity and to the apportionment of benefits and burdens throughout the polity split the citizenry into a multiplicity of selves pitted against numerous others, the common self that binds all citizens to the unity of the polity remains glued together and shows no danger of unravelling. In ordinary times, neither self nor other may be fully satisfied with their fate and may be likely to struggle continuously to ameliorate their respective positions. Neither of them, however, is likely to become so dissatisfied with his or her status or with the existing institutional framework for processing conflicts as to want to withdraw from the polity.

Times of crisis, in contrast, occur when the common identity or the very life of the polity are in imminent peril. The cause of the peril may be external, as in the case of a foreign war, or internal, as in the case of civil war or violent secession. In times of crisis, the conception of the good of self or other is so little integrated or accommodated within the polity that all possible institutional resolutions of the conflict between self and other will strike one or both of them as deeply insufficient, unsatisfactory and unjust.

Times of stress stand halfway between ordinary times and times of crisis. In times of stress, there is less extensive and less successful accommodation and integration of significantly represented conceptions of the good within the polity. Self and other are less likely than in ordinary times to consider institutional processes of conflict resolution to be just or fair. The identity or unity of the common self that is supposed

---

[8] It is important, however, to distinguish the long-term aftermath from the immediate impact and short-term consequences of a terrorist attack. For example, the day of the 11 September attacks, which resulted in around 3,000 deaths, and subsequent days in which the United States had to cope with the shock of the sudden and unexpected attacks and with the prospect of imminent future attacks, can be characterised fairly as a time of crisis. The long period of disquiet that followed those first few weeks, however, seems better described as one of stress than of crisis.

to bind together the citizenry is not disintegrating, but it is destabilised and under various pressures. Whereas a conventional war may cause a crisis, terrorism and the war on terror seem more likely to create stress. Indeed, unlike a military invasion, terrorist acts are likely to be sporadic and widespread, causing more psychological than physical harm. Having terrorists hidden within the polity's population is undoubtedly unnerving and can easily lead to overreactions, undue suppression of fundamental rights or an exacerbation of ethnic or racial prejudice such that certain selves and the conceptions of the good they endorse may become increasingly unhinged. At some point, erosion of accommodation of certain conceptions of the good may place increasing strain on the working unity of the polity's citizenry. In short, both the threat posed by the terrorist – be he or she a foreign or a domestic one – and the dangers posed by overreaction may fray the common glue that binds the polity together.

That the current war on terror gives rise to conditions of stress rather than of crisis is well captured in the following passage from Lord Hoffmann's opinion in the *A (Belmarsh Detainees)* case:

[The United Kingdom] is a nation that has been tested in adversity, which has survived physical destruction and catastrophic loss of life. I do not underestimate the ability of fanatical groups of terrorists to kill and destroy, but they do not threaten the life of the nation. Whether we would survive Hitler hung in the balance, but there is no doubt that we shall survive Al-Qaeda. The Spanish people have not said that what happened in Madrid, hideous crime as it was, threatened the life of their nation. Their legendary pride would not allow it. Terrorist violence, serious as it is, does not threaten our institutions of government or our existence as a civil community.[9]

B. The Criminal Law, Law of War and Police Power Law Paradigms

Both ordinary criminals and soldiers in the armies of foreign enemies can pose threats to the lives and security of the members of a polity. The law, however, treats suspected criminals and captured enemy soldiers very differently. Following arrest, suspected criminals must be charged, tried, convicted and sentenced before they can be legitimately confined to prison for a determinate maximum period of time. Moreover, in constitutional democracies, such as the United States for example, criminal defendants are afforded certain categorical constitutionally protected

---

[9] *A (Belmarsh Detainees)* [2005] 2 AC 68 at para 96, per Lord Hoffmann, concurring.

rights, such as the right against self-incrimination,[10] the right to counsel[11] and the right to confront witnesses who testify against them,[12] to secure an acceptable minimum of procedural fairness. Such rights frame the 'criminal law paradigm'. In contrast, captured foreign enemy soldiers who are not in violation of the laws of war can only be detained consistent with applicable norms of the international law so as to prevent them from further participation in the military conflict on the side of the captor's foreign enemies.[13] Such prisoners of war must be treated humanely, are exempt from all but a minimum of clearly defined interrogation and are to be released without undue delay upon termination of hostilities.[14] In short, these, as well as other legally binding norms that set the legitimate bounds for the treatment of prisoners of war in the context of conventional military hostilities among two or more nation-states, circumscribe the 'law of war paradigm'.

In addition to requiring neutralisation of criminals and foreign soldiers fighting against the country's armed forces, the security of that country's citizenry may require further restraints impinging on the citizenry as a whole or on some distinct groups within it. For example, a city plagued by rampant youth gang violence may improve security for its inhabitants by imposing a general curfew or one confined to all residents below a certain age. More generally, special security needs arising because of certain specific threats – for instance, threats posed by terrorists, the spread of deadly contagious disease, a natural disaster, organised crime – call for government measures for the protection of the citizenry that are bound to impinge on the protection or exercise of certain fundamental rights, such as freedom of movement or assembly, privacy and so on. In these circumstances, the constitutional state must seek to harmonise liberty and security through a balancing process. The legal-constitutional underpinnings of such a balancing process as well as the specific legal norms it engenders give shape to the 'police power law paradigm'.

C. Proportionality and Balancing

In all three jurisdictions, judicial balancing played a key role in the disposition of the claims arising in the context of the war on terror. The Israeli Supreme Court applied a proportionality test, the Law Lords relied on both proportionality and balancing, and the US Supreme Court

---

[10] See US Constitution, amend V.
[11] See *ibid*, amend VI.
[12] *Ibid*.
[13] See generally Geneva Convention Relative to the Treatment of Prisoners of War, 12 August 1949, 6 UST 3316, 75 UNTS 135.
[14] *Ibid*, Arts 13, 17 and 118.

used balancing.[15] Proportionality and balancing are not synonymous, but they overlap significantly, particularly since balancing proper forms part of proportionality tests such as that used by the Israeli Court.[16]

Judicial balancing would work best if the social goods subjected to balancing were both quantifiable and comparable. Thus, if total liberty weighed as much in units of good as total security; and if each unit of added cost or benefit to liberty would be the equivalent to the correlative unit with respect to security; and finally, if the aggregate of liberty and security were always zero-sum; then judicial balancing could be thoroughly principled and accurate as well as completely transparent. Actually, however, judicial balancing involving liberty and security is anything but simple, straightforward or transparent. The benefits of liberty or security may not be quantifiable, and even if quantifiable, they may not be comparable. Finally, it is highly questionable that the relation between the two is a zero-sum one: most likely, there is no liberty without security, and security without liberty is not a worthy pursuit.

A further objection against balancing liberty against security stems from the fact that liberty interests are, to a significant degree, protected as constitutional rights – for example, freedom of speech, of assembly and against arbitrary detention – whereas security interests constitute, to a large extent, a collective social good. Consistent with this, if constitutional liberty rights could be simply weighed against non-constitutional interests, such as a societal interest in maximising security, they would fall victim to ordinary legislative policy-making, which consists of working out trade-offs among competing collective interests. To avoid this, constitutional rights may be exempted from weighing and only subject to categorical limitations – for example, pornography is not speech, speech can only be prohibited if it incites to violence – or, following Dworkin, they may be subjected to weighing, but susceptible to being outweighed only by the most weighty social policy goals.[17] In other words, in Dworkin's view, limitations of constitutional rights can only be justified if their costs to rights holders are *far* outweighed by the benefit to be produced through the institution of pressing social policy. Consistent with this, the conflict between liberty and security may not be susceptible to resolution through simple balancing, although it may be amenable to some kind of comparative weighing with some handicapping of the weights of non-constitutional interests as against constitutional interests.

From a theoretical standpoint, the concept of proportionality can be traced back to Aristotle's conception of justice and equality, which

---

[15] See n 2 above.
[16] See Section IV below.
[17] See R Dworkin, *Taking Rights Seriously* (Cambridge, MA, Harvard University Press, 1977) 92 at 95–6.

requires that equals be treated equally and unequals unequally.[18] Treating equals unequally or unequals equally is disproportionate, as is treating unequals more unequally than they are unequal.[19] From the standpoint of the application of a proportionality standard to resolve conflicts between constitutional rights and social policies for the collective good, on the other hand, two factors loom as paramount: (1) constitutional rights and social policies embodied in legislation or executive decrees are of unequal value such that trade-offs based on a simple calculus of utilities would be disproportionate; and (2) even when a particular social policy is of such vast importance that curtailing conflicting constitutional rights would not be disproportionate – for example, when an executive decree issued in the context of a struggle for national survival during an emergency partially restricts freedom of movement and assembly – the resulting limitations on, or suspensions of, the constitutional rights involved must not be themselves disproportionate.

Consistent with the first of the factors above, proportionality in relation to constitutional rights requires treating these rights and conflicting collective goods as unequals. How unequally the rights and goods must be treated so that they are proportionately rather than disproportionately unequal cannot be determined without reference to substantive normative criteria that lie outside of the realm of proportionality. For example, racist speech is likely to be deeply offensive to a large majority within the polity, but mere discomfort with it, standing alone, would not justify its suppression. On the other hand, in some countries it is constitutional— and hence deemed proportional—to prohibit racist speech that incites racial *hatred*, whereas in the United States, only speech that incites racial *violence* may be thus prohibited.[20] Assuming the racist's right to communicate racist views and the discomfort of the audience reached by such views to involve equivalent costs and benefits absent the input of constitutional considerations; and assuming that incitement to violence imposes a greater collective cost on the polity than does incitement to hatred;[21] then limiting free speech because of discomfort would be

---

[18] See Aristotle, *Nicomachean Ethics, Book V* (trs Martin Ostwald) (Cambridge, MA, Prentice Hall, 1962).

[19] For example, if stealing $100 is punishable by 10 days in prison and stealing $300 by 30 days, it is disproportionate to punish stealing $200 by a year in prison.

[20] Compare *The Queen v Keegstra* [1990] 3 SCR 697 (Can) (upholding criminal conviction of high school teacher who taught anti-Semitic propaganda to his students) with *Collin v Smith*, 578 F.2d 1197 (7th Cir), cert denied, 439 US 916 (1978) (holding that proposed Neo-Nazi march in Nazi military uniforms including swastika in suburb heavily populated by Jewish Holocaust survivors does not amount to incitement to violence and hence cannot be prohibited).

[21] This assumption is by no means self-evident. Arguably, incitement to hatred is in the long run as, or more, pernicious than incitement to violence as it may spread undetected evils that may prove eventually more destructive of a polity's social fabric.

disproportionate. However, whether either incitement to hatred or incitement to violence or else both of these would render such limitations disproportionate would depend on values extrinsic to proportionality. Such values may be embodied in a constitutional text,[22] found in the collective identity of a polity[23] or elaborated by judges in the course of adjudicating constitutional claims.[24]

Consistent with the second factor listed above, on the other hand, proportionality concerns the means employed to achieve constitutionally permissible ends. In this context, proportionality requires a 'fit' between means and ends. When some important collective objective justifies limitation of some constitutional right, the permissible intrusion on that right should be the minimum possible consistent with achieving the objective.

In the real world, it is rarely, if ever, possible to achieve a perfect fit between means and ends. For example, if one could predict with accuracy who will perpetrate a terrorist act unless restrained, it would be possible to assure security from terrorism by means of restrictions on all those and only those determined to carry out terrorist acts. But since that is impossible, the best *possible* fit is bound to be one that is both under- and over-inclusive, one that will not sufficiently restrict all would-be terrorists and that will inevitably target some who would never engage in terrorist acts.

In our imperfect world, the best fit is one that, though over- and under-inclusive, is nonetheless least restrictive of liberty and equality rights. Indeed, all relevant rights in relation to the war on terror and to the cases examined below, namely, besides liberty and equality rights proper, due process rights, habeas corpus rights, privacy rights and the right to use and enjoy one's property are at a higher level of abstraction

---

[22] See, eg, Art 10 of the European Convention on Human Rights (ECHR), which protects freedom of expression but allows for such 'restrictions or penalties as are prescribed by law and are necessary in a democratic society, in the interests of national security, territorial integrity, or public safety': European Convention on Human Rights, 4 November 1950, 213 UNTS 221, Art 10. ECHR rights are formally treaty-based ones, but they are nonetheless the functional equivalents of constitutional rights. See N Dorsen *et al*, *Comparative Constitutionalism: Cases and Materials* (Upper Saddle River, NJ, West Publishing Company, 2003) 2.

[23] The difference between the Canadian and US treatment of hate speech, see n 20 above, may be due to the contrast between Canadian multiculturalism and American individualism. See M Rosenfeld, *Just Interpretations: Law Between Ethics and Politics* (Los Angeles, CA, University of California Press, 1998) 186–7.

[24] Thus, the US Supreme Court has held that limitation of freedom of speech cannot be justified unless in furtherance of a 'compelling' state interest. See, eg, *Burson v Freeman*, 504 US 191 (1992). Similarly, racial classifications cannot be upheld absent compliance with a 'strict scrutiny test'. This test requires that there be a compelling state interest and the means used in pursuit of that interest be 'necessary'. See *Korematsu v United States*, 323 US 214 (1944).

reducible to liberty and/or equality rights.[25] Moreover, liberty and equality rights are sometimes complementary and sometimes in conflict with one another. For example, if most international terrorists happen to be Muslim, then imposing restrictions on the rights of Muslims alone may be less restrictive from the standpoint of liberty than extending such restrictions to all persons within the polity. But since the vast majority of Muslims have no ties to terrorism, imposing the restrictions on them as a group would disproportionately impinge on their rights to equality.

A proportionate fit in an imperfect world, therefore, is one that is the least practically restrictive of liberty and equality rights, and that strikes a balance between restrictions on liberty rights and those on equality rights when the two are in conflict. To perform these tasks, moreover, requires comparing alternative means to determine which provide a better fit, and weighing the costs of restrictions on liberty against those on equality to strike a proper balance and to avoid excessive restrictions on either of them.

In short, the first factor of proportionality involves balancing, but it is balancing on a scale that is weighted in favor of constitutional rights. The second factor is likely to include comparisons of the costs and benefits of alternative means to the same end, but these are unlikely to involve straightforward balancing in as much as they relate to trade-offs between restrictions on liberty and restrictions on equality for purposes of achieving something else, such as, in the cases that concern us here, security. Balancing proper, however, has a place within broader proportionality analysis. Such balancing is appropriate in two kinds of situations: those involving direct conflicts between two rights; and those relating to the uncertainties surrounding the likelihood that, and degree to which, legislative or executive means will significantly advance a collective end that is of such great importance as to justify some limitations on constitutional rights.

In the case of a conflict between liberty and equality in the pursuit of security, the rights are pitted against one another indirectly. The object is to achieve security without undue impingements on liberty or equality and without disproportionate sacrifice of one to the other. The primary goal, however, is the achievement of security with the least possible overall limitation on rights, and that goal may well be best achieved with a greater limitation on equality than on liberty, or vice versa. In a direct conflict, in contrast, benefits and burdens related to one right are measured exclusively against those pertaining to another conflicting right and

---

[25] For example, privacy involves liberty to make decisions within the sphere of intimate decisions: see *Griswold v Connecticut*, 381 US 479 (1965), while dignity requires both liberty to make choices for oneself, and equality inasmuch as treatment of any person as an inferior results in a deprivation of dignity.

the resolution of the conflict in question is properly reached through balancing proper. For example, if a journalist's freedom of the press right clashes with a private person's privacy right, as where the journalist wants to publish a story about that person's intimate life, the burden on freedom of the press that prohibition of publication would entail would have to be weighed directly against the burden on privacy that such publication would cause.

Concerning the second situation identified above, the probability that a particular means will lead to the achievement of a targeted end plays an important role in determining proportionality and often calls for balancing proper. For example, capture and detention of a person who one knows with 100 per cent certainty is about to detonate a dirty bomb in the centre of a city that would cause at least 100,000 deaths would provide a huge boost to security. In that case, the benefit to security far outweighs any corresponding burden on liberty. But what if there is only one chance in one thousand that the person in indefinite detention is a would-be bomber? And what if the chance of any such bomb detonating and causing serious casualties is only one in ten thousand? More generally, are significant restrictions on everyone's liberty in order to be in a slightly stronger position in the war on terror justified, assuming that, at worst, terrorism will cause a number of fatalities amounting to a fraction of those due to highway accidents?

To answer these questions properly, the gravity of a threat to security must be measured in relation to its degree of probability, and any relevant net decrease in liberty must be weighed against the corresponding net increase in security – that is, the aimed level of increased security discounted by the probability of its achievement. Thus, actual achievement of collective security may be proportionate to even extensive limitation of rights. In contrast, a slight increase in security would not suffice to justify curtailment of rights. Furthermore, even conceding that the war on terror involves weighty security objectives that justify significant restrictions on constitutional rights, policies that would only marginally improve security against terrorists would be outweighed by any significant corresponding burden on liberty rights.

In the last analysis, proportionality analysis comprises measuring, 'fitting', comparing and balancing in relation to normative standards or values that transcend proportionality itself. Responsibility for proportionality can be entrusted to legislators, members of the executive branch or to judges, or it can be apportioned among all of them. How much of proportionality analysis and balancing is left to judges depends on many factors, including the particular constitutional order involved and the particular nature of the legislation and/or executive decrees at stake. Furthermore, how much of, and what kind of, proportionality analysis and balancing should be optimally left to judges is also context-dependent, as will be illustrated by examination of the cases below. Finally, when proportionality standards have been set by the legislature and when balancing is embodied in legislation, whether ordinary or constitutional, a judge applying such legislation or evaluating it in connection with a constitutional challenge may be pretty much limited to performing a categorical determination.[26]

D. Background Conditions: Contrasting the War on Terror in the United States, Israel and the United Kingdom

The factual circumstances of the cases in the three relevant jurisdictions were quite varied, as were the experiences with terrorism of each of the three countries. Moreover, at least from a formal standpoint, the legal issues differed significantly from one country to the next. The US cases dealt mainly with the constitutional rights of persons being detained for long and indeterminate periods; the Israeli cases with the rights of Palestinian civilians under the international law of occupation and Israeli administrative law in the context of Israeli military operations in the Occupied Territories; and the UK case, with the rights of detained foreign nationals who could not be deported to their home countries under the European Convention on Human Rights (ECHR) and the United Kingdom's Human Rights Act 1998 granting the ECHR domestic effect. Specifically, the US cases involve claims arising under the US Constitution, federal law and international law. Israel does not have a written constitution, and the Palestinians whose rights were at stake in the two cases involved live in occupied territory governed by laws of belligerent occupation. Consequently, the Israeli cases arise under the law of belligerent occupation, Israeli administrative law and international law. In spite of these differences, in both Israel and the United States similarly conceived fundamental rights[27] are in conflict with military policies and actions designed to promote the paramount security interests of the country. For their part, the relevant legal norms applicable in the UK case

---

[26] A clear example of such categorical determination is provided by Justice Scalia's dissenting opinion in the *Hamdi* case. As Justice Scalia sees it, the balance between liberty interests protected through the right of habeas corpus as against collective security interests are balanced within the US Constitution itself in as much as the latter prescribes criteria for when habeas corpus claims should prevail against conflicting security claims, and in as much as it specifies the conditions under which the right to habeas corpus may be suspended: see US Constitution, Art I, § 9, cl 2.

[27] The humanitarian rights at stake in Israel are for present purposes functionally equivalent to US due process rights. The main difference is that the US cases deal mainly with procedural due process whereas the Israeli ones focus on rights that are roughly equivalent to US substantive due process rights.

come from the ECHR, an international treaty, and from the Human Rights Act 1998, a domestic statute. Nonetheless, functionally, these applicable norms involve basic liberty, equality and due process rights. From the standpoint of judicial balancing, therefore, the three legal regimes are sufficiently congruent to allow for fruitful comparison.

III. JUDICIAL BALANCING AND THE US DECISIONS

In only one of the three US decisions, *Hamdi v Rumsfeld*, is judicial balancing explicitly used, and even in that case, only by a plurality of four justices.[28] The other two decisions, although consistent with *Hamdi*, do not rely on balancing as they concentrate on threshold issues. In *Rasul v Bush*, the Supreme Court's focus was on whether the foreign alleged 'enemy combatants' held in Guantanamo were entitled to the same rights to challenge their detention as those of their US counterparts held in the United States.[29] Finally, although *Rumsfeld v Padilla* raised the same substantive issues as *Hamdi*, the Court decided the case on procedural grounds.[30]

The Bush Administration came close to embracing executive supremacy as its position in all three cases.[31] The Court, however, squarely rejected that position by subjecting Hamdi's claims to judicial

[28] See *Hamdi v Rumsfeld*, 542 US 507 at 539 (2004). Justices Ginsburg and Souter, who concurred in part and dissented in part, can be said to have implicitly agreed to the plurality's balancing, as their disagreement with the latter was over whether the Congress had given the executive branch authority to detain alleged 'enemy combatants' indefinitely, and not over the right to challenge detentions actually authorised by Congress: *ibid* at 540.

[29] See *Rasul v Bush*, 542 US 466 at 484 (2004).

[30] Padilla had sued the Secretary of Defense, Donald Rumsfeld, for his allegedly unconstitutional detention. The Court held that the commander of the navy brig where Padilla was being held was the proper party for such a lawsuit, and hence dismissed the case against Rumsfeld, without prejudice as to Padilla's constitutional claims: see *Rumsfeld v Padilla*, 542 US 426 at 432 (2004).

[31] This position was not pressed all the way, for although the Bush Administration argued that it was within the exclusive power of the President as Commander-in-Chief during a time of war to designate a person as an 'enemy combatant' and to detain the latter until the end of hostilities (which, in the case of the war against terror with potentially no certain end, may mean permanently), it did concede that the courts had limited jurisdiction to determine whether a contested detention was *within the authority* of the executive branch, but not whether the decision of the executive branch was right or wrong based on disputed facts: see Brief for Respondents at 26, *Hamdi v Rumsfeld*, 542 US 507 (2004) (No 03–6696). Thus, the courts would be limited to an initial categorical inquiry. For example, the courts could decide that it is not within the President's war powers to designate as 'enemy combatants' students on US campuses who criticise his war policies. On the other hand, the government assertion that Hamdi was initially detained in Afghanistan where the United States was engaged in a war against the Taliban would be all the information that a court would be entitled to before having to accept the President's exclusive power to determine whether or not to label Hamdi an enemy combatant.

balancing[32] and acted consistent with that rejection in *Rasul* by refusing to accept the government's position that, when it came to foreign enemy combatant detainees, Guantanamo was beyond the reach of US courts.[33] For the plurality in *Hamdi*, the finding that detention of enemy combatants was authorised by Congress is but the first of two steps necessary to reach a proper decision. The second step is to determine through judicial balancing whether the exercise of the congressionally backed authority unduly tramples on constitutionally protected liberties.

Because the US Constitution does not provide for special emergency powers, the Bush Administration's argument for minimal judicial intervention in connection with the enemy combatant detentions is not predicated on the proposition that the President could disregard constitutional liberties when fighting the war on terror. Instead, the argument in question relies on a balancing approach, but insists that only the executive is competent and constitutionally empowered to conduct such balancing.[34]

According to the Bush Administration, continued detention of Hamdi more than two years after his initial capture in Afghanistan was justified because it was a necessary means to achieving two compelling government interests: gathering crucial intelligence in the war on terror and preventing suspected terrorists in US custody from rejoining the armed struggle against the United States.[35] Moreover, the balancing in question is similar to that employed by courts when they adjudicate other conflicts between government policy and fundamental rights claims. The only significant difference consistent with the Bush Administration's position is that in one case balancing is for the executive branch, while in the other it is for the courts. Does that matter much? Is the executive as capable or as accountable as the judiciary regarding such balancing? Does it matter that most cases occur in ordinary times, whereas the war on terror occurs under conditions of crisis or stress? Finally, is the requisite balancing associated with the war on terror beyond the competence of courts?

---

[32] See *Hamdi*, 542 US 507 at 529.

[33] See *Rasul*, 542 US 426 at 483.

[34] Cf *Hamdi*, 542 US 507 at 536 (even in the case of war, the 'United States Constitution ... most assuredly envisions a role for all three branches when individual liberties are at stake').

[35] The Bush Administration argued that it had virtually complete exclusive authority regarding enemy combatants because of the President's Commander-in-Chief power: see US Constitution, Art II, § 2, cl 1. This might justify the inference that the Bush Administration's claims of exclusivity are ultimately based on a categorical assertion rather than on implementation of a balancing approach were it not for the duty of the executive branch, even when acting unilaterally, to give fundamental liberties their due: see n 34 above. Although both the categorical interpretation and that reliance on balancing are plausible, given the executive's constitutional obligation regarding fundamental liberties, the latter interpretation clearly emerges as the better one.

Ordinary judicial balancing is most transparent and best institutionally equipped to reconcile compelling government interests and fundamental liberties, but may be ill equipped to properly assess threats to security or to cope with the complex and rapidly changing circumstances prevalent in emergencies or special circumstances such as those prompted by the war on terror. *Hamdi* affords an excellent opportunity to explore how judicial balancing may fare in practice, particularly since a dissenting opinion relies on a categorical approach rather than on judicial balancing,[36] thus affording a glimpse into the contrast between these two approaches to judicial decision-making.

Yasser Hamdi, born in Louisiana, moved to Saudi Arabia as a child and was captured in 2001 in Afghanistan by the Northern Alliance, a coalition of Afghan military groups opposed to the Taliban government, which subsequently turned him over to the US military.[37] The latter detained and interrogated Hamdi in Afghanistan and then transported him to Guantanamo.[38] In 2002, upon learning that Hamdi was a US citizen, the military transferred him to the United States, where he remained in indefinite military detention.[39] The government's position was that Hamdi was an 'enemy combatant' and that as such he could be held indefinitely without formal charges or a hearing until such time as the government determined that access to counsel or further proceedings would be warranted.[40] Hamdi's father filed a petition for a writ of habeas corpus, alleging that his son was being illegally detained in violation of the Fifth and Fourteenth Amendments,[41] and international law, including the Geneva Conventions on Prisoners of War.[42] The petition asked the court to order the government to cease interrogating Hamdi, to declare Hamdi's detention unconstitutional and to require that the government either press charges against Hamdi and provide him with counsel or release him from detention.[43] The petition also requested that the court order an evidentiary hearing to deal with the conflicting factual assertions of the parties concerning the circumstances surrounding Hamdi's capture and his transfer to the US military.[44]

The facts were indeed disputed. The government asserted that Hamdi had received military training from the Taliban and that he became part

---

[36] See the dissenting opinion of Justice Scalia: *Hamdi v Rumsfeld*, 542 US 507 at 554–79 (2004).

[37] *Ibid* at 510.

[38] *Ibid*.

[39] *Ibid*.

[40] *Ibid*, at 510–11.

[41] *Ibid* at 511.

[42] *Ibid* at 515. Although some of the opinions in the case discussed the claims under international law, evaluation of these claims is beyond the scope of the present undertaking.

[43] *Ibid* at 511.

[44] *Ibid*.

of a Taliban unit with which he remained after 11 September 2001, when the United States commenced armed conflict against the Taliban and Al Qaeda in Afghanistan.[45] Hamdi was captured when his Taliban unit surrendered to the Northern Alliance forces.[46] Upon being turned over to the US military, Hamdi was designated an 'enemy combatant'. For his part, Hamdi asserted that he had travelled to Afghanistan to do 'relief work' and that he was 'trapped' there once the military hostilities began. The Court's plurality opinion by Justice O'Connor hones in on the factual dispute concerning the propriety of Hamdi's designation as an enemy combatant and provides the most comprehensive account of the appropriate role of judicial balancing in the context of the conflict between security and liberty in an ongoing war against terror.

The plurality acknowledged that dealing with enemy combatant designations in the war on terror would raise thorny problems as the enemy may not be visible or clearly defined and as the end of such war may be elusive and unlikely to be marked by a clear-cut event, such as a formal ceasefire agreement.[47] Nevertheless, these difficulties did not affect Hamdi's case, as conventional military hostilities were taking place in late 2001 in Afghanistan when Hamdi was captured, and as such armed conflict between the United States and the Taliban was still occurring in Afghanistan in 2004 at the time the case was heard by the Court.[48]

The bulk of the plurality's analysis was devoted to Hamdi's challenge to his designation as an enemy combatant. The only evidence the government introduced in the courts in support of its contention that Hamdi was properly being detained as an enemy combatant was the declaration of an officer of the Defense Department who had reviewed relevant documentation and was familiar with military policy and procedure relating to designation as an enemy combatant, but who had no first-hand information concerning Hamdi's capture by the Northern Alliance, or the evidence the military had considered in concluding that Hamdi was an enemy combatant.[49] The government's position before the Court was that the above-cited declaration was all the evidence that Hamdi was entitled to; for, as noted above,[50] the government insisted that the courts were limited to the determination of whether Hamdi's

---

[45]   *Ibid* at 512–13.

[46]   *Ibid* at 513.

[47]   *Ibid* at 520.

[48]   *Ibid* at 521. Contrast the circumstances surrounding the detention of another US citizen, Jose Padilla, upon his arrival in a commercial airplane in Chicago from a trip to Pakistan: see *Rumsfeld v Padilla*, 524 US 426 at 426 (2004). Determining whether Padilla was properly designated as an 'enemy combatant' would have necessitated dealing with the difficult questions left open in *Hamdi*. By disposing of the case on procedural grounds, the Court avoided dealing with these questions: see *ibid* at 426.

[49]   See *Hamdi*, 542 US 507 at 512–13.

[50]   See n 31 above.

detention was within the authority of the executive branch. For that purpose, the government argued it was sufficient that it present 'some evidence', and the declaration satisfied that requirement.[51] Consistent with this argument, the courts would have been limited to determining, from the face of such declaration, whether Hamdi's detention was consistent with the executive branch's authority to detain enemy combatants. This determination, however, would have to have been made without regard to the veracity of the declaration or to the weight of the evidence on which it purported to rely. Accordingly, the judiciary would have been limited to a determination, based solely on a declaration made by the government, of whether the asserted government authority fell within the legitimate realm of authority of the executive branch. Under these circumstances, virtually complete executive supremacy would prevail.

Hamdi, on the other hand, wanted a full judicial hearing in compliance with constitutional safeguards and the law of evidence to determine whether he was properly designated as an enemy combatant.[52] Had Hamdi been charged with a criminal offence, he would have been entitled to the full panoply of constitutional protections afforded criminal defendants and to the government's having to prove the charges against him beyond a reasonable doubt. As the Court's plurality emphasised, Congress contemplated that habeas corpus petitioners would have an opportunity to present facts and rebut facts introduced against them.[53] Moreover, the plurality specified that it was up to the courts to adjust the ways in which the due process requirements associated with habeas corpus petitions may be handled depending on the particular context of the challenged detention.[54] Rejecting executive supremacy, the plurality declared that resolution of the conflict over what process was due to Hamdi had to be achieved on the basis of 'constitutional balancing'.[55] What had to be balanced, moreover, was Hamdi's procedural due process right not to be deprived of his liberty without notice and an opportunity to be heard, on the one hand, and the government's compelling interest in waging the war in Afghanistan in the most efficient way possible with the least possible danger to US troops and (because the war in Afghanistan is part of the war on terror and the Taliban is linked to Al Qaeda) to US civilians at home and abroad, on the other hand.

---

[51] *Hamdi*, 542 US 507 at 526.
[52] *Ibid* at 524–5.
[53] *Ibid* at 526.
[54] *Ibid*.
[55] *Ibid* at 532.

Such constitutional balancing is quite customary in judicial determinations of the limits of substantive constitutional rights, but quite problematic when used to specify procedural rights in cases such as Hamdi's. For
example, free speech rights do not extend to utterances that incite to
violence.[56] This means that the state's interest in protecting those who are
likely to become victims of violence as a consequence of inflammatory
utterances that urge aggression against them clearly outweighs whatever
communicative benefit may flow from the inciting utterance. Accordingly, the balancing involved sets the limits of the substantive rights at
stake. In contrast, in at least certain settings, such as criminal prosecutions of serious crimes that may result in long prison terms, the confines
of the applicable procedural rights cannot fluctuate depending on the
circumstances of the crime at stake. For example, the criminal trial of a
person accused of being a serial killer cannot be conducted with fewer
procedural safeguards than the trial of someone accused of a white-collar
crime who poses no danger of violence whatsoever. The Constitution
guarantees the same procedural rights to all accused of having committed a serious crime; this is appropriate because they all have an equal
stake in determination of innocence or guilt.

Hamdi was neither accused of a crime nor subjected to a criminal
proceeding, but his detention, which the plurality acknowledged could
potentially have lasted throughout his entire lifetime,[57] was comparable
to that of a convicted criminal sentenced to a long prison term. The
determinative issue in *Hamdi* is not whether the security interests of the
United States far outweigh the liberty interests of enemy combatants, but
whether or not Hamdi was an enemy combatant. And, with respect to
this latter issue, while there may be no need to adhere to the formalities
of a criminal trial, it is difficult to understand why Hamdi should not
have been entitled to procedural safeguards that are as efficacious and as
fair as those afforded criminal defendants. Balancing in the context of
procedural due process rights is certainly warranted in many civil cases
in which the threatened deprivation of liberty or property is relatively
minor. Whereas temporary suspension of a state-granted licence or
denial of a state permit resulting in a loss of business must comply with
the due process requirements of notice and an opportunity to be heard, it
is clear that insisting on the formalities of a criminal trial in such cases
would be completely disproportionate.[58]

---

[56]   See *Brandenburg v Ohio*, 395 US 444 at 447–8 (1969).

[57]   *Hamdi*, 542 US 507 at 520.

[58]   Cf *Cleveland Board of Education v Loudermill*, 470 US 532 at 546 (1985) (holding that
tenured public employee facing dismissal was entitled to a pre-termination notice, oral or
written, of charges, an explanation of employer's evidence, and an opportunity to present
his side of the story).

To determine what process is necessary to comply with due process under given circumstances, the courts resort to judicial balancing consistent with the criteria set in *Mathews v Eldridge*,[59] a case involving termination of disability benefits. The test articulated in *Mathews* and implemented by the plurality in *Hamdi* requires weighing the private interest affected by state action against the government's asserted interest, taking into proper account the added burden the government would have to assume were it to afford greater process.[60] More specifically, what the judicial balancing test must address is 'the risk of an erroneous deprivation' of the private interest affected if the process were reduced against the 'probable value, if any, of additional or substitute safeguards'.[61]

The plurality recognised that Hamdi's interest in being free from physical detention by the government is 'the most elemental of liberty interests'[62] and that the danger of erroneous deprivation of liberty in the absence of sufficient process is very high.[63] In particular, the plurality noted that the danger of mistaken military detention of journalists and humanitarian relief workers in a war such as that fought in Afghanistan is quite high.[64] On the other hand, the military's need to detain captured enemy combatants to prevent their return to the theatre of war to fight alongside the enemy is compelling, as is the freedom to pursue strategic military objectives with utmost flexibility.[65] Equally paramount is that the military not get bogged down with trial-like processes that would distract them from their military mission and might compromise military secrets by making them subject to discovery.[66]

Under these circumstances, the plurality found that neither the criminal-trial-like process proposed by Hamdi nor the declaration offered by the government struck the proper balance.[67] The former would be too burdensome on the military; the latter would not allow a meaningful challenge to an erroneous detention. The proper balance, according to the plurality, required that a citizen detained as an enemy combatant be given notice of the factual basis for such detention and be entitled to rebut the government's factual assertion before a neutral decision-maker. To alleviate the burden on the government while the executive is engaged in active military operations, the plurality specified that hearsay

---

[59]   424 US 319 (1976).
[60]   *Hamdi*, 542 US 507 at 529 (citing *Mathews*, 424 US 319 at 335).
[61]   *Ibid* (quoting *Mathews*, 424 US 319 at 335).
[62]   *Ibid*.
[63]   *Ibid*.
[64]   *Ibid* at 530 (citing Brief for AmeriCares *et al* as Amici Curiae Supporting Petitioner).
[65]   *Ibid* at 531.
[66]   *Ibid* at 531–2.
[67]   *Ibid* at 532–3.

evidence was acceptable, and that once the government made out a prima facie case for detention, it would be appropriate to grant the government's evidence a presumption of validity: the burden of persuasion would then shift to the detainee to rebut that presumption and to demonstrate that he or she did not fall within the relevant criteria.[68] This burden-shifting procedure would ensure, in the plurality's estimation, that 'the errant tourist, embedded journalist, or local aid worker has a chance to prove military error'.[69]

The 'balance' struck by the plurality imposes little additional burden on the government, and it may be adequate for an erroneously detained journalist, but not for someone in a predicament such as Hamdi's. The government's initial burden would be satisfied by a simple declaration without factual verification, but the shifting of the burden of proof would make it very difficult and burdensome to overcome that declaration's presumption of validity. It is well known that the determination of which party bears the burden of proof is often decisive in litigation.[70] In the case of a journalist, bearing the burden of proof may not amount to an insurmountable obstacle if the detainee is employed by a large news organisation that can vouch for the journalist's employment and for his or her assignment to cover the war. But what if someone like Hamdi had been turned over to the Northern Alliance by local Afghan villagers who acted to receive a ransom?

In the last analysis, the plurality accorded too little weight to the serious deprivation of liberty associated with the designation as an enemy combatant and too much weight to security concerns relating to the war on terrorism. The plurality's handling of balancing in *Hamdi* thus raises the question of whether it would be better to use a categorical approach in enemy combatant cases. Justice Scalia's dissenting opinion in *Hamdi* does offer a categorical solution to the conflict between the government and Hamdi. According to Justice Scalia, the government could only continue to detain Hamdi indefinitely without pressing charges against him if Congress were to suspend the right to habeas corpus, which it can only do in case of an invasion or rebellion.[71] Otherwise, the government could either press charges against Hamdi or release him, as the Constitution would then require that his habeas corpus petition be granted.[72] Justice Scalia further stressed that there

---

[68]   *Ibid* at 534.
[69]   *Ibid.*
[70]   See, eg, *Armstrong v Manzo*, 380 US 545 at 551 (1965).
[71]   See *Hamdi*, 542 US 507 at 562. Congress would have to decide whether the 11 September 2001 attacks constituted an 'invasion' and whether these attacks still justified suspension several years later: *ibid* at 578.
[72]   *Ibid* at 576–8.

were several criminal laws already enacted by Congress that the executive could invoke to press charges against someone like Hamdi, including laws against treason, against providing material support to terrorists and against 'enlistment to serve in armed hostility against the United States'.[73]

Another important factor further complicates the task of striking a proper balance between security and liberty in cases such as Hamdi's. That factor is that the war on terror is fought at once as a conventional military war and as a national and international operation designed to bring criminals to justice. Indeed, the military campaign conducted by the United States and its allies against the Taliban in Afghanistan was regarded by the Bush Administration as a war against a state army.[74] At the same time, the President made clear that Al Qaeda members and other terrorists would not be treated as fighters and that he would not afford them rights under the Geneva Conventions.[75] The problem caused by this bifurcated approach without clear lines of demarcation was that issues relating to those designated as enemy combatants did not fit neatly within either of the two well-defined distinct legal paradigms. In cases of conventional war, captured enemy soldiers are to be subjected to the categorical prescriptions of the Geneva Conventions and of other relevant bodies of international law.[76] In contrast, criminal suspects must be charged with a crime or released from detention within a relatively short time.[77] Also, if charged they must be afforded the full set of constitutionally guaranteed procedural protections regardless of the crime involved.[78] The government attempted to straddle the line between these two regimes in order not to fall within the strictures of the criminal law system while also escaping from the requirements of the Geneva Conventions. Neither the US citizens, Hamdi and Padilla, nor those Guantanamo detainee plaintiffs in *Rasul* – who were citizens of countries friendly to the United States, such as Australia and Kuwait[79] – fell within the ordinary definition of enemy combatants. Moreover, they all contested their designations as enemy combatants. The government sought

---

[73] *Ibid* at 561.

[74] See 'Bush: Geneva Treaty Applies to Taliban Detainees', CNN.Com, 7 February 2002, available at <http://archives.cnn.com/2002/US/02/07/ret.bush.detainees/>. Although President Bush specified that the Taliban had not been recognised by the United States as the legitimate government of Afghanistan, he declared that he would apply the Geneva Conventions to Taliban fighters.

[75] *Ibid*.

[76] See Geneva Convention Relative to the Treatment of Prisoners of War, Art 118, 12 August 1949, 6 UST 3316, 75 UNTS 135.

[77] See Justice Scalia's dissenting opinion in *Hamdi* 542 US 507 at 554–8.

[78] See nn 10–18 above.

[79] *Rasul v Bush*, 542 US 426 at 466, 470–71 (2004).

to avoid legal responsibility for the detentions by seeking to carve out as best it could a no-man's-land between the two regimes.[80]

In the end, both the need for balancing and the kind of balancing needed depend on which legal regime is properly brought to bear on these cases. And, neither of the two familiar paradigms, that of criminal law or that of the law of war, seems adequate.

IV. BALANCING, PROPORTIONALITY AND THE ISRAELI DECISIONS

Not only is the Israeli Court's balancing as broad as the US Court's is narrow, but the Israeli cases are much more directly related to an ongoing war than their US counterparts. Whereas the US cases dealt with procedural rights of detainees far removed from theatres of war, the Israeli cases concerned substantive rights pressed by civilian non-combatants affected by ongoing military activity, including active combat within the very core of the relevant theatre of war.[81] Moreover, whereas in the United States balancing did not result in a dramatic departure from the government's position, in Israel, balancing led the Court to order the government to make substantial changes to the location of the separation barrier built for security and to make changes in the conduct of an ongoing military operation in Gaza.

If, from the standpoint of security, the circumstances surrounding the Israeli cases seem much less amenable to balancing than their US counterparts, from the standpoint of the respective rights involved, the opposite appears to be true. The Israeli cases involve substantive liberty, property and dignity rights – which are usually subjected to judicial balancing. The Israeli cases relate to military action claimed to be necessary for the security of the country and for the safety of its citizens. At the same time, these military undertakings adversely affected the legitimate and recognised liberty, property and dignity interests of Palestinian civilians residing in the occupied territory areas affected. In a

---

[80] The US Supreme Court further limited the government's asserted unilateral power two years after the decisions discussed above. The Court held in *Hamdan v Rumsfeld*, 126 S Ct 2749 (2006), a 5-to-3 decision, that the President did not have the exclusive power to set military commissions to try Guantanamo detainees or to refuse compliance with obligations imposed by the Geneva Conventions. Since Hamdan was first subjected to a proceeding before a military commission, the Congress authorised the latter and sought to deprive the US federal courts of jurisdiction to hear habeas corpus petitions by those subjected to military commission trials. At the time of writing, the US Supreme Court has not issued a decision on the constitutionality of these congressional measures. (See Military Commissions Act, Pub L No 109–360, 120 Stat.2600 (17 October 2006).

[81] See *Mara'abe v The Prime Minister of Israel* HCJ7957/04 (2005) (separation fence erected to thwart would-be suicide bombers coming from the West Bank); *Beit Sourik*, n 1 above (same); see also *Physicians for Human Rights*, n 1 above (military operation, including hostile combat in Gaza).

constitutional democracy, the military has an obligation – enhanced in Israel by the legal responsibilities imposed by the international laws of belligerent occupation applicable to the West Bank and Gaza[82] – to take into account, and to ascribe proper weight to, the needs, legitimate interests, rights and liberties of the civilians who will be inevitably adversely affected by implementation of military policy.[83] Beyond that, however, should ongoing military operations be subjected to judicial balancing? And if they are, are judges competent to perform the requisite balancing operations?

The Israeli decisions rest on a seeming paradox. As Chief Justice Barak starkly stated in *Beit Sourik*: 'We, Justices of the Supreme Court are not experts in military affairs.'[84] Yet, he also hastened to add that his Court is competent to review the Israeli military commander's decision concerning the location of the barrier because judges are *the* experts in applying the principle of proportionality.[85] This sense of paradox is heightened, moreover, by the Court's refusal to enter into the battle among military experts. The Palestinian plaintiffs whose land was seized, mobility curtailed and communal life disrupted were joined by the Council for Peace and Security (Council), an Israeli non-governmental organisation that included high-ranking reserve officers of the Israeli Defence Forces (IDF) and that had expertise in military security.[86] The Council joined the Palestinian plaintiffs as amici curiae[87] and argued that, in their expert opinion, better security for Israel and less intrusive incursion into Palestinian lands and community life could be achieved by moving the barrier closer to Israel.[88] The defendant, the IDF's military commander in the West Bank, acknowledged the expertise of the Council but disagreed with their judgment, insisting that the actual location for the barrier decided upon by the IDF was the optimal security option after giving proper weight to political considerations and to the legitimate interests of Palestinian civilians.[89] Faced with this disagreement among experts, the Court recognised that the conflicting positions involved were 'based upon contradictory military views',[90] but went on to declare 'we must grant special weight to the military opinion of the official who is

---

[82] See *Beit Sourik* at para 23.
[83] *Ibid* at para 13 (discussing the military's assertion that in planning the separation barrier 'great weight was given' to the interests of Palestinians affected).
[84] *Ibid* at para 46.
[85] *Ibid* at para 48.
[86] *Ibid* at para 16.
[87] *Ibid* at para 18.
[88] *Ibid* at paras 18–19.
[89] *Ibid* at para 20.
[90] *Ibid* at para 47.

responsible for security'.[91] Yet, for all its unwillingness to enter the battle of the military experts, the Court engaged in a weighing of the trade-offs between security and liberty struck by the barrier, concluded that the IDF had acted in a disproportionate manner,[92] and ordered the military commander to come up with changes regarding the barrier in order to ensure compliance with the requirements of proportionality.[93]

The Court's recourse to balancing and proportionality analysis in its adjudication of the controversy over the separation barrier is grounded both in the relevant application of substantive law and in the Court's established practice of using balancing to resolve conflicts between competing interests. From the standpoint of substantive law, the international law of belligerent occupation allows the occupying country to protect its security and that of its citizens, but also requires that country to balance its security needs against the rights, needs and interests of the population residing in the occupied territory.[94] More generally, proportionality is a key principle of the law of war, which requires establishing a balance between 'military needs and humanitarian considerations'.[95] Proportionality is also a general principle of Israeli administrative law and has more recently become a constitutional principle incorporated in Article 8 of Israel's Basic Law on human dignity and freedom.[96]

The IDF, which is an administrative body under Israeli law, had performed its substantive legal obligation to balance security concerns against the rights and interests of affected Palestinians before settling on the location of the barrier. The Court's exercise in judicial balancing started after this initial determination, thus raising the question of the extent to which it merely supplements the non-judicial balancing performed by the military commander as opposed to engaging in a de novo balancing of its own. To elucidate this question, it is first necessary to inquire briefly into the proportionality test used by the Court.

The proportionality test used by the Court, applicable under both international law and Israeli administrative law, is divided into three subtests.[97] The first subtest requires that the administrative means used be rationally related to the realisation of the state's objective.[98] The

---

[91]   *Ibid*. While the court refused to weigh the respective strengths and weakness of the two contending military positions, it did indicate that the military commander's position was not beyond challenge. The commander was entitled to a presumption that his 'professional reasons are sincere reasons': *ibid*. This presumption can only be overcome by 'very convincing evidence'.

[92]   *Ibid* at paras 60–62.

[93]   *Ibid* at para 86.

[94]   *Ibid* at para 34.

[95]   *Ibid* at para 37.

[96]   *Ibid* at para 38.

[97]   *Ibid* at para 40.

[98]   *Ibid*.

second subtest prescribes that the means used to realise the objective be those that are 'least injurious' to adversely affected individuals.[99] Finally, the third subtest, that of 'proportionality in the narrow sense', requires that the harm to the relevant individuals be proportionate to the benefit to the state.[100] The third subtest can be satisfied in one of two possible ways: either by directly weighing the benefits against the harms of the proposed administrative course of action, or by comparing different administrative alternatives to one another to determine whether the decrease in benefit caused by shifting from the most beneficial alternative to a somewhat less beneficial one is accompanied by a greater decrease in harm. If it is, then, proportionality requires that the somewhat less beneficial but significantly less harmful alternative be adopted.[101]

All three subtests require balancing, albeit different kinds of balancing. The rationality requirement of the first subtest calls for minimal balancing in that only such means that are so disproportionate as to be irrational are excluded.[102] The second subtest requires a balancing among the respective injuries that would result from adoption of the various possible means toward the relevant administrative objective. This requires applying a proportionality standard that includes comparison and may involve 'balancing' in a purely formal sense, as when one alternative calling for the expropriation of 100 landowners is 'weighed' against another alternative involving only 50 such expropriations. On the other hand, more problematic balancing would become necessary if one alternative involved land expropriations and the other restrictions on the affected population's freedom of movement. Finally, the third subtest, that of proportionality proper, requires extensive balancing, either between military benefits and civilian harms, or between the ratios of harm to benefit for various plausible alternatives.

Notwithstanding the Court's declarations to the contrary, the military dispute between the Council and the military commander concerning which of their proposed routes for the barrier would be best for security did figure prominently in the Court's application of the three-part proportionality test. The dispute centered on whether the barrier would make Israel more secure if built away from Israel's population or if built away from the Palestinian population. The Council maintained that a barrier close to Israel's population would be more easily defended as it would provide time and space to intercept terrorists before they could

---

[99] *Ibid.*

[100] *Ibid.*

[101] *Ibid.*

[102] Minimal 'rationality' analysis does not, strictly speaking, always require balancing. Whether or not it does depends on whether the relevant means are 'irrational' because grossly disproportionate, or 'irrational' because illogical, contradictory, or inherently absurd.

harm Israeli soldiers or civilians.[103] The military commander's view, on the other hand, was that a barrier closer to the Palestinian population would be safer for Israeli soldiers and would give the latter a better opportunity to run down or capture terrorists before they could reach Israeli civilians.[104] Furthermore, the military commander and the Council agreed that a barrier closer to the Palestinian population would be more injurious to that population than one right next to the Israeli population,[105] and also, according to the Council, a closer barrier would further embitter the Palestinians and thus eventually foment greater terrorism.[106] The dispute between military experts had a significant bearing on the Court's application of the third subtest under the proportionality standard. The Court resorted to the second alternative, namely, comparing different plans for the location of the barrier with respect to the ratio of harm to benefit that each of these plans would produce. Accordingly, the Court did not engage in a direct weighing of harms and benefits of the IDF plan, but it did take into account the plan proposed by the Council for purposes of weighing the IDF plan against plausible alternatives.[107]

The specific finding of the Court was that even though it accepted that the IDF plan led to greater security than the Council's, the IDF plan also led to much greater injury than the Council's. Therefore, concluded the Court, since the difference in security between the plans was 'minute', the IDF plan failed the third subtest and had to be rejected as disproportionate.[108] Based on that conclusion, the Court ordered the military commander to draw a new plan for the barrier.[109]

In the end, the Court did not engage in a direct comparison of military plans, but it did perform an indirect comparison. The Court struck down the IDF's plan not because it did not arrive at a proper *military* balance between security and liberty, but because it failed to strike that very same balance as required by humanitarian considerations.

From a substantive point of view, the balancing engaged in by the Court in *Beit Sourik* is certainly de novo balancing rather than a review of the adequacy of an administrative agency's balancing. The Israeli Court's balancing seems to be the equivalent of the kind of balancing that courts

---

[103]   *Beit Sourik* at para 18.
[104]   *Ibid* at para 20.
[105]   *Ibid* at paras 18, 29.
[106]   *Ibid* at para 18.
[107]   *Ibid* at para 61.
[108]   *Ibid* at para 61. *Cf Mara'abe*, n 81 above at para 116. If no plausible alternative proves viable, then without the disputed segment 'there is no security for the Israelis', and with it 'there is a severe injury to the fabric of life of the residents of the [Palestinian] villages'. Applying the third subtest under such circumstances will be 'the most difficult of the questions'.
[109]   *Beit Sourik* at para 71.

routinely perform in ordinary civilian settings.[110] This squarely raises the question of whether different criteria concerning balancing should apply in the context of military affairs than in that of civilian ones. This question will be examined in Section VI below.

In the end, the Israeli Court leaves unanswered the following questions. First, is there any cogent way to draw or maintain the distinction between zones of military discretion and zones where such discretion ought to be balanced against humanitarian concerns? Second, even if there were a cogent way to maintain the latter distinction, is judicial intervention into day-to-day military operations ever justified? And if not, is there any plausible alternative to unmitigated military discretion in the face of an ongoing war on terror? For all its insistence that it did not second-guess military policy, the Israeli Court came close in *Beit Sourik* to engaging in complete de novo review. In the application of the proportionality test 'in the narrow sense', the Court gave some deference, but not much, to the military judgement of the relevant IDF commander.

V. UK PROPORTIONALITY ANALYSIS AND THE DISTINCTION BETWEEN TIMES OF CRISIS AND TIMES OF STRESS

Like the US cases, the main issue in the *A (Belmarsh Detainees)* case decided by the Law Lords was whether indefinite detention without charge of persons suspected of having links to terrorism was compatible with fundamental liberty and due process rights. As viewed by the Law Lords, the answer to this question depended on one or both of two key considerations: whether the war on terror as gauged from the vantage point of the United Kingdom created a state of emergency or merely conditions of stress; and whether different treatment of the detainees who were non-deportable foreigners as compared to that of otherwise similarly situated deportable foreigners and British nationals not subject to deportation violated applicable anti-discrimination standards. Eight of the nine Law Lords found the challenged detentions to be in violation of the ECHR and the 1998 UK Human Rights Act.[111]

In reaching their decision, the Law Lords applied a proportionality standard to determine whether the war on terror created a state of emergency:[112] they balanced the detainees' liberty interests against the nation's security interests,[113] much as the plurality in *Hamdi* had done,

---

[110] In the United States, such balancing is routinely used in relation to certain federalism issues concerning regulation of commerce: see *Pike v Bruce Church, Inc*, 397 US 137 (1970).

[111] Lord Walker of Gestingthorpe was the lone dissenter. See *A (Belmarsh Detainees)* [2004] UKHL 56, [2005] 2 AC 68 at paras 191–218.

[112] See *ibid* at paras 30–44.

[113] *Ibid*.

and they considered whether the different treatment accorded foreign suspected terrorists in comparison with domestic ones was dispropor-tionate.[114] The eight Law Lords who found the challenged detentions illegitimate diverged on the precise grounds for their conclusions. There was disagreement over how much deference the courts owed Parliament and the executive, over whether the United Kingdom's war on terror was fought under emergency conditions or conditions of stress, and over whether the challenged detentions were illegitimate because unduly discriminatory (the prevalent view) or because there was no state of emergency (Lord Hoffmann's view).[115]

After the 11 September 2001 attacks, the UK Parliament adopted anti-terrorist legislation that provides in relevant part that a 'suspected international terrorist may be detained' as someone subject to deporta-tion even if he or she cannot be deported due to some legal or factual impediment.[116] Consistent with this legislation, the United Kingdom deported certain foreign suspected terrorists to their country of citizen-ship, but could not do so with respect to others whose deportation would have been in violation of UK obligations under international law because of the danger that the would-be deportees would be tortured upon their return home. The latter challenged their indefinite detention without charge under the ECHR, incorporated into UK domestic law by the Human Rights Act 1998.

The relevant provisions of the ECHR were: Article 5, which, guarantees the 'right to liberty and security of the person' and provides basic due process rights to those under arrest;[117] Article 14, which prohibits dis-crimination with respect to the rights secured by the ECHR; and Article 15, which allows a country to derogate from its obligations under the ECHR in times of emergency. Article 15.1 provides in relevant part:

> 'In time of war or other public emergency *threatening the life of the nation* any High Contracting Party may take measures derogating from its obligations under this Convention to the extent strictly required by the exigencies of the situation'.[118]

In November 2001, the United Kingdom derogated from its obligations under the ECHR, citing the 11 September attacks and the subsequent UN Security Council resolutions recognising those attacks as a threat to world peace and security, and referring to an existing threat posed by

[114]   *Ibid* at paras 132, 138.
[115]   *Ibid* at para 97.
[116]   See *ibid* at para 14 (citing Anti-terrorism, Crime and Security Act 2001, c 49, s 23(1)); see also *ibid* at para 8.
[117]   See ECHR, Art 5(2), (3) and (4).
[118]   *Ibid*, Art 15(1).

international terrorists against the United Kingdom in which foreign nationals within its borders were playing a pivotal role.[119]

Within this framework, the key issues were: whether the threat of international terrorism was proportionate so as to justify derogation; whether, assuming it was, the means used to combat such terrorism were the least restrictive possible with respect to the relevant liberty (Article 5) and equality (Article 14) rights; and who, as between the political branches and the courts, had the ultimate power to determine the proportionality of derogation. Moreover, these inquiries had to be placed in the context of an overall concern for striking a proper balance between liberty and security in the United Kingdom's war against international terror.[120]

The standard for derogation, the existence of a state of crisis, was provided by the ECHR. Furthermore, since derogation must be affirmatively instituted by a country, the initial decision and, hence, determination of the existence of a state of crisis in the first instance, is the responsibility of the political branches. As mentioned above, the Law Lords were divided over whether this determination by the political branches was binding on the judiciary.

The question of whether it is proper for judges to review the proportionality of derogation, which involves deciding whether the United Kingdom is actually in a state of crisis, parallels the question of the propriety of judicial balancing in the US cases in significant respects, but with one major difference: under UK law, the judiciary can declare derogation or the means used to combat the crisis that prompted derogation to be contrary to the Human Rights Act 1998, but it cannot order relief or invalidate the challenged laws or executive decrees. It remains up to Parliament to initiate changes or to remain with the status quo notwithstanding the judicial declaration.[121] As a consequence, an erroneous assessment of the balance between liberty and security by UK judges seems less ominous than one by US judges, since the UK Parliament can ignore such an assessment, whereas the US political branches cannot.[122]

In the *A (Belmarsh Detainees)* case, there were at least three reasons that bolster the conclusion that judicial review of the initial political decision was desirable and that it could be performed in a principled way. The first reason is that although the United Kingdom faced a similar threat from international terrorism as other Western European nations, it was

---

[119] See *A (Belmarsh Detainees)* [2005] 2 AC 68 at paras 10–11.

[120] See *ibid* at para 191.

[121] See *ibid* at para 220.

[122] This is not to say that a decision by the Law Lords may not result in strong political pressure on Parliament to make the law conform to the judicial decision. Nonetheless, from an institutional standpoint, Parliament remains free to ignore the judicial decision.

the only country to have derogated from its obligations under the ECHR.[123] Even Spain, after the attack perpetrated by Al Qaeda on 11 March 2004 in Madrid, did not derogate.[124]

The second reason is that the United Kingdom did have a period within living memory during World War Two in which the life of the nation was definitely threatened, and as Lord Hoffmann pointed out in the passage cited above,[125] the current threat posed by international terrorism is nothing comparable. The threat of international terrorism does cause fear, and such fear may lead to exaggeration of the actual dangers confronting the citizenry or of the probability that such dangers will materialise.[126] Precisely because of this, the circumstances surrounding derogation should be closely scrutinised, and it seems proper for judges to perform that function.[127] As Lord Hoffmann observed, neither the United Kingdom nor Spain conducted public affairs as if their institutions were threatened or the life of the country was in peril.[128] That alone should suffice to lift the presumption of validity of the derogation.

The third reason that buttresses the case for judicial review is that the means devised to deal with the threat that supposedly justified derogation bolster security minimally if at all. This suggests that the UK political branches are not taking the terrorist threat as seriously as they claim they are.

The disproportionate means selected by the United Kingdom provide an independent ground for a judicial finding that the challenged detentions were illegitimate. As these means bordered on the irrational,[129] alternative means that treated all those suspected of having links to international terrorism the same would not only have been more equitable, but in all likelihood more efficient and, hence, far more rational.[130] Moreover, focus on the means rather than on the decision to derogate

---

[123]   See *A (Belmarsh Detainees)* [2005] 2 AC 68 at paras 23–25.
[124]   *Ibid* at para 25.
[125]   See n 9 above.
[126]   See *A (Belmarsh Detainees)* [2005] 2 AC 68 at para 115.
[127]   *Ibid* at para 116.
[128]   *Ibid* at para 97. Moreover, that concern was not altered by the July 2005 attacks: see R Frammolino, 'By Foot or by Bus, Londoners 'Get On With It', *LA Times* (US), 23 July 2005, at A9 (reporting on the resilience of London commuters after the attacks).
[129]   *Ibid* at para 132.
[130]   Detaining *all* terrorist suspects would overcome objections on equality grounds, but still leave the policy vulnerable to challenges on liberty grounds. As Lord Hoffmann emphasised, 'suspicion of being a supporter [of international terrorism] is one thing and proof of wrongdoing is another': *ibid* at para 87. Indeed, the policy would be grossly over-inclusive and hence disproportionately restrictive of liberty if everyone who expressed sympathy for Al Qaeda in a discussion overheard in a pub was subject to indefinite detention.

arguably has the advantage of confining the judicial role to what is clearly a matter of law as opposed to something that is above all a matter of politics.[131]

VI. ASSESSING US BALANCING AND UK AND ISRAELI PROPORTIONALITY AS JUDICIAL TOOLS IN THE WAR ON TERROR

As seen thus far, US balancing appears too narrow as the Court's *Hamdi* plurality's repudiation of executive supremacy did not result in an adequate protection of liberty. By the same token, Israeli balancing seems too broad, for although in form it professes to leave a zone of exclusivity to the executive,[132] in practice virtually no military action or policy remains beyond the reach of judicial balancing. Finally, it is difficult to gauge the scope of UK balancing, given the blatant disproportionality of the means used to implement the derogation.

An important difference between the three jurisdictions relates to how they respectively chose to place issues arising out of the war on terror within one of the three legal paradigms identified above. The justices in *Hamdi* were divided into four different legal positions ranging from the paradigm of war to that of criminal law. The position of the four justices in the plurality is best viewed as almost fitting completely within the paradigm of the law of (conventional) war. Indeed, the plurality agreed to the legitimacy of the detention of enemy combatants for security reasons for the duration of the hostilities. Its only concession to the unconventional nature of the war on terror was that it recognised that, given the unusual nature of the enemy and the extraordinary difficulty in pinpointing the end of such a war, risks of mistaken detention and of the detentions remaining unnoticed were much greater than in the context of ordinary war. Accordingly, the plurality concluded, detainees ought to have a right to challenge their status, but because it was essentially working from a paradigm of war, it granted procedural due process rights adequate in the context of civil, not criminal law. Because Hamdi's two-year detention, which could have plausibly extended for decades, fits better within a criminal law paradigm, however, the procedural rights carved out by the plurality are bound to seem inadequate and disproportionate.

Unlike the US Court, which seems caught between two paradigms, the Israeli Court perceives itself as firmly grounded in a war paradigm, and a very conventional one for that matter. The Israeli Court was quite explicit

---

[131] This view was that of Lord Bingham of Cornhill: see *ibid* at para 29.
[132] The IDF is an administrative body, but it is under the command of the Prime Minister and Minister of Defense: *Beit Sourik* at para 23.

that it was applying the law of war and of belligerent occupation. What is surprising under these circumstances is how little deference the Israeli Court has actually given to the military. Moreover, although the Court specified that the judicially challenged military actions were directed against Palestinian terrorism, nothing specific to the war on terror seems to figure in either the paradigm explicitly embraced by the Court or in its actual decisions.

There is an incongruity between the Israeli Court's unanimous embrace of the war paradigm and its seeming under-weighing of the military security objectives at stake in the cases before it. Whereas these cases concern the rights and interests of Palestinian civilians, the Court also stressed that, both in the West Bank and Gaza, terrorists often mingle with the civilian population, thus posing a constant hidden and unpredictable danger.[133] Under these circumstances, the under-weighing of, or lack of sufficient deference to, military security objectives is puzzling unless one hypothesises that alongside or underneath the war paradigm lies a different paradigm.

This second paradigm is the police power law paradigm. The occupying Israeli military administration is indeed the guarantor of public order and rights in those portions of the occupied territories that it controls or substantially affects. From the standpoint of this second paradigm, moreover, the IDF is exercising what amounts to police powers vis-à-vis the Palestinian civilians affected by its activities in the West Bank and Gaza. Just as any state bears responsibility for maintaining order and providing essential services to its citizenry, the IDF as military occupier had similar obligations toward Palestinian civilians over whose lives it exercised substantial control.

Viewed from the standpoint of the police power law paradigm, most of the claims of the Palestinian civilians ought to have been treated by the Israeli Court as requiring a balancing between what are essentially IDF police power claims[134] and what substantially amount to Palestinian civilians' constitutional rights claims. Consistent with this requirement of balancing, the Israeli Court would be in the same position as any court confronting constitutional cases presenting a conflict between the exercise of state police powers and the vindication of fundamental individual rights.

---

[133]   The very purpose of the separation barrier was to contain terrorism by separating the Palestinian population in the midst of which terrorists were easily concealed from the Israeli population that they targeted: *ibid.*

[134]   In a democracy, police powers are used to foster collective goals that are majoritarian in origin. In an occupation, in contrast, the collective goals involved are not majoritarian, but instead imposed by international law. Nevertheless, in terms of the content of these goals and of their clashes with individual rights, the two situations are largely equivalent and hence the police power law paradigm can extend to both.

In the end, the seeming incongruity of the Israeli decisions can be traced back to the Court's concurrent reliance on two separate paradigms. From the standpoint of Israel's interests and Israeli administrative law, the Court was operating under a war paradigm, and hence, its deferential declarations regarding discretion in the pursuit of military objectives. From the standpoint of the international law of belligerent occupation and of its institutional role as guarantor of the Palestinian population's fundamental rights as recognised under applicable humanitarian standards, on the other hand, the Court placed itself within a police power law paradigm. Moreover, effectively, given the little deference it accorded to military discretion, the Court remained principally within the police power law paradigm.

The Law Lords in *A (Belmarsh Detainees)*, much like the US Court, seem to straddle between the law of war paradigm and the criminal law paradigm. Those Law Lords who agreed that the derogation from ECHR rights was warranted because the life of the United Kingdom was under threat would undoubtedly have agreed to the indefinite detention of suspected terrorists were it not for the discriminatory manner in which it was being implemented.

The question of the legitimacy of derogation, which figures prominently in *A (Belmarsh Detainees)*, puts into question whether the United Kingdom's war on terror is being fought under conditions of crisis. Assuming, consistent with some views among the Law Lords, that it is not being fought under such conditions, is the war paradigm still appropriate? As will be argued below, so long as the war on terror is fought under conditions of stress rather than of crisis, neither the war paradigm nor the criminal law one is likely to be adequate.

The first question that consideration of balancing in relation to the war on terror poses is whether it would be optimal to rely exclusively on extra-judicial balancing. In cases of extra-judicial balancing, such as those that arise under the constitutional guarantees afforded criminal defendants under the US Constitution, courts are limited to categorical determinations. Arguably, categorical adjudication is preferable to judicial balancing, because it presumably allows for less judicial discretion or judicial politics.[135]

In spite of the possible benefits of extra-judicial balancing or of those of categorical judicial determinations, the preceding analysis clearly counsels against doing away with judicial balancing. Executive balancing is likely to be skewed owing to that branch's special responsibility for

---

[135] This is, in fact, a debatable point. Certain adjudications seem to bear this point out, but not others: see HLA Hart, *The Concept of Law* (Oxford, Oxford University Press, 1961) 125.

security.[136] Furthermore, the institutional process-based approach requiring both executive and legislative action provides greater safeguards than the executive branch acting alone. As evinced by the US Congress's broad delegation of power after 11 September 2001, by the sweeping powers it granted the executive by enacting the USA PATRIOT Act,[137] and by the equally sweeping UK legislation, however, the latter approach, whatever additional balancing it promotes, does not do away with the need for judicial protection of constitutional rights or their equivalents.[138]

To better appreciate the need for judicial balancing, it may be useful to look at the alternative offered by a categorical approach such as that found in Justice Scalia's opinion in *Hamdi*. That approach would not have been appropriate for the Israeli cases dealing with substantive rights of civilians. Indeed, a categorical approach to substantive rights provides too blunt a tool to allow for as much enjoyment of such rights as would be compatible with the state's realisation of its vital security needs. Furthermore, even under the assumption that a categorical approach is unequivocally superior with respect to the procedural rights of criminal defendants, Justice Scalia's approach seems too rigid in the context of the war on terror. Because Hamdi's plight was similar to that of a criminal suspect, and because the plurality in *Hamdi* gave too much weight to the government's security interests, a categorical approach may seem to have been superior in the context of that case. But the numerous other kinds of situations in which liberty and security are bound to clash in the war on terror will inevitably be varied and different. Accordingly, the more flexible balancing approach would be better. For example, even under the circumstances surrounding Padilla's detention, and assuming that after two years of detention proper judicial balancing would grant him essentially the same rights as those of a criminal defendant, there may still be a need for flexibility. Thus, if the government arrested Padilla on the basis of intelligence it could not reveal, it might be appropriate to allow it to introduce hearsay testimony or present secret evidence in camera allowing for review and challenge by the judge but not by the detainee's counsel.

---

[136] The same argument applies, perhaps even more strongly, with respect to the administrative power represented by the IDF in the Israeli cases.

[137] See Uniting and Strengthening America by Providing Appropriate Tools Required to Intercept and Obstruct Terrorism (USA PATRIOT Act), Act of 2001, Pub L No 107–56, 115 Stat 272 (codified in scattered sections of the USC).

[138] As parliamentary democracies, rather than presidential ones like the United States, Israel and the United Kingdom have less of a separation between legislative and executive power than does the United States. Since even the arguably stronger separation prevalent in the United States does not suffice to adequately protect rights in the war on terror, separation of powers differences between the three countries can be left aside for present purposes.

Balancing affords greater flexibility, but is it reliable? Can it be made to conform to standards? Or, does balancing in the end rest solely on the unfettered discretion of judges? The Israeli proportionality test makes for significantly more intrusive judicial intervention into policy, including military policy, than does the US strict scrutiny test or the UK proportionality standard.[139] This difference is important and it must be kept in mind while considering whether judicial balancing is appropriate or desirable in cases involving military affairs. More specifically, the question that needs to be addressed in relation to this latter difference between the US and the Israeli approach – which may be conveniently referred to as a difference between 'balancing means' and 'balancing ends' – is whether the Israeli approach goes too far, and if it does, whether that is due to lack of judicial expertise in weighing military policy or to the conclusion that such weighing is impolitic and potentially damaging to the judiciary's institutional interests.

There are strong arguments against courts weighing ends in such a way that squarely thrusts them into policy-making – a power that constitutions generally grant to legislative and administrative bodies.[140] Assuming, nonetheless, that such balancing is institutionalised in a particular country, is there any reason to single out military policy for exemption from judicial balancing?

In terms of lack of judicial expertise, military policy seems no different than environmental, economic or police policy aimed at securing public order. Moreover, whether or not balancing of ends is considered appropriate, it is difficult to see how courts could avoid balancing means in the context of military affairs. On the other hand, the relevant difference between military policy and other policies such as environmental policy, for example, is that the former requires much more secrecy than the latter, and that military issues may have a different kind of political sensitivity than environmental or most other non-military issues. Indeed, military affairs tend to have foreign as well as domestic implications, and a serious impact on national security and diplomacy.

From the standpoint of inter-institutional balancing, therefore, it is preferable to avoid or greatly limit judicial balancing of ends in general, and especially in the realm of military policy. Moreover, although balancing of means generally is crucial from an inter-institutional standpoint, as purely non-judiciary balancing is often insufficient, certain precautionary

---

[139] If the UK standard is interpreted as requiring judicial review of a political determination that the nation is in a state of crisis, it would more closely approximate to the Israeli standard than the US one.

[140] See, eg, US Constitution, Arts I (legislative powers granted to Congress) and II (executive powers delegated to President); 1958 French Constitution, Art 34 (Parliament makes laws); German Basic Law, Arts 70–78 (Parliament and government make federal law).

limitations with little substantial effect on affected fundamental rights should be permissible in the context of military affairs. For example, greater tolerance of hearsay evidence, or recourse to in camera review to preserve confidentiality of sensitive military information, ought to be allowed even if that would slightly weaken actual protection of fundamental rights.

In the last analysis, there ought to be no automatic ban on judicial balancing of ends. In some cases, as the discussion of *A (Belmarsh Detainees)* indicated, judicial balancing of ends may be both clearly feasible and desirable. Even in the military context, there may be rare cases where no other institutional balancing of security and rights takes place at all, and where, accordingly, fundamental rights would be left completely unprotected absent judicial balancing. In the remaining cases, however, judicial balancing of ends should be avoided and balancing of means pursued with appropriate adjustments to avoid compromising military security.

VII. CONCLUDING OBSERVATIONS: BALANCING AND TERROR

Although judicial balancing should not be eliminated in cases arising from the war on terror, its shortcomings, which have emerged in the course of the preceding analysis, call for a determination of whether it is possible to structure and guide such balancing so as to minimise unsatisfactory outcomes. Should that be impossible, use of judicial balancing would still be preferable to its abandonment, but its benefits would remain modest and unpredictable.

The problems concerning judicial balancing discussed thus far arise in substantial part because the legal issues that emerge from the war on terror do not fit neatly within any of the three existing legal paradigms discussed throughout. Consistent with this, it seems appropriate to aim for a new paradigm, the 'war-on-terror law paradigm'. This new paradigm should incorporate aspects of the three other paradigms but recast the relationships among them. The war-on-terror law paradigm should also account for the tensions that pit conditions of stress against conditions of crisis.

The war-on-terror law paradigm should be conceived as a dynamic one, evolving and adapting to the needs and problems of the war on terror. The war on terror is in many ways different from ordinary war. It is different in terms of the enemy it confronts, of how it is fought, of the dangers it poses and of its duration. Whereas conventional wars are generally limited in duration, the war on terror must be *conceived* as a war without end. This, in turn, should have a strong bearing on how extraordinary powers are conceived and institutionalised in the context of the war on terror. In the context of a conventional war of limited duration, emergency powers can be conceived and implemented as temporary extraordinary measures. In the war on terror, extraordinary measures must be conceived as permanent, and as such require a different and more careful balancing of security and rights – one that is tailored to the concerns of times of stress rather than to the exigencies of times of crisis.

By its very nature, terrorism is intended to cause fear, panic and insecurity to a degree that is often disproportionate to the damage inflicted or the real danger posed. To be sure, some of the imaginable acts of terrorism, such as dirty bombs or biological or chemical contamination, could cause mass disasters. Others, such as suicide bombings or truck-bombing incidents, may cause only dozens of casualties, certainly an unacceptable toll and nothing to be taken lightly, but something much smaller than the casualties suffered in conventional wars. It is important for the institutions of government, including the judiciary, not to be swayed by the most frightening imaginary scenarios without first inquiring into the feasibility or probability of particular kinds of acts of terror.[141] Otherwise, both inter-institutional and judicial balancing will inevitably become skewed.

In the last analysis, suggesting systematic ways to circumvent the danger of judicial overreaching may prove particularly difficult. It is clear that judicial intrusions into military policy and action, even if not absolutely barred, ought to be few and far between. It seems preferable to curtail the scope of judicial balancing either through the administrative process, if the military carries out the law-and-order function, or through legislation, if civilian authorities do. Some of the issues raised in the cases discussed above, such as clarification of the category of 'enemy combatant', are better left to legislators. Other tasks can be entrusted to judicial balancing as properly circumscribed within an emerging paradigm of the war on terror. This will inevitably involve some experimentation and some discretion to choose among various open paths. This does not mean that judicial balancing in the area need be unconstrained or undisciplined. Given a commonality of values and objectives when it comes to the war on terror, and given that successful judicial balancing requires openness toward all plausible positions, it is quite possible that a cogent, fair and balanced jurisprudence on the war of terror will emerge. We are

---

[141] See *Chemical, Biological, Radiological And Nuclear (CBRN) Terrorism*, The Wednesday Report, <http://www.thewednesdayreport.com/twr/CBRN.htm> (last visited 6 March 2006) (stating that the 'popular scenario involving poisoning the water supply of a major metropolitan area does not appear very feasible' and that use of many chemical or biological agents would depend on a perfect combination of various atmospheric conditions to be successful).

at the beginning of this process, and hopefully development of the new legal paradigm of the war on terror will provide useful tools to handle these novel, constantly changing and always daunting challenges.

12

International Law, Counterterrorism and the Quest for Checks and Balances:

Why the Calling Sirens of Constitutionalism Should Be Resisted

ANDREA BIANCHI

I. INTRODUCTION

THE INSPIRING MOTIF behind this research project is an inquiry into the extent to which the fight against terrorism has affected Western democratic principles of good governance, traditionally thought of in terms of constitutionalism. The overarching ambition, overtly acknowledged in the title of this section, is whether a new set of paradigms is needed. In fact, the reference to paradigms that the editors have made in this context may have been ill advised. What are paradigms but the 'disciplinary matrix' – that complex set of intellectual categories and semantic connotations – which we use in our day-to-day practice and which shape the contours of our own tiny fields of expertise?[1] They are what make us distinct, by providing us with a professional identity. This holds true also for law and its sub-disciplines. How many times have we felt alienated while attending a luncheon talk at the invitation of our colleague from the Department of Administrative Law?[2] How many times have we thought: 'What is this person talking about?' This is not the case when we listen to our own colleagues. However boring the speaker or the topic may be, in our dizziness we are cradled

---

[1] On the concept of 'disciplinary matrix' and the relevance of 'paradigms' see T Kuhn, 'Second Thoughts on Paradigms' in F Suppe (ed), *The Structure of Scientific Theories* (Urbana/Chicago/London, University of Illinois Press, 1974) 459–82.

[2] Presumably the same holds true for administrative lawyers attending luncheon talks organised by the International Law Department.

by a familiar lullaby, which plays well known and reassuring tunes. Eventually, we may end up falling asleep anyway, but, at least, we do so with a deep sense of serenity.

Why then do we pursue an interdisciplinary approach? In fact, the appeal of interdisciplinarity lies in the ambition to put to work different areas of knowledge to draw a grand, all-encompassing interdisciplinary map where the current realities will be firmly grasped by our intellect. Science will finally make progress by overcoming the hurdle of frag-mented epistemological communities, incapable by definition to have a grasp of the greater whole.

As I set out on this adventurous path of borrowing the central paradigm from the fellow-discipline of constitutional law and trying to adjust it to international law, I had the enthusiasm of a neophyte. I immediately perceived the tension that Thomas Kuhn considers to be at the basis of scientific research. I speak of that friction between the professional skills that make you work along the lines of tradition and on the basis of established rules and practices, accepted as orthodoxy by the profession, and the professional ideology of the real researcher, always looking ahead with a view to bringing about novelty and change and attempting to free himself from the shackles of professional convention.[3] The academic hubris, which we all possess in different doses, surrepti-tiously suggested that I could eventually come up with a holistic, hopefully interdisciplinary, aspirationally universal vision, where all the strands of analysis previously used would naturally come together in a grand synthesis of sorts, whose paradigms would be intelligible and acceptable to everyone. This is the spirit in which I started playing with constitutionalism and the doctrine of checks and balances.

II. THE DEBATE ON CONSTITUTIONALISM IN INTERNATIONAL LAW: A MISLEADING START?

If one were to think that there is no room in international law for a discourse on constitutionalism, he or she ought to see the number of recent writings which directly bear on such a topic.[4] Indeed, the sudden

---

[3] See T Kuhn, 'The Function of Dogma in Scientific Research', in AC Crombie (ed), *Scientific Change* (London, Heinemann, 1963) 347–69; and more generally T Kuhn, *The Structure of Scientific Revolution* (Chicago, IL, University of Chicago Press, 1962).

[4] See, recently, the impressive collection of essays in R St. John Macdonald and D Johnston (eds), *Towards World Constitutionalism, Issues in the Legal Ordering of the World Community* (Leiden, Martinus Nijhoff, 2005).

proliferation of constitutionalism studies in international law – admittedly not an entirely new subject[5] – coincides, quite paradoxically, with an increasing number of challenges being posed to the unity of the system. It is quite interesting to note that the International Law Commission, for instance, has not decided to take up a study on constitutionalism but rather one on fragmentation and specialisation.[6]

To be fair, it should be pointed out at the outset that the debate on constitutionalism in international law has always had a distinctly European flavour.[7] US democratic constitutionalism, as aptly explained by some commentators, revolves around the 'nation's democratically self-given legal and political commitments' and is little prone to seek and find limitations to government in the sphere of international law.[8] After all, such a different sensitivity is as much a legacy of history as it is of legal culture.[9] With the notable exception of the New Haven School and its grand idea of world public order based on human dignity,[10] US scholars have contributed less to the debate on international constitutionalism than their European counterparts.

To present a cursory account of the way in which recent international legal scholarship has addressed the issue of constitutionalism is no easy task and, presumably, for the purposes of this chapter a fairly irrelevant exercise. Suffice to mention that different strands of scholarship can be traced, each of which emphasise varying aspects of what could be

---

[5] See the seminal work of A Verdross, *Die Verfassung der Völkerrechtsgemeinschaft* (Wien/Berlin, J. Springer, 1926) (on this and other aspects of Verdross's work see B Simma, 'The Contribution of Alfred Verdross to the Theory of International Law' (1995) 6 *European Journal of International Law* 33). See also G Scelle, 'Le droit constitutionnel international', in *Mélanges Carré de Malberg* (Paris, Librairie du Recueil Sirey, 1933) 501 *ff*; H. Lauterpacht, 'The Covenant as the 'Higher Law'' (1936) 16 *British Yearbook of International Law* 54; and W Friedman, *The Changing Structure of International Law* (London, Stevens & Sons, 1964) at 293 *ff*.

[6] See the Report of the Study Group of the ILC finalised by M Koskenniemi on 'Fragmentation of International Law: Difficulties Arising from the Diversification and Expansion of International Law', UN Doc A/CN.4/L.682 (2006).

[7] At the point of raising the suspicion of being a hegemonic discourse: see M Koskenniemi, 'International Law and Hegemony: a Reconfiguration' (2004) 17 *Cambridge Review of International Affairs* 202–3. On the European international law mindset see the provocative remarks made by the same author in 'International Law in Europe: Between Tradition and Renewal' (2005) 16 *European Journal of International Law* 111.

[8] J Rubenfeld, 'The Two World Orders' (2003) 27 *The Wilson Quarterly* 28.

[9] See A Bianchi 'International Law and US Courts: the Myth of Lohengrin Revisited' (2004) 15 *European Journal of International Law* 751. From a political, rather than legal and judicial, perspective the differences between Europe and the United States are evaluated by R Kagan, 'Power and Weakness' (June 2002) 113 *Policy Review* 3–28; see also by the same author, *Of Paradise and Power* (New York, Knopf, 2003).

[10] See MS McDougal, *Human Rights and World Public Order* (New Haven, CT, Yale University Press, 1980); and MS McDougal, HD Lasswell and WM Reisman, 'The World Constitutive Process of Authoritative Decision', in McDougal and Reisman (eds), *International Law Essays: a Supplement to International Law in Contemporary Perspective* (Mineola, NY, Foundation Press, 1981) 191.

roughly defined as the emergence of a constitutional order in international law. The obvious temptation for mainstream scholarship lay in looking at the UN Charter as an international constitution of sorts, either standing prominently as the only international document resembling a constitution,[11] or approaching such status although falling short of some fundamental requirements usually associated with national constitutions. Attempts to transform the Charter into a world constitution have also been made on the premise that the Charter is not a constitution at present.[12]

By and large, however, the normative, as opposed to the institutional, dimension of international constitutionalism has been emphasised. Thriving on an ever-increasing consolidation of the notion of international community and its foundational normative tenets, such as *jus cogens* and obligations *erga omnes*, numerous scholars have identified fundamental norms with the distinguishing traits of the constitutionalisation process.[13] Hierarchically ordered norms, even without the backing of adequate institutional mechanisms, could fulfil constitutional functions.[14] Although the issue of legitimacy is a cause for concern, the existence of universal values that can be enforced at international, regional and domestic law level is tantamount to a constitutional structure in which different but complementary components may be looked at as a whole.[15] Other eclectic versions have been proposed with a view to reconciling the institutional and normative elements.[16] The interaction of different layers of normative authority and levels of governance, which already present varying degrees of constitutionalisation, is advocated as

[11]   See PM Dupuy, 'The Constitutional Dimension of the Charter of the United Nations Revisited', in A von Bogdandy and R Wolfrum (eds), *Max Planck Yearbook of UN Law Vol 1* (Leiden, Martinus Nijhoff, 1997) 1; B Fassbender, 'The United Nations Charter as World Constitution' (1998) 36 *Columbia Journal of Transnational Law* 529.

[12]   EU Petersmann, 'Constitutionalism, International Law and We the people of the United Nations' in HJ Cremet *et al* (eds), *Tradition und Weltoffenheit des Rechts: Festschrift für Helmut Steinberg*, (Berlin, Springer, 2002) at 291*ff*.

[13]   See, among others, H Mosler, 'The International Society as a Legal Community' (1974) IV, 140 *Recueil des Cours* 1; C Tomuschat, 'Obligations Arising for States Without or Against their Will' (1993) IV, 241 *Recueil des Cours* 195; B Simma, 'From Bilateralism to Community Interest in International Law', (1994) VI, 250 *Recueil des Cours* 217.

[14]   See A Peters, 'Compensatory Constitutionalism: the Function and Potential of Fundamental International Norms and Structures' (2006) 19 *Leiden Journal of International Law* 579.

[15]   See E de Wet, 'The International Constitutional Order' (2006) 55 ICLQ 51, and by the same author, 'The Emergence of International and Regional Value Systems as a Manifestation of the Emerging International Constitutional Order' (2006) 19 *Leiden Journal of International Law* 611.

[16]   See J Frowein, 'Reactions by Not Directly Affected States to Breaches of Public International Law' (1994) IV, 248 *Recueil des Cours*.

the paradigm for twenty-first-century constitutionalism.[17] Integration of such constitutional elements as human rights protection into existing allegedly self-contained regimes is also perceived as a way of constitutionalising international law.[18] Imaginative models of would-be international orders continue to blossom, and never has the debate on constitutionalism been so alive.[19]

While the existence of conflicting interpretive trends makes the international community no different than any other organised society, emphasis on such contradicting visions of the same society may look, at first sight, somewhat disconcerting. Looking at the international legal order as one developing towards inchoate forms of constitutionalisation or, rather, as a system which can be broken down into countless regimes, each of which would have their own set of applicable rules and processes, may be a sign of schizophrenia.[20] At closer scrutiny, however, it cannot be by chance that the interest in constitutionalisation is revived at a time of increasing perplexity about the capacity of international law to stand on its own as a complete and autonomous system.[21] It is both an outcry of rage and an act of faith.

III. A SIMPLIFIED PARADIGM: AGGLOMERATION OF POWER AND THE QUEST FOR ITS CONTROL

Overall, the impression one is left with is that the current debate on constitutionalism in international law might lead us astray. The panoply of interpretive canons that have been used to make the current realities of

---

[17] See T Cottier and M Hertig, 'The Prospects of 21st Century Constitutionalism' in A von Bogdandy and R Wolfrum (eds), *Max Planck Yearbook of International Law Vol 7* (Leiden, Martinus Nijhoff, 2003) 261.

[18] See EU Petersmann, 'Human Rights, Constitutionalism and the World Trade Organization: Challenges for World Trade Organization Jurisprudence and Civil Society' (2006) 19 *Leiden Journal of International Law* 633.

[19] See A von Bogdandy, 'Constitutionalism in International Law: Comment on a Proposal from Germany' (2006) 47 *Harvard International Law Journal* 223, thoroughly examining the works of Tomuschat, particularly his general course at The Hague Academy, 'International Law: Ensuring the Survival of Mankind on the Eve of a New Century' (1999) 281 *Recueil des Cours* 10, and the recent book by J Habermas, *Der gespaltene Westen* [*The Divided West*] (Suhrkamp, Auflage, 2004), in which an eclectic model for world order based on a strong supranational institution, the Security Council, with extensive enforcement powers, and on a network of transnational policy-formulating and coordinating regimes is envisaged.

[20] On the limits of the constitutionalism discourse in the contemporary international community see C Walter, 'Constitutionalizing (Inter)national Governance – Possibilities for and Limits to the Development of an International Constitutional Law' (2001) 44 *German Yearbook of International Law* 170.

[21] See J Klabbers, 'Constitutionalism Lite' (2004) 1 *International Organizations Law Review* 31.

international law amenable within the boundaries of a quasi-constitutional framework is impressive. Each strand of thought may contain bits of truth. What is slightly confusing is that even the most evidently irreconcilable theories seem all to rely on plausible, if not entirely convincing, arguments. One cannot help noticing, however, that the interpretive paradigm underlying our research efforts hardly fits into any of the proposed intellectual schemes. The doctrine of separation of powers remains alien to an international legal order, in which such a distinction risks being an imperfect score for a different musical performance. To try and trace how the three functions are performed at international law may have some intellectual interest and pedagogical value but risks contributing little to the comprehension of how international law works.[22] Not too dissimilar considerations apply to the corollary of the separation of powers doctrine: checks and balances. However varied in its manifold applications at the level of municipal legal system, the doctrine of checks and balances does presuppose a higher degree of institutionalisation than international law currently has. Attempts to project long-established and well-tested domestic institutional mechanisms are doomed to create frustration, for the practical impossibility of making them fit the different realities of international law.[23]

In fact, the perspective used in this study is much narrower in scope. The remarks that follow are primarily inspired by a fairly pragmatic approach. The main issue is that the resurgence of international terrorism on a grand scale has caused, among other things, an agglomeration of power in the UN Security Council. Given the fairly tenuous textual constraints existing in the Charter it would have been difficult to prevent such an agglomeration of power. The Charter was not designed to look like a national constitution. No particular care was taken to carefully balance the powers of the different organs, let alone to introduce checks and balances. It was a multilateral treaty in which the foundations of a new international order were laid down after the horror and devastation brought about by World War Two. War had to be banned from international relations, and extensive powers were given to the organ that was to act as the watchdog for the international community: the Security Council (SC).[24] In an odd reversal of perspective and roles, the entity which

---

[22] See G Abi-Saab, 'Cours general de droit international public', (1987) VII, 207 *Recueil des Cours* 29, especially at 127–318.

[23] See, for instance, the sceptical remarks made by J Klabbers as regards the suitability and desirability of having judicial review at international law: 'Straddling Law and Politics: Judicial Review in International Law', in R St John Macdonald and D Johnston (eds), *Towards World Constitutionalism. Issues in the Legal Ordering of the World Community* (Leiden, Martinus Nijhoff, 2005) at 809ff.

[24] See the interesting essay by G Arangio-Ruiz, 'On the Security Council's "Law-Making"' (2000) 3 *Rivista di diritto internazionale* 609–725.

was meant to exercise control on (state) power has turned itself into the power to be controlled (by states and other actors).

Before taking this argument any further, an effort to demonstrate the soundness of the premise upon which this chapter hinges, namely that there has been an agglomeration of power in the SC in the aftermath of the terrorist attacks of 11 September 2001, seems to be in order.

IV. THE SECURITY COUNCIL'S PIVOTAL ROLE IN THE FIGHT AGAINST INTERNATIONAL TERRORISM

Shortly after the 11 September attacks, the SC took up a pivotal role in the fight against international terrorism. This should come as no surprise. The SC's expanded reading of the notion of 'threat to international peace and security' had already allowed for inclusion of international terrorism in the range of issues potentially triggering Chapter VII powers. Furthermore, targeted sanctions had already been used against the Taliban. In particular, by Resolution 1267 a ban on travel, an arms embargo and the freezing of the Taliban's assets worldwide had been imposed.[25] A Sanctions Committee was also established with a view to administering the list of individuals and entities against which the sanctions had to be applied. The Committee also had the task of reviewing the national reports that states were to submit pursuant to the resolution. By Resolution 1333 the freezing measures were expanded to reach out to Osama bin Laden, Al Qaeda and its affiliates.

After the Taliban were overthrown by the US-led military invasion, the SC passed Resolution 1390, which reiterated the sanctions previously enacted. Resolution 1390 does not refer to any particular state and has an open-ended character, quite unprecedented in the practice of the SC. In order to ameliorate the implementation of the relevant resolutions, the SC later imposed on states the obligation to submit a list of individuals and entities whose assets have been frozen.[26] An analytical Support and Sanctions Monitoring Team was also set up to provide technical assistance in the management of the sanctions regime.[27]

Another strand of action under Chapter VII was undertaken by the SC by way of Resolution 1373. As is well known, Resolution 1373 lays down a series of general obligations that states must fulfil. These obligations range from the prevention and repression of the financing of terrorism

---

[25] These measures were regularly renewed (see SC Res 1333 (2000), para 23; SC Res 1390 (2002), para 3; SC Res 1455 (2003), para 2; SC Res 1526 (2004), para 3; SC Res 1617 (2005), para 21).

[26] SC Res 1455 (2003), para 6.

[27] The mandate of the Monitoring Team has been recently extended by Resolution 1735 (see § 32 of the Resolution and Annex II attached thereto).

and the prevention and criminalisation of acts of terrorism in domestic legal orders to international cooperation in judicial matters. Unlike previous resolutions, this resolution has a general scope and is not connected to any specific situation. Furthermore, the obligations therein contained have the generality and abstract character that statutory law usually presents in a domestic law setting. This is why many commentators have characterised Resolution 1373 as an instance of general law-making by the SC.[28]

The implementation of Resolution 1373 largely relies on UN member states. The SC, however, created a monitoring body, the Counter-terrorism Committee (CTC) to supervise the implementation process by the member states and to enhance their capacity to effectively fight international terrorism. The difficulties encountered by the CTC in discharging its mandate caused the SC to pass Resolution 1535, by which a CTC Executive Directorate was created, with a view to improving the capacity of the CTC to continue monitoring the implementation of Resolution 1373 and to assisting states in their capacity-building efforts.

If one is ready to include in the category of relevant SC measures those that do not appear to have been adopted under Chapter VII, mention should also be made of Resolution 1624. In Resolution 1624 states are called upon 'to prohibit by law incitement to commit a terrorist act or acts', 'to prevent such conduct' and to deny safe haven to any person with respect to whom there is credible and reliable information giving serious reasons for considering that they have been guilty of such conduct. The rather indeterminate character of the proscribed conduct and the broad scope of the prohibitions laid down in the resolution are a cause for concern. All the more so, if one considers the fairly ambiguous nature of Resolution 1624. Despite the absence of any reference to Chapter VII and the use of a verbal mode which is not the one used for binding decisions,[29] to have directed states to report on the implementation of the resolution to the CTC and to have directed the CTC to include

[28] See P Szasz, 'The Security Council Starts Legislating' (2002) 96 *American Journal of International Law* 901–5. See also PM Dupuy: 'un cas très exceptionnel de législation unilatérale internationale à portée immédiatement obligatoire pour tous les Etats membres de l'ONU': 'La communauté internationale et le terrorisme', in Société Française de Droit International, *New Threats to International Peace and Security*, Journée franco-allemande, (Paris, Pedone, 2004) at 36.

[29] As regards the determination of the binding nature of the SC's resolutions some caution seems to be required. See, for instance, what the ICJ held in the *Namibia* case: 'The language of a resolution of the Security Council should be carefully analysed before a conclusion can be made as to its binding effect. In view of the nature of the powers under Article 25, the question whether they have been in fact exercised is to be determined in each case, having regard to the terms of the resolution to be interpreted, the discussions leading to it, the Charter provisions invoked and, in general, all circumstances that might assist in determining the legal consequences of the resolution of the Security Council' (*Legal Consequences for States of the Continued Presence of South Africa in Namibia (South West Africa)*

in its dialogue with member states their efforts to implement this resolution carries with it some ambiguity and risks blurring the line between mandatory and non-mandatory measures.[30] Be that as it may, it is beyond controversy that the SC's pivotal role in the fight against international terrorism makes it look as if it were acting in a government-like fashion.

V. THE NOVELTY OF THE APPROACH

To assess the extent to which the above-mentioned activities of the SC can be characterised as novel is open to some controversy. Surely the inclusion of international terrorism within the notion of 'threat to the peace' is the result of the expanded interpretation of the latter fostered by the practice of the SC in the 1990s. A few inconsistencies notwithstanding, the SC extended the notion of 'threat', originally limited to situations involving the threat of use of military violence, to cover fairly heterogeneous grounds such as the safe delivery of humanitarian aid and the prevention of massive flows of refugees.[31] Such broad interpretation can hardly be contested, given the wide measure of discretion enjoyed by the SC under Article 39 of the Charter. It is of some significance that not even after the Lockerbie bombing, when the SC characterised as a threat to the peace the refusal by Libya to surrender for prosecution two of its nationals – arguably the boldest qualification of all by the SC of a situation amounting to a threat to the peace – states did not voice strong objections.[32] The International Court of Justice (ICJ) for its part sanctioned the relevant resolution in the name of the parallelism of power doctrine and confirmed its previous practice of non-interference with the way in which the SC had used its discretionary power.[33]

---

notwithstanding Security Council Resolution 276 (1970), ICJ Reports (1971) 16, at 53, para 114). By applying this test the Court concluded that the decisions made by the SC in paras 2 and 5 of Resolution 276 (1970) which begin respectively with 'Declares ...' and 'Calls upon all States ...' were of a legally binding nature (*ibid* at 53, para 115).

[30] See the interesting declaration made by the representative of South Africa at the occasion of the adoption by consensus of GA Res 60/288 on 'The United Nations Global Counter-Terrorism Strategy'; also, para 4 of s 1 of the Plan of Action on terror incitement referred to 'our obligations under international law to prohibit by law incitement to commit a terrorist act or acts and prevent such conduct'. Such an international law obligation, if it existed, did not arise from SC Resolution 1624 (2005), which was non-binding. (see UN Doc GA/10488).

[31] Somalia (SC Res 733 (1992)) and Haiti (SC Res 841 (1993)) are the outstanding examples.

[32] See SC Res 748 (1992) adopting sanctions against Libya for its non-compliance with SC Res 731 (1992). Resolution 748 was adopted by 10 votes to none, with 5 abstentions (Cape Verde, China, India, Morocco and Zimbabwe).

[33] See, however, the dissenting opinion of Judge Gros in the advisory opinion on the *Legal Consequences for States of the Continued Presence of South Africa in Namibia (South West*

What appears to be new is that, after 11 September 2001, the SC started characterising any act of international terrorism as a 'threat to international peace and security', a qualification that has since been reiterated after the occurrence of every single attack.[34] This is a marked departure from previous practice, when the SC had considered as a threat the attitude of particular countries vis-à-vis terrorist groups or activities.[35] The post-11 September 2001 practice clearly purports that international terrorism as such belongs to the category of 'threats to international peace and security', which may trigger Chapter VII powers.

The combination of targeted sanctions addressed to private individuals and entities and the imposition of general obligations on states represents the normative strategy pursued by the SC in fighting against international terrorism. If the enactment of targeted sanctions is not exactly new, as precedents can be traced to the practice of the SC in the 1990s,[36] the modalities of their implementation as well as their administration by the relevant Sanctions Committee have turned out to be far more challenging than past experiences. It suffices to mention the difficulties of administering the 'blacklist' to realise what sort of challenges the Sanctions Committee is exposed to. On the one hand, inclusion on the list is still the object of much controversy, given the enduring lack of transparency of the process as well as the absence of any procedural guarantee for the person or entity to be listed.[37] On the other, the de-listing procedure remains firmly under the grasp of states, with individuals being at their mercy and having no directly enforceable means of redress.[38] The fact that the

---

Africa) notwithstanding Security Council Resolution 276 (1970): '[T]hat is another attempt to modify the principles of the Charter as regards the powers vested by States in the organs they instituted. To assert that a matter may have a distant repercussion on the maintenance of peace is not enough to turn the Security Council into a world government', *ICJ Reports* (1971) 323, at 340, para 34. See also the dissenting opinion of Judge Sir Gerald Fitzmaurice in the same case: 'limitations on the powers of the Security Council are necessary because of the all too great ease with which any acutely controversial international situation can be represented as involving a latent threat to peace and security, even where it is really too remote genuinely to constitute one. Without these limitations, the functions of the Security Council could be used for purposes never originally intended' (*ibid* at 294, para 116).

[34]   See SC Res 1438 (2002) concerning the bomb attacks in Bali on 12 October 2002; SC Res 1440 (2002) concerning the taking of hostages in Moscow on 23 October 2002; SC Res 1530 (2004) concerning the bomb attacks in Madrid on 11 March 2004; SC Res 1611 (2005) concerning the terrorist attacks in London on 7 July 2005.

[35]   See SC Res 731 (1992), SC Res 1054 (1996), SC Res 1267 (1999).

[36]   See the sanctions enacted against the members of UNITA: SC Res 1127 (1997) and SC Res 1173 and 1176 (1998).

[37]   Guidelines of the Committee for the Conduct of its work (adopted on 7 November 2002, as amended on 10 April 2003 and revised on 21 December 2005).

[38]   *Ibid.*

measures must be enforced at the domestic law level creates an additional hurdle, given the different ways in which the list is incorporated into municipal legal systems and the varying status it is accorded under domestic law.[39]

Different considerations apply to Resolution 1373, undoubtedly a normative tool of a novel character. If one takes the main elements of the definition of legislative acts given by E Yemin, that is that they be 'unilateral in form, that they create or modify some element of a legal norm, and the legal norm in question is general in nature, that is directed to indeterminate addressees and capable of repeated application in time',[40] it would be difficult indeed not to characterise Resolution 1373 as a piece of legislation. The need to incorporate several provisions taken by the UN Convention on the financing of terrorism with the purpose of making them generally obligatory in spite of their original conventional nature, further attests to the willingness by the SC of acting in a general law-making capacity.

Yet another distinct feature of SC anti-terror measures is that they do not seem to have been inspired by the need to face a contingency or specific situation. Hence, the temporary character that should characterise the SC's measures – traditionally geared towards preventing situations or restoring a state of normalcy – is simply not there. Anti-terror measures have been taken for an indefinite period of time and, given that they need be implemented into domestic legal systems, they will not easily be removed. Once again, the original role of the SC as peace enforcer using police powers in specific situations stands in sharp contrast with the function taken up lately in the context of the fight against international terrorism, namely that of a general law-maker, adjudicator and enforcer in respect of a situation which could be aptly characterised as an indeterminate threat of indefinite duration.[41]

VI. ... AND ITS PRACTICAL IMPLICATIONS

The practical implications of the approach used by the SC in fighting international terrorism are far from negligible. In the first place the issue of whether the SC can act as law-maker comes to the fore. To what extent may an organ which was originally conceived as the 'peace enforcer' act

[39] See A Bianchi, 'Security Council's Anti-terror Resolutions and their Implementation by Member States: an Overview' (2006) 4 *Journal of International Criminal Justice* 1044–73.

[40] E Yemin, *Legislative Powers in the United Nations and Specialized Agencies*, (Leiden, Sijthoff, 1969) at 6.

[41] See A Bianchi, 'Assessing the Effectiveness of the UN SC's Anti-terrorism Measures: the Quest for Legitimacy and Cohesion' (2006) 17 *European Journal of International Law* 881–919.

by way of general legislation? As is known, the SC enjoys a wide measure of discretion under Chapter VII with regards both to the determination of the existence of one of the situations that may trigger its powers and to the choice of the measures envisaged in the Chapter. In fact, despite scholarly efforts to demonstrate the contrary, the textual constraints imposed by the Charter are not strict. The drafting of the Charter was marked by 'the predominance of the political over the legal approach'[42] and to constrain the SC within legalistic constructions may well lead to 'claims of illegality which simply do not square with reality'.[43] The ultimate test of the legitimacy of the SC's action remains the level of acceptance by UN member states.

It is an irony of sorts that the SC has taken on itself the task of discharging legislative functions. The uneven representation of the international community within the SC, which goes hand in hand with the flagrant discrimination between the five permanent members enjoying a veto power and the other members, the lack of transparency of its procedures and, most of all, the absence of a legal culture within it, makes the SC particularly unsuitable for the job.[44] However, it would be unfair to look at the attempt by the SC to impose on the UN member states obligations of a general character as a whim or, even worse, as an act of arbitrariness prompted by the will of the prevailing political forces. At closer scrutiny, the exercise of the powers enjoyed by the SC under Chapter VII has come in handy to react to a situation largely perceived as one requiring a timely normative response.

It has to be acknowledged that international law is not particularly well equipped to produce general law in a short timespan.[45] The only two law-making mechanisms apt to produce general law are multilateral treaties and custom. The former requires a long and cumbersome procedure to be adopted, particularly in a community of nearly 200 states. Moreover, multilateral treaty negotiations in such an enlarged community are likely to produce outcomes which are negatively affected by package deals and compromise on important issues. The ensuing process of national ratification is also time consuming, and the overall effectiveness of the legal regime on the global scale will inevitably depend on the

---

[42] H Kelsen, *The Law of the United Nations. A Critical Analysis of Its Fundamental Problems* (New Jersey, The Lawbook Exchange, Second Reprinting, 2001) at 735.

[43] M Wood, 'Comment on Erika de Wet's Contribution "The Security Council as a Law Maker: The Adoption of (Quasi)-Judicial Decisions"' in R Wolfrum and V Röben (eds), *Developments of International Law in Treaty Making* (Berlin, Springer, 2005) 227–35 at 228.

[44] M Koskenniemi, 'The Police in the Temple. Order, Justice and the UN: A Dialectical View', (1995) 6 *European Journal of International Law* 1–25 at 3.

[45] See my considerations in 'Enforcing International Law Norms against Terrorism: Achievements and Prospects' in A Bianchi (ed), *Enforcing International Law Norms against Terrorism* (Oxford/Portland, OR, Hart Publishing, 2004), 491–534 at 516–17.

number of parties to the treaty, let alone the number and scope of reservations attached to it. By the same token, the development of customary law – technically the only universally accepted means to produce general law – is an even lengthier process, given the need to establish generality of practice and *opinio juris*. In addition to that, customary law rules are often characterised by general normative standards, hardly apt to provide effective regulation in areas where precise normative standards are required.

This is why it should not come as a surprise that the SC has taken advantage of its powers under Chapter VII to promptly produce general law to face a situation, such as the threat to international peace and security represented by international terrorism, perceived by large sectors of the international community as a global threat requiring a prompt normative response. Abstract considerations and legalistic preoccupations about the proper role of the SC have therefore yielded to the prevailing conviction that action by the SC was expedient to effectively counter the threat of international terrorism.

Yet another practical implication of the measures taken by the SC in the context of the fight against international terrorism is their encroachment on human rights.[46] Quite paradoxically, the use of targeted sanctions by the SC, which had been hailed by many, after the fairly disastrous experience with the Iraqi sanctions,[47] as a way to avoid the accusation of violating the fundamental human rights of the civilian population, has turned out to be quite controversial from the standpoint of human rights protection. The listing and de-listing of individuals onto and off the blacklist pose problems in terms of the right to fair trial and the right to an effective remedy. If one were to characterise the inclusion of an individual on the blacklist and the ensuing sanctions to which he or she is subjected as a criminal charge – as it would be perfectly plausible to do[48] – such fundamental guarantees of fair trial as the right to be

---

[46] See Bianchi, n 39 above.

[47] On the effects of the Iraqi sanctions regime see the Symposium on: 'The Impact on International Law of a Decade of Sanctions Against Iraq', with contributions by different authors, published in (2002) 13 *European Journal of International Law* 1–321.

[48] Quite understandably, the 1526 Monitoring Team resists the view that the list be considered a criminal list (see *Third Report of the Analytical Support and Sanctions Monitoring Team appointed pursuant to resolution 1526 (2004), concerning Al-Qaida and the Taliban and associated individuals and entities*, UN Doc S/2005/572, paras 39–43). However, the ECHR has held that a criminal charge 'may in some instances take the form of other measures which carry the implication of such an allegation and which likewise substantially affect the situation of the suspect' (*Foti and others v Italy*, ECHR (1982), Series A, No 56, para 52). The Court takes 'criminal charge' *stricto sensu* to mean 'the official notification given to an individual by the competent authority of an allegation that he has committed a criminal offence' (*Ibid.* See also *Eckle v Allemagne*, ECHR (1982), Series A, No 51, para 73).

presumed innocent,[49] the right to be judged by an impartial tribunal after a 'fair and public hearing' would be applicable.[50] It is hardly necessary to underscore that the inclusion of a person on the list outside any judicial proceedings against him or her in which charges are discussed is a flagrant violation of the presumption of innocence, let alone the temerity of maintaining that the SC is an impartial tribunal. The lack of transparency of the procedure leading to the inclusion of the individual on the blacklist equally falls short of the requirements of a 'fair and public hearing' inherent in the notion of fair trial.

Other human rights are affected by the SC's measures, including the right to property, the exercise of which is undoubtedly hampered, if not prejudiced, by asset-freezing measures. Even such a fundamental principle as *nullum crimen, nulla poena sine lege* could be called into question, if one looks at the way in which the SC has required states to bring to justice any person who 'attempts to participate in the financing, planning, preparation or commission of terrorist acts'. It is self-evident that the rather indeterminate contours of the notion 'attempt to participate' hardly meet the requirements of precision and legal certainty which lie at the core of the principle of legality.[51] Along similar lines, the implementation by member states of the general obligations laid down in Resolution 1373 has given rise to an expansion of the reach of national criminal law in the name of the fight against terrorism, which may come to clash with internationally accepted human rights standards.[52] International human rights monitoring bodies have already expressed their concern

[49] It is worth remembering that the principle of presumption of innocence must be applied not only by the judiciary, but also by any other public authorities: see General Comment No 13 of the Human Rights Committee, HRI\GEN\1\Rev.1 (1994), para 7. See also, in the context of the ECHR, *Allenet de Ribemont v France*, ECHR (1995) Series A, No 308, para 36.

[50] For the test of impartiality as applied by the ECtHR see *De Cubber v Belgique*, ECHR (1984) Series A, No 86, para 24; *Hauschildt v Danemark*, ECHR (1989) Series A, No 154, para 46.

[51] The principle, characterised by the ECtHR as 'an essential element of the rule of law' and considered as a non-derogable right under all human rights treaties derogation clauses, is meant 'to provide effective safeguards against arbitrary prosecution, conviction and punishment' (see *SW v UK*, ECHR (1995), Series A, No 335-B, para 34). The most obvious implication of the principle is that 'an offence must be clearly defined in law' (see *Kokkinakis v Greece*, ECHR (1993), Series A, No 260-A, para 52). As far as the ICCPR is concerned see M Nowak, *UN Covenant on Civil and Political Rights. CCRP Commentary*, 2nd edn (Kehl, NP Engel, 2005) 360: '[Article 15] gives rise not only to the prohibition of retroactive criminal laws in the narrow sense but also to a general duty on States parties to define precisely by law all *criminal offences* in the interest of *legal certainty* and to preclude the application of criminal laws from being extended by *analogy*': 'Accord Report' of the Special Rapporteur on the Promotion and Protection of Human Rights and Fundamental Freedoms While Countering Terrorism, E/CN.4/2006/98, para 46).

[52] See the 'Accord Report' of the Special Rapporteur, n 51 above, para 47.

about the risk of treating ordinary crimes as terrorist offences, thus subjecting them to counterterrorism exceptions and derogations.

VII. INTERNATIONAL JUDICIAL SCRUTINY AND ITS LIMITS

The issue of whether judicial scrutiny can be exercised over SC resolutions has traditionally been addressed with reference to the ICJ, the main judicial organ of the UN. As is well known, no express power of judicial review is vested in the ICJ by the UN Charter. The institutional arrangement provided by the Charter was one in which the main organs could freely act within the boundaries of the powers attributed to them by the Charter. The system had not been conceived by the drafters in constitutional terms, and no coordination mechanism (let alone checks and balances), with the exception of Article 12, was included in the text. Nevertheless, this has not prevented the Court from exercising, in an incidental fashion, a sort of judicial scrutiny over the acts of other UN organs. The exercise of such judicial control has most of the time been surreptitiously denied by the Court, which, despite its stated intentions, eventually ended up upholding General Assembly (GA) or SC resolutions.

It is not unprecedented, however, that the task of exercising judicial scrutiny over the acts of the SC is exercised by other international tribunals. One may remember that the two *ad hoc* criminal tribunals on former Yugoslavia and Rwanda dealt with the issue of the legitimacy of their creation by way of SC resolutions in their early case-law. In the *Tadic* and *Kanyabashi* cases,[53] the two *ad hoc* tribunals eventually upheld the validity/legitimacy of the resolutions creating them, by resorting to Article 41 of the Charter, which empowers the SC to take measures to restore international peace and security.[54] One may agree or not agree with the outcome, but surely these were instances in which judicial review was exercised, albeit in a somewhat incestuous way, over SC resolutions by international tribunals other than the ICJ.

Recently, the Court of First Instance of the European Communities (CFI) has passed judgment on a number of cases, which potentially implied an indirect exercise of judicial control over SC anti-terror resolutions. In the cases of *Kadi* and *Yusuf* the CFI broached the issue for the first time in the context of an action for the annulment of the EC Regulations imposing financial sanctions against the Taliban, Osama bin

---

[53] *The Prosecutor v Dusco Tadic*, ICTY Appeals Chamber Decision of 2 October 1995 on the Defence Motion for Interlocutory Appeal on Jurisdiction, IT-94-I-AR 72; *The Prosecutor v Joseph Kanyabashi*, ICTR Trial Chamber Decision of 18 June 1997 on the Defence Motion on Jurisdiction, Case No ICTR -96–15-T.

[54] *The Prosecutor v Dusco Tadic*, para 35; *The Prosecutor v Joseph Kanyabashi*, para 27.

Laden and the Al Qaeda network.[55] The Court expounded the reasons why in principle it would not be allowed to exercise judicial review over SC resolutions, as a matter of both international and community law.[56] However, the Court looked at itself as being

> empowered to check, indirectly, the lawfulness of the resolutions of the Security Council in question with regard to *jus cogens*, understood as a body of higher rules of public international law binding on all subjects of international law, including the bodies of the Untied Nations, and from which no derogation is possible.[57]

The Court went on to consider whether the alleged breach of such fundamental rights as the right to make use of one's property, the right to a fair hearing and the right to an effective judicial remedy amounted to a violation of *jus cogens*. In a somewhat erratic and not particularly persuasive reasoning, the Court eventually found that no violation of any of the above norms had occurred, and on those grounds it rejected the claims of the applicants. As regards the right to property, the CFI held that only such arbitrary deprivations of property as confiscatory measures could have been regarded as contrary to *jus cogens*.[58] Furthermore the right to be heard, considered by the Court as the only aspect of the right to fair trial actually invoked by the applicants, had not been violated. In the view of the Court, the underlying circumstances of the case would not warrant

> the facts and evidence adduced against them [the applicants] to be communicated to them, once the Security Council or its Sanctions Committee is of the view that there are grounds concerning the international community's security that militate against it.[59]

Finally the lack of a judicial remedy and the impossibility for the applicants to have their case heard in court could not 'outweigh the essential public interest in the maintenance of international peace and security'.[60] All the more so, given that the Sanctions Committee has in any event provided for a review mechanism of the measures.

---

[55]   *Yassin Abdullah Kadi v Council of the European Union and Commission of the European Communities*, Case T-315/01, Judgment of the Court of First Instance, 21 September 2005, paras 209–31; *Ahmed Ali Yusuf and Al Barakaat International Foundation v Council of the European Union and Commission of the European Communities*, Case T-306/01, Judgment of the Court of First Instance, 21 September 2005, paras 260–82.

[56]   *Yassin Abdullah Kadi*, para 225; *Ahmed Ali Yusuf*, para 276.

[57]   *Yassin Abdullah Kadi*, para 226; *Ahmed Ali Yusuf*, para 277.

[58]   *Yassin Abdullah Kadi*, para 242; *Ahmed Ali Yusuf*, para 293.

[59]   *Yassin Abdullah Kadi*, para 274; *Ahmed Ali Yusuf*, para 320.

[60]   *Yassin Abdullah Kadi*, para 289; *Ahmed Ali Yusuf*, para 344.

The CFI reiterated its approach in two later cases: *Ayadi* and *Hassan*.[61] After having confirmed the assessment previously made on the entitlement to review indirectly the lawfulness of SC measures against the background of peremptory norms, the CFI, prompted by the applicants' more specific arguments on the ineffective character of the review machinery (that is, the de-listing procedure) set up by the SC, held that EU member states have an obligation to initiate the review procedure before the SC. In particular, EU member states must act 'promptly to ensure that such persons' cases are presented without delay and fairly and impartially to the [Sanctions] Committee'.[62] If the state does not fulfil this obligation, the individual concerned should be allowed to bring an action for judicial review before national courts against the refusal by the competent national authority to submit their case to the Sanctions Committee for re-examination. The somewhat shaky foundation for the obligation to exercise diplomatic protection on behalf of the listed individual by the state of nationality or residence, traced by the Court to Article 6 of the EU Treaty,[63] hardly allowed the Court to divert attention from the alleged violation by the EC organs, and indirectly, by the SC of the fundamental rights of the applicants. Be that as it may, to have inferred from Article 6 of the EU Treaty an obligation to exercise diplomatic protection attests to a certain *malaise* of the Court vis-à-vis the mechanical implementation of SC's anti-terror measures, particularly when their effects can be detrimental to human rights.

Although the legal analysis carried out by the CFI is far from being persuasive, it does remain significant that an international tribunal actually exercised judicial scrutiny of SC resolutions against the background of peremptory norms. Even intuitively, reference to rules of *jus cogens* as some sort of international public order is vaguely reminiscent of judicial review. At the very least, it represents an instance of judicial control on the agglomeration of power in the light of fundamental community values. Presumably, national courts would be more reluctant to follow suit. In the *Al Jeddah* case, the English Court of Appeal showed a great deal of caution in this respect, and underscored the impropriety for a national court to review SC resolutions. Ironically, the Court, while denying altogether that it was empowered to assess the lawfulness of SC resolutions, did not abstain from judgment and indirectly upheld the validity of Resolution 1546, applying it to the facts of the case.[64]

---

[61] *Chafiq Ayadi v Council of the European Union* (Judgment of the Court of First Instance of 12 July 2006), para 149; and *Faraj Hassan v Council of the European Union and Commission of the European Communities* (Judgment of the Court of First Instance of 12 July 2006), para 119.
[62] *Chafiq Ayadi*, para 149, and *Faraj Hassan*, para 119.
[63] *Chafiq Ayadi*, para 146, and *Faraj Hassan*, para 116.
[64] *R (on the application of Al-Jeddah) v Secretary of State for Defence*, Court of Appeal, Civil Division, Judgment of 29 March 2006.

In a highly decentralised system such as that of international law, forms of judicial control of the kind examined above remain sporadic and their impact is limited on specific cases. If to frame the above developments in terms of constitutionalism may appear utopian for the time being, their relevance ought not to be underestimated. Regardless of the cultural attitudes taken by courts and taking into account the greater difficulties that municipal courts may face in this respect, nothing prevents tribunals, at both international and national level, from exercising judicial scrutiny over SC resolutions in an incidental way. However episodic and inorganic such judicial interventions may be, their impact on perceptions of legitimacy of SC resolutions might be greater than expected. Irrespective of any institutionalised form of judicial review, such an informal judicial communicative process may lead to an evaluation of the normative action of the SC under the traditional dichotomy legal/illegal, which the SC as political organ may not ignore.[65]

VIII. OTHER FORMS OF CONTROL AT THE INTERFACE OF LAW AND POLITICS

It may be apt to recall that the Appeals Chamber of the International Criminal Tribunal for the former Yugoslavia (ICTY), while discussing the legality of its own creation by the SC, noted in passing that 'the legislative, executive and judicial division of powers which is largely followed in most municipal legal systems does not apply to the international setting nor, more specifically, to the setting of an international organisation such as the United Nations'.[66] The fundamental tenets of this proposition may appear to many as a truism. The UN Charter laid down an institutional design which provided for separation of functions rather than powers. Each and every organ of the organisation was supposed to operate independently from the other organs, and they all enjoyed a wide measure of discretion as regards the determination of their own competence. Even the ICJ, by developing the parallelism of powers and functions doctrine subscribed to this view and carefully avoided using language reminiscent of constitutional analysis in its case-law.[67] Arguably, for the first time in the recent Advisory Opinion on the Israeli wall,

---

[65] A Bianchi, 'Globalization of Human Rights: the Role of Non-State Actors', in G Teubner (ed), *Global Law without a State* (Aldershot, Dartmouth, 1997) 179–212, at 192 *ff*.

[66] *Prosecutor v Dusko Tadic a/k/a 'Dule'*, ICTY, Decision of the Appeals Chamber on the Defence Motion for Interlocutory Appeal on Jurisdiction, 2 October 1995, para 43.

[67] *United States Diplomatic and Consular Staff in Tehran* (United States/Iran), ICJ Reports (1980), 3 at 21–2 (para 40); *Military and Paramilitary Activities in and against Nicaragua*, ICJ Reports (1984) 392, at 434–5 (para 95); *Case Concerning Application of the Convention on the Prevention and Punishment of the Crime of Genocide (Bosnia and Herzegovina v Yugoslavia (Serbia and Montenegro))*, ICJ Reports (1993), 3, at 18–19 (para 33).

the Court seemed to be ready and willing to tamper with this long-established institutional balance, by providing a fairly expansive reading of Article 12 of the Charter.[68] Admittedly, the Court's considerations were too ambiguous to be taken as an instance of judicial activism likely to have altered once and for all the interpretation of Article 12. Be that as it may, although the system does not lend itself to be interpreted against the background of the traditional separation of powers and checks and balances doctrines, mutual interference among the main organs is far from being a mere hypothetical case.

Evidence of this can be traced to the complex dynamics between the SC and the GA. For instance, to look at the SC's anti-terror policy and the exercise of legislative powers associated with it in isolation from the attitude of the GA would be simplistic indeed. If at the time of adoption of Resolution 1373 no major dissent was voiced internationally, this is because the GA had largely approved of the measures that the SC would take. This is hardly surprising as the political backing of the GA is essential to provide the legitimacy, in terms of political representation, that the SC does not possess. By the same token, the GA has probably greatly contributed to spurring the SC on, shifting its attitude in terms of respect for human rights. In a series of resolutions adopted since 2003,[69] the GA has stressed the need to respect human rights and fundamental freedoms recognised in the Universal Declaration of Human Rights while countering terrorism. In its latest resolution the GA endorsed the statement made in the Report of the Secretary-General (SG) that states must 'work to uphold and protect the dignity of individuals and their fundamental freedoms'.[70] The action undertaken in concert with the SG led to the adoption of the United Nations Global Counter-terrorism Strategy, adopted by consensus by the GA on 20 September 2006.[71] The attached Plan of Action emphasises that human rights protection and counterterrorism measures 'are not conflicting goals, but complementary and mutually reinforcing', reaffirming the need that measures taken by states in the context of the fight against terrorism must comply with their human rights obligations. The resolutions of the defunct Commission of Human Rights as well as the works undertaken in the context of special procedures by different rapporteurs, including the Special Rapporteur on

---

[68]   *Legal Consequences of the Construction of a Wall in the Occupied Palestinian Territory*, ICJ Reports (2004) 136, at 149–50, paras 27–8. See on this point, A Bianchi, 'Dismantling the Wall: the ICJ's Advisory Opinion and Its Likely Impact on International Law' (2004) 47 *German Yearbook of International Law* 343–91 at 363*ff.*

[69]   See A/RES/57/219, A/RES/58/187, A/RES/59/191, A/RES/60/158.

[70]   See A/RES/60/168, para 7.

[71]   See A/RES/60/288.

the promotion and protection of human rights while countering terrorism, are also noteworthy in terms of showing the mobilisation of UN monitoring bodies.[72]

The response of the GA and other subsidiary UN organs to human rights protection concerns reflects a much wider preoccupation that the fight against terrorism may justify resorting to policies and practices which are detrimental to human rights. Such concerns have been expressed in international fora as well as in non-governmental ones. For instance, within the Council of Europe, since as early as 2002, after the enactment of the Guidelines of the Committee of Ministers of the Council of Europe on human rights and the fight against terrorism,[73] constant attention has been paid to specific aspects of counterterrorism policies. Recently an independent report on due process and the SC's anti-terror measures has been produced under the auspices of the Council of Europe, which draws attention to several shortcomings of the SC's anti-terror measures against the background of European Convention standards.[74] Countless examples can be given of non-governmental organisations (NGOs) voicing concern about counterterrorism measures and their impact on human rights. It suffices, by way of example, to mention the activities of the International Commission of Jurists, which has formed an Eminent Jurists Panel whose mandate is to

> examine the compatibility of laws, policies and practices, which are justified expressly or implicitly as necessary to counter terrorism, with international human rights law and, where applicable, with international humanitarian law.[75]

Academic circles and professional associations have also contributed to drawing attention to the detrimental effects of anti-terror policies on human rights.[76] The interaction of governmental as well as non-governmental actors contributes to creating a communicative process at the trans-national level whereby the perception of legitimacy of anti-terror policies and practices is assessed either in legal terms or, often, on

---

[72]   This practice is carefully assessed in the Report of the Secretary-General on 'Protecting human rights and fundamental freedoms while countering terrorism' (A/61/353), submitted to the GA pursuant to Resolution 60/158.

[73]   See <CM/Del/Dec(2002)804/4.3/appendix3E / 11 July 2002>.

[74]   See 'The European Convention on Human Rights, Due Process and United Nations Security Council Counter-Terrorism Sanctions', Report prepared by Professor Iain Cameron (Council of Europe, 2006).

[75]   On the mandate and activities of the Eminent Jurists Panel consult the ICJ website at <http://ejp.icj.org/>.

[76]   See the recently adopted 'Ottawa Principles on Anti-terrorism and Human Rights', available at <http://www.rightsandantiterrorism.ca>.

the basis of 'some basic understanding of certain human values the respect of which is perceived to be fundamental'.[77]

Finally, one may note that some built-in mechanisms exist within the SC which could be regarded as a form of control. Ultimately, the whole SC decision-making process relies on the agreement of its members, with the well-known distinctions that the veto power entails. It is noteworthy that, at the time of the adoption of Resolution 1540 on the acquisition of weapons of mass destruction by non-state actors,[78] many states qualified their consent. Despite the fact that the resolution was adopted by consensus, several states, including one permanent member, made it clear that their acceptance of yet another law-making resolution was not an instance of acquiescence in the recent practice of the SC acting as law-maker. They expressly stated that their acceptance depended on the extant gaps of international regulation and the need for a prompt normative response to the clear and present danger of weapons of mass destruction being acquired by non-state actors.[79] Self-limitation by the SC itself may turn out to be an effective instrument of control, albeit heavily dependent on political contingencies.

IX. THE SHIFT OF ATTITUDE BY THE SECURITY COUNCIL

It is a fair speculation to make that the normative response adopted by the SC in the aftermath of 11 September 2001 was prompted by such compelling security concerns that its side-effects, particularly in terms of human rights protection, were hardly a consideration. The urge to counter the terrorist threat by appropriate preventative and repressive measures did not allow pondering the extent to which the measures allegedly taken to defend society from evil could themselves have detrimental effects on the members of the society they were meant to protect. It might be worth recalling that this attitude was universally shared at the time and that no particular objection was voiced by the UN member states. Over time, however, both states and the UN realised that the fight against international terrorism could not be pursued to the

---

[77] Bianchi, n 65 above at 190.

[78] See SC Res 1540 (2004).

[79] See the statement of the representative of Algeria: 'In the absence of binding international standards, and because of the seriousness and the urgent nature of the threat, the response to it needs to be articulated and formulated by the Security Council': S/PV 4950 at 5. See also S/PV 4956, particularly the statements of France (at 2), Pakistan (at 3) and Spain (at 8).

detriment of human rights. As early as October 2002 the Secretary-General warned that 'to pursue security at the expense of human rights is short-sighted, self-contradictory and, in the long run, self-defeating'.[80]

The pressure mounting from the different components of the international societal body led the SC to eventually stress the obligation that states

> ensure that any measure taken to combat terrorism comply with all their obligations under international law, and should adopt such measures in accordance with international law, in particular international human rights, refugee and humanitarian law.

What had previously found its place in a Declaration annexed to Resolution 1456 and in the preamble of Resolution 1566 was eventually sanctioned in the *dispositif* of Resolution 1624.[81] Resolution 1624 represents a benchmark insofar as the SC directed the CTC to include in its dialogue with the member states their efforts to implement the resolution, which expressly provides for the duty to respect human rights, refugee and humanitarian law while implementing SC measures.[82] Pursuant to this directive the SC has recently taken the commitment to incorporate human rights considerations into its communication strategies.[83] This is indeed a remarkable departure from the early practice of the CTC, whose first Chairman had publicly and quite bluntly declared that monitoring the implementation of SC measures against the background of international human rights treaties was outside the scope of the CTC.[84]

It is obviously quite difficult to establish a causal link between the development of judicial and political controls sketched out above and the shift in the attitude of the SC. Ultimately, however, it seems reasonable to assume that the SC felt compelled to adjust its counterterrorism normative strategy to an increasing pressure, coming from within the UN as

[80]   See UN Doc SG/SM/8417-SC/7523.
[81]   See para 6 of the Declaration attached to SC Res 1456 (2003), preamble of SC Res 1566 (2004) and para 4 of SC Res 1624 (2005).
[82]   SC Res 1624 (2005), para 6.
[83]   See Conclusions for policy guidance regarding human rights and the CTC, S/AC.40/2006/PG.2, 25 May 2006: 'The CTC and CTED, under direction of the Committee, should incorporate human rights into their communications strategy, as appropriate, noting the importance of States ensuring that in taking counter-terrorism measures they do so consistent with their obligations under international law, in particular human rights law, refugee law and humanitarian law, as reflected in the relevant Security Council resolutions'.
[84]   'The Counter-Terrorism Committee is mandated to monitor the implementation of resolution 1373 (2001). Monitoring performance against other international conventions, including human rights law, is outside the scope of the Counter-Terrorism Committee's mandate. But we will remain aware of the interaction with human rights concerns, and we will keep ourselves briefed as appropriate. It is, of course, open to other organizations to study States' reports and take up their content in other forums', Briefing of the first Chair of the CTC to the Security Council on 18 January 2002, S/PV.4453, at 5.

well as from outside, to subject the implementation of anti-terror measures to human rights considerations. The tension at UN headquarters in New York must have been indeed tangible and compelling for the Office of the Legal Counsel to commission a study on 'Targeted Sanctions and Due Process',[85] and for three governments to mandate a research institute to produce a report on how to strengthen targeted sanctions through fair and clear procedures, a report subsequently presented to the SC itself.[86]

In a recent speech given on behalf of the Secretary-General before the SC, the UN Legal Counsel considered at length and in considerable detail the issue of how to guarantee fundamental due process rights to individuals targeted by SC measures.[87] In particular, the suggestion was made that targeted individuals should be informed of the case against them and be heard within a reasonable time, by way of written submissions. Furthermore, an effective and impartial review mechanism should be set up and the measures regularly reviewed. The fact that the Legal Counsel addressed this issue in the broader context of how to strengthen the role of law in international affairs is evidence of the particular importance attributed to the issue of the fairness and legitimacy of SC anti-terror measures.

Eventually, the SC passed Resolution 1735, which has introduced some changes to the listing and de-listing procedures.[88] States must substantiate their case to enter an individual or corporate entity in the list by providing factual information about the reasons for listing individuals, groups, undertakings or any other entity, part of the information may even be forwarded to the individual, and the states of nationality and/or residence must be notified of the listing. If these amendments have the merit of addressing, at least partly, the concerns expressed about the lack of fairness of the sanctions regime vis-à-vis individuals and their rights, it can hardly be said that they have solved the problem. Nor has the establishment, under Resolution 1730,[89] of a 'focal point' made available to all the addressees of the sanctions regime. Any targeted individual or entity may directly petition the focal point and submit a de-listing request. The focal point is simply meant to act as a broker, redirecting individual requests to concerned governments. A consultation procedure

---

[85] See B Fassbender, 'Targeted Sanctions and Due Process', Study commissioned by the United Nations Office of Legal Affairs, 20 March 2006.

[86] See the Watson Institute's report on, 'Strengthening Targeted Sanctions through Clear and Fair Procedures' (2006), commissioned by the governments of Germany, Sweden and Switzerland, making recommendations to the SC for the improvement of targeted sanctions.

[87] See 'Strengthening international law: rule of law and maintenance of international peace and security', S/PV 5474 at 5.

[88] SC Res 1735 (2006).

[89] SC Res 1730 (2006).

among the states concerned (including the designating state) is then envisaged, with a view to determining whether the de-listing request should be recommended to the relevant Sanctions Committee. Ultimately, the procedural changes brought about by these two resolutions do not affect the nature of the process, which remains firmly in the grasp of states.

X. THE SPONTANEOUS EMERGENCE OF AN INCHOATE SYSTEM OF 'CHECKS AND BALANCES' AND ITS SIGNIFICANCE

The relativity and rather unsystematic character of the 'checks and balances' triggered by the SC's anti-terror measures attests to the existence, even in international law, of forms of control over the agglomeration of power. In this very basic connotation, the use of the expression 'checks and balances' does not seem preposterous. Perhaps it would be misleading to interpret these instances of practice as reliable evidence of a trend towards the 'constitutionalisation' of international law in the traditional domestic law patterns. It is hard to discern any structured, let alone institutionally preordained, scheme geared towards the control over power exercised in government-like fashion.

However, the spontaneous triggering of forms of control over the action of the SC is a cause for reflection. It surely attests to the limits of the functionalist doctrine within the United Nations. The Charter does not assure any degree of systematic reciprocal control in the case of one of the organs trespassing on its functions. Admittedly, this has allowed the SC to agglomerate power. The incidental interventions made by the ICJ are hardly enough to substantiate an effective mechanism of judicial review in such circumstances. Self-restraint by the SC cannot be regarded as a 'check', for it emanates from the very same organ in which power has agglomerated. More interesting is the role played by the GA, whose constant efforts to state that human rights must be protected while countering terrorism, has probably been of critical importance to induce a change in the attitude of the SC. Interestingly enough, however, the GA never indulged direct criticism of the SC, rather stressing that it is the duty of states to assure conformity of anti-terror measures with human rights standards. This can be interpreted as additional evidence that there is no institutional system of checks and balances within the UN organisation.

Most of all, however, it is of significance that the scrutiny which has been exercised over SC's anti-terror measures and their national implementation hinges primarily on the assessment of their conformity with human rights standards. Admittedly, the forms of control analysed above emerged somewhat belatedly. This can be explained on several grounds, including the post-11 September 2001 emotional shock which caused many to think that security concerns should be given absolute priority. Be that as it may, the concurrent operation of the various formal and informal checks has probably induced the SC to reconsider its overall strategy to include respect for human rights as part and parcel of its anti-terror normative policy.

Furthermore, it is quite striking that reference to human rights is often unqualified, which leaves one to wonder which particular human rights are perceived by the international community as having a fundamental character. This finding may inspire different considerations. On the one hand, respect for human rights, regardless of any further qualifications, could be seen as an essential component of the rule of law. Moreover, its invocation as an insurmountable limit to the exercise of power in international law can be taken to attest to the existence of a 'discrete public order system'.[90] The rhetorical force of the invocation performs a systemic function that is different from that of identifying which particular human rights are applicable to anti-terror measures. The latter issue can only be broached in context. Human rights violations may be considered before domestic courts or before international judicial or monitoring bodies operating on the basis of treaty law, and the applicable standards may vary to some extent.

The fairly indeterminate character of the reference to human rights would hardly be a source of concern were it not for the fact that, recently, the set of values on which the international community had previously structured itself have been increasingly called into question. In fact, the contingencies of our time and, in particular, the impact that the fight against terrorism seems to have had on the perception of the role of the law in domestic and international affairs, clearly purport that some of the values which until recently were readily identifiable as fundamental are now being challenged. The attempt by some states to redefine the notion of torture and, later, to call into question its scope of application is evidence of this attitude.[91] Along similar lines, other domains of international law, such as the international regulation of the use of force, international humanitarian law and the international law of jurisdiction –

---

[90] The expression is Ian Brownlie's: International Law at the Fiftieth Anniversary of the United Nations, 255 *Recueil des Cours* (1995) at 77. For the proposition that international law can be evaluated through the main conceptual tenets of the rule of law see G Fitzmaurice, The General Principles of International Law Considered from the Standpoint of the Rule of Law, 92 *Recueil des Cours* (1957, II).

[91] See, for instance, the Second periodic report of the United States of America to the Committee against torture of May 6, 2005 (CAT/C/48/Add.3/Rev.1), and the CAT Conclusions and Recommendations of 25 July 2006 (CAT/C/USA/CO/2).

to mention just a few – have been challenged with a view to bringing about major changes in their respective legal regimes.[92]

As regards more specifically human rights, the lack of a common understanding of which particular human rights should be protected and subject to what conditions in different circumstances, may make it difficult in the future to effectively identify which values should be given priority and be protected accordingly. The normative category of *jus cogens* is but a tool to reflect the expression of an order of values allegedly emerging from the societal body. The fact that the European CFI has used *jus cogens* as the relevant legal parameter to assess the validity of SC resolutions is highly significant. Similar considerations apply to the reference to non-derogable rights under Article 4 of the ICCPR which appears in some documents, most notably the recent resolutions of the GA.[93]

It may well be true that values in any organised society can be contradictory, which is the reason why 'the nature of governmental structure through which decisions are arrived at is critically important for the actual content of these decisions'.[94] However, in the highly decentralised international community where institutions are scant and power diffused, the risk of agglomeration of power in any given entity is a greater source of concern. The only checks and balances that are likely to be triggered are themselves not numerous and highly heterogeneous. Their aggregate efficacy depends heavily on the sharing of some fundamental values that the relevant actors are committed to foster. Western political thought, when domestic constitutionalism doctrines were developed, could rely on a set of values such as justice, liberty and equality, which, however loosely defined, provided a common ground for constitutionalism doctrines to thrive. Values may not be self-executing and need institutions to be implemented, but their existence is a prerequisite for the identity of the community. Short of that common understanding, there can be no meaningful sense of organised society, let alone one moving forward towards constitutionalisation. To what extent the reaction of the societal body to the agglomeration of power in the SC is a step in that direction may be too premature to tell, but surely to have generated a widespread moral intuition that fundamental rights should

---

[92] For a study on the impact of international terrorism on the different areas of international law see A Bianchi (ed), *Enforcing International Law Norms against Terrorism* (Oxford/Portland, OR, Hart Publishing, 2004).

[93] See, for instance, para 3 of A/RES/60158.

[94] See MCJ Vile, *Constitutionalism and the Separation of Powers*, 2nd edn (Indianapolis, Liberty Fund, 1998) 1.

be respected and to have translated it into the language of legal obligation in relevant legal instruments is a sign that the rhetorical discourse,
once duly set in place, may also have practical implications.

A final remark on the highly heterogeneous character of the spontaneous mechanisms of control which have emerged in international society
seems to be apt. In a famous piece of writing, Roberto Ago said in the
1950s that the formation of international law may occur spontaneously,
without any source or law-making process attributing the quality of law
to it.[95] The analogy is an appealing one. If it is admitted that law may
spring in spontaneous form and be regarded by the societal body as law,
why would it not be possible to conceive a system of checks and balances
that originate spontaneously without any necessary connection to an
institutional arrangement of sort? After all, what matters is that power be
controlled when it tends to aggregate and that the control be effective.
Whether it is embedded in a constitutionally posited order or manifests
itself loosely as the result of the dynamic among the different actors
operating in contemporary international society may be too abstract a
preoccupation and lead us astray from the core of the matter. Once again,
rather than characterising international society as primitive, invertebrate
or in the process of approaching the completeness of domestic legal
orders and their constitutional structures, it would be good to acknowledge its being different from a state community and explain its peculiarities not against the background of domestic constitutional doctrines but
as a distinct social and legal phenomenon. In this context, the formation
of spontaneous law and the emergence of spontaneous checks against the
agglomeration of power may be looked at not just as fancy intellectual
constructs of international lawyers but as a fairly accurate description of
the social and legal realities of the contemporary international community. If it does not look like any domestic constitutional order and is not
even remotely reminiscent of any historically rooted constitutionalism
doctrine, this is the tribute we have to pay to the diversity of legal
phenomena and to the peculiarities of international law.

XI. CONCLUSION

At this point I should have liked to conclude by paraphrasing Kapler, the
great mathematician and astronomer of the seventeenth century, who
once said that 'the diversity of the phenomena of nature is so great in
order that the human mind shall never be lacking in fresh nourishment'.

---

[95] R Ago, 'Positive Law and International Law' (1957) 51 *American Journal of International Law* 691.

One could then say after him that 'the diversity of legal phenomena is so great in order that the legal analyst's mind shall never be lacking in fresh nourishment'.

What better conclusion could ever be found? In diversity lies richness and the potential for scientific progress. How self-reassuring to think that, after all, we all may be right. The problem with that conclusion is that I found it too much like a self-fulfilling prophecy. I have thus opted for another one.

At the outset of this chapter, cursory reference was made to what Thomas Kuhn considers to be the constant tension underlying the work of researchers. This tension is between, on the one hand, the professional skills of the researcher, whose problem-solving talents are developed on the basis of established rules and professional practices, and, on the other, the ideology of the profession.[96] This ideology consists of fostering the image of the gifted explorer, who knows no rules than those dictated by nature and empiric observation. Even legal scholars, whom one may wish to think of as more constrained than others by their epistemology, are often inspired by the desire to explore and design new patterns of enquiry, even to the detriment of those rules they are supposed to administer and preserve. According to Kuhn, this tension and the ability to sustain it are important to science's success. Presumably, this is also a source of frustration to many. How can this tension be resolved? Does the solution lie – as Kuhn seems to purport – in shifting paradigms?

Would the import of paradigms from constitutional law be tantamount to such a shift? I am instinctively sceptical that this would be the case. As Stanley Fish has aptly noted, whenever two disciplines come close to each other 'it will be the case either that one is trading on the prestige or vocabulary of the other or one has swallowed the other'.[97] It seems to me that international law is anxiously trading on the prestige and vocabulary of constitutional law. This is problematic because it may lead to drawing an interdisciplinary map where constitutional law categories gain prominence at the expense of the international law shapes, which risk being rendered invisible.[98] In my view, this would be as much a setback for the profession as a mystification of reality.

What I have attempted to do in this chapter is perhaps a good illustration of the intellectual tensions I have just described. On the one hand, I have, more or less consciously, attempted to preserve the integrity

---

[96] See T Kuhn, 'The Function of Dogma in Scientific Research' in AC Crombie (ed), *Scientific Change* (London, Heinemann, 1963) at 368–9.

[97] See S Fish, *Professional Correctness. Literary Studies and Political Change* (Oxford, Clarendon Press, 1995) 83.

[98] *Ibid* at 81.

of the discipline of international law, refusing the application of paradigms borrowed from constitutional law doctrine. Fish was right: I did
not want to trade on the prestige of constitutional law at the risk of being
swallowed. On the other, I have worked with the professional tools of my
own discipline to make sense of the reality I was investigating. At the
same time I attempted to bring about innovation by thinking in terms of
spontaneous forms of control over the agglomeration of power, surely
not an orthodox form of thinking for a lawyer. In doing so, however, I
eventually reverted to traditional professional skills by invoking the
authority of one of the greatest international law scholars of all times,
Roberto Ago. It is hard indeed to escape the tension between professional
skills and professional ideology, the two indissolubly linked attitudes of
the researcher.

At this point, one may legitimately wonder whether these considerations matter at all. Are they not doomed to scientific irrelevance? Do they
not simply reinforce the view that we exist, professionally, as international, constitutional lawyers, political scientists or whatever else only
because we can distinguish ourselves from the others? Are we not bound
to preserve the intelligibility of our specific paradigms? Is interdisciplinarity not a myth? Are our distinct epistemologies ever to meet? And
finally ... have I described an inchoate, proto-constitutional system of
checks and balances or a spontaneous reaction of the societal body to a
fairly unprecedented agglomeration of power?

Here is the duck/rabbit optical illusion used by Wittgenstein and other philosophers of science to demonstrate the critical relevance of paradigms.[99] In looking at this image, our brain shifts between different perceptions and catches sight of a rabbit – or more properly a hare – and a duck. This is traditionally presented as an optical illusion. But is it really so? It is not an illusion. It isn't. It is a reality. This is both a hare and a duck. Or is it not?

---

[99] See L Wittgenstein, *Philosophical Investigations* (Oxford, Basil Blackwell, 1974). In fact, Wittgenstein used a hand-sketched, less refined drawing than the one reproduced in the text.

Index